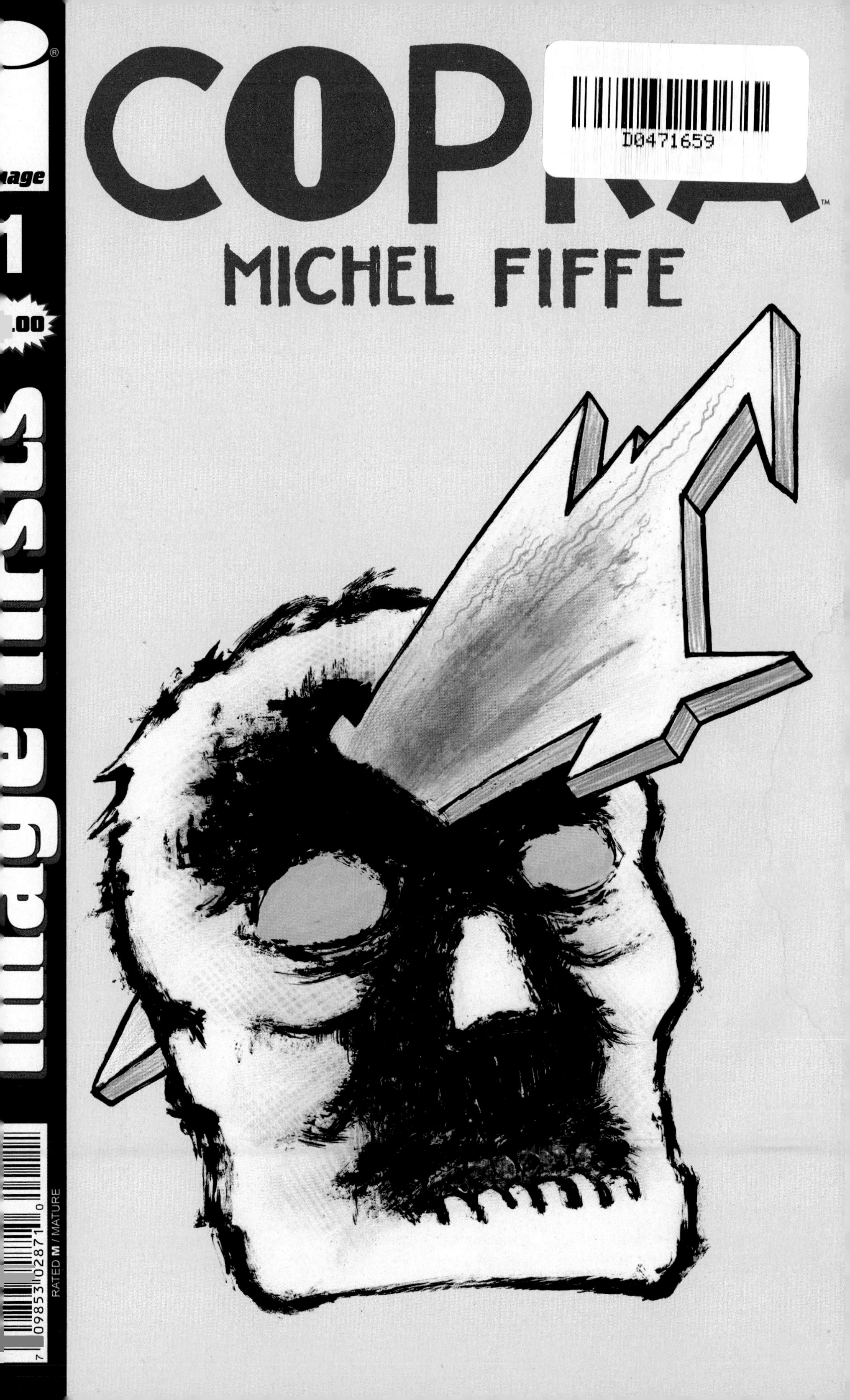
COPRA™
MICHEL FIFFE
image
1
.00
image firsts
RATED M / MATURE

COPRA

ISSUE ONE

CREATED AND PRODUCED BY MICHEL FIFFE

"RAGING WRATH"

MICHELFIFFE.COM • IMAGECOMICS.COM • DESIGN: Michel Fiffe and Adam Pruett • PRODUCTION ARTIST: Erika Schnatz

IMAGE COMICS, INC. • Robert Kirkman: Chief Operating Officer • Erik Larsen: Chief Financial Officer • Todd McFarlane: President • Marc Silvestri: Chief Executive Officer • Jim Valentino: Vice President • Eric Stephenson: Publisher / Chief Creative Officer • Jeff Boison: Director of Publishing Planning & Book Trade Sales • Chris Ross: Director of Digital Sales • Jeff Stang: Director of Direct Market Sales • Kat Salazar: Director of PR & Marketing • Drew Gill: Art Director • Heather Doornink: Production Director • Nicole Lapalme: Controller

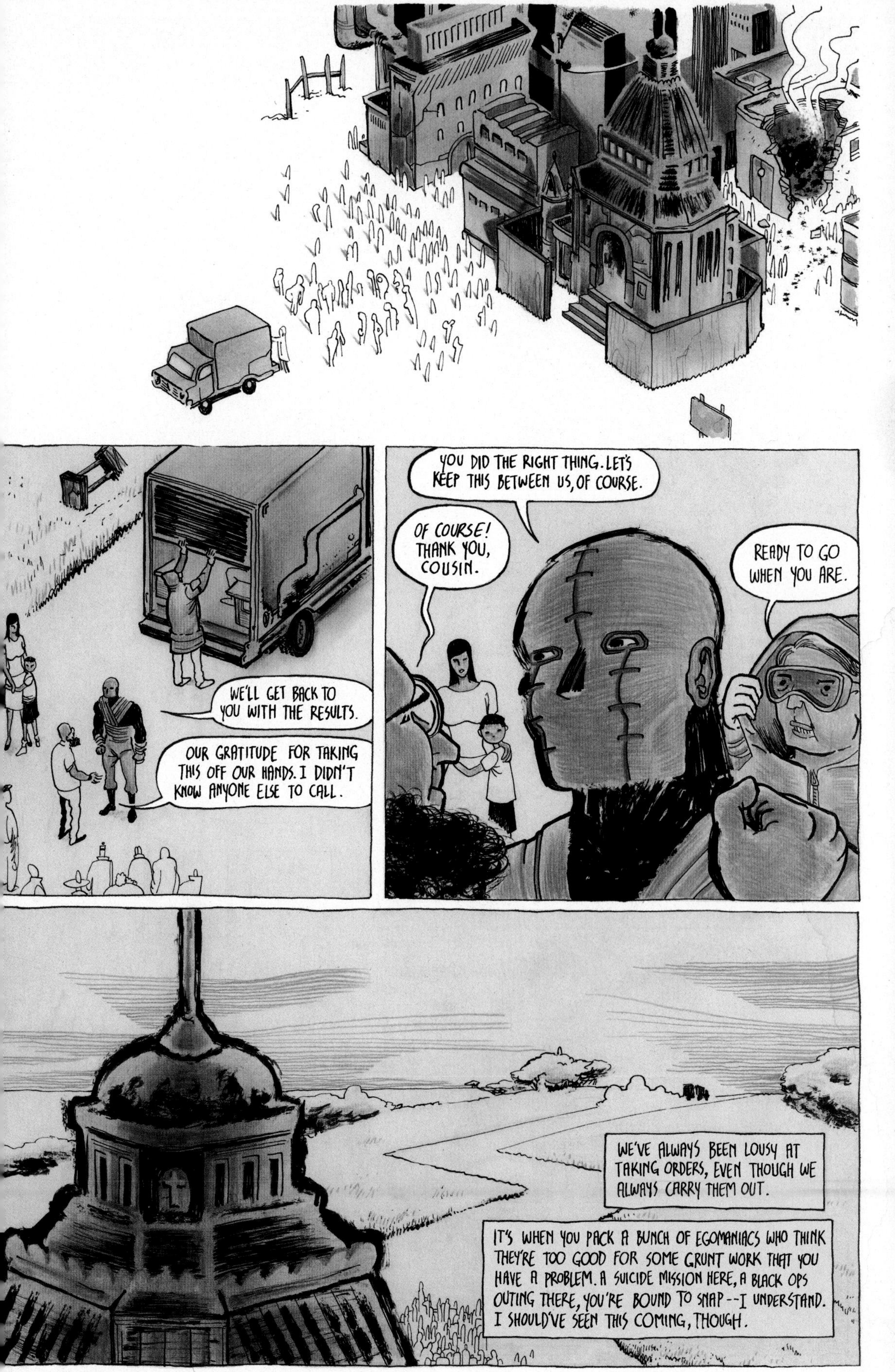
WE'LL GET BACK TO YOU WITH THE RESULTS.
OUR GRATITUDE FOR TAKING THIS OFF OUR HANDS. I DIDN'T KNOW ANYONE ELSE TO CALL.
YOU DID THE RIGHT THING. LET'S KEEP THIS BETWEEN US, OF COURSE.
OF COURSE! THANK YOU, COUSIN.
READY TO GO WHEN YOU ARE.
WE'VE ALWAYS BEEN LOUSY AT TAKING ORDERS, EVEN THOUGH WE ALWAYS CARRY THEM OUT.
IT'S WHEN YOU PACK A BUNCH OF EGOMANIACS WHO THINK THEY'RE TOO GOOD FOR SOME GRUNT WORK THAT YOU HAVE A PROBLEM. A SUICIDE MISSION HERE, A BLACK OPS OUTING THERE, YOU'RE BOUND TO SNAP--I UNDERSTAND. I SHOULD'VE SEEN THIS COMING, THOUGH.

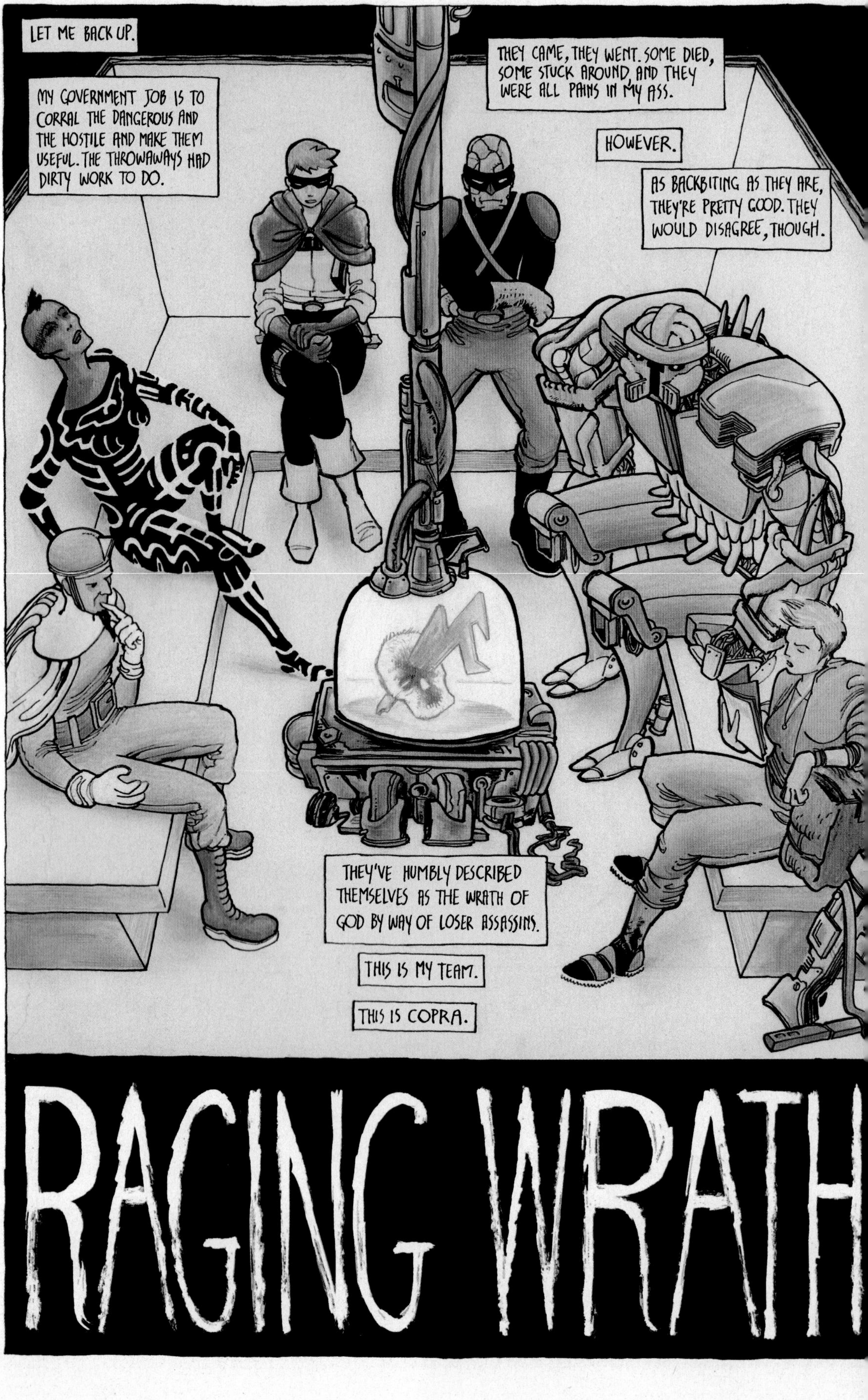
LET ME BACK UP.
MY GOVERNMENT JOB IS TO CORRAL THE DANGEROUS AND THE HOSTILE AND MAKE THEM USEFUL. THE THROWAWAYS HAD DIRTY WORK TO DO.
THEY CAME, THEY WENT. SOME DIED, SOME STUCK AROUND, AND THEY WERE ALL PAINS IN MY ASS.
HOWEVER.
AS BACKBITING AS THEY ARE, THEY'RE PRETTY GOOD. THEY WOULD DISAGREE, THOUGH.
THEY'VE HUMBLY DESCRIBED THEMSELVES AS THE WRATH OF GOD BY WAY OF LOSER ASSASSINS.
THIS IS MY TEAM.
THIS IS COPRA.
RAGING WRATH

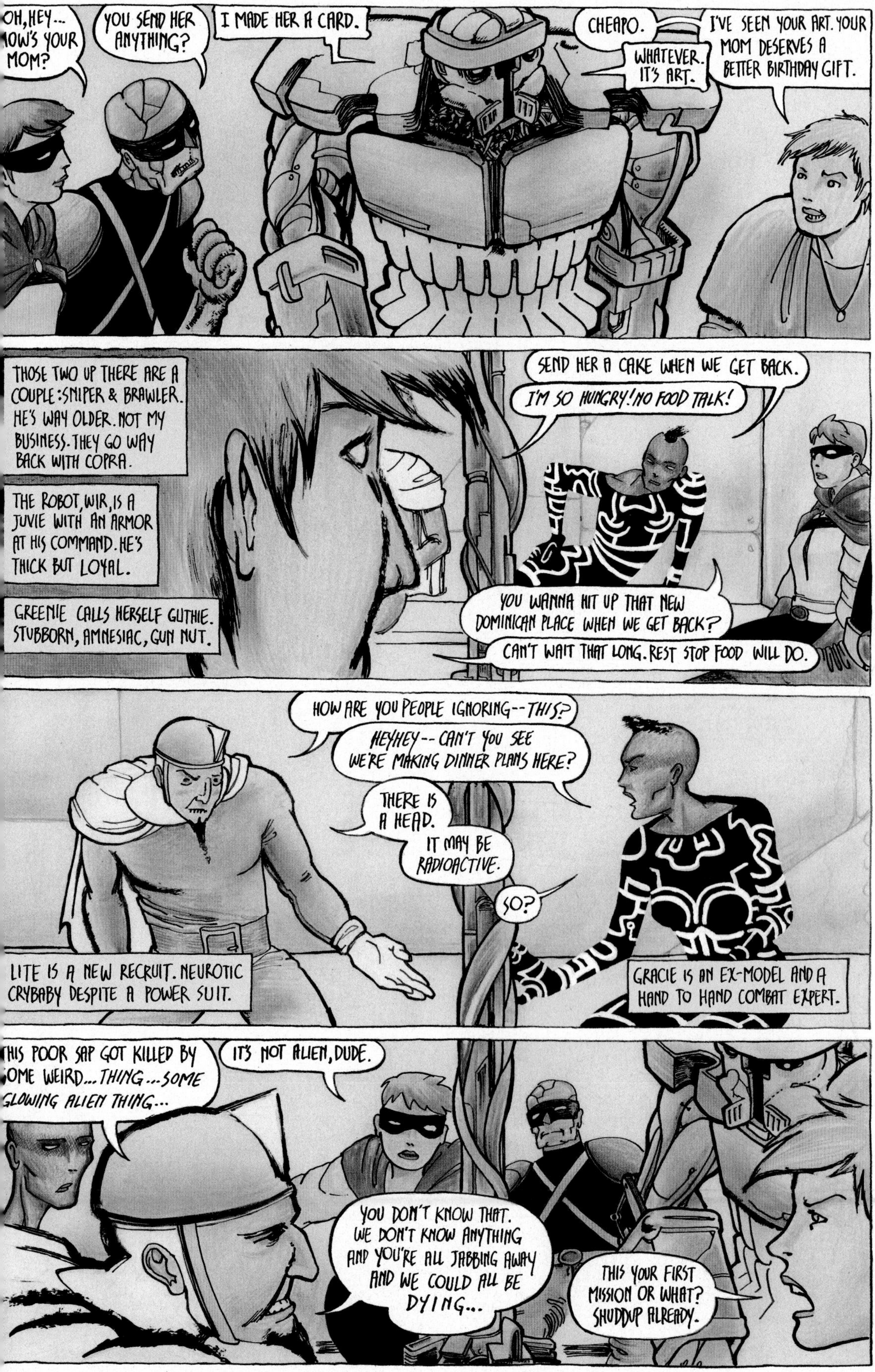
OH, HEY... HOW'S YOUR MOM?
YOU SEND HER ANYTHING?
I MADE HER A CARD.
CHEAPO.
WHATEVER. IT'S ART.
I'VE SEEN YOUR ART. YOUR MOM DESERVES A BETTER BIRTHDAY GIFT.
THOSE TWO UP THERE ARE A COUPLE: SNIPER & BRAWLER. HE'S WAY OLDER. NOT MY BUSINESS. THEY GO WAY BACK WITH COPRA.
THE ROBOT, WIR, IS A JUVIE WITH AN ARMOR AT HIS COMMAND. HE'S THICK BUT LOYAL.
GREENIE CALLS HERSELF GUTHIE. STUBBORN, AMNESIAC, GUN NUT.
SEND HER A CAKE WHEN WE GET BACK.
I'M SO HUNGRY! NO FOOD TALK!
YOU WANNA HIT UP THAT NEW DOMINICAN PLACE WHEN WE GET BACK?
CAN'T WAIT THAT LONG. REST STOP FOOD WILL DO.
HOW ARE YOU PEOPLE IGNORING--THIS?
HEYHEY--CAN'T YOU SEE WE'RE MAKING DINNER PLANS HERE?
THERE IS A HEAD.
IT MAY BE RADIOACTIVE.
SO?
LITE IS A NEW RECRUIT. NEUROTIC CRYBABY DESPITE A POWER SUIT.
GRACIE IS AN EX-MODEL AND A HAND TO HAND COMBAT EXPERT.
THIS POOR SAP GOT KILLED BY SOME WEIRD... THING... SOME GLOWING ALIEN THING...
IT'S NOT ALIEN, DUDE.
YOU DON'T KNOW THAT. WE DON'T KNOW ANYTHING AND YOU'RE ALL JABBING AWAY AND WE COULD ALL BE DYING...
THIS YOUR FIRST MISSION OR WHAT? SHUDDUP ALREADY.

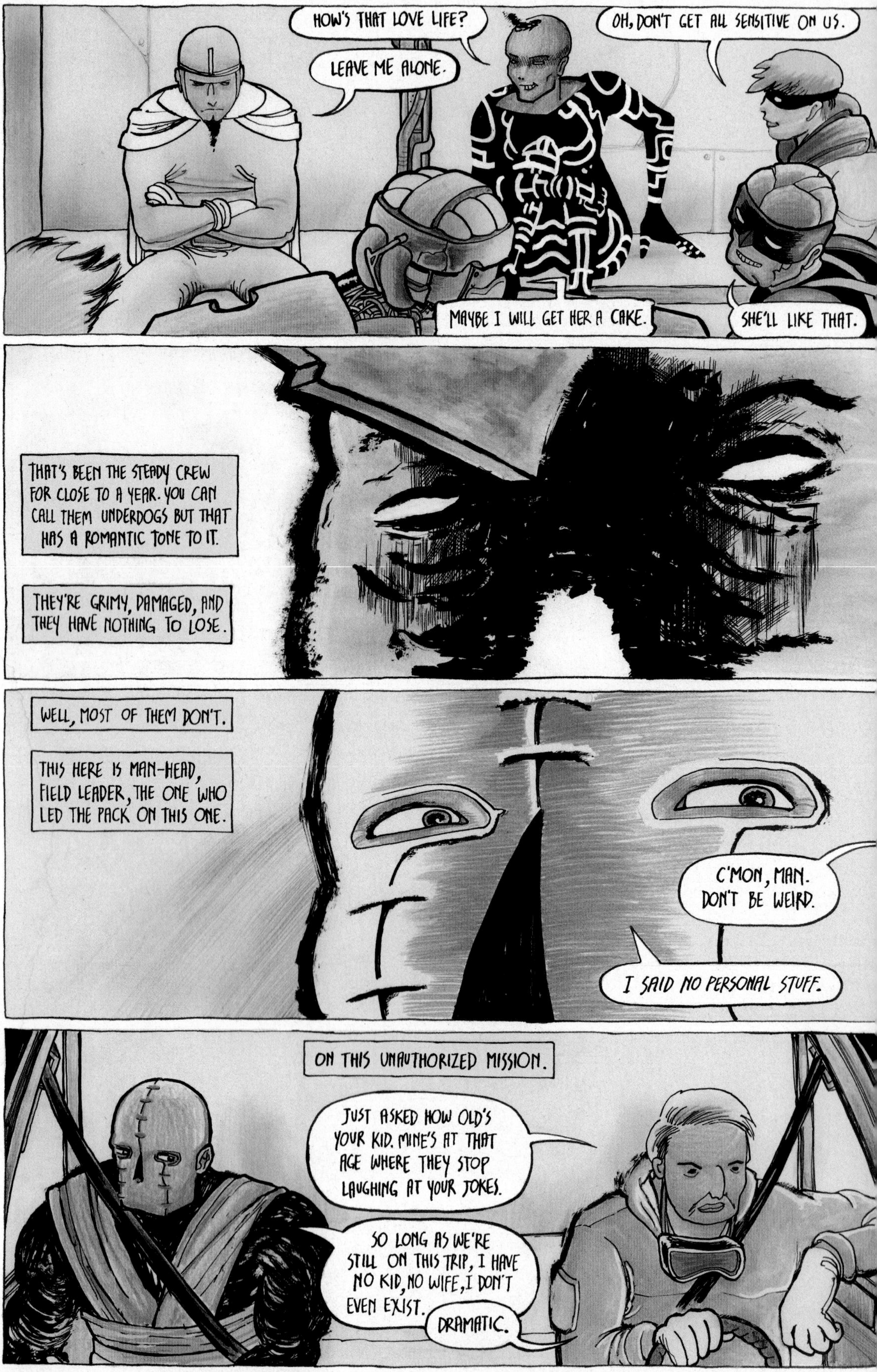
HOW'S THAT LOVE LIFE?
LEAVE ME ALONE.
OH, DON'T GET ALL SENSITIVE ON US.
MAYBE I WILL GET HER A CAKE.
SHE'LL LIKE THAT.
THAT'S BEEN THE STEADY CREW FOR CLOSE TO A YEAR. YOU CAN CALL THEM UNDERDOGS BUT THAT HAS A ROMANTIC TONE TO IT.
THEY'RE GRIMY, DAMAGED, AND THEY HAVE NOTHING TO LOSE.
WELL, MOST OF THEM DON'T.
THIS HERE IS MAN-HEAD, FIELD LEADER, THE ONE WHO LED THE PACK ON THIS ONE.
C'MON, MAN. DON'T BE WEIRD.
I SAID NO PERSONAL STUFF.
ON THIS UNAUTHORIZED MISSION.
JUST ASKED HOW OLD'S YOUR KID. MINE'S AT THAT AGE WHERE THEY STOP LAUGHING AT YOUR JOKES.
SO LONG AS WE'RE STILL ON THIS TRIP, I HAVE NO KID, NO WIFE, I DON'T EVEN EXIST.
DRAMATIC.

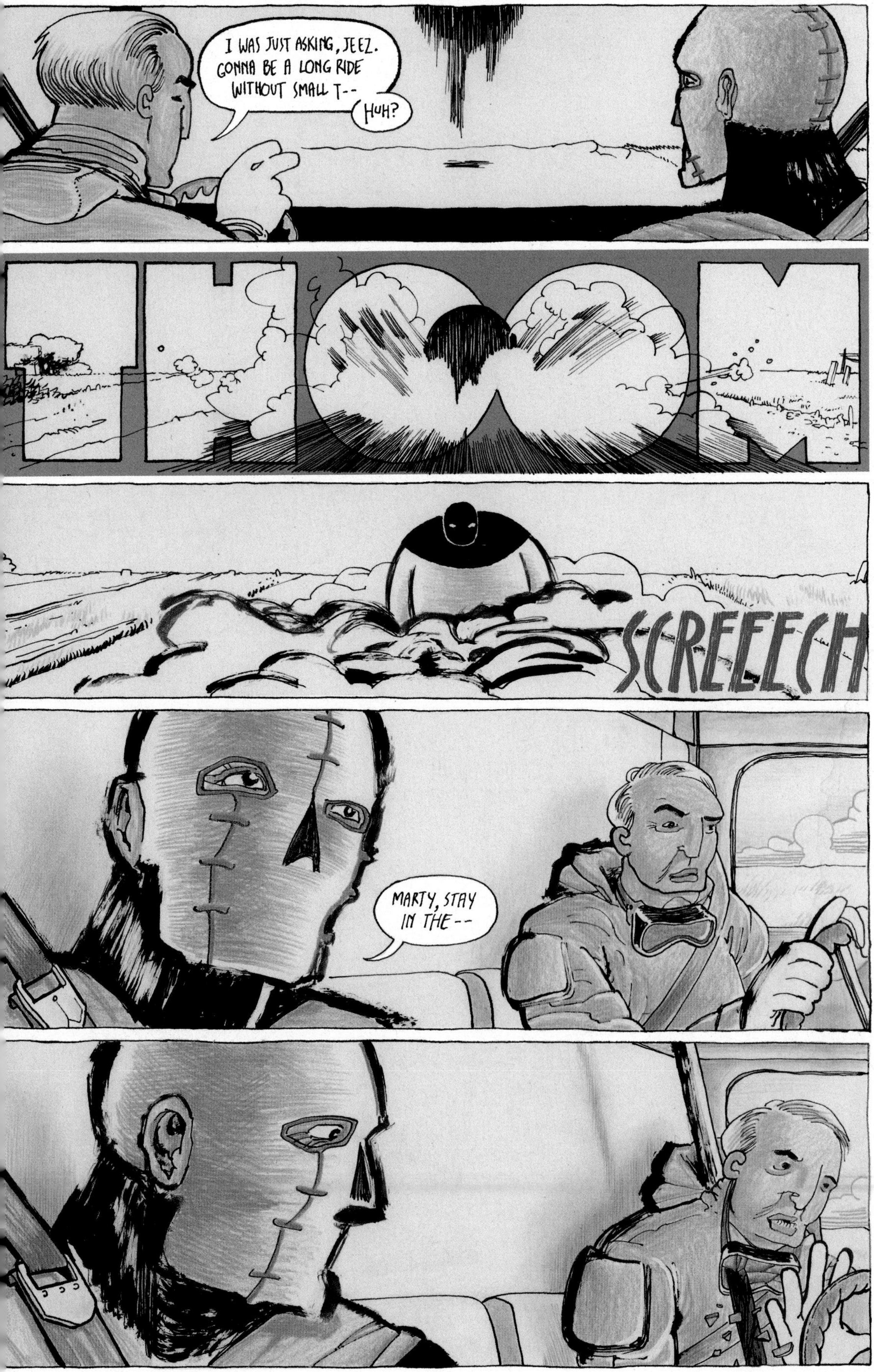
I WAS JUST ASKING, JEEZ. GONNA BE A LONG RIDE WITHOUT SMALL T--
HUH?
THOOOM
SCREEECH
MARTY, STAY IN THE--

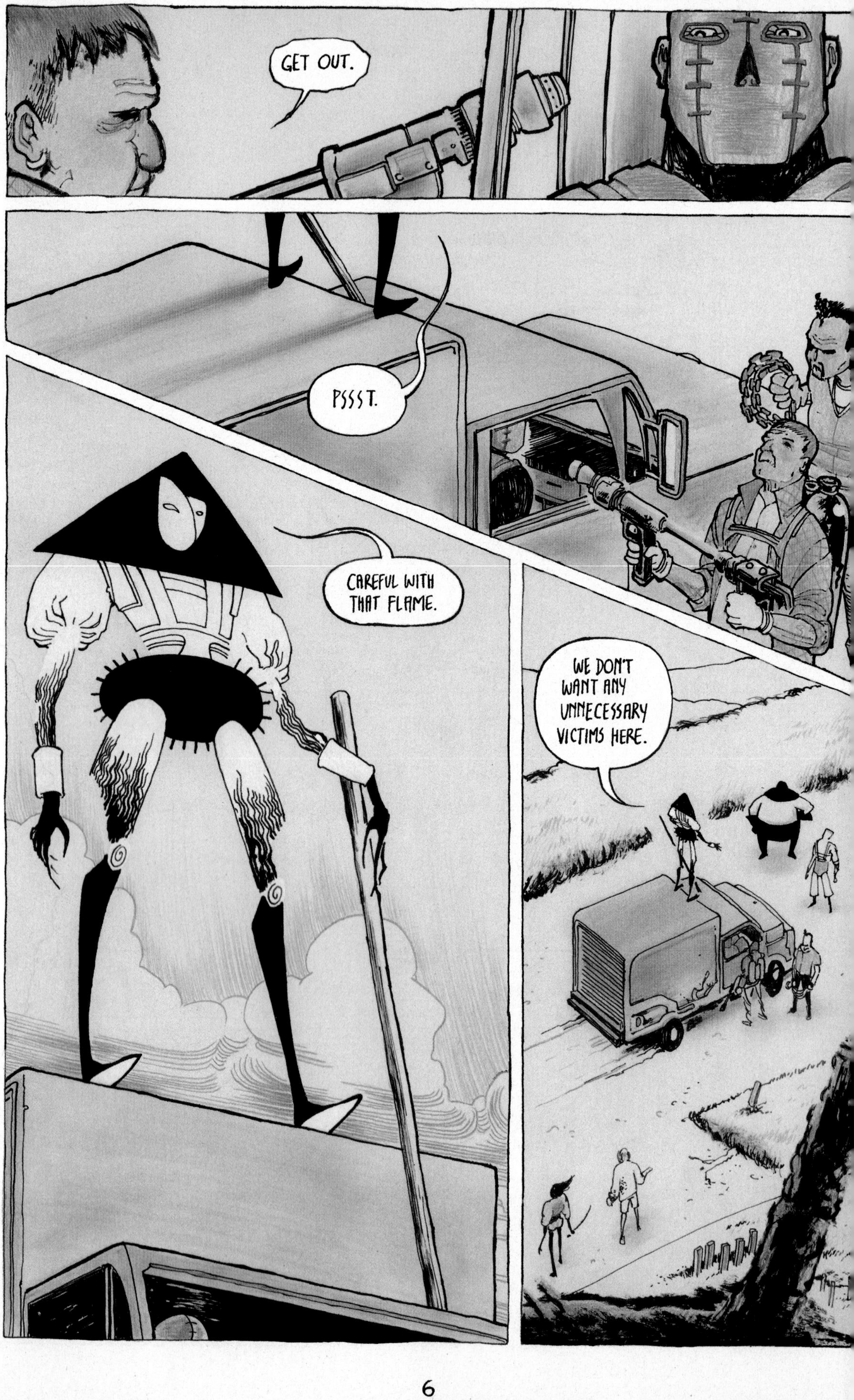
GET OUT.
PSSST.
CAREFUL WITH THAT FLAME.
WE DON'T WANT ANY UNNECESSARY VICTIMS HERE.

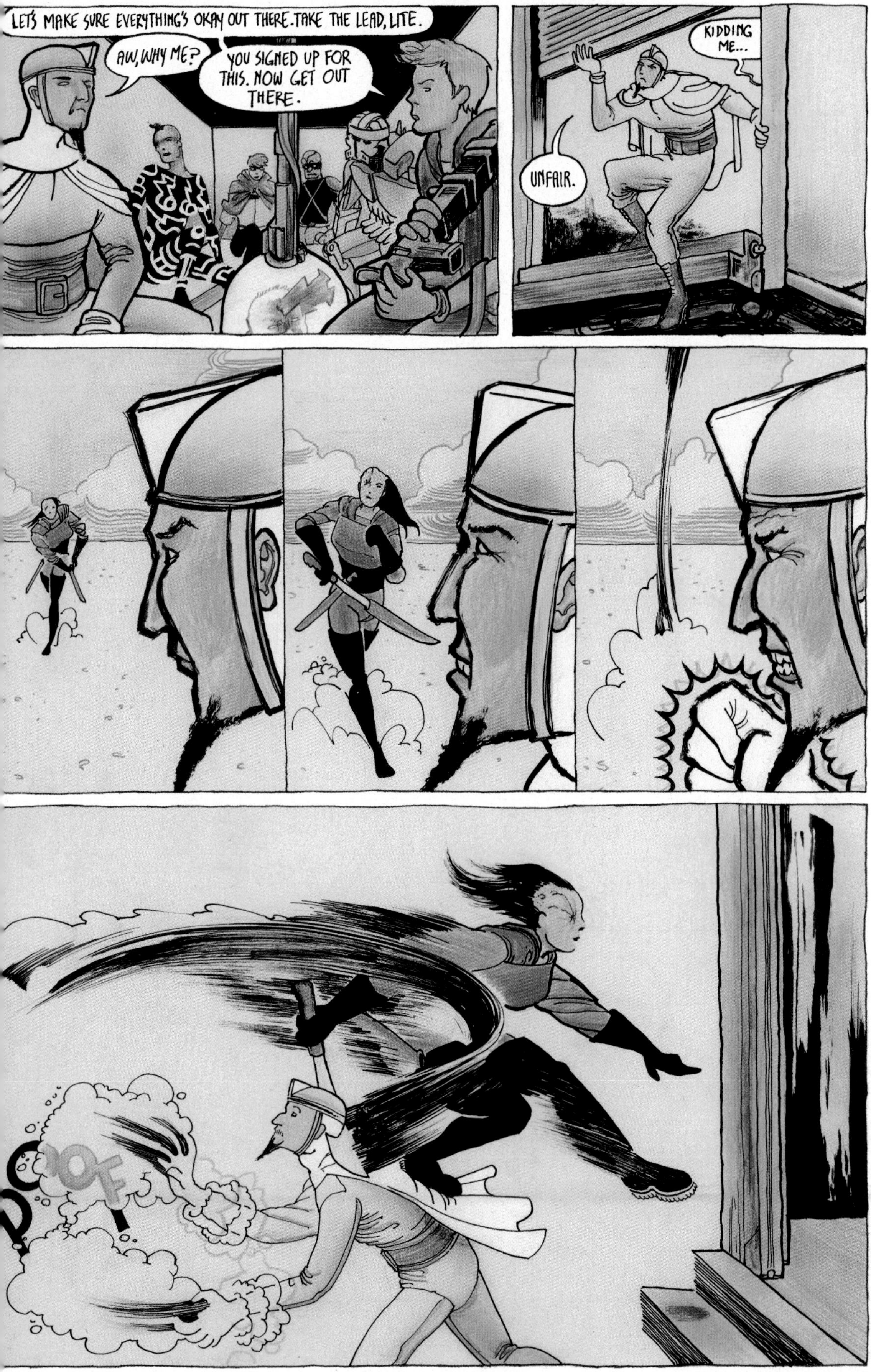
LET'S MAKE SURE EVERYTHING'S OKAY OUT THERE. TAKE THE LEAD, LITE.
AW, WHY ME?
YOU SIGNED UP FOR THIS. NOW GET OUT THERE.
KIDDING ME...
UNFAIR.

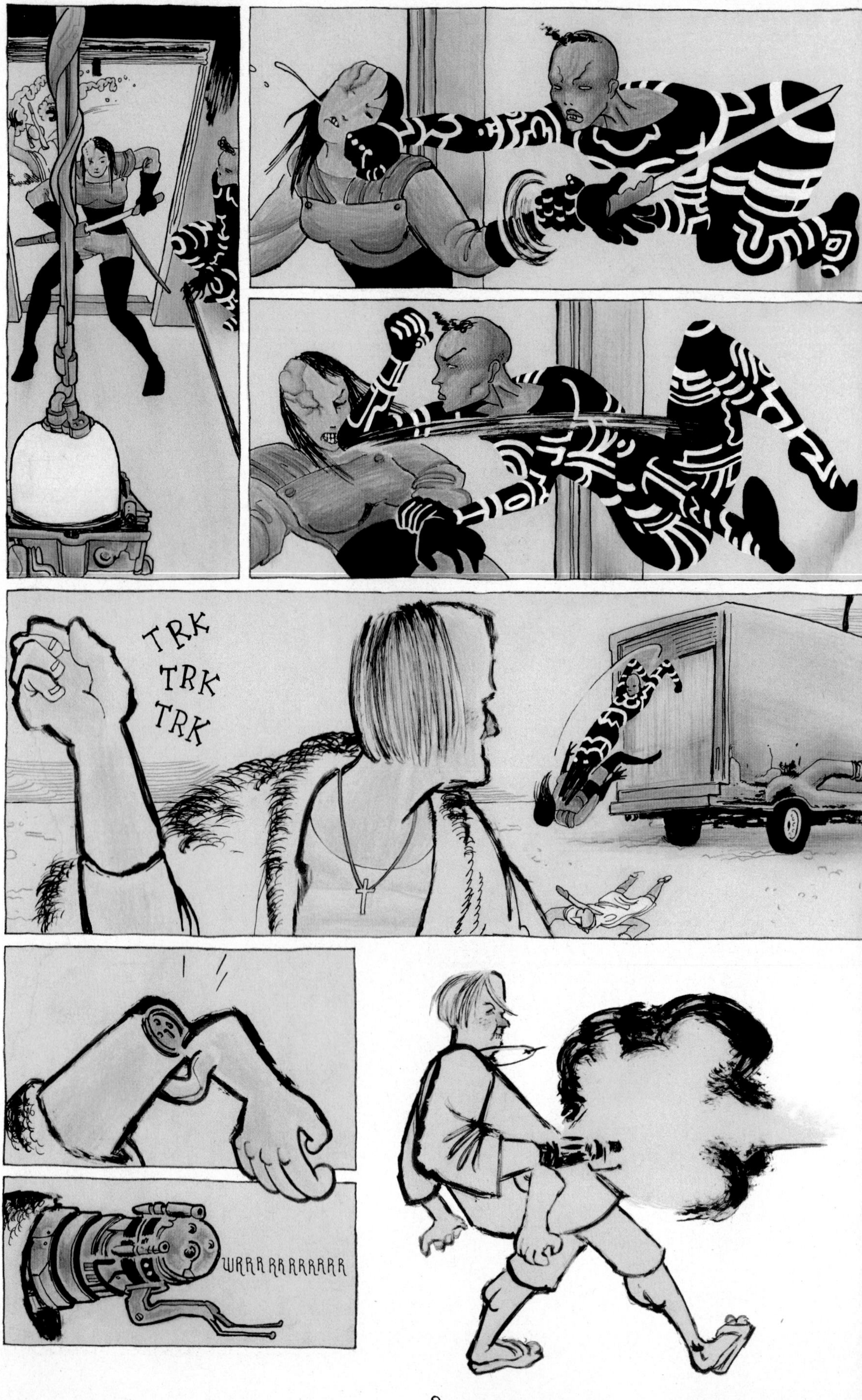
TRK
TRK
TRK
WRRR RRRRRRRR

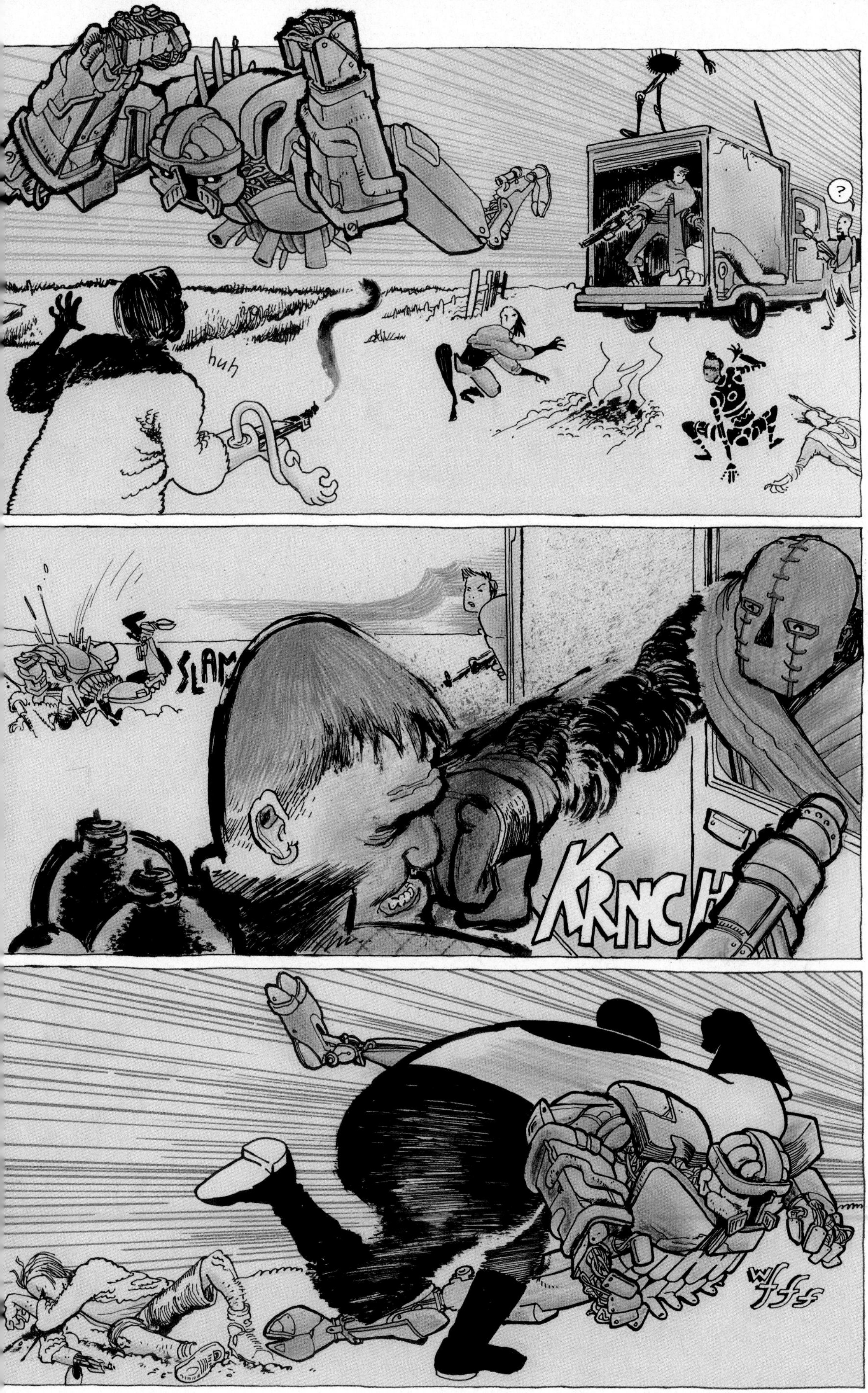
?
huh
SLAM
KRNCH
wfff

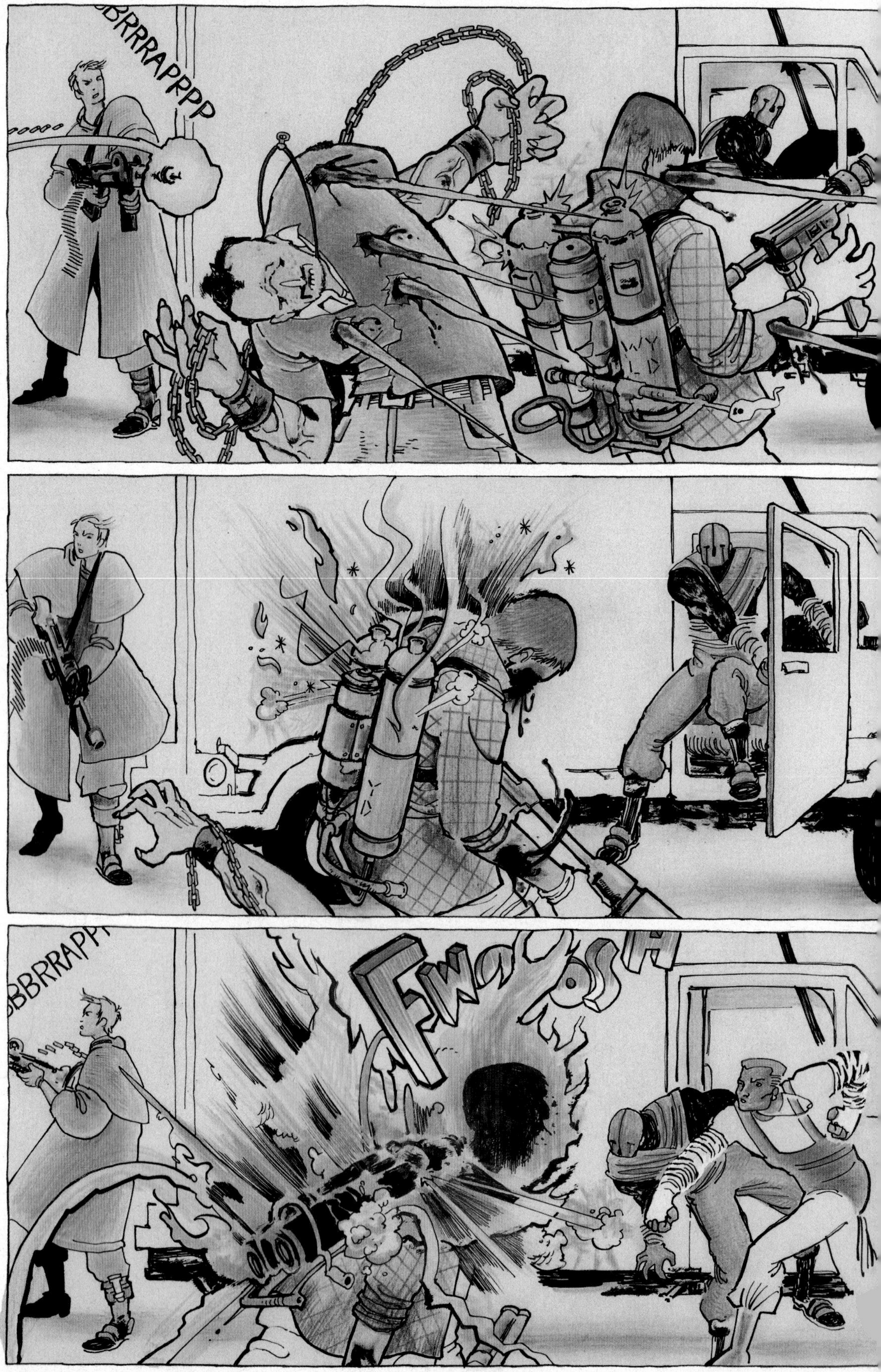
BBRRRRAPPPP
BBBRRAPP
FWOOOSH

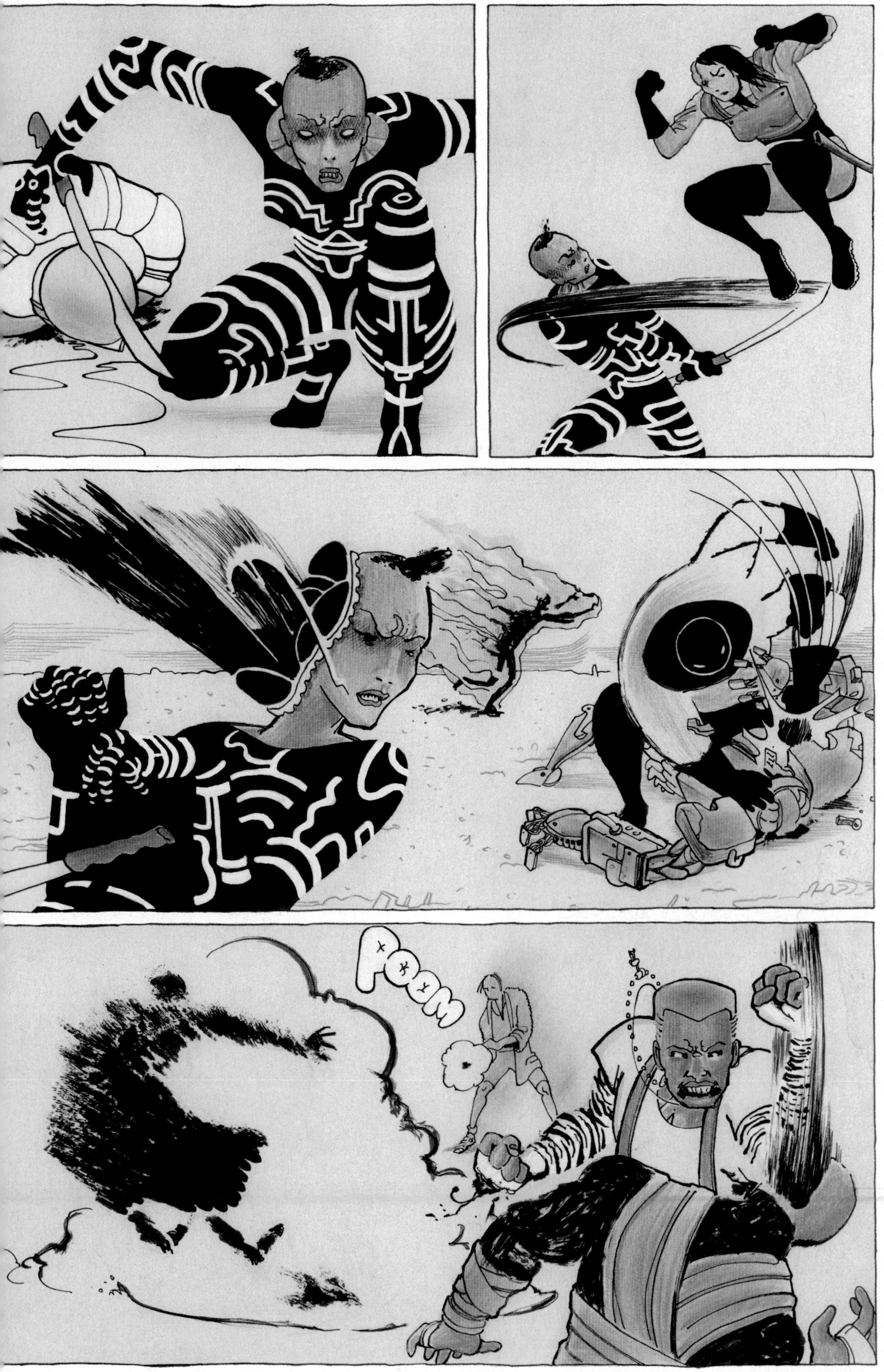
POOM

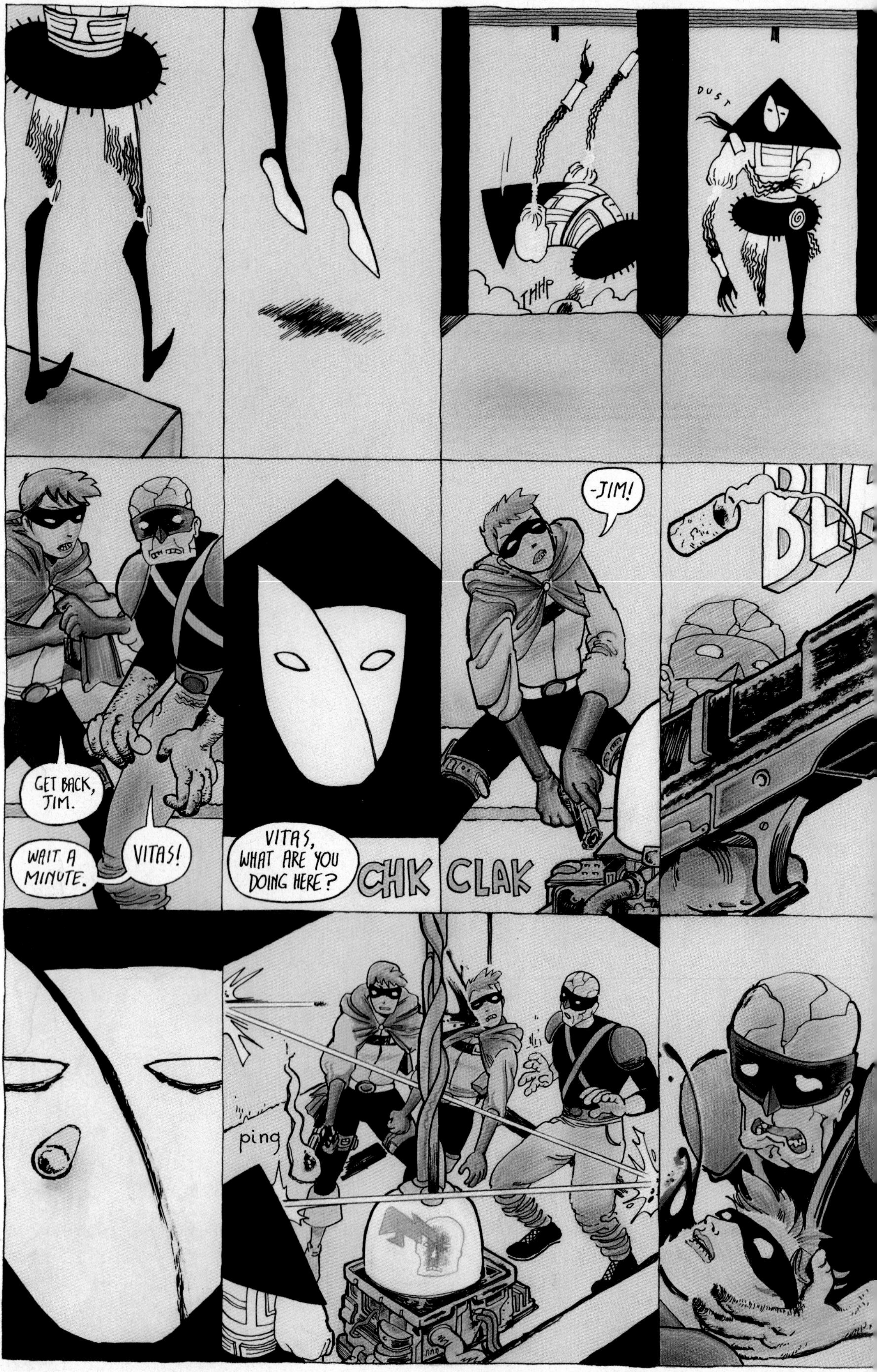
THHP
DUST
GET BACK, JIM.
VITAS!
WAIT A MINUTE.
VITAS, WHAT ARE YOU DOING HERE?
CHK
CLAK
-JIM!
ping

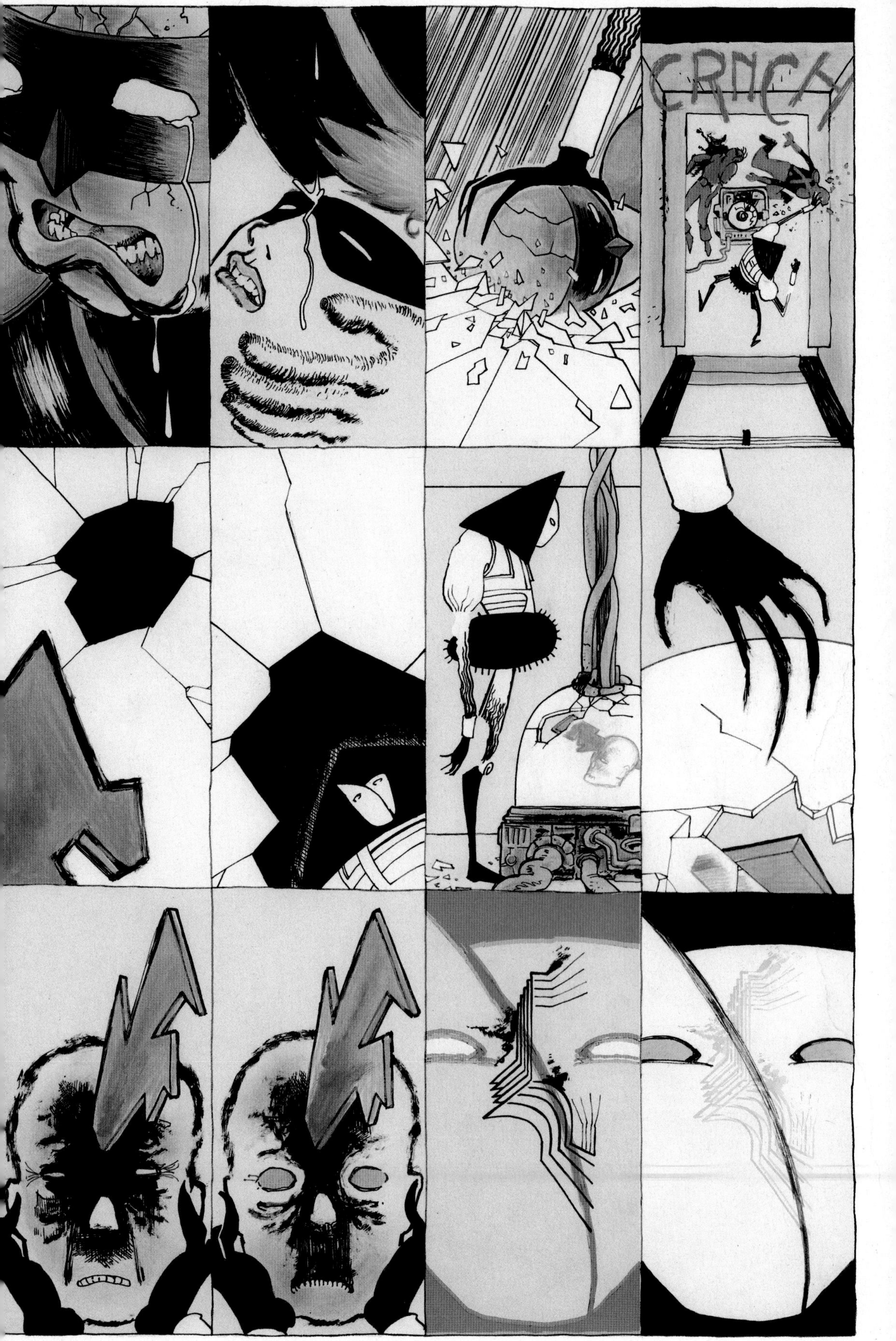
CRNCH

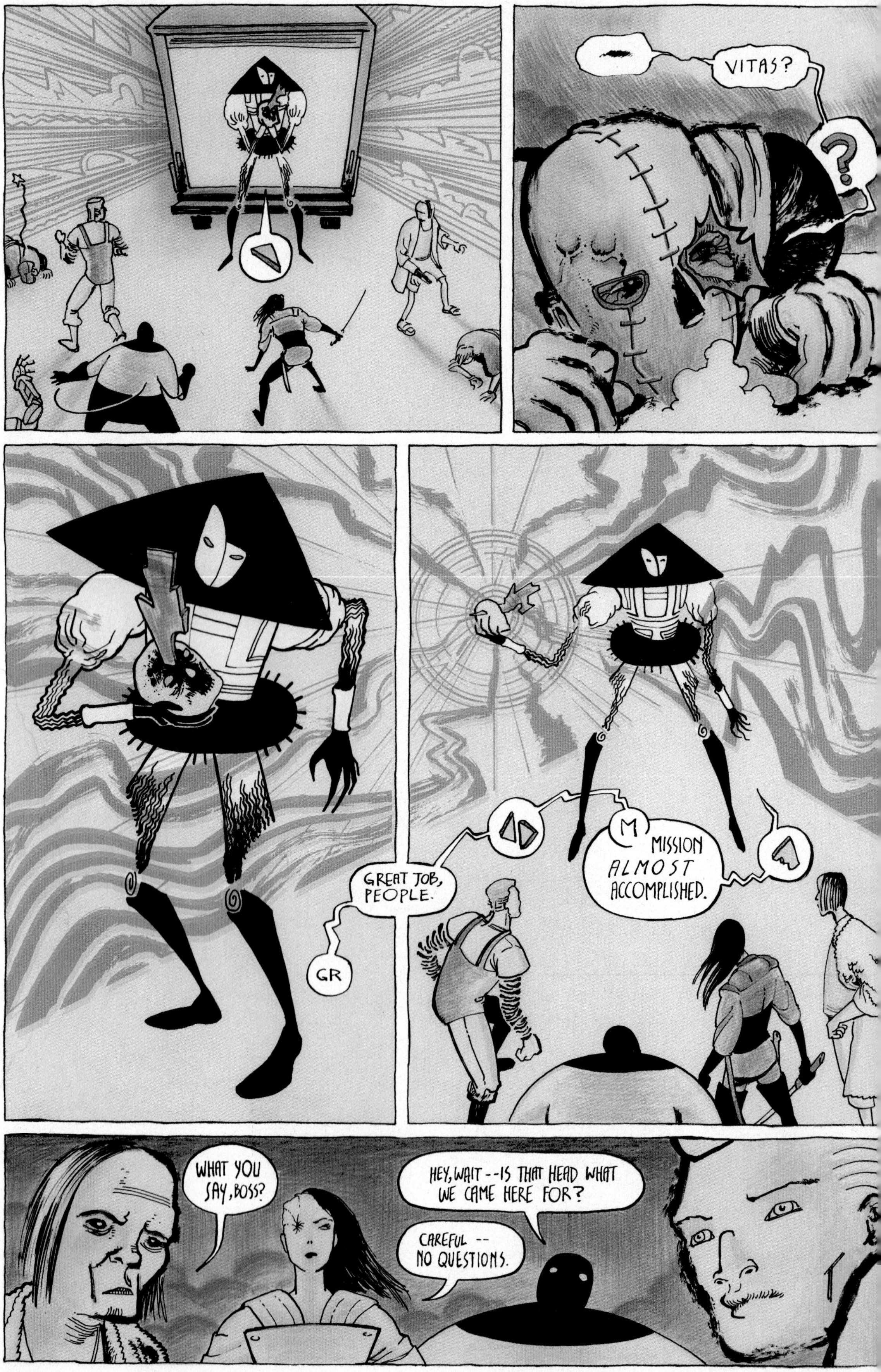
VITAS?
?
GREAT JOB, PEOPLE.
GR
M
MISSION ALMOST ACCOMPLISHED.
WHAT YOU SAY, BOSS?
HEY, WAIT --IS THAT HEAD WHAT WE CAME HERE FOR?
CAREFUL -- NO QUESTIONS.

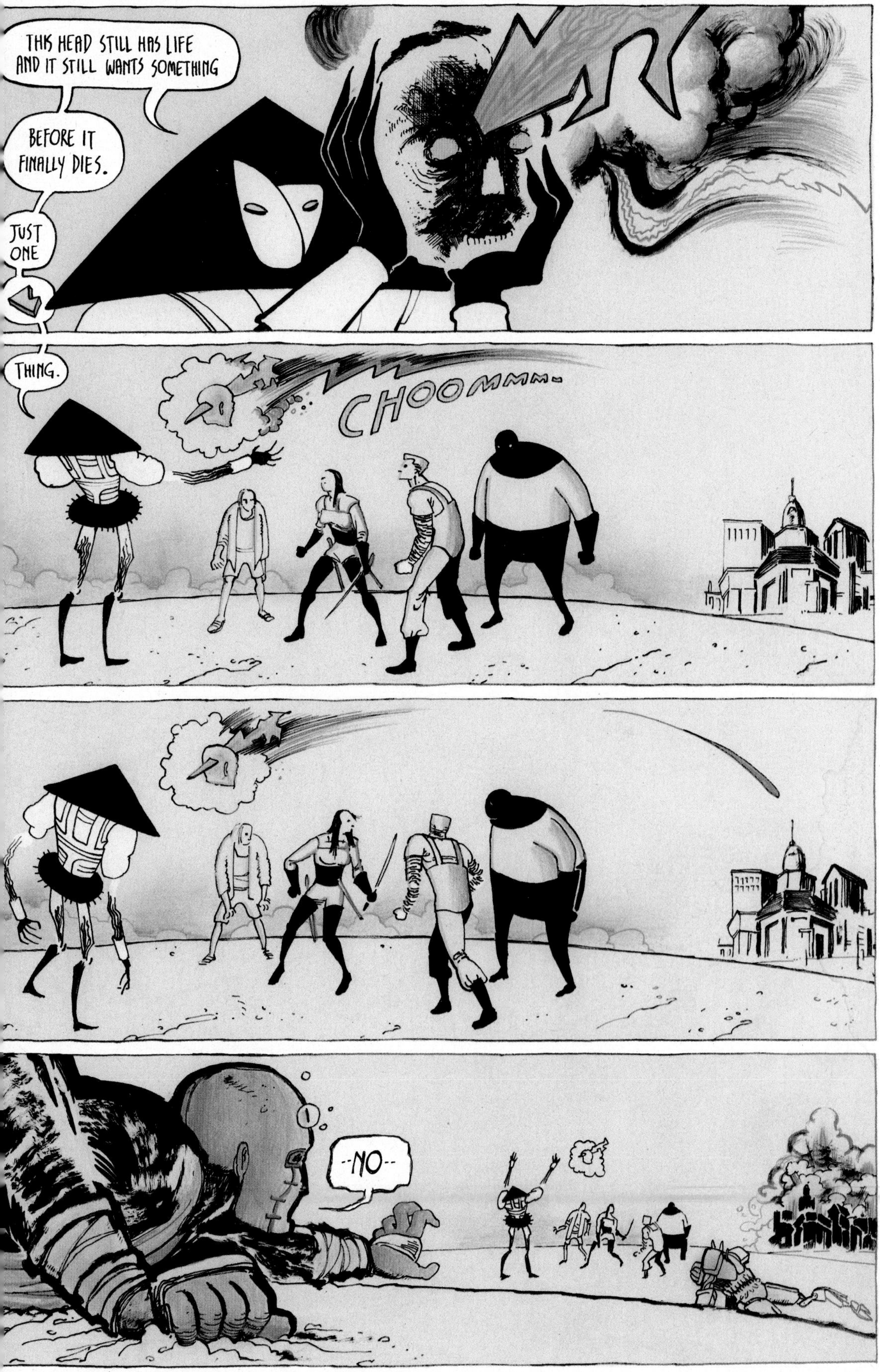
THIS HEAD STILL HAS LIFE AND IT STILL WANTS SOMETHING
BEFORE IT FINALLY DIES.
JUST ONE
THING.
CHOOMMM-
-NO-

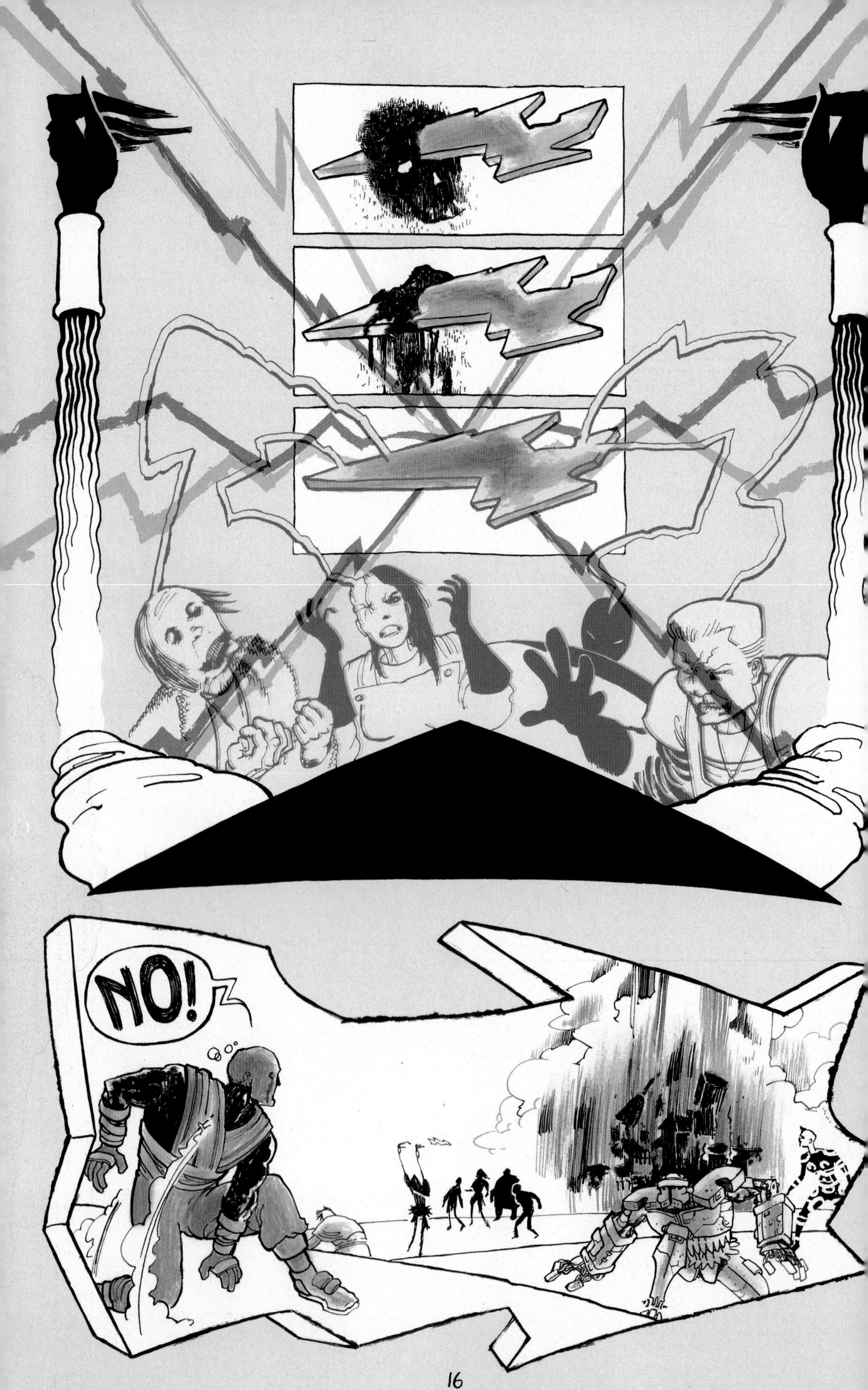
NO!

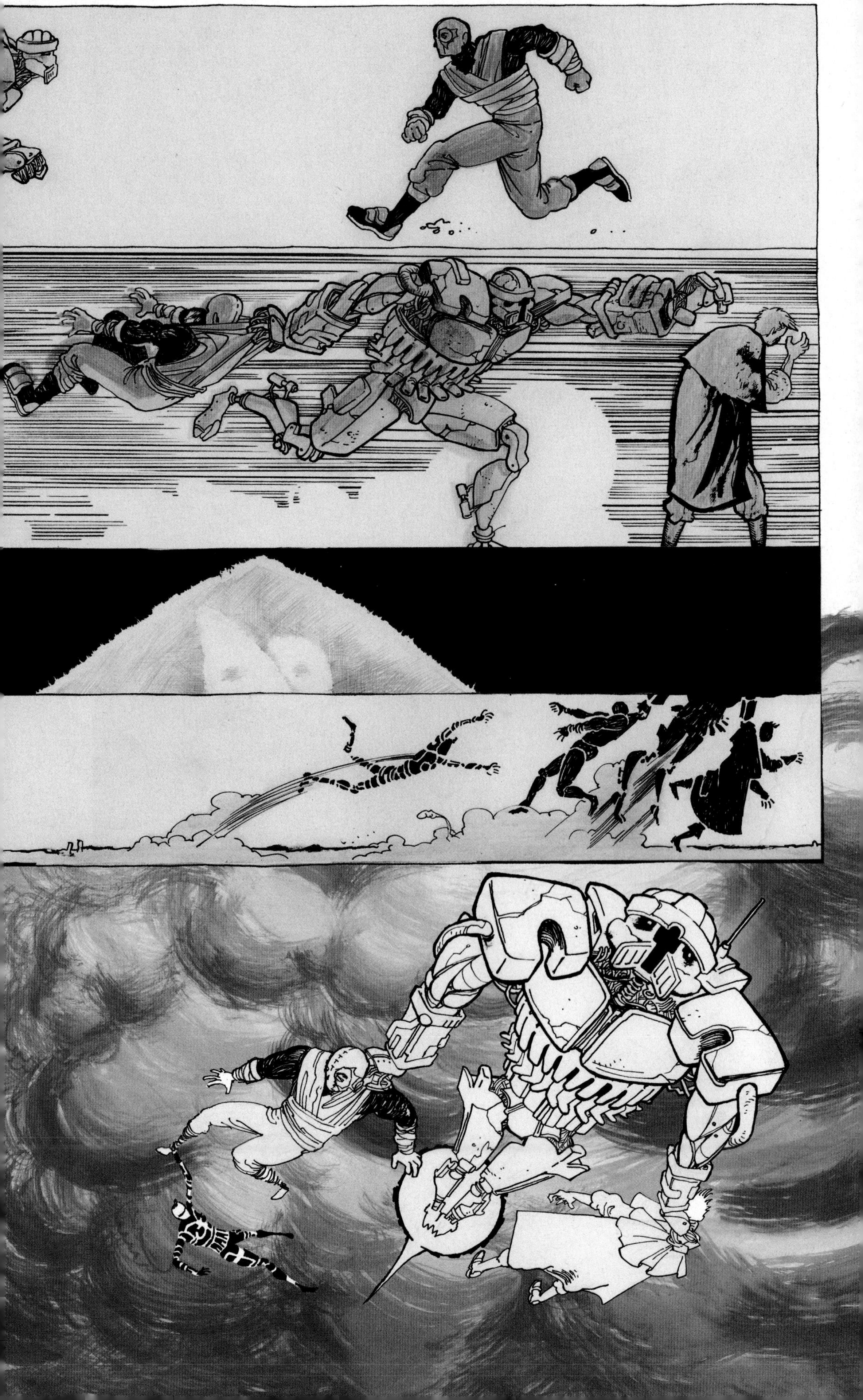

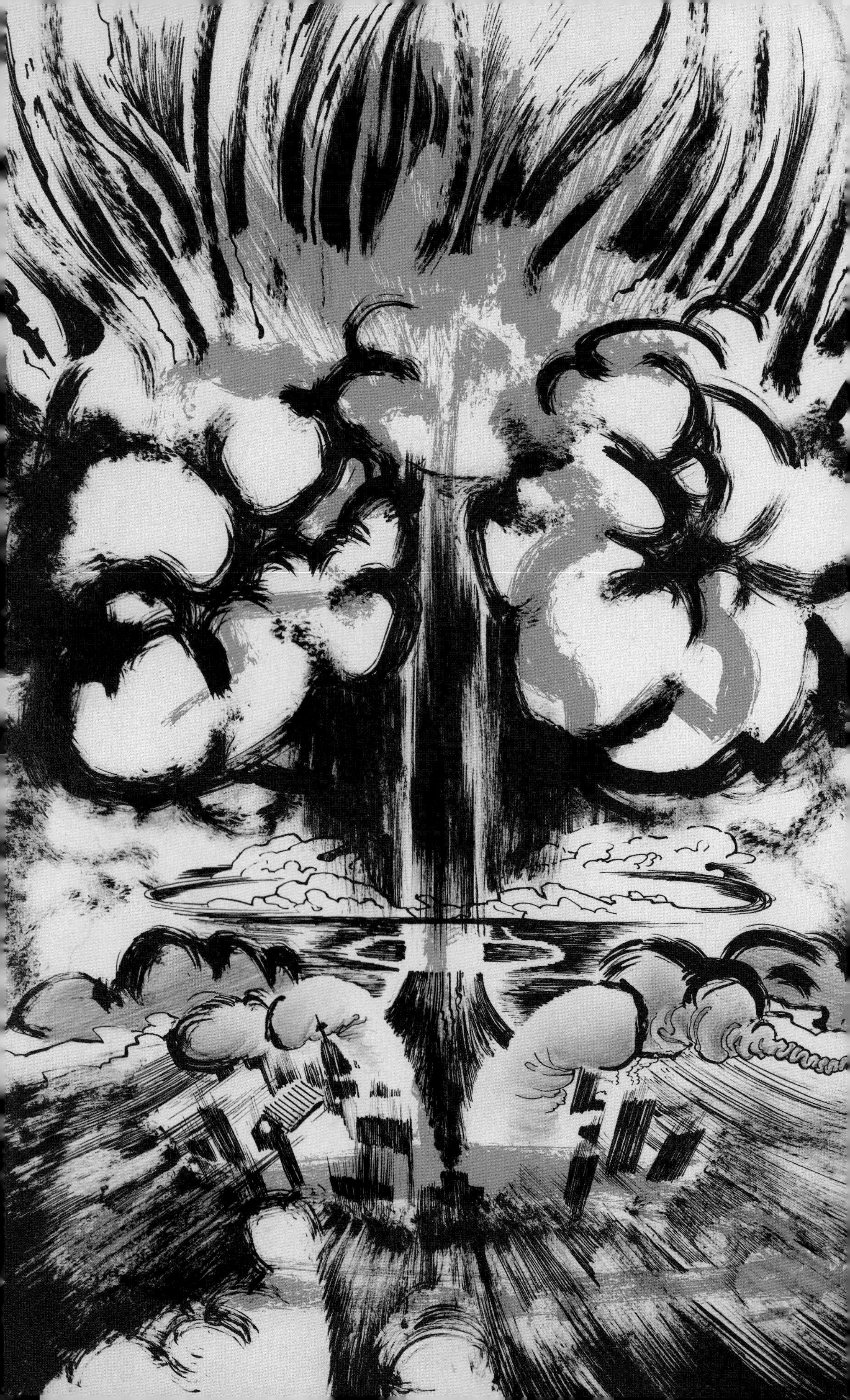

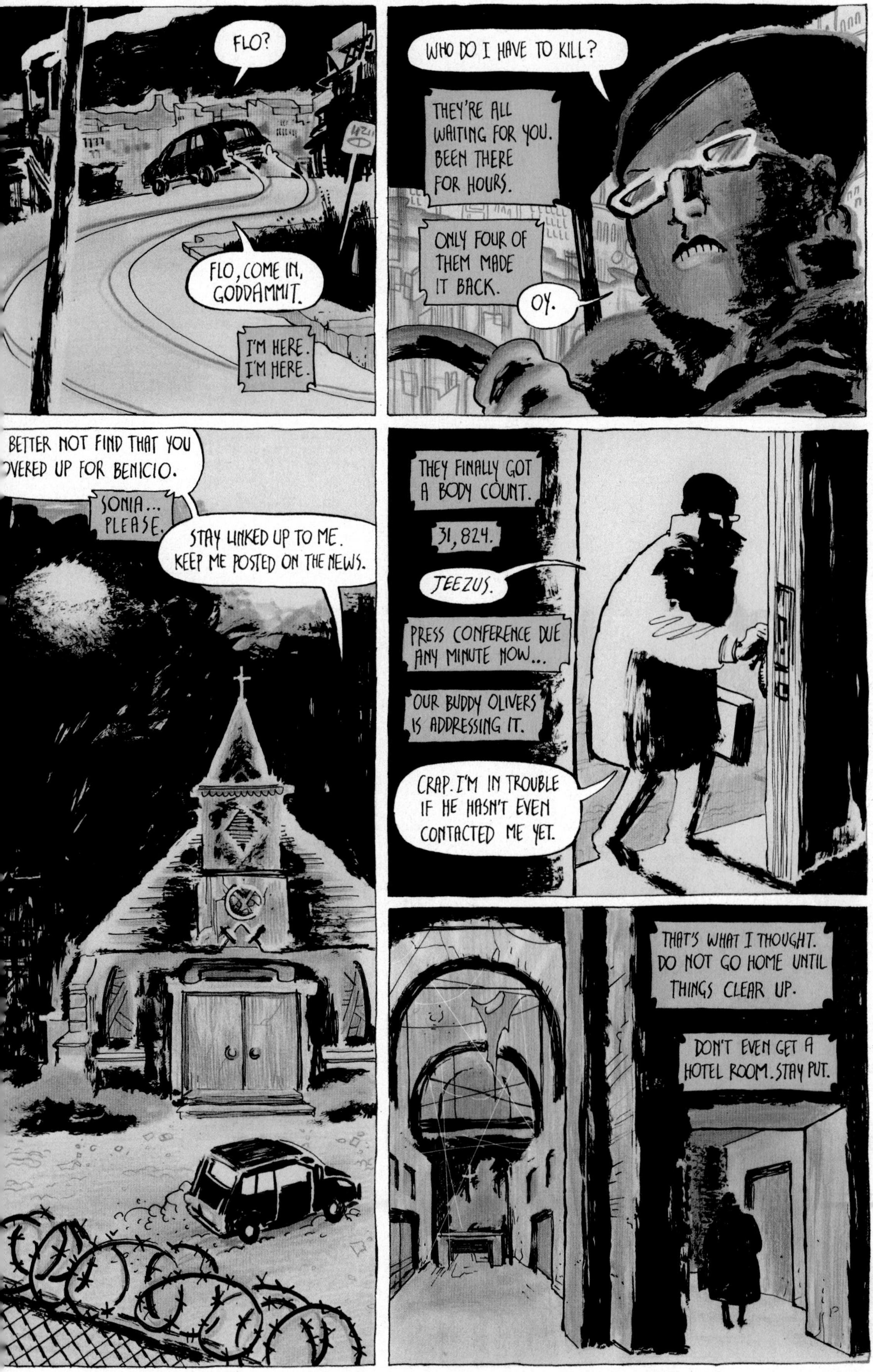
FLO?
FLO, COME IN, GODDAMMIT.
I'M HERE. I'M HERE.
WHO DO I HAVE TO KILL?
THEY'RE ALL WAITING FOR YOU. BEEN THERE FOR HOURS.
ONLY FOUR OF THEM MADE IT BACK.
OY.
BETTER NOT FIND THAT YOU COVERED UP FOR BENICIO.
SONIA... PLEASE.
STAY LINKED UP TO ME. KEEP ME POSTED ON THE NEWS.
THEY FINALLY GOT A BODY COUNT.
31,824.
JEEZUS.
PRESS CONFERENCE DUE ANY MINUTE NOW...
OUR BUDDY OLIVERS IS ADDRESSING IT.
CRAP. I'M IN TROUBLE IF HE HASN'T EVEN CONTACTED ME YET.
THAT'S WHAT I THOUGHT. DO NOT GO HOME UNTIL THINGS CLEAR UP.
DON'T EVEN GET A HOTEL ROOM. STAY PUT.

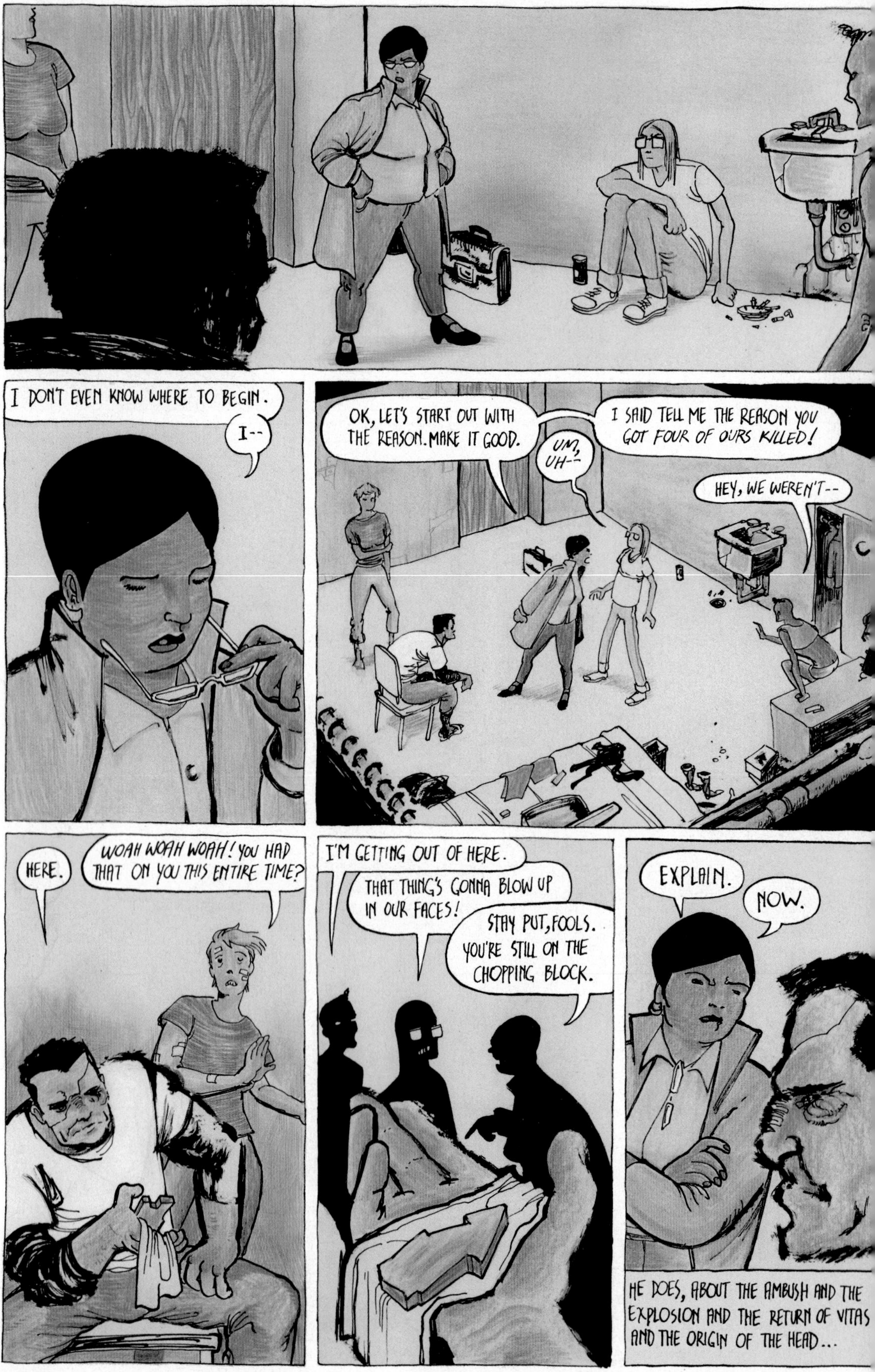
I DON'T EVEN KNOW WHERE TO BEGIN.
I--
OK, LET'S START OUT WITH THE REASON. MAKE IT GOOD.
UM, UH--
I SAID TELL ME THE REASON YOU GOT FOUR OF OURS KILLED!
HEY, WE WEREN'T--
HERE.
WOAH WOAH WOAH! YOU HAD THAT ON YOU THIS ENTIRE TIME?
I'M GETTING OUT OF HERE.
THAT THING'S GONNA BLOW UP IN OUR FACES!
STAY PUT, FOOLS. YOU'RE STILL ON THE CHOPPING BLOCK.
EXPLAIN.
NOW.
HE DOES, ABOUT THE AMBUSH AND THE EXPLOSION AND THE RETURN OF VITAS AND THE ORIGIN OF THE HEAD...

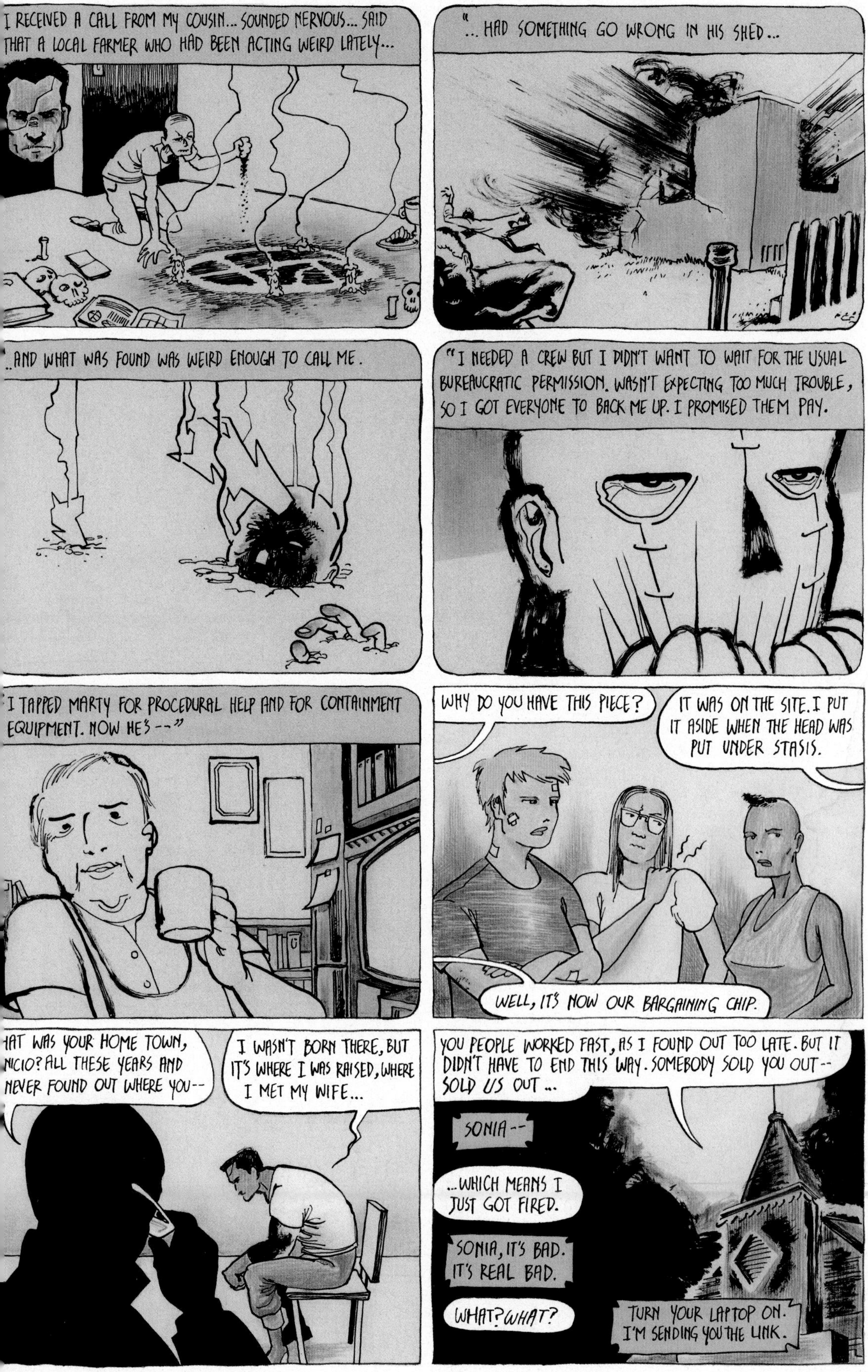
I RECEIVED A CALL FROM MY COUSIN... SOUNDED NERVOUS... SAID THAT A LOCAL FARMER WHO HAD BEEN ACTING WEIRD LATELY...
"...HAD SOMETHING GO WRONG IN HIS SHED...
..AND WHAT WAS FOUND WAS WEIRD ENOUGH TO CALL ME.
"I NEEDED A CREW BUT I DIDN'T WANT TO WAIT FOR THE USUAL BUREAUCRATIC PERMISSION. WASN'T EXPECTING TOO MUCH TROUBLE, SO I GOT EVERYONE TO BACK ME UP. I PROMISED THEM PAY.
"I TAPPED MARTY FOR PROCEDURAL HELP AND FOR CONTAINMENT EQUIPMENT. NOW HE'S --"
WHY DO YOU HAVE THIS PIECE?
IT WAS ON THE SITE. I PUT IT ASIDE WHEN THE HEAD WAS PUT UNDER STASIS.
WELL, IT'S NOW OUR BARGAINING CHIP.
HAT WAS YOUR HOME TOWN, NICIO? ALL THESE YEARS AND NEVER FOUND OUT WHERE YOU--
I WASN'T BORN THERE, BUT IT'S WHERE I WAS RAISED, WHERE I MET MY WIFE...
YOU PEOPLE WORKED FAST, AS I FOUND OUT TOO LATE. BUT IT DIDN'T HAVE TO END THIS WAY. SOMEBODY SOLD YOU OUT-- SOLD US OUT...
SONIA--
...WHICH MEANS I JUST GOT FIRED.
SONIA, IT'S BAD. IT'S REAL BAD.
WHAT? WHAT?
TURN YOUR LAPTOP ON. I'M SENDING YOU THE LINK.

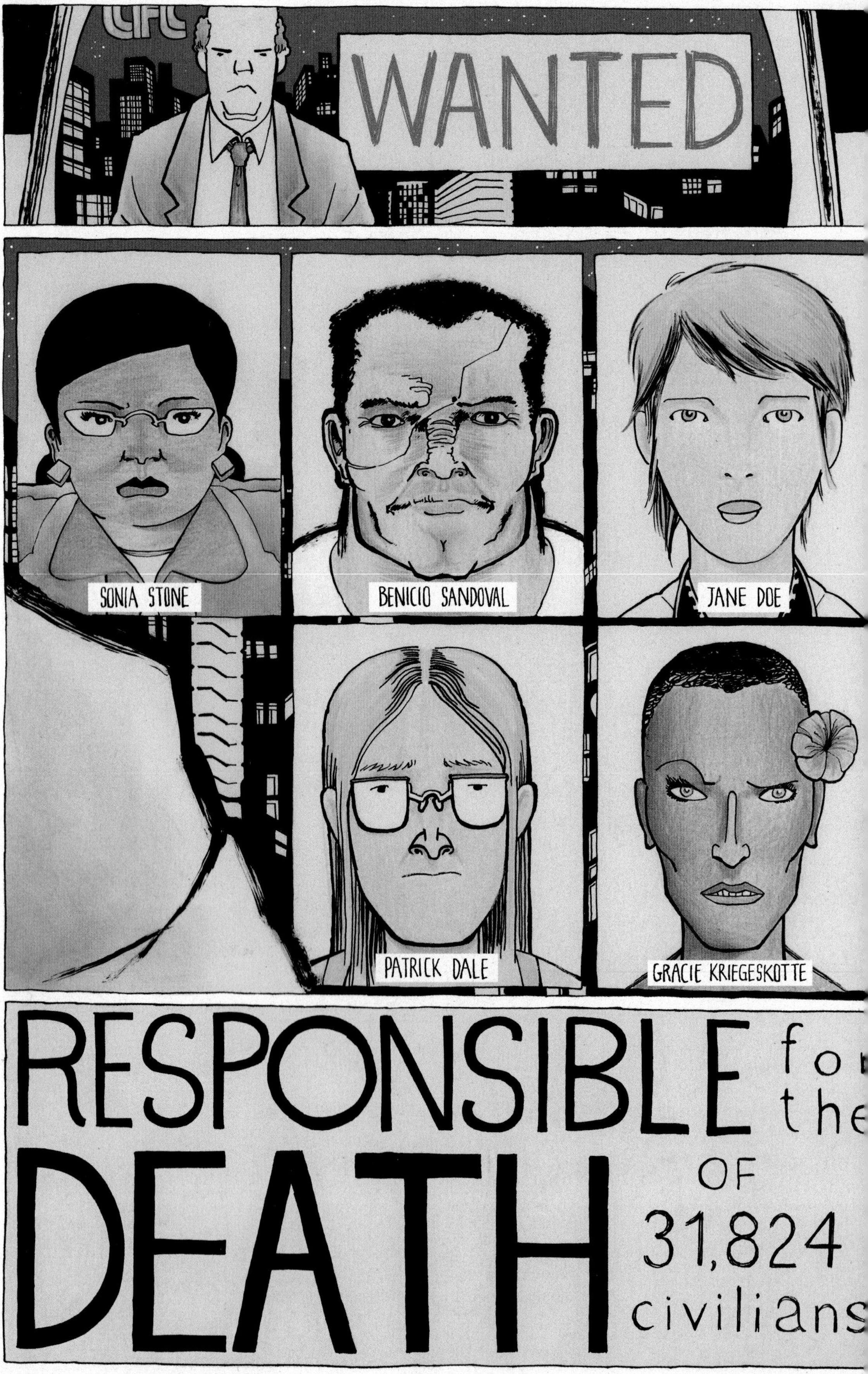
WANTED
SONIA STONE
BENICIO SANDOVAL
JANE DOE
PATRICK DALE
GRACIE KRIEGESKOTTE
RESPONSIBLE for the
DEATH OF 31,824 civilians

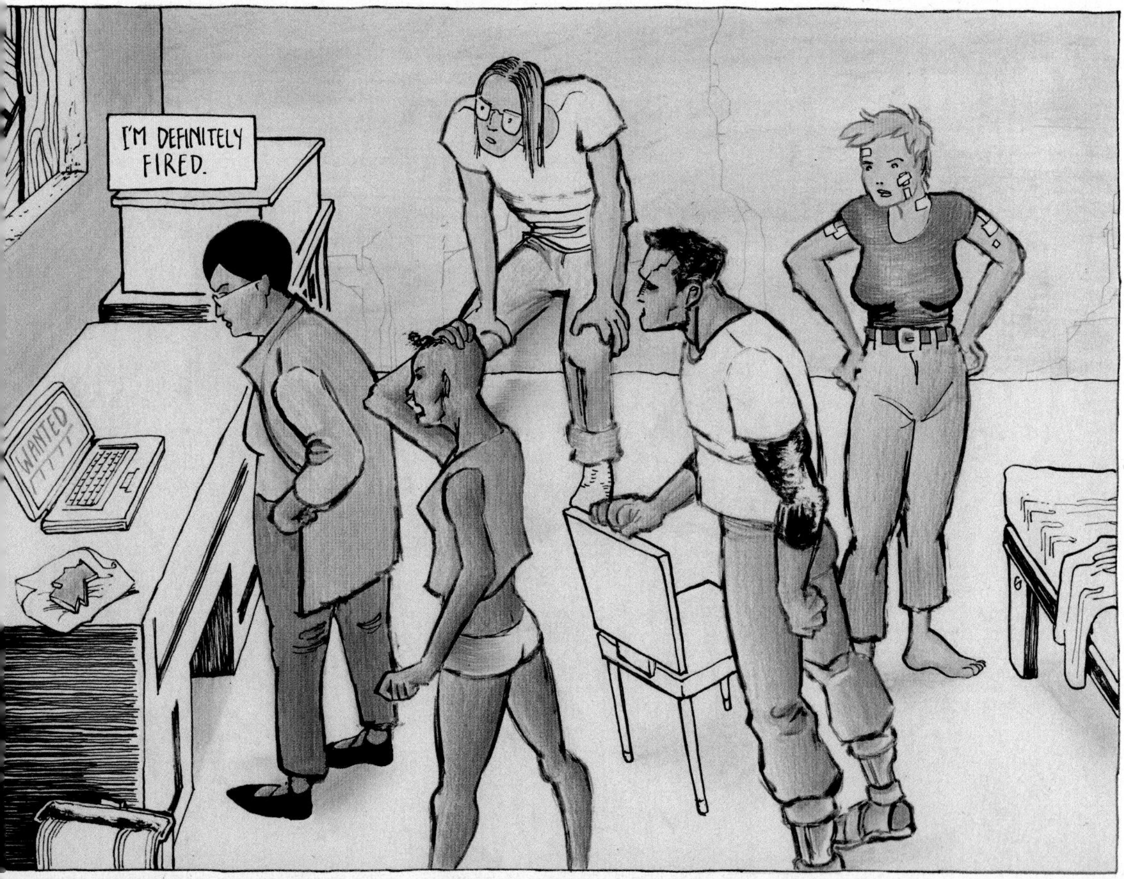
I'M DEFINITELY FIRED.
WANTED

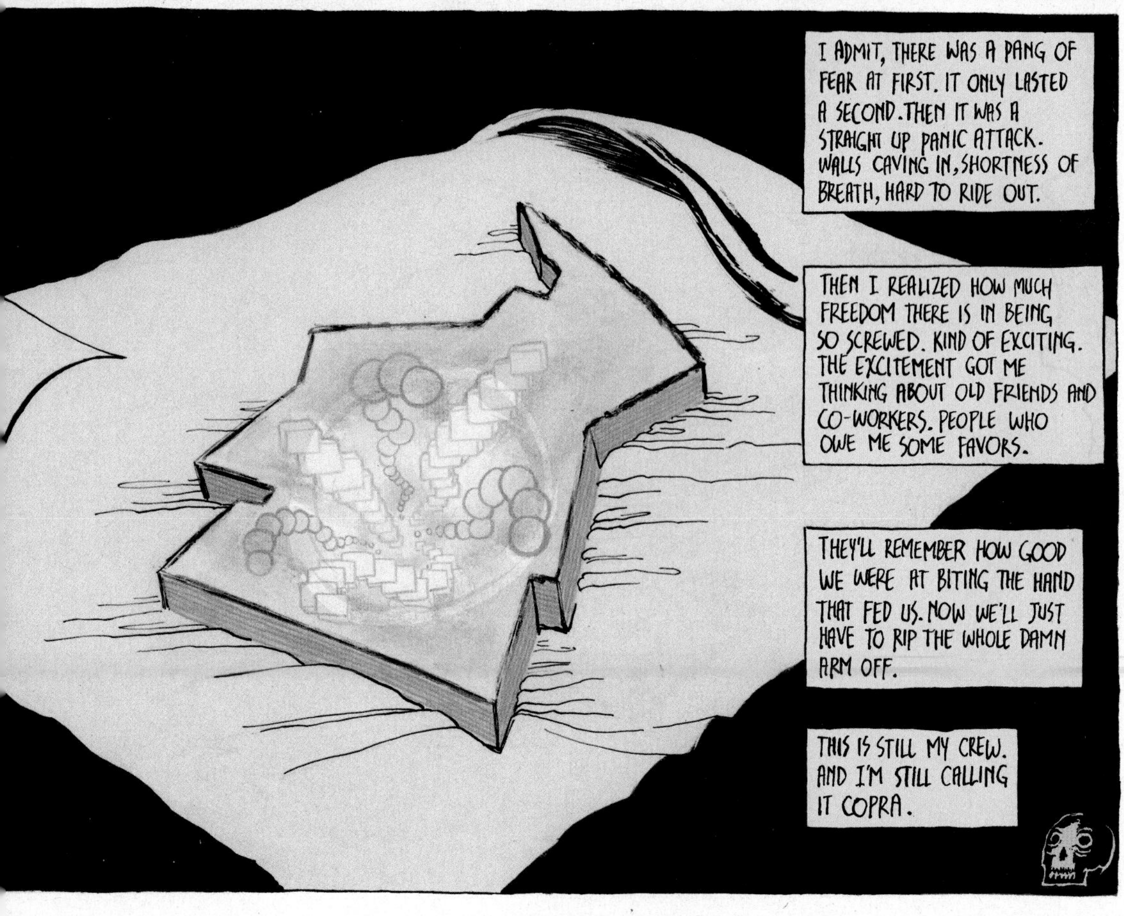
I ADMIT, THERE WAS A PANG OF FEAR AT FIRST. IT ONLY LASTED A SECOND. THEN IT WAS A STRAIGHT UP PANIC ATTACK. WALLS CAVING IN, SHORTNESS OF BREATH, HARD TO RIDE OUT.
THEN I REALIZED HOW MUCH FREEDOM THERE IS IN BEING SO SCREWED. KIND OF EXCITING. THE EXCITEMENT GOT ME THINKING ABOUT OLD FRIENDS AND CO-WORKERS. PEOPLE WHO OWE ME SOME FAVORS.
THEY'LL REMEMBER HOW GOOD WE WERE AT BITING THE HAND THAT FED US. NOW WE'LL JUST HAVE TO RIP THE WHOLE DAMN ARM OFF.
THIS IS STILL MY CREW. AND I'M STILL CALLING IT COPRA.

COMING SOON IN COPRA

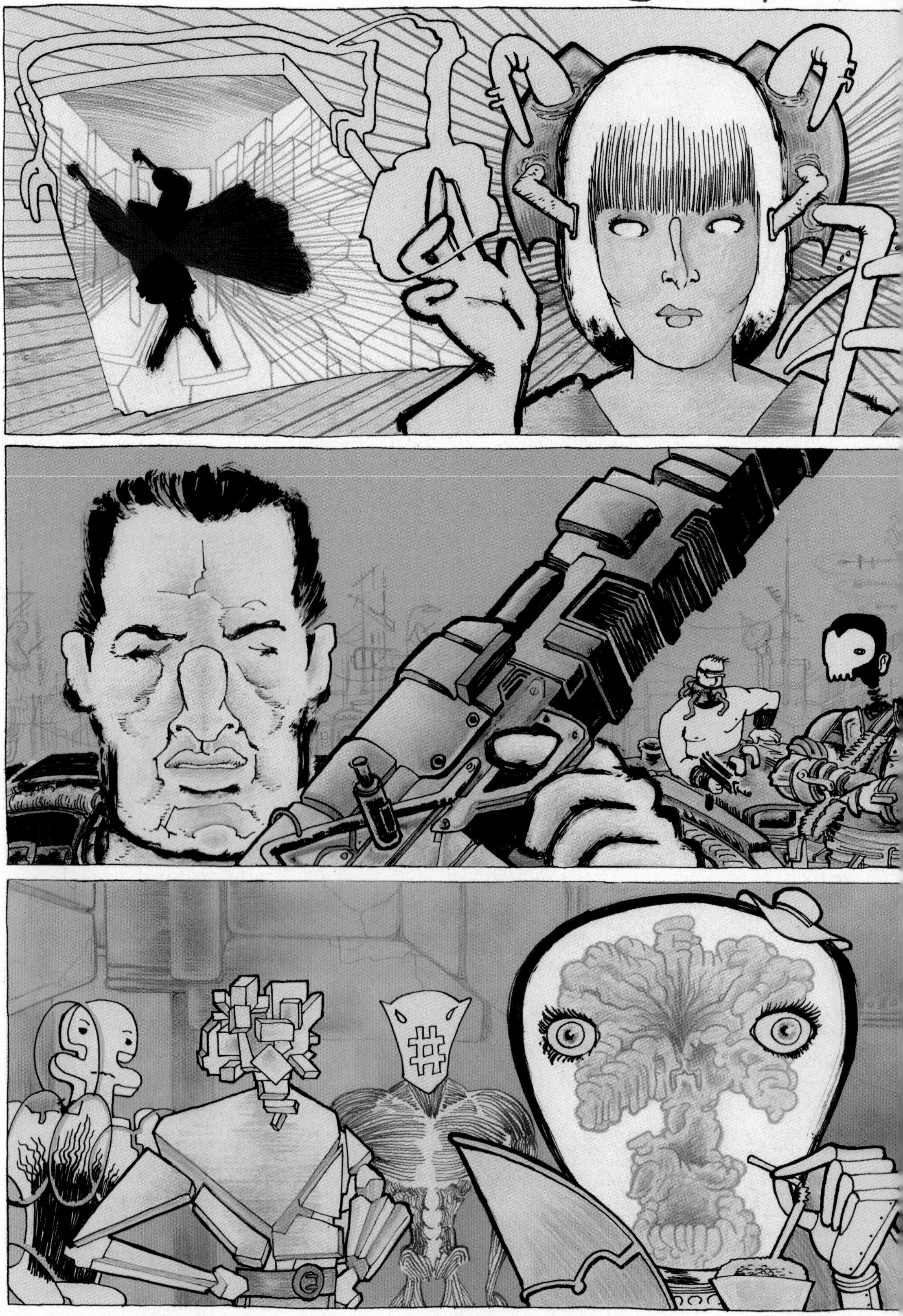

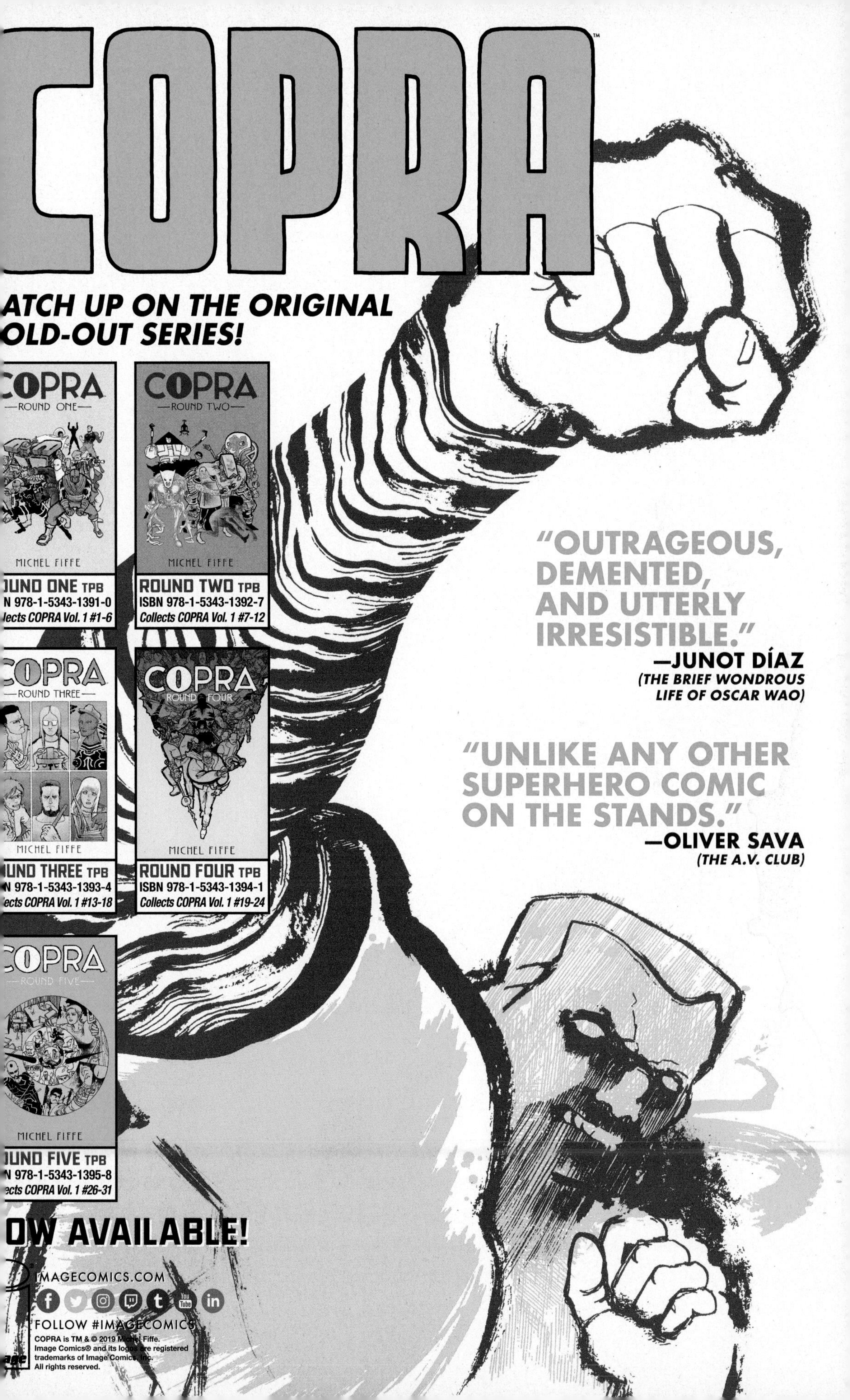
COPRA™
ATCH UP ON THE ORIGINAL
OLD-OUT SERIES!
COPRA
—ROUND ONE—
MICHEL FIFFE
UND ONE TPB
N 978-1-5343-1391-0
lects COPRA Vol. 1 #1-6
COPRA
—ROUND TWO—
MICHEL FIFFE
ROUND TWO TPB
ISBN 978-1-5343-1392-7
Collects COPRA Vol. 1 #7-12
COPRA
—ROUND THREE—
MICHEL FIFFE
UND THREE TPB
N 978-1-5343-1393-4
lects COPRA Vol. 1 #13-18
COPRA
ROUND FOUR
MICHEL FIFFE
ROUND FOUR TPB
ISBN 978-1-5343-1394-1
Collects COPRA Vol. 1 #19-24
COPRA
—ROUND FIVE—
MICHEL FIFFE
UND FIVE TPB
N 978-1-5343-1395-8
lects COPRA Vol. 1 #26-31
"OUTRAGEOUS, DEMENTED, AND UTTERLY IRRESISTIBLE."
—JUNOT DÍAZ
(THE BRIEF WONDROUS LIFE OF OSCAR WAO)
"UNLIKE ANY OTHER SUPERHERO COMIC ON THE STANDS."
—OLIVER SAVA
(THE A.V. CLUB)
OW AVAILABLE!
IMAGECOMICS.COM
FOLLOW #IMAGECOMICS
COPRA is TM & © 2019 Michel Fiffe.
Image Comics® and its logos are registered trademarks of Image Comics, Inc.
All rights reserved.

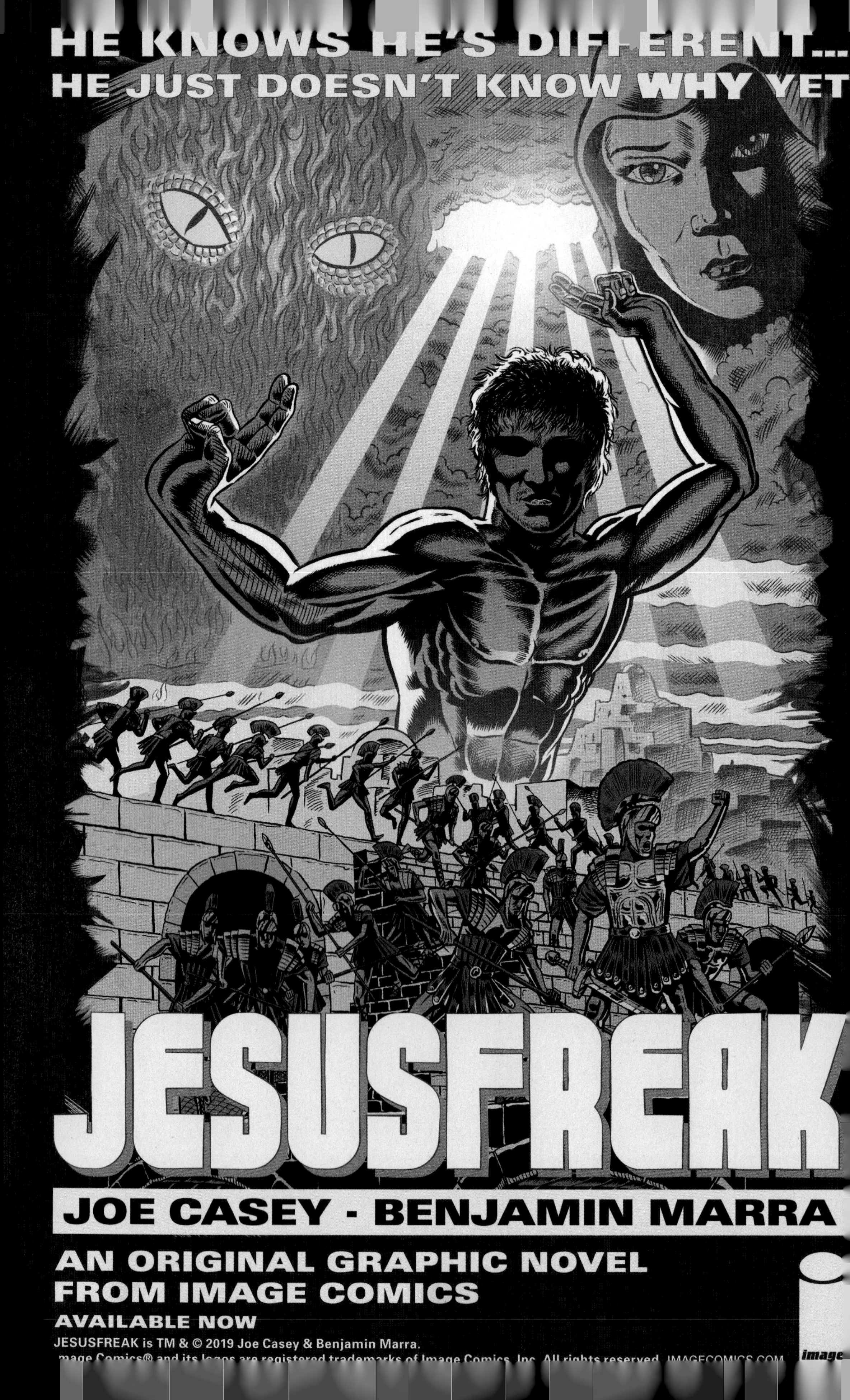
HE KNOWS HE'S DIFFERENT...
HE JUST DOESN'T KNOW WHY YET
JESUSFREAK
JOE CASEY - BENJAMIN MARRA
AN ORIGINAL GRAPHIC NOVEL
FROM IMAGE COMICS
AVAILABLE NOW
JESUSFREAK is TM & © 2019 Joe Casey & Benjamin Marra.
image

ADVENTURE AWAITS IN ANDREW MACLEAN'

HEAD LOPPER

MICHEL FIFFE
BLOODSTRIKE
BRUTALISTS

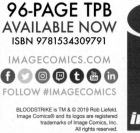

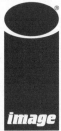

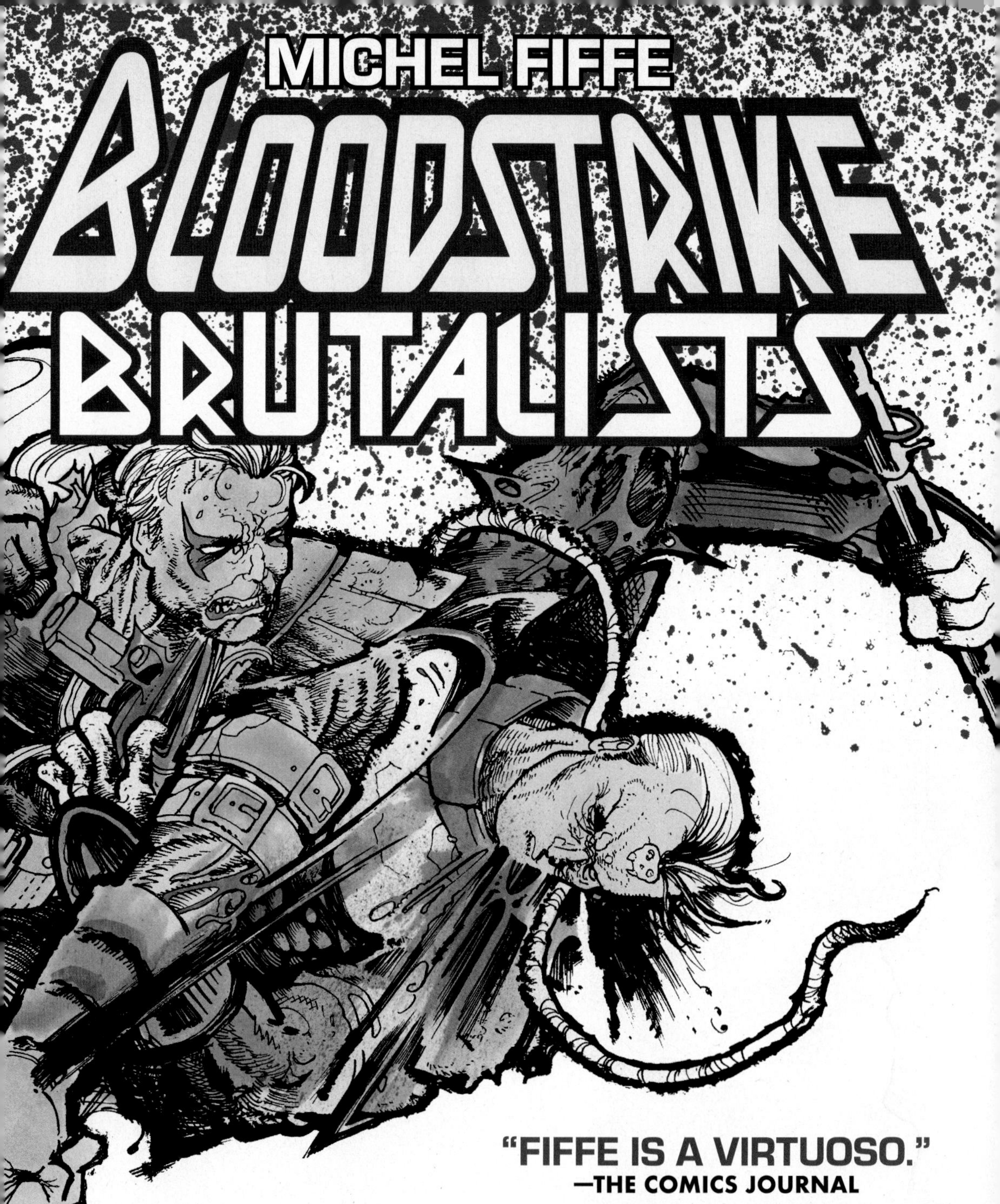

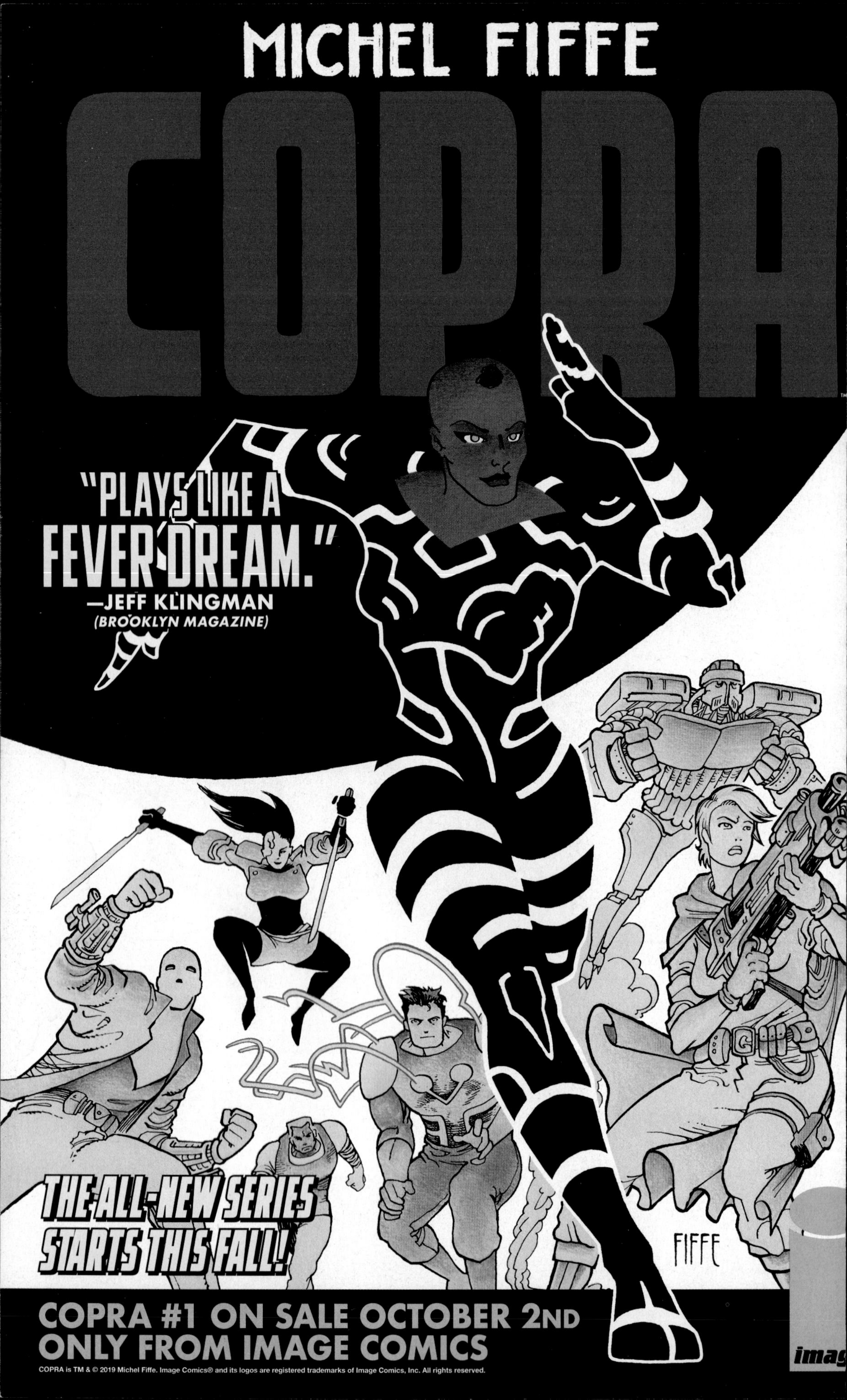
MICHEL FIFFE
COPRA™
"PLAYS LIKE A FEVER DREAM."
—JEFF KLINGMAN
(BROOKLYN MAGAZINE)
FIFFE
THE ALL-NEW SERIES STARTS THIS FALL!
COPRA #1 ON SALE OCTOBER 2ND
ONLY FROM IMAGE COMICS
COPRA is TM & © 2019 Michel Fiffe. Image Comics® and its logos are registered trademarks of Image Comics, Inc. All rights reserved.

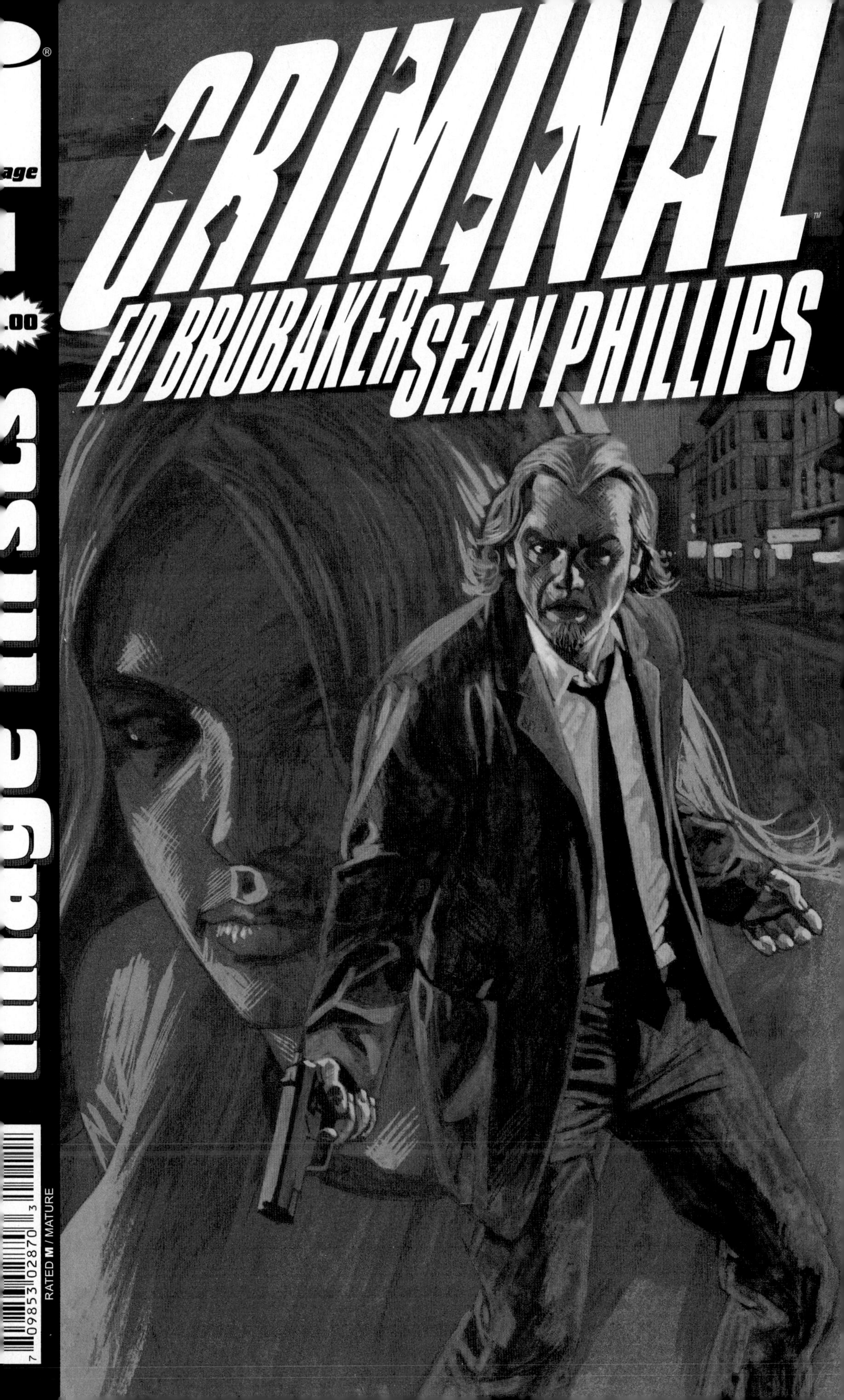
CRIMINAL
ED BRUBAKER
SEAN PHILLIPS
RATED M / MATURE

by
**Ed Brubaker and
Sean Phillips**

**Colors by
Val
Staples**

IMAGE COMICS, INC.
Robert Kirkman: Chief Operating Officer
Erik Larsen: Chief Financial Officer
Todd McFarlane: President
Marc Silvestri: Chief Executive Officer
Jim Valentino: Vice President
Eric Stephenson: Publisher / Chief Creative Officer
Jeff Boison: Director of Publishing Planning & Book Trade Sales
Chris Ross: Director of Digital Sales
Jeff Stang: Director of Direct Market Sales
Kat Salazar: Director of PR & Marketing
Drew Gill: Art Director
Heather Doornink: Production Director
Nicole Lapalme: Controller
IMAGECOMICS.COM

 Publication design by Sean Phillips

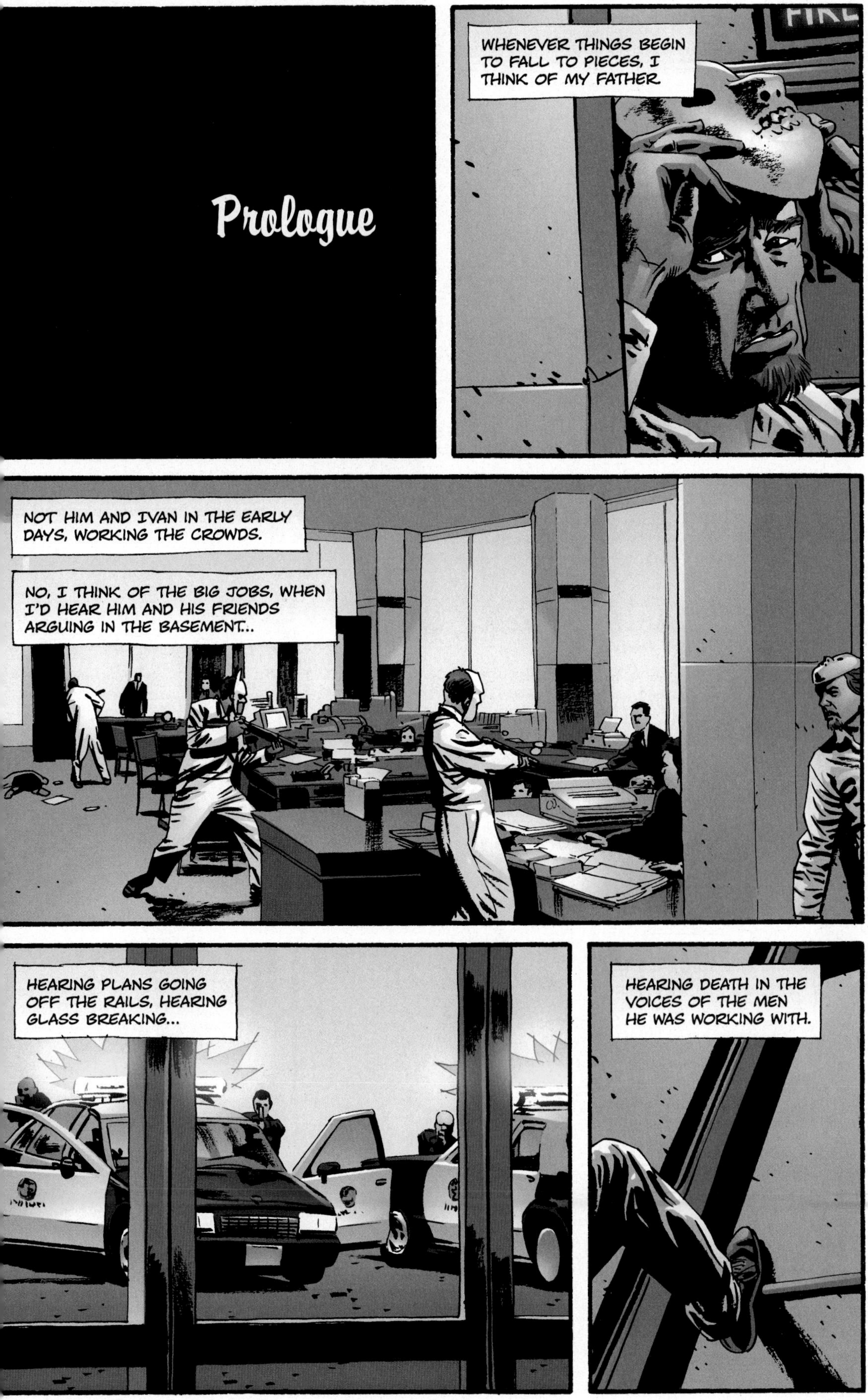
Prologue
WHENEVER THINGS BEGIN TO FALL TO PIECES, I THINK OF MY FATHER
NOT HIM AND IVAN IN THE EARLY DAYS, WORKING THE CROWDS.
NO, I THINK OF THE BIG JOBS, WHEN I'D HEAR HIM AND HIS FRIENDS ARGUING IN THE BASEMENT...
HEARING PLANS GOING OFF THE RAILS, HEARING GLASS BREAKING...
HEARING DEATH IN THE VOICES OF THE MEN HE WAS WORKING WITH.

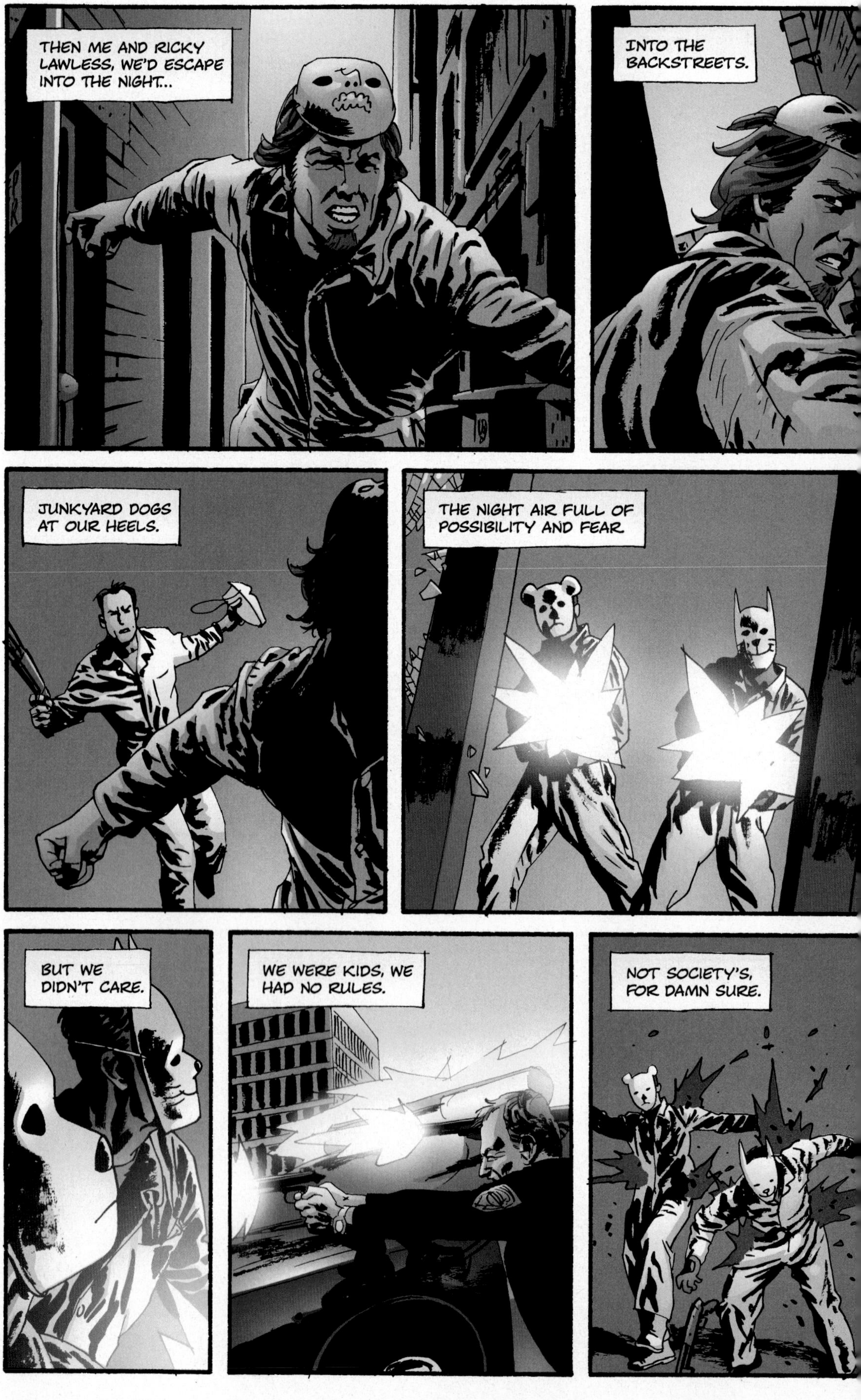
THEN ME AND RICKY LAWLESS, WE'D ESCAPE INTO THE NIGHT...
INTO THE BACKSTREETS.
JUNKYARD DOGS AT OUR HEELS.
THE NIGHT AIR FULL OF POSSIBILITY AND FEAR.
BUT WE DIDN'T CARE.
WE WERE KIDS, WE HAD NO RULES.
NOT SOCIETY'S, FOR DAMN SURE.

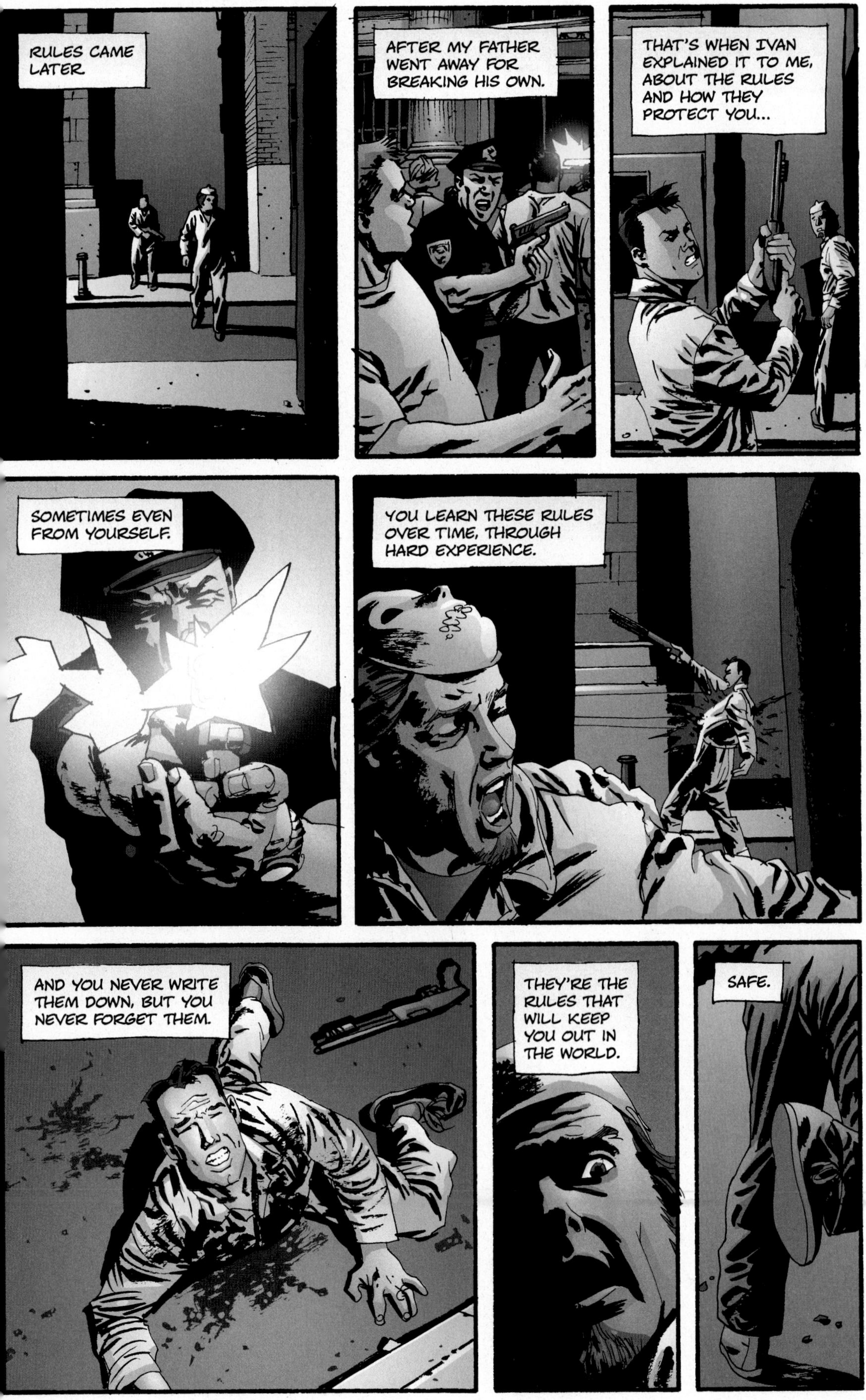
RULES CAME LATER
AFTER MY FATHER WENT AWAY FOR BREAKING HIS OWN.
THAT'S WHEN IVAN EXPLAINED IT TO ME, ABOUT THE RULES AND HOW THEY PROTECT YOU...
SOMETIMES EVEN FROM YOURSELF.
YOU LEARN THESE RULES OVER TIME, THROUGH HARD EXPERIENCE.
AND YOU NEVER WRITE THEM DOWN, BUT YOU NEVER FORGET THEM.
THEY'RE THE RULES THAT WILL KEEP YOU OUT IN THE WORLD.
SAFE.

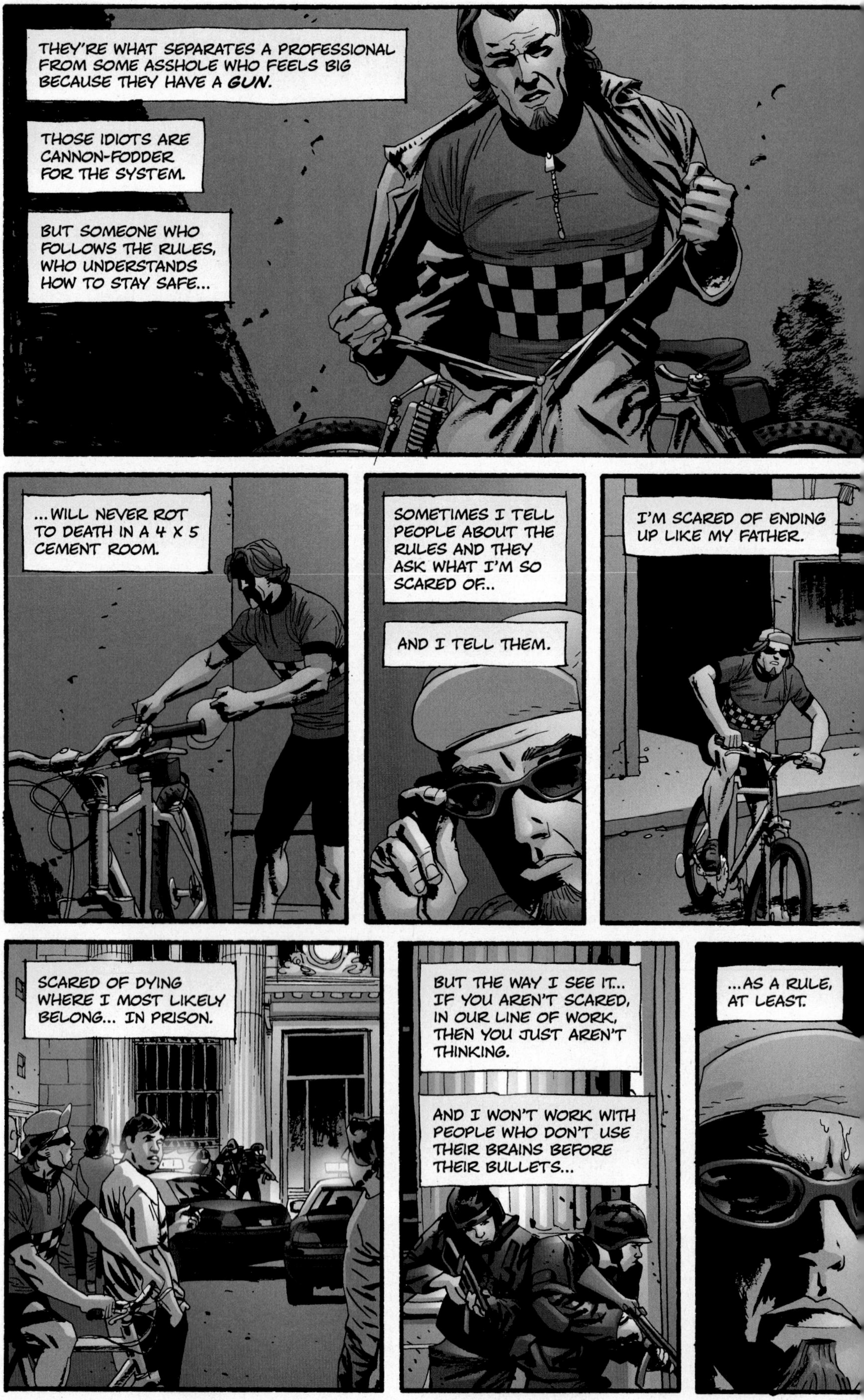
THEY'RE WHAT SEPARATES A PROFESSIONAL FROM SOME ASSHOLE WHO FEELS BIG BECAUSE THEY HAVE A *GUN*.
THOSE IDIOTS ARE CANNON-FODDER FOR THE SYSTEM.
BUT SOMEONE WHO FOLLOWS THE RULES, WHO UNDERSTANDS HOW TO STAY SAFE...
...WILL NEVER ROT TO DEATH IN A 4 X 5 CEMENT ROOM.
SOMETIMES I TELL PEOPLE ABOUT THE RULES AND THEY ASK WHAT I'M SO SCARED OF..
AND I TELL THEM.
I'M SCARED OF ENDING UP LIKE MY FATHER.
SCARED OF DYING WHERE I MOST LIKELY BELONG... IN PRISON.
BUT THE WAY I SEE IT... IF YOU AREN'T SCARED, IN OUR LINE OF WORK, THEN YOU JUST AREN'T THINKING.
AND I WON'T WORK WITH PEOPLE WHO DON'T USE THEIR BRAINS BEFORE THEIR BULLETS...
...AS A RULE, AT LEAST.

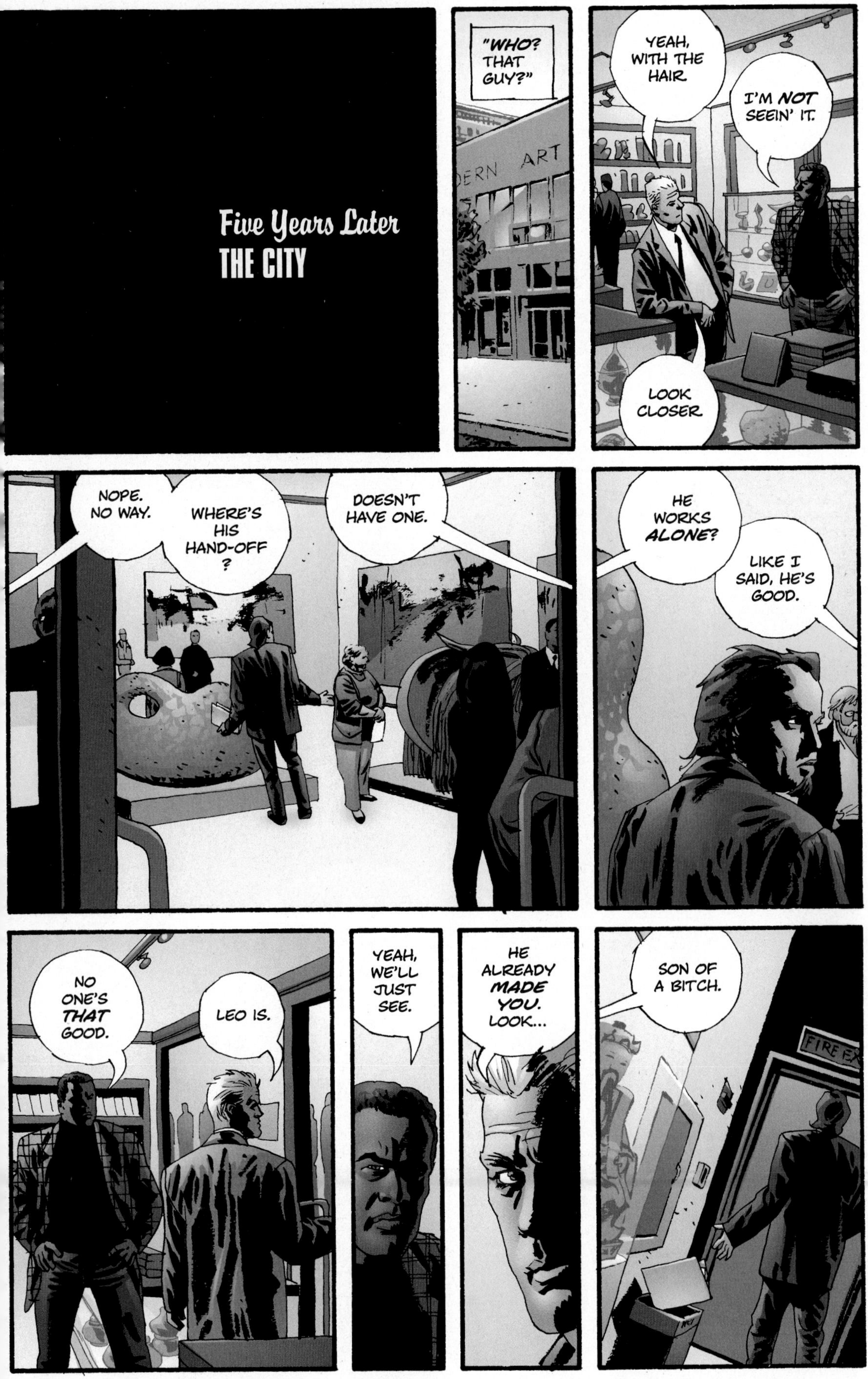
Five Years Later
THE CITY
"WHO? THAT GUY?"
YEAH, WITH THE HAIR
I'M NOT SEEIN' IT.
LOOK CLOSER
NOPE. NO WAY.
WHERE'S HIS HAND-OFF ?
DOESN'T HAVE ONE.
HE WORKS ALONE?
LIKE I SAID, HE'S GOOD.
NO ONE'S THAT GOOD.
LEO IS.
YEAH, WE'LL JUST SEE.
HE ALREADY MADE YOU. LOOK...
SON OF A BITCH.
FIRE EX

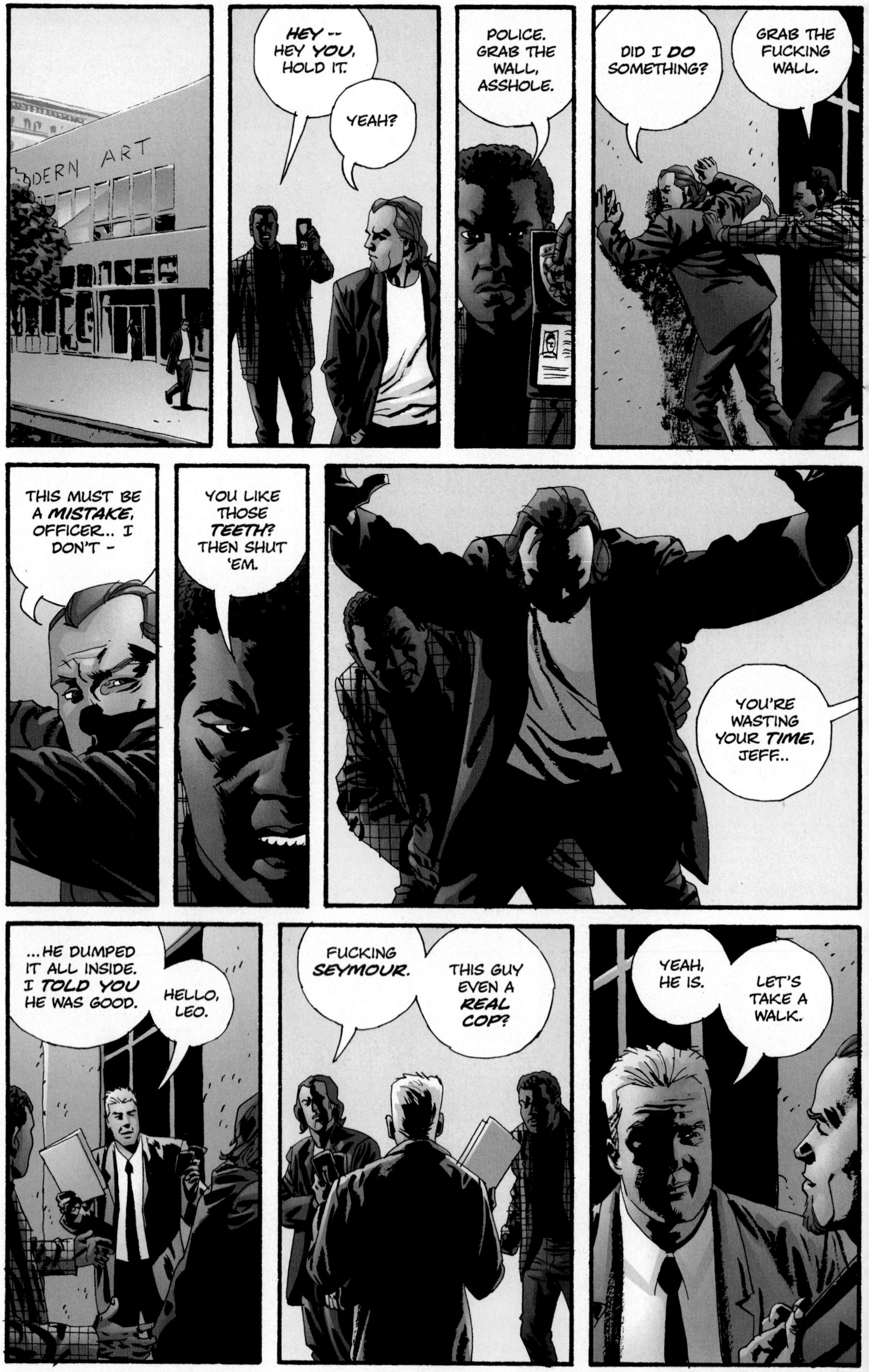

DERN ART
HEY -- HEY YOU, HOLD IT.
YEAH?
POLICE. GRAB THE WALL, ASSHOLE.
DID I DO SOMETHING?
GRAB THE FUCKING WALL.
THIS MUST BE A MISTAKE, OFFICER... I DON'T -
YOU LIKE THOSE TEETH? THEN SHUT 'EM.
YOU'RE WASTING YOUR TIME, JEFF...
...HE DUMPED IT ALL INSIDE. I TOLD YOU HE WAS GOOD.
HELLO, LEO.
FUCKING SEYMOUR.
THIS GUY EVEN A REAL COP?
YEAH, HE IS.
LET'S TAKE A WALK.

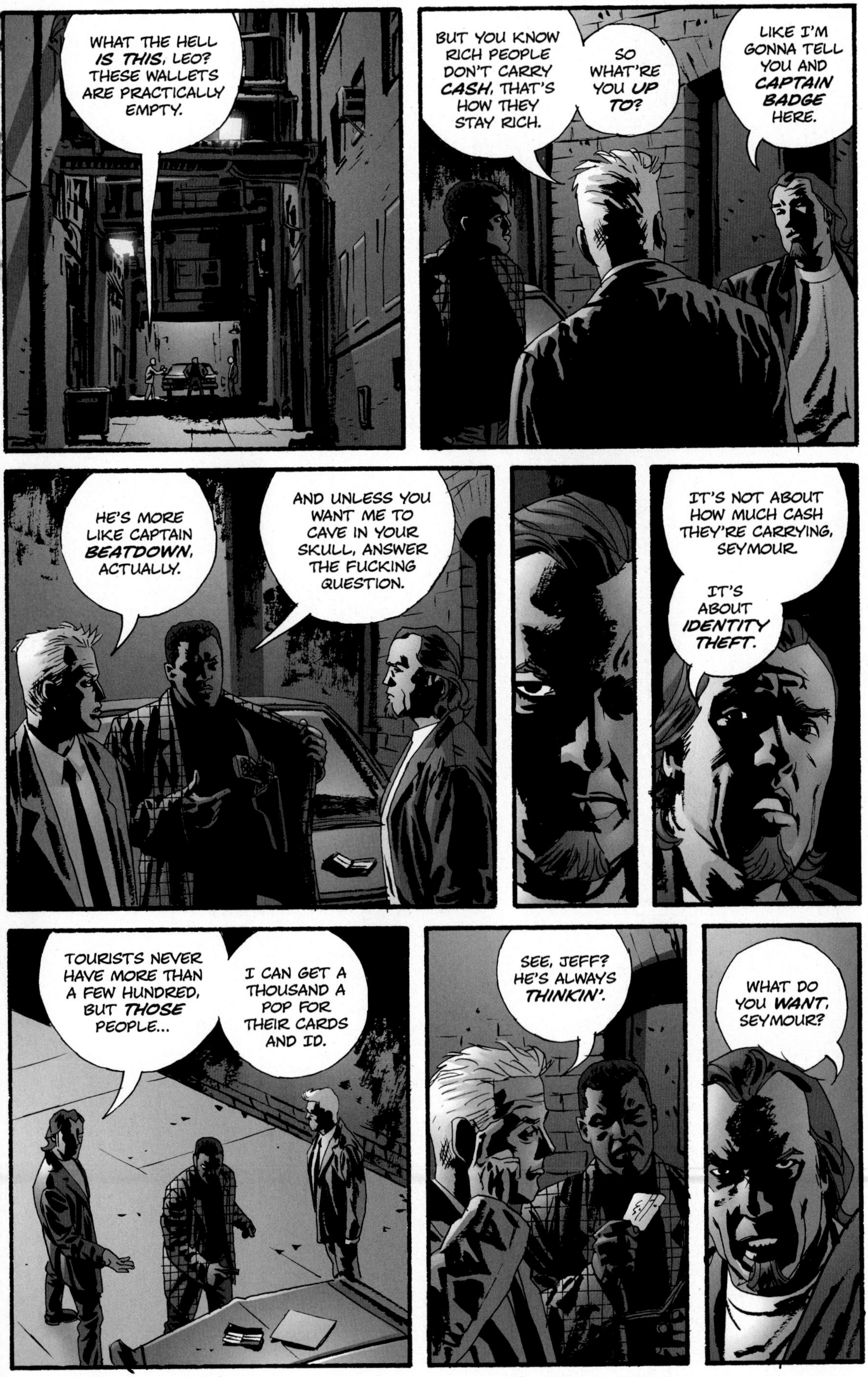
WHAT THE HELL IS THIS, LEO? THESE WALLETS ARE PRACTICALLY EMPTY.
BUT YOU KNOW RICH PEOPLE DON'T CARRY CASH, THAT'S HOW THEY STAY RICH.
SO WHAT'RE YOU UP TO?
LIKE I'M GONNA TELL YOU AND CAPTAIN BADGE HERE.
HE'S MORE LIKE CAPTAIN BEATDOWN, ACTUALLY.
AND UNLESS YOU WANT ME TO CAVE IN YOUR SKULL, ANSWER THE FUCKING QUESTION.
IT'S NOT ABOUT HOW MUCH CASH THEY'RE CARRYING, SEYMOUR.
IT'S ABOUT IDENTITY THEFT.
TOURISTS NEVER HAVE MORE THAN A FEW HUNDRED, BUT THOSE PEOPLE...
I CAN GET A THOUSAND A POP FOR THEIR CARDS AND ID.
SEE, JEFF? HE'S ALWAYS THINKIN'.
WHAT DO YOU WANT, SEYMOUR?

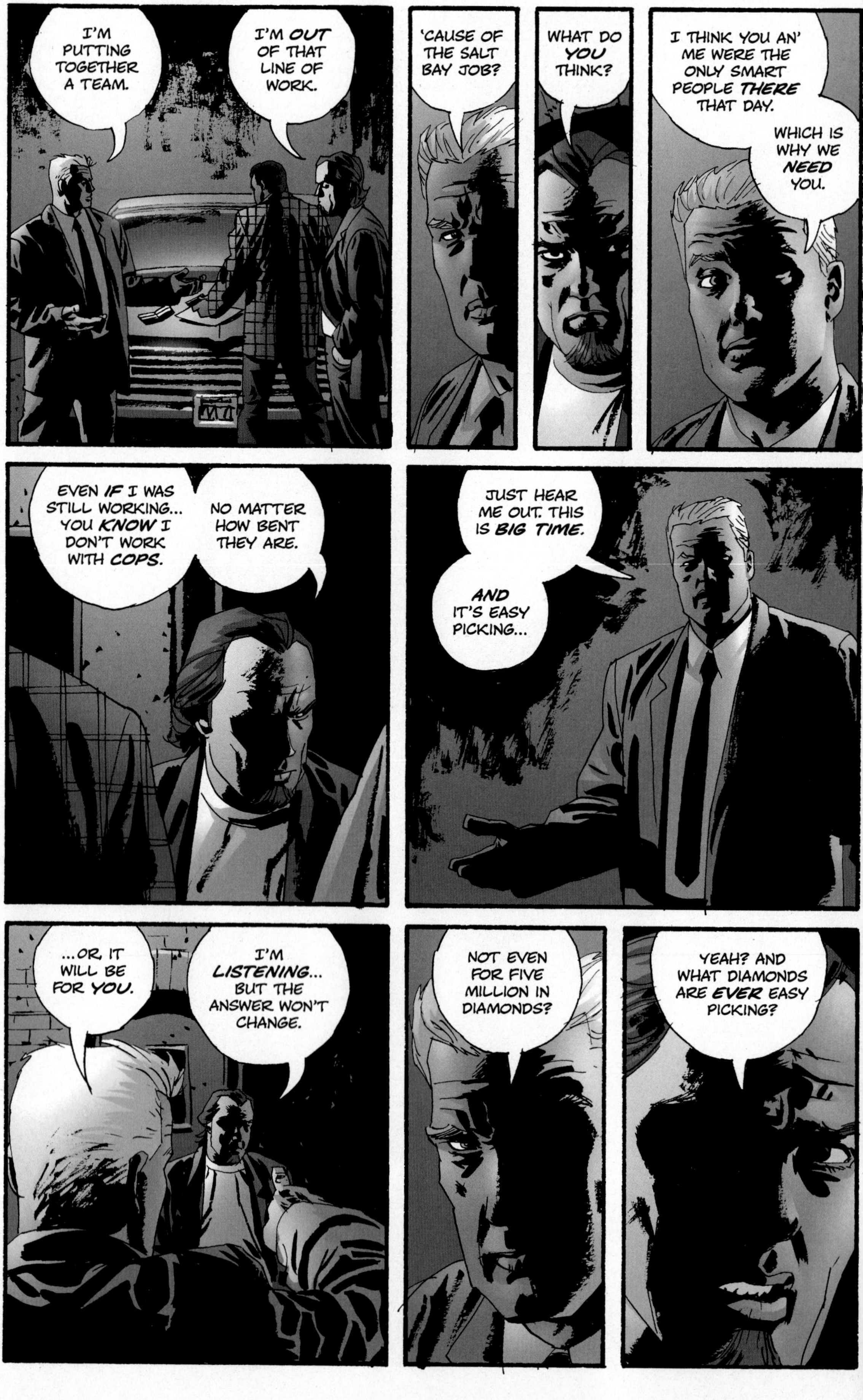
I'M PUTTING TOGETHER A TEAM.
I'M OUT OF THAT LINE OF WORK.
'CAUSE OF THE SALT BAY JOB?
WHAT DO YOU THINK?
I THINK YOU AN' ME WERE THE ONLY SMART PEOPLE THERE THAT DAY.
WHICH IS WHY WE NEED YOU.
EVEN IF I WAS STILL WORKING... YOU KNOW I DON'T WORK WITH COPS.
NO MATTER HOW BENT THEY ARE.
JUST HEAR ME OUT. THIS IS BIG TIME.
AND IT'S EASY PICKING...
...OR, IT WILL BE FOR YOU.
I'M LISTENING... BUT THE ANSWER WON'T CHANGE.
NOT EVEN FOR FIVE MILLION IN DIAMONDS?
YEAH? AND WHAT DIAMONDS ARE EVER EASY PICKING?

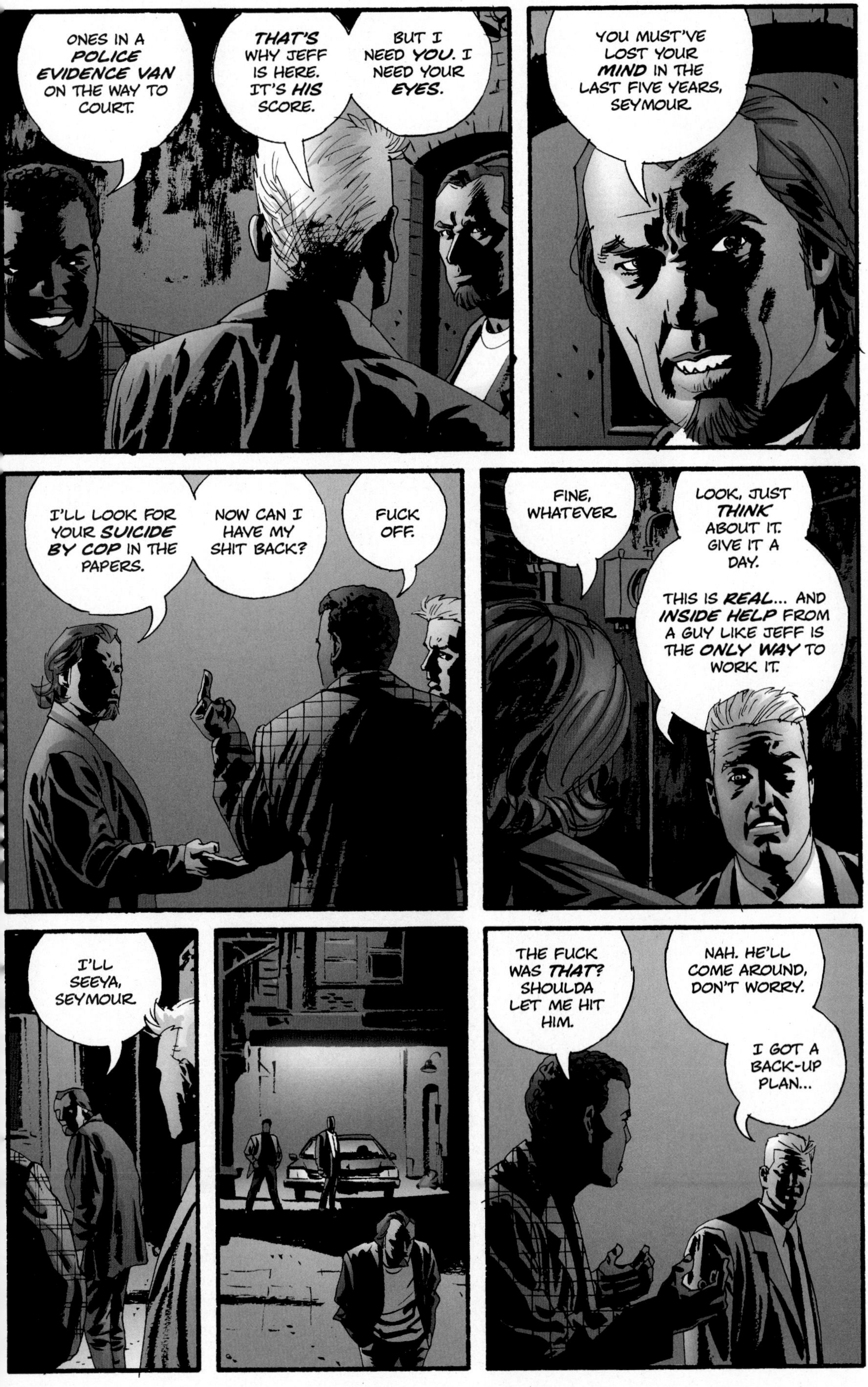
ONES IN A POLICE EVIDENCE VAN ON THE WAY TO COURT.
THAT'S WHY JEFF IS HERE. IT'S HIS SCORE.
BUT I NEED YOU. I NEED YOUR EYES.
YOU MUST'VE LOST YOUR MIND IN THE LAST FIVE YEARS, SEYMOUR
I'LL LOOK FOR YOUR SUICIDE BY COP IN THE PAPERS.
NOW CAN I HAVE MY SHIT BACK?
FUCK OFF.
FINE, WHATEVER
LOOK, JUST THINK ABOUT IT. GIVE IT A DAY.
THIS IS REAL... AND INSIDE HELP FROM A GUY LIKE JEFF IS THE ONLY WAY TO WORK IT.
I'LL SEEYA, SEYMOUR
THE FUCK WAS THAT? SHOULDA LET ME HIT HIM.
NAH. HE'LL COME AROUND, DON'T WORRY.
I GOT A BACK-UP PLAN...

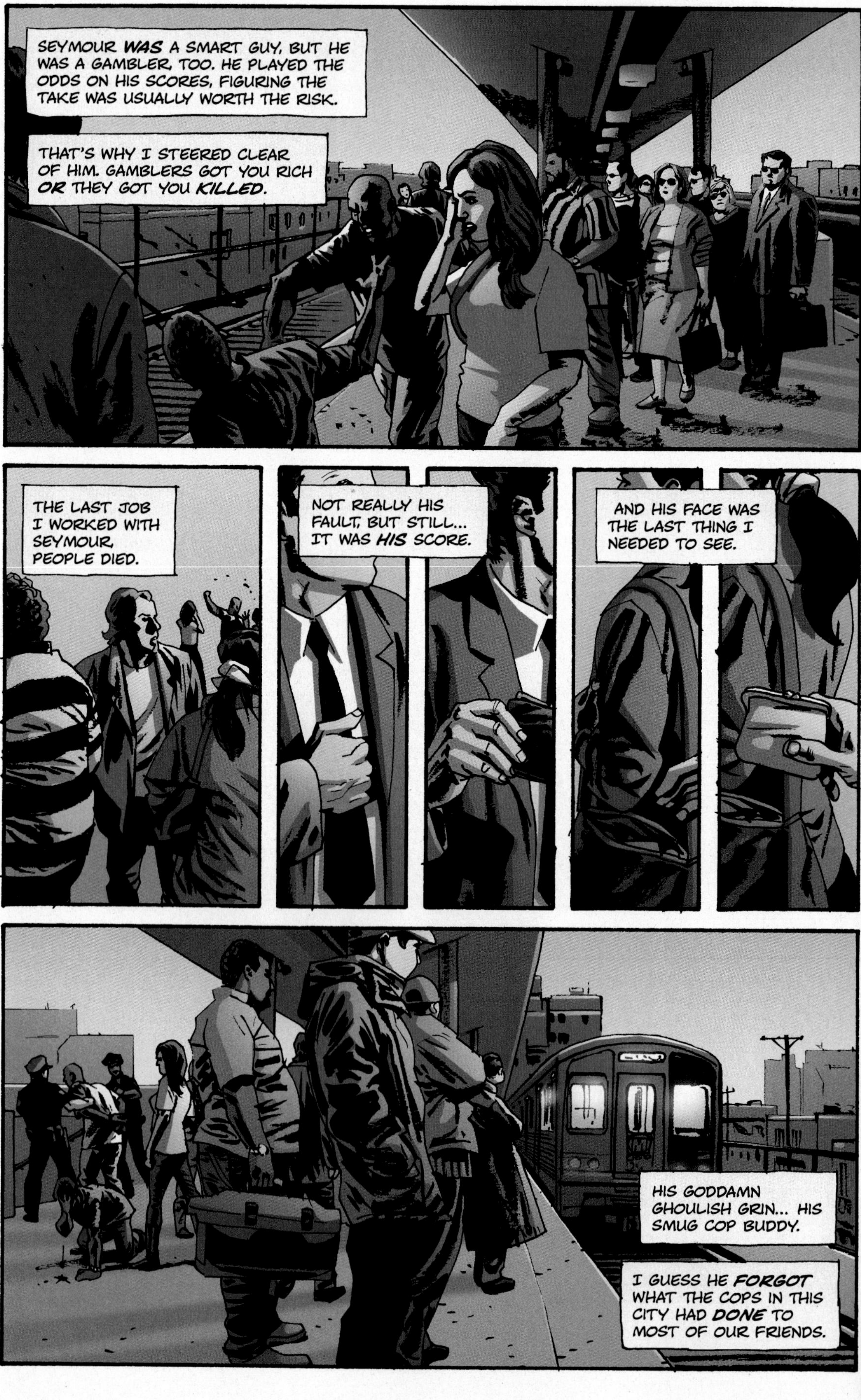
SEYMOUR WAS A SMART GUY, BUT HE WAS A GAMBLER, TOO. HE PLAYED THE ODDS ON HIS SCORES, FIGURING THE TAKE WAS USUALLY WORTH THE RISK.
THAT'S WHY I STEERED CLEAR OF HIM. GAMBLERS GOT YOU RICH OR THEY GOT YOU KILLED.
THE LAST JOB I WORKED WITH SEYMOUR, PEOPLE DIED.
NOT REALLY HIS FAULT, BUT STILL... IT WAS HIS SCORE.
AND HIS FACE WAS THE LAST THING I NEEDED TO SEE.
HIS GODDAMN GHOULISH GRIN... HIS SMUG COP BUDDY.
I GUESS HE FORGOT WHAT THE COPS IN THIS CITY HAD DONE TO MOST OF OUR FRIENDS.

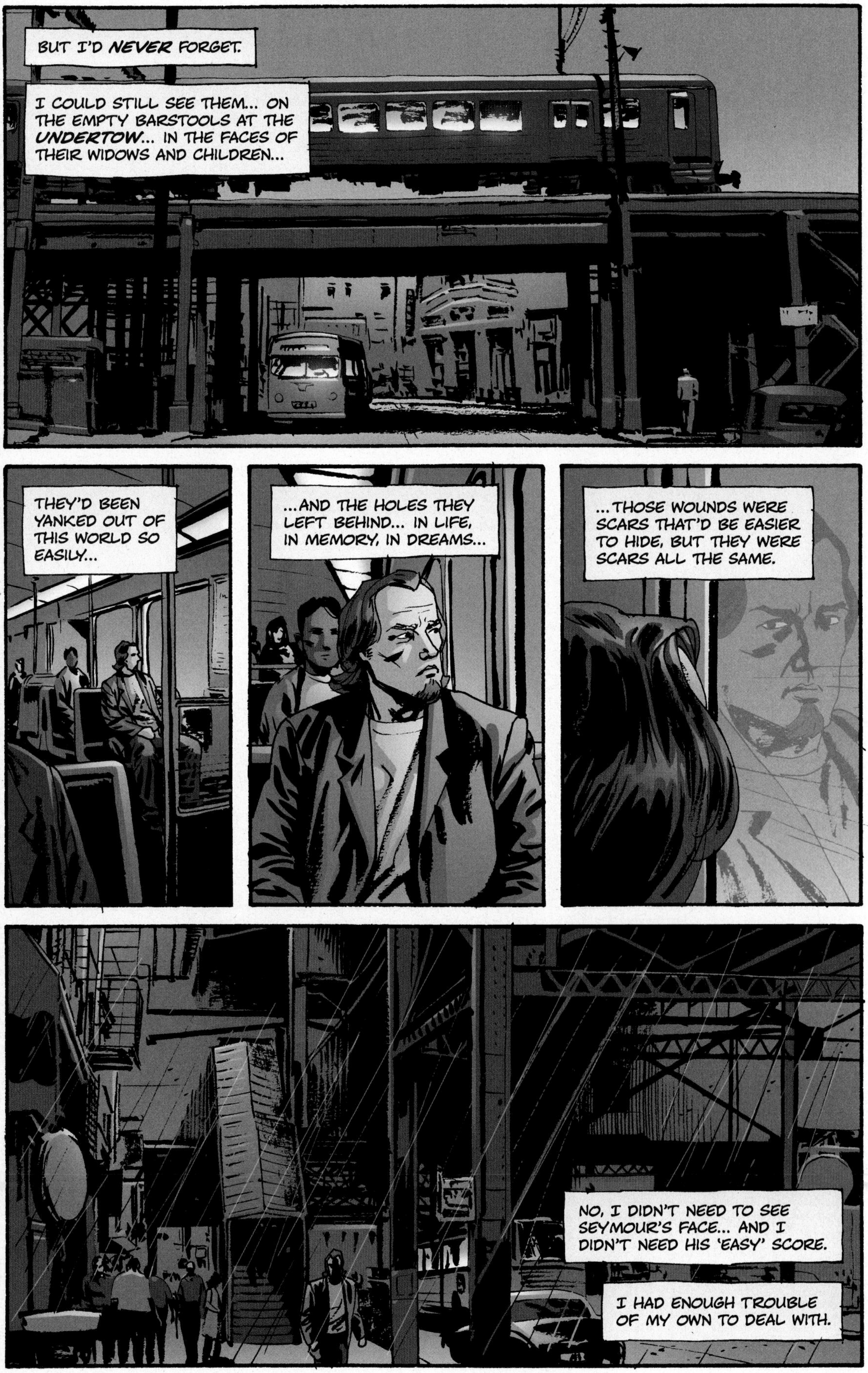
BUT I'D *NEVER* FORGET.
I COULD STILL SEE THEM... ON THE EMPTY BARSTOOLS AT THE *UNDERTOW*... IN THE FACES OF THEIR WIDOWS AND CHILDREN...
THEY'D BEEN YANKED OUT OF THIS WORLD SO EASILY...
...AND THE HOLES THEY LEFT BEHIND... IN LIFE, IN MEMORY, IN DREAMS...
...THOSE WOUNDS WERE SCARS THAT'D BE EASIER TO HIDE, BUT THEY WERE SCARS ALL THE SAME.
NO, I DIDN'T NEED TO SEE SEYMOUR'S FACE... AND I DIDN'T NEED HIS 'EASY' SCORE.
I HAD ENOUGH TROUBLE OF MY OWN TO DEAL WITH.

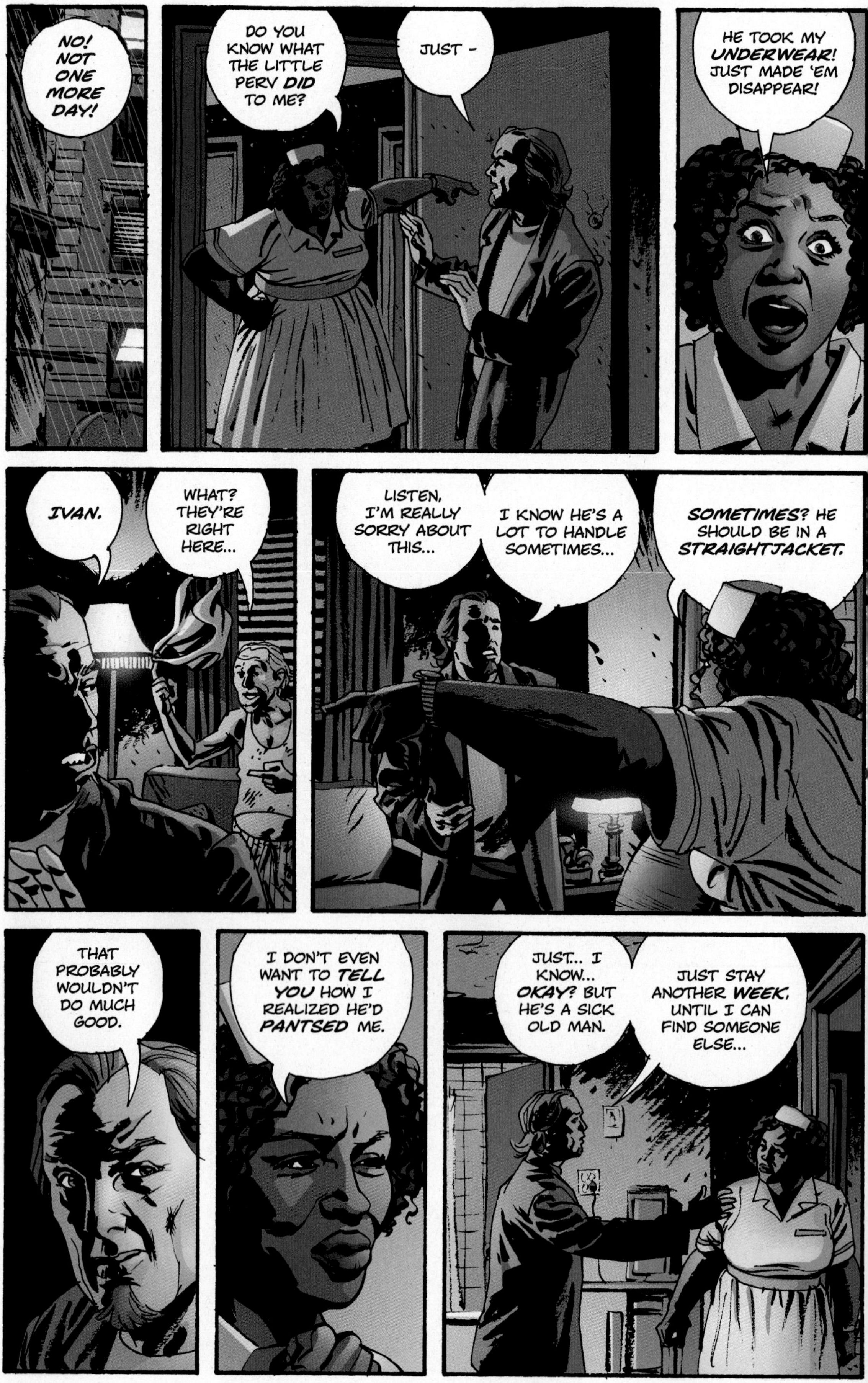
NO! NOT ONE MORE DAY!
DO YOU KNOW WHAT THE LITTLE PERV DID TO ME?
JUST -
HE TOOK MY UNDERWEAR! JUST MADE 'EM DISAPPEAR!
IVAN.
WHAT? THEY'RE RIGHT HERE...
LISTEN, I'M REALLY SORRY ABOUT THIS...
I KNOW HE'S A LOT TO HANDLE SOMETIMES...
SOMETIMES? HE SHOULD BE IN A STRAIGHTJACKET.
THAT PROBABLY WOULDN'T DO MUCH GOOD.
I DON'T EVEN WANT TO TELL YOU HOW I REALIZED HE'D PANTSED ME.
JUST... I KNOW... OKAY? BUT HE'S A SICK OLD MAN.
JUST STAY ANOTHER WEEK, UNTIL I CAN FIND SOMEONE ELSE...

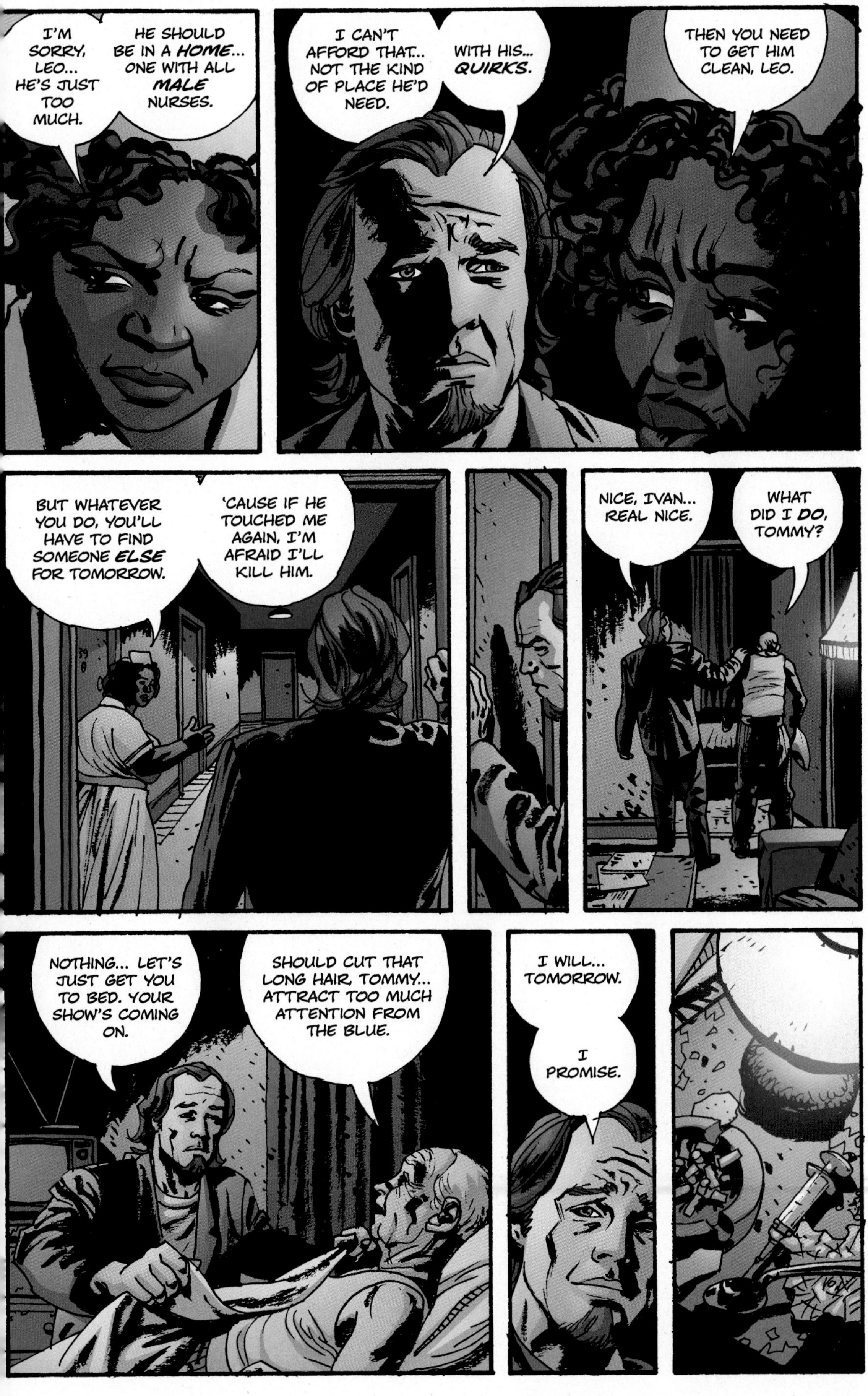
I'M SORRY, LEO... HE'S JUST TOO MUCH.
HE SHOULD BE IN A HOME... ONE WITH ALL MALE NURSES.
I CAN'T AFFORD THAT... NOT THE KIND OF PLACE HE'D NEED.
WITH HIS... QUIRKS.
THEN YOU NEED TO GET HIM CLEAN, LEO.
BUT WHATEVER YOU DO, YOU'LL HAVE TO FIND SOMEONE ELSE FOR TOMORROW.
'CAUSE IF HE TOUCHED ME AGAIN, I'M AFRAID I'LL KILL HIM.
NICE, IVAN... REAL NICE.
WHAT DID I DO, TOMMY?
NOTHING... LET'S JUST GET YOU TO BED. YOUR SHOW'S COMING ON.
SHOULD CUT THAT LONG HAIR, TOMMY... ATTRACT TOO MUCH ATTENTION FROM THE BLUE.
I WILL... TOMORROW.
I PROMISE.

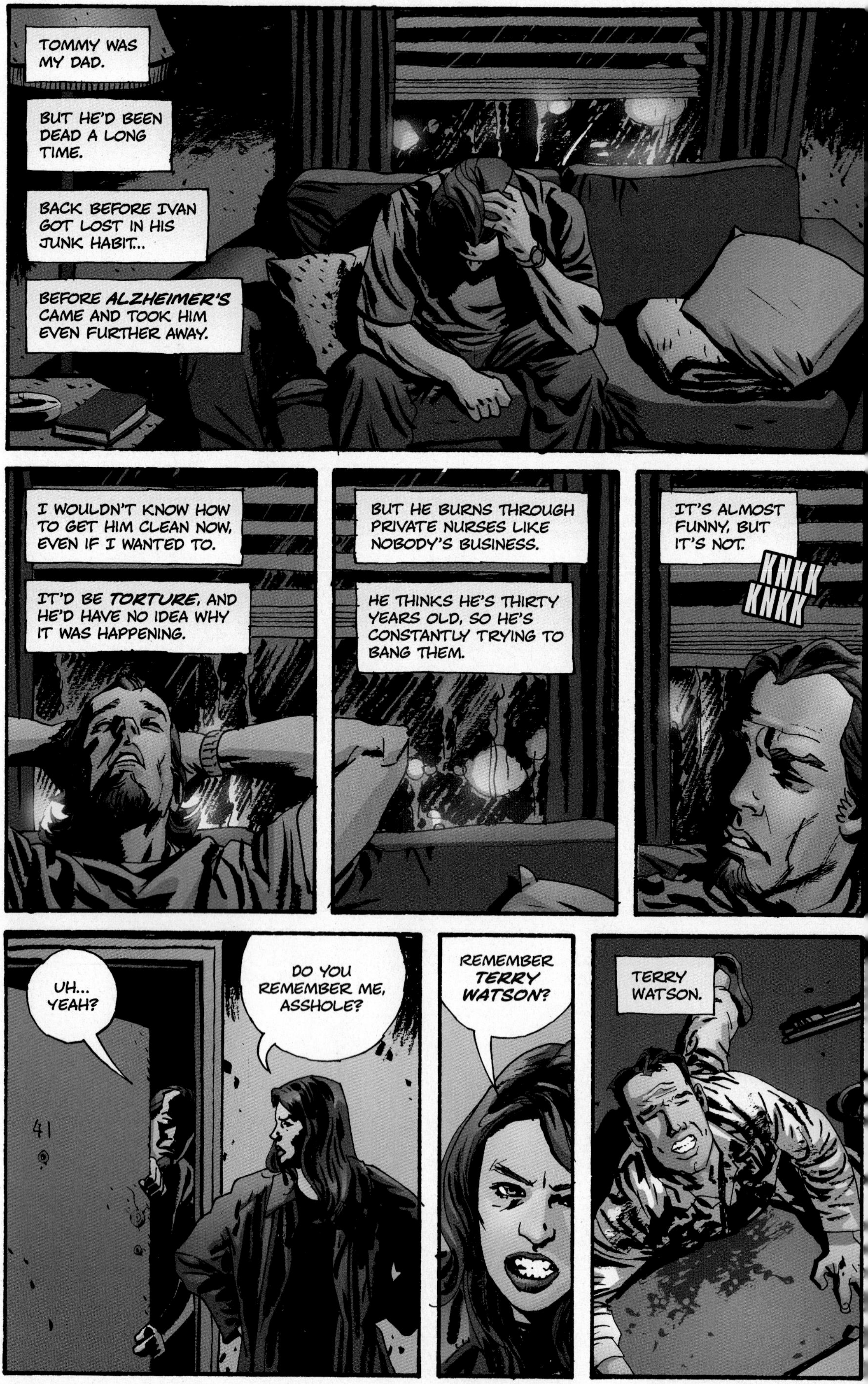
TOMMY WAS MY DAD.
BUT HE'D BEEN DEAD A LONG TIME.
BACK BEFORE IVAN GOT LOST IN HIS JUNK HABIT...
BEFORE ALZHEIMER'S CAME AND TOOK HIM EVEN FURTHER AWAY.
I WOULDN'T KNOW HOW TO GET HIM CLEAN NOW, EVEN IF I WANTED TO.
IT'D BE TORTURE, AND HE'D HAVE NO IDEA WHY IT WAS HAPPENING.
BUT HE BURNS THROUGH PRIVATE NURSES LIKE NOBODY'S BUSINESS.
HE THINKS HE'S THIRTY YEARS OLD, SO HE'S CONSTANTLY TRYING TO BANG THEM.
IT'S ALMOST FUNNY, BUT IT'S NOT.
KNKK KNKK
UH... YEAH?
DO YOU REMEMBER ME, ASSHOLE?
41
REMEMBER TERRY WATSON?
TERRY WATSON.

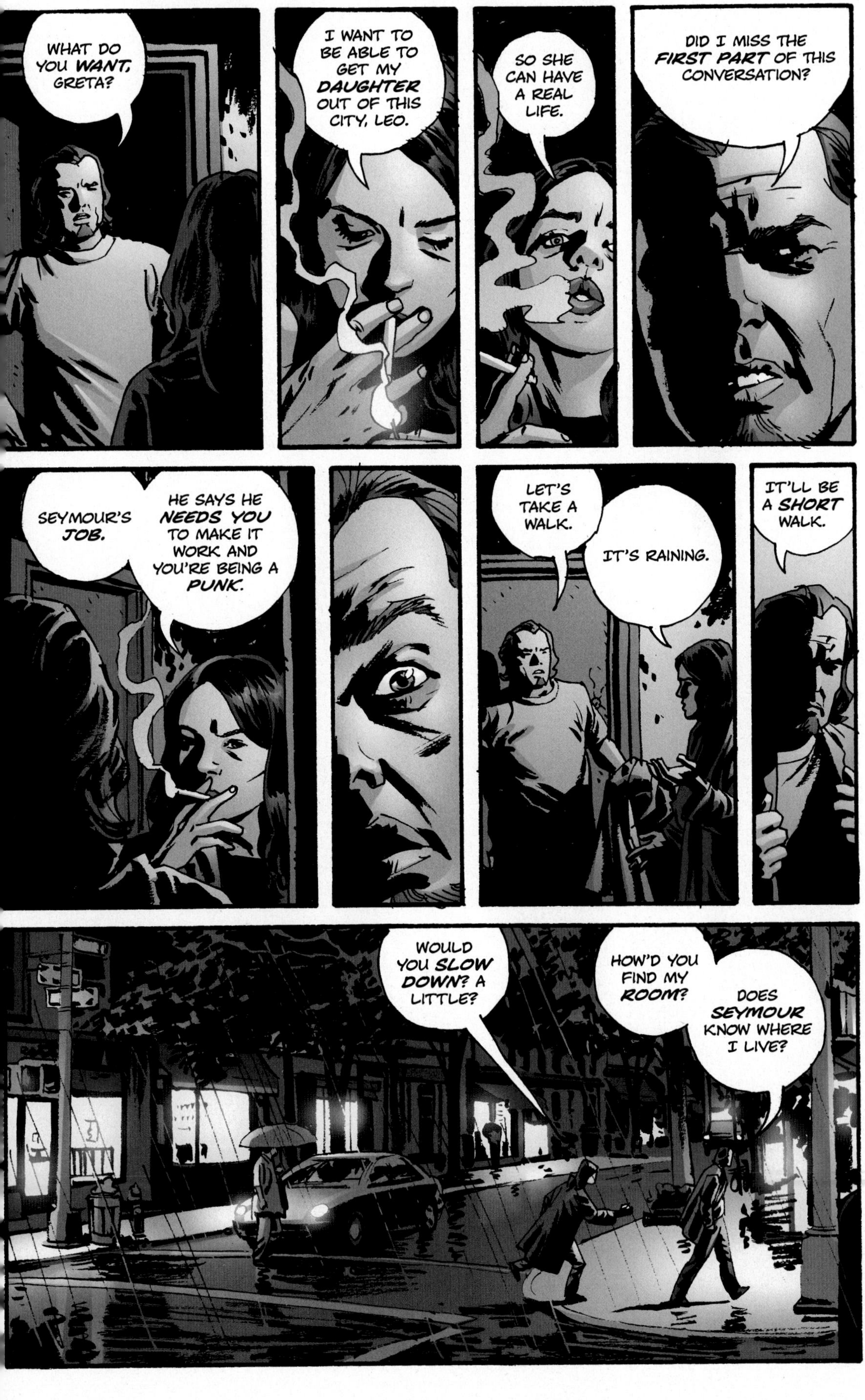
WHAT DO YOU WANT, GRETA?
I WANT TO BE ABLE TO GET MY DAUGHTER OUT OF THIS CITY, LEO.
SO SHE CAN HAVE A REAL LIFE.
DID I MISS THE FIRST PART OF THIS CONVERSATION?
SEYMOUR'S JOB.
HE SAYS HE NEEDS YOU TO MAKE IT WORK AND YOU'RE BEING A PUNK.
LET'S TAKE A WALK.
IT'S RAINING.
IT'LL BE A SHORT WALK.
WOULD YOU SLOW DOWN? A LITTLE?
HOW'D YOU FIND MY ROOM?
DOES SEYMOUR KNOW WHERE I LIVE?

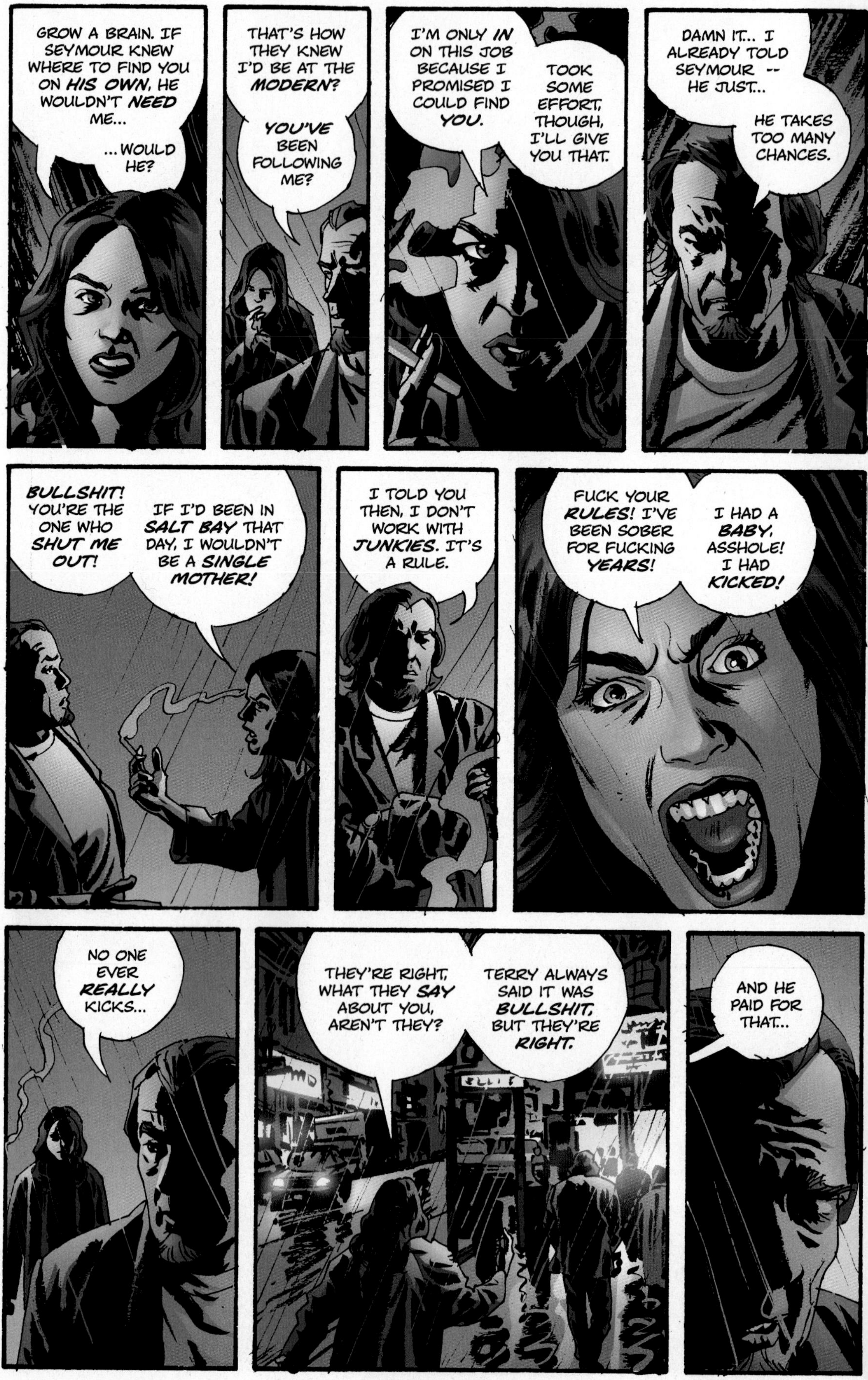
GROW A BRAIN. IF SEYMOUR KNEW WHERE TO FIND YOU ON HIS OWN, HE WOULDN'T NEED ME...
...WOULD HE?
THAT'S HOW THEY KNEW I'D BE AT THE MODERN?
YOU'VE BEEN FOLLOWING ME?
I'M ONLY IN ON THIS JOB BECAUSE I PROMISED I COULD FIND YOU.
TOOK SOME EFFORT, THOUGH, I'LL GIVE YOU THAT.
DAMN IT... I ALREADY TOLD SEYMOUR -- HE JUST...
HE TAKES TOO MANY CHANCES.
BULLSHIT! YOU'RE THE ONE WHO SHUT ME OUT!
IF I'D BEEN IN SALT BAY THAT DAY, I WOULDN'T BE A SINGLE MOTHER!
I TOLD YOU THEN, I DON'T WORK WITH JUNKIES. IT'S A RULE.
FUCK YOUR RULES! I'VE BEEN SOBER FOR FUCKING YEARS!
I HAD A BABY, ASSHOLE! I HAD KICKED!
NO ONE EVER REALLY KICKS...
THEY'RE RIGHT, WHAT THEY SAY ABOUT YOU, AREN'T THEY?
TERRY ALWAYS SAID IT WAS BULLSHIT, BUT THEY'RE RIGHT.
AND HE PAID FOR THAT...

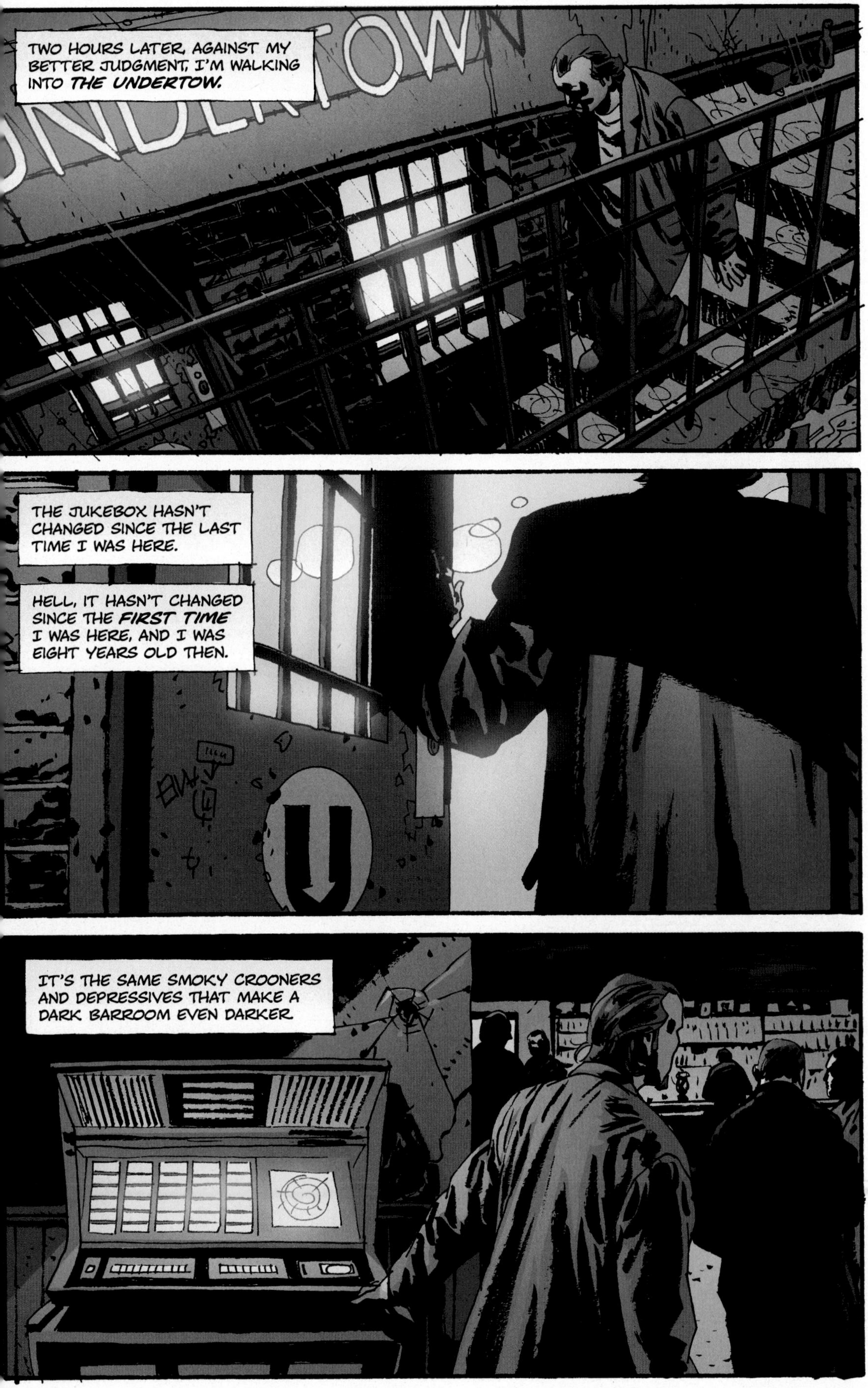
TWO HOURS LATER, AGAINST MY BETTER JUDGMENT, I'M WALKING INTO *THE UNDERTOW.*
THE JUKEBOX HASN'T CHANGED SINCE THE LAST TIME I WAS HERE.
HELL, IT HASN'T CHANGED SINCE THE *FIRST TIME* I WAS HERE, AND I WAS EIGHT YEARS OLD THEN.
IT'S THE SAME SMOKY CROONERS AND DEPRESSIVES THAT MAKE A DARK BARROOM EVEN DARKER.

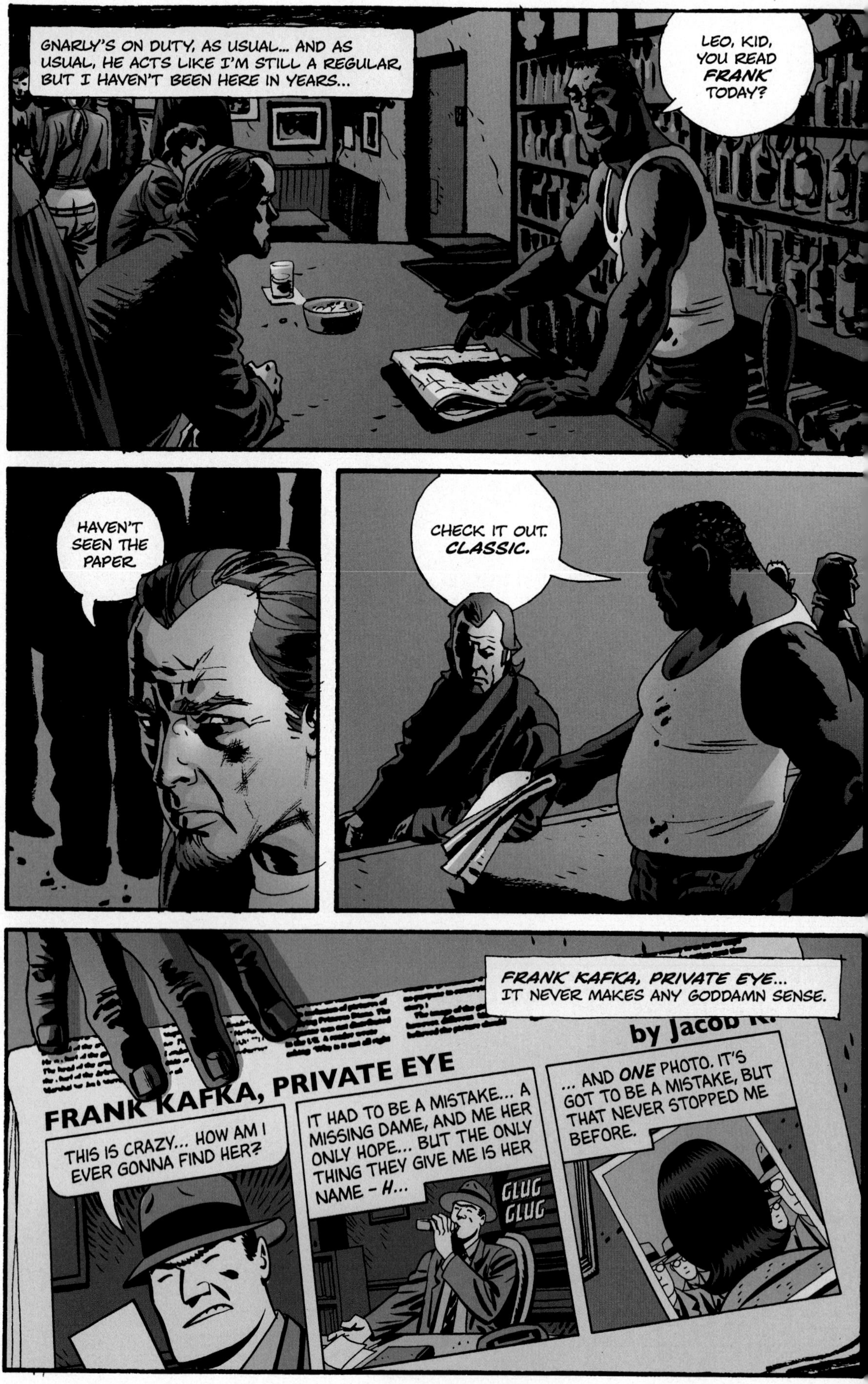

GNARLY'S ON DUTY, AS USUAL... AND AS USUAL, HE ACTS LIKE I'M STILL A REGULAR BUT I HAVEN'T BEEN HERE IN YEARS...
LEO, KID, YOU READ *FRANK* TODAY?
HAVEN'T SEEN THE PAPER
CHECK IT OUT. *CLASSIC.*
FRANK KAFKA, PRIVATE EYE... IT NEVER MAKES ANY GODDAMN SENSE.
by Jacob K.
FRANK KAFKA, PRIVATE EYE
THIS IS CRAZY... HOW AM I EVER GONNA FIND HER?
IT HAD TO BE A MISTAKE... A MISSING DAME, AND ME HER ONLY HOPE... BUT THE ONLY THING THEY GIVE ME IS HER NAME – *H*...
GLUG GLUG
... AND *ONE* PHOTO. IT'S GOT TO BE A MISTAKE, BUT THAT NEVER STOPPED ME BEFORE.

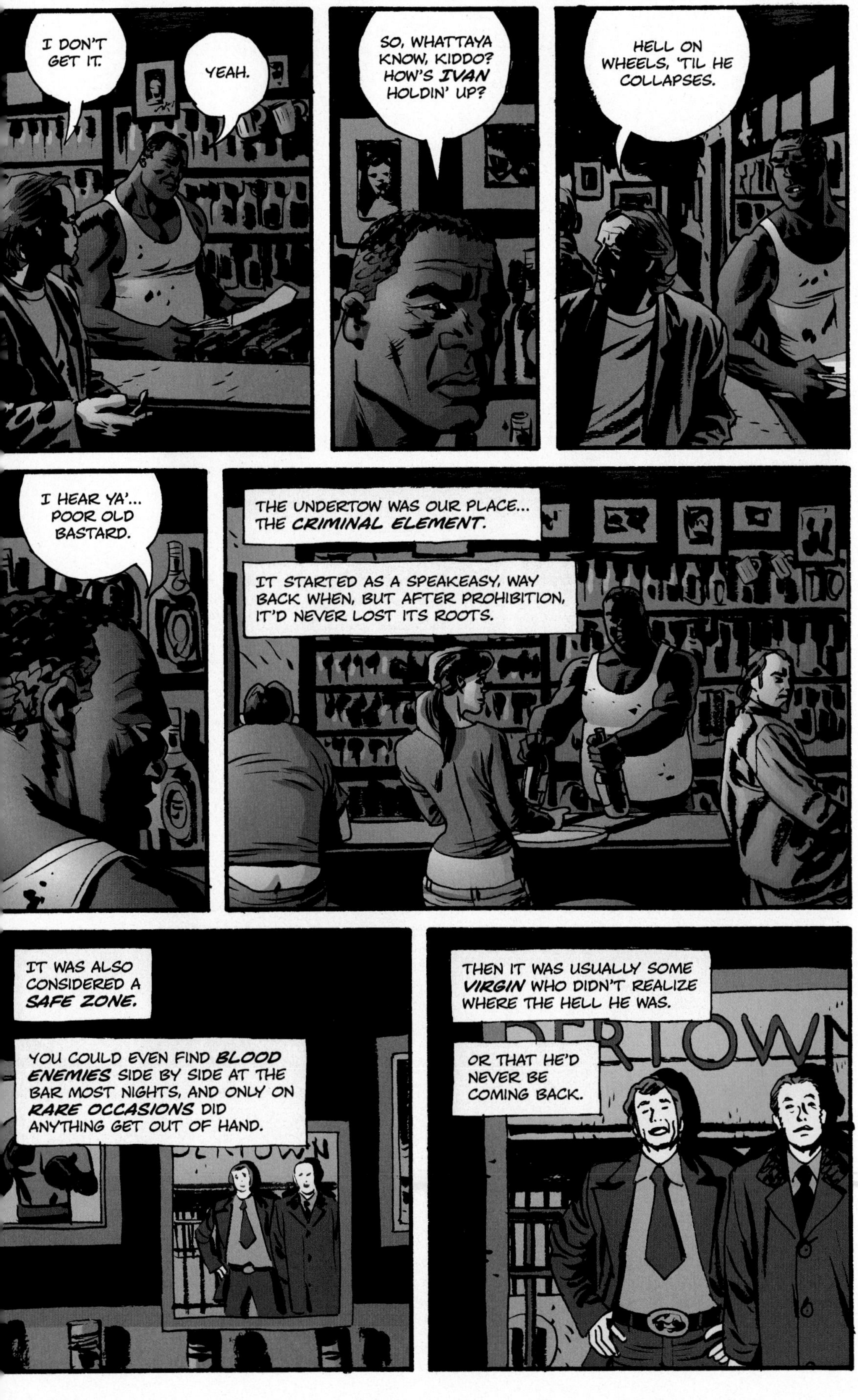

I DON'T GET IT.
YEAH.
SO, WHATTAYA KNOW, KIDDO? HOW'S IVAN HOLDIN' UP?
HELL ON WHEELS, 'TIL HE COLLAPSES.
I HEAR YA'... POOR OLD BASTARD.
THE UNDERTOW WAS OUR PLACE... THE CRIMINAL ELEMENT.
IT STARTED AS A SPEAKEASY, WAY BACK WHEN, BUT AFTER PROHIBITION, IT'D NEVER LOST ITS ROOTS.
IT WAS ALSO CONSIDERED A SAFE ZONE.
YOU COULD EVEN FIND BLOOD ENEMIES SIDE BY SIDE AT THE BAR MOST NIGHTS, AND ONLY ON RARE OCCASIONS DID ANYTHING GET OUT OF HAND.
THEN IT WAS USUALLY SOME VIRGIN WHO DIDN'T REALIZE WHERE THE HELL HE WAS.
OR THAT HE'D NEVER BE COMING BACK.

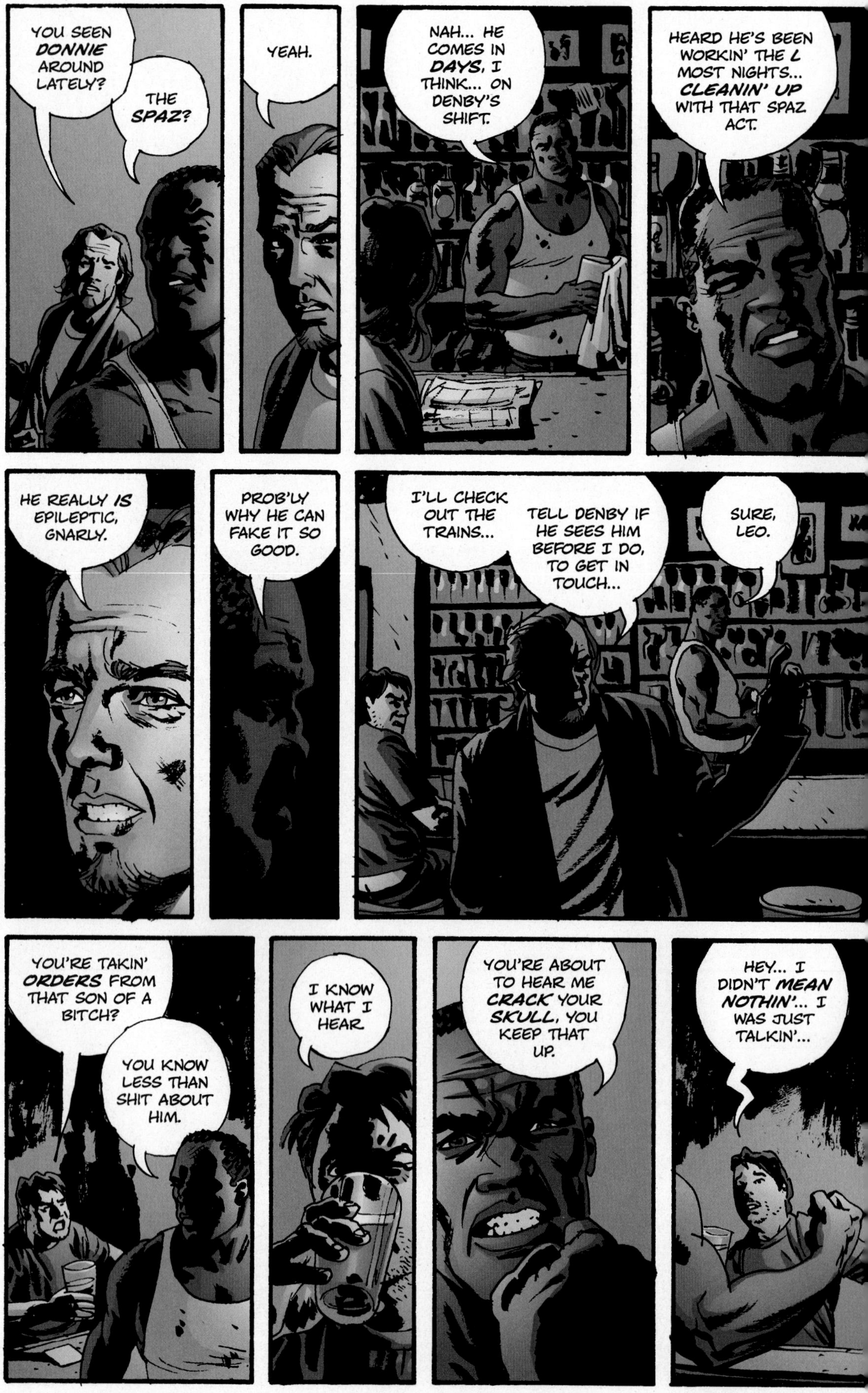
YOU SEEN DONNIE AROUND LATELY?
THE SPAZ?
YEAH.
NAH... HE COMES IN DAYS, I THINK... ON DENBY'S SHIFT.
HEARD HE'S BEEN WORKIN' THE L MOST NIGHTS... CLEANIN' UP WITH THAT SPAZ ACT.
HE REALLY IS EPILEPTIC, GNARLY.
PROB'LY WHY HE CAN FAKE IT SO GOOD.
I'LL CHECK OUT THE TRAINS...
TELL DENBY IF HE SEES HIM BEFORE I DO, TO GET IN TOUCH...
SURE, LEO.
YOU'RE TAKIN' ORDERS FROM THAT SON OF A BITCH?
YOU KNOW LESS THAN SHIT ABOUT HIM.
I KNOW WHAT I HEAR.
YOU'RE ABOUT TO HEAR ME CRACK YOUR SKULL, YOU KEEP THAT UP.
HEY... I DIDN'T MEAN NOTHIN'... I WAS JUST TALKIN'...

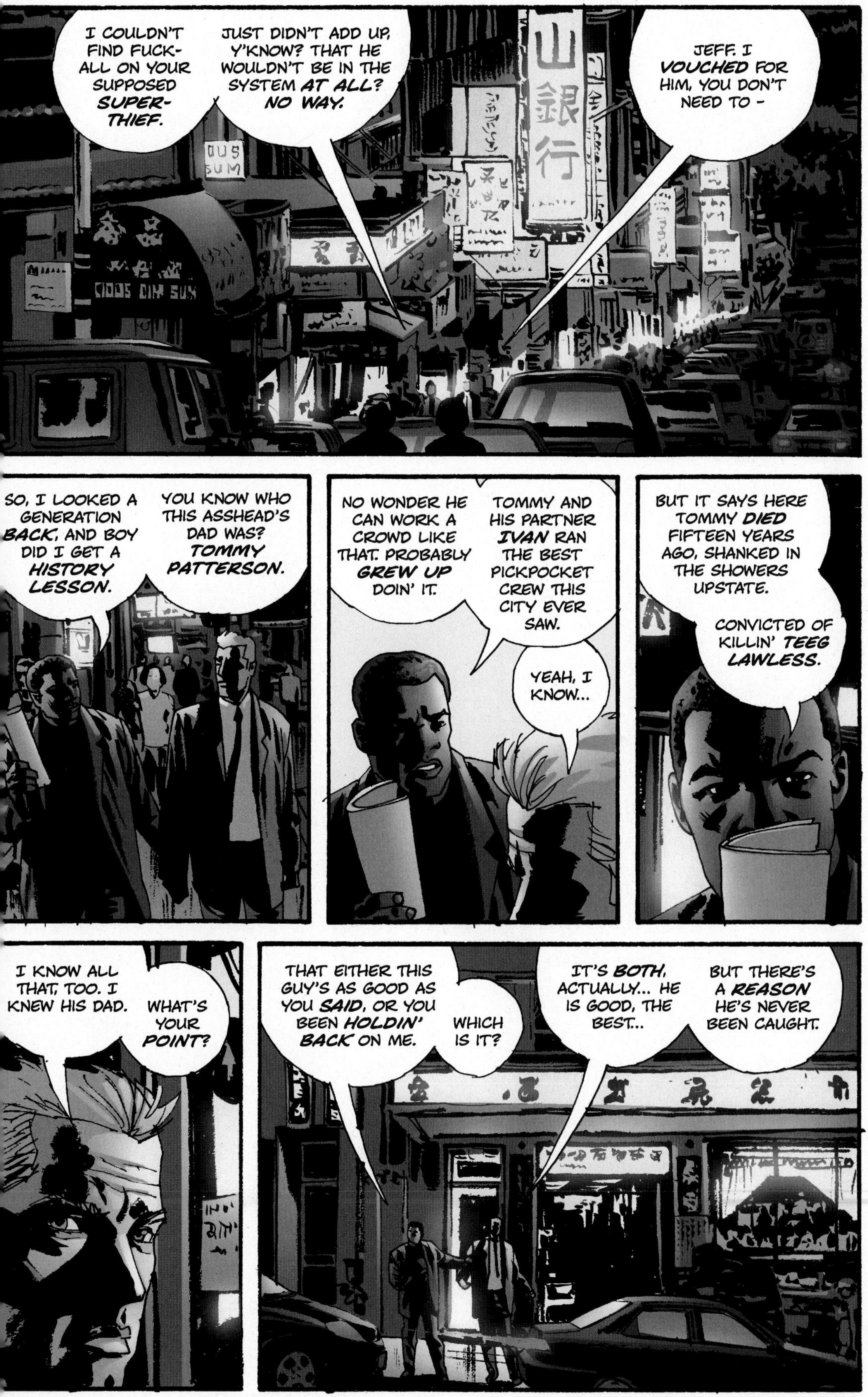
I COULDN'T FIND FUCK-ALL ON YOUR SUPPOSED SUPER-THIEF.
JUST DIDN'T ADD UP, Y'KNOW? THAT HE WOULDN'T BE IN THE SYSTEM AT ALL? NO WAY.
JEFF. I VOUCHED FOR HIM, YOU DON'T NEED TO -
SO, I LOOKED A GENERATION BACK, AND BOY DID I GET A HISTORY LESSON.
YOU KNOW WHO THIS ASSHEAD'S DAD WAS? TOMMY PATTERSON.
NO WONDER HE CAN WORK A CROWD LIKE THAT. PROBABLY GREW UP DOIN' IT.
TOMMY AND HIS PARTNER IVAN RAN THE BEST PICKPOCKET CREW THIS CITY EVER SAW.
YEAH, I KNOW...
BUT IT SAYS HERE TOMMY DIED FIFTEEN YEARS AGO, SHANKED IN THE SHOWERS UPSTATE.
CONVICTED OF KILLIN' TEEG LAWLESS.
I KNOW ALL THAT, TOO. I KNEW HIS DAD.
WHAT'S YOUR POINT?
THAT EITHER THIS GUY'S AS GOOD AS YOU SAID, OR YOU BEEN HOLDIN' BACK ON ME.
WHICH IS IT?
IT'S BOTH, ACTUALLY... HE IS GOOD, THE BEST...
BUT THERE'S A REASON HE'S NEVER BEEN CAUGHT.

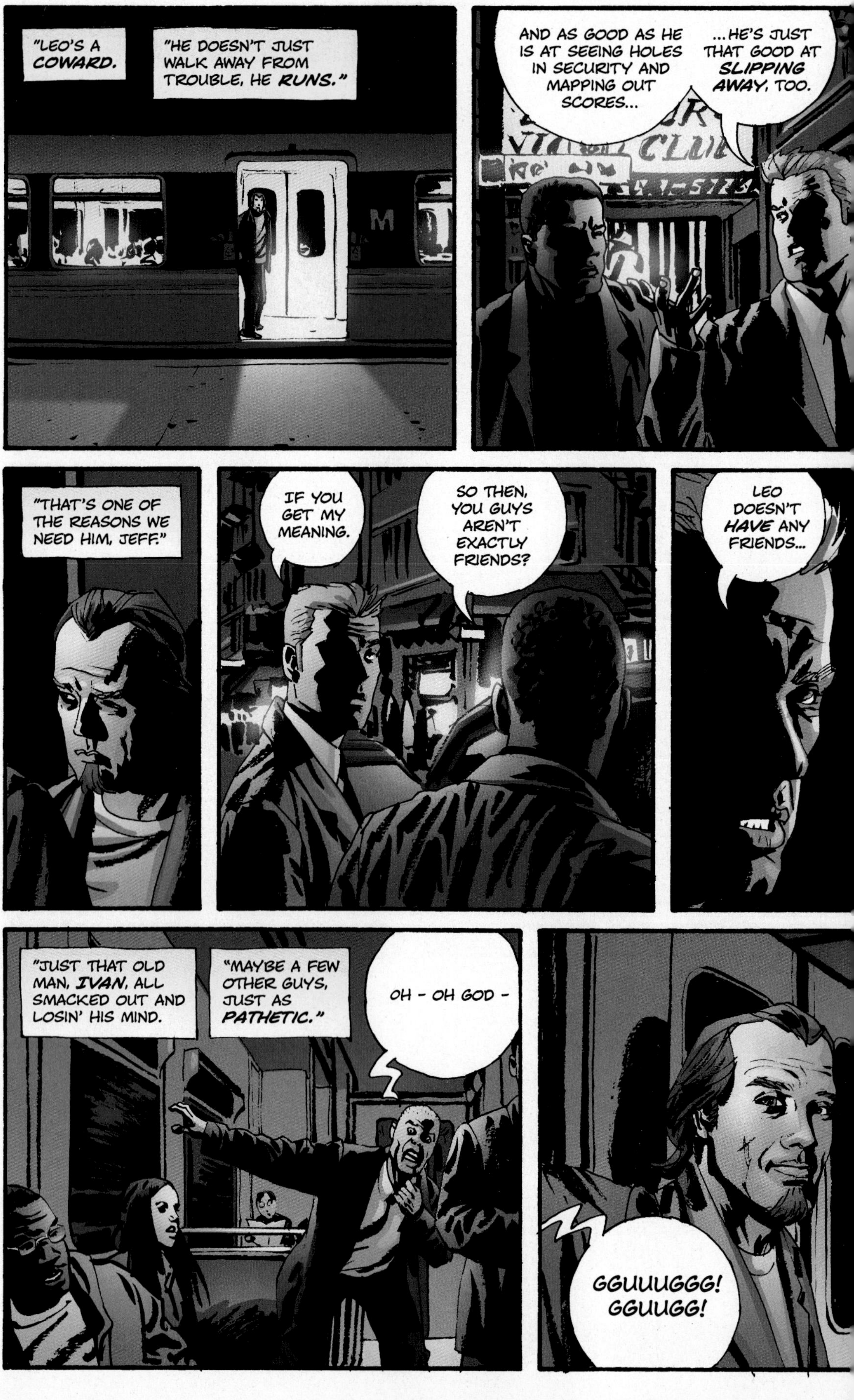
"LEO'S A COWARD.
"HE DOESN'T JUST WALK AWAY FROM TROUBLE, HE RUNS."
AND AS GOOD AS HE IS AT SEEING HOLES IN SECURITY AND MAPPING OUT SCORES...
...HE'S JUST THAT GOOD AT SLIPPING AWAY, TOO.
"THAT'S ONE OF THE REASONS WE NEED HIM, JEFF."
IF YOU GET MY MEANING.
SO THEN, YOU GUYS AREN'T EXACTLY FRIENDS?
LEO DOESN'T HAVE ANY FRIENDS...
"JUST THAT OLD MAN, IVAN, ALL SMACKED OUT AND LOSIN' HIS MIND.
"MAYBE A FEW OTHER GUYS, JUST AS PATHETIC."
OH - OH GOD -
GGUUUGGG! GGUUGG!

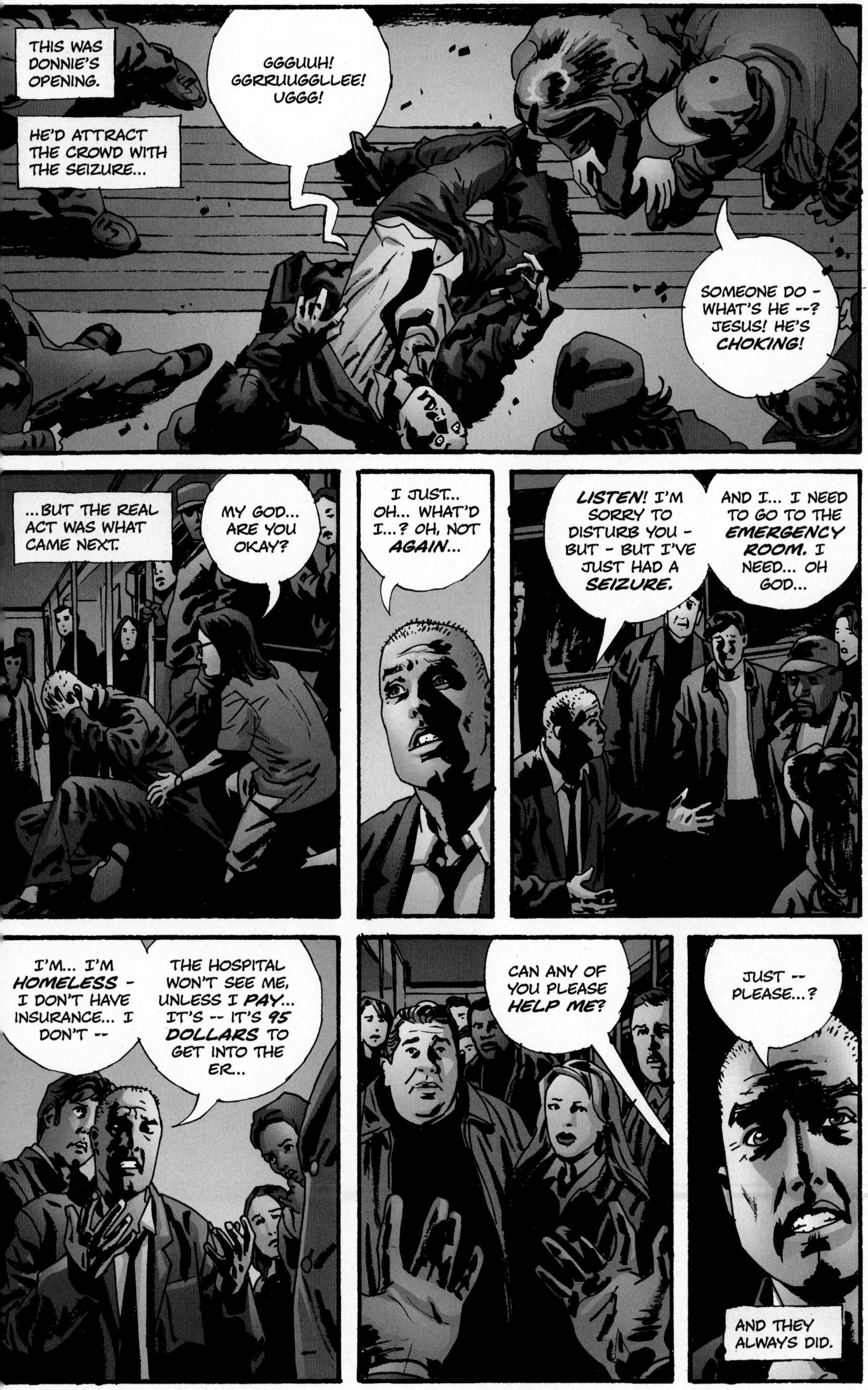
THIS WAS DONNIE'S OPENING.
HE'D ATTRACT THE CROWD WITH THE SEIZURE...
GGGUUH! GGRRUUGGLLEE! UGGG!
SOMEONE DO - WHAT'S HE --? JESUS! HE'S CHOKING!
...BUT THE REAL ACT WAS WHAT CAME NEXT.
MY GOD... ARE YOU OKAY?
I JUST... OH... WHAT'D I...? OH, NOT AGAIN...
LISTEN! I'M SORRY TO DISTURB YOU - BUT - BUT I'VE JUST HAD A SEIZURE.
AND I... I NEED TO GO TO THE EMERGENCY ROOM. I NEED... OH GOD...
I'M... I'M HOMELESS - I DON'T HAVE INSURANCE... I DON'T --
THE HOSPITAL WON'T SEE ME, UNLESS I PAY... IT'S -- IT'S 95 DOLLARS TO GET INTO THE ER...
CAN ANY OF YOU PLEASE HELP ME?
JUST -- PLEASE...?
AND THEY ALWAYS DID.

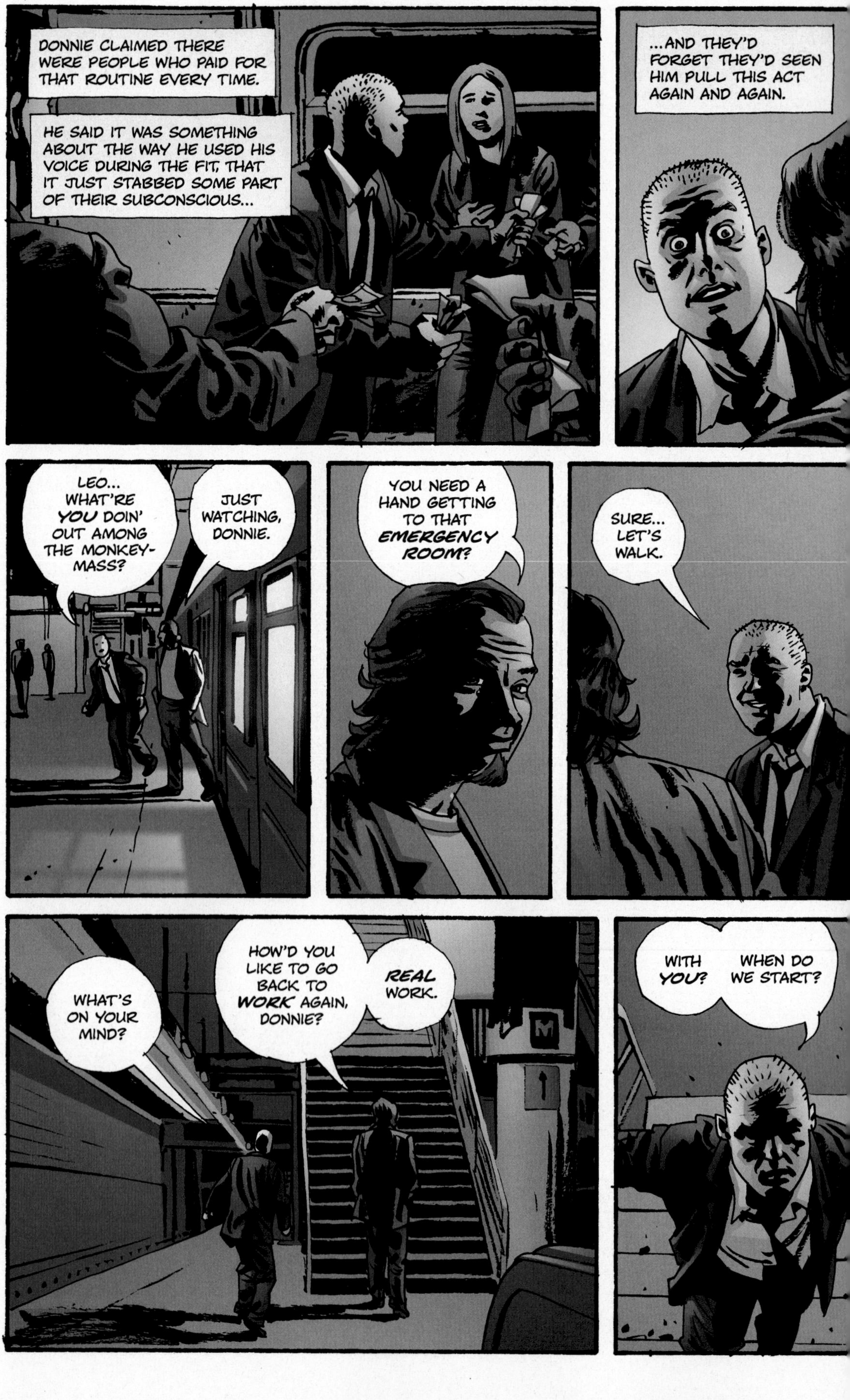
DONNIE CLAIMED THERE WERE PEOPLE WHO PAID FOR THAT ROUTINE EVERY TIME.
HE SAID IT WAS SOMETHING ABOUT THE WAY HE USED HIS VOICE DURING THE FIT, THAT IT JUST STABBED SOME PART OF THEIR SUBCONSCIOUS...
...AND THEY'D FORGET THEY'D SEEN HIM PULL THIS ACT AGAIN AND AGAIN.
LEO... WHAT'RE *YOU* DOIN' OUT AMONG THE MONKEY-MASS?
JUST WATCHING, DONNIE.
YOU NEED A HAND GETTING TO THAT *EMERGENCY ROOM*?
SURE... LET'S WALK.
WHAT'S ON YOUR MIND?
HOW'D YOU LIKE TO GO BACK TO *WORK* AGAIN, DONNIE?
REAL WORK.
WITH *YOU*?
WHEN DO WE START?

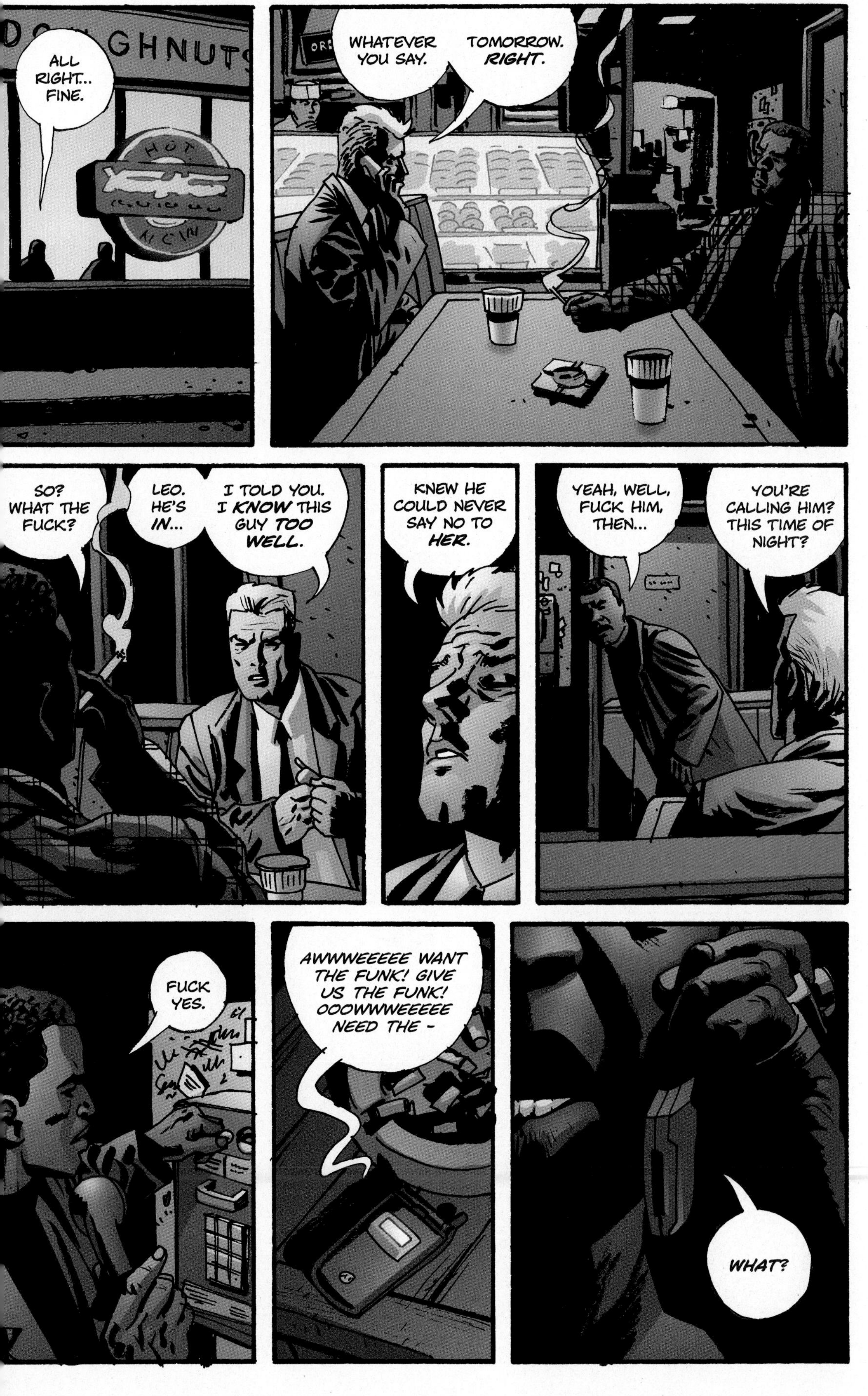
DOUGHNUTS
ALL RIGHT... FINE.
WHATEVER YOU SAY.
TOMORROW. RIGHT.
SO? WHAT THE FUCK?
LEO. HE'S IN...
I TOLD YOU. I KNOW THIS GUY TOO WELL.
KNEW HE COULD NEVER SAY NO TO HER.
YEAH, WELL, FUCK HIM, THEN...
YOU'RE CALLING HIM? THIS TIME OF NIGHT?
FUCK YES.
AWWWEEEEE WANT THE FUNK! GIVE US THE FUNK! OOOWWWEEEEE NEED THE -
WHAT?

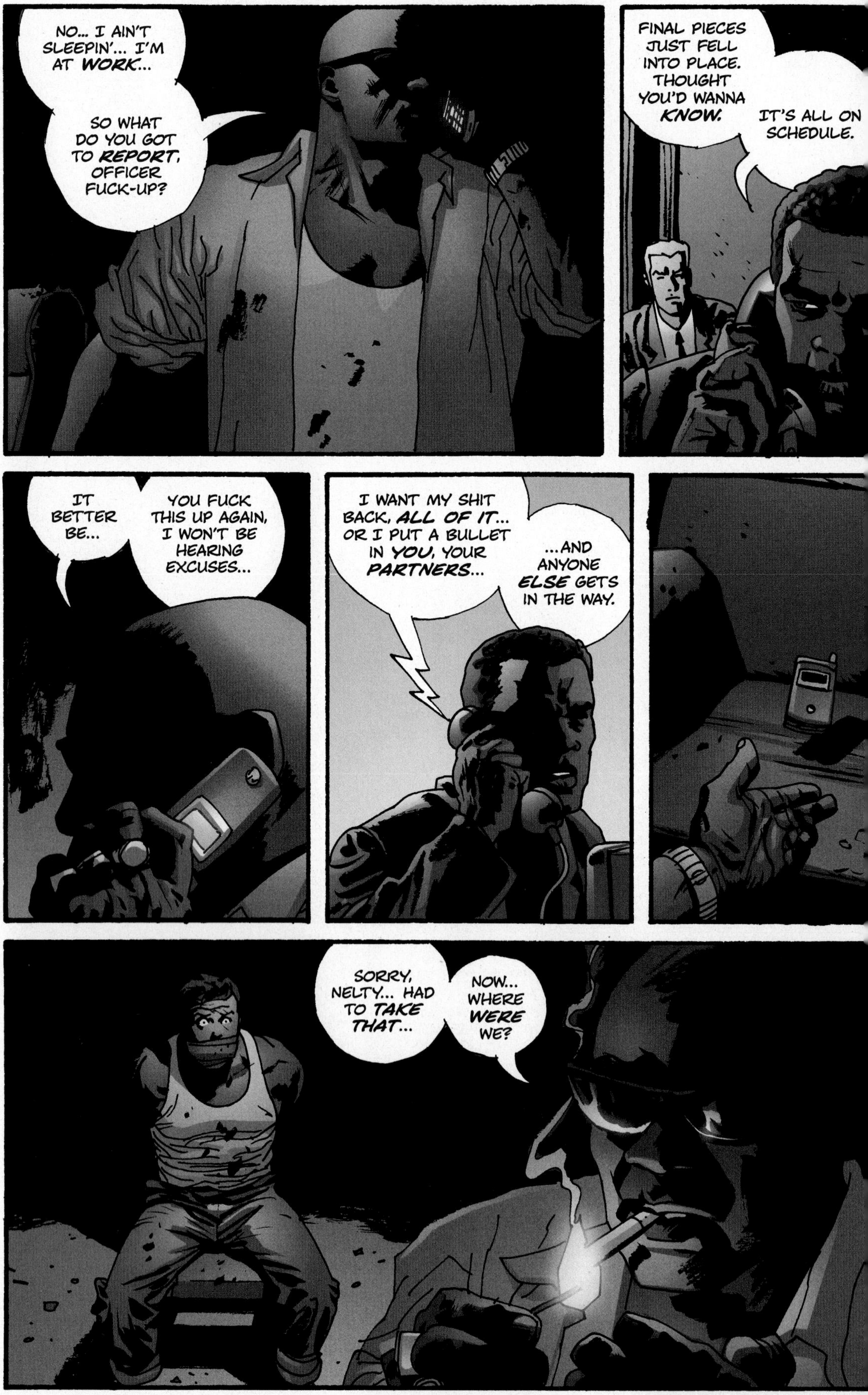
NO... I AIN'T SLEEPIN'... I'M AT WORK...
SO WHAT DO YOU GOT TO REPORT, OFFICER FUCK-UP?
FINAL PIECES JUST FELL INTO PLACE. THOUGHT YOU'D WANNA KNOW.
IT'S ALL ON SCHEDULE.
IT BETTER BE...
YOU FUCK THIS UP AGAIN, I WON'T BE HEARING EXCUSES...
I WANT MY SHIT BACK, ALL OF IT... OR I PUT A BULLET IN YOU, YOUR PARTNERS...
...AND ANYONE ELSE GETS IN THE WAY.
SORRY, NELTY... HAD TO TAKE THAT...
NOW... WHERE WERE WE?

To Be Continued

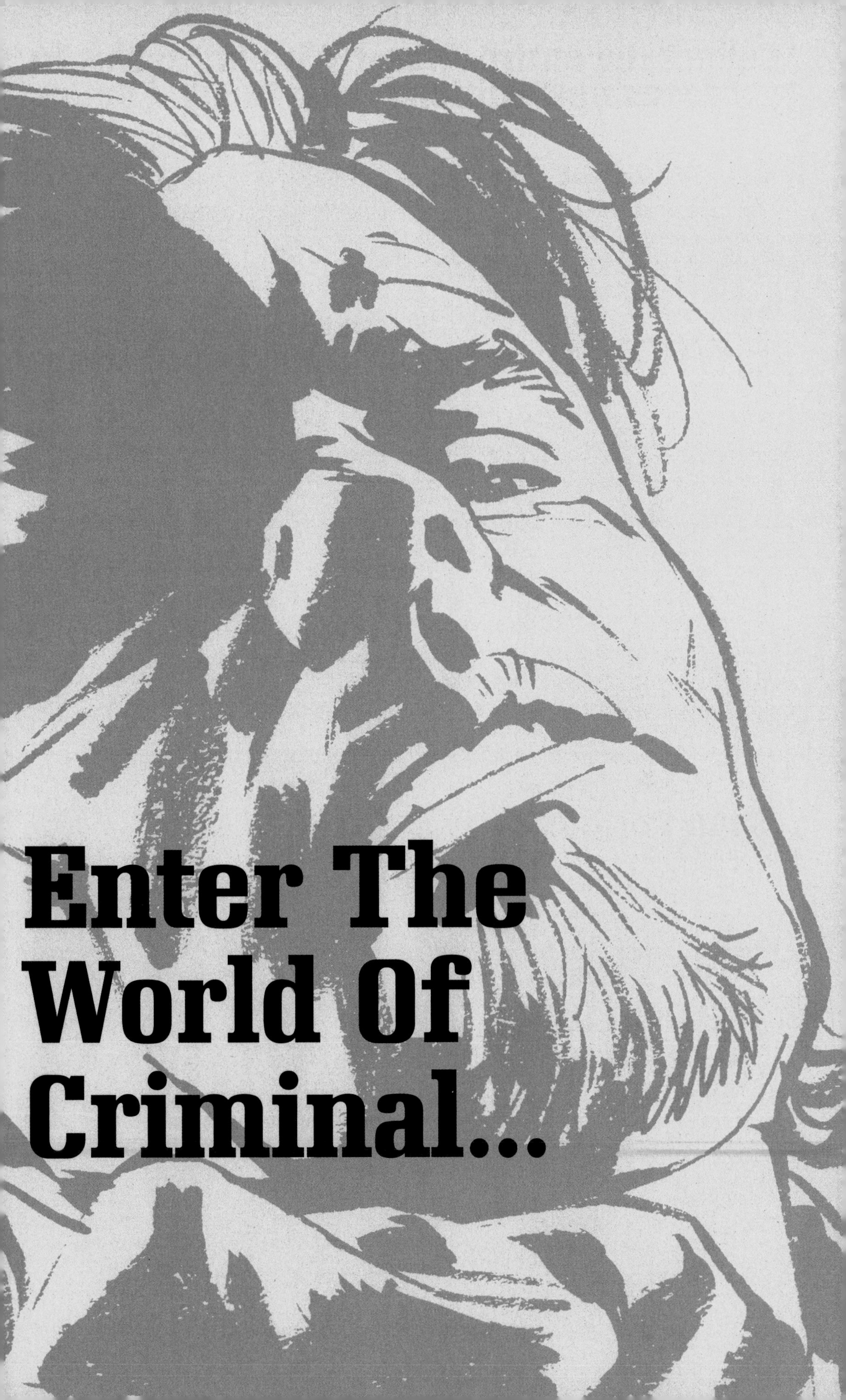

Enter The World Of Criminal...

Collect the entire Award-Winning series in gorgeous new editions from Image Comics

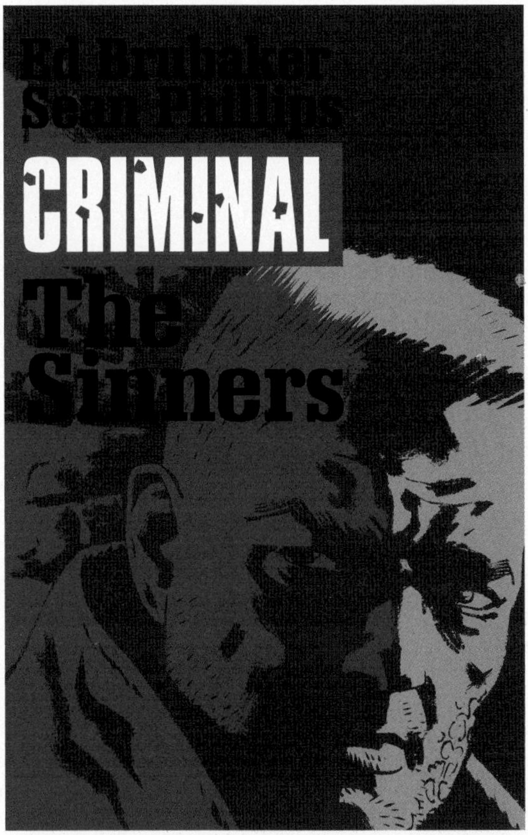
Ed Brubaker
Sean Phillips
CRIMINAL
The Sinners

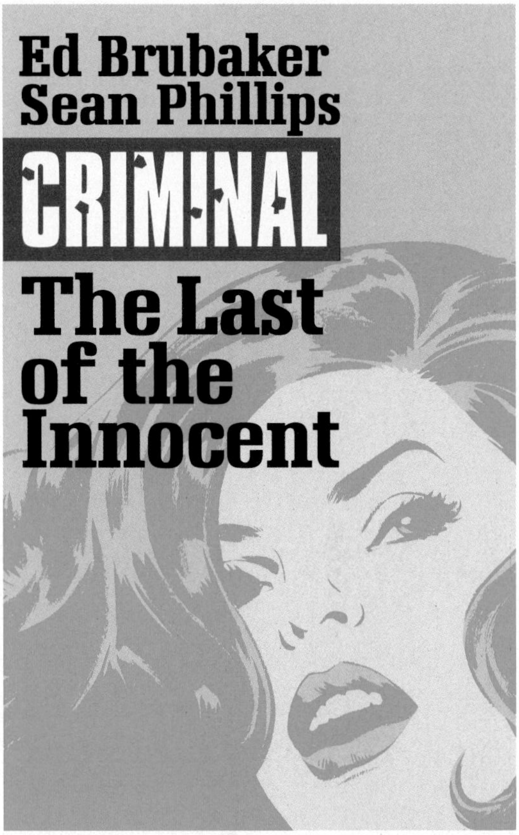
Ed Brubaker
Sean Phillips
CRIMINAL
The Last of the Innocent

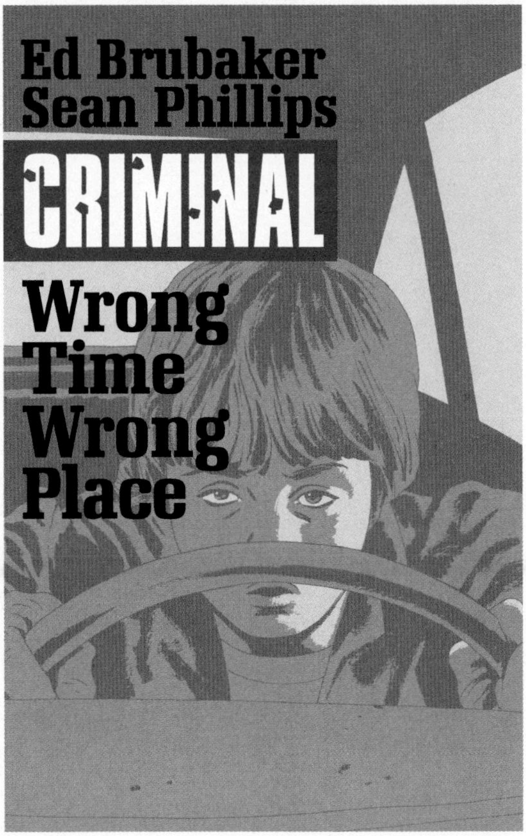
Ed Brubaker
Sean Phillips
CRIMINAL
Wrong Time Wrong Place

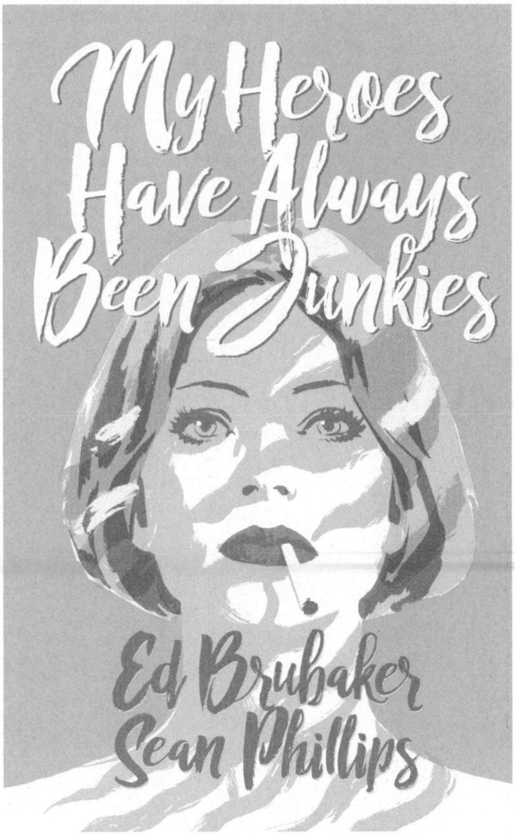
My Heroes Have Always Been Junkies
Ed Brubaker
Sean Phillips

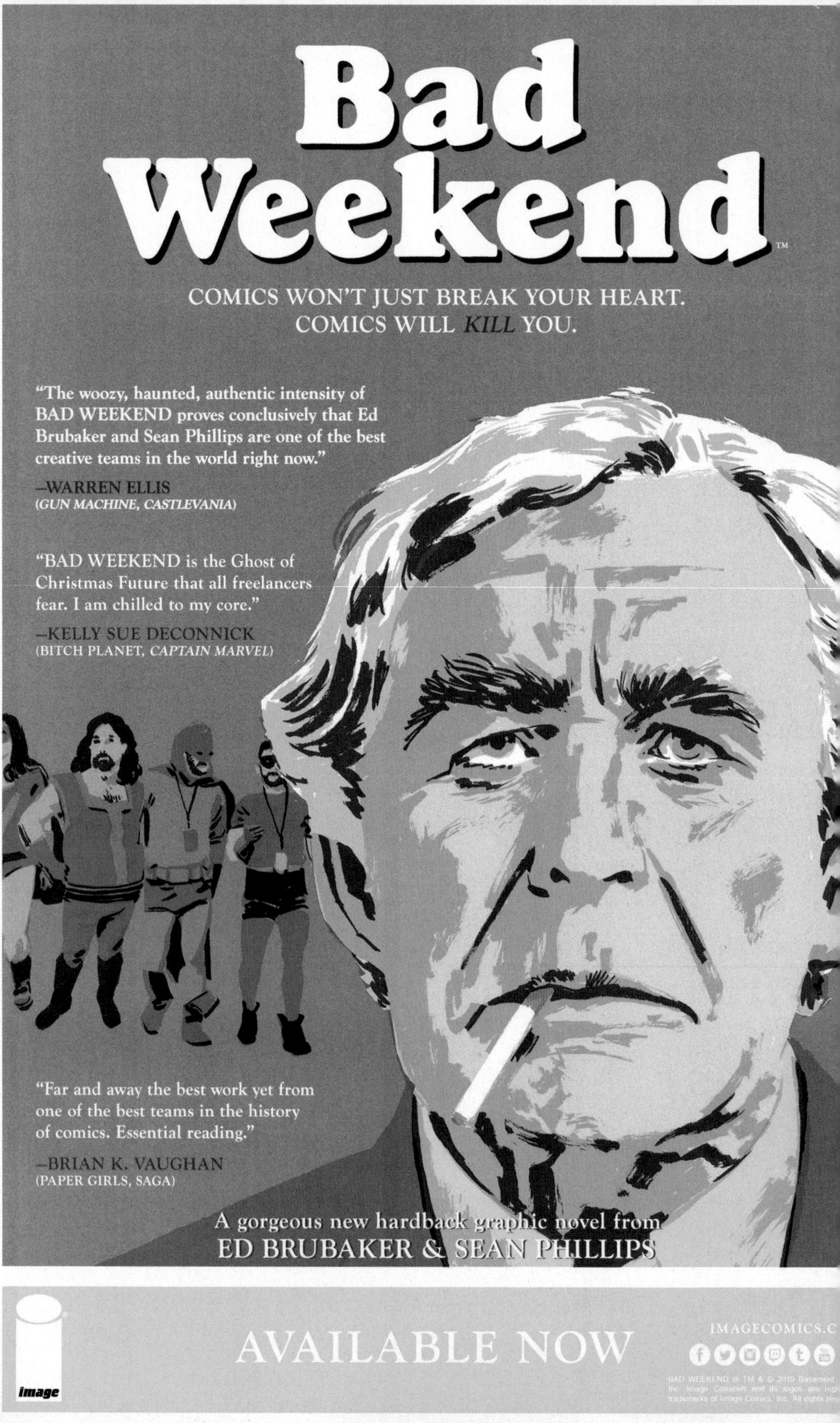
Bad
Weekend
™
COMICS WON'T JUST BREAK YOUR HEART.
COMICS WILL *KILL* YOU.
"The woozy, haunted, authentic intensity of BAD WEEKEND proves conclusively that Ed Brubaker and Sean Phillips are one of the best creative teams in the world right now."
–WARREN ELLIS
(*GUN MACHINE, CASTLEVANIA*)
"BAD WEEKEND is the Ghost of Christmas Future that all freelancers fear. I am chilled to my core."
–KELLY SUE DECONNICK
(BITCH PLANET, *CAPTAIN MARVEL*)
"Far and away the best work yet from one of the best teams in the history of comics. Essential reading."
–BRIAN K. VAUGHAN
(PAPER GIRLS, SAGA)
A gorgeous new hardback graphic novel from
ED BRUBAKER & SEAN PHILLIPS
image
AVAILABLE NOW
IMAGECOMICS.C
BAD WEEKEND is TM & © 2019 Basement
Inc. Image Comics® and its logos are reg
trademarks of Image Comics, Inc. All rights res

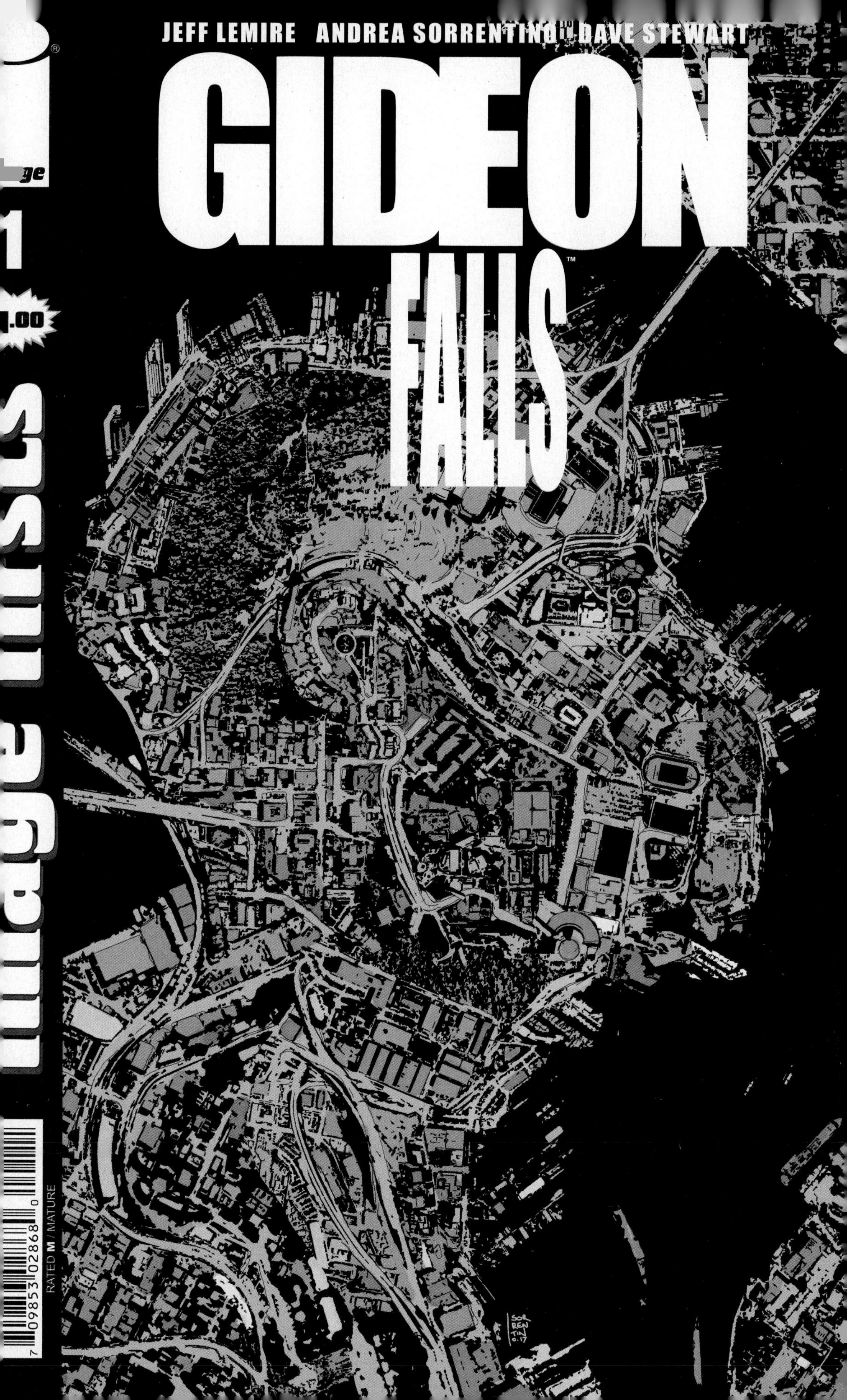
JEFF LEMIRE ANDREA SORRENTINO DAVE STEWART
GIDEON FALLS™
1
image firsts
RATED M / MATURE

IMAGE COMICS, INC. • **Robert Kirkman**: Chief Operating Officer • **Erik Larsen**: Chief Financial Officer • **Todd McFarlane**: President • **Marc Silvestri**: Chief Executive Officer • **Jim Valentino**: Vice President • **Eric Stephenson**: Publisher / Chief Creative Officer • **Jeff Boison**: Director of Publishing Planning & Book Trade Sales • **Chris Ross**: Director of Digital Sales • **Jeff Stang**: Director of Direct Market Sales • **Kat Salazar**: Director of PR & Marketing • **Drew Gill**: Art Director • **Heather Doornink**: Production Director • **Nicole Lapalme**: Controller • **IMAGECOMICS.COM**

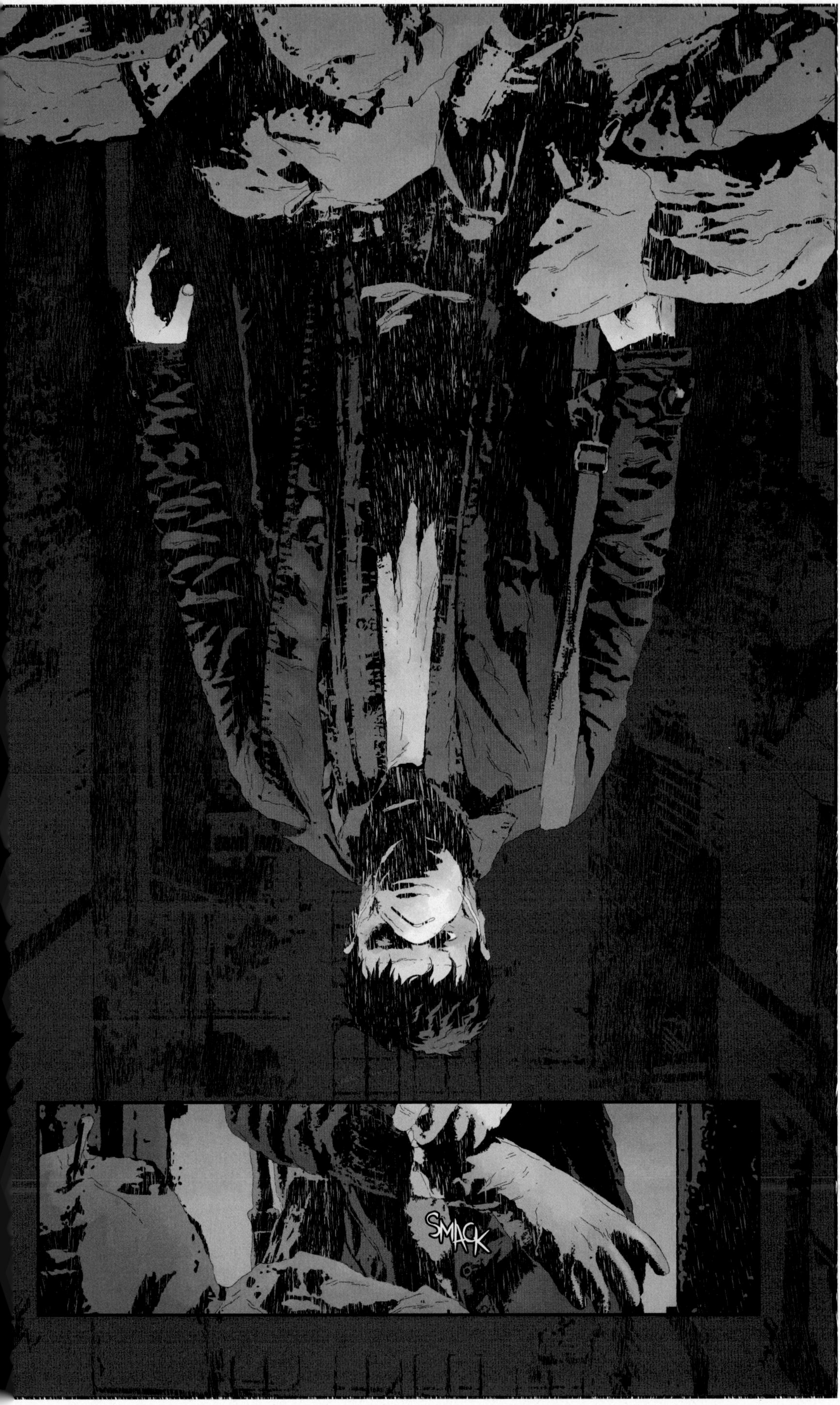
SMACK

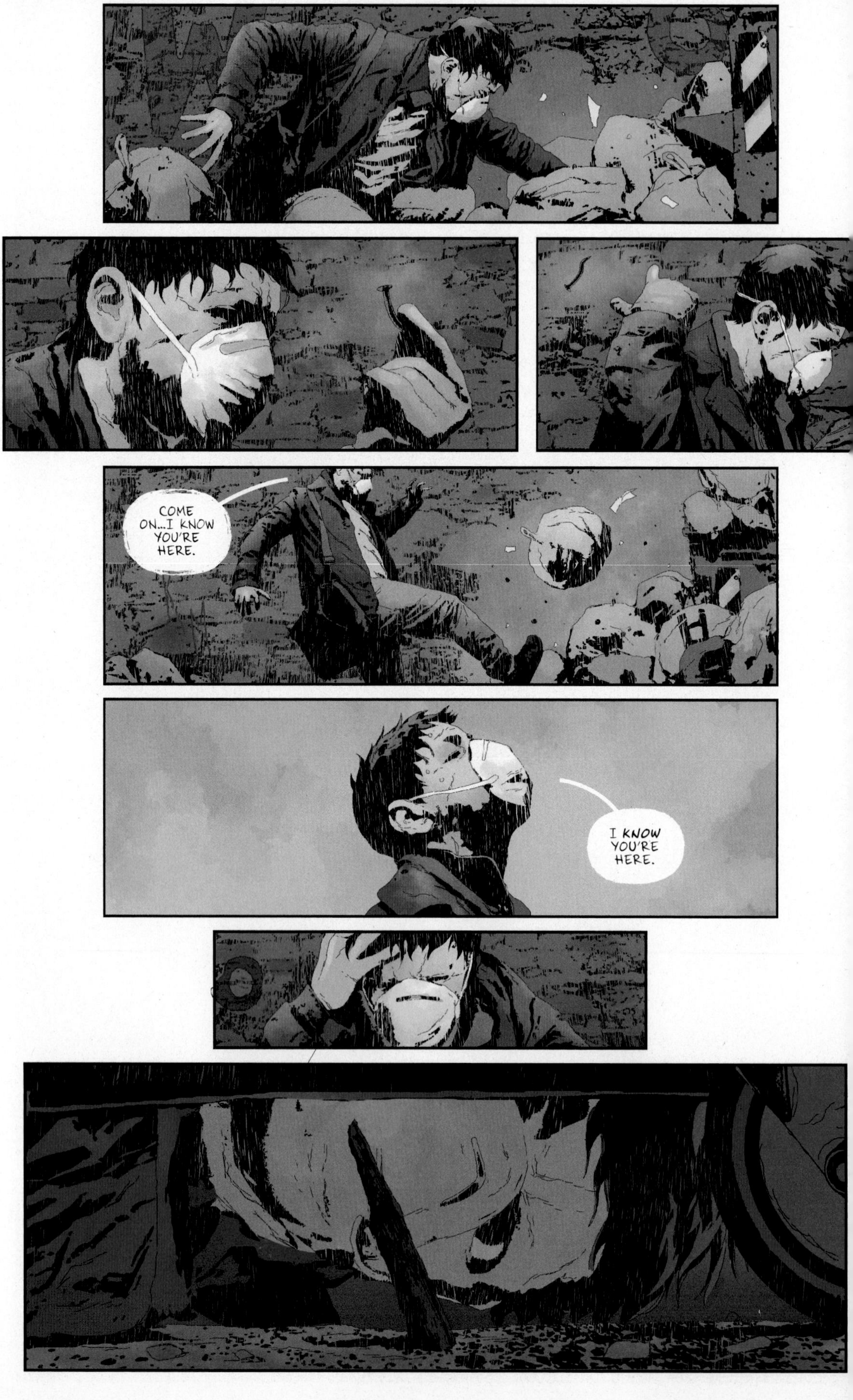
COME ON...I KNOW YOU'RE HERE.
I KNOW YOU'RE HERE.

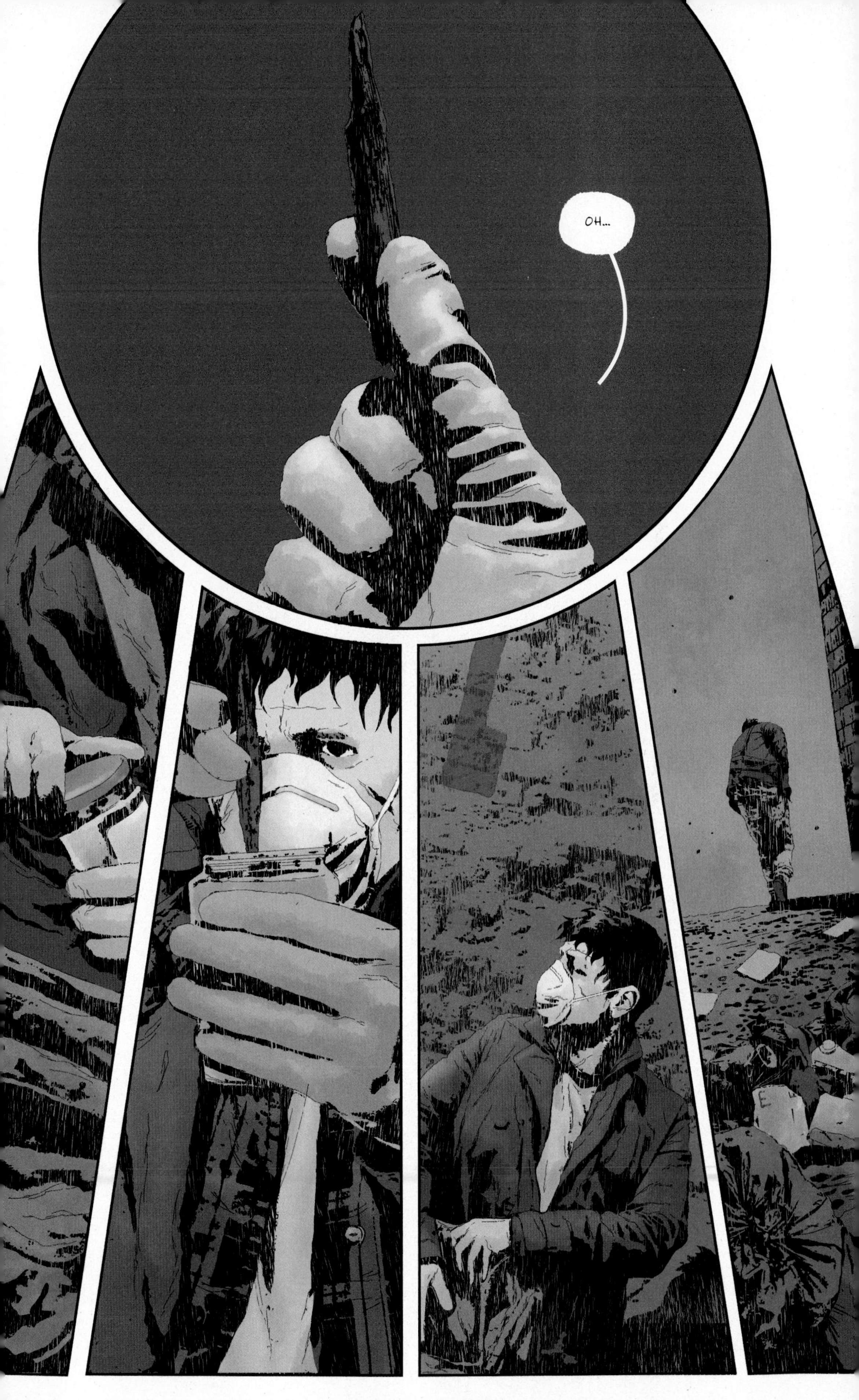
OH...

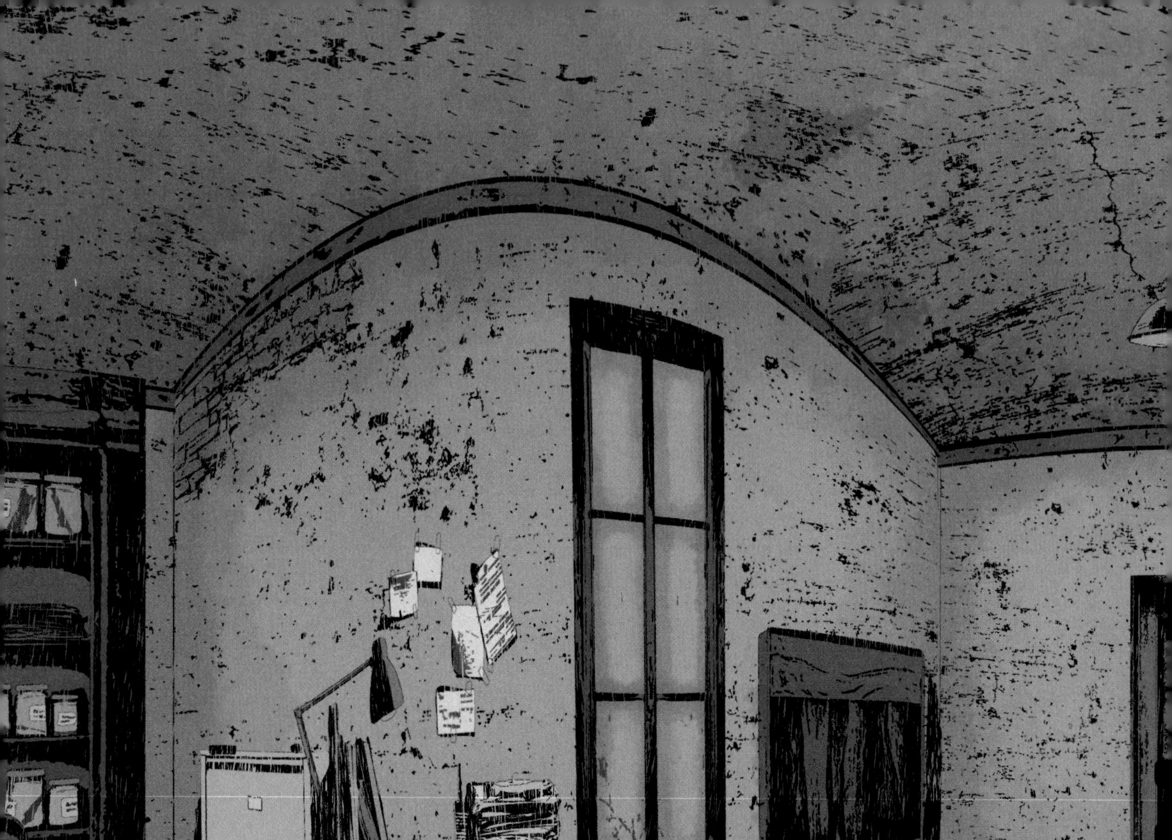

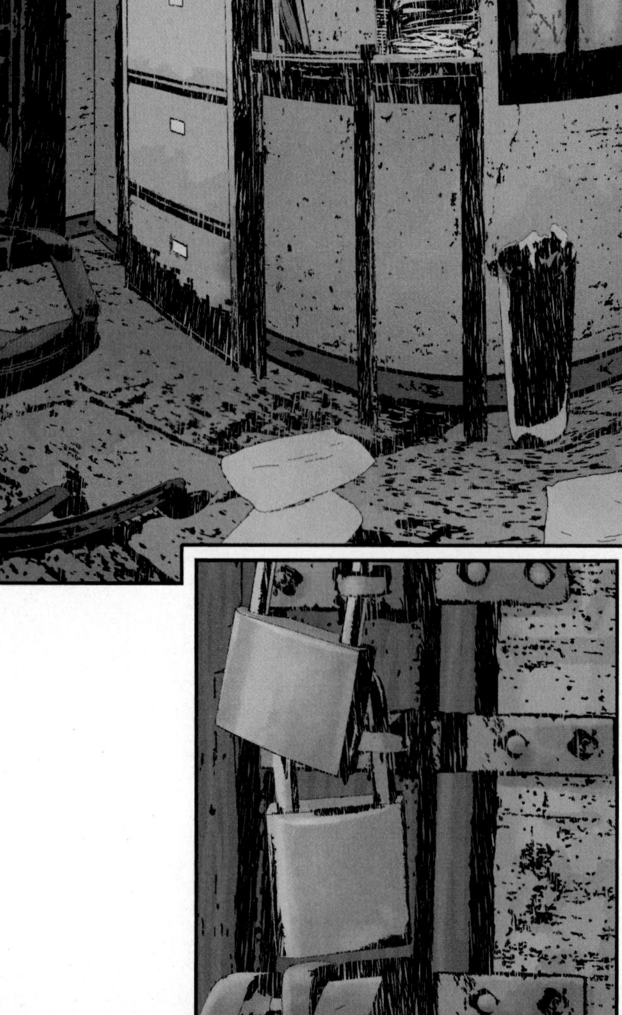

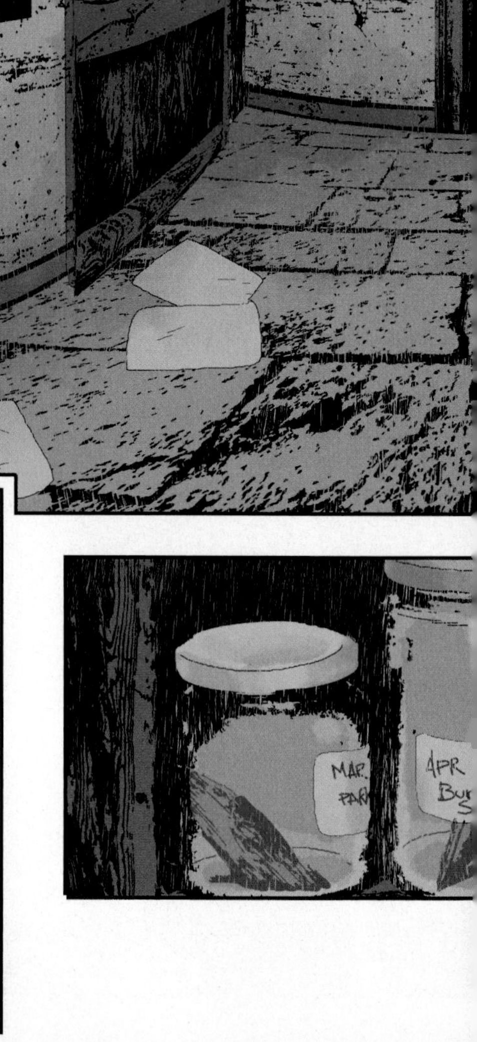
MAR.
APR

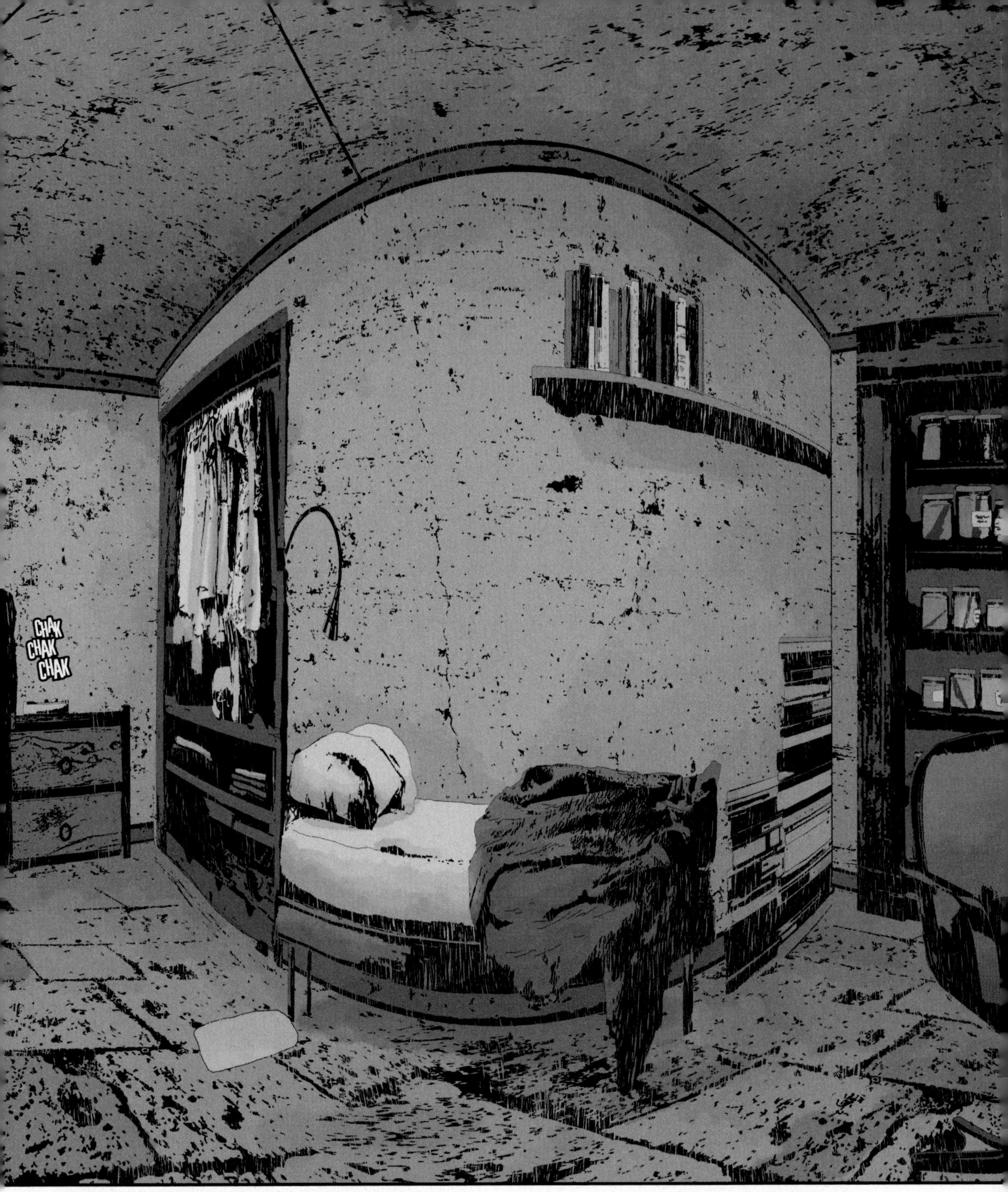
CHAK
CHAK
CHAK

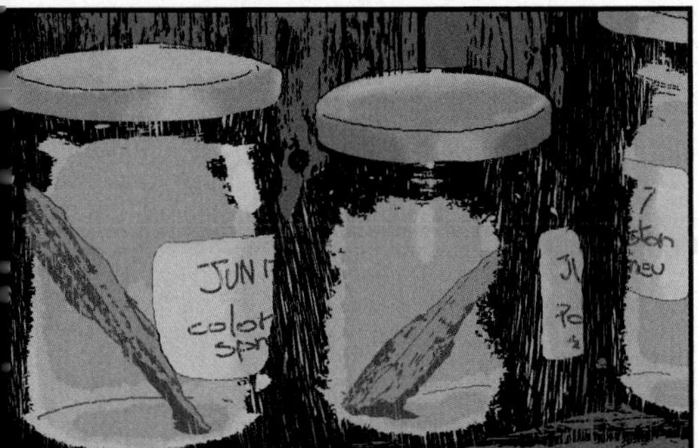

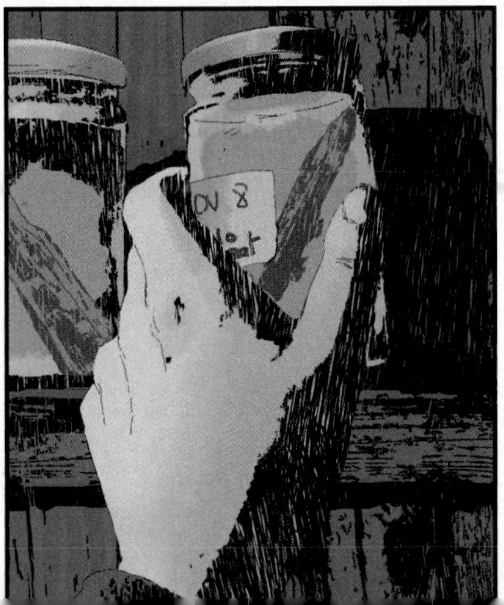

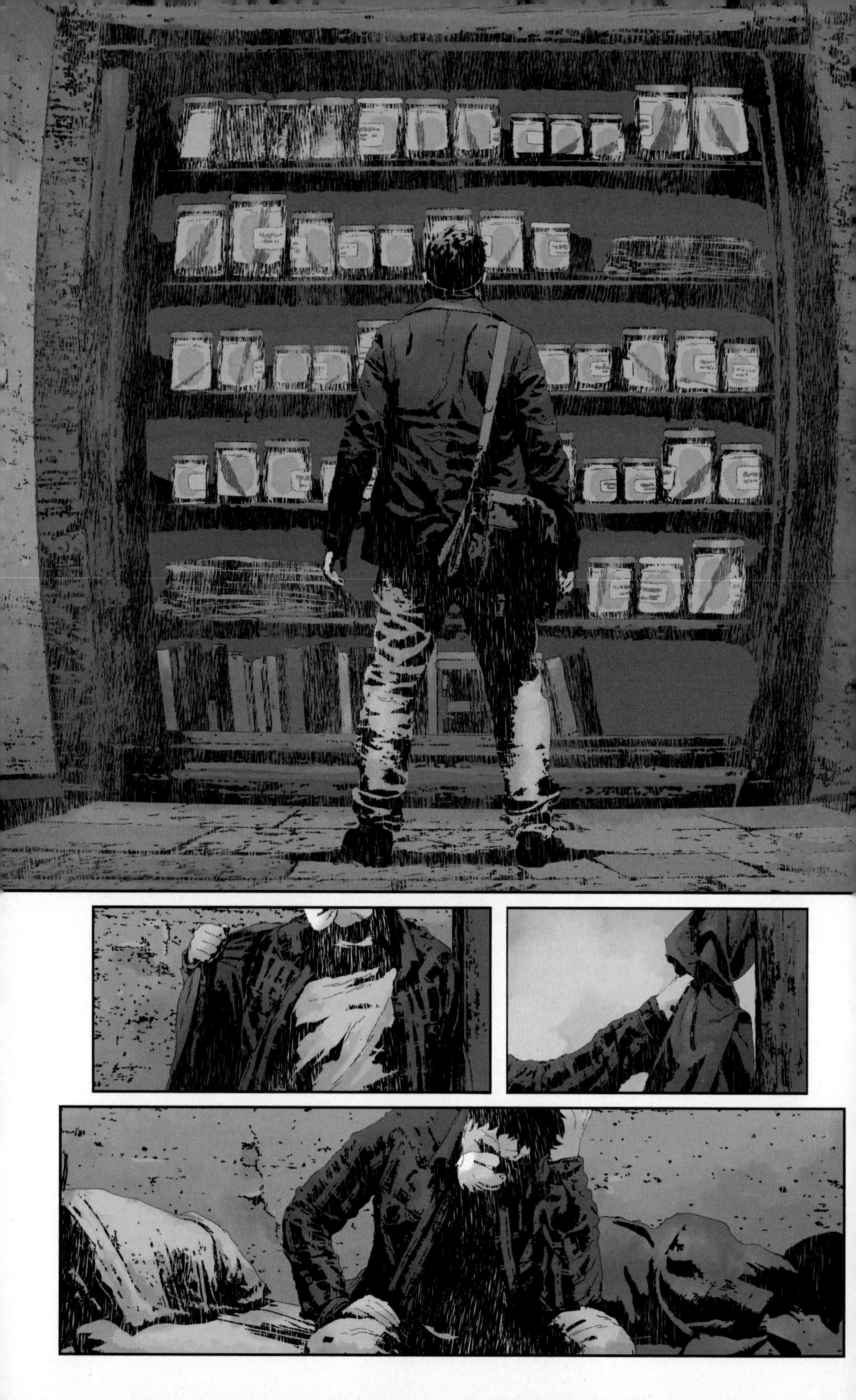

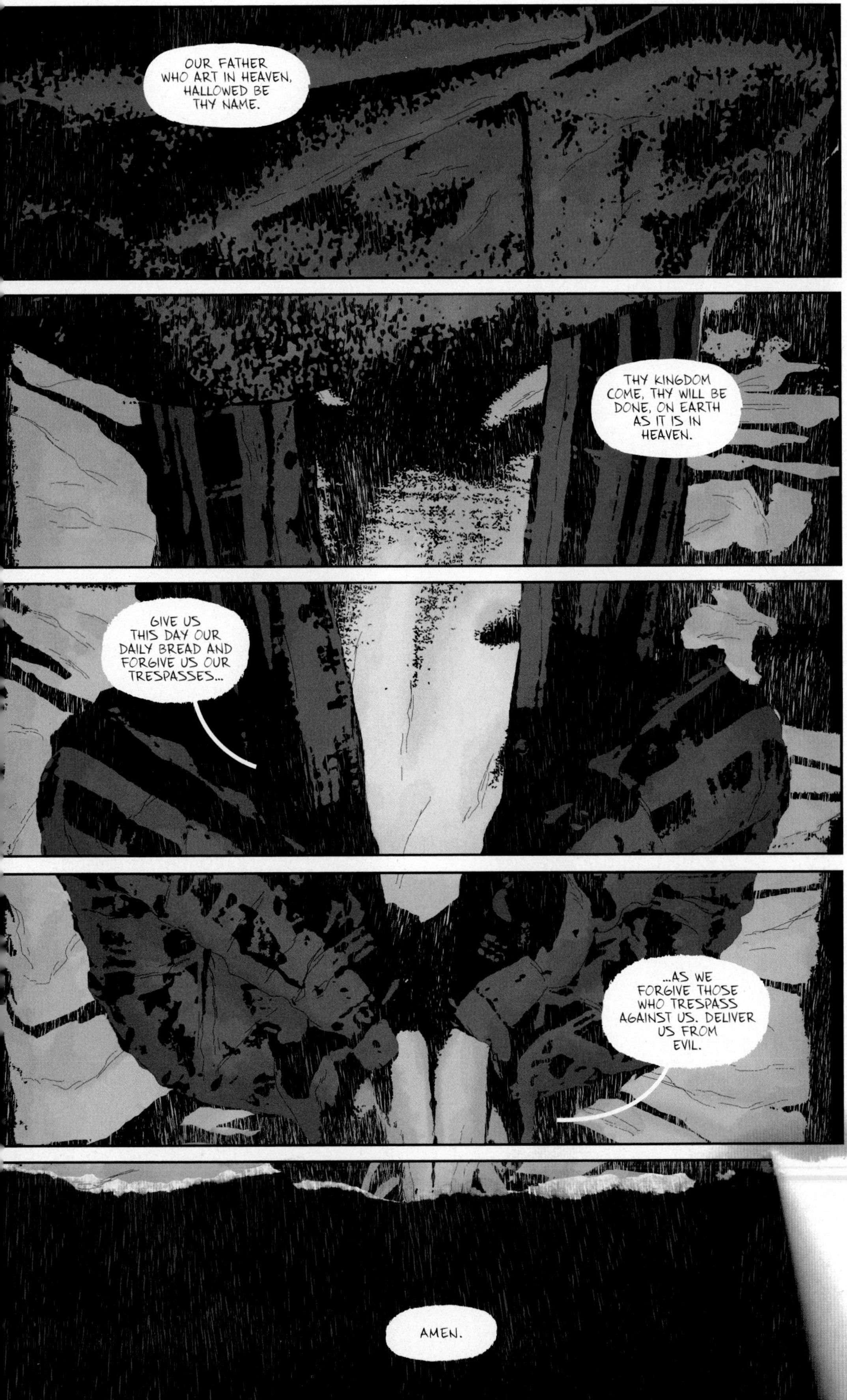
OUR FATHER WHO ART IN HEAVEN, HALLOWED BE THY NAME.
THY KINGDOM COME, THY WILL BE DONE, ON EARTH AS IT IS IN HEAVEN.
GIVE US THIS DAY OUR DAILY BREAD AND FORGIVE US OUR TRESPASSES...
...AS WE FORGIVE THOSE WHO TRESPASS AGAINST US. DELIVER US FROM EVIL.
AMEN.

Jeff Lemire
Andrea Sorrentino

with colors by:
Dave Stewart

lettering and design by:
Steve Wands

and edited by:
Will Dennis

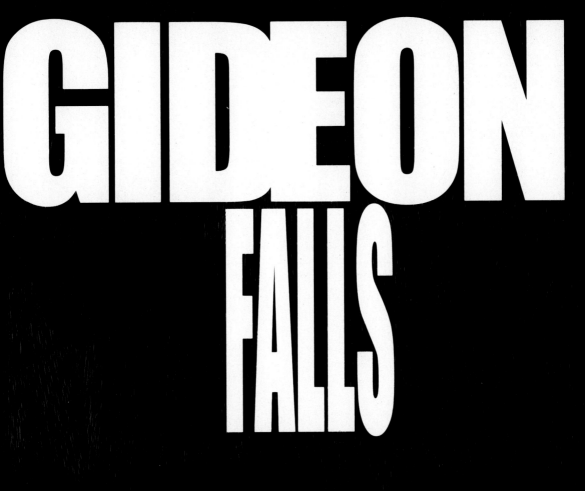

GIDEON
FALLS

1.01
the speed of pain

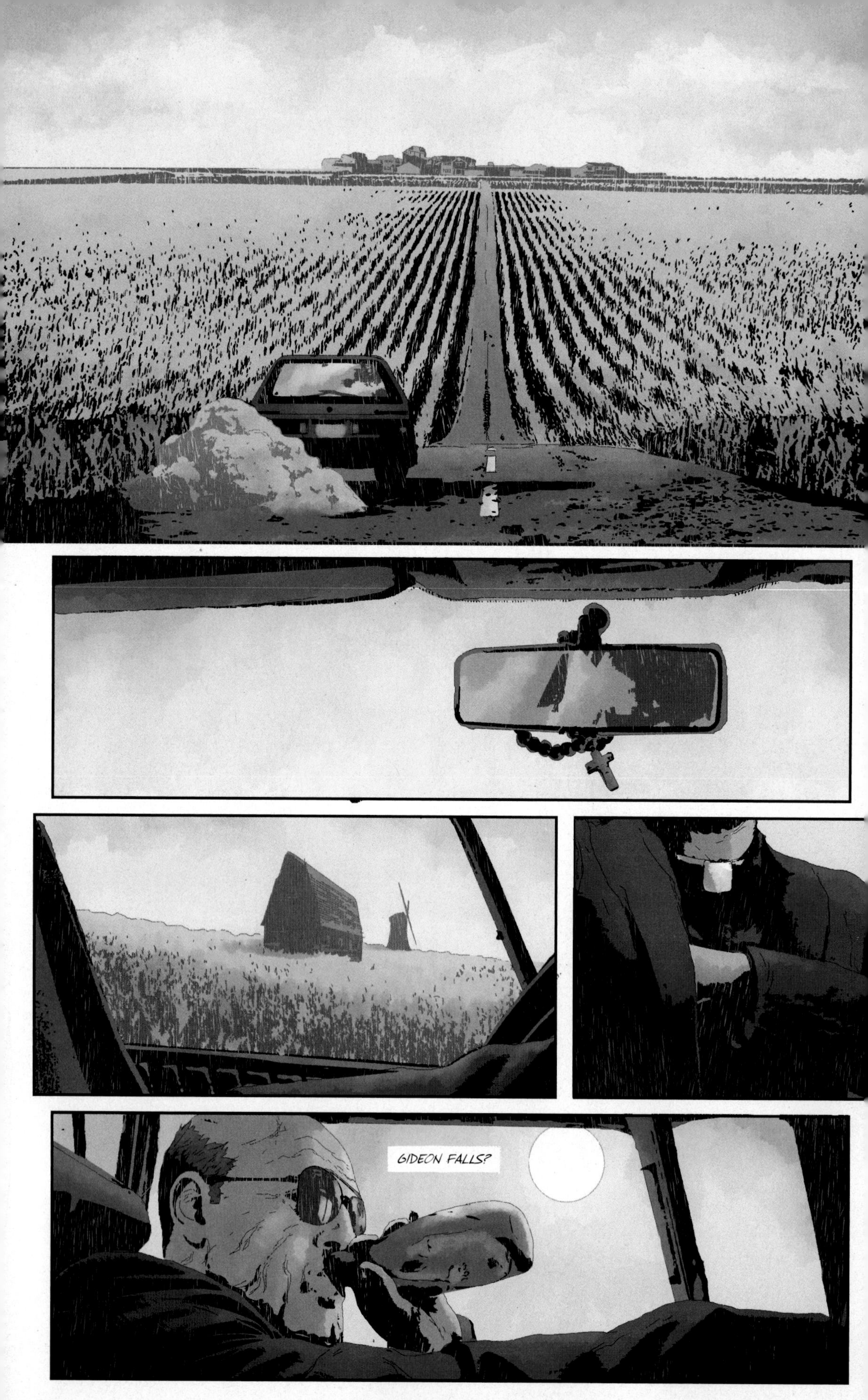
GIDEON FALLS?

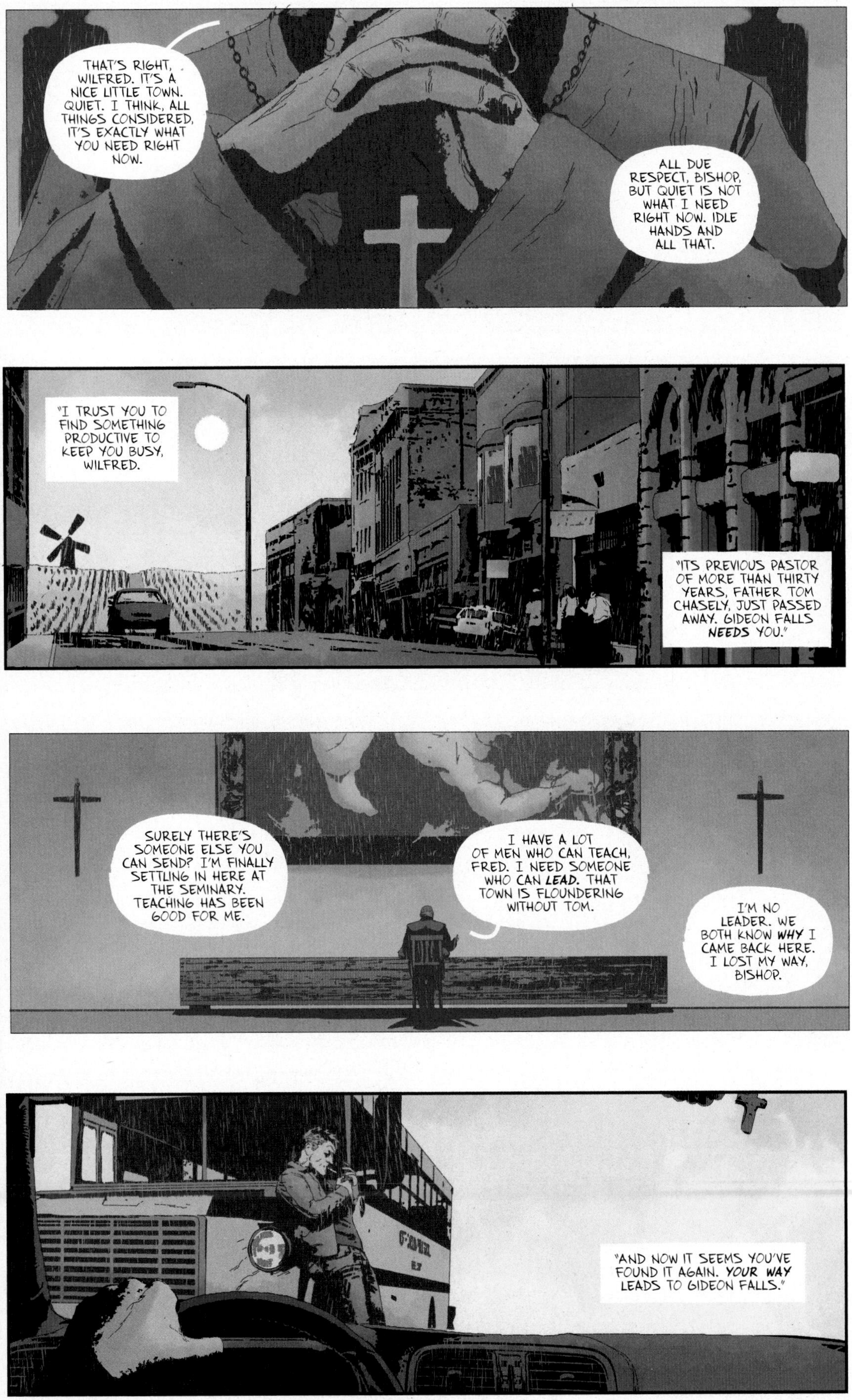
THAT'S RIGHT, WILFRED. IT'S A NICE LITTLE TOWN. QUIET. I THINK, ALL THINGS CONSIDERED, IT'S EXACTLY WHAT YOU NEED RIGHT NOW.
ALL DUE RESPECT, BISHOP, BUT QUIET IS NOT WHAT I NEED RIGHT NOW. IDLE HANDS AND ALL THAT.
"I TRUST YOU TO FIND SOMETHING PRODUCTIVE TO KEEP YOU BUSY, WILFRED.
"ITS PREVIOUS PASTOR OF MORE THAN THIRTY YEARS, FATHER TOM CHASELY, JUST PASSED AWAY. GIDEON FALLS **NEEDS** YOU."
SURELY THERE'S SOMEONE ELSE YOU CAN SEND? I'M FINALLY SETTLING IN HERE AT THE SEMINARY. TEACHING HAS BEEN GOOD FOR ME.
I HAVE A LOT OF MEN WHO CAN TEACH, FRED. I NEED SOMEONE WHO CAN ***LEAD.*** THAT TOWN IS FLOUNDERING WITHOUT TOM.
I'M NO LEADER. WE BOTH KNOW ***WHY*** I CAME BACK HERE. I LOST MY WAY, BISHOP.
"AND NOW IT SEEMS YOU'VE FOUND IT AGAIN. ***YOUR WAY*** LEADS TO GIDEON FALLS."

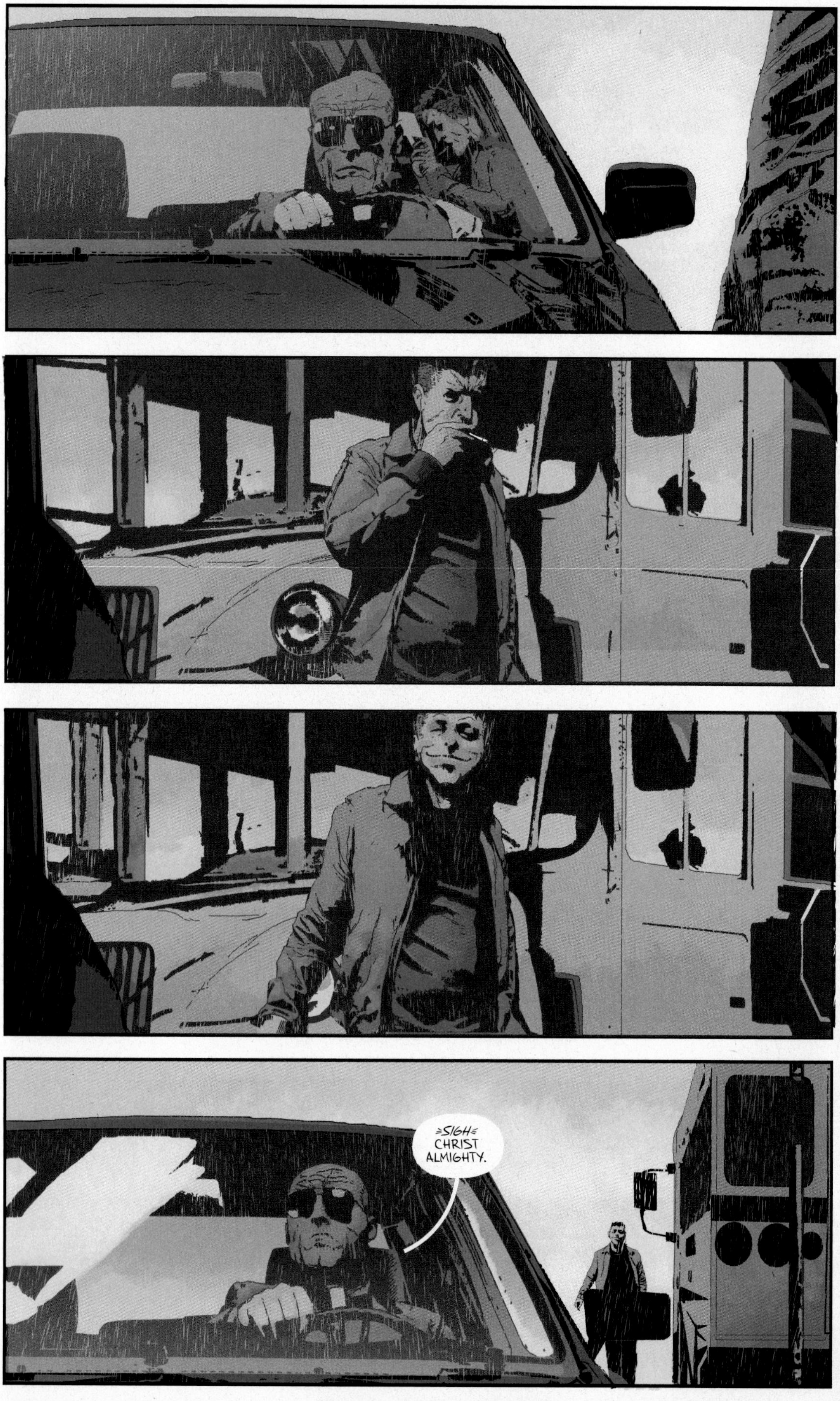
SIGH
CHRIST ALMIGHTY.

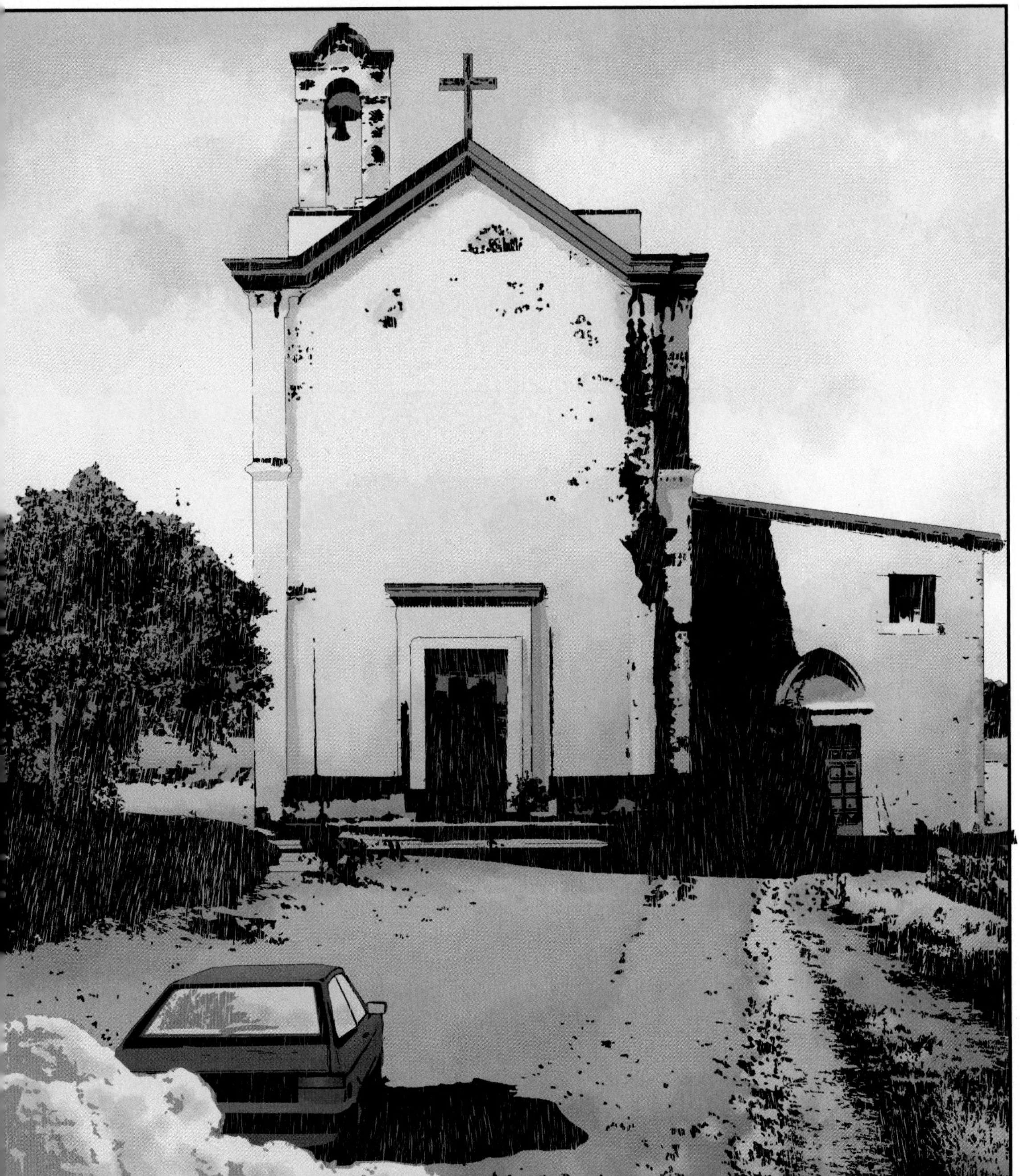

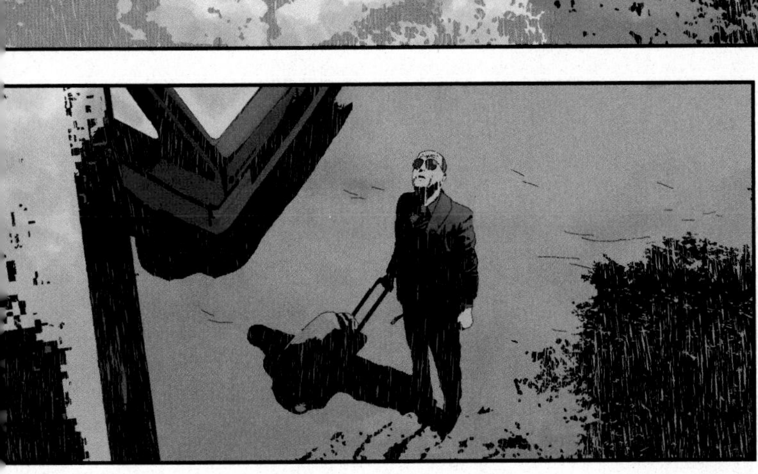

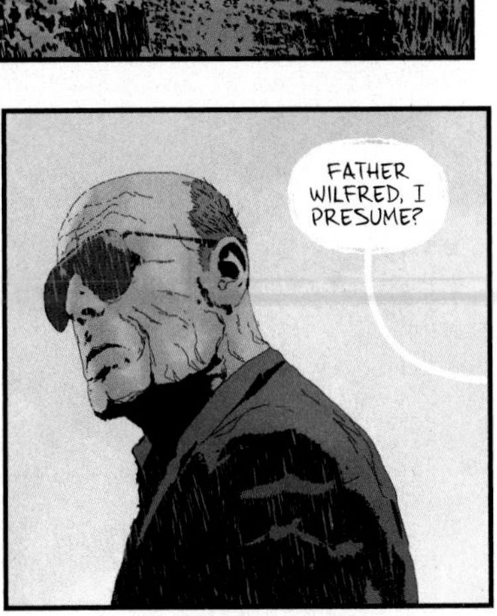
FATHER WILFRED, I PRESUME?

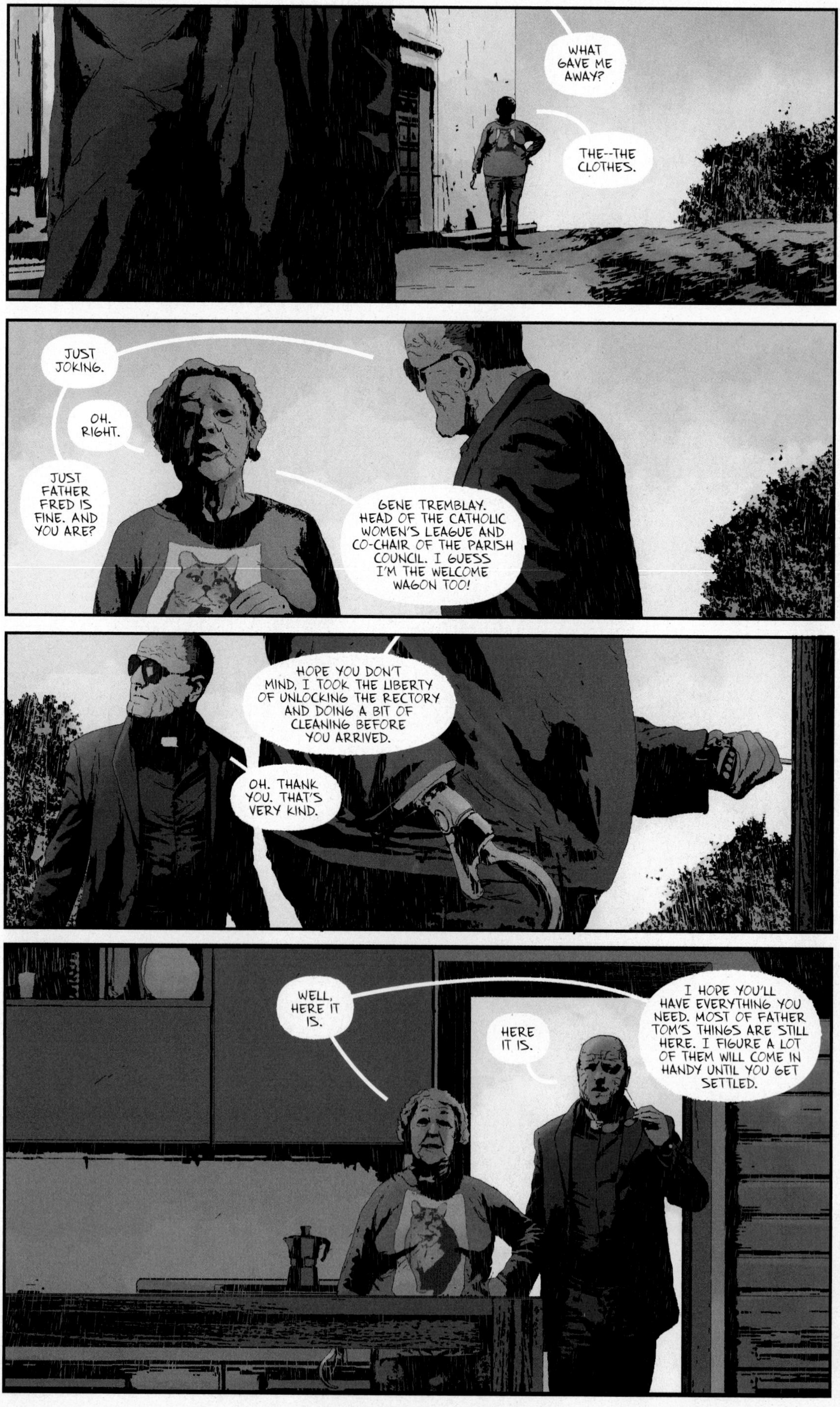
WHAT GAVE ME AWAY?
THE--THE CLOTHES.
JUST JOKING.
OH. RIGHT.
JUST FATHER FRED IS FINE. AND YOU ARE?
GENE TREMBLAY. HEAD OF THE CATHOLIC WOMEN'S LEAGUE AND CO-CHAIR OF THE PARISH COUNCIL. I GUESS I'M THE WELCOME WAGON TOO!
HOPE YOU DON'T MIND, I TOOK THE LIBERTY OF UNLOCKING THE RECTORY AND DOING A BIT OF CLEANING BEFORE YOU ARRIVED.
OH. THANK YOU. THAT'S VERY KIND.
WELL, HERE IT IS.
I HOPE YOU'LL HAVE EVERYTHING YOU NEED. MOST OF FATHER TOM'S THINGS ARE STILL HERE. I FIGURE A LOT OF THEM WILL COME IN HANDY UNTIL YOU GET SETTLED.
HERE IT IS.

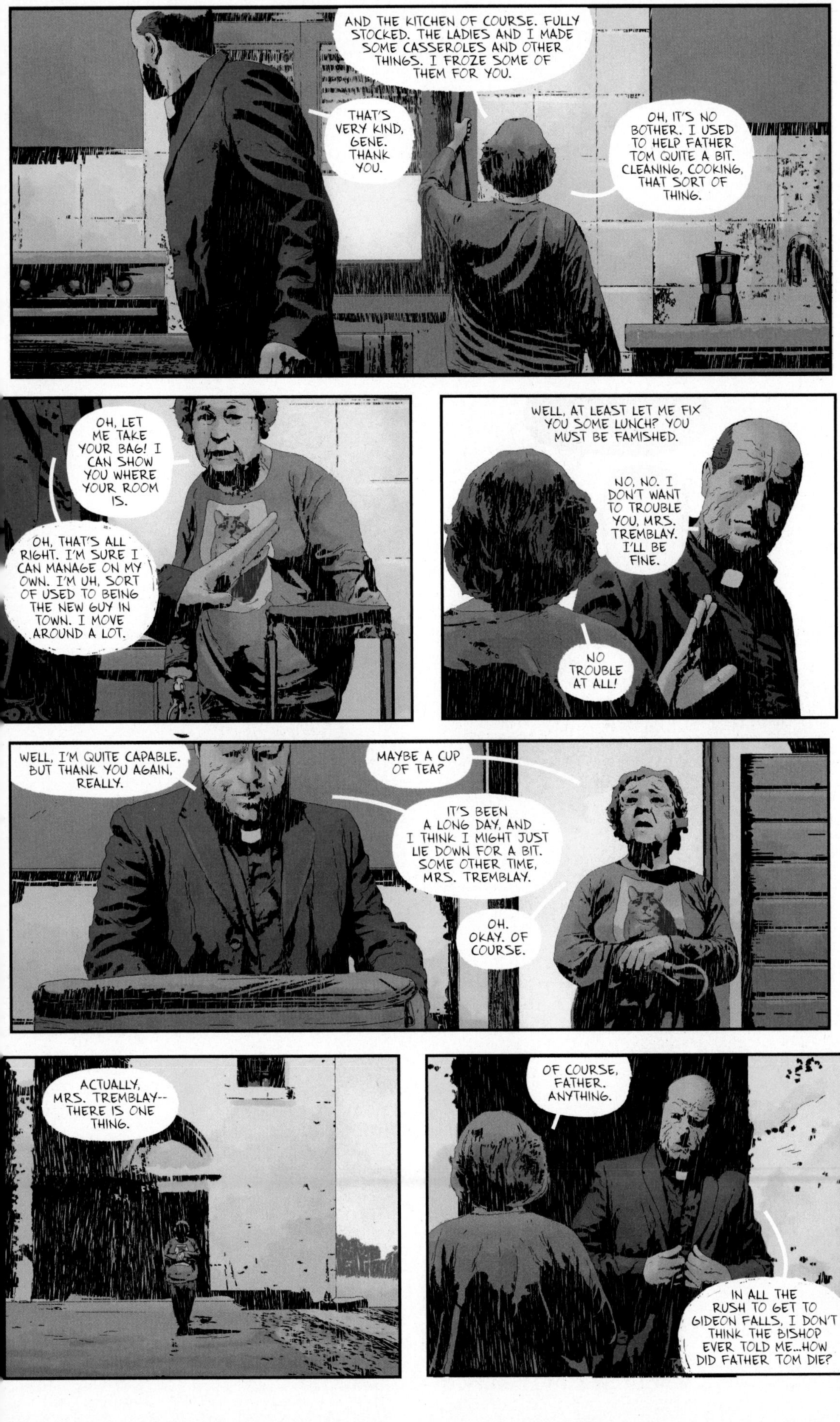
AND THE KITCHEN OF COURSE. FULLY STOCKED. THE LADIES AND I MADE SOME CASSEROLES AND OTHER THINGS. I FROZE SOME OF THEM FOR YOU.
THAT'S VERY KIND, GENE. THANK YOU.
OH, IT'S NO BOTHER. I USED TO HELP FATHER TOM QUITE A BIT. CLEANING, COOKING, THAT SORT OF THING.
OH, LET ME TAKE YOUR BAG! I CAN SHOW YOU WHERE YOUR ROOM IS.
OH, THAT'S ALL RIGHT. I'M SURE I CAN MANAGE ON MY OWN. I'M UH, SORT OF USED TO BEING THE NEW GUY IN TOWN. I MOVE AROUND A LOT.
WELL, AT LEAST LET ME FIX YOU SOME LUNCH? YOU MUST BE FAMISHED.
NO, NO. I DON'T WANT TO TROUBLE YOU, MRS. TREMBLAY. I'LL BE FINE.
NO TROUBLE AT ALL!
WELL, I'M QUITE CAPABLE. BUT THANK YOU AGAIN, REALLY.
MAYBE A CUP OF TEA?
IT'S BEEN A LONG DAY, AND I THINK I MIGHT JUST LIE DOWN FOR A BIT. SOME OTHER TIME, MRS. TREMBLAY.
OH. OKAY. OF COURSE.
ACTUALLY, MRS. TREMBLAY-- THERE IS ONE THING.
OF COURSE, FATHER. ANYTHING.
IN ALL THE RUSH TO GET TO GIDEON FALLS, I DON'T THINK THE BISHOP EVER TOLD ME...HOW DID FATHER TOM DIE?

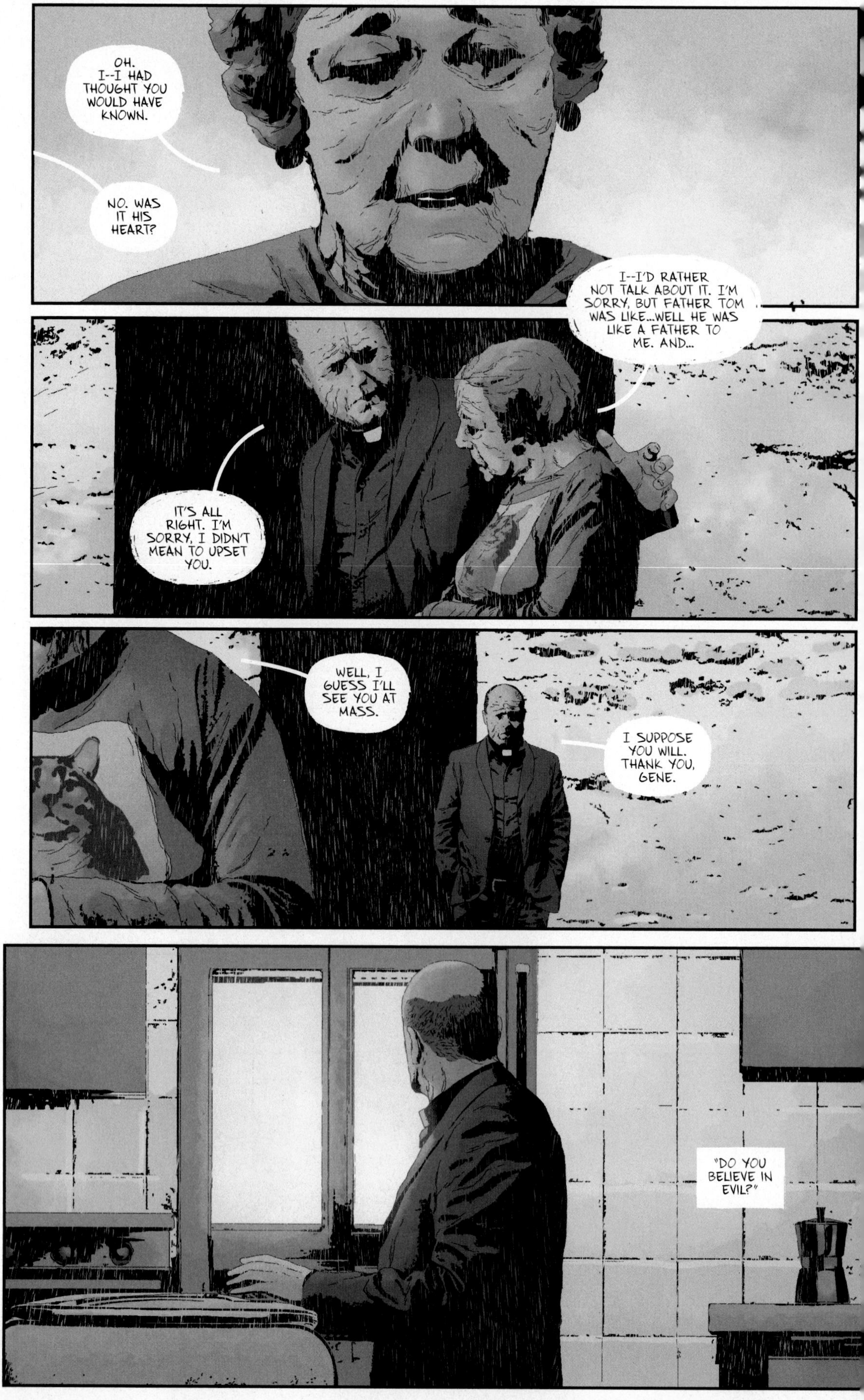
OH. I--I HAD THOUGHT YOU WOULD HAVE KNOWN.
NO. WAS IT HIS HEART?
I--I'D RATHER NOT TALK ABOUT IT. I'M SORRY, BUT FATHER TOM WAS LIKE...WELL HE WAS LIKE A FATHER TO ME. AND...
IT'S ALL RIGHT. I'M SORRY, I DIDN'T MEAN TO UPSET YOU.
WELL, I GUESS I'LL SEE YOU AT MASS.
I SUPPOSE YOU WILL. THANK YOU, GENE.
"DO YOU BELIEVE IN EVIL?"

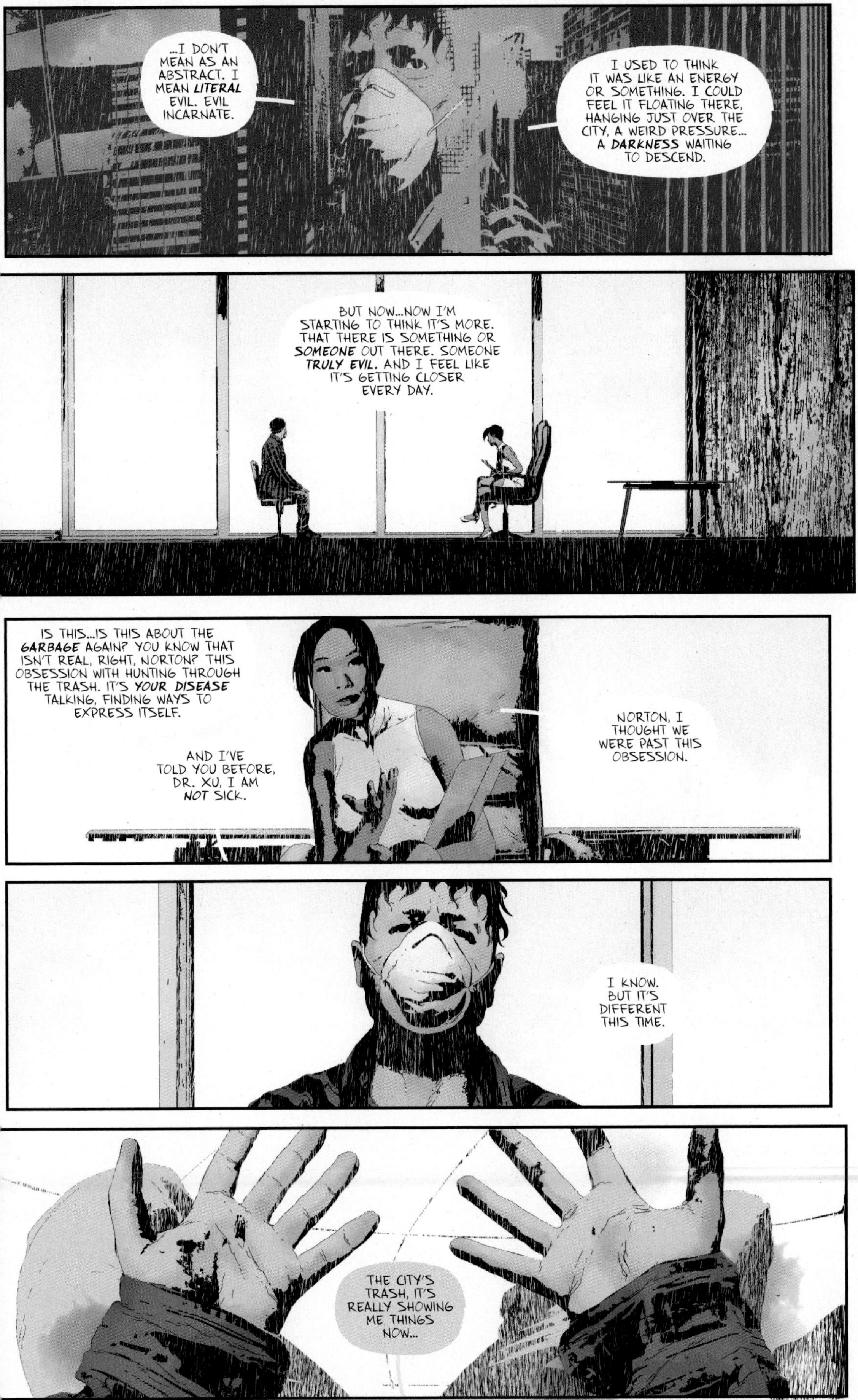
...I DON'T MEAN AS AN ABSTRACT. I MEAN LITERAL EVIL. EVIL INCARNATE.
I USED TO THINK IT WAS LIKE AN ENERGY OR SOMETHING. I COULD FEEL IT FLOATING THERE, HANGING JUST OVER THE CITY, A WEIRD PRESSURE... A DARKNESS WAITING TO DESCEND.
BUT NOW...NOW I'M STARTING TO THINK IT'S MORE. THAT THERE IS SOMETHING OR SOMEONE OUT THERE. SOMEONE TRULY EVIL. AND I FEEL LIKE IT'S GETTING CLOSER EVERY DAY.
NORTON, I THOUGHT WE WERE PAST THIS OBSESSION.
AND I'VE TOLD YOU BEFORE, DR. XU, I AM NOT SICK.
IS THIS...IS THIS ABOUT THE GARBAGE AGAIN? YOU KNOW THAT ISN'T REAL, RIGHT, NORTON? THIS OBSESSION WITH HUNTING THROUGH THE TRASH. IT'S YOUR DISEASE TALKING, FINDING WAYS TO EXPRESS ITSELF.
I KNOW. BUT IT'S DIFFERENT THIS TIME.
THE CITY'S TRASH, IT'S REALLY SHOWING ME THINGS NOW...

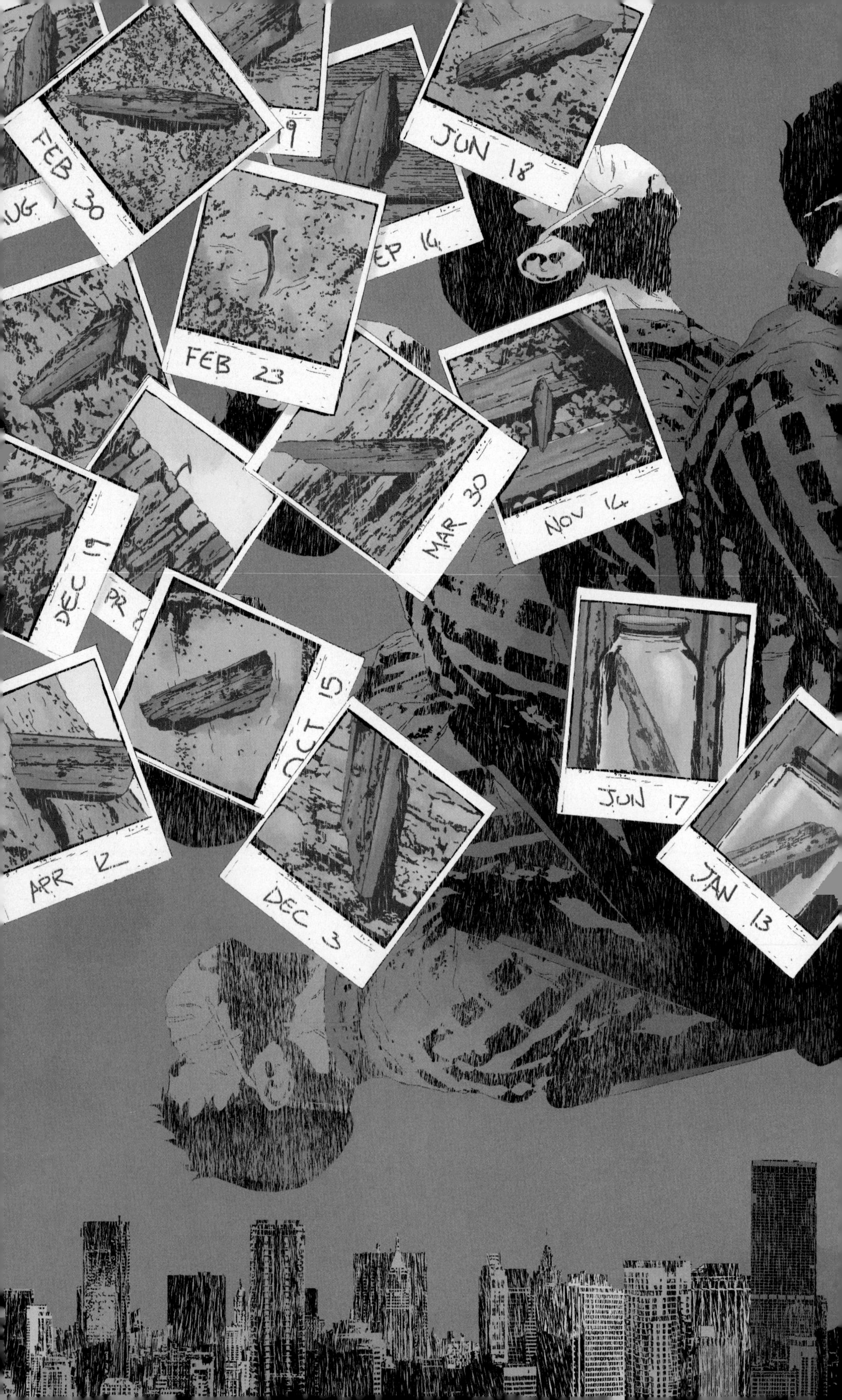
FEB 30
JUN 18
FEB 23
MAR 30
NOV 14
DEC 19
OCT 15
JUN 17
APR 12
DEC 3
JAN 13

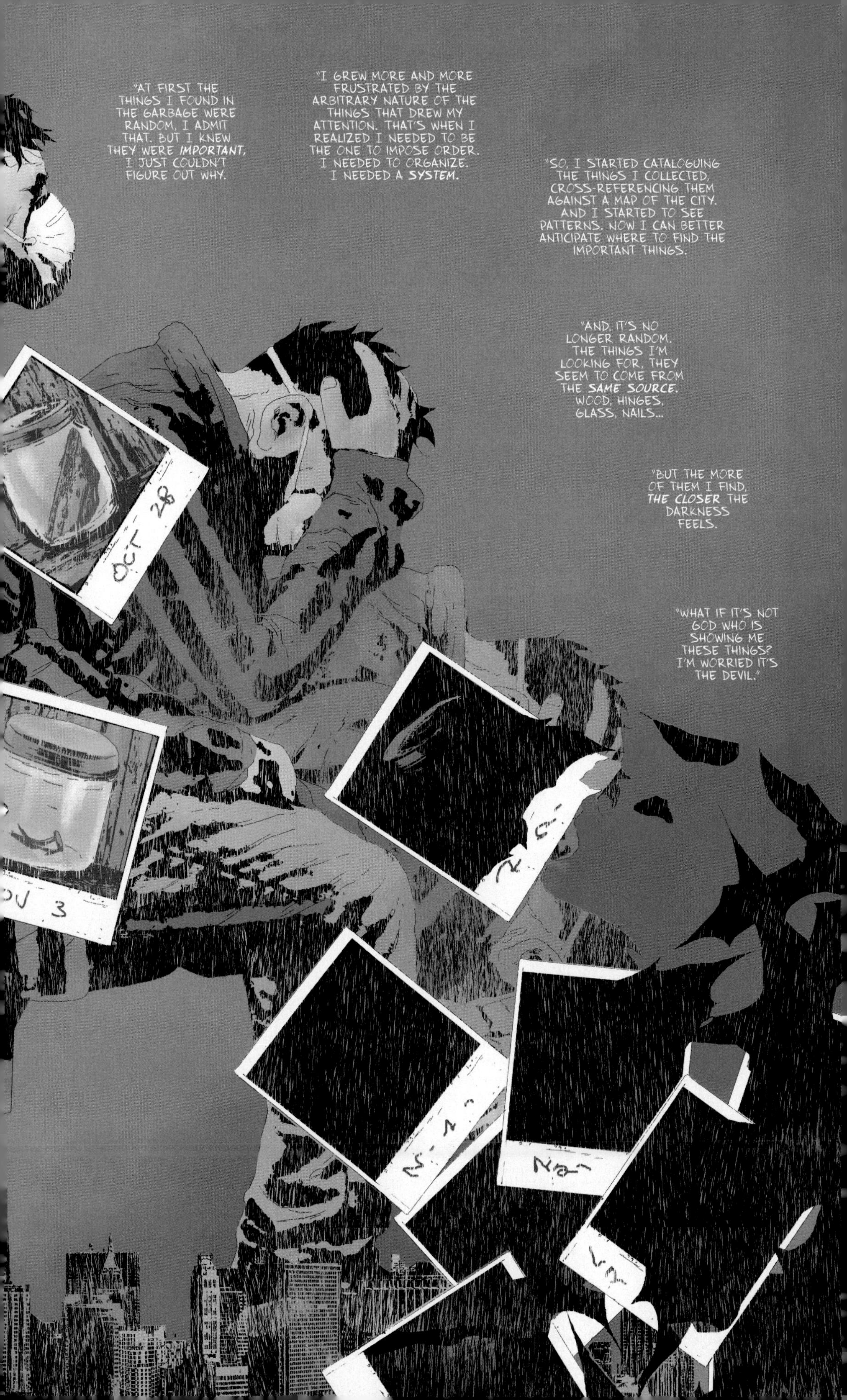
"AT FIRST THE THINGS I FOUND IN THE GARBAGE WERE RANDOM, I ADMIT THAT. BUT I KNEW THEY WERE *IMPORTANT*, I JUST COULDN'T FIGURE OUT WHY.
"I GREW MORE AND MORE FRUSTRATED BY THE ARBITRARY NATURE OF THE THINGS THAT DREW MY ATTENTION. THAT'S WHEN I REALIZED I NEEDED TO BE THE ONE TO IMPOSE ORDER. I NEEDED TO ORGANIZE. I NEEDED A **SYSTEM.**
"SO, I STARTED CATALOGUING THE THINGS I COLLECTED, CROSS-REFERENCING THEM AGAINST A MAP OF THE CITY. AND I STARTED TO SEE PATTERNS. NOW I CAN BETTER ANTICIPATE WHERE TO FIND THE IMPORTANT THINGS.
"AND, IT'S NO LONGER RANDOM. THE THINGS I'M LOOKING FOR, THEY SEEM TO COME FROM THE ***SAME SOURCE.*** WOOD, HINGES, GLASS, NAILS...
"BUT THE MORE OF THEM I FIND, ***THE CLOSER*** THE DARKNESS FEELS.
"WHAT IF IT'S NOT GOD WHO IS SHOWING ME THESE THINGS? I'M WORRIED IT'S THE DEVIL."
OCT 28

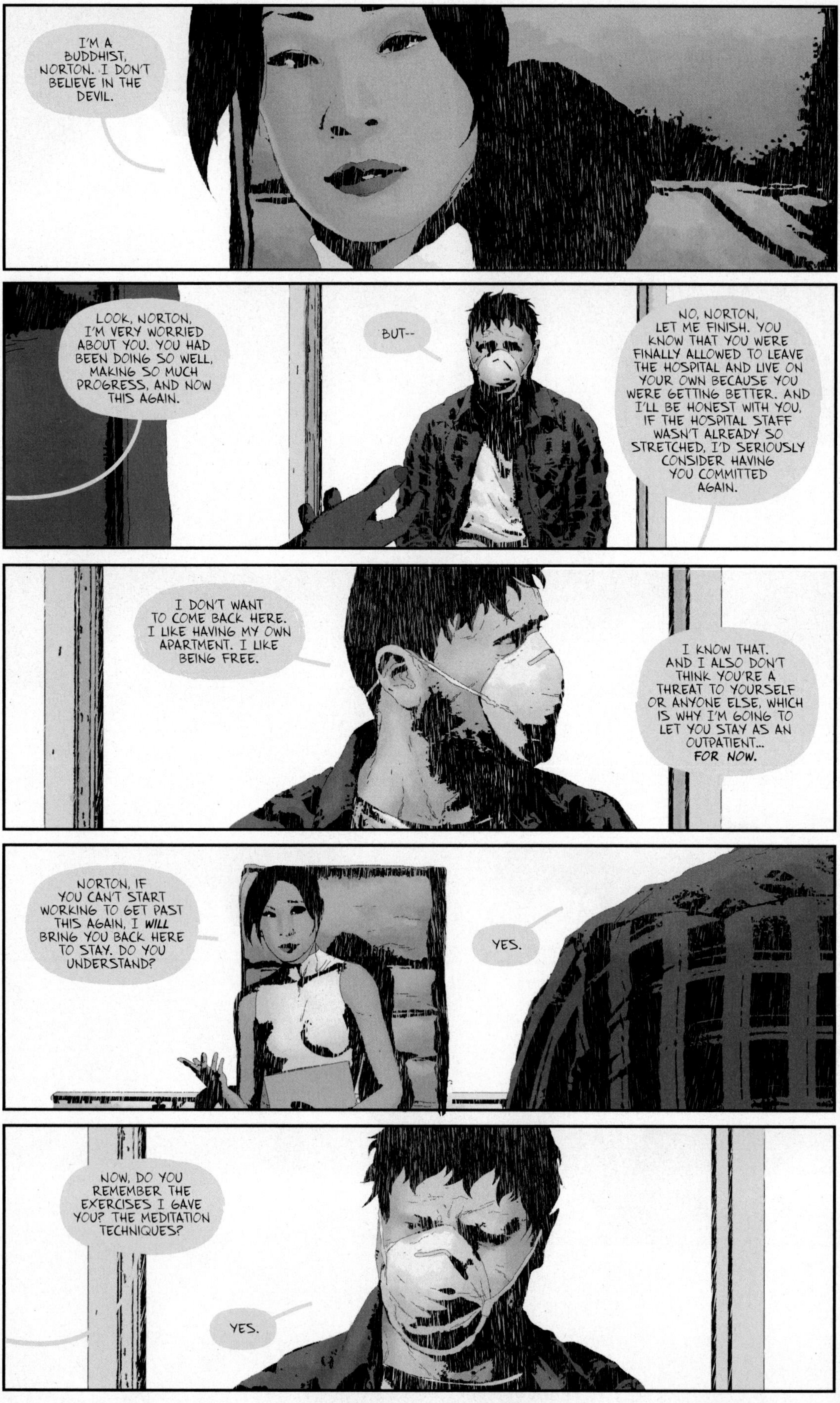
I'M A BUDDHIST, NORTON. I DON'T BELIEVE IN THE DEVIL.
LOOK, NORTON, I'M VERY WORRIED ABOUT YOU. YOU HAD BEEN DOING SO WELL, MAKING SO MUCH PROGRESS, AND NOW THIS AGAIN.
BUT--
NO, NORTON, LET ME FINISH. YOU KNOW THAT YOU WERE FINALLY ALLOWED TO LEAVE THE HOSPITAL AND LIVE ON YOUR OWN BECAUSE YOU WERE GETTING BETTER. AND I'LL BE HONEST WITH YOU, IF THE HOSPITAL STAFF WASN'T ALREADY SO STRETCHED, I'D SERIOUSLY CONSIDER HAVING YOU COMMITTED AGAIN.
I DON'T WANT TO COME BACK HERE. I LIKE HAVING MY OWN APARTMENT. I LIKE BEING FREE.
I KNOW THAT. AND I ALSO DON'T THINK YOU'RE A THREAT TO YOURSELF OR ANYONE ELSE, WHICH IS WHY I'M GOING TO LET YOU STAY AS AN OUTPATIENT... **FOR NOW.**
NORTON, IF YOU CAN'T START WORKING TO GET PAST THIS AGAIN, I ***WILL*** BRING YOU BACK HERE TO STAY. DO YOU UNDERSTAND?
YES.
NOW, DO YOU REMEMBER THE EXERCISES I GAVE YOU? THE MEDITATION TECHNIQUES?
YES.

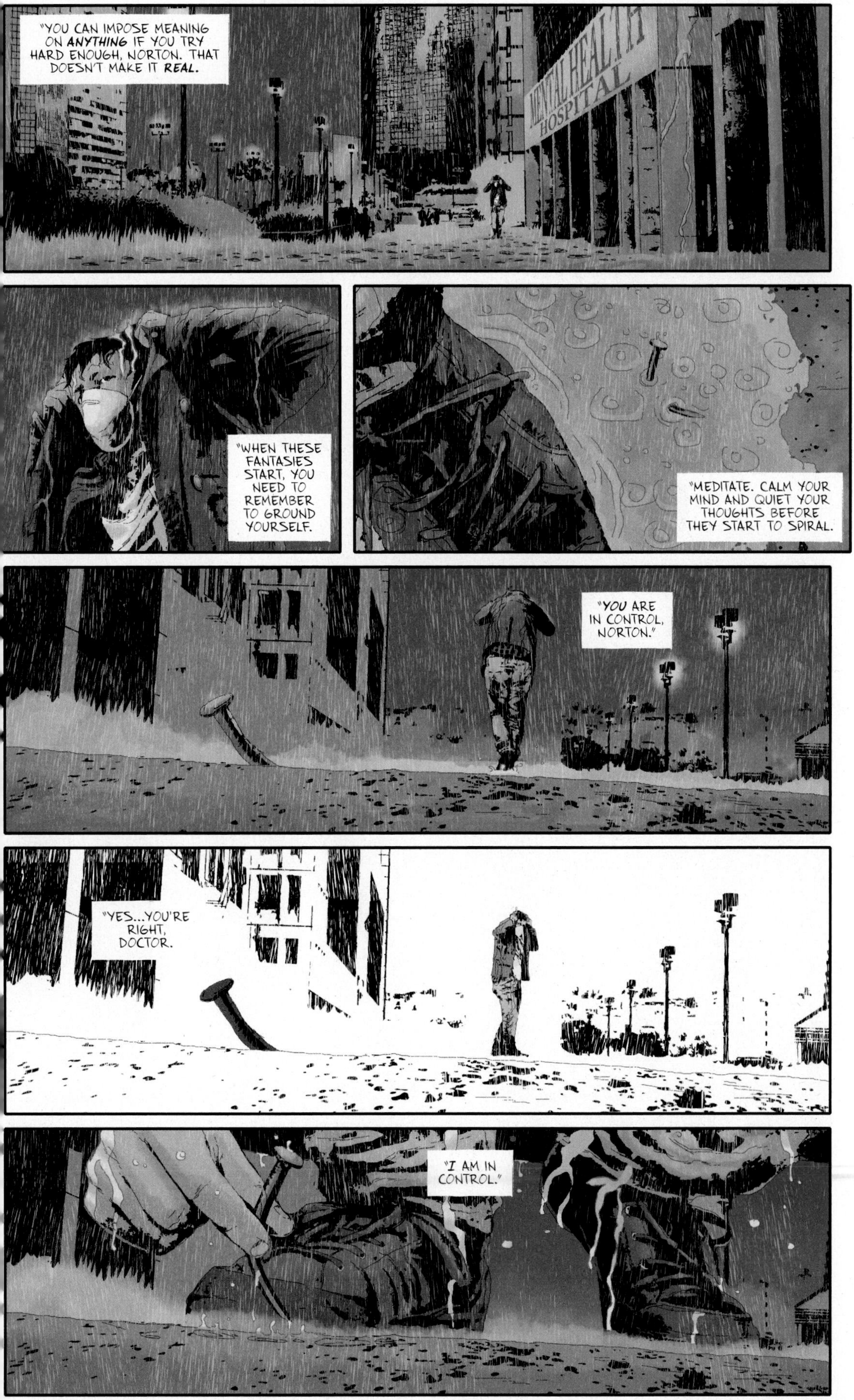
"YOU CAN IMPOSE MEANING ON ANYTHING IF YOU TRY HARD ENOUGH, NORTON. THAT DOESN'T MAKE IT REAL.
MENTAL HEALTH HOSPITAL
"WHEN THESE FANTASIES START, YOU NEED TO REMEMBER TO GROUND YOURSELF.
"MEDITATE. CALM YOUR MIND AND QUIET YOUR THOUGHTS BEFORE THEY START TO SPIRAL.
"YOU ARE IN CONTROL, NORTON."
"YES...YOU'RE RIGHT, DOCTOR.
"I AM IN CONTROL."

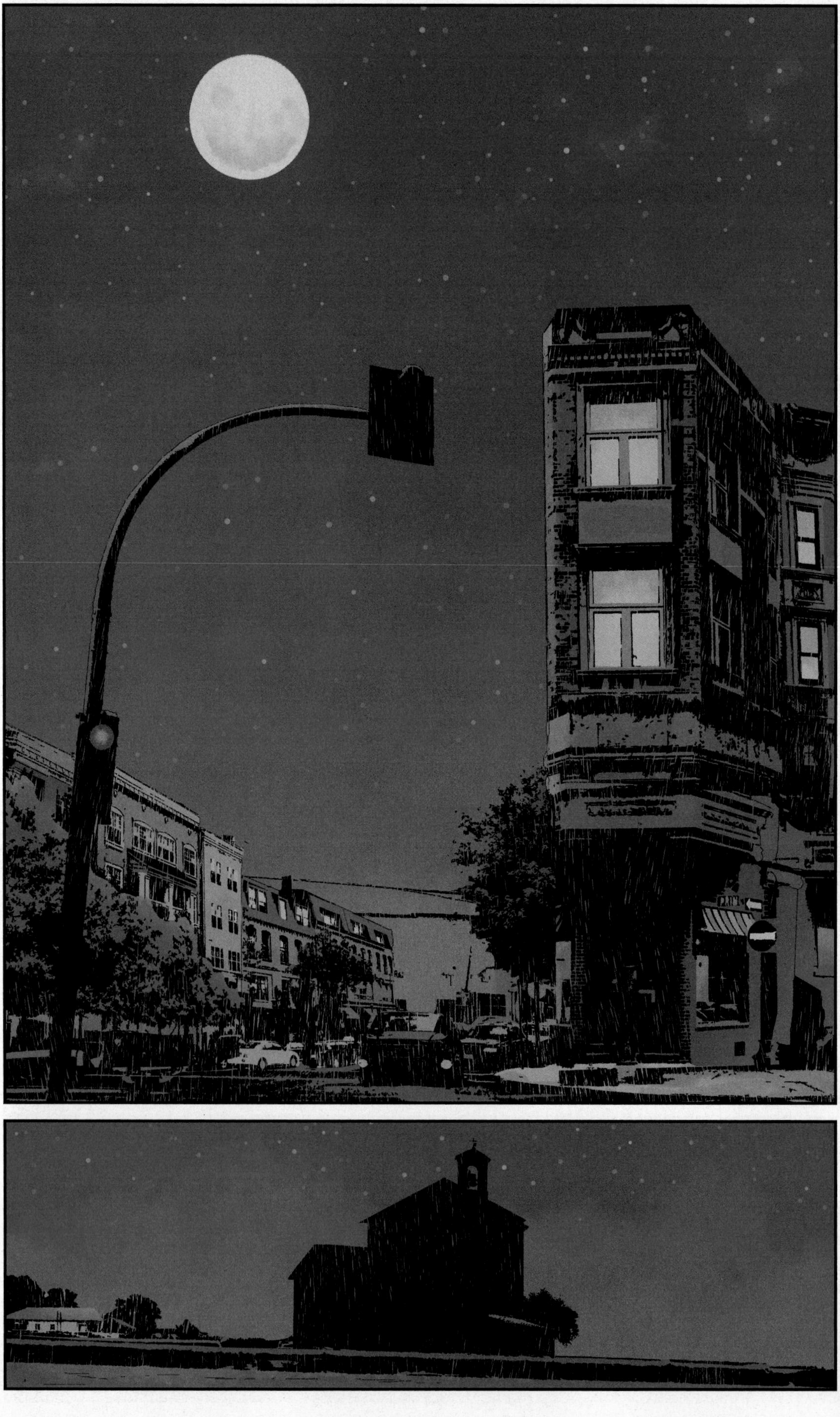

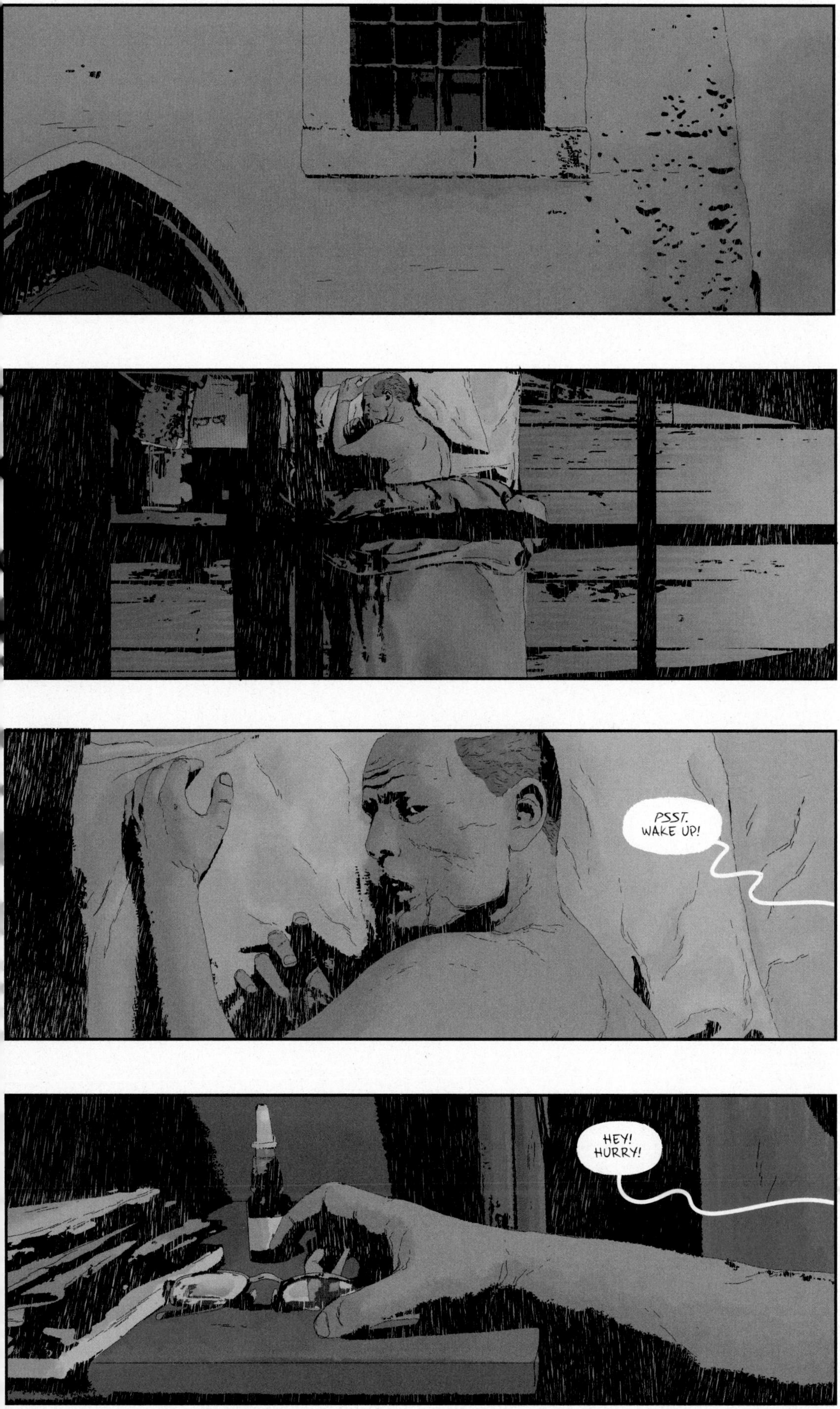
PSST. WAKE UP!
HEY! HURRY!

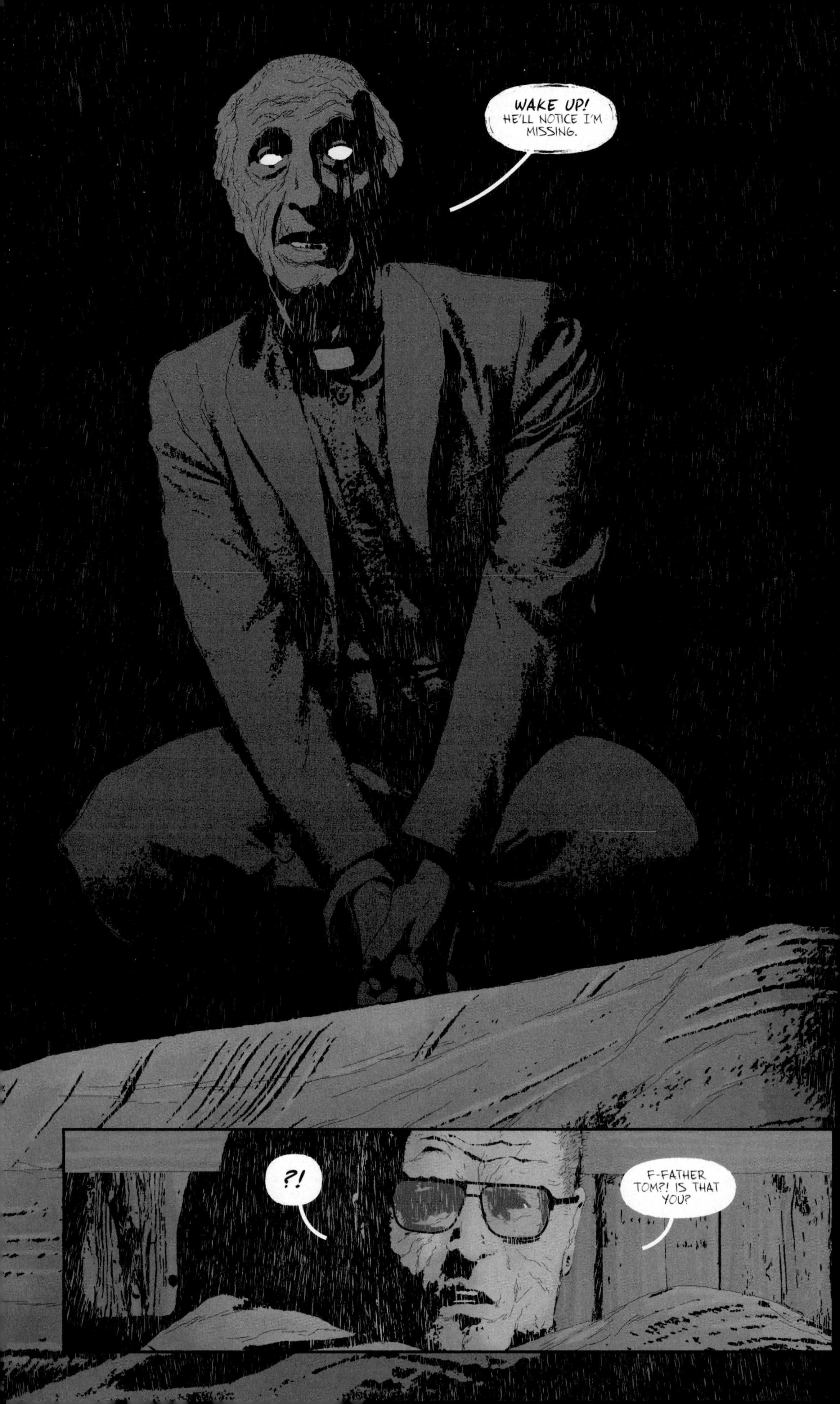
WAKE UP! HE'LL NOTICE I'M MISSING.
?!
F-FATHER TOM?! IS THAT YOU?

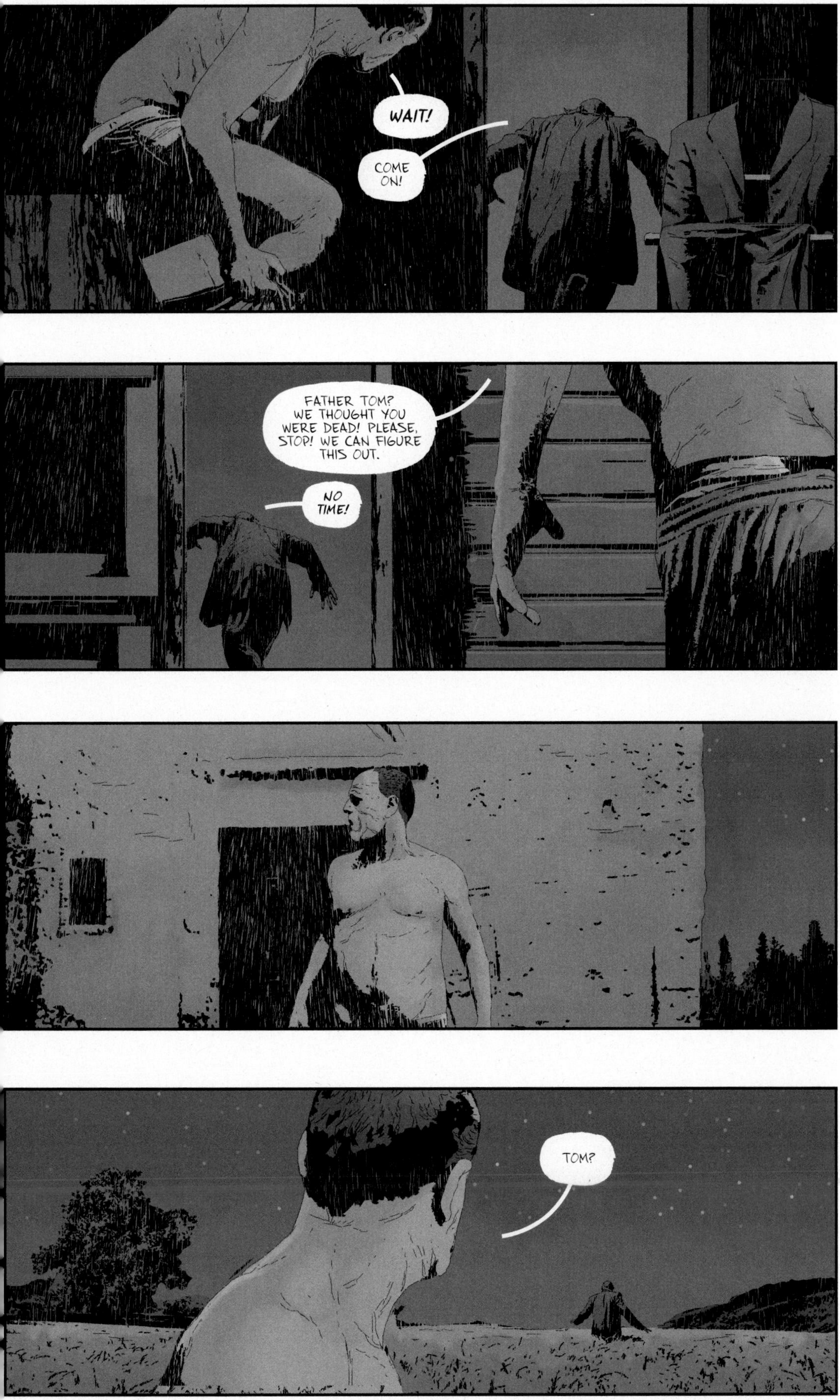
WAIT!
COME ON!
FATHER TOM? WE THOUGHT YOU WERE DEAD! PLEASE, STOP! WE CAN FIGURE THIS OUT.
NO TIME!
TOM?

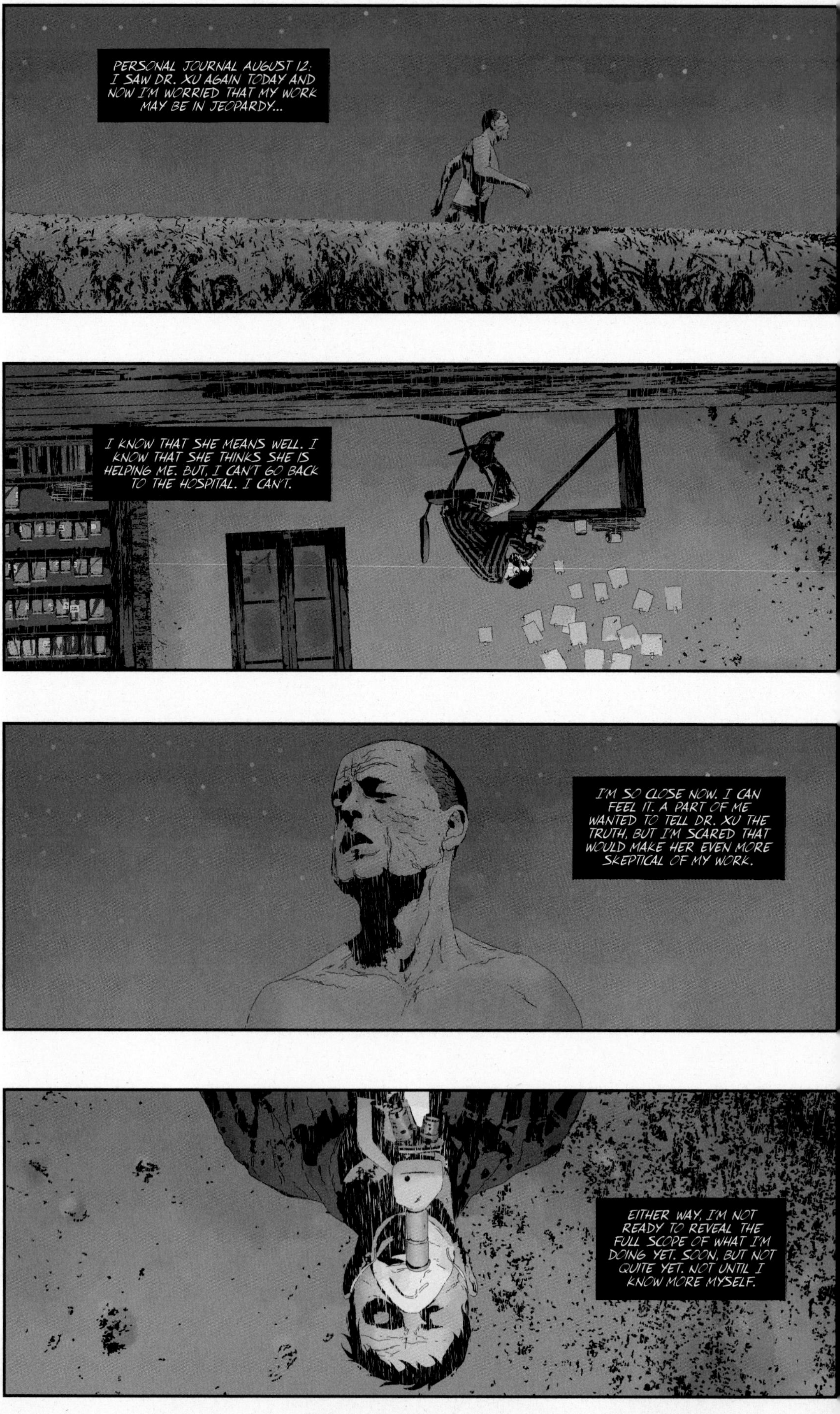
PERSONAL JOURNAL AUGUST 12: I SAW DR. XU AGAIN TODAY AND NOW I'M WORRIED THAT MY WORK MAY BE IN JEOPARDY...
I KNOW THAT SHE MEANS WELL. I KNOW THAT SHE THINKS SHE IS HELPING ME. BUT, I CAN'T GO BACK TO THE HOSPITAL. I CAN'T.
I'M SO CLOSE NOW. I CAN FEEL IT. A PART OF ME WANTED TO TELL DR. XU THE TRUTH, BUT I'M SCARED THAT WOULD MAKE HER EVEN MORE SKEPTICAL OF MY WORK.
EITHER WAY, I'M NOT READY TO REVEAL THE FULL SCOPE OF WHAT I'M DOING YET. SOON, BUT NOT QUITE YET. NOT UNTIL I KNOW MORE MYSELF.

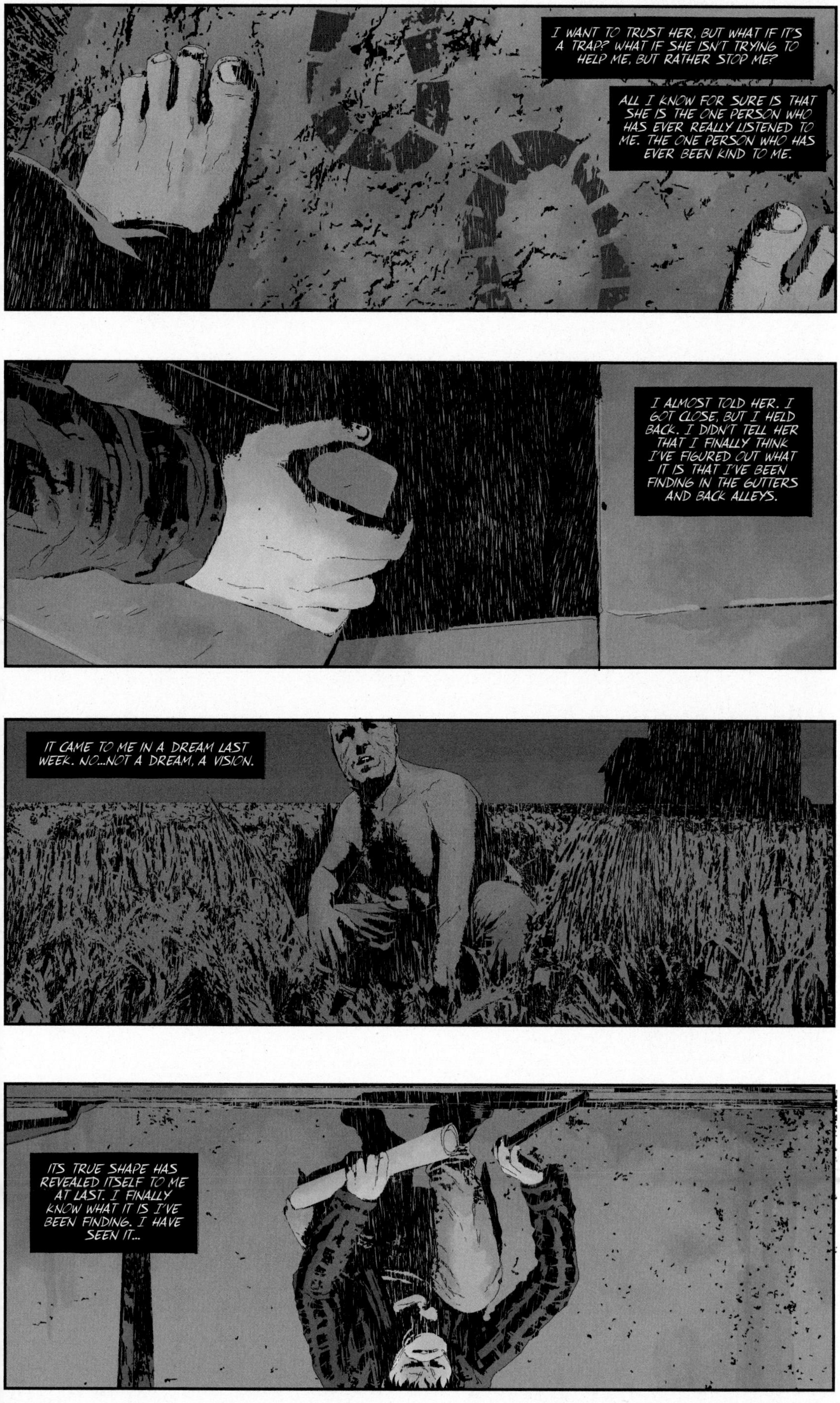
I WANT TO TRUST HER, BUT WHAT IF IT'S A TRAP? WHAT IF SHE ISN'T TRYING TO HELP ME, BUT RATHER STOP ME?
ALL I KNOW FOR SURE IS THAT SHE IS THE ONE PERSON WHO HAS EVER REALLY LISTENED TO ME. THE ONE PERSON WHO HAS EVER BEEN KIND TO ME.
I ALMOST TOLD HER. I GOT CLOSE, BUT I HELD BACK. I DIDN'T TELL HER THAT I FINALLY THINK I'VE FIGURED OUT WHAT IT IS THAT I'VE BEEN FINDING IN THE GUTTERS AND BACK ALLEYS.
IT CAME TO ME IN A DREAM LAST WEEK. NO...NOT A DREAM, A VISION.
ITS TRUE SHAPE HAS REVEALED ITSELF TO ME AT LAST. I FINALLY KNOW WHAT IT IS I'VE BEEN FINDING. I HAVE SEEN IT...

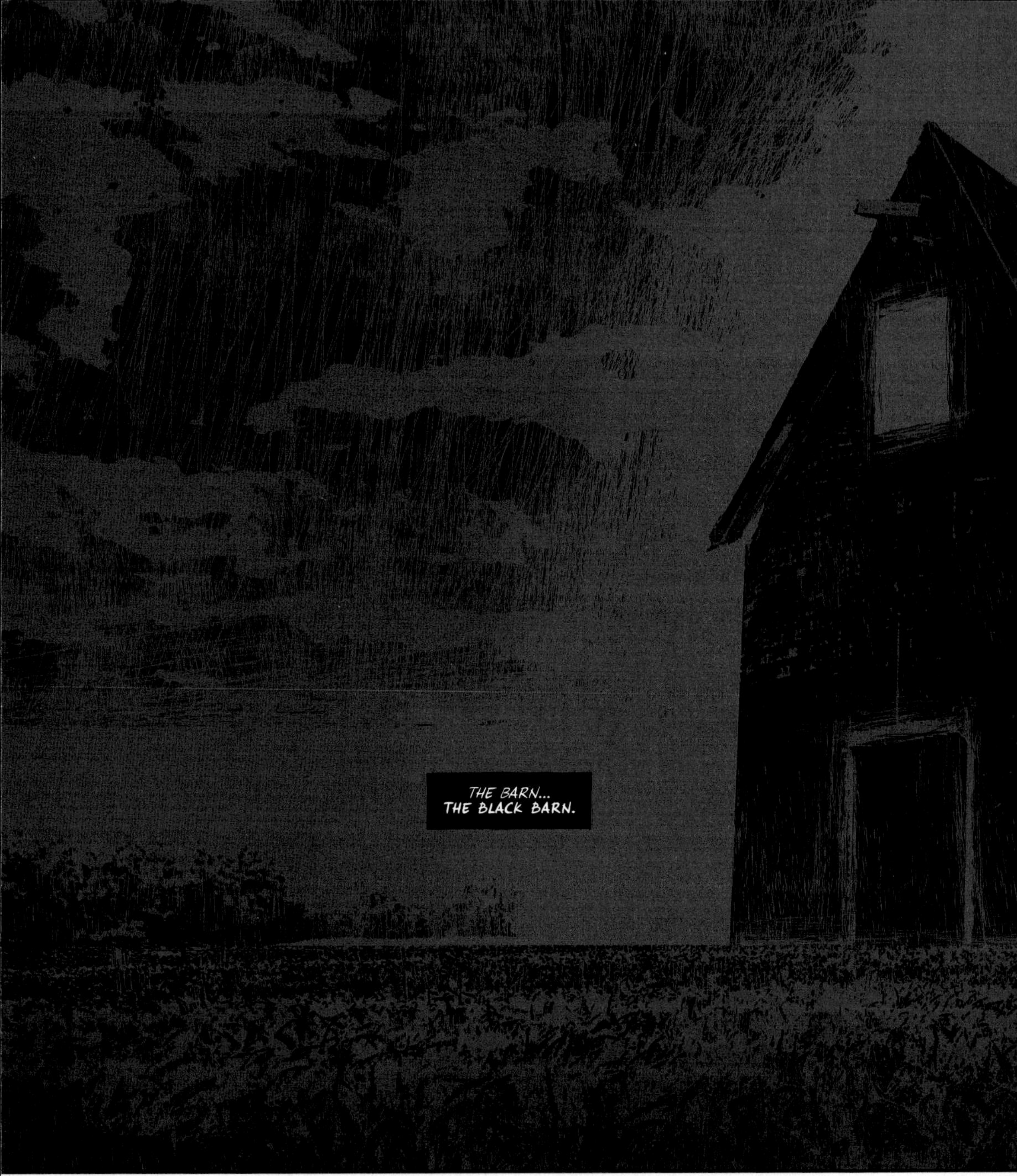
THE BARN...
THE BLACK BARN.

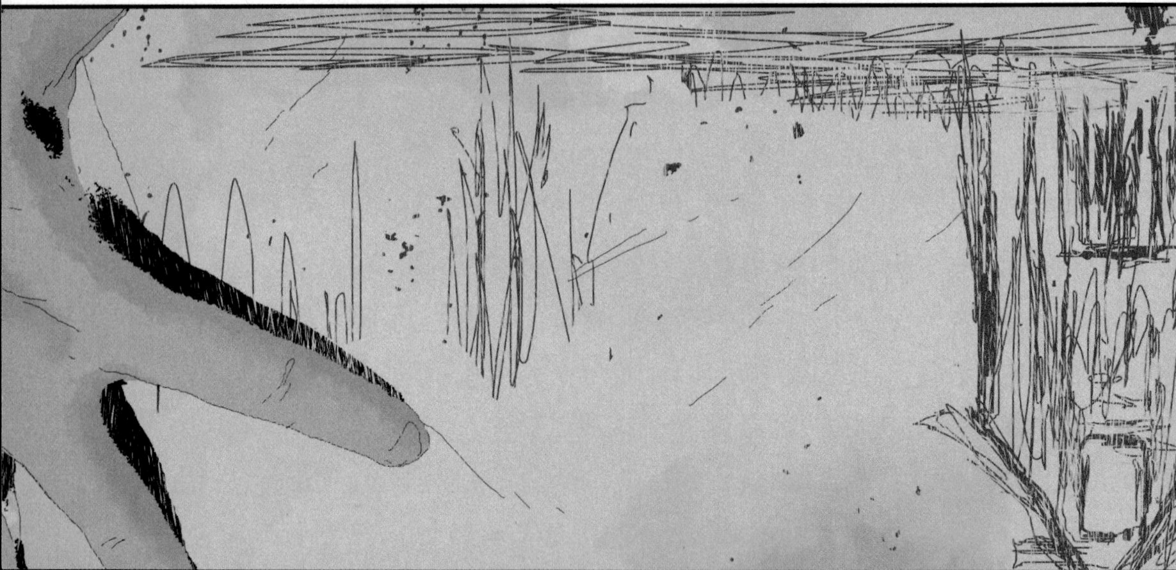

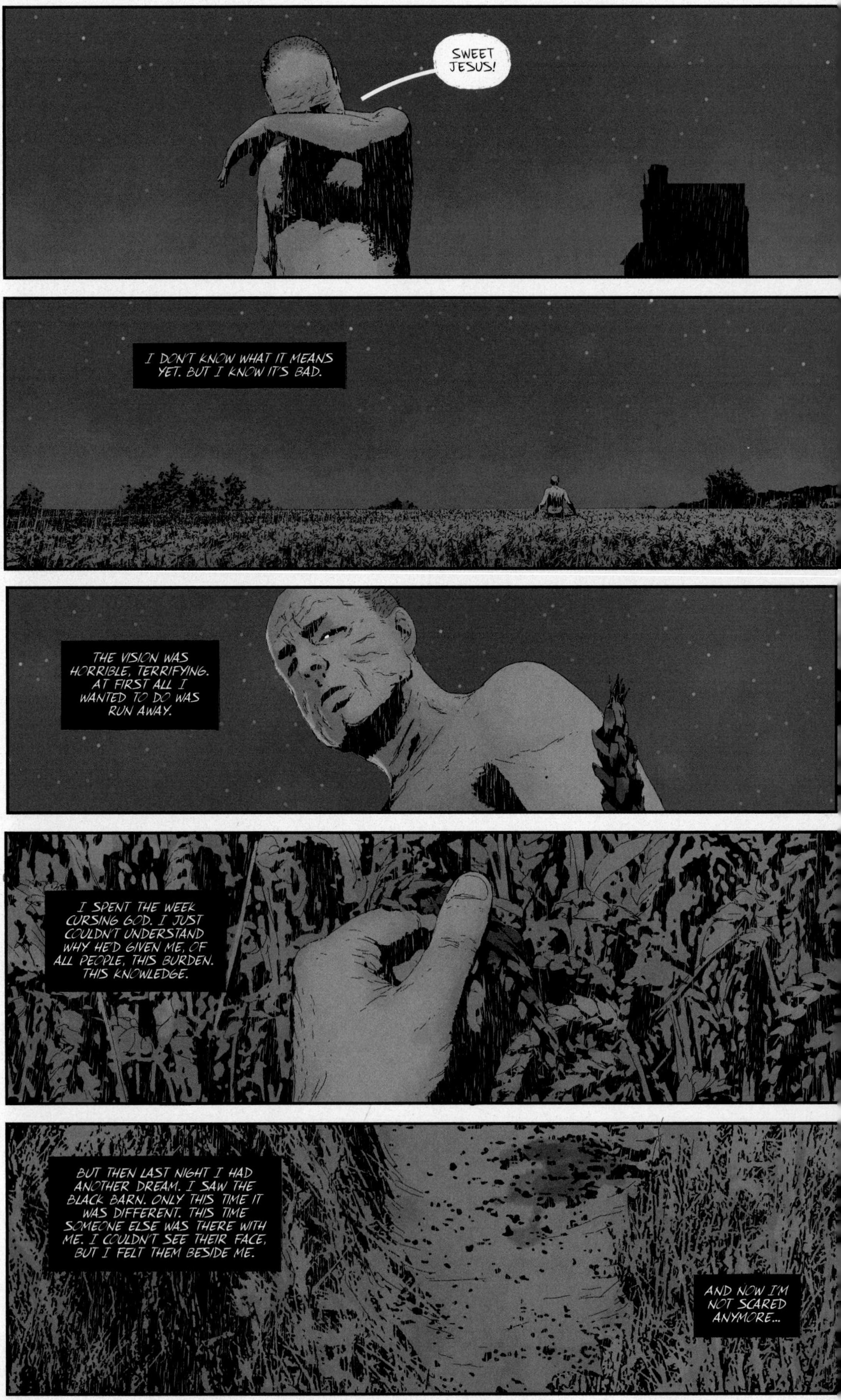
SWEET JESUS!
I DON'T KNOW WHAT IT MEANS YET. BUT I KNOW IT'S BAD.
THE VISION WAS HORRIBLE, TERRIFYING. AT FIRST ALL I WANTED TO DO WAS RUN AWAY.
I SPENT THE WEEK CURSING GOD. I JUST COULDN'T UNDERSTAND WHY HE'D GIVEN ME, OF ALL PEOPLE, THIS BURDEN. THIS KNOWLEDGE.
BUT THEN LAST NIGHT I HAD ANOTHER DREAM. I SAW THE BLACK BARN. ONLY THIS TIME IT WAS DIFFERENT. THIS TIME SOMEONE ELSE WAS THERE WITH ME. I COULDN'T SEE THEIR FACE, BUT I FELT THEM BESIDE ME.
AND NOW I'M NOT SCARED ANYMORE...

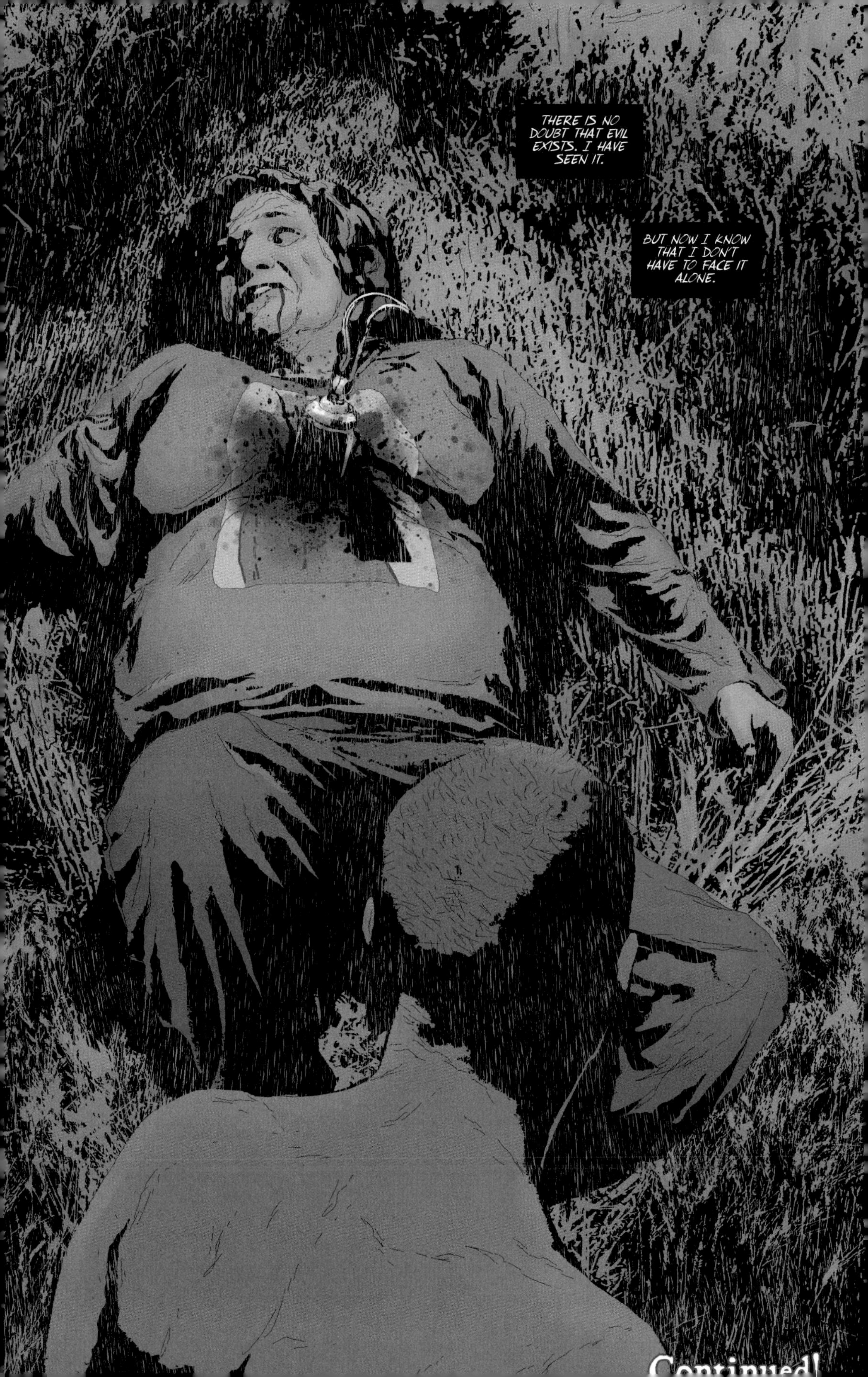
THERE IS NO DOUBT THAT EVIL EXISTS. I HAVE SEEN IT.
BUT NOW I KNOW THAT I DON'T HAVE TO FACE IT ALONE.
Continued!

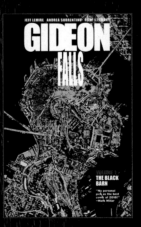

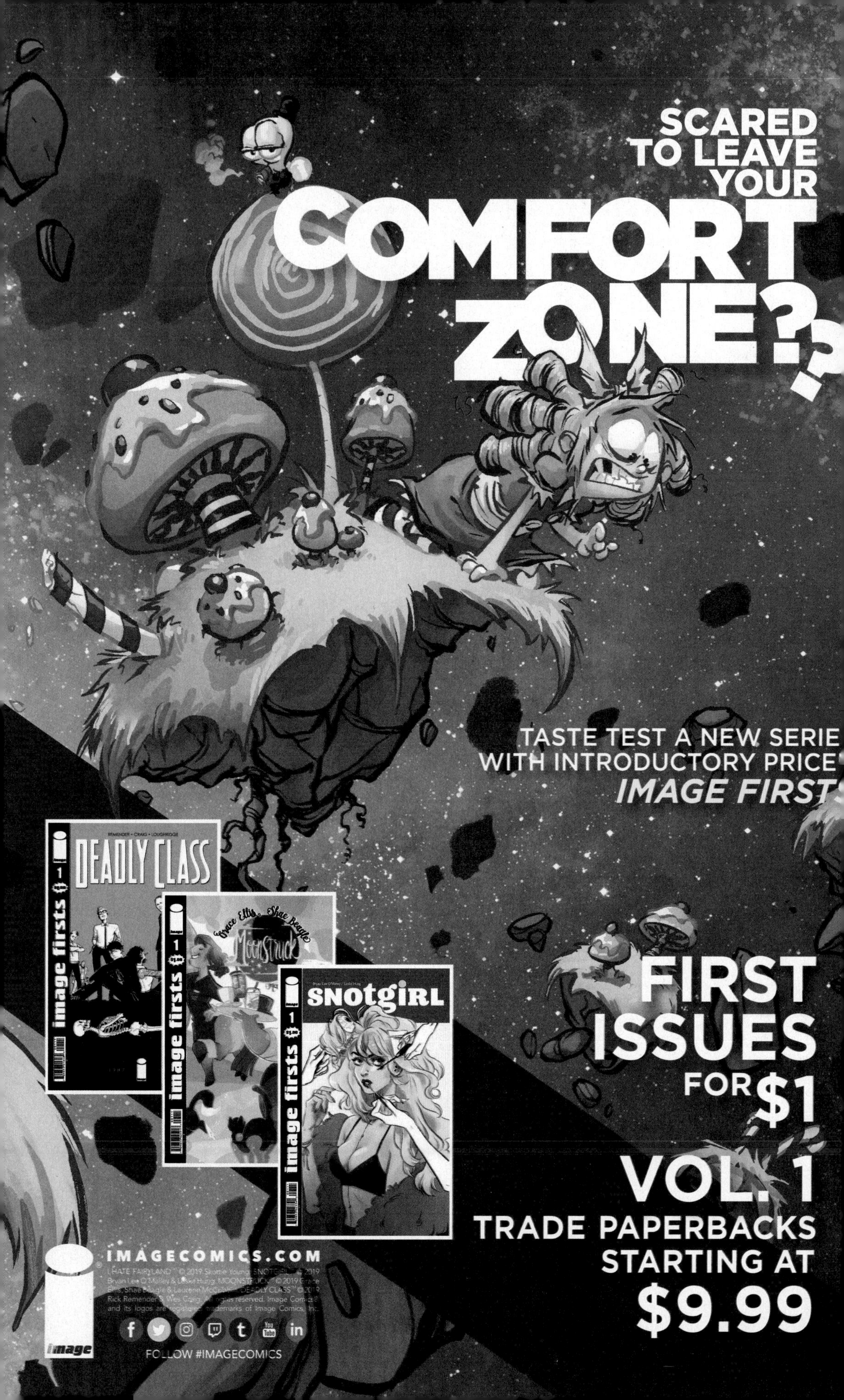

SCARED TO LEAVE YOUR
COMFORT ZONE??
TASTE TEST A NEW SERIE
WITH INTRODUCTORY PRICE
IMAGE FIRST
DEADLY CLASS
image firsts
Moonstruck
SNOTGIRL
FIRST ISSUES FOR $1
VOL. 1
TRADE PAPERBACKS
STARTING AT
$9.99
IMAGECOMICS.COM
FOLLOW #IMAGECOMICS

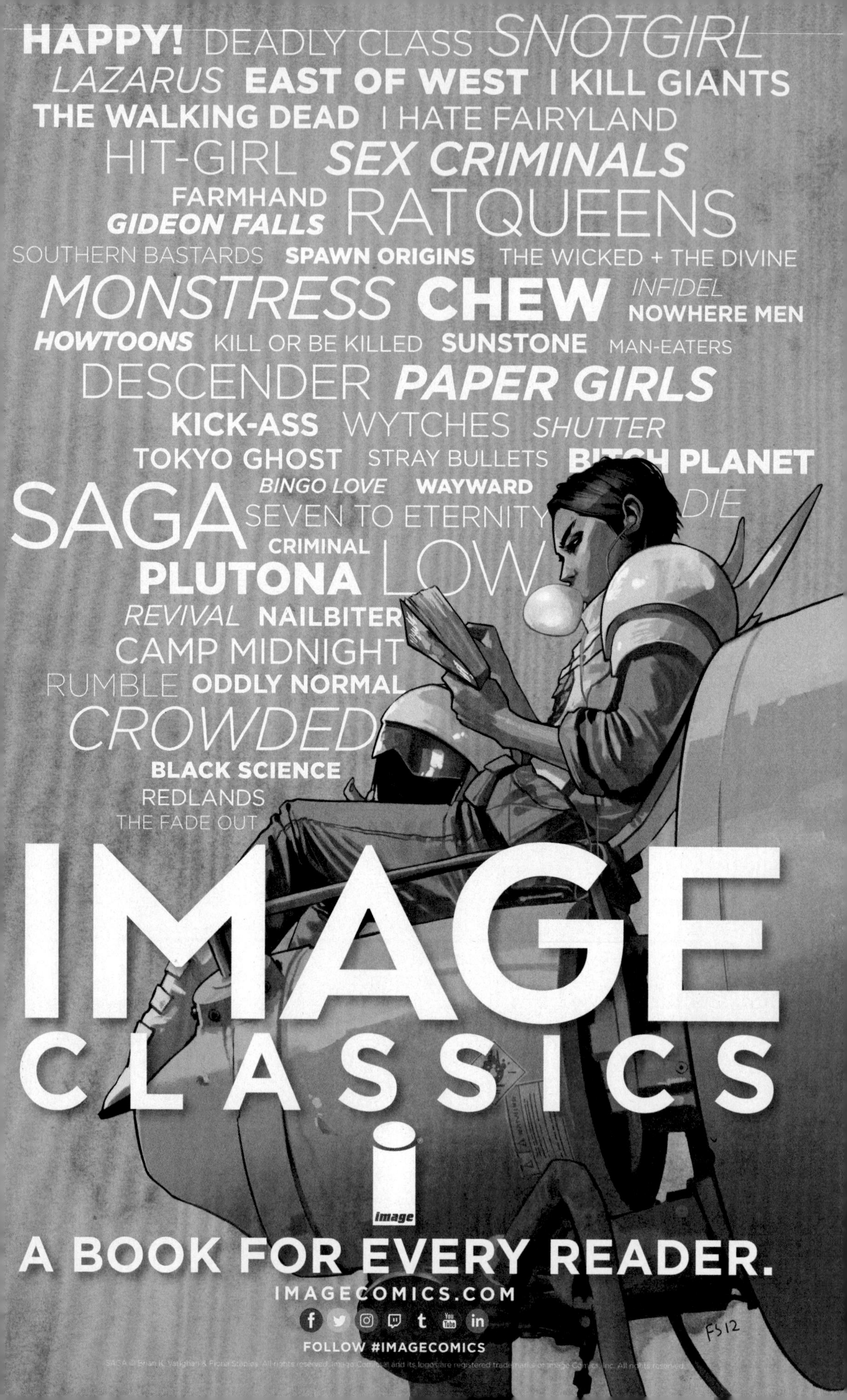
HAPPY! DEADLY CLASS SNOTGIRL
LAZARUS EAST OF WEST I KILL GIANTS
THE WALKING DEAD I HATE FAIRYLAND
HIT-GIRL SEX CRIMINALS
FARMHAND RATQUEENS
GIDEON FALLS
SOUTHERN BASTARDS SPAWN ORIGINS THE WICKED + THE DIVINE
MONSTRESS CHEW INFIDEL
NOWHERE MEN
HOWTOONS KILL OR BE KILLED SUNSTONE MAN-EATERS
DESCENDER PAPER GIRLS
KICK-ASS WYTCHES SHUTTER
TOKYO GHOST STRAY BULLETS BITCH PLANET
SAGA BINGO LOVE WAYWARD
SEVEN TO ETERNITY DIE
CRIMINAL
PLUTONA LOW
REVIVAL NAILBITER
CAMP MIDNIGHT
RUMBLE ODDLY NORMAL
CROWDED
BLACK SCIENCE
REDLANDS
THE FADE OUT
IMAGE CLASSICS
image
A BOOK FOR EVERY READER.
IMAGECOMICS.COM
FOLLOW #IMAGECOMICS
FS12
SAGA © Brian K. Vaughan & Fiona Staples. All rights reserved. Image Comics® and its logos are registered trademarks of Image Comics, Inc. All rights reserved.

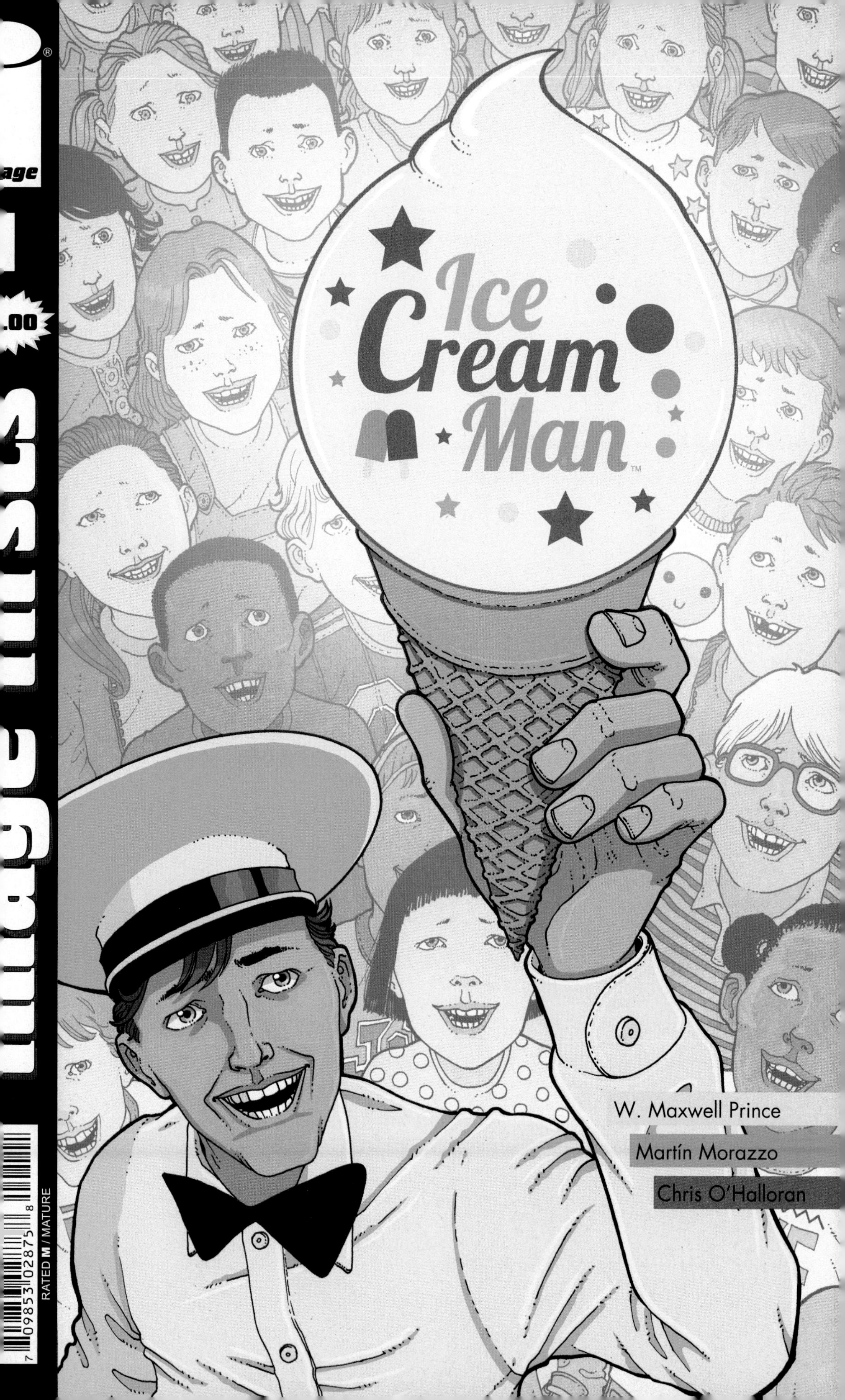
Ice Cream Man
W. Maxwell Prince
Martín Morazzo
Chris O'Halloran
RATED M / MATURE

1

Ice Cream Man

• RASPBERRY SURPRISE •

WRITTEN BY **W. MAXWELL PRINCE**   ART BY **MARTÍN MORAZZO**

COLORS BY **CHRIS O'HALLORAN**   LETTERING BY **GOOD OLD NEON**

COVER A **MORAZZO & O'HALLORAN**   COVER B **FRAZER IRVING**

DESIGN BY **ASHLEY WALKER**

What's your favorite flavor? Email wmaxwellprince@gmail.com

IMAGE FIRSTS: ICE CREAM MAN #1. August 2019. Published by Image Comics, Inc. Office of publication: 2701 NW Vaughn St., Suite 780, Portland, OR 97210. Copyright © 2019 **W. Maxwell Prince & Martín Morazzo**. All rights reserved. "Ice Cream Man," its logos, and the likenesses of all characters herein are trademarks of **W. Maxwell Prince & Martín Morazzo**, unless otherwise noted. "Image" and the Image Comics logos are registered trademarks of Image Comics, Inc. No part of this publication may be reproduced or transmitted, in any form or by any means (except for short excerpts for journalistic or review purposes), without the express written permission of **W. Maxwell Prince & Martín Morazzo**, or Image Comics, Inc. All names, characters, events, and locales in this publication are entirely fictional. Any resemblance to actual persons (living or dead), events, or places, without satiric intent, is coincidental. Printed in the USA. For information regarding the CPSIA on this printed material call: 203-595-3636. For international rights, contact: foreignlicensing@imagecomics.com.

IMAGE COMICS, INC. Robert Kirkman **Chief Operating Officer** • Erik Larsen **Chief Financial Officer** • Todd McFarlane **President** • Marc Silvestri **Chief Executive Officer** • Jim Valentino **Vice President** • Eric Stephenson **Publisher / Chief Creative Officer** • Jeff Boison **Director of Publishing Planning & Book Trade Sales** • Chris Ross **Director of Digital Sales** • Jeff Stang **Director of Direct Market Sales** • Kat Salazar **Director of PR & Marketing** • Drew Gill **Art Director** • Heather Doornink **Production Director** • Nicole Lapalme **Controller**

IMAGECOMICS.COM

image

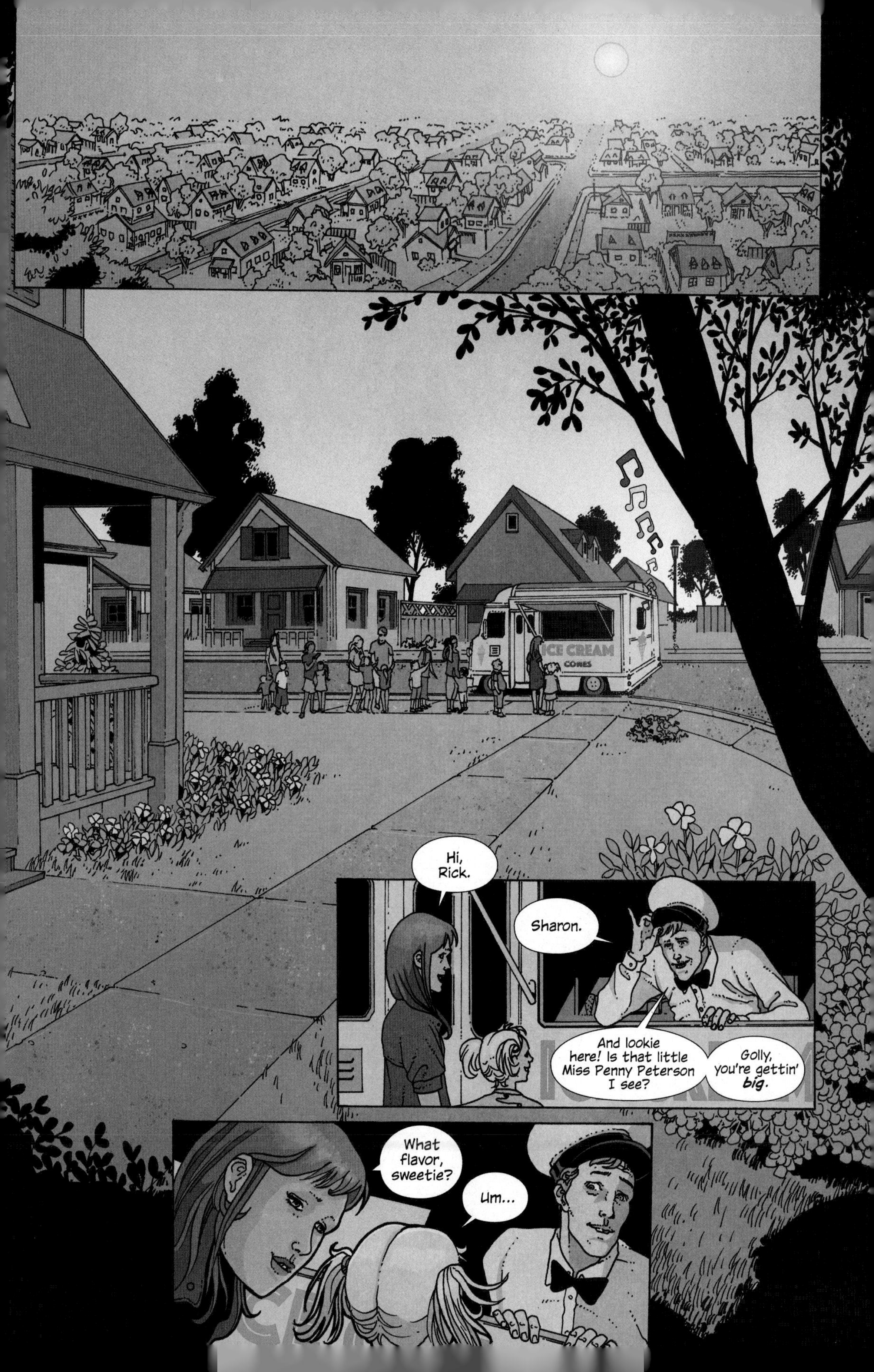
ICE CREAM
CONES
Hi, Rick.
Sharon.
And lookie here! Is that little Miss Penny Peterson I see?
Golly, you're gettin' *big*.
What flavor, sweetie?
Um...

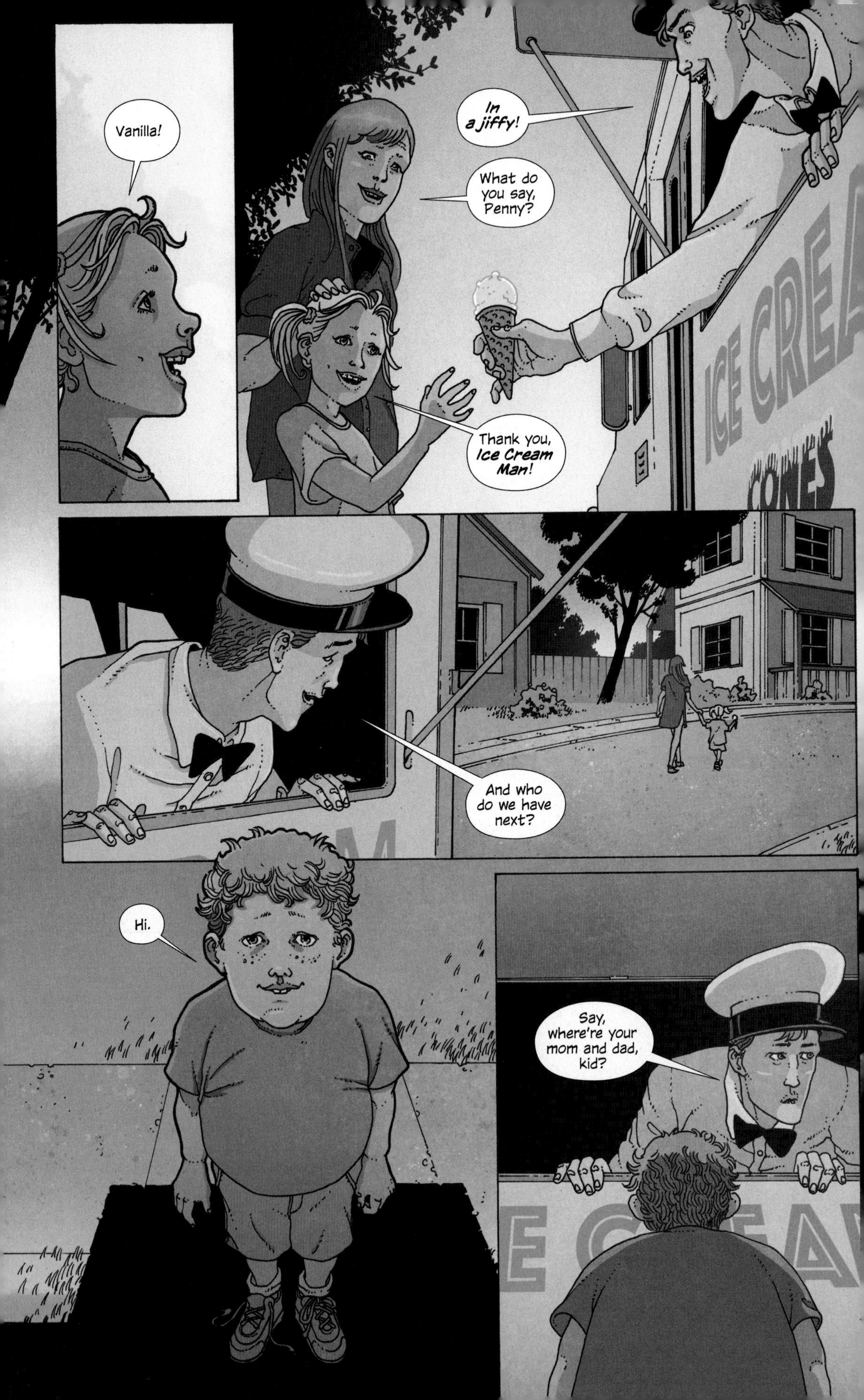
Vanilla!
What do you say, Penny?
In a jiffy!
Thank you, Ice Cream Man!
ICE CREAM
CONES
And who do we have next?
Hi.
Say, where're your mom and dad, kid?

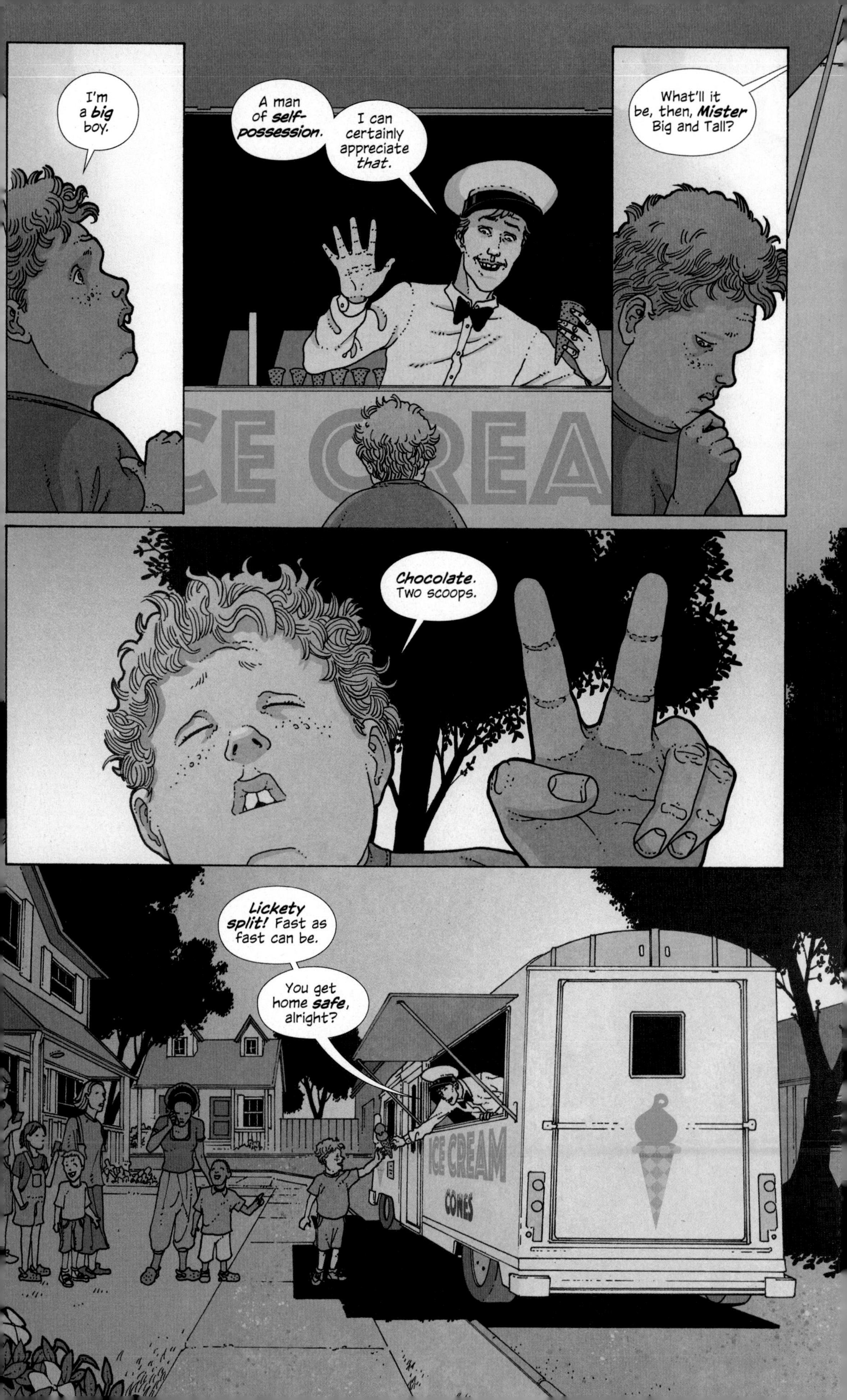

I'm a **big** boy.
A man of **self-possession**.
I can certainly appreciate *that*.
What'll it be, then, **Mister** Big and Tall?
ICE CREA
Chocolate. Two scoops.
Lickety split! Fast as fast can be.
You get home **safe**, alright?
ICE CREAM
CONES

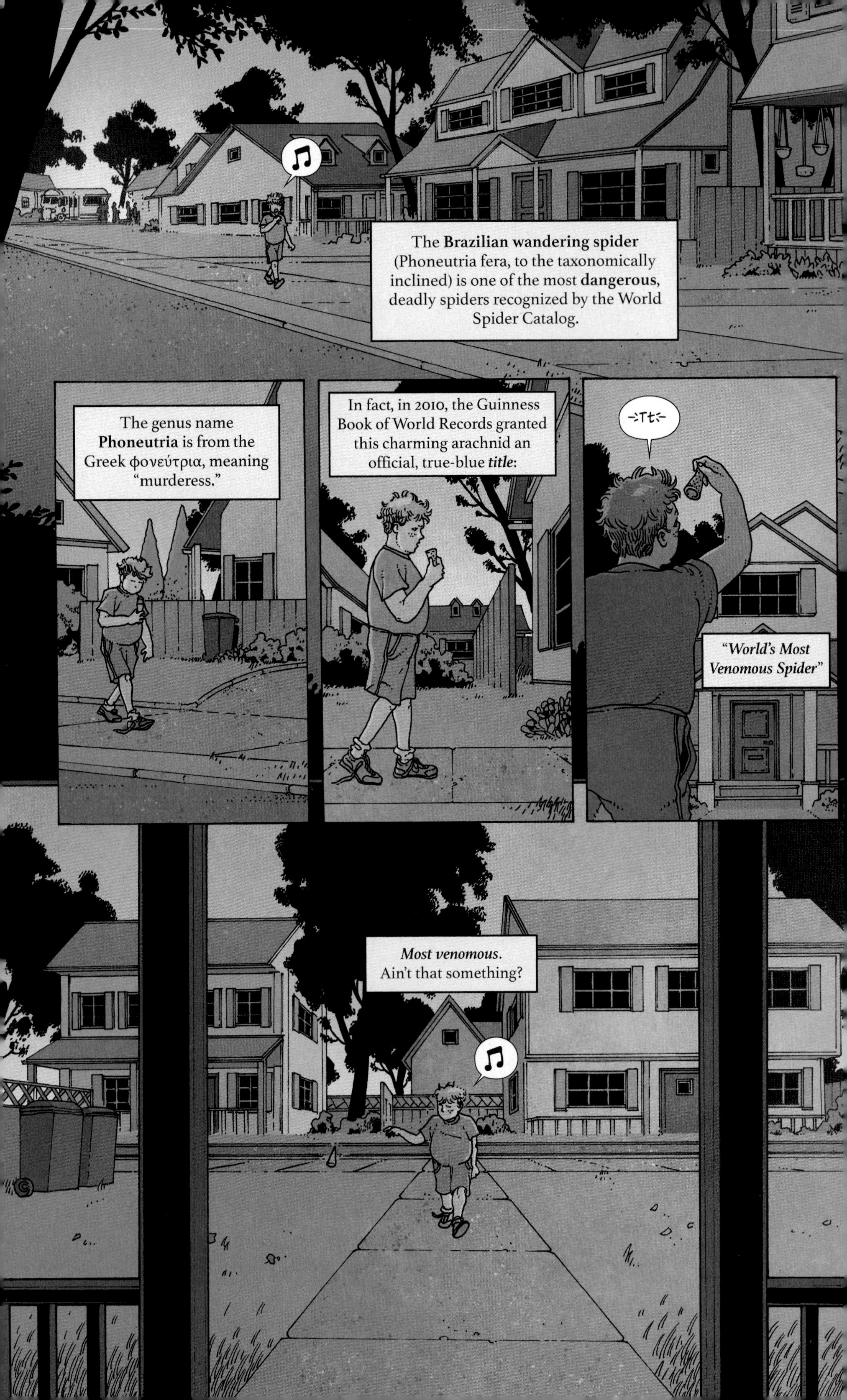

The **Brazilian wandering spider** (Phoneutria fera, to the taxonomically inclined) is one of the most **dangerous**, deadly spiders recognized by the World Spider Catalog.
The genus name **Phoneutria** is from the Greek φονεύτρια, meaning "murderess."
In fact, in 2010, the Guinness Book of World Records granted this charming arachnid an official, true-blue *title*:
Tt
"World's Most Venomous Spider"
Most venomous. Ain't that something?

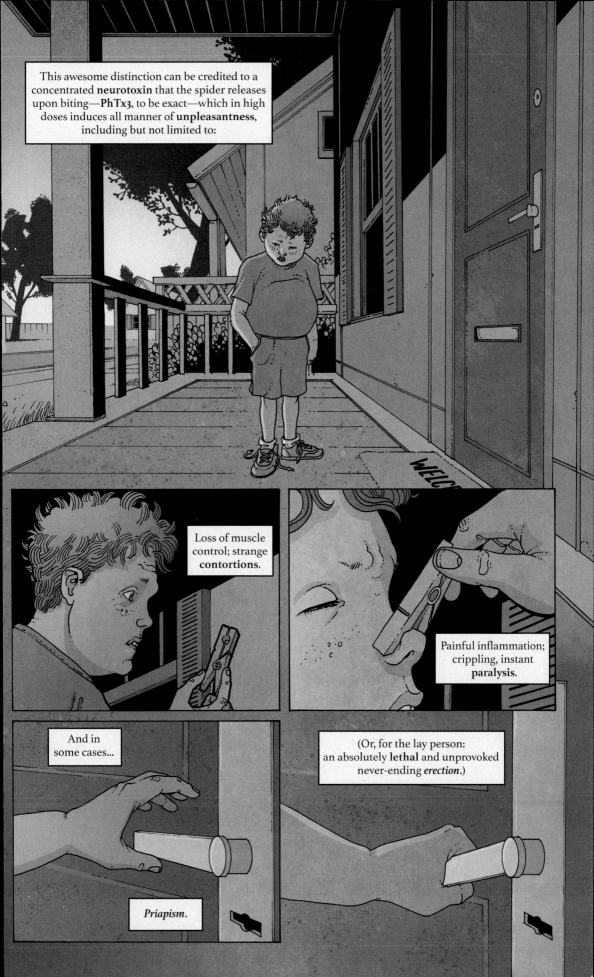

This awesome distinction can be credited to a concentrated **neurotoxin** that the spider releases upon biting—**PhTx3**, to be exact—which in high doses induces all manner of **unpleasantness**, including but not limited to:

Loss of muscle control; strange **contortions**.

Painful inflammation; crippling, instant **paralysis**.

And in some cases...

(Or, for the lay person: an absolutely **lethal** and unprovoked never-ending *erection*.)

Priapism.

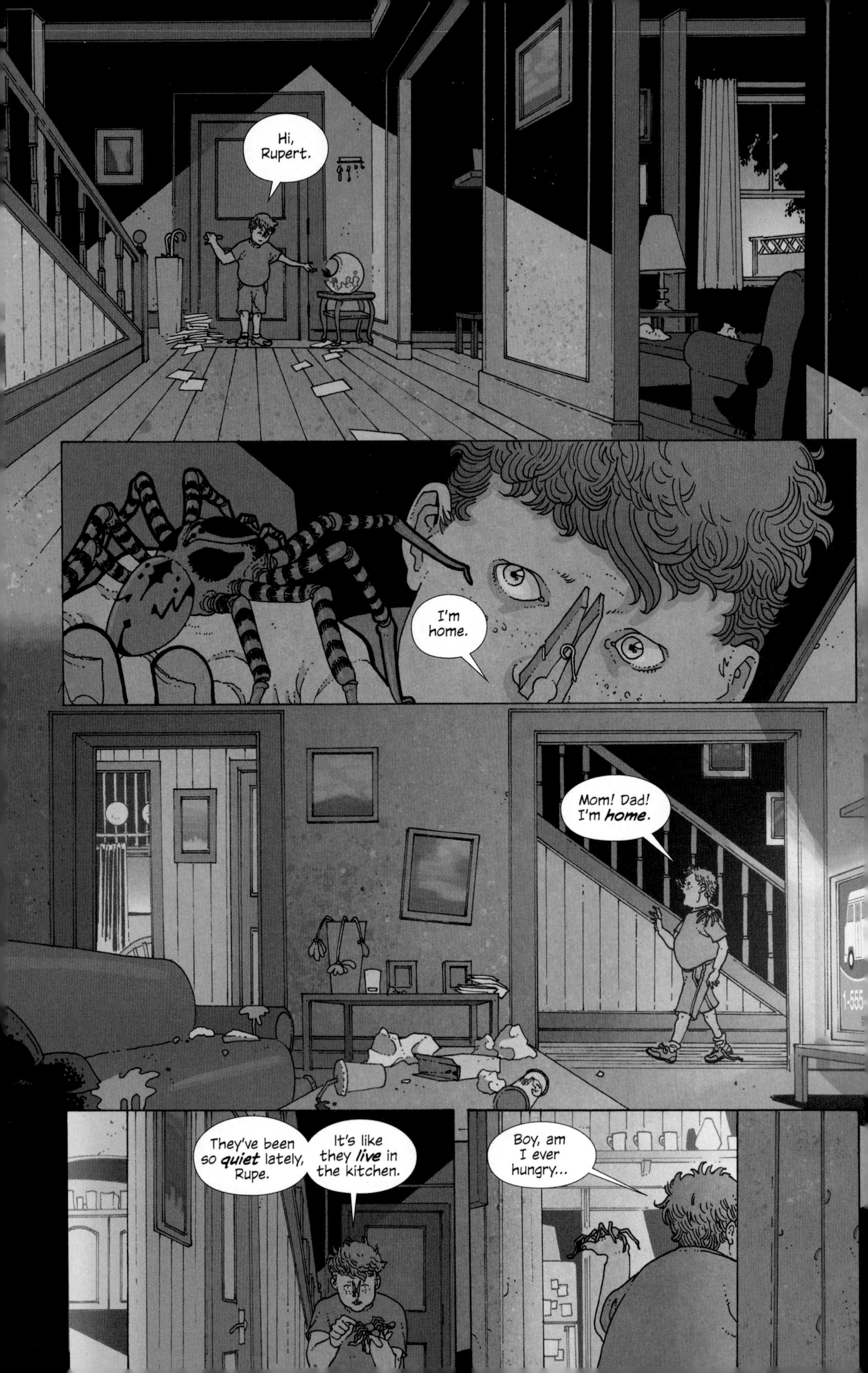
Hi, Rupert.
I'm home.
Mom! Dad! I'm **home**.
1-555
They've been so **quiet** lately, Rupe.
It's like they **live** in the kitchen.
Boy, am I ever hungry...

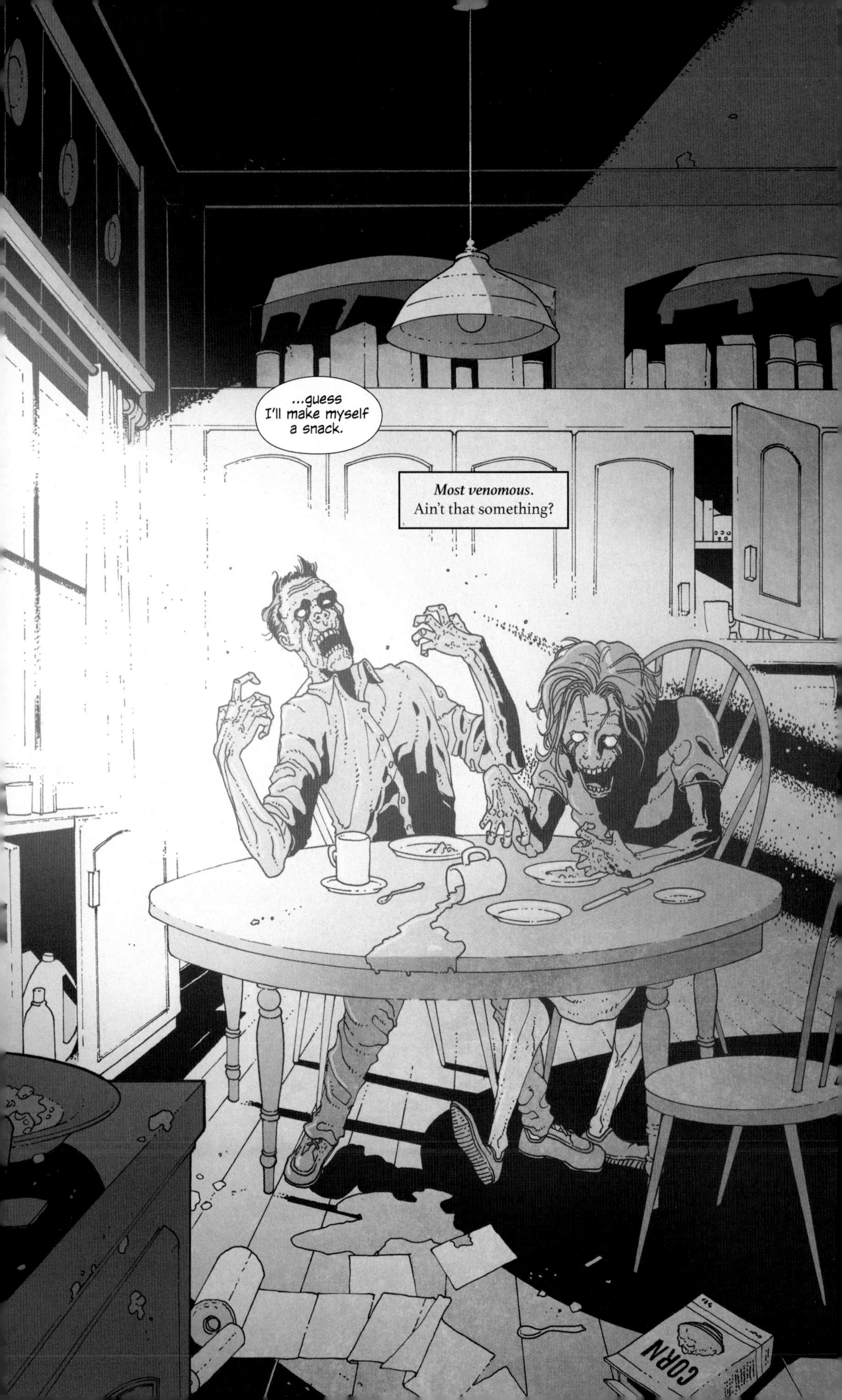
...guess I'll make myself a snack.
Most venomous. Ain't that something?
CORN

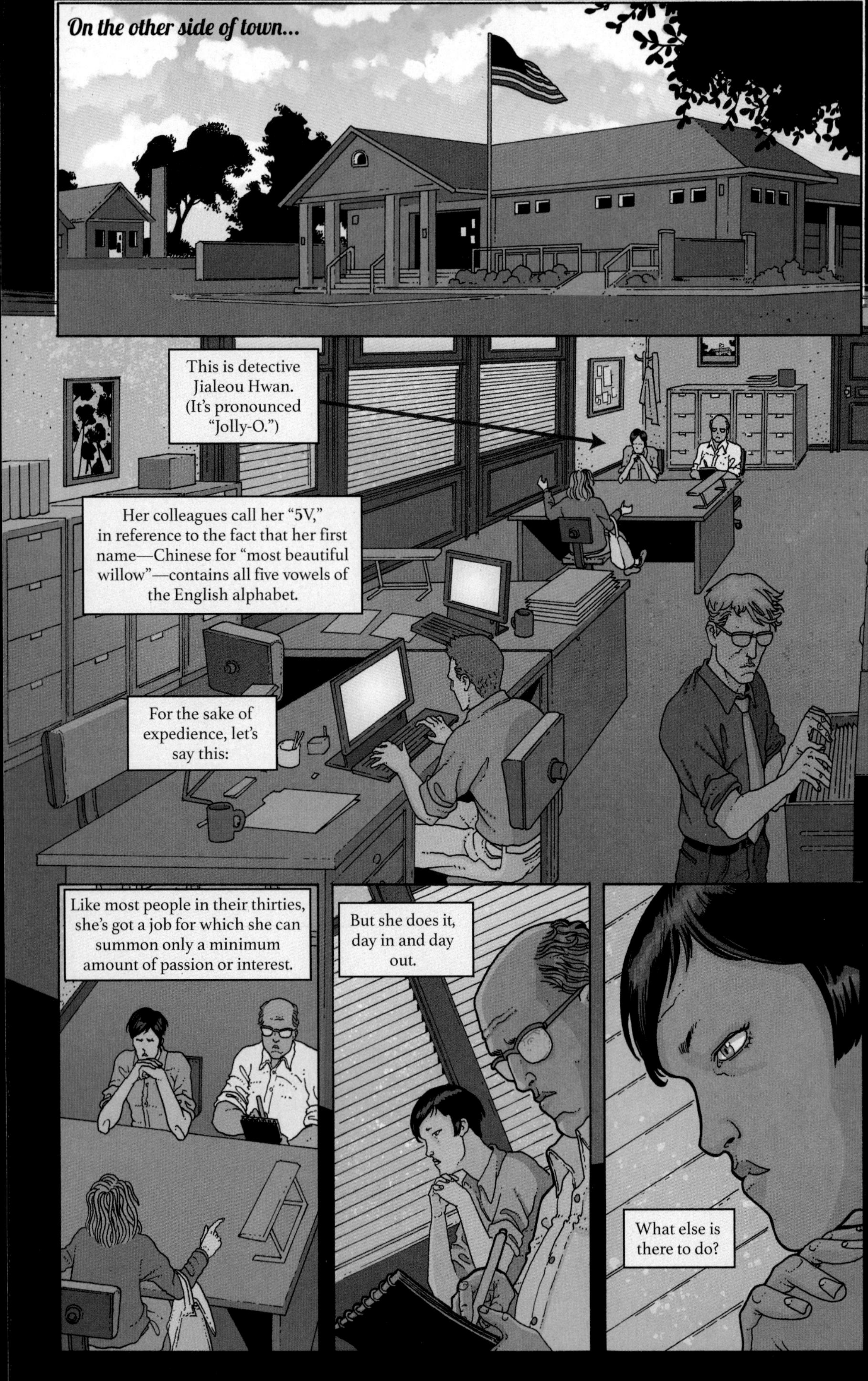
On the other side of town...
This is detective Jialeou Hwan. (It's pronounced "Jolly-O.")
Her colleagues call her "5V," in reference to the fact that her first name—Chinese for "most beautiful willow"—contains all five vowels of the English alphabet.
For the sake of expedience, let's say this:
Like most people in their thirties, she's got a job for which she can summon only a minimum amount of passion or interest.
But she does it, day in and day out.
What else is there to do?

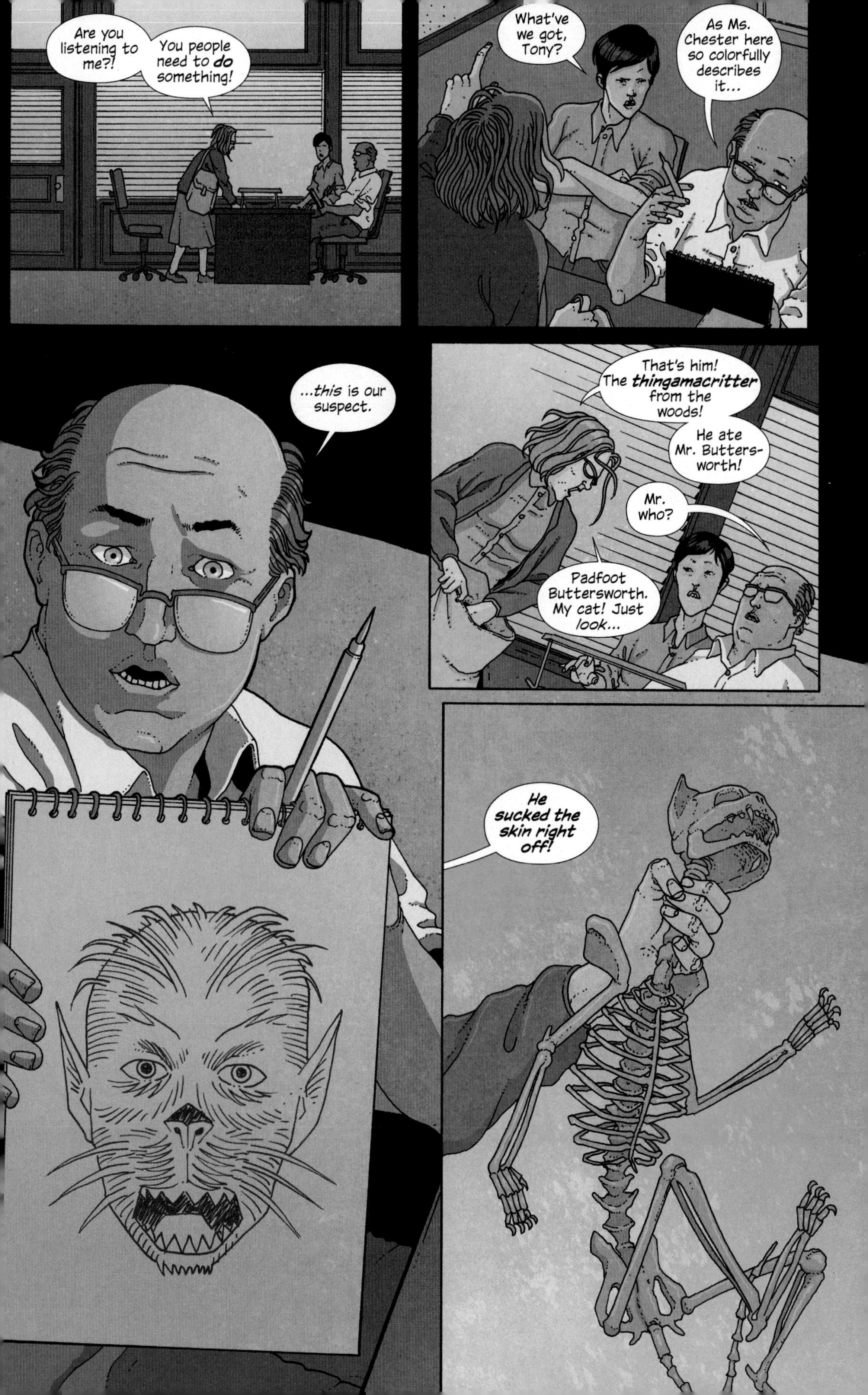
Are you listening to me?!
You people need to **do** something!
What've we got, Tony?
As Ms. Chester here so colorfully describes it...
...*this* is our suspect.
That's him! The ***thingamacritter*** from the woods!
He ate Mr. Butters-worth!
Mr. who?
Padfoot Buttersworth. My cat! Just look...
He sucked the skin right off!

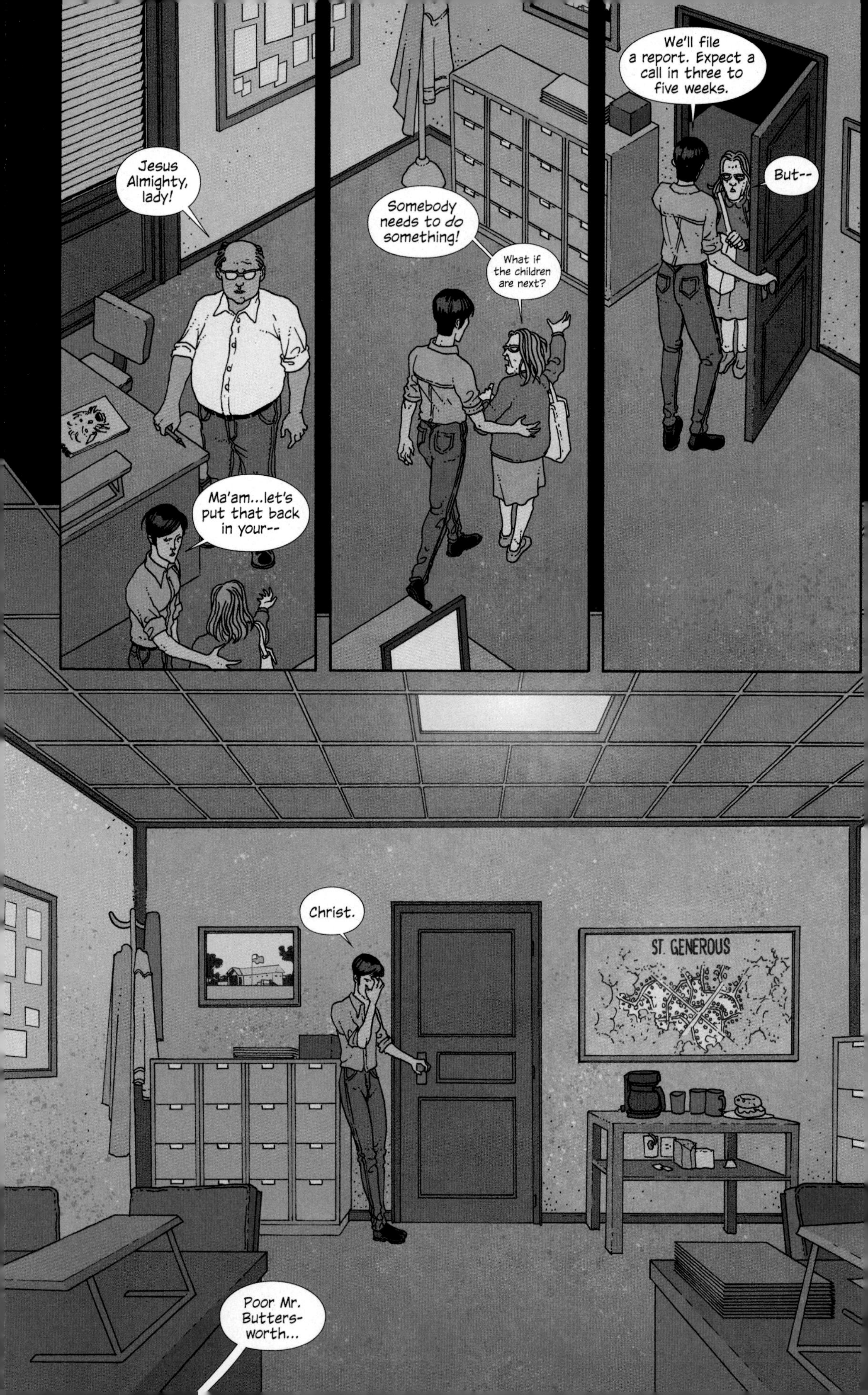
Jesus Almighty, lady!
Ma'am...let's put that back in your--
Somebody needs to do something!
What if the children are next?
We'll file a report. Expect a call in three to five weeks.
But--
Christ.
ST. GENEROUS
Poor Mr. Butters-worth...

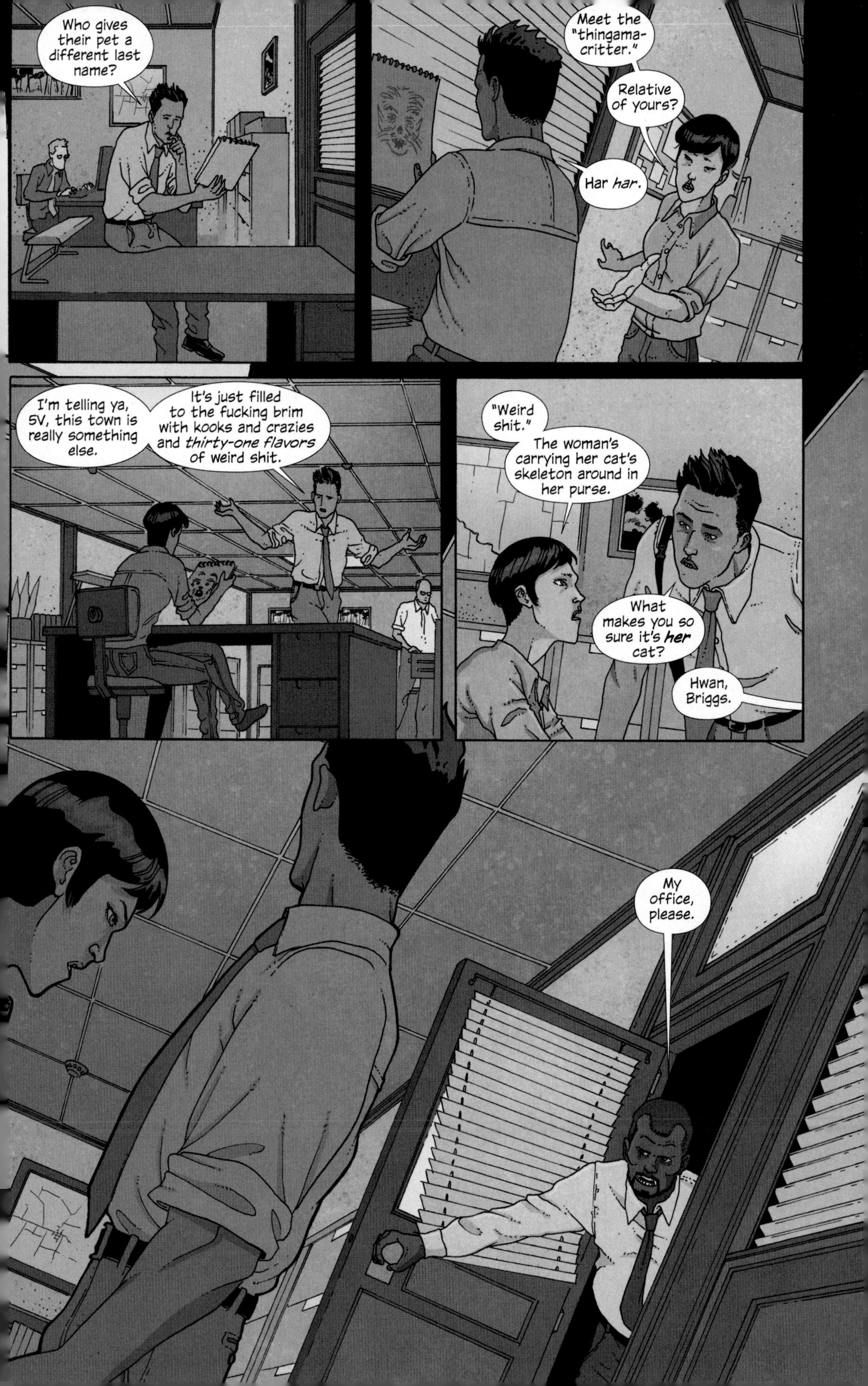

Who gives their pet a different last name?
Meet the "thingama-critter."
Relative of yours?
Har *har*.
I'm telling ya, SV, this town is really something else.
It's just filled to the fucking brim with kooks and crazies and *thirty-one flavors* of weird shit.
"Weird shit."
The woman's carrying her cat's skeleton around in her purse.
What makes you so sure it's ***her*** cat?
Hwan, Briggs.
My office, please.

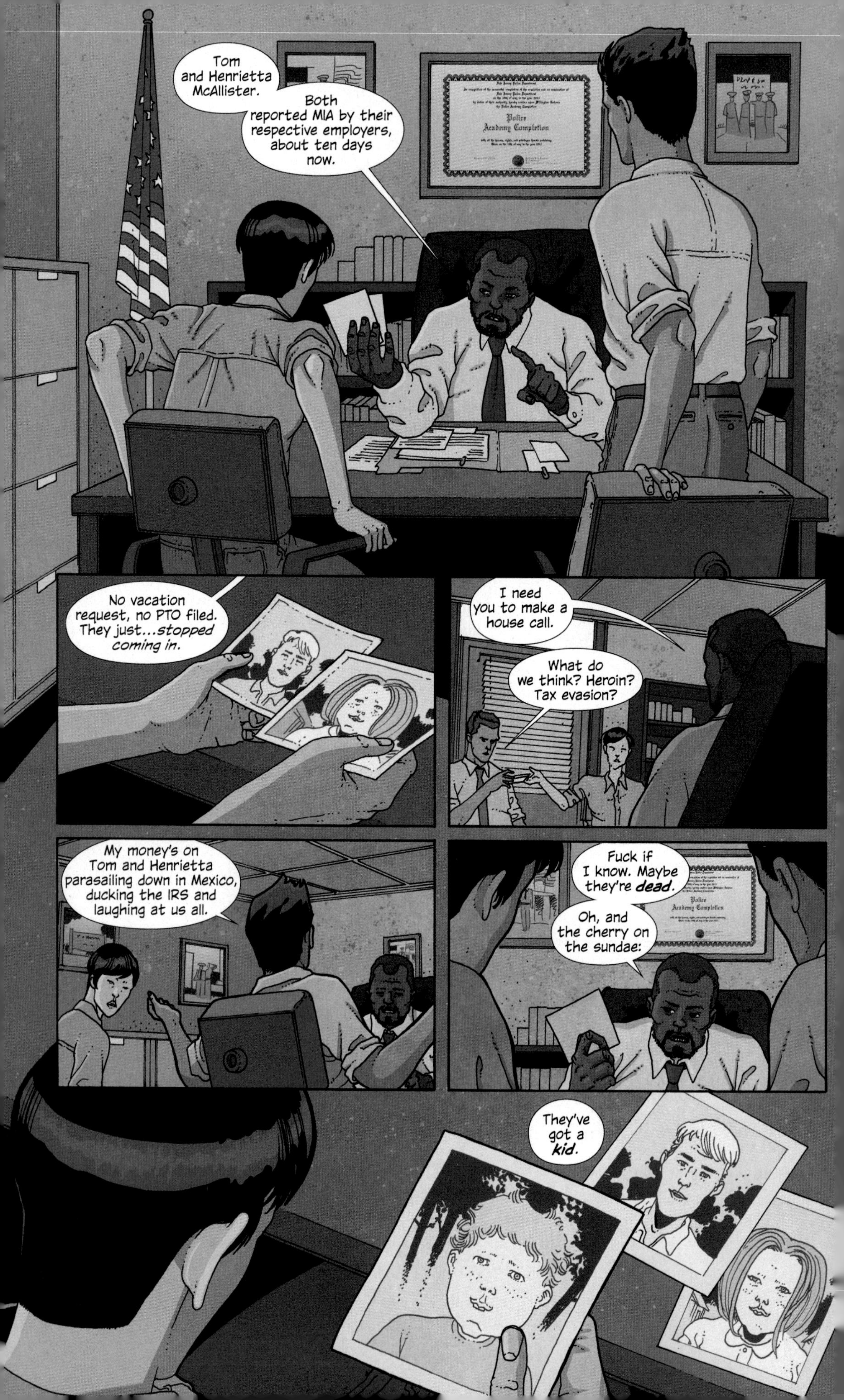
Tom and Henrietta McAllister.
Both reported MIA by their respective employers, about ten days now.
No vacation request, no PTO filed. They just...*stopped coming in*.
I need you to make a house call.
What do we think? Heroin? Tax evasion?
My money's on Tom and Henrietta parasailing down in Mexico, ducking the IRS and laughing at us all.
Fuck if I know. Maybe they're ***dead***.
Oh, and the cherry on the sundae:
They've got a ***kid***.

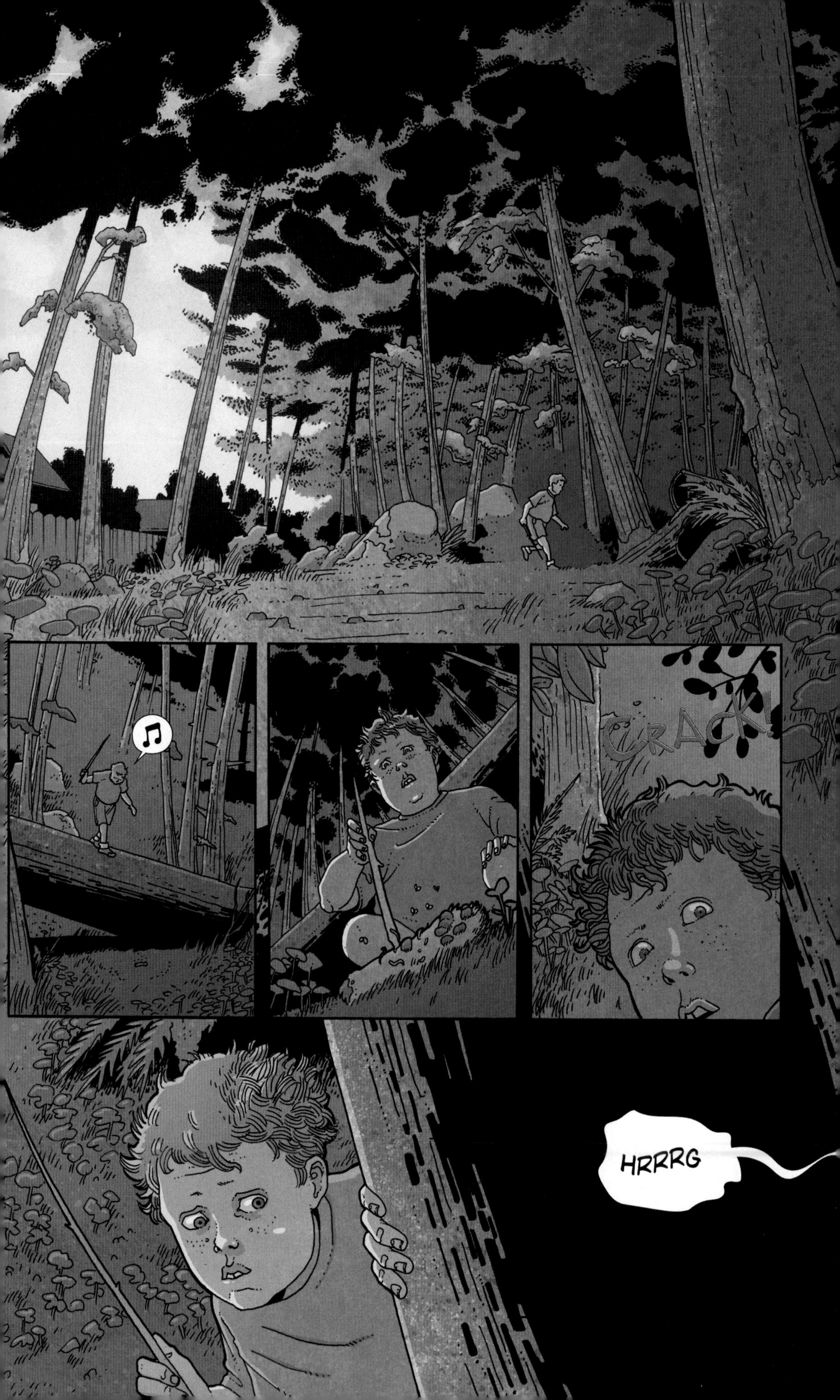

♫
CRACK!
HRRRG

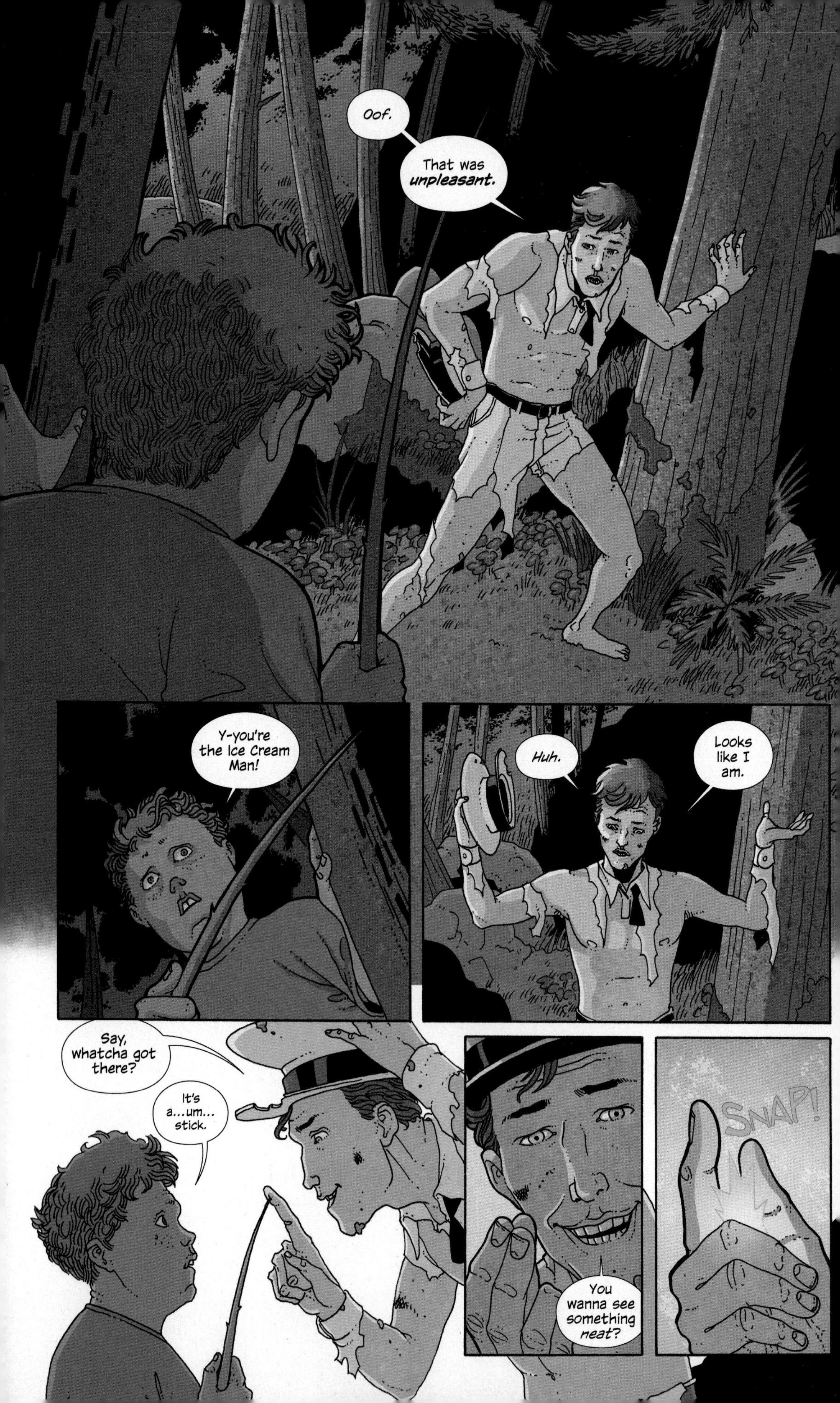

Oof.
That was *unpleasant.*
Y-you're the Ice Cream Man!
Huh.
Looks like I am.
Say, whatcha got there?
It's a...um... stick.
You wanna see something *neat?*
SNAP!

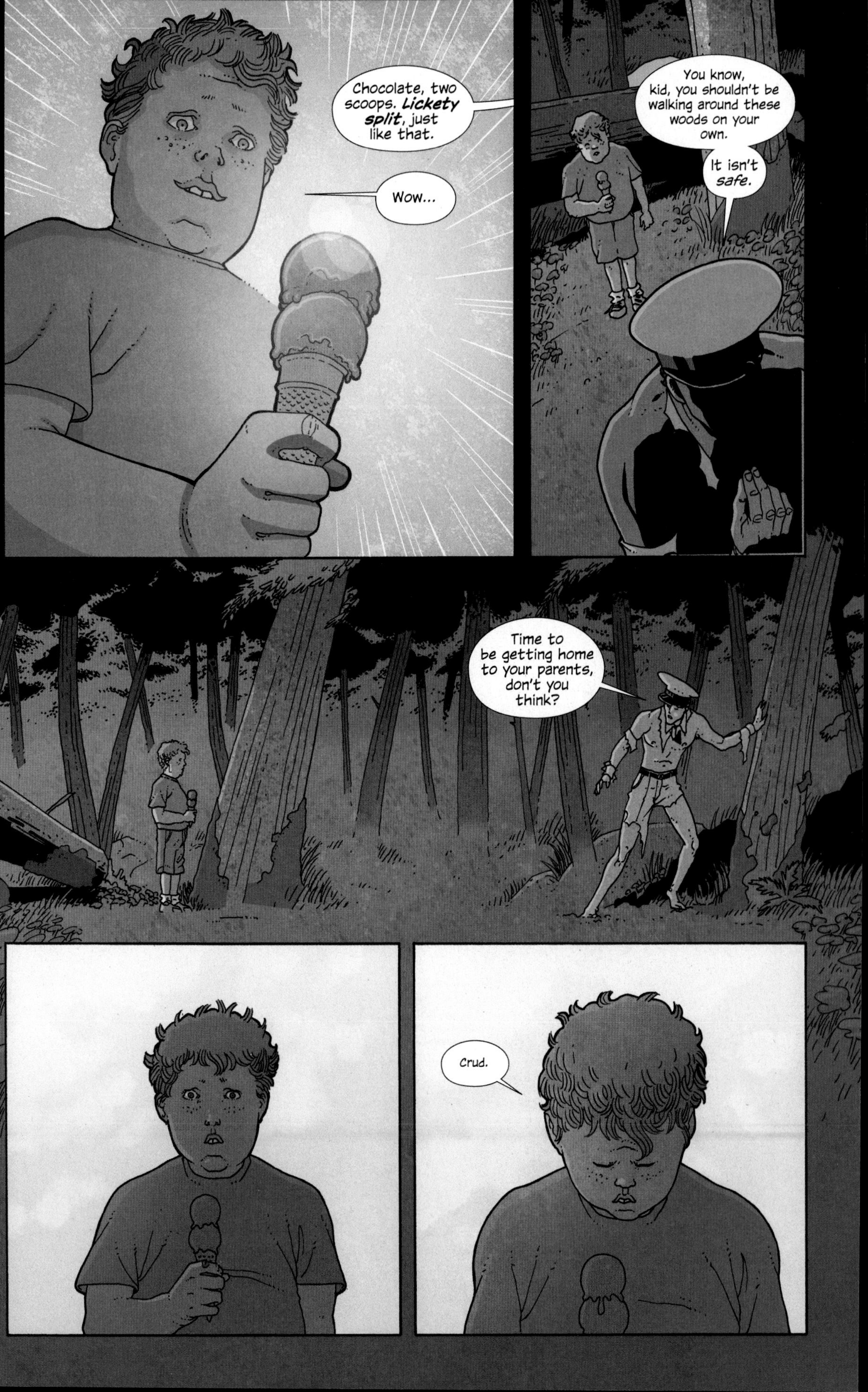
Chocolate, two scoops. Lickety split, just like that.
Wow...
You know, kid, you shouldn't be walking around these woods on your own.
It isn't safe.
Time to be getting home to your parents, don't you think?
Crud.

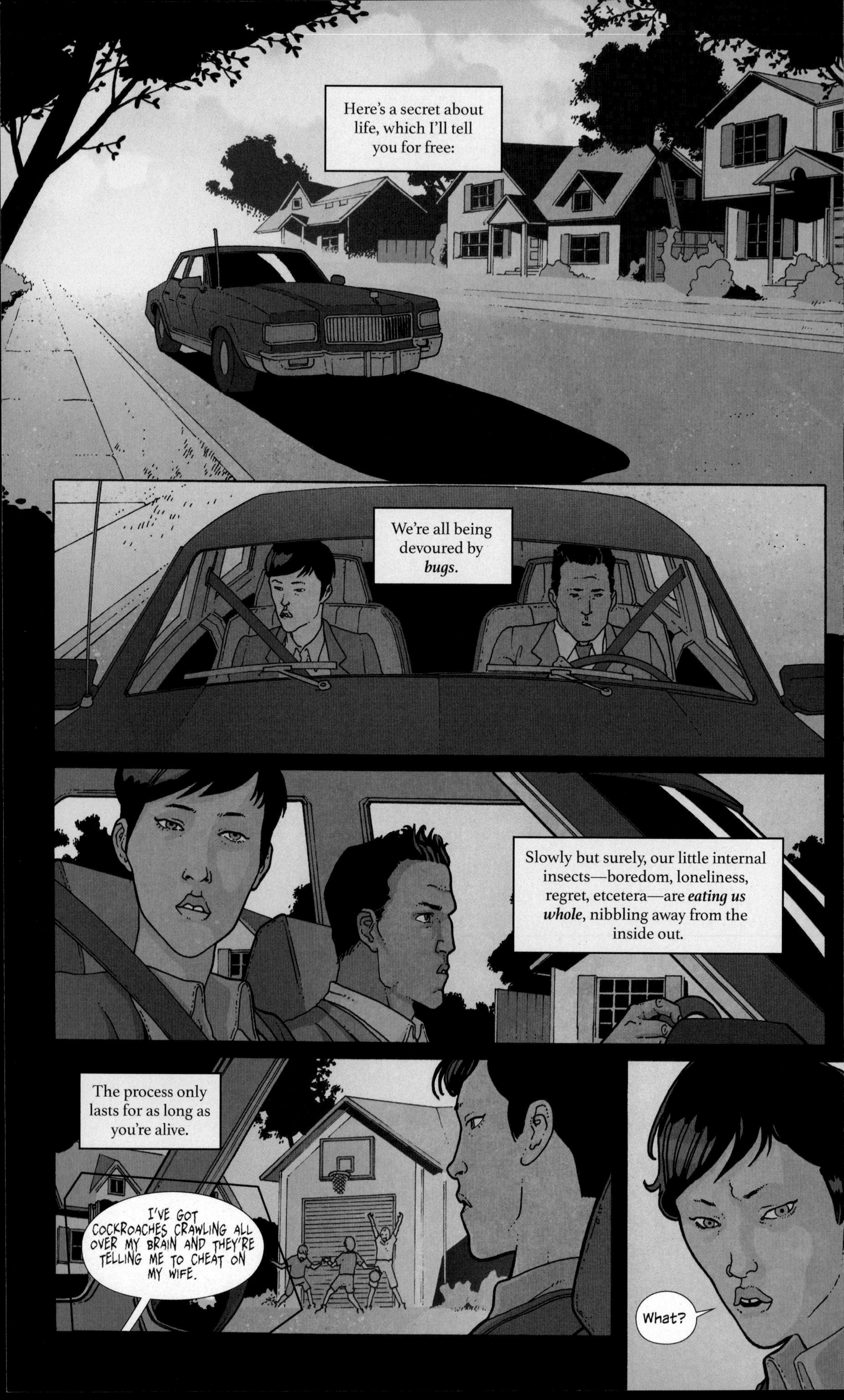
Here's a secret about life, which I'll tell you for free:
We're all being devoured by *bugs*.
Slowly but surely, our little internal insects—boredom, loneliness, regret, etcetera—are *eating us whole*, nibbling away from the inside out.
The process only lasts for as long as you're alive.
I'VE GOT COCKROACHES CRAWLING ALL OVER MY BRAIN AND THEY'RE TELLING ME TO CHEAT ON MY WIFE.
What?

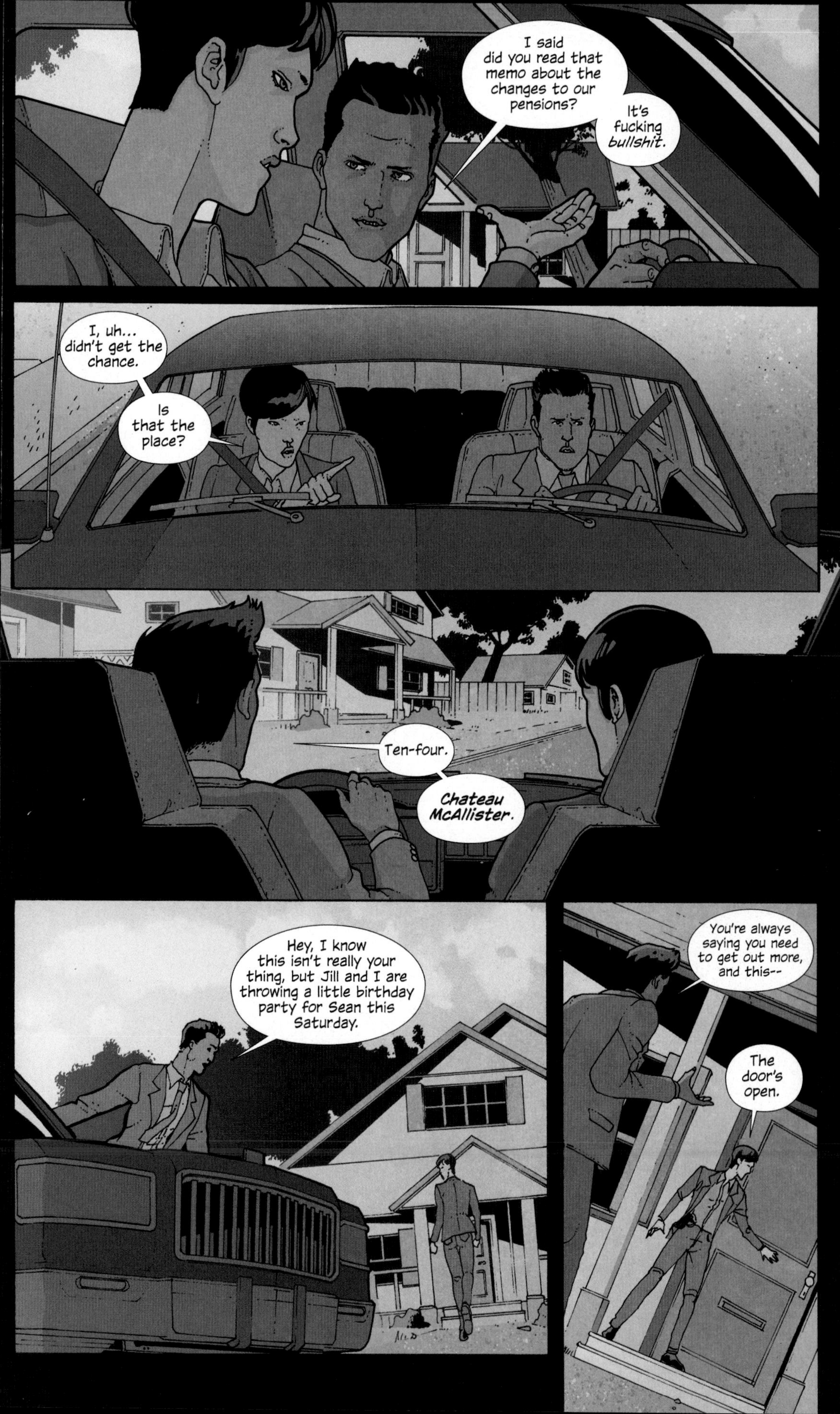
I said did you read that memo about the changes to our pensions?
It's fucking *bullshit*.
I, uh... didn't get the chance.
Is that the place?
Ten-four.
Chateau McAllister.
Hey, I know this isn't really your thing, but Jill and I are throwing a little birthday party for Sean this Saturday.
You're always saying you need to get out more, and this--
The door's open.

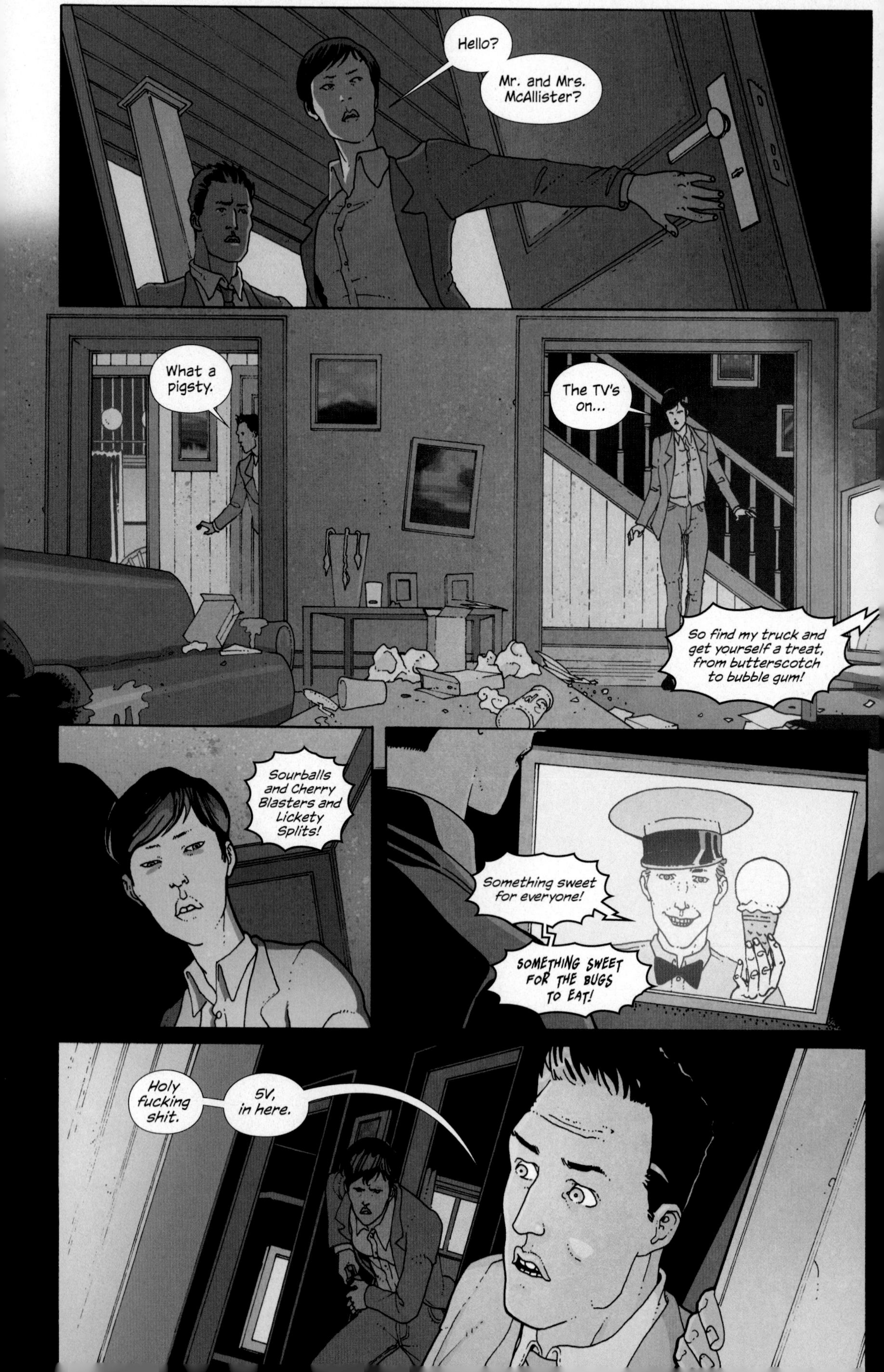
Hello?
Mr. and Mrs. McAllister?
What a pigsty.
The TV's on...
So find my truck and get yourself a treat, from butterscotch to bubble gum!
Sourballs and Cherry Blasters and Lickety Splits!
Something sweet for everyone!
SOMETHING SWEET FOR THE BUGS TO EAT!
Holy fucking shit.
5V, in here.

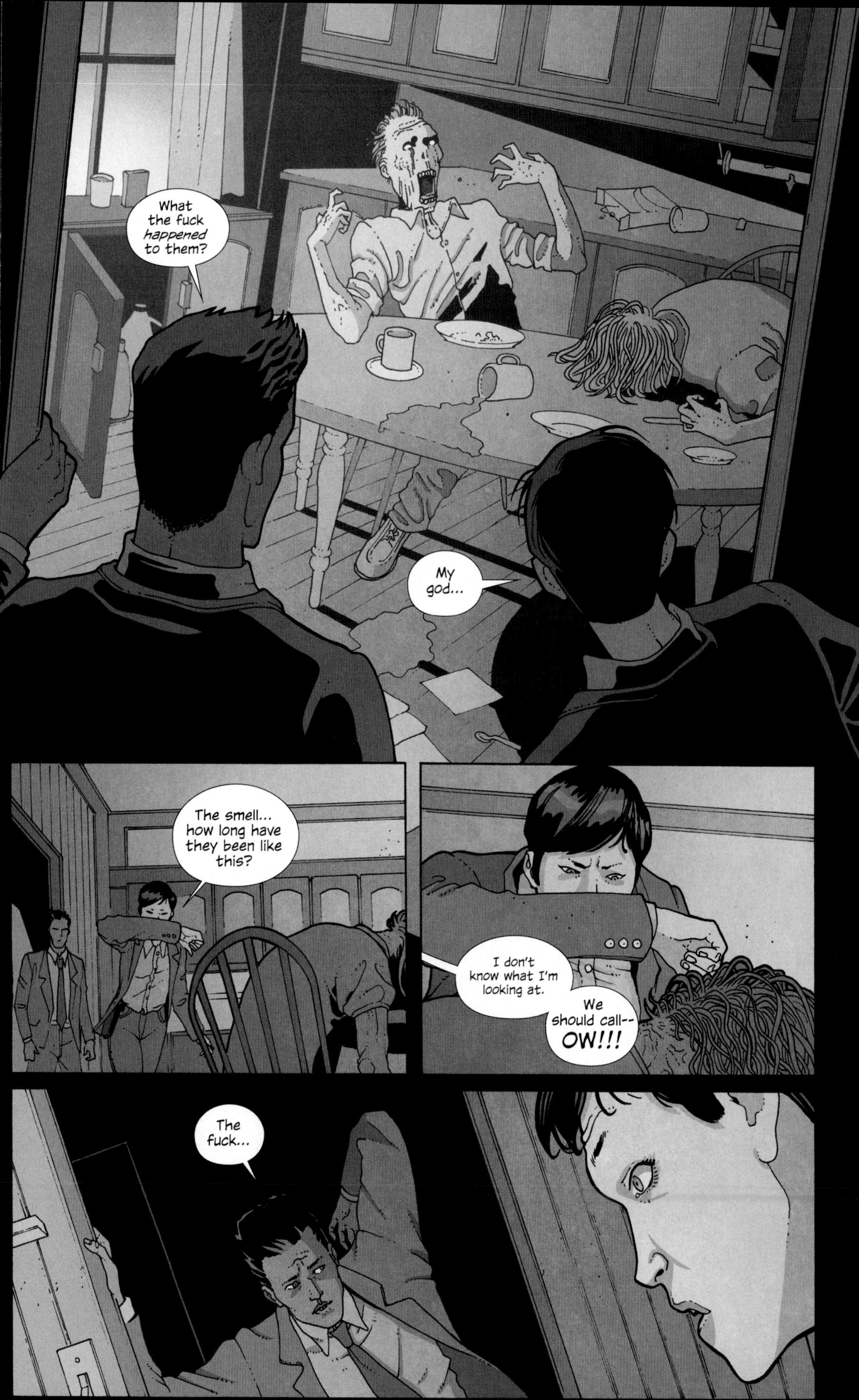
What the fuck *happened* to them?
My god...
The smell... how long have they been like this?
I don't know what I'm looking at.
We should call-- OW!!!
The fuck...

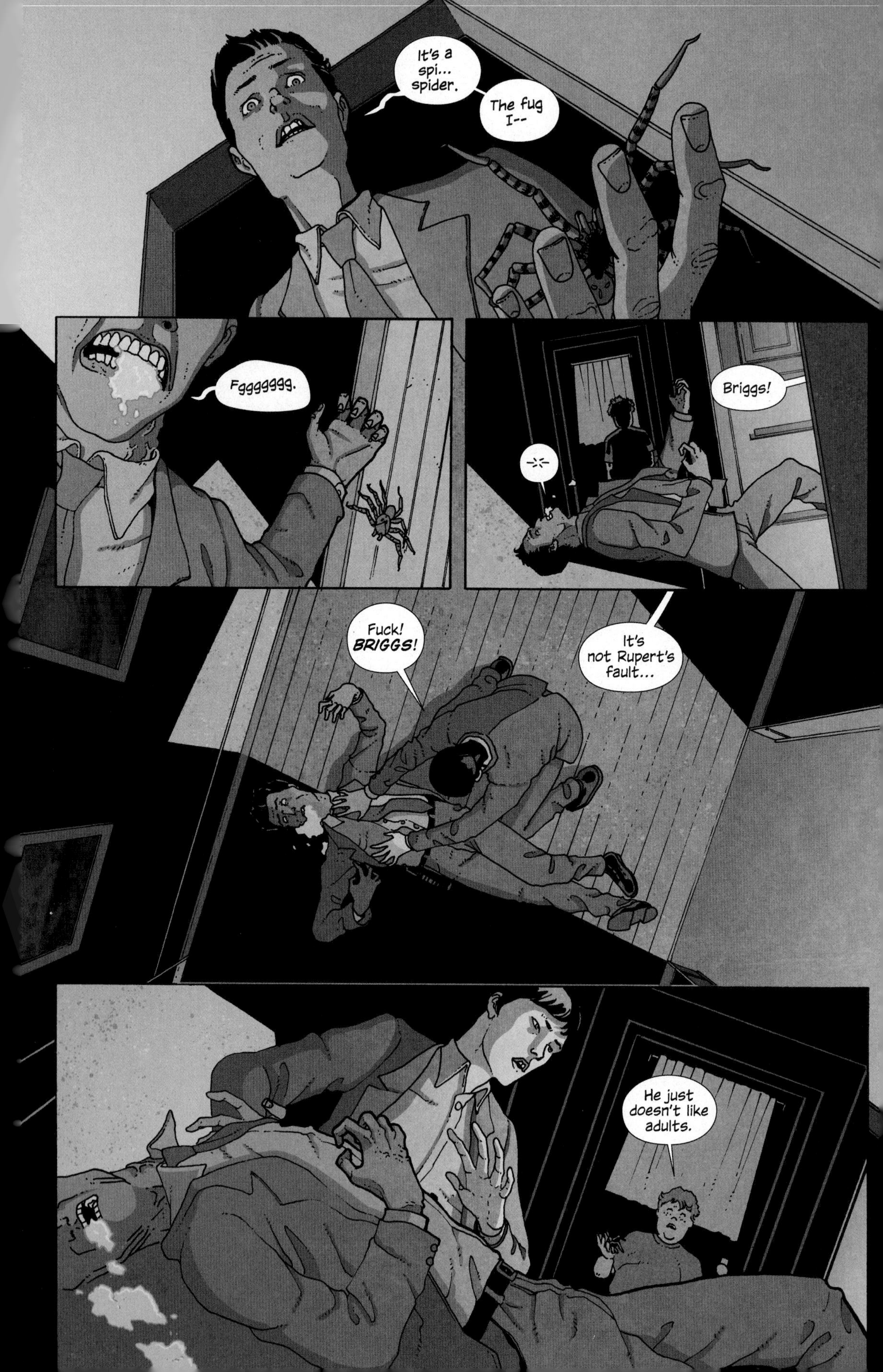
It's a spi... spider.
The fug I--
Fggggggg.
Briggs!
Fuck! BRIGGS!
It's not Rupert's fault...
He just doesn't like adults.

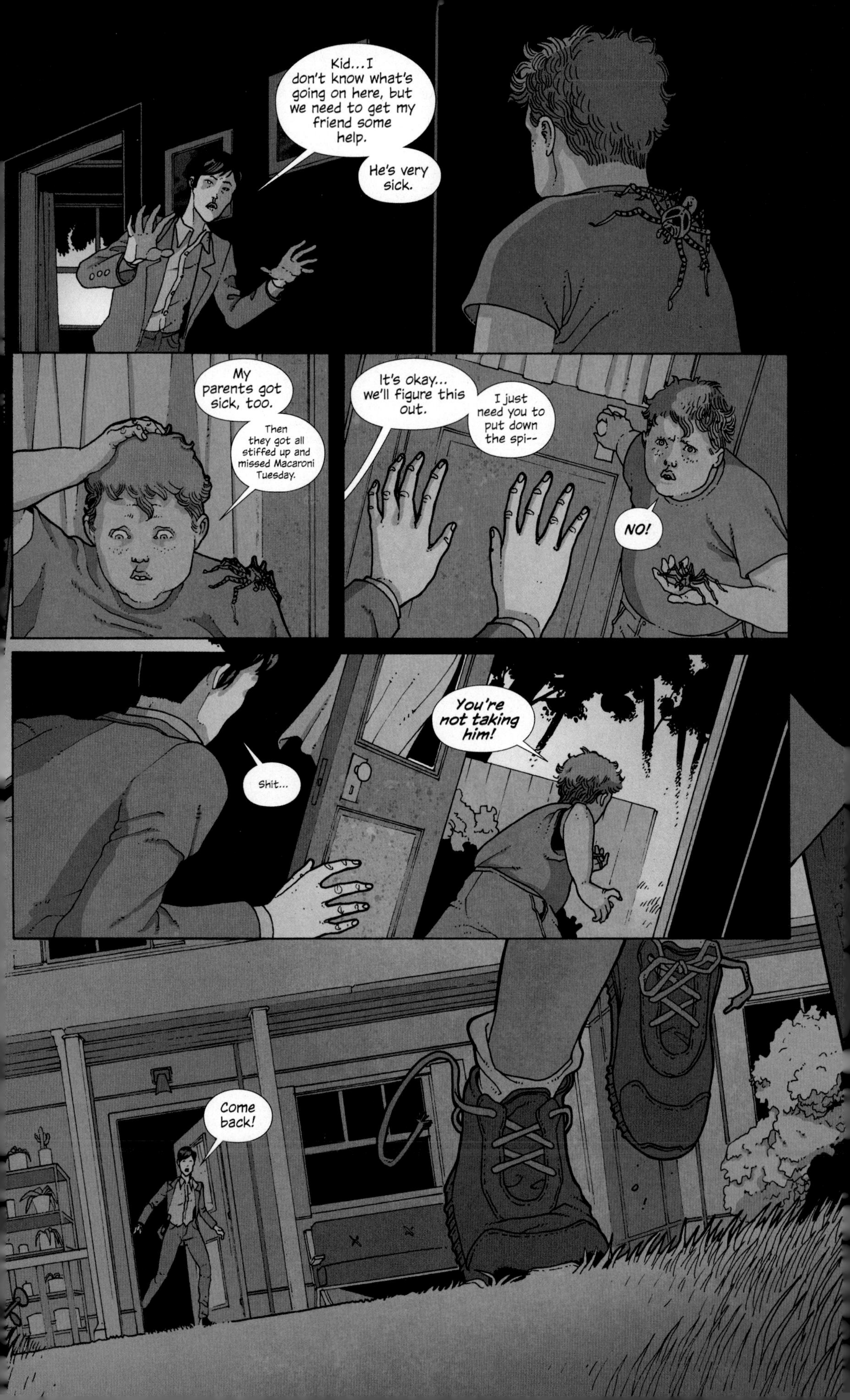
Kid...I don't know what's going on here, but we need to get my friend some help.
He's very sick.
My parents got sick, too.
Then they got all stiffed up and missed Macaroni Tuesday.
It's okay... we'll figure this out.
I just need you to put down the spi--
NO!
Shit...
You're not taking him!
Come back!

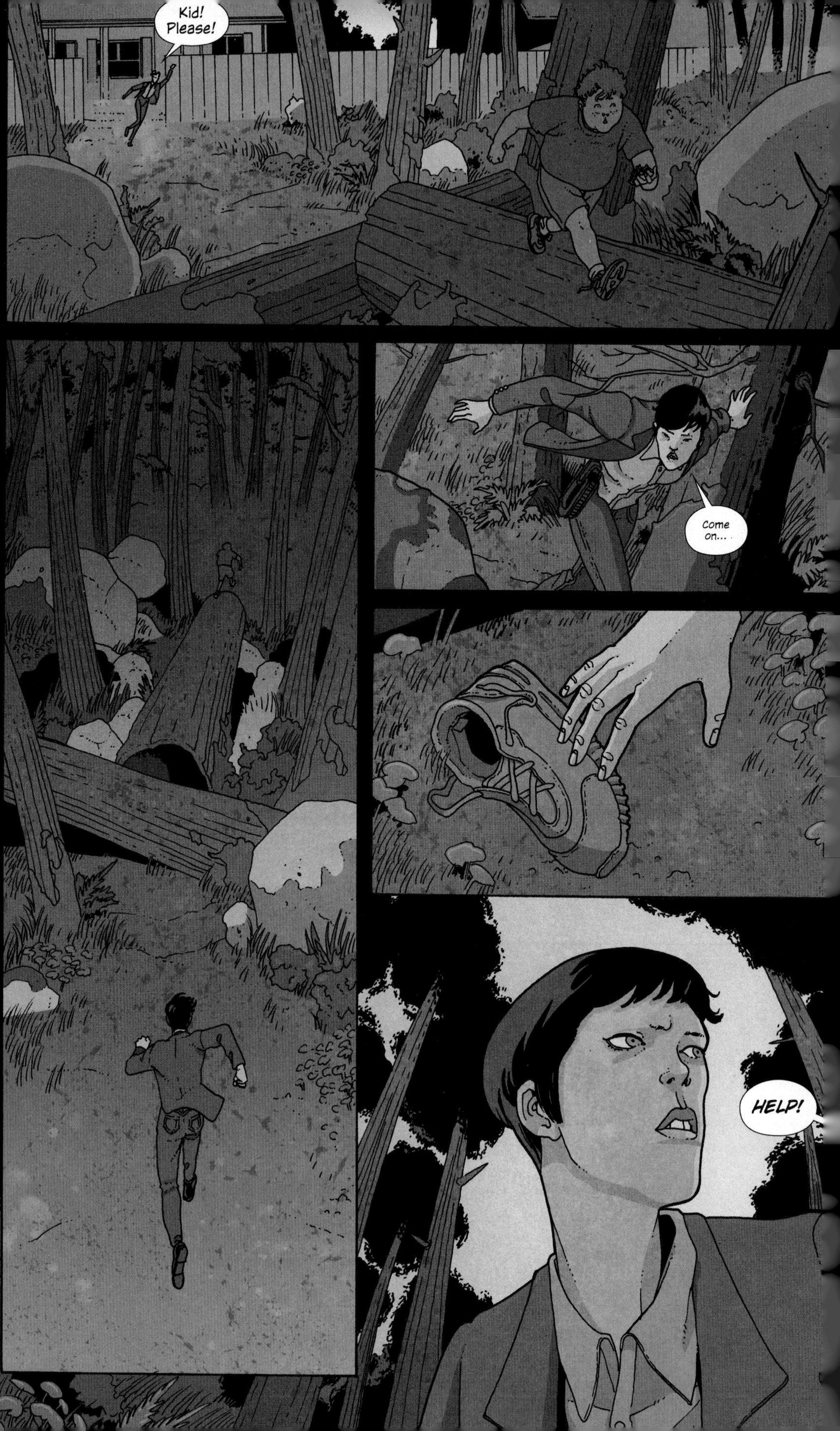
Kid! Please!
Come on...
HELP!

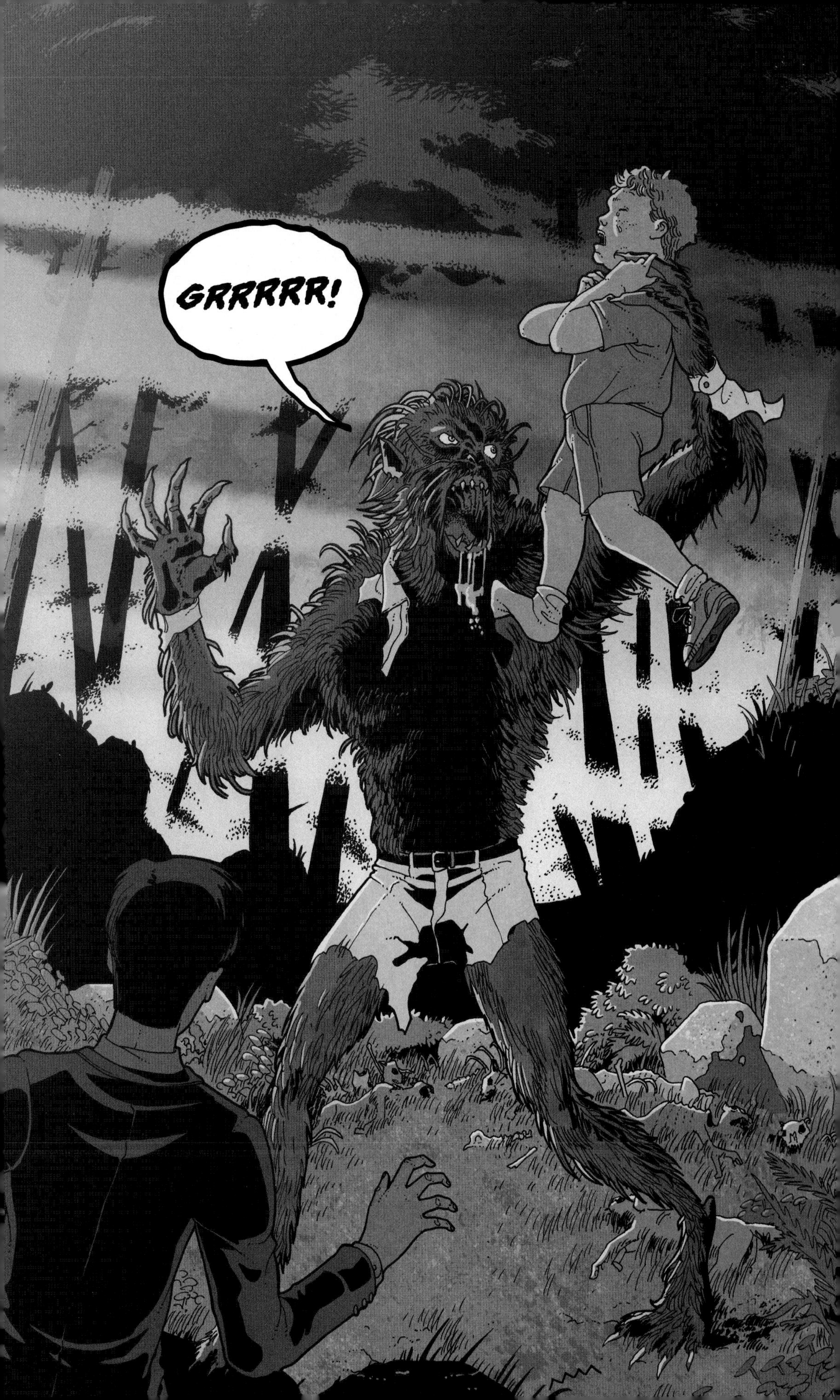
GRRRRR!

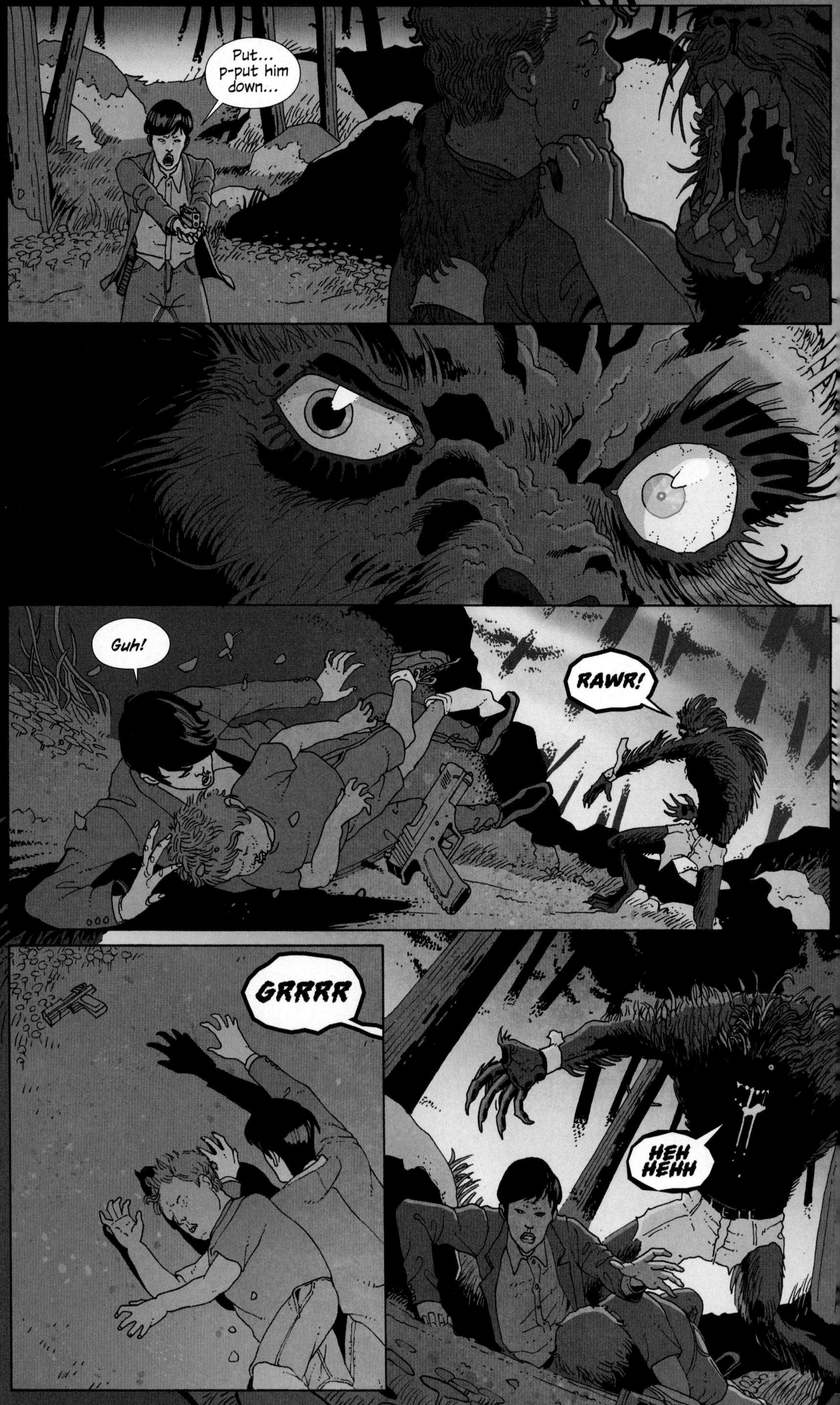
Put...
p-put him
down...
Guh!
RAWR!
GRRRR
HEH
HEHH

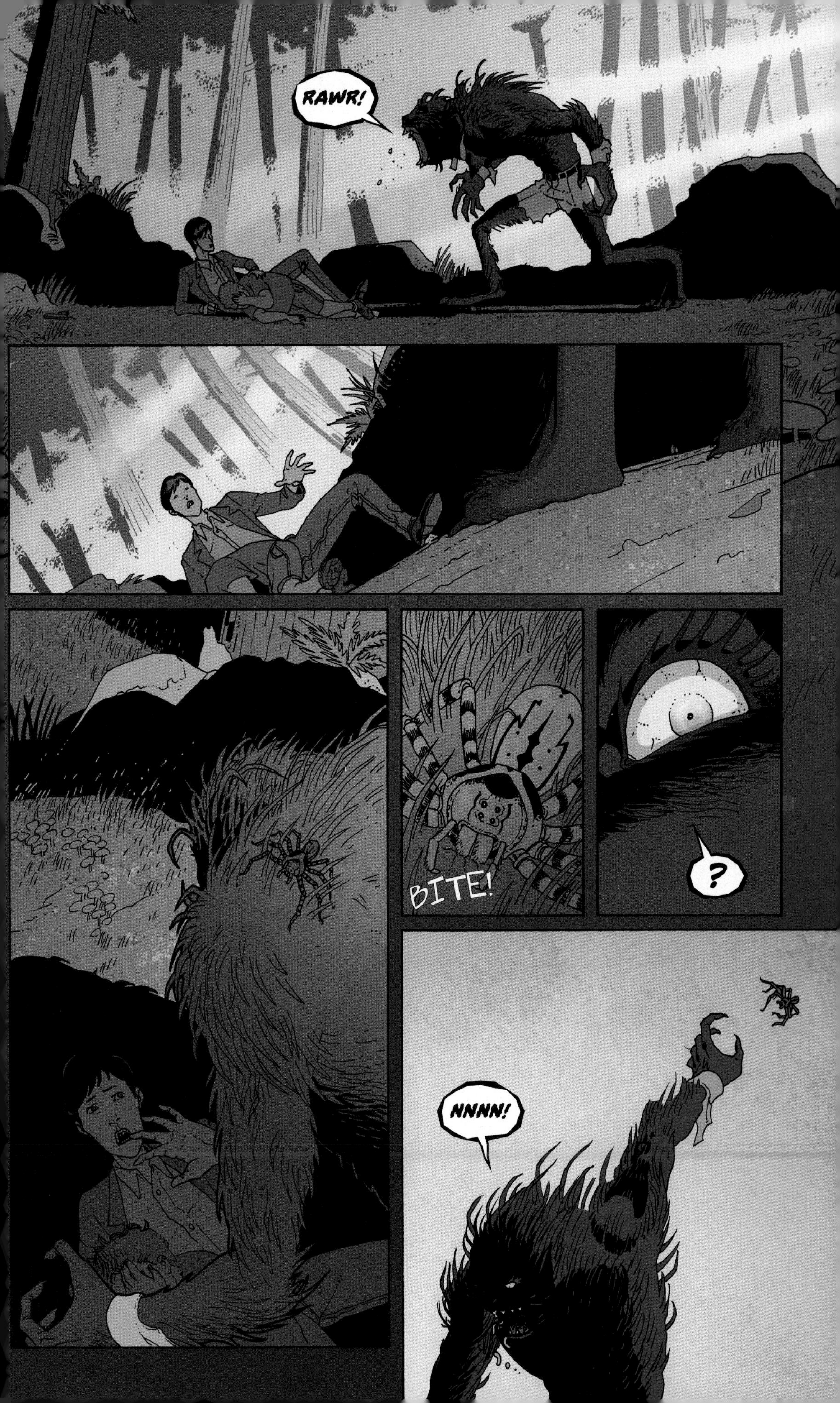
RAWR!
BITE!
?
NNNN!

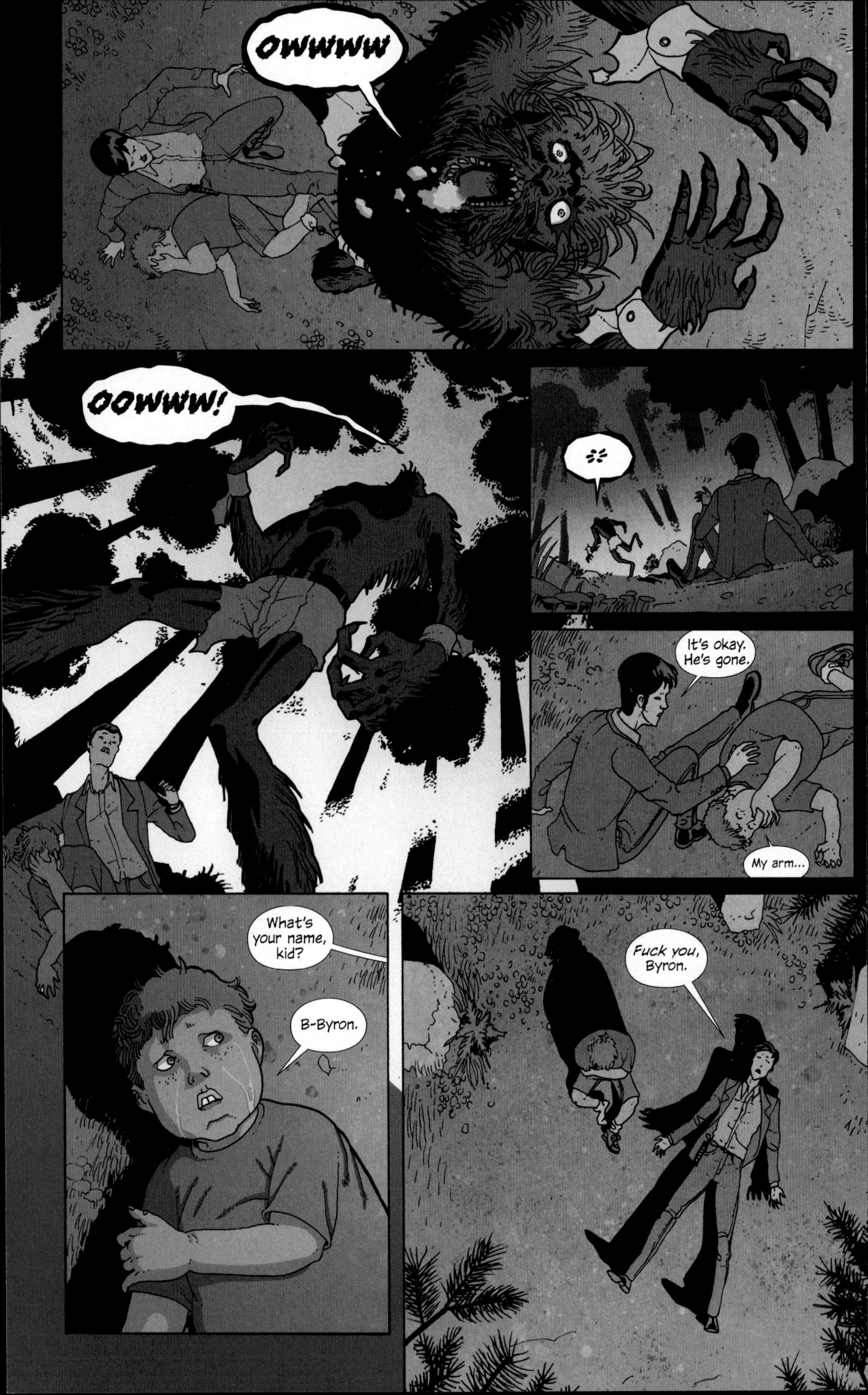
OWWWW
OOWWW!
It's okay. He's gone.
My arm...
What's your name, kid?
B-Byron.
Fuck you, Byron.

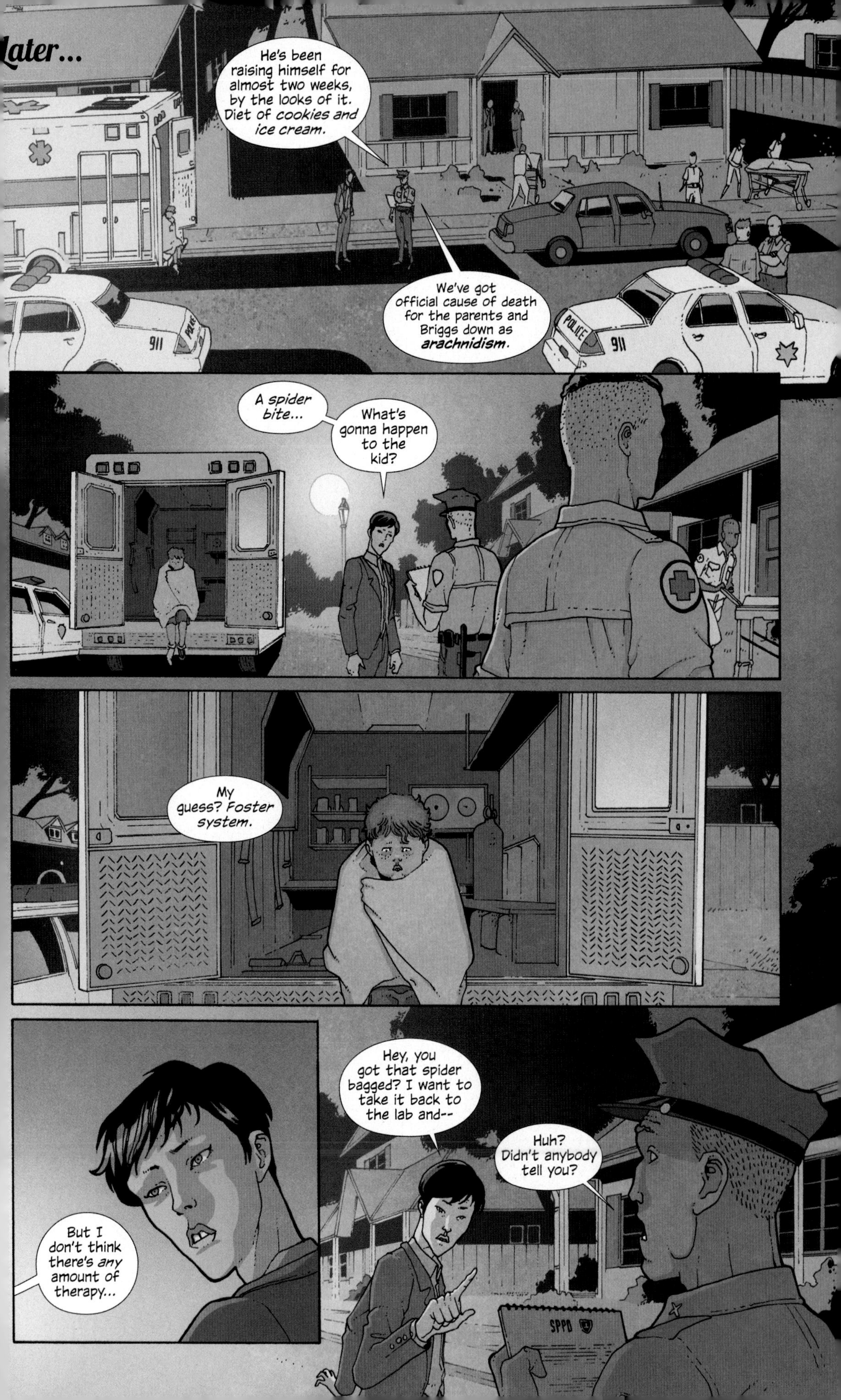
Later...
He's been raising himself for almost two weeks, by the looks of it. Diet of cookies and ice cream.
We've got official cause of death for the parents and Briggs down as arachnidism.
911
POLICE
911
POLICE
A spider bite...
What's gonna happen to the kid?
My guess? Foster system.
Hey, you got that spider bagged? I want to take it back to the lab and--
Huh? Didn't anybody tell you?
SPPD
But I don't think there's any amount of therapy...

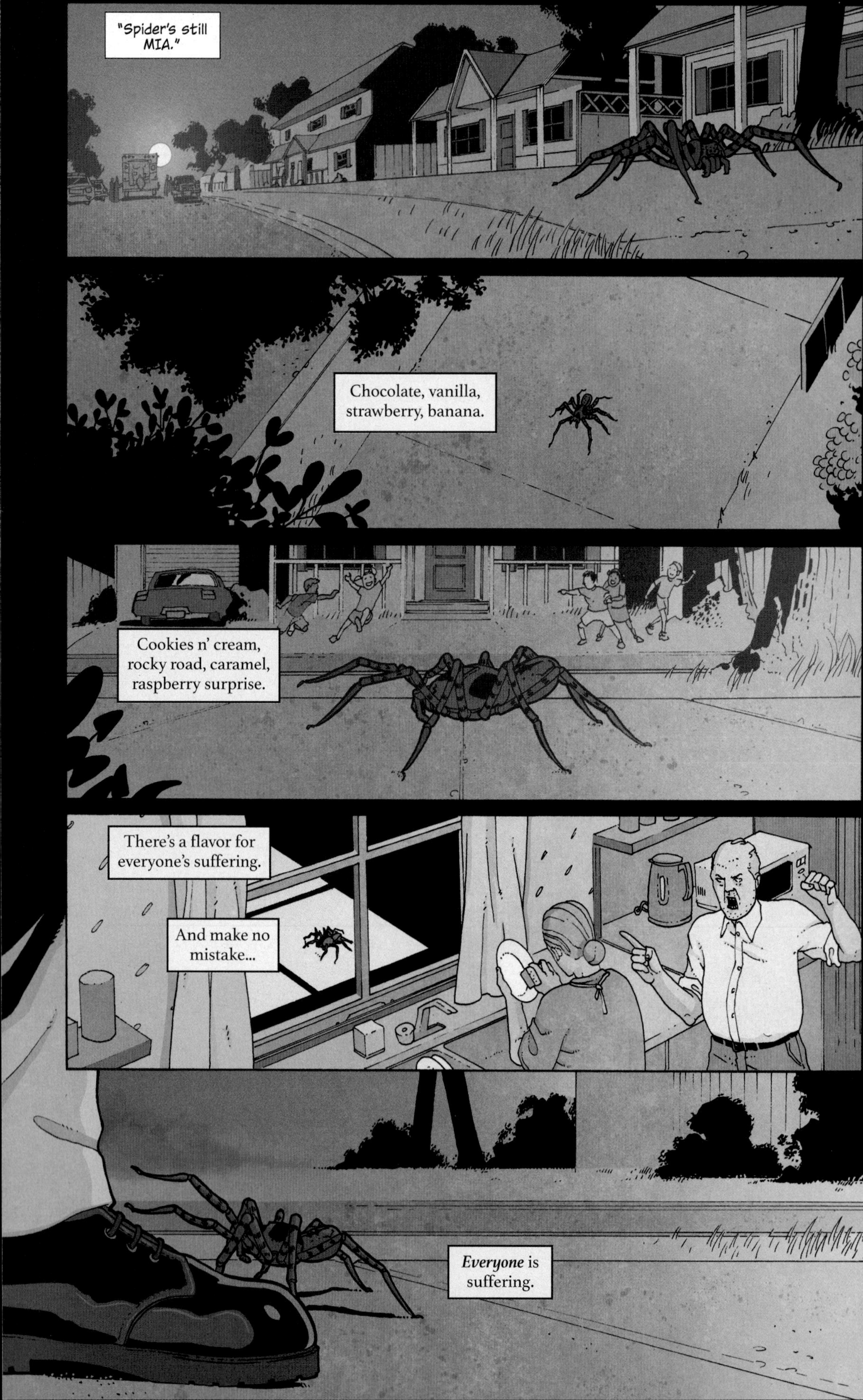
"Spider's still MIA."
Chocolate, vanilla, strawberry, banana.
Cookies n' cream, rocky road, caramel, raspberry surprise.
There's a flavor for everyone's suffering.
And make no mistake...
Everyone is suffering.

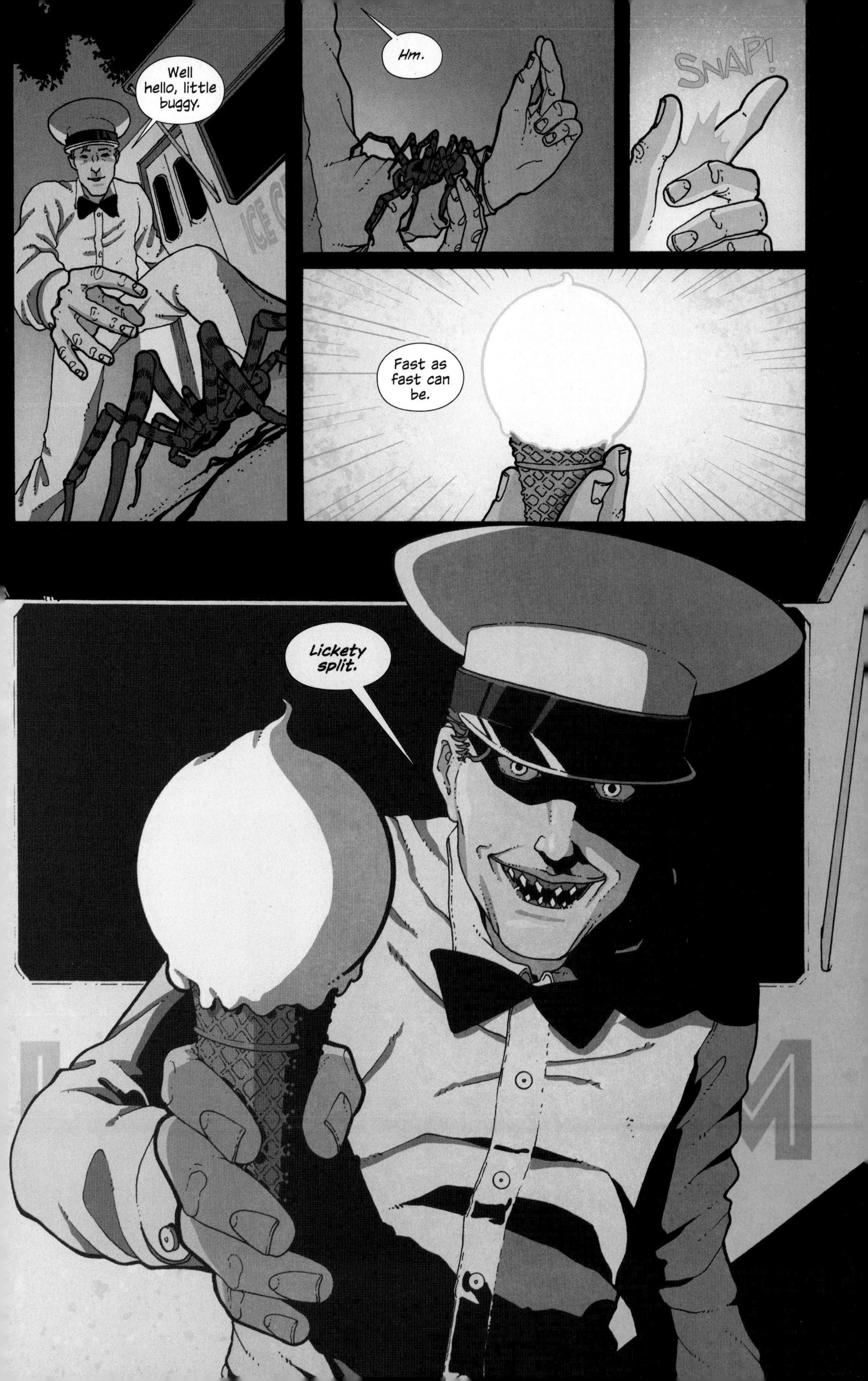
Well hello, little buggy.
Hm.
SNAP!
Fast as fast can be.
Lickety split.

Chocolate, vanilla, existential horror...
There's a flavor for everyone's miser

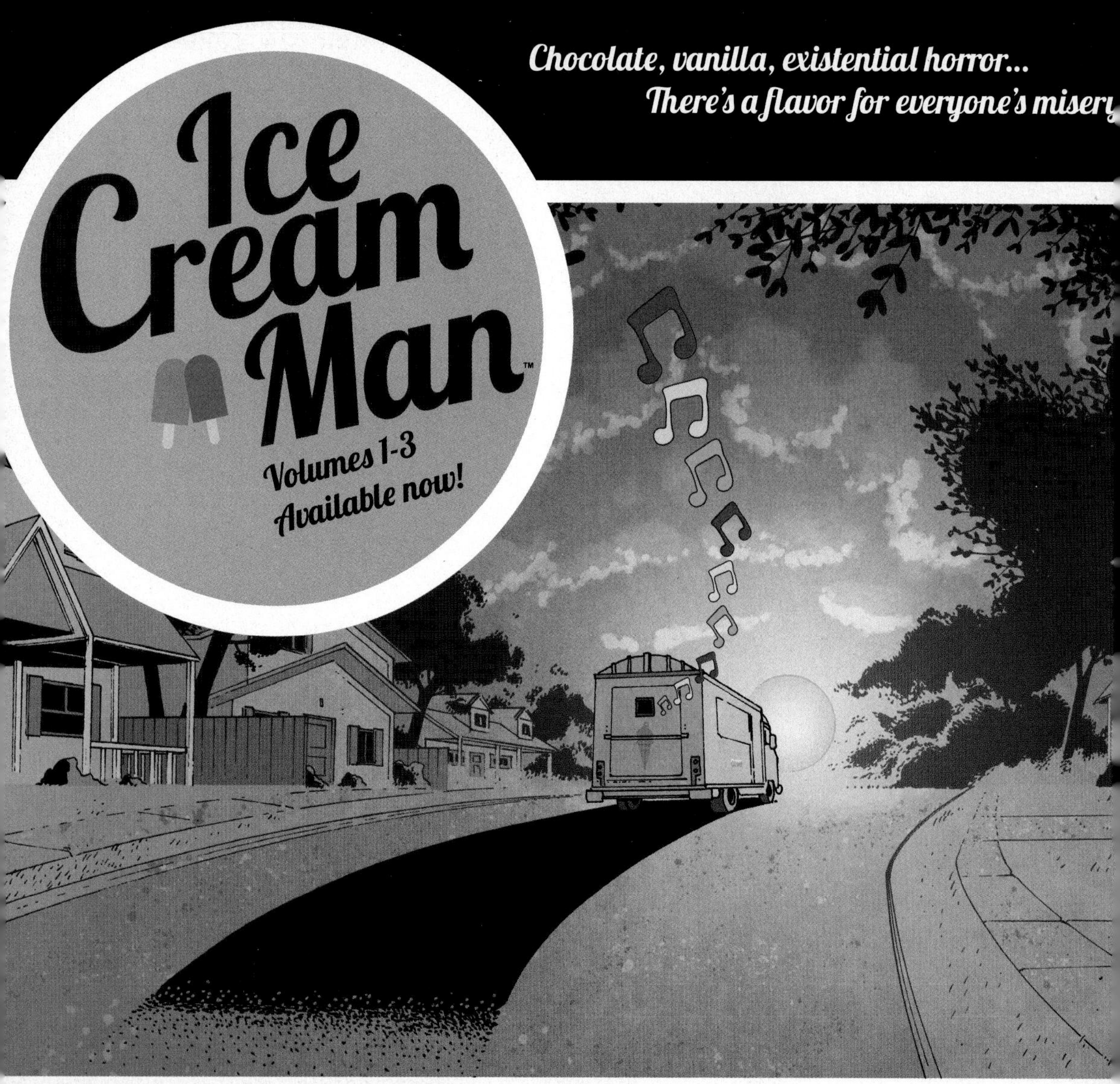
Ice Cream Man™
Volumes 1-3
Available now!

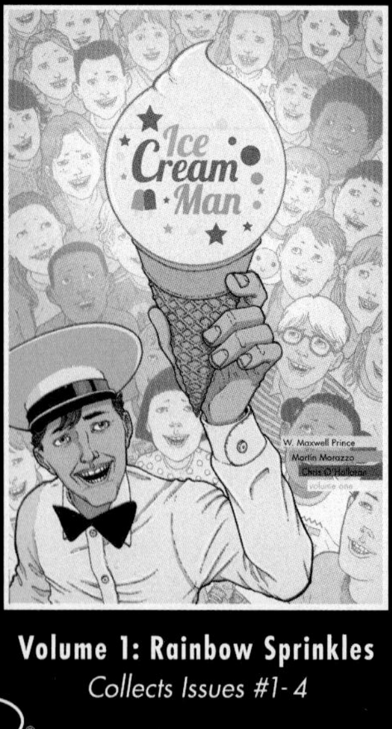
Ice Cream Man
W. Maxwell Prince
Martin Morazzo
Chris O'Halloran

Volume 1: Rainbow Sprinkles
Collects Issues #1- 4

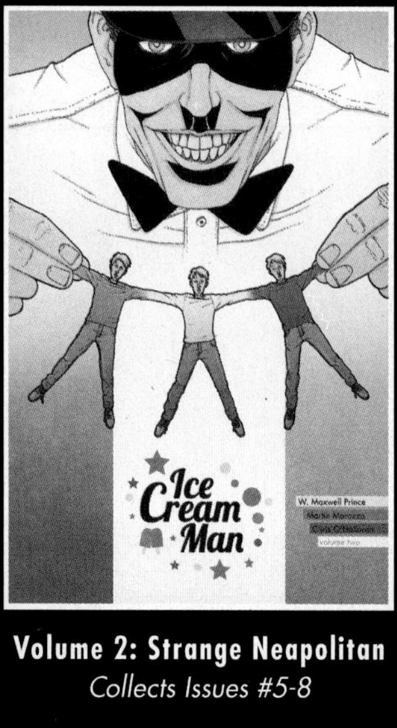
Ice Cream Man
W. Maxwell Prince
Martin Morazzo
Chris O'Halloran

Volume 2: Strange Neapolitan
Collects Issues #5-8

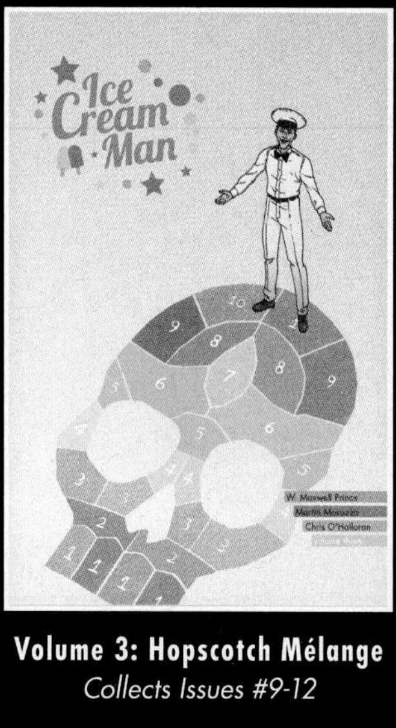
Ice Cream Man
W. Maxwell Prince
Martin Morazzo
Chris O'Halloran

Volume 3: Hopscotch Mélange
Collects Issues #9-12

IMAGECOMICS.C
FOLLOW #IMAGECOM

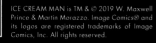

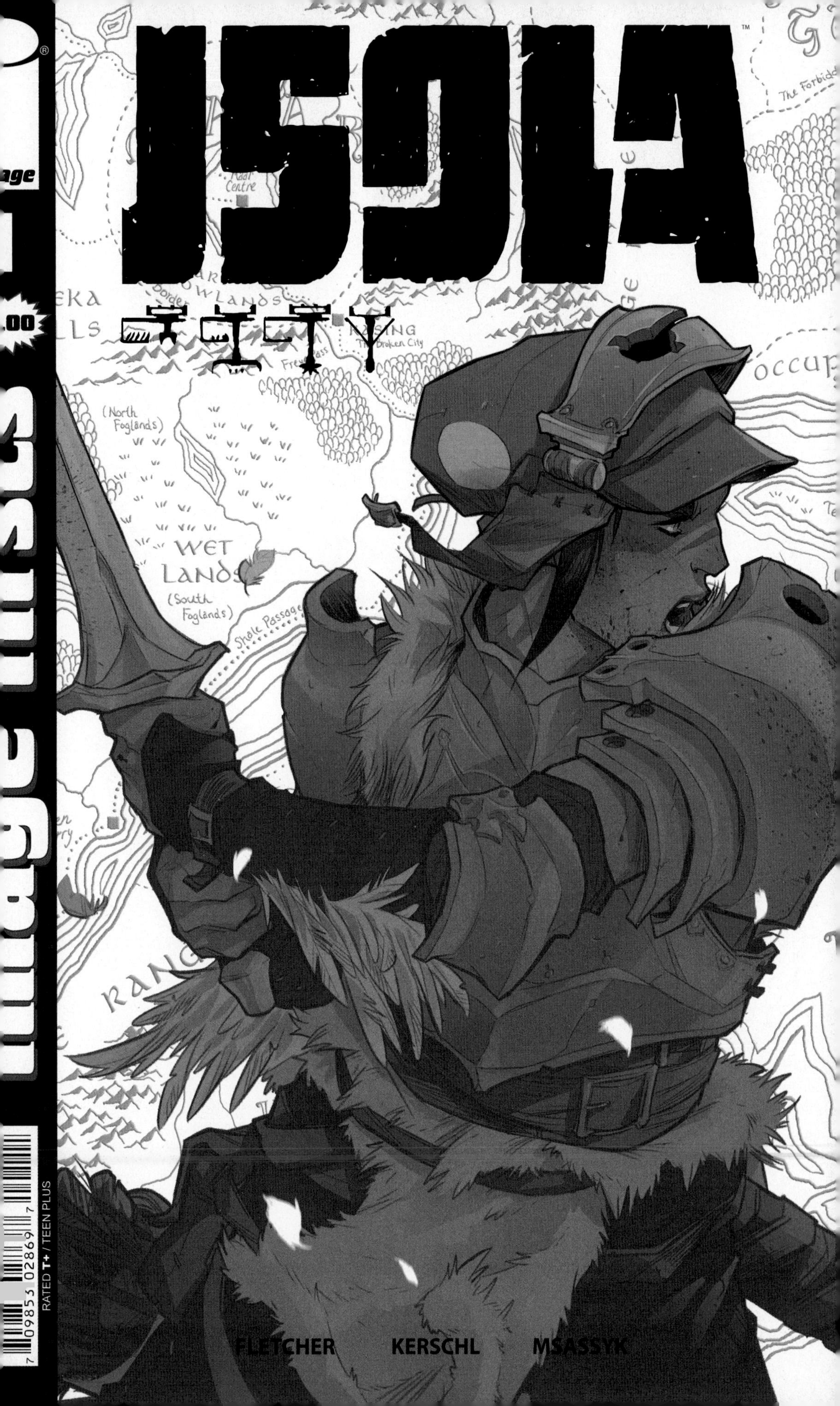

ISOLA
image firsts
RATED T+ / TEEN PLUS
(North Foglands)
WET LANDS
(South Foglands)
Shale Passage
The Broken City
FLETCHER
KERSCHL
MSASSYK

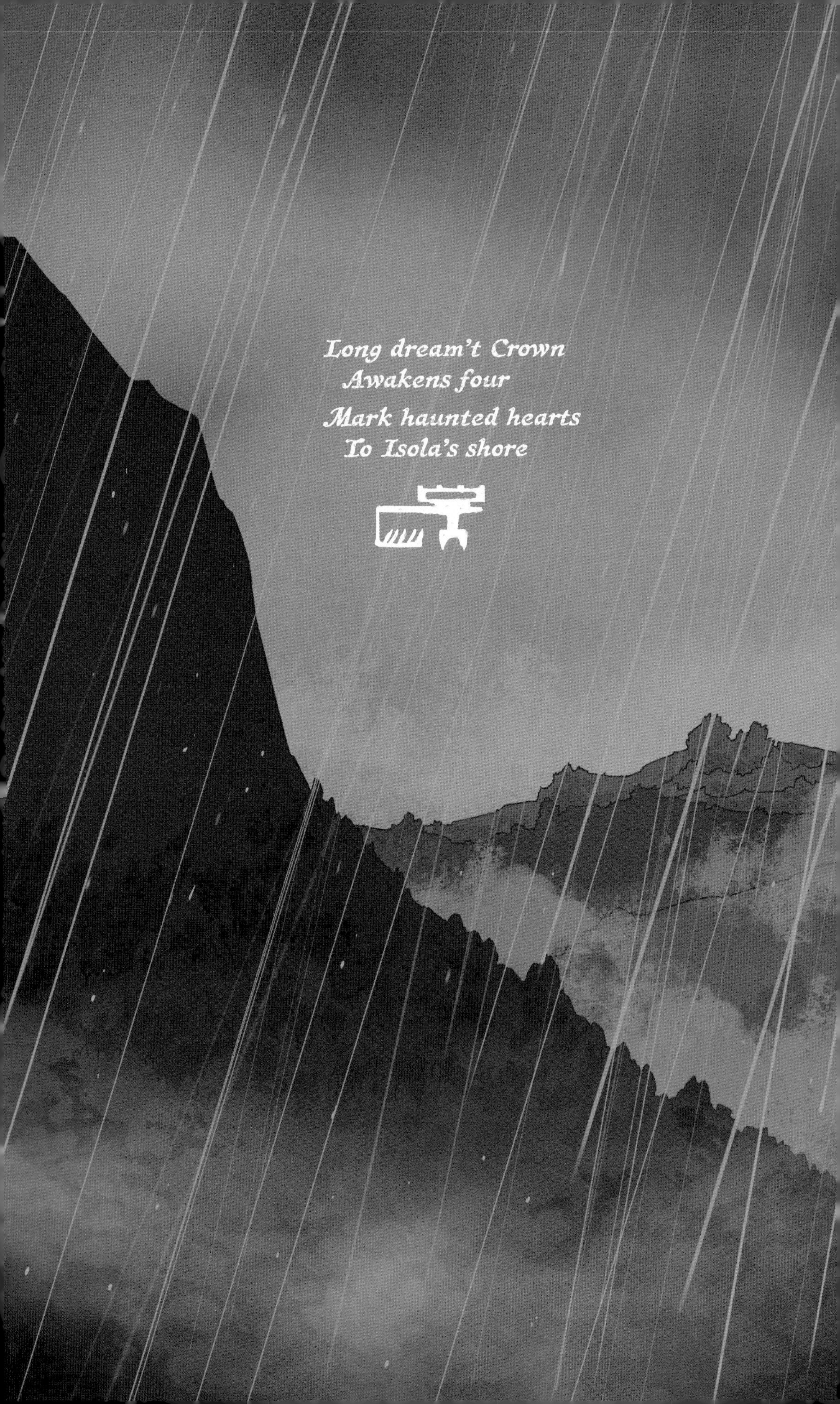
Long dream't Crown
Awakens four
Mark haunted hearts
To Isola's shore

ISSSS-SSSSSSSS

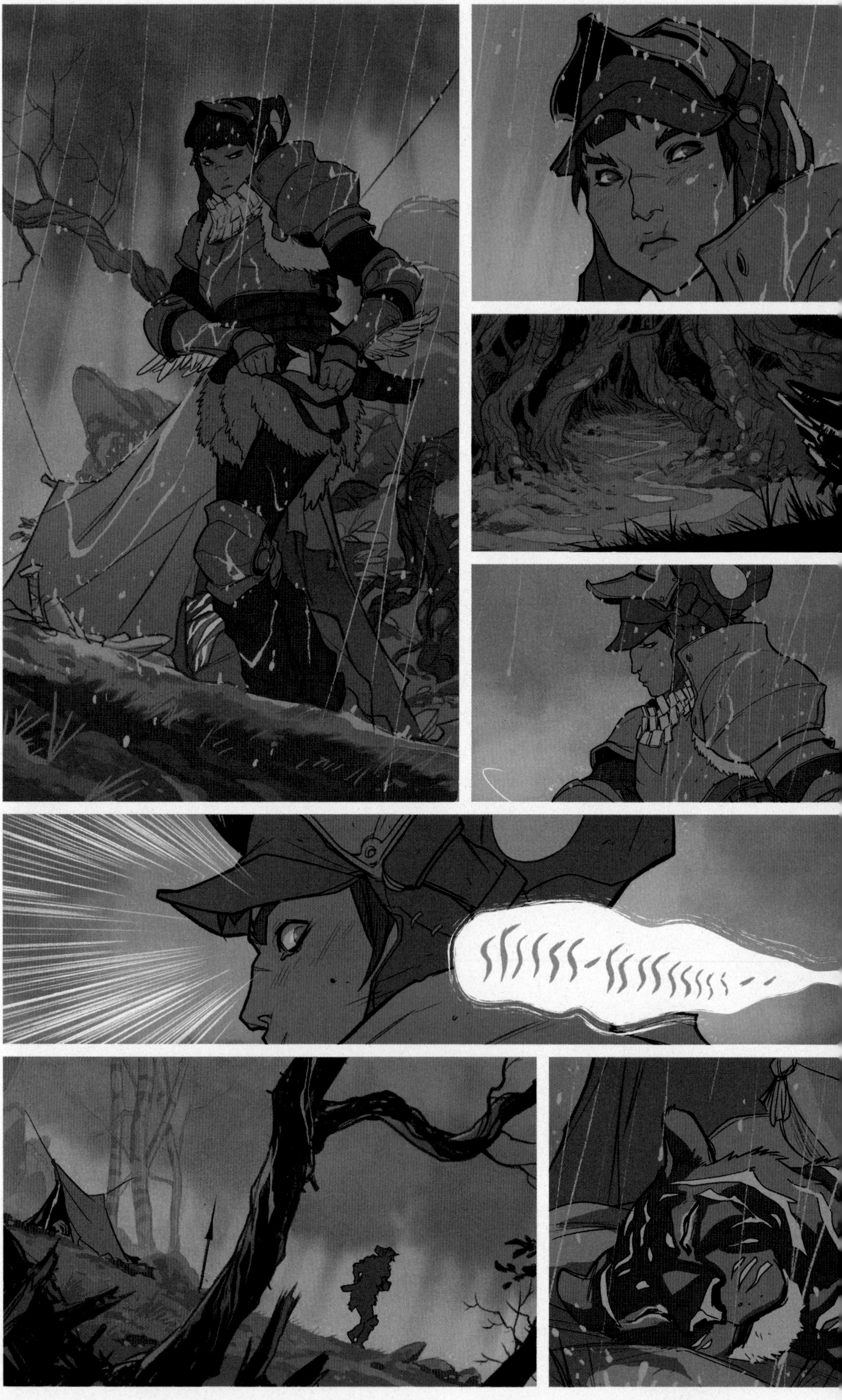

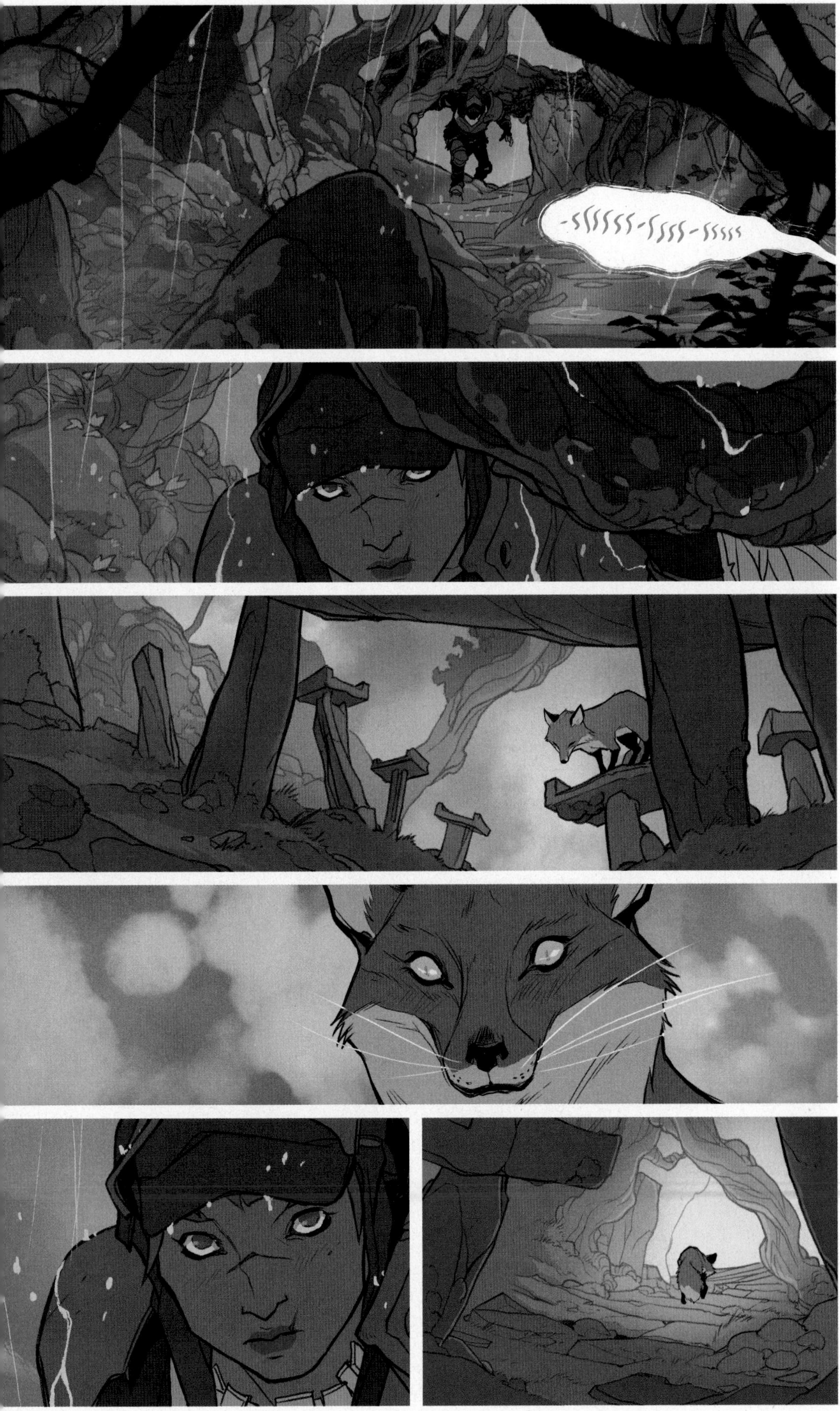

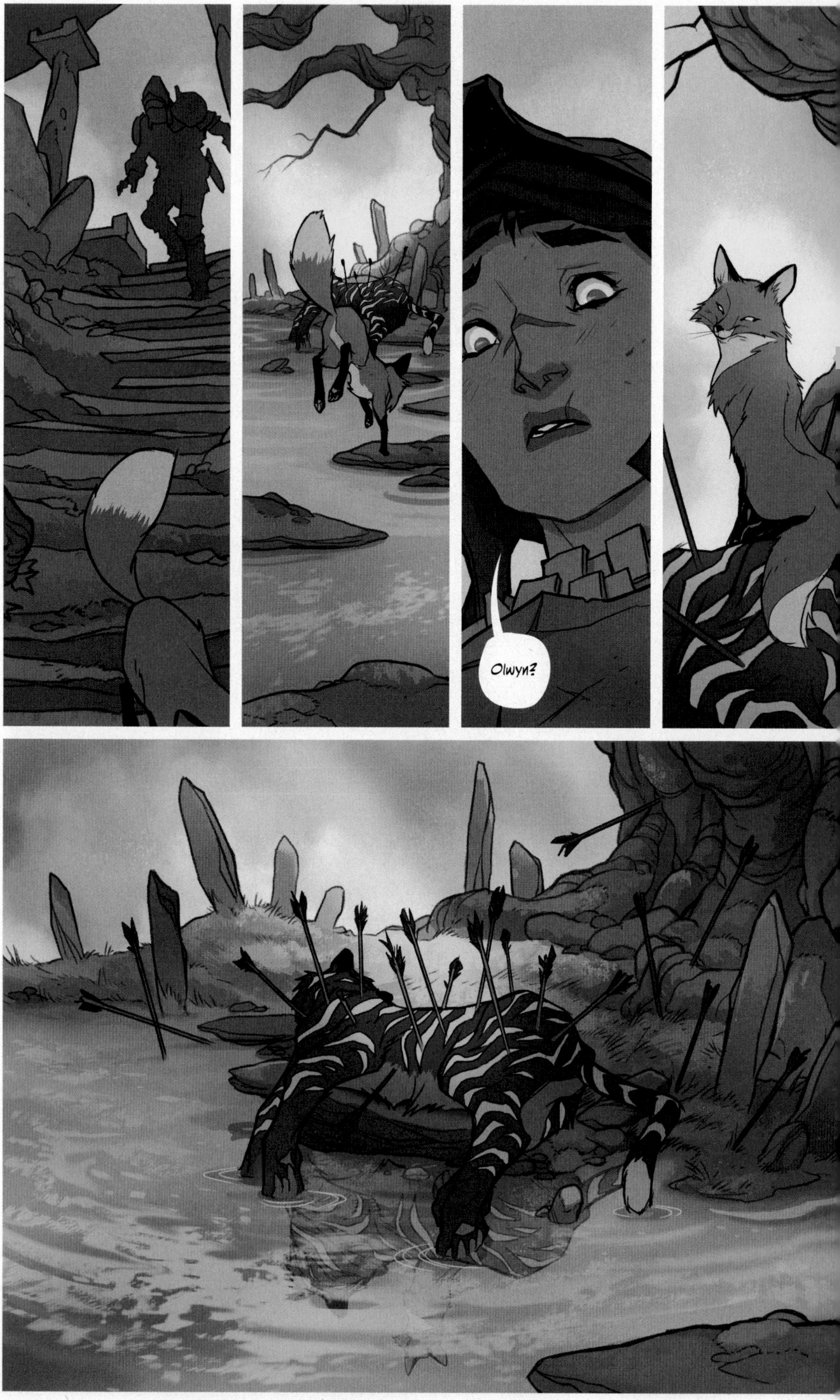
Olwyn?

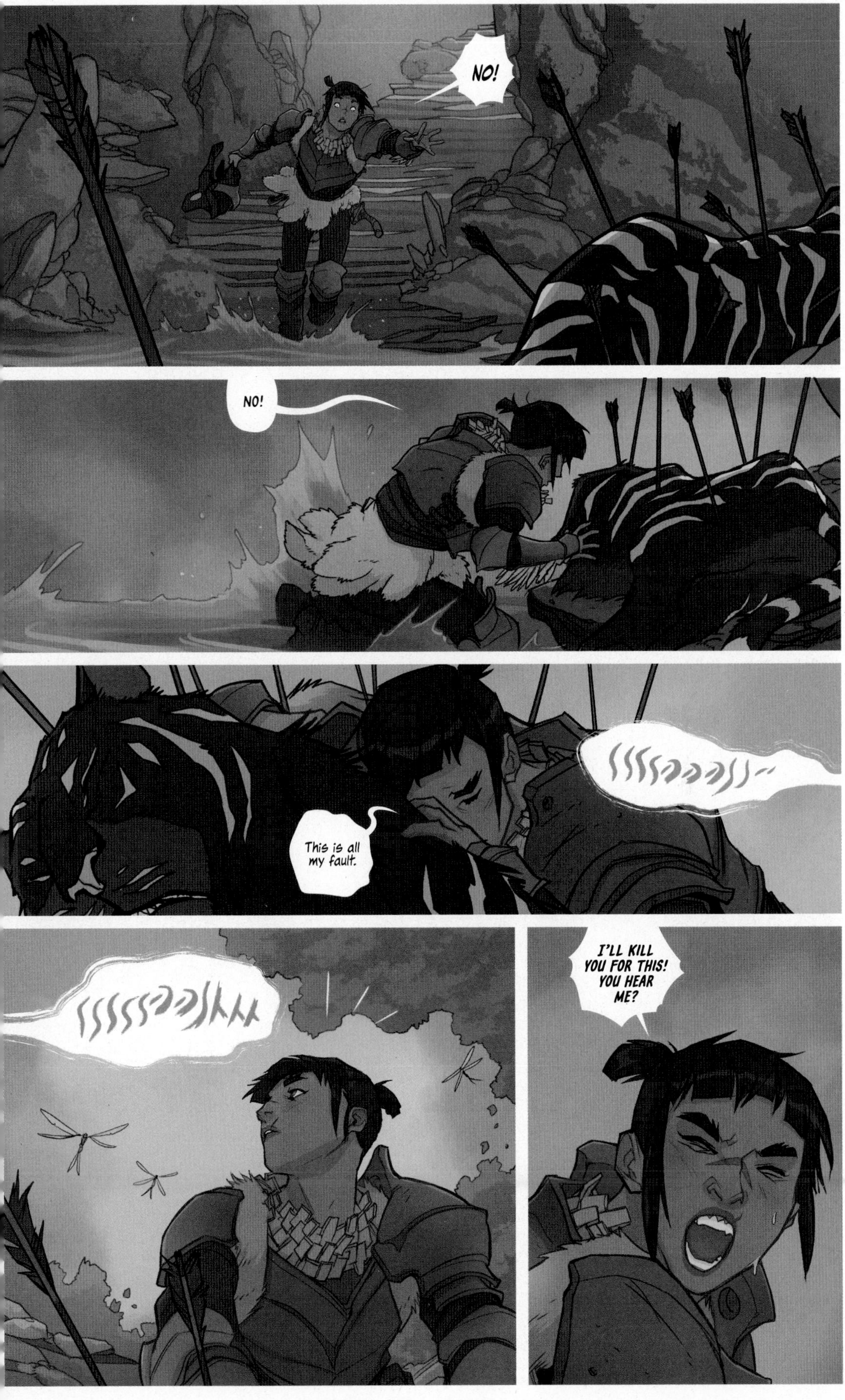
NO!
NO!
This is all my fault.
I'LL KILL YOU FOR THIS! YOU HEAR ME?

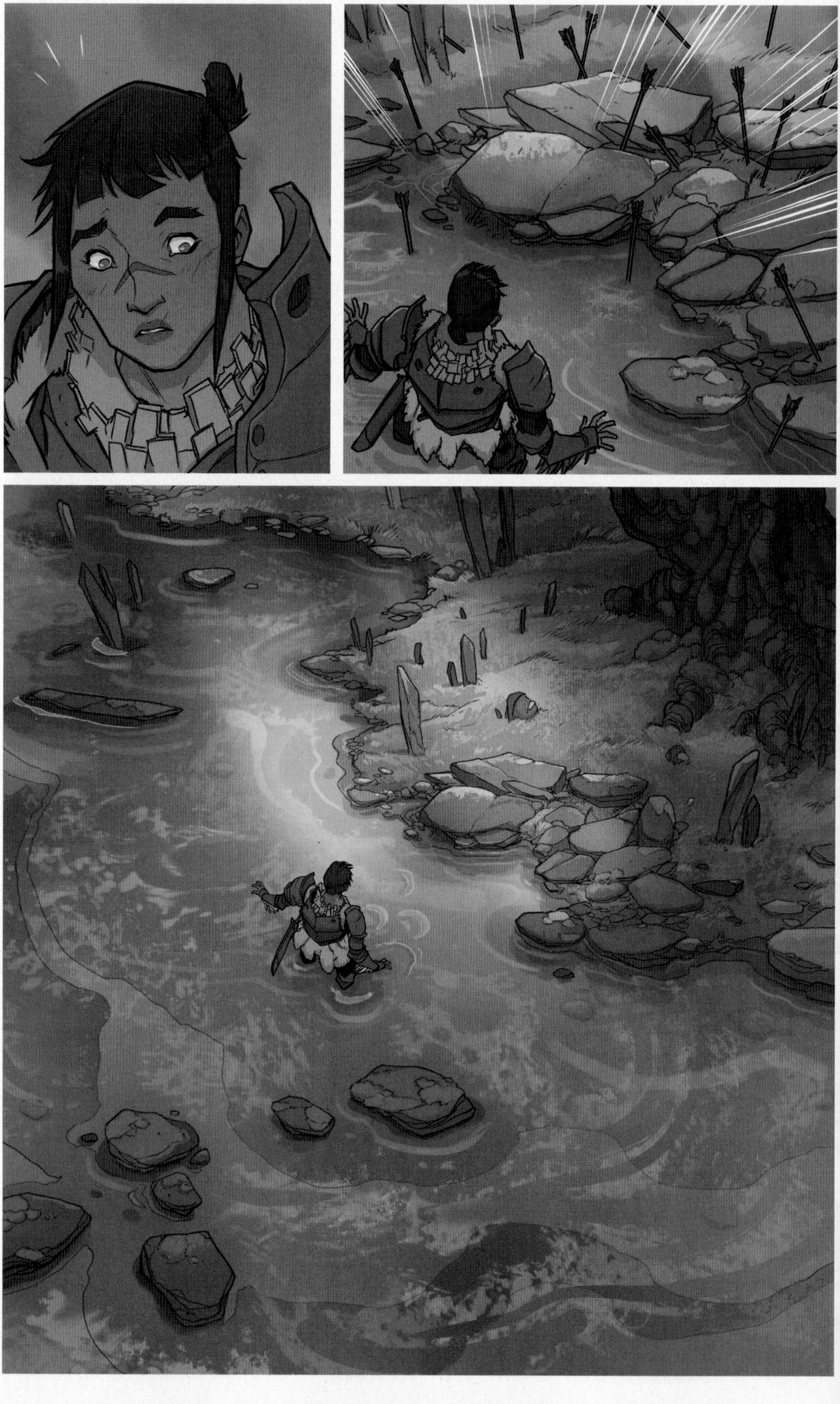

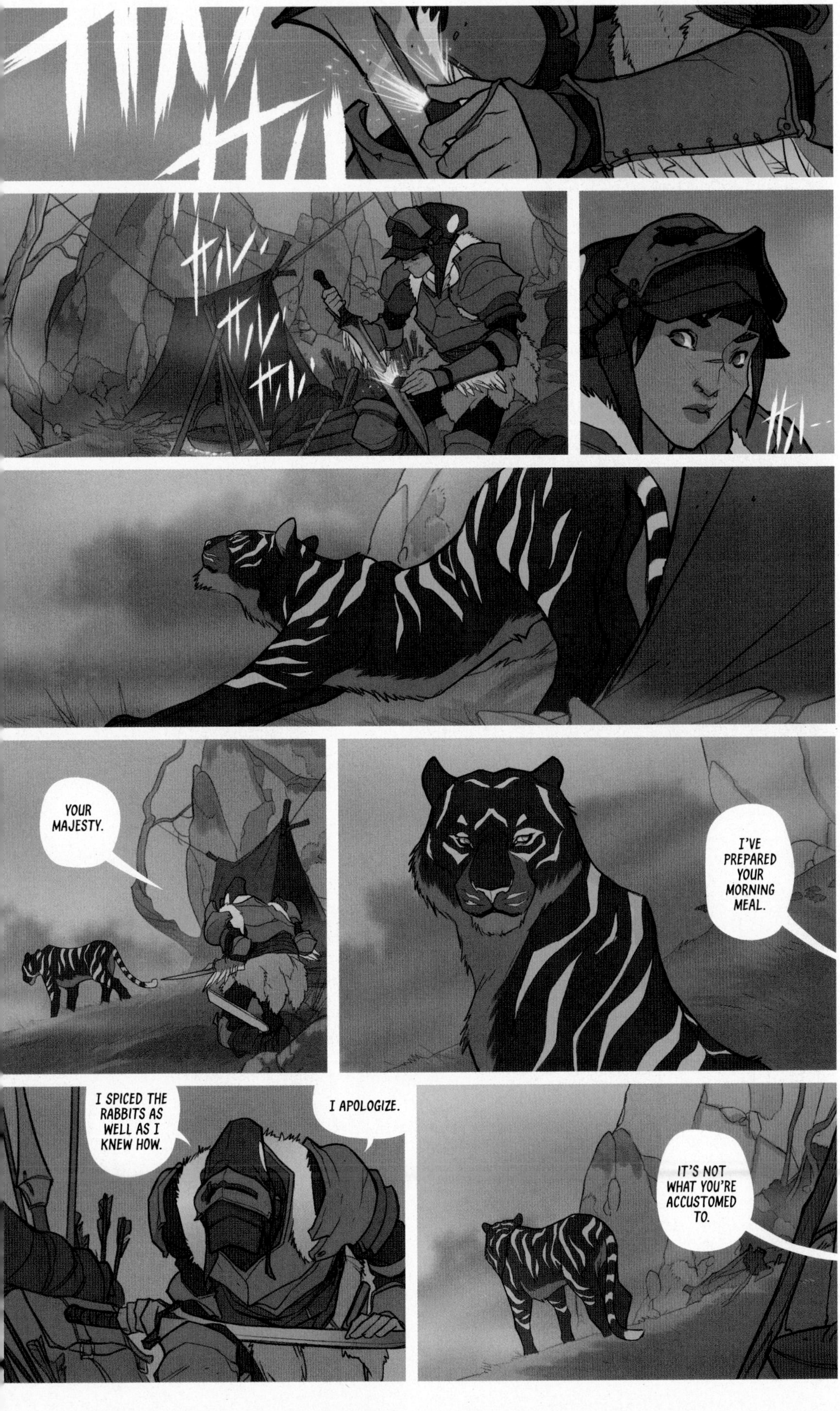
YOUR MAJESTY.
I'VE PREPARED YOUR MORNING MEAL.
I SPICED THE RABBITS AS WELL AS I KNEW HOW.
I APOLOGIZE.
IT'S NOT WHAT YOU'RE ACCUSTOMED TO.

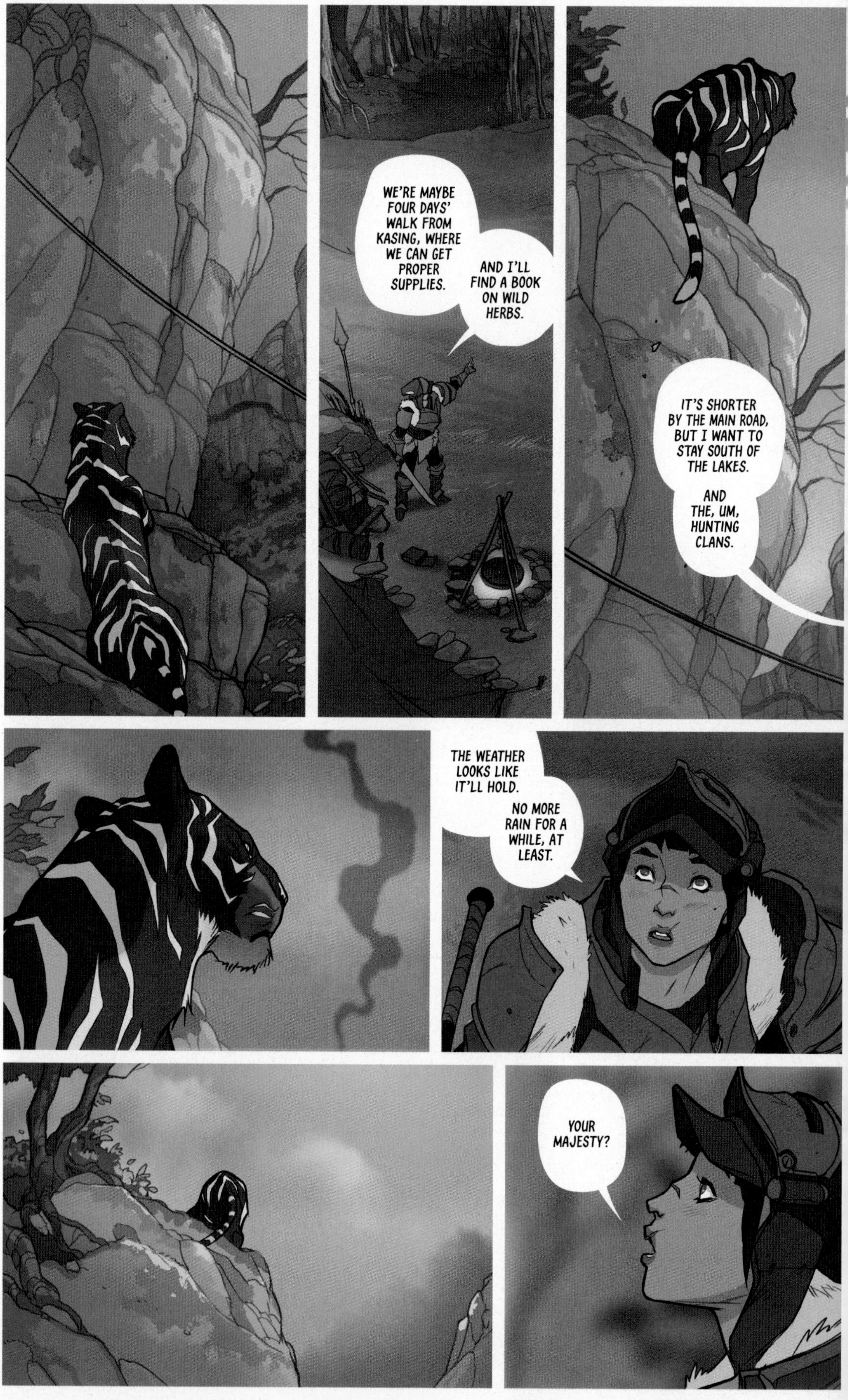
WE'RE MAYBE FOUR DAYS' WALK FROM KASING, WHERE WE CAN GET PROPER SUPPLIES.
AND I'LL FIND A BOOK ON WILD HERBS.
IT'S SHORTER BY THE MAIN ROAD, BUT I WANT TO STAY SOUTH OF THE LAKES.
AND THE, UM, HUNTING CLANS.
THE WEATHER LOOKS LIKE IT'LL HOLD.
NO MORE RAIN FOR A WHILE, AT LEAST.
YOUR MAJESTY?

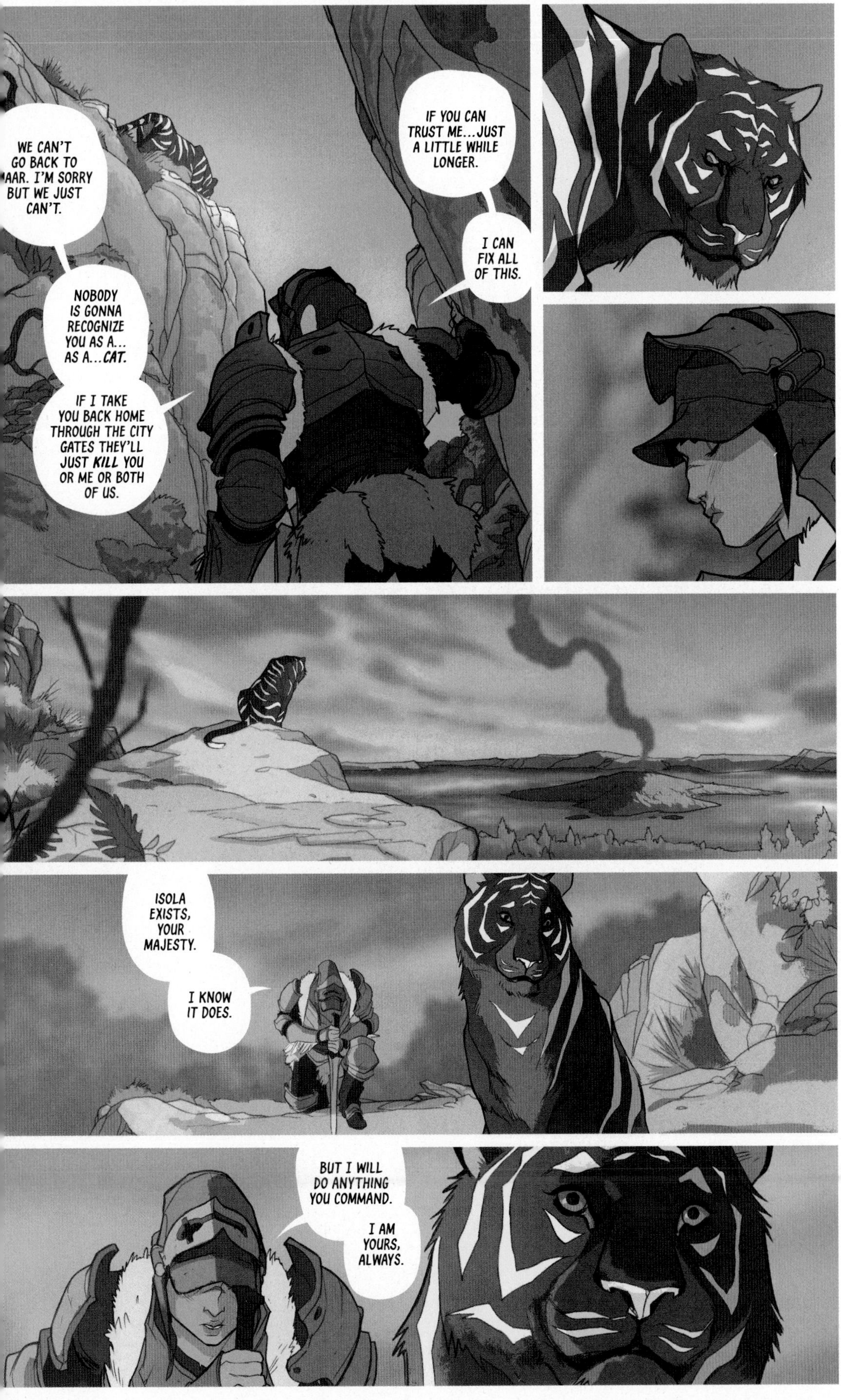
WE CAN'T GO BACK TO AAR. I'M SORRY BUT WE JUST CAN'T.
NOBODY IS GONNA RECOGNIZE YOU AS A... AS A...CAT.
IF I TAKE YOU BACK HOME THROUGH THE CITY GATES THEY'LL JUST KILL YOU OR ME OR BOTH OF US.
IF YOU CAN TRUST ME...JUST A LITTLE WHILE LONGER.
I CAN FIX ALL OF THIS.
ISOLA EXISTS, YOUR MAJESTY.
I KNOW IT DOES.
BUT I WILL DO ANYTHING YOU COMMAND.
I AM YOURS, ALWAYS.

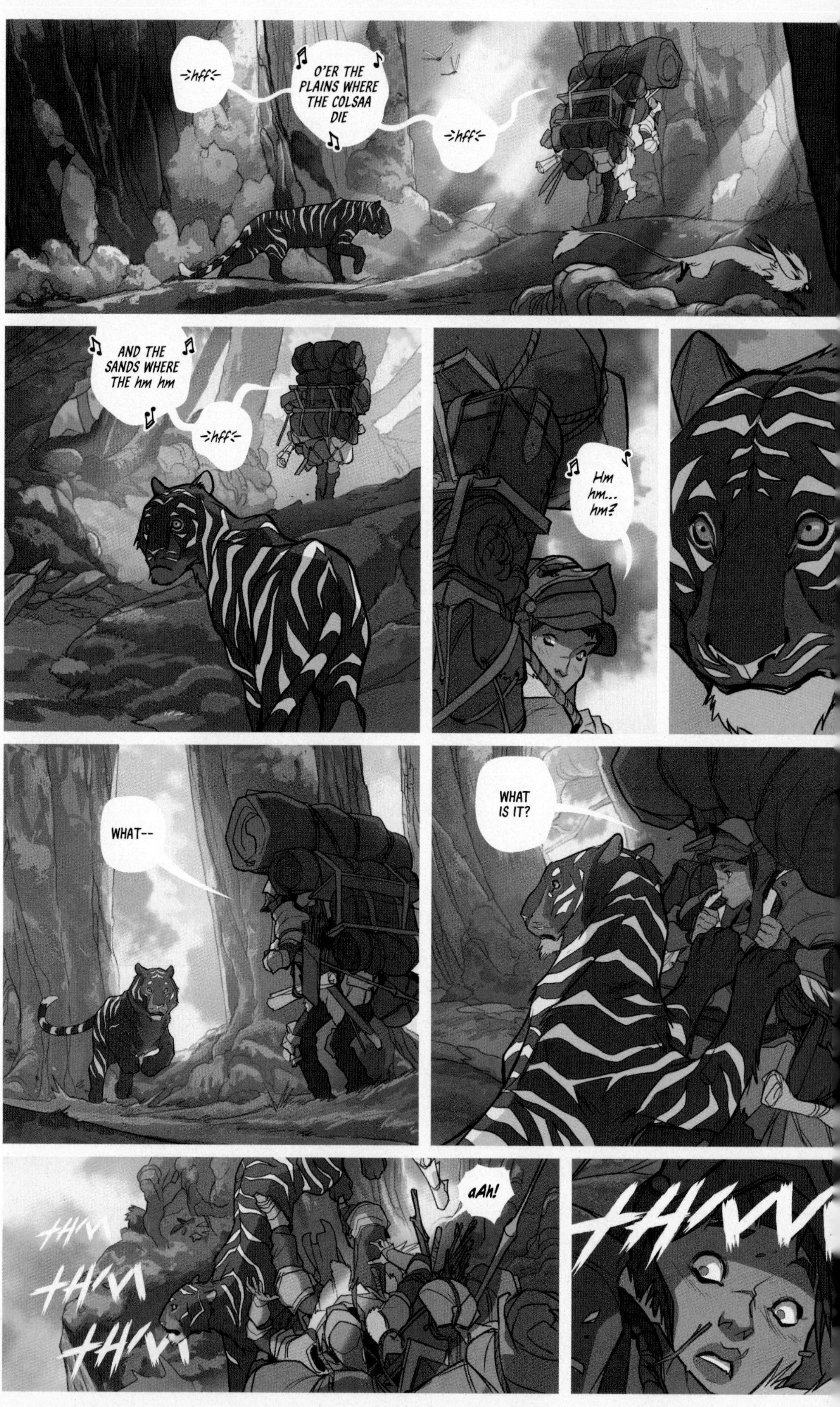
~hff~
O'ER THE PLAINS WHERE THE COLSAA DIE
~hff~
AND THE SANDS WHERE THE hm hm
~hff~
Hm hm... hm?
WHAT--
WHAT IS IT?
THW
THW
THW
aAh!
THWW

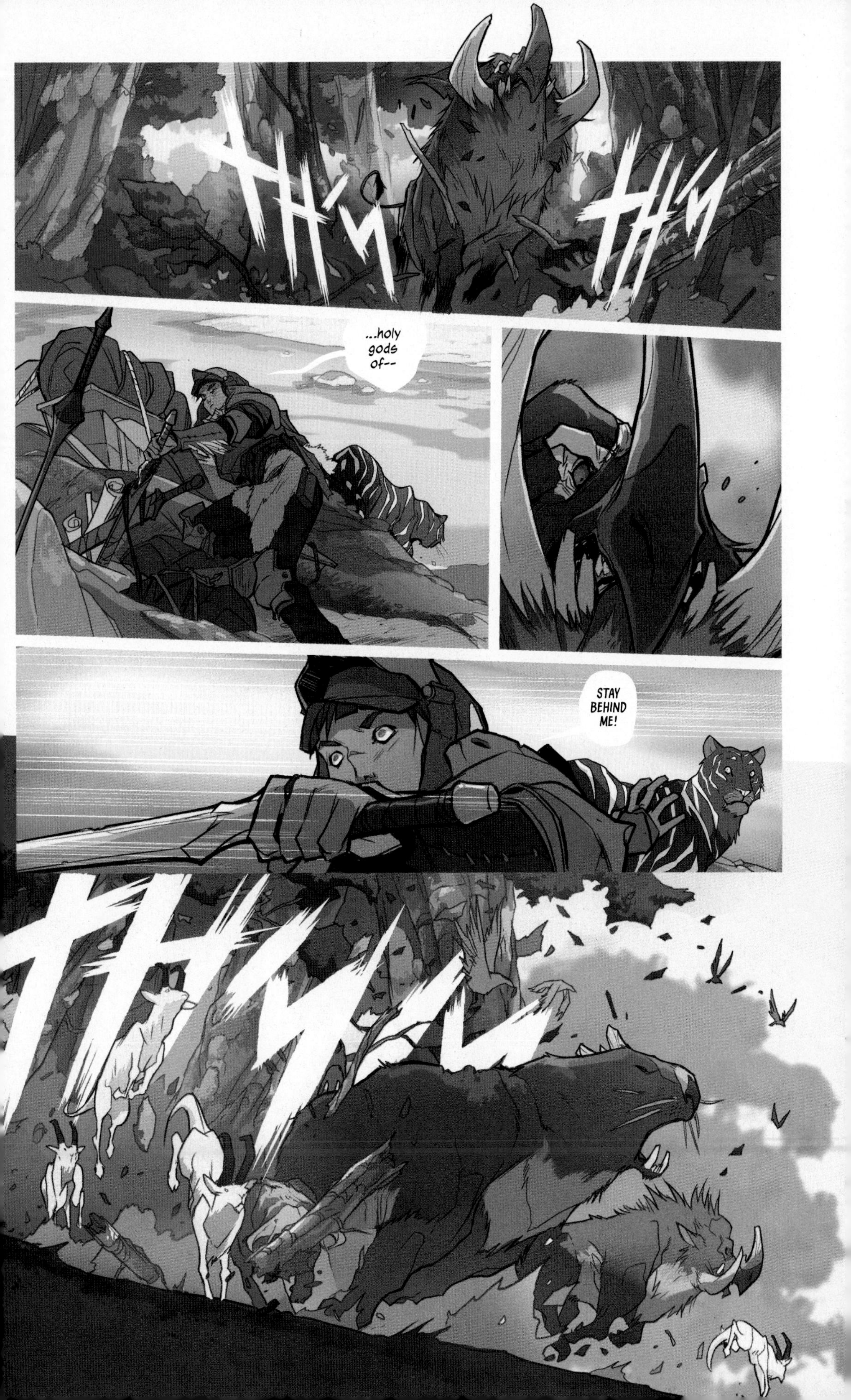
THWN
THWN
...holy gods of--
STAY BEHIND ME!
THWUNK

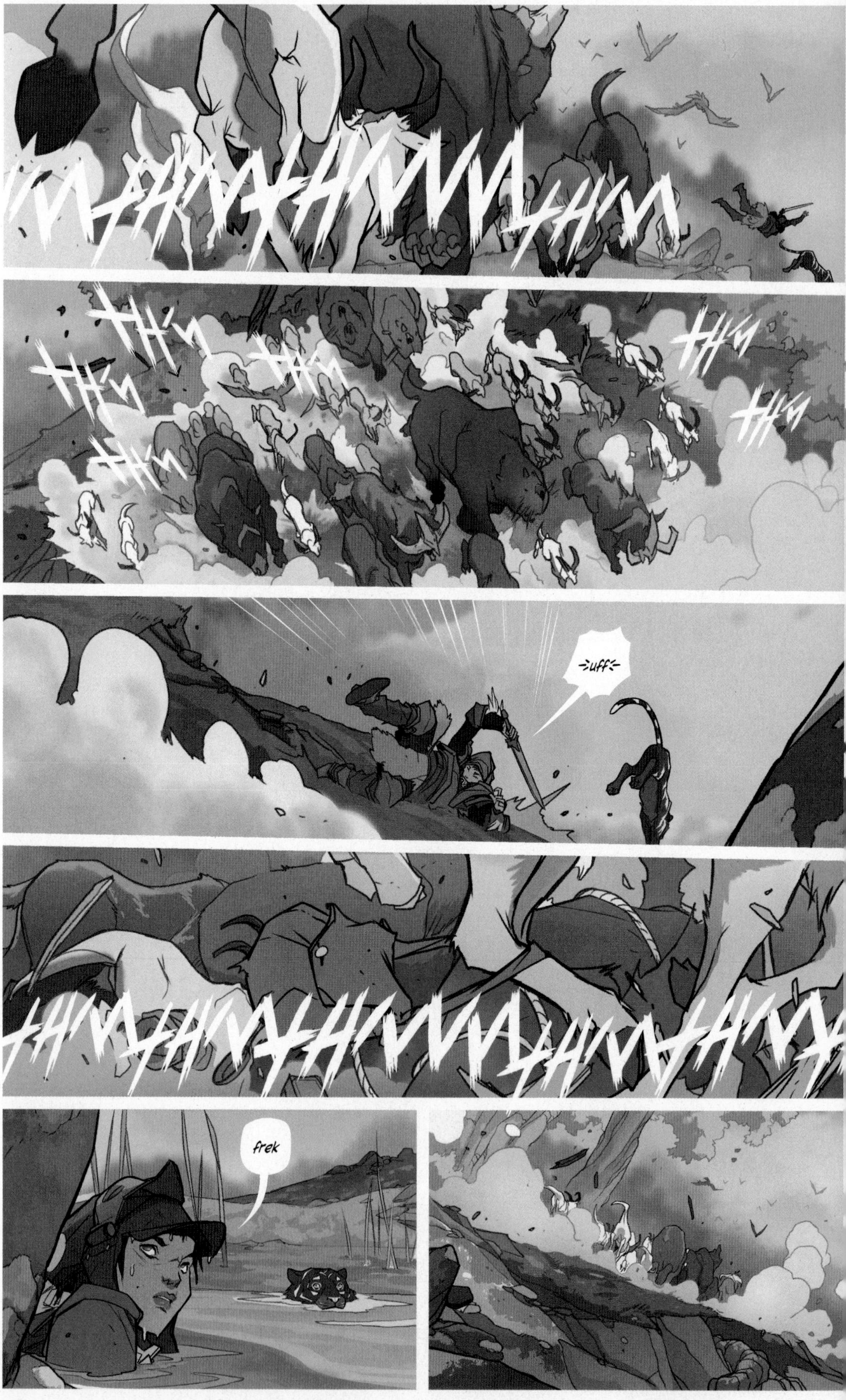
uff
frek

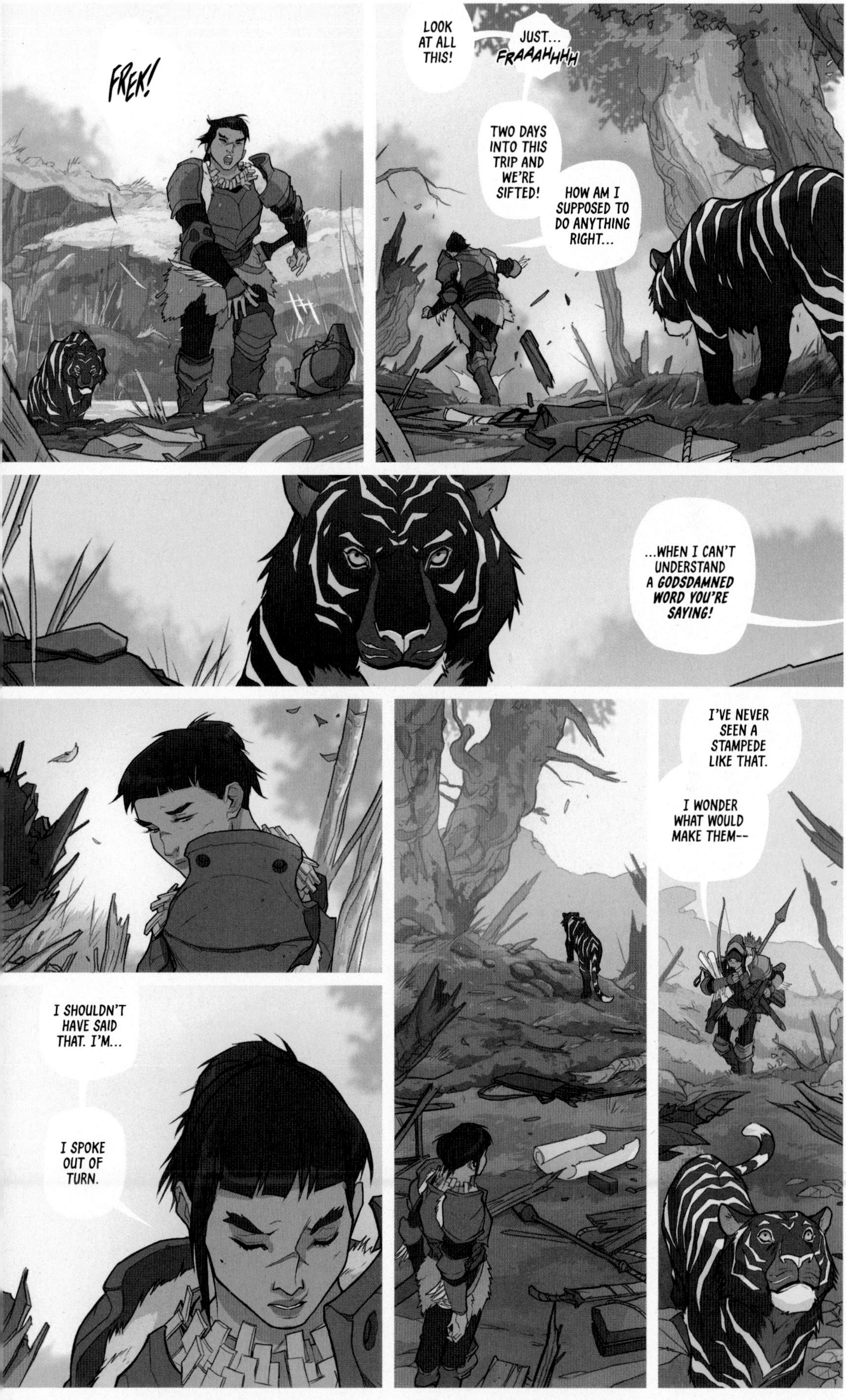
FREK!
LOOK AT ALL THIS!
JUST... FRAAAHHHH
TWO DAYS INTO THIS TRIP AND WE'RE SIFTED!
HOW AM I SUPPOSED TO DO ANYTHING RIGHT...
...WHEN I CAN'T UNDERSTAND A *GODSDAMNED WORD YOU'RE SAYING!*
I SHOULDN'T HAVE SAID THAT. I'M...
I SPOKE OUT OF TURN.
I'VE NEVER SEEN A STAMPEDE LIKE THAT.
I WONDER WHAT WOULD MAKE THEM--

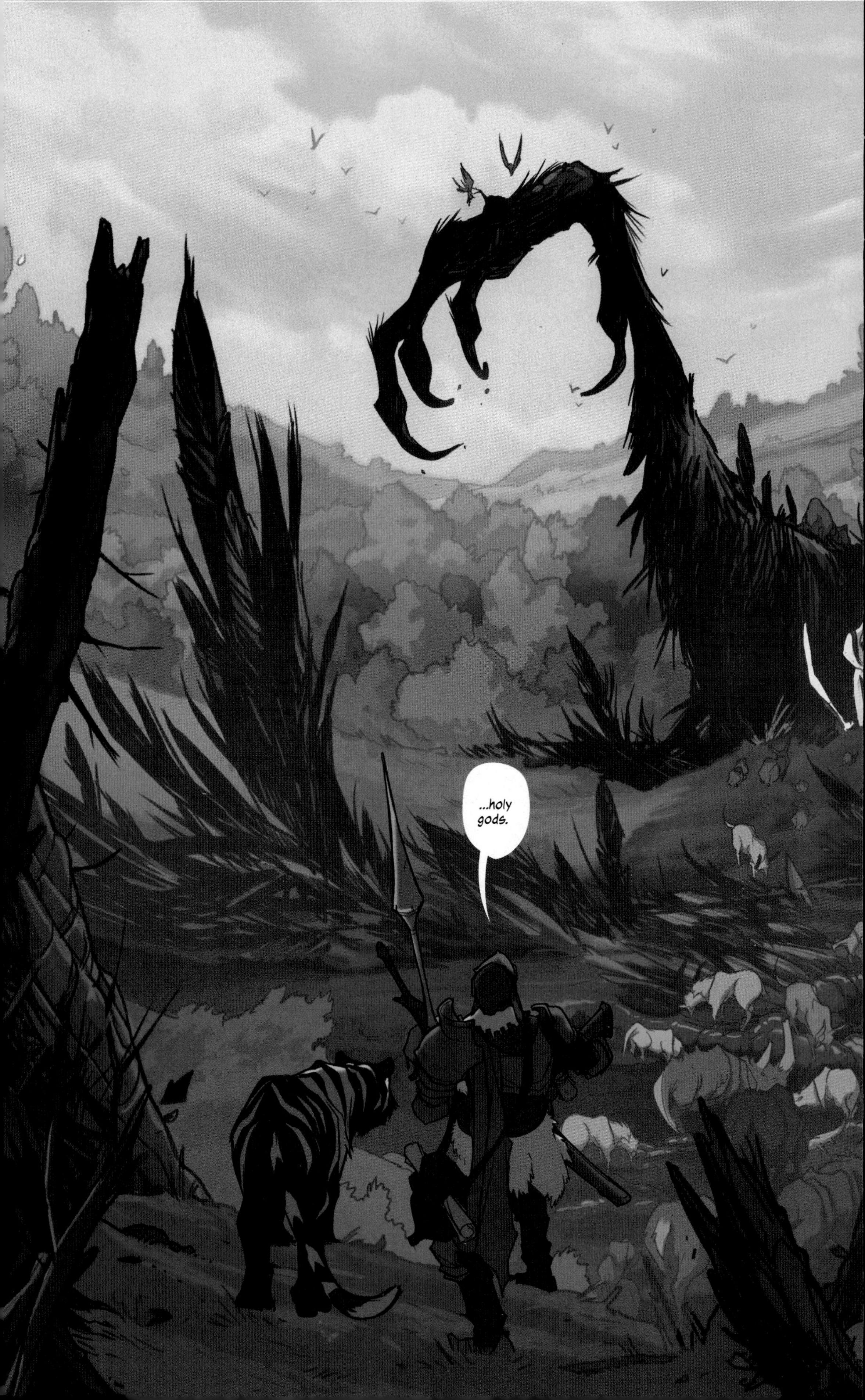
...holy gods.

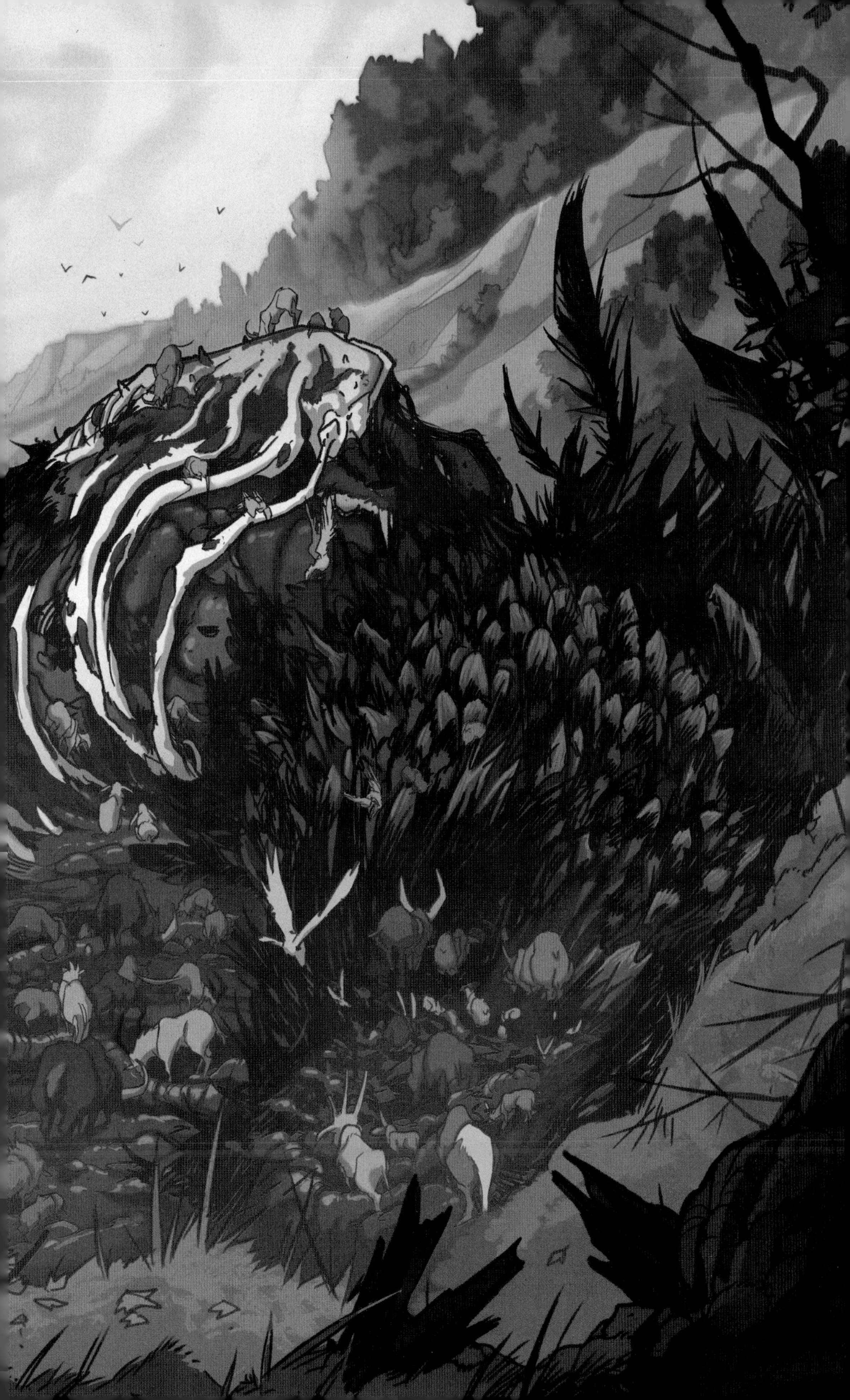

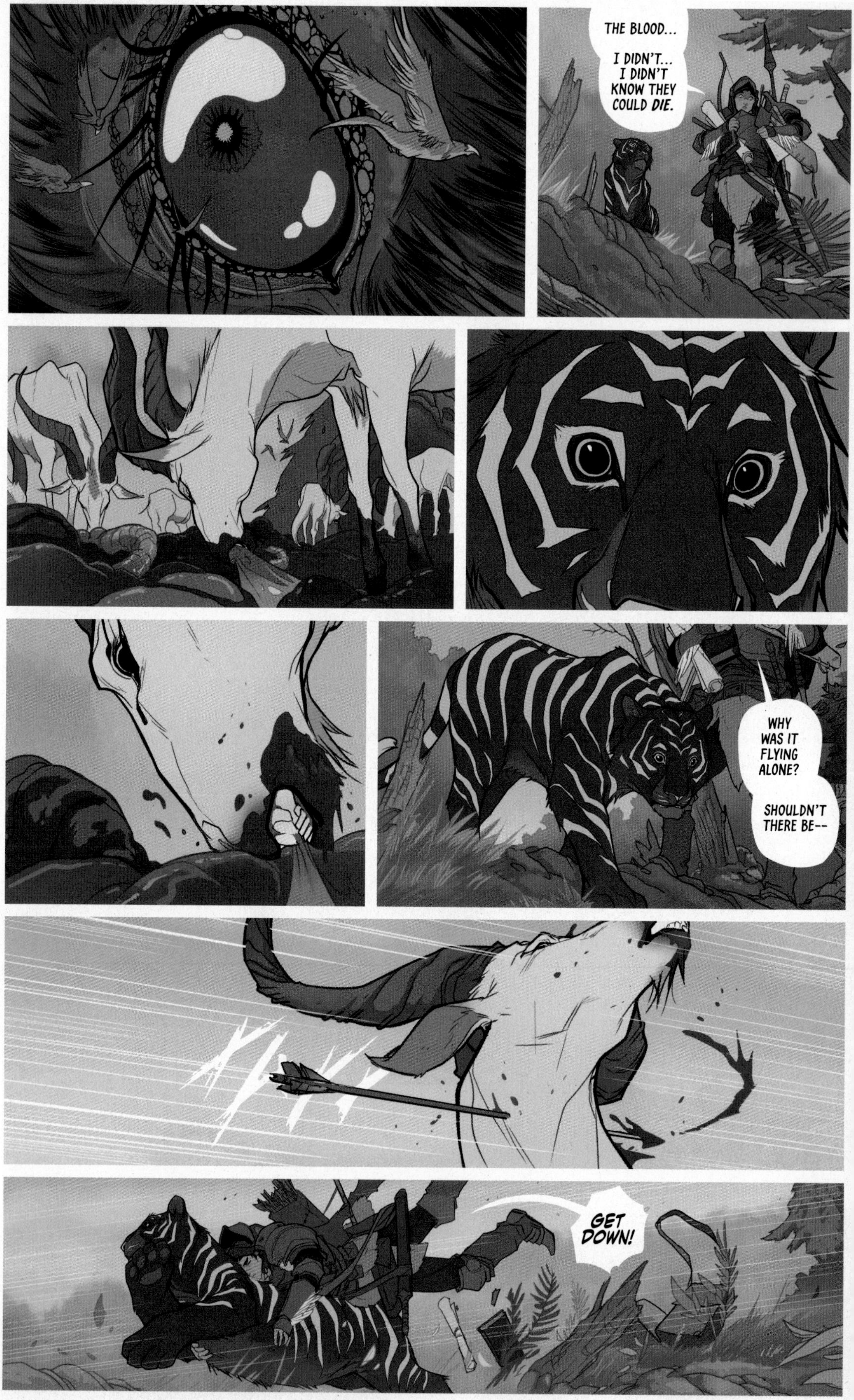
THE BLOOD...
I DIDN'T... I DIDN'T KNOW THEY COULD DIE.
WHY WAS IT FLYING ALONE?
SHOULDN'T THERE BE--
GET DOWN!

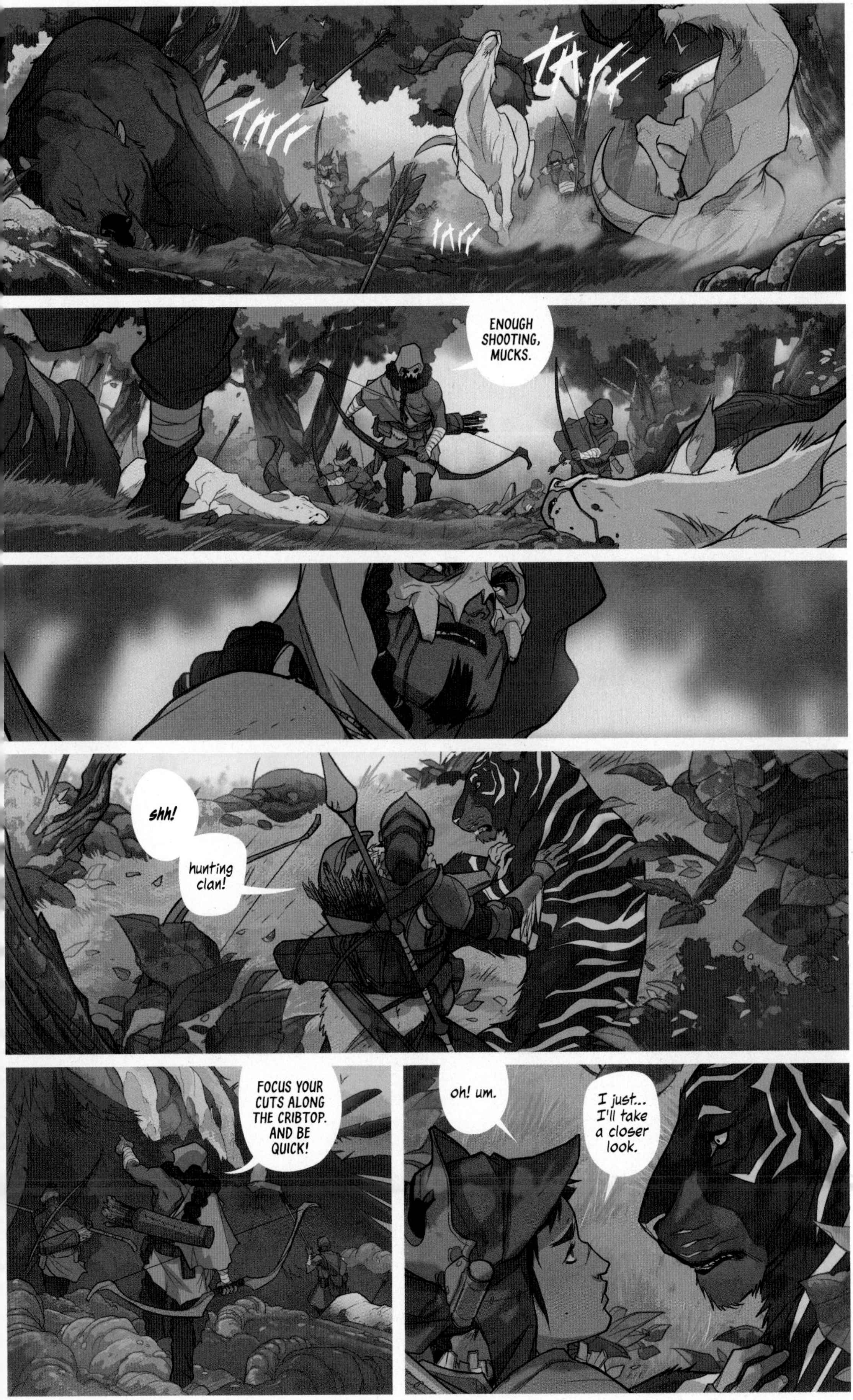

THK
THKK
THK
ENOUGH SHOOTING, MUCKS.
shh!
hunting clan!
FOCUS YOUR CUTS ALONG THE CRIBTOP. AND BE QUICK!
oh! um.
I just... I'll take a closer look.

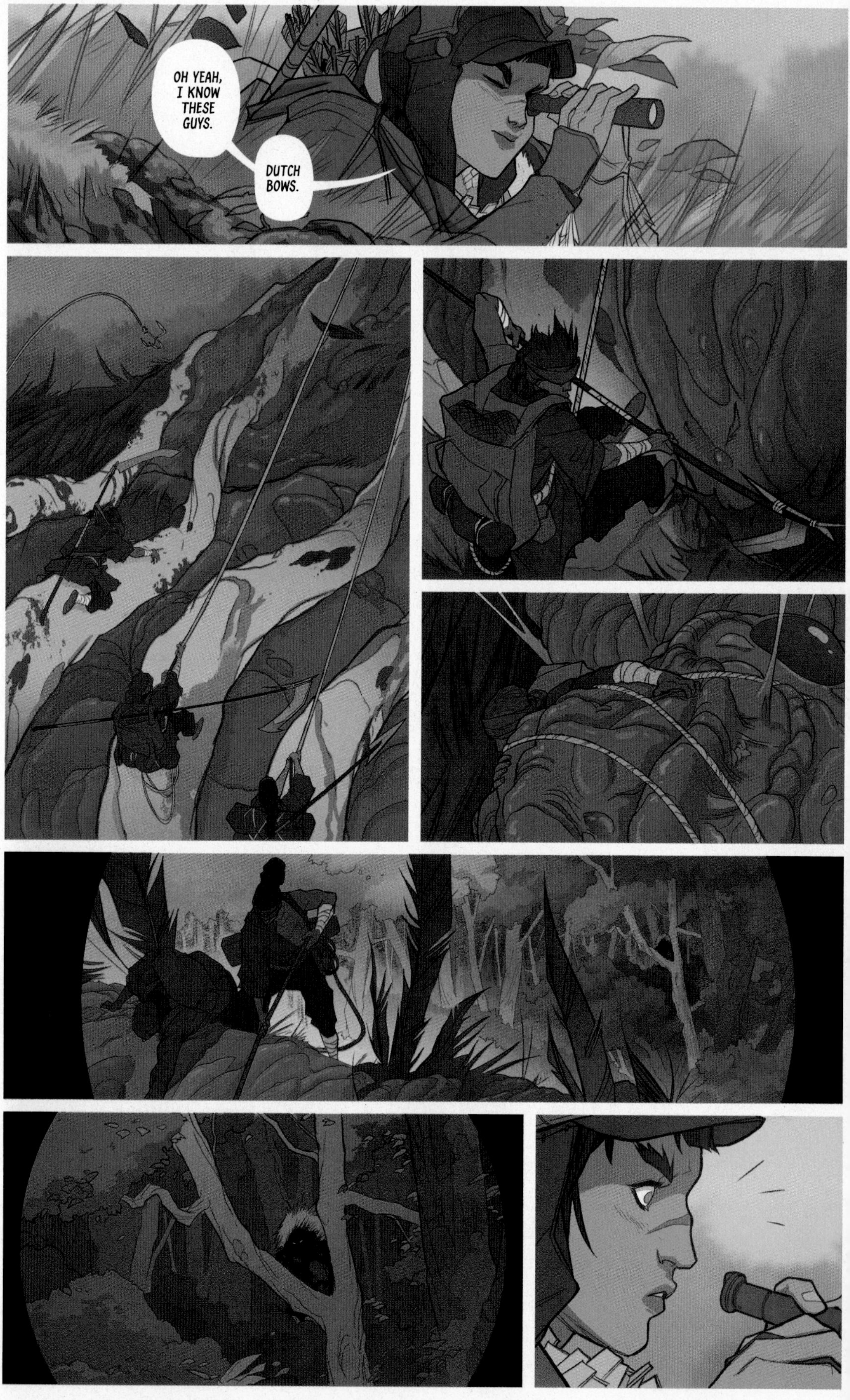
OH YEAH, I KNOW THESE GUYS.
DUTCH BOWS.

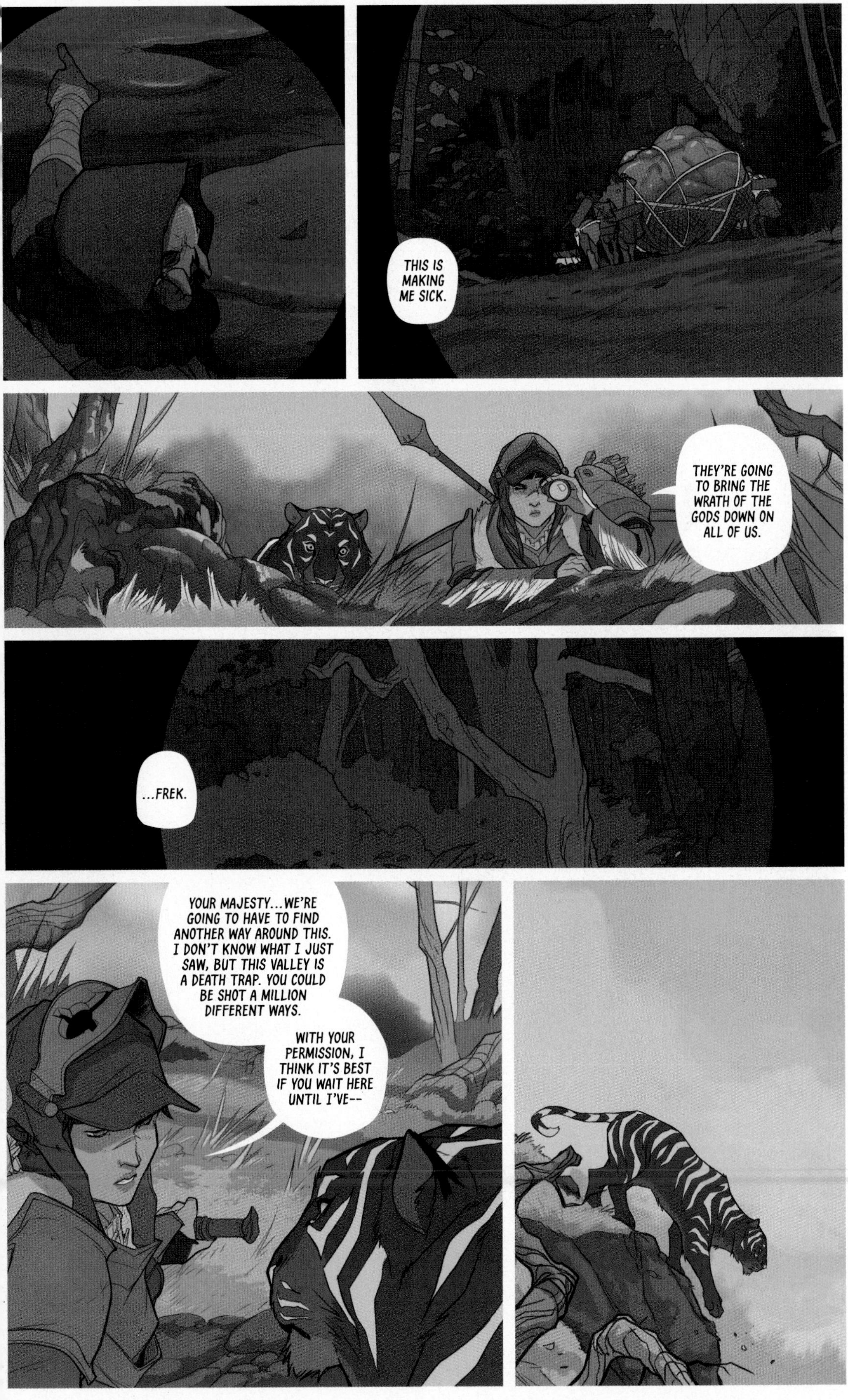
THIS IS MAKING ME SICK.
THEY'RE GOING TO BRING THE WRATH OF THE GODS DOWN ON ALL OF US.
...FREK.
YOUR MAJESTY...WE'RE GOING TO HAVE TO FIND ANOTHER WAY AROUND THIS. I DON'T KNOW WHAT I JUST SAW, BUT THIS VALLEY IS A DEATH TRAP. YOU COULD BE SHOT A MILLION DIFFERENT WAYS.
WITH YOUR PERMISSION, I THINK IT'S BEST IF YOU WAIT HERE UNTIL I'VE--

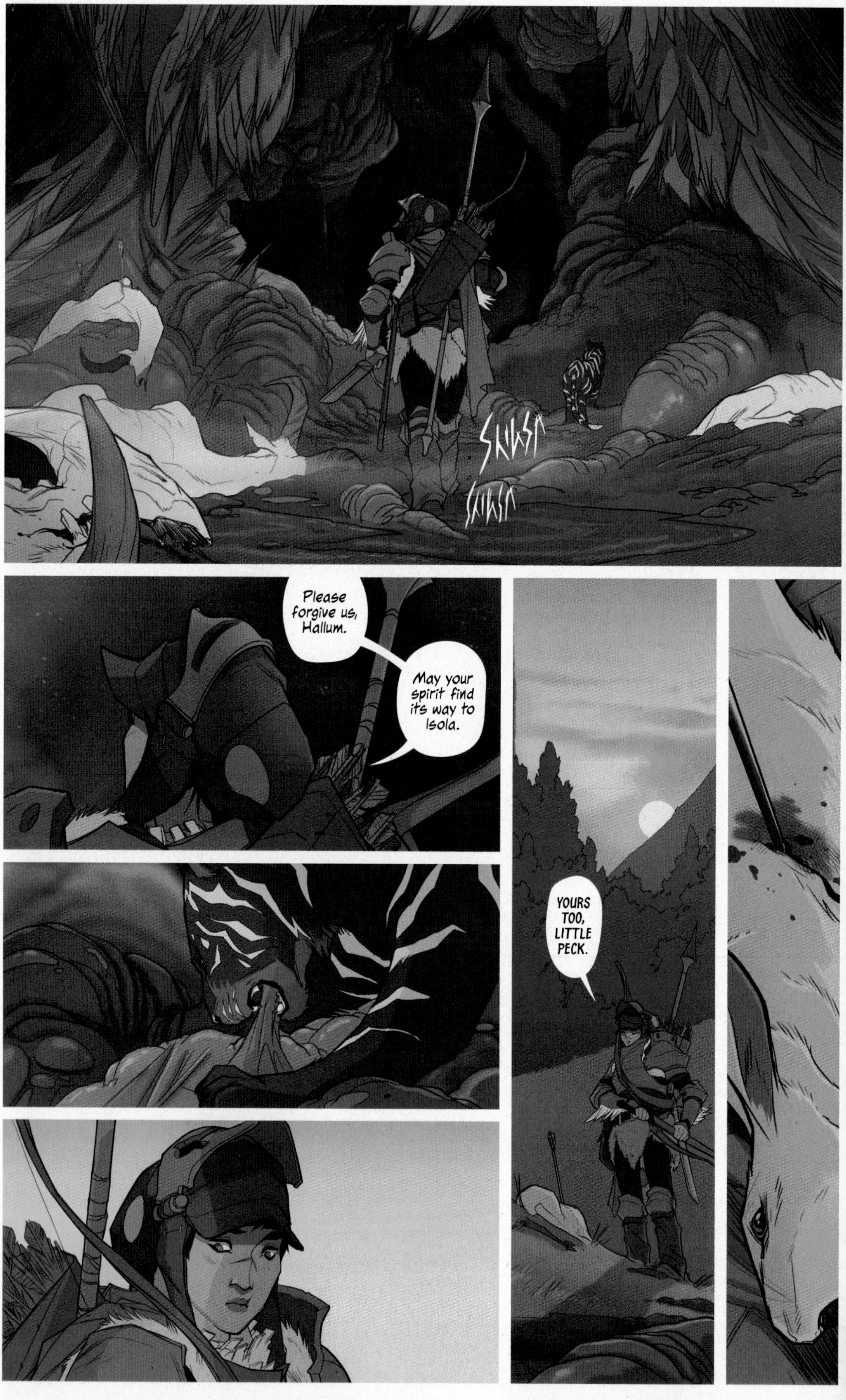
SHWSH
SHWSH
Please forgive us, Hallum.
May your spirit find its way to Isola.
YOURS TOO, LITTLE PECK.

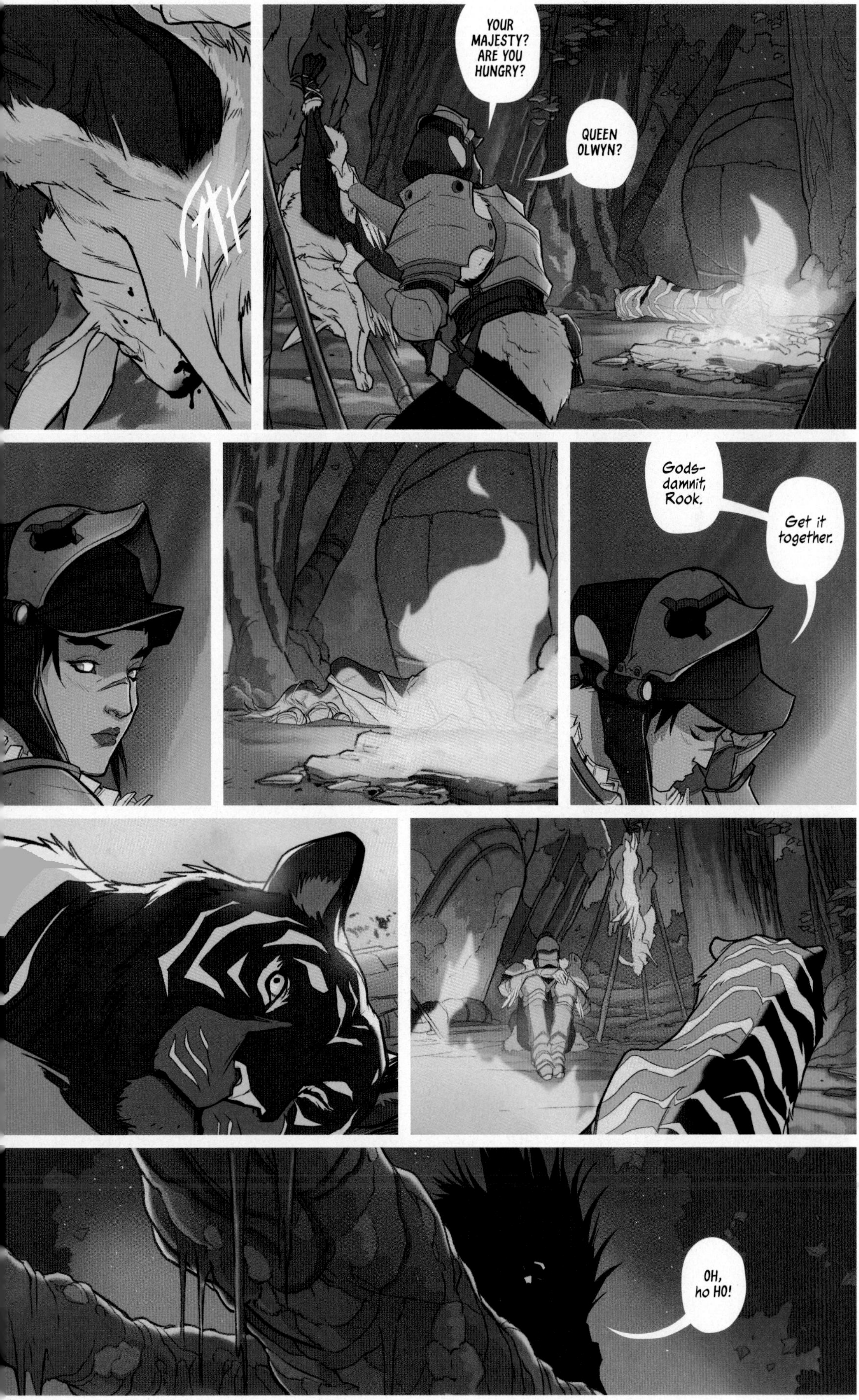
YOUR MAJESTY? ARE YOU HUNGRY?
QUEEN OLWYN?
Gods-damnit, Rook.
Get it together.
OH, ho HO!

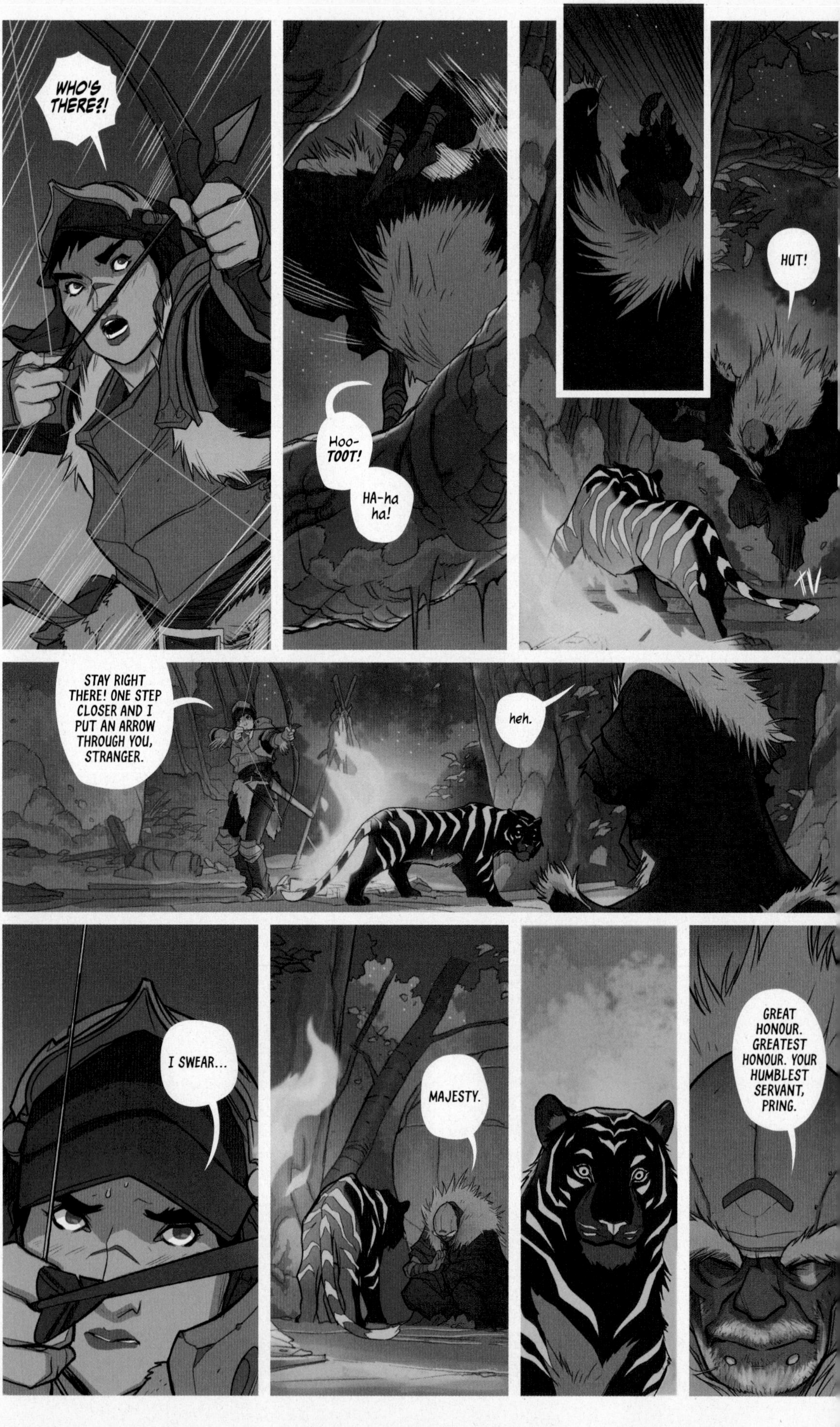
WHO'S THERE?!
Hoo-TOOT!
HA-ha ha!
HUT!
STAY RIGHT THERE! ONE STEP CLOSER AND I PUT AN ARROW THROUGH YOU, STRANGER.
heh.
I SWEAR...
MAJESTY.
GREAT HONOUR. GREATEST HONOUR. YOUR HUMBLEST SERVANT, PRING.

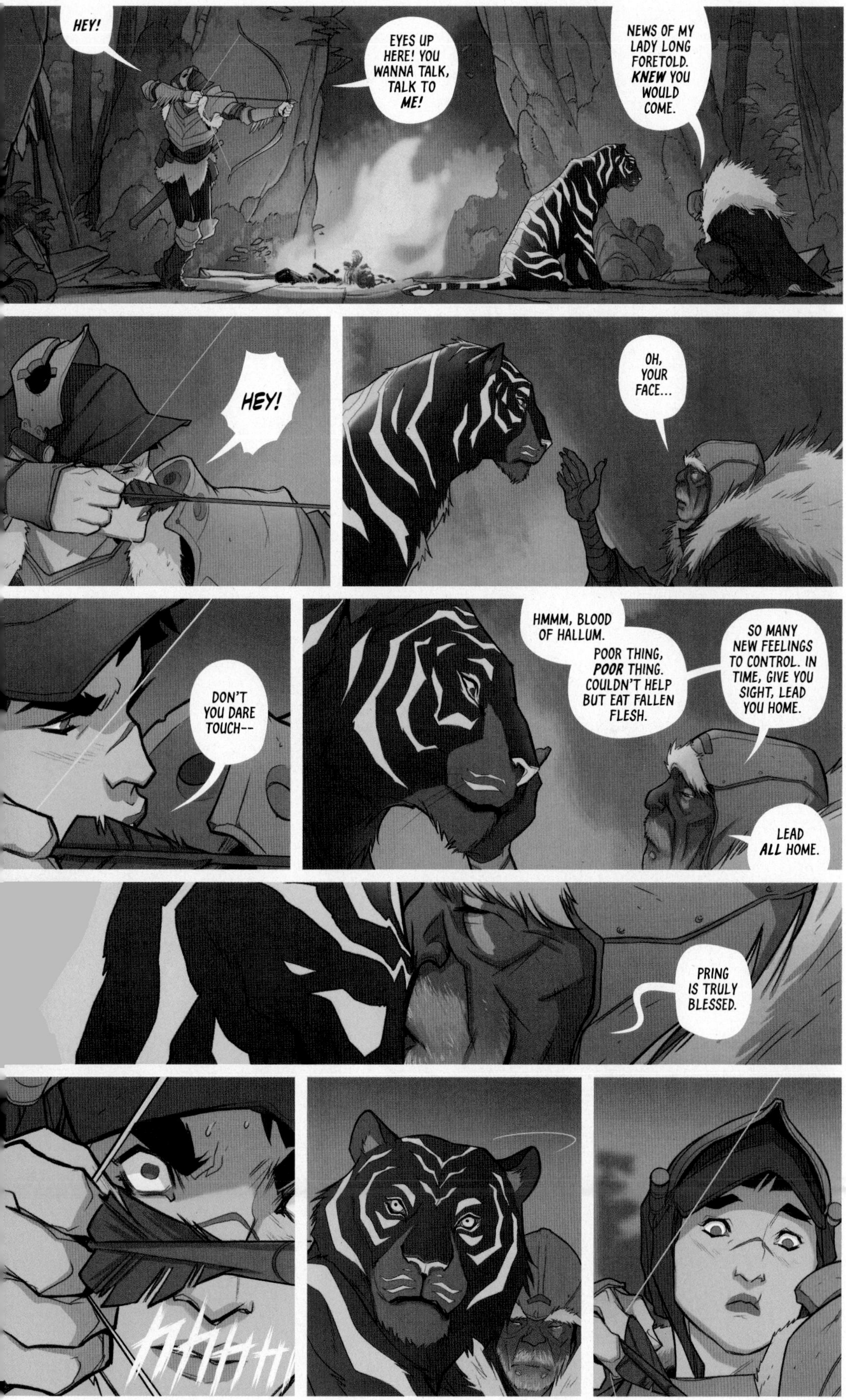
HEY!
EYES UP HERE! YOU WANNA TALK, TALK TO *ME!*
NEWS OF MY LADY LONG FORETOLD. ***KNEW*** YOU WOULD COME.
HEY!
OH, YOUR FACE...
DON'T YOU DARE TOUCH--
HMMM, BLOOD OF HALLUM.
POOR THING, ***POOR*** THING. COULDN'T HELP BUT EAT FALLEN FLESH.
SO MANY NEW FEELINGS TO CONTROL. IN TIME, GIVE YOU SIGHT, LEAD YOU HOME.
LEAD ***ALL*** HOME.
PRING IS TRULY BLESSED.
hhhhh

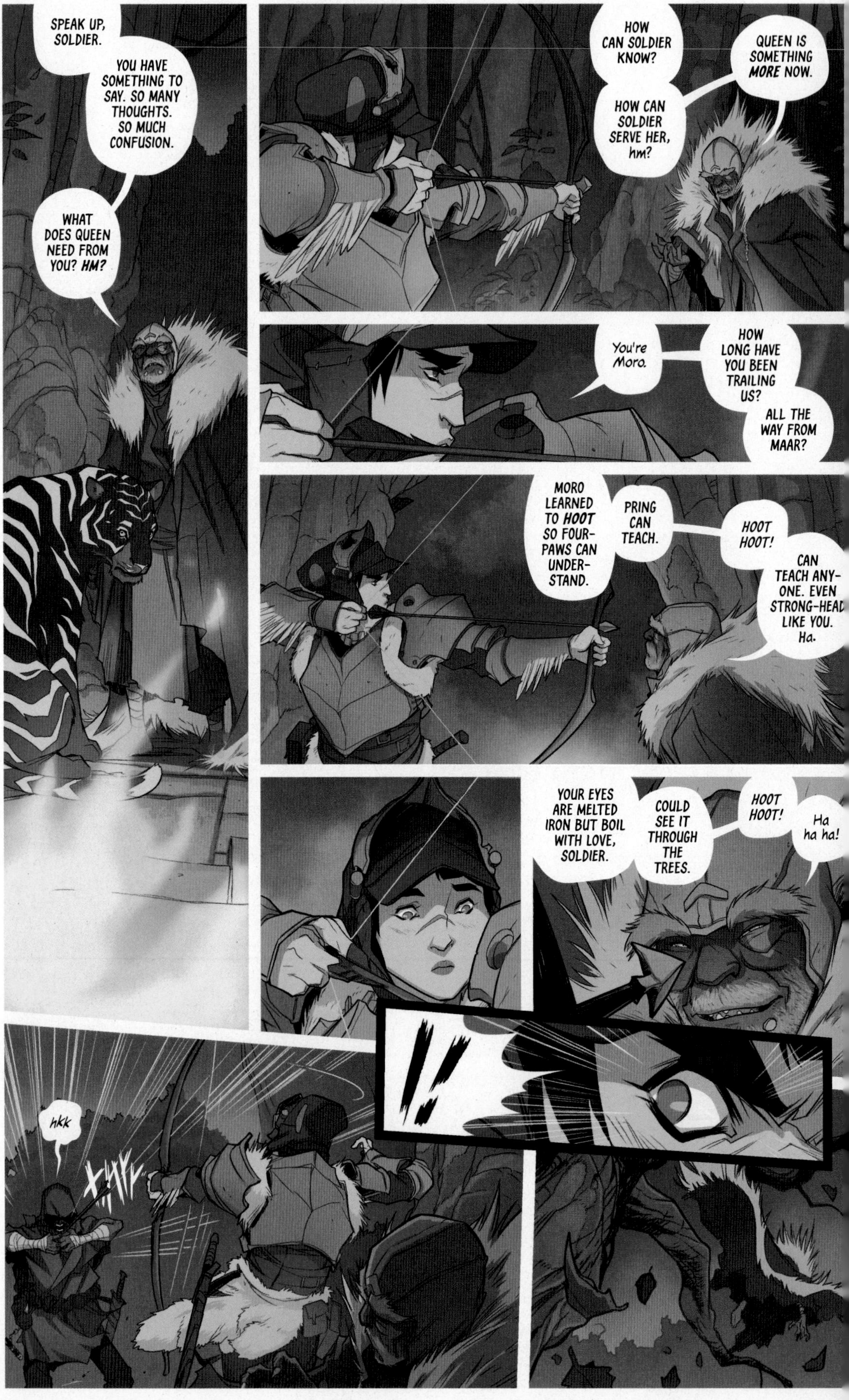
SPEAK UP, SOLDIER.
YOU HAVE SOMETHING TO SAY. SO MANY THOUGHTS. SO MUCH CONFUSION.
WHAT DOES QUEEN NEED FROM YOU? HM?
HOW CAN SOLDIER KNOW?
HOW CAN SOLDIER SERVE HER, hm?
QUEEN IS SOMETHING MORE NOW.
You're Moro.
HOW LONG HAVE YOU BEEN TRAILING US?
ALL THE WAY FROM MAAR?
MORO LEARNED TO HOOT SO FOUR-PAWS CAN UNDER-STAND.
PRING CAN TEACH.
HOOT HOOT!
CAN TEACH ANY-ONE. EVEN STRONG-HEAD LIKE YOU. Ha.
YOUR EYES ARE MELTED IRON BUT BOIL WITH LOVE, SOLDIER.
COULD SEE IT THROUGH THE TREES.
HOOT HOOT!
Ha ha ha!
!!
hkk

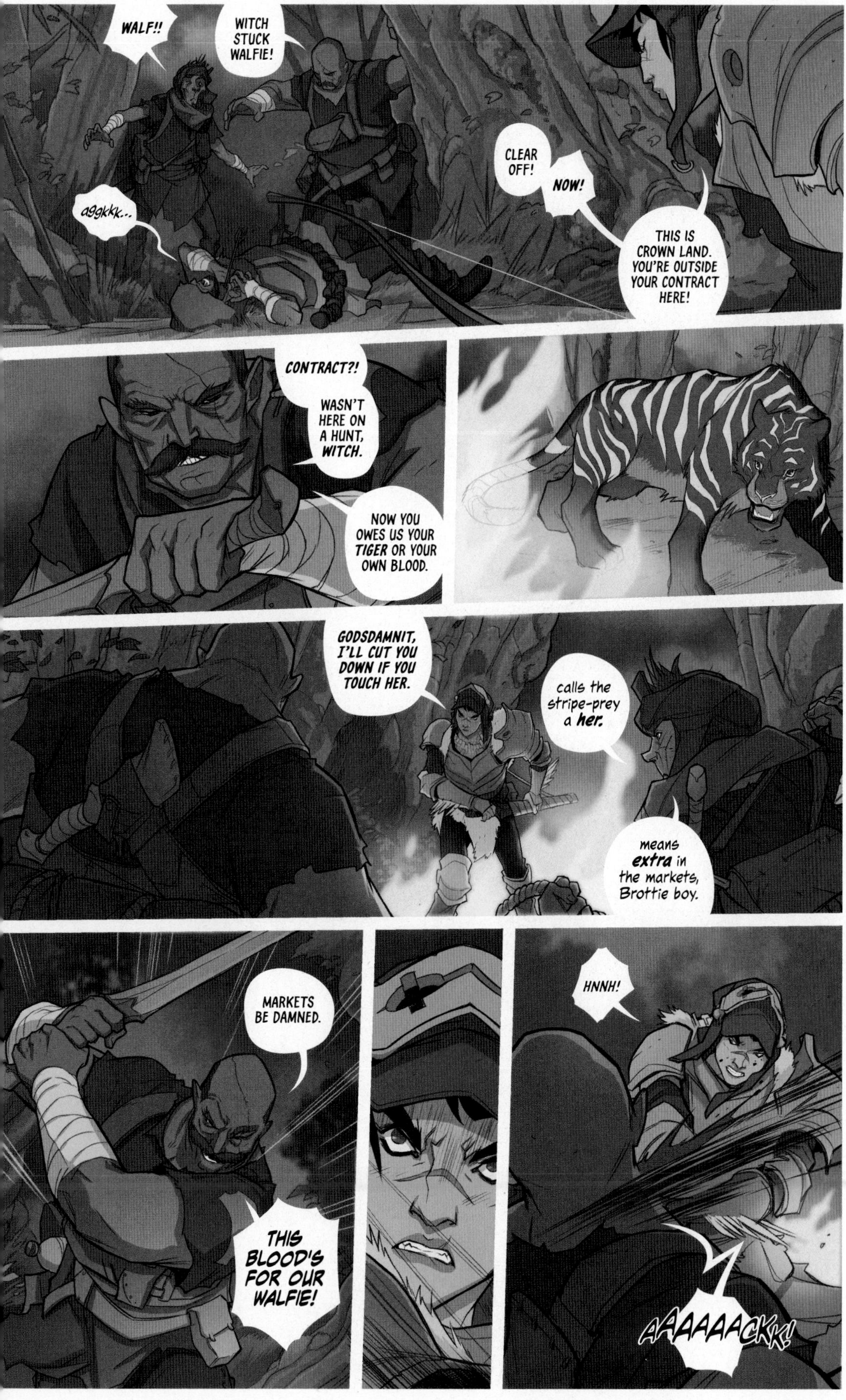
WALF!!
WITCH STUCK WALFIE!
aggkkk...
CLEAR OFF!
NOW!
THIS IS CROWN LAND. YOU'RE OUTSIDE YOUR CONTRACT HERE!
CONTRACT?!
WASN'T HERE ON A HUNT, WITCH.
NOW YOU OWES US YOUR TIGER OR YOUR OWN BLOOD.
GODSDAMNIT, I'LL CUT YOU DOWN IF YOU TOUCH HER.
calls the stripe-prey a her.
means extra in the markets, Brottie boy.
MARKETS BE DAMNED.
THIS BLOOD'S FOR OUR WALFIE!
HNNH!
AAAAAACKK!

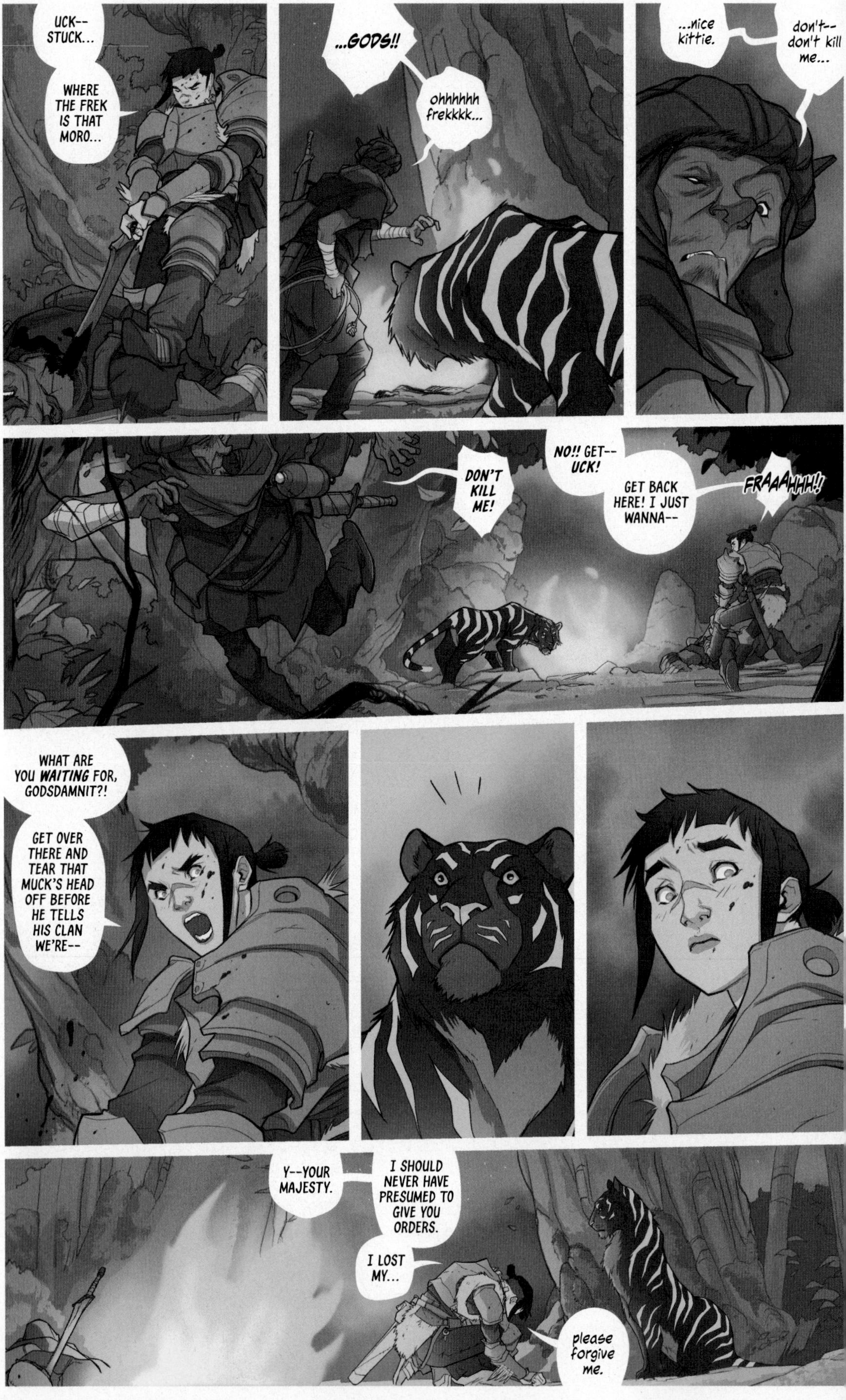
UCK--
STUCK...
WHERE THE FREK IS THAT MORO...
...GODS!!
ohhhhhh frekkkk...
...nice kittie.
don't--
don't kill me...
DON'T KILL ME!
NO!! GET--
UCK!
GET BACK HERE! I JUST WANNA--
FRAAAHHH!!
WHAT ARE YOU WAITING FOR, GODSDAMNIT?!
GET OVER THERE AND TEAR THAT MUCK'S HEAD OFF BEFORE HE TELLS HIS CLAN WE'RE--
Y--YOUR MAJESTY.
I SHOULD NEVER HAVE PRESUMED TO GIVE YOU ORDERS.
I LOST MY...
please forgive me.

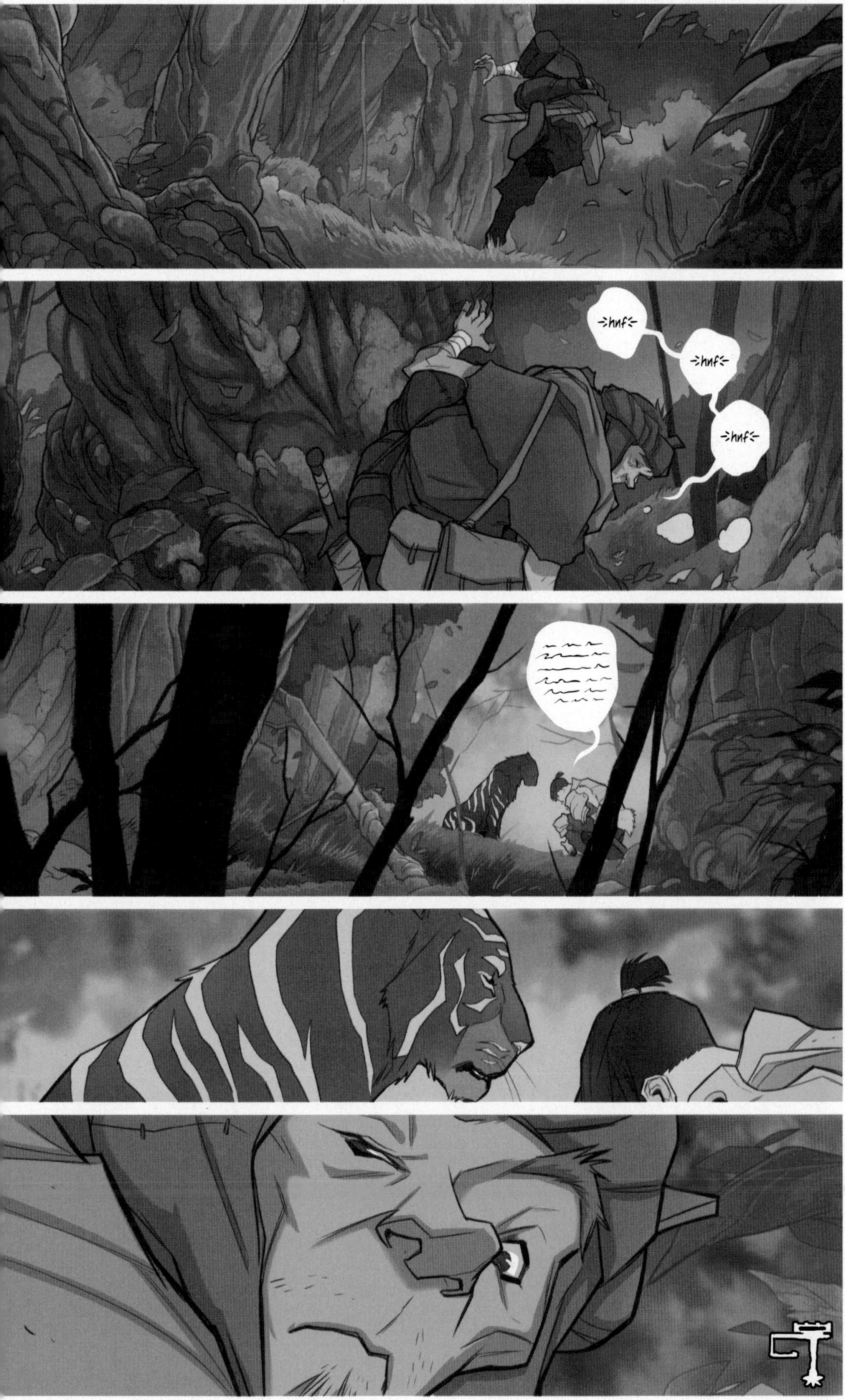

hnf
hnf
hnf

1

BRENDEN FLETCHER / KARL KERSCHL
STORY

KARL KERSCHL / MSASSYK
ART

ADITYA BIDIKAR
LETTERS

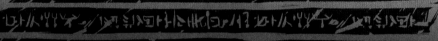

IMAGE COMICS, INC. • **Robert Kirkman**: Chief Operating Officer • **Erik Larsen**: Chief Financial Officer • **Todd McFarlane**: President • **Marc Silvestri**: Chief Executive Officer • **Jim Valentino**: Vice President • **Eric Stephenson**: Publisher / Chief Creative Officer • **Jeff Boison**: Director of Publishing Planning & Book Trade Sales • **Chris Ross**: Director of Digital Sales • **Jeff Stang**: Director of Direct Market Sales • **Kat Salazar**: Director of PR & Marketing • **Drew Gill**: Art Director • **Heather Doornink**: Production Director • **Nicole Lapalme**: Controller • **IMAGECOMICS.COM**

image

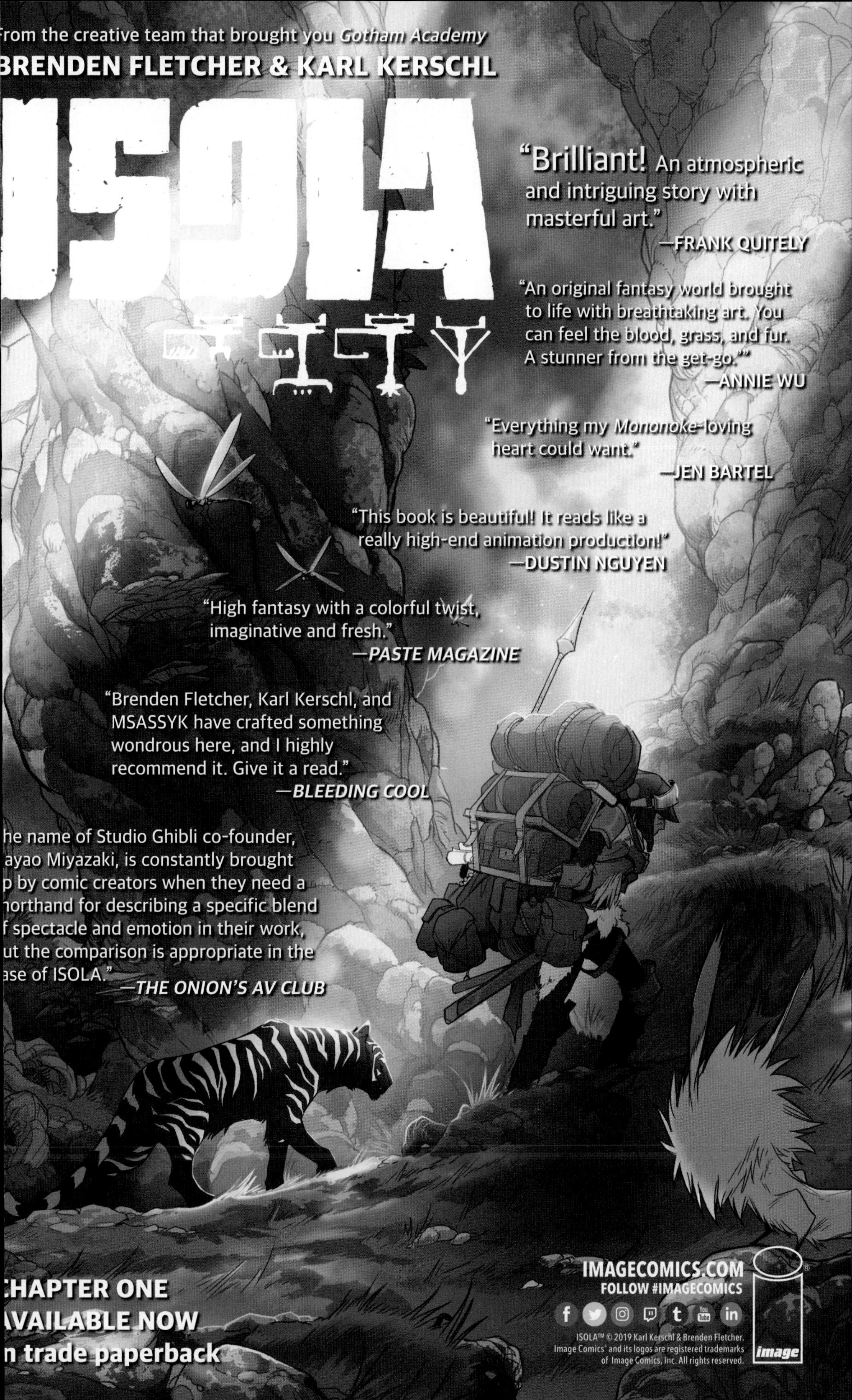

rom the creative team that brought you *Gotham Academy*
BRENDEN FLETCHER & KARL KERSCHL
"Brilliant! An atmospheric and intriguing story with masterful art." —FRANK QUITELY
"An original fantasy world brought to life with breathtaking art. You can feel the blood, grass, and fur. A stunner from the get-go." —ANNIE WU
"Everything my *Mononoke*-loving heart could want." —JEN BARTEL
"This book is beautiful! It reads like a really high-end animation production!" —DUSTIN NGUYEN
"High fantasy with a colorful twist, imaginative and fresh." —*PASTE MAGAZINE*
"Brenden Fletcher, Karl Kerschl, and MSASSYK have crafted something wondrous here, and I highly recommend it. Give it a read." —*BLEEDING COOL*
he name of Studio Ghibli co-founder, ayao Miyazaki, is constantly brought p by comic creators when they need a horthand for describing a specific blend f spectacle and emotion in their work, ut the comparison is appropriate in the ase of ISOLA." —*THE ONION'S AV CLUB*
HAPTER ONE
VAILABLE NOW
n trade paperback
IMAGECOMICS.COM
FOLLOW #IMAGECOMICS
ISOLA™ © 2019 Karl Kerschl & Brenden Fletcher. Image Comics® and its logos are registered trademarks of Image Comics, Inc. All rights reserved.

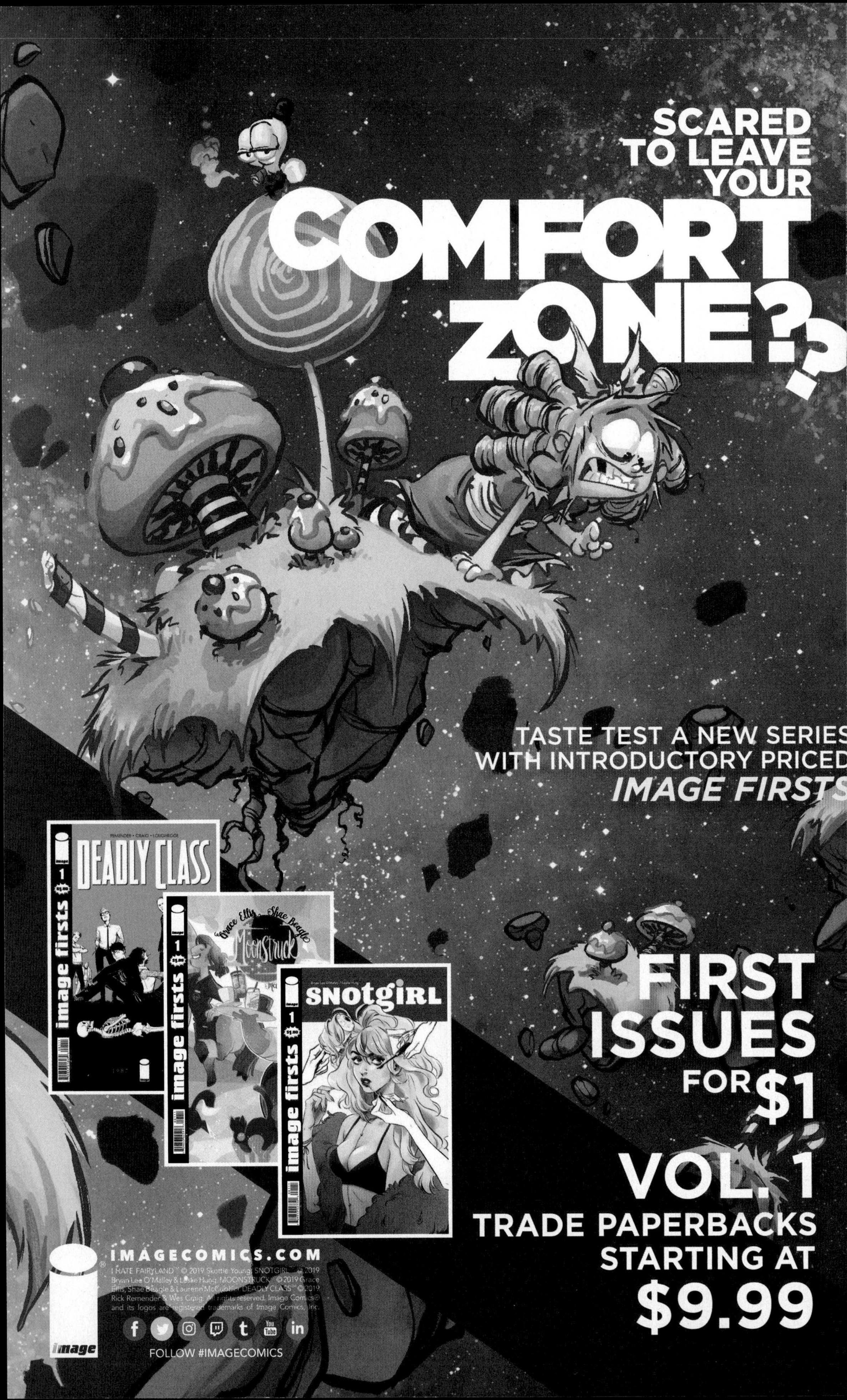
SCARED TO LEAVE YOUR
COMFORT ZONE??
TASTE TEST A NEW SERIES WITH INTRODUCTORY PRICED
IMAGE FIRSTS
DEADLY CLASS
image firsts
1
Moonstruck
SNOTGIRL
FIRST ISSUES FOR $1
VOL. 1 TRADE PAPERBACKS STARTING AT $9.99
IMAGECOMICS.COM
I HATE FAIRYLAND™ © 2019 Skottie Young. SNOTGIRL™ © 2019 Bryan Lee O'Malley & Leslie Hung. MOONSTRUCK™ © 2019 Grace Ellis, Shae Beagle & Laurenn McCubbin. DEADLY CLASS™ © 2019 Rick Remender & Wes Craig. All rights reserved. Image Comics® and its logos are registered trademarks of Image Comics, Inc.
FOLLOW #IMAGECOMICS

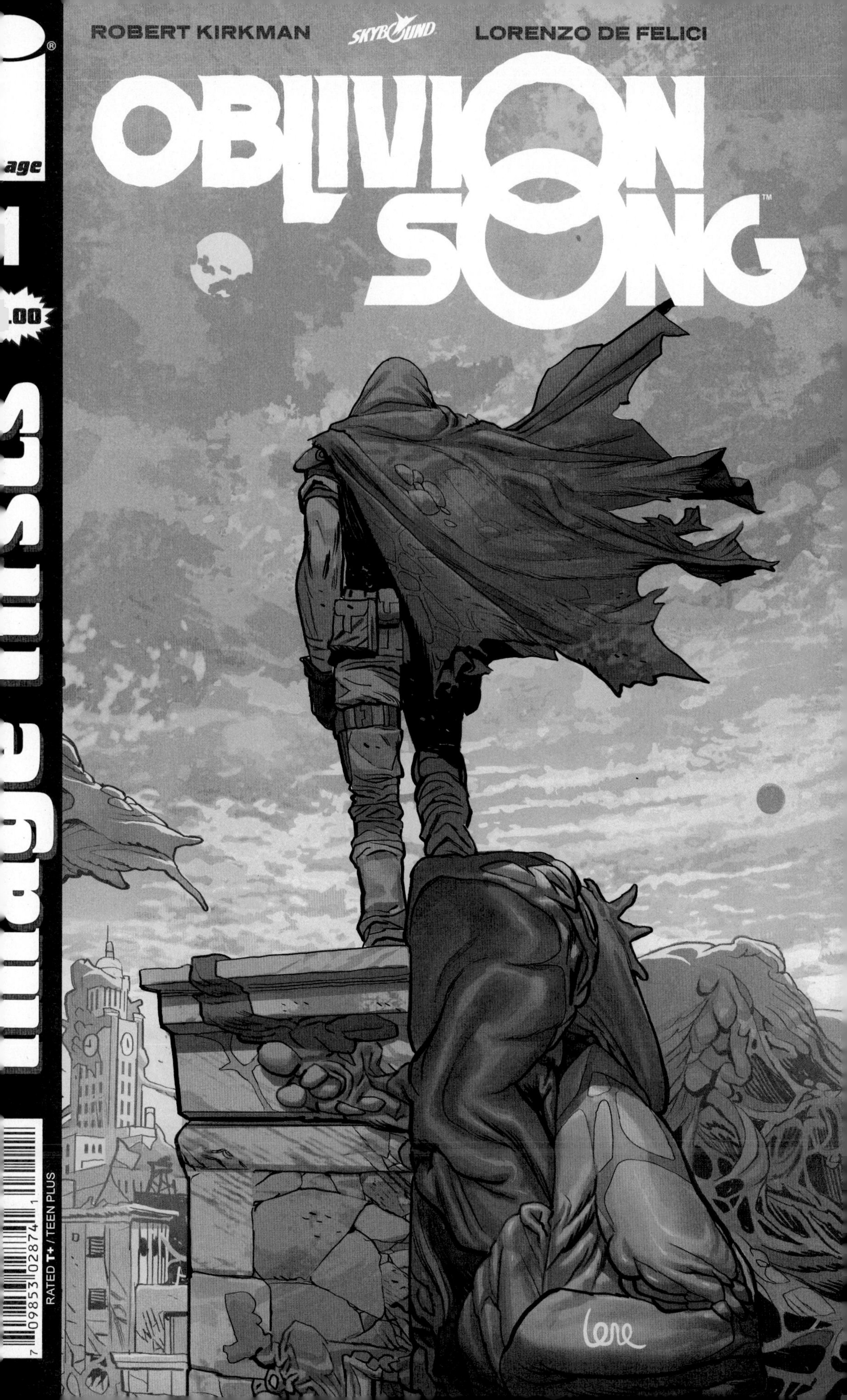
ROBERT KIRKMAN
SKYBOUND
LORENZO DE FELICI
OBLIVION SONG
image firsts
RATED T+ / TEEN PLUS

ROBERT KIRKMAN
WRITER/CREATOR

LORENZO DE FELICI
ARTIST/CREATOR

ANNALISA LEONI
COLORIST

RUS WOOTON
LETTERER

ARIELLE BASICH
ASSOCIATE EDITOR

SEAN MACKIEWICZ
EDITOR

LORENZO DE FELICI
COVER

ANDRES JUAREZ
LOGO · PRODUCTION DESIGN

CARINA TAYLOR
PRODUCTION

FOR SKYBOUND ENTERTAINMENT

ROBERT KIRKMAN *Chairman* • DAVID ALPERT *CEO* • SEAN MACKIEWICZ *SVP, Editor-in-Chief* • SHAWN KIRKHAM *SVP, Business Development* • BRIAN HUNTINGTON *VP of Online Content* • SHAUNA WYNNE *Publicity Director* • ANDRES JUAREZ *Art Director* • JON MOISAN *Editor* • ARIELLE BASICH *Associate Editor* • KATE CAUDILL *Assistant Editor* • CARINA TAYLOR *Production Artist* • PAUL SHIN *Business Development Manager* • JOHNNY O'DELL *Social Media Manager* • DAN PETERSEN *Sr. Director of Operations & Events*

Foreign Rights Inquiries: ag@sequentialrights.com
Other Licensing Inquiries: contact@skybound.com
WWW.SKYBOUND.COM

IMAGE COMICS, INC.

ROBERT KIRKMAN *Chief Operating Officer* • ERIK LARSEN *Chief Financial Officer* • TODD MCFARLANE *President* • MARC SILVESTRI *Chief Executive Officer* • JIM VALENTINO *Vice President* • ERIC STEPHENSON *Publisher / Chief Creative Officer* • JEFF BOISON *Director of Publishing Planning & Book Trade Sales* • CHRIS ROSS *Director of Digital Sales* • JEFF STANG *Director of Specialty Sales* • KAT SALAZAR *Director of PR & Marketing* • DREW GILL *Art Director* • HEATHER DOORNINK *Production Director* • NICOLE LAPALME *Controller*
WWW.IMAGECOMICS.COM

□□□□□□□□□□□□

THE BREEZE, THE CREATURES IN THE DISTANCE,
INSECTS... IT ALL CAME TOGETHER LIKE... IT SOUNDED
LIKE NOTHING I'D EVER HEARD BEFORE...

...IT WAS LIKE **MUSIC**.

□□□□□□□□□□□□

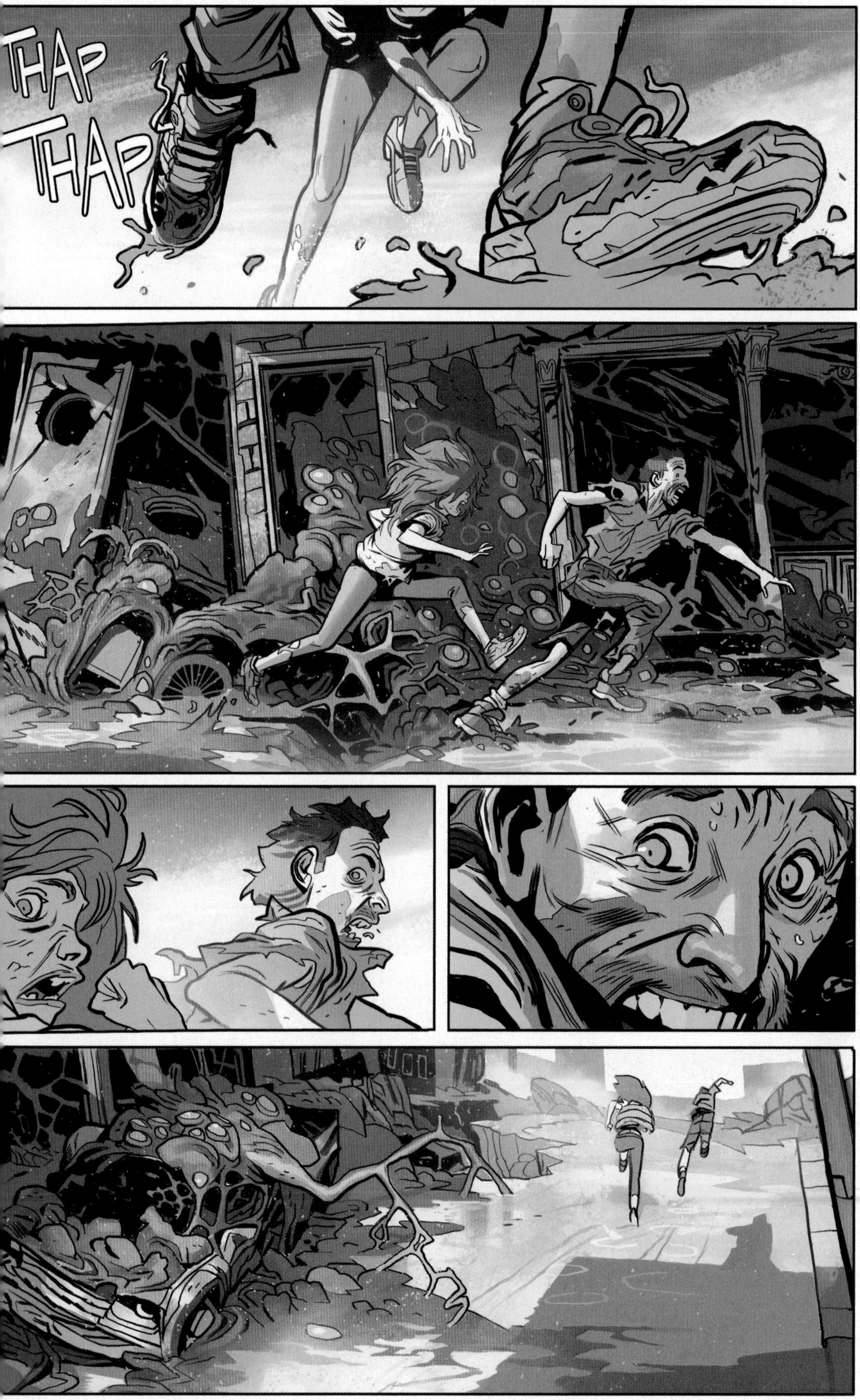
THAP
THAP

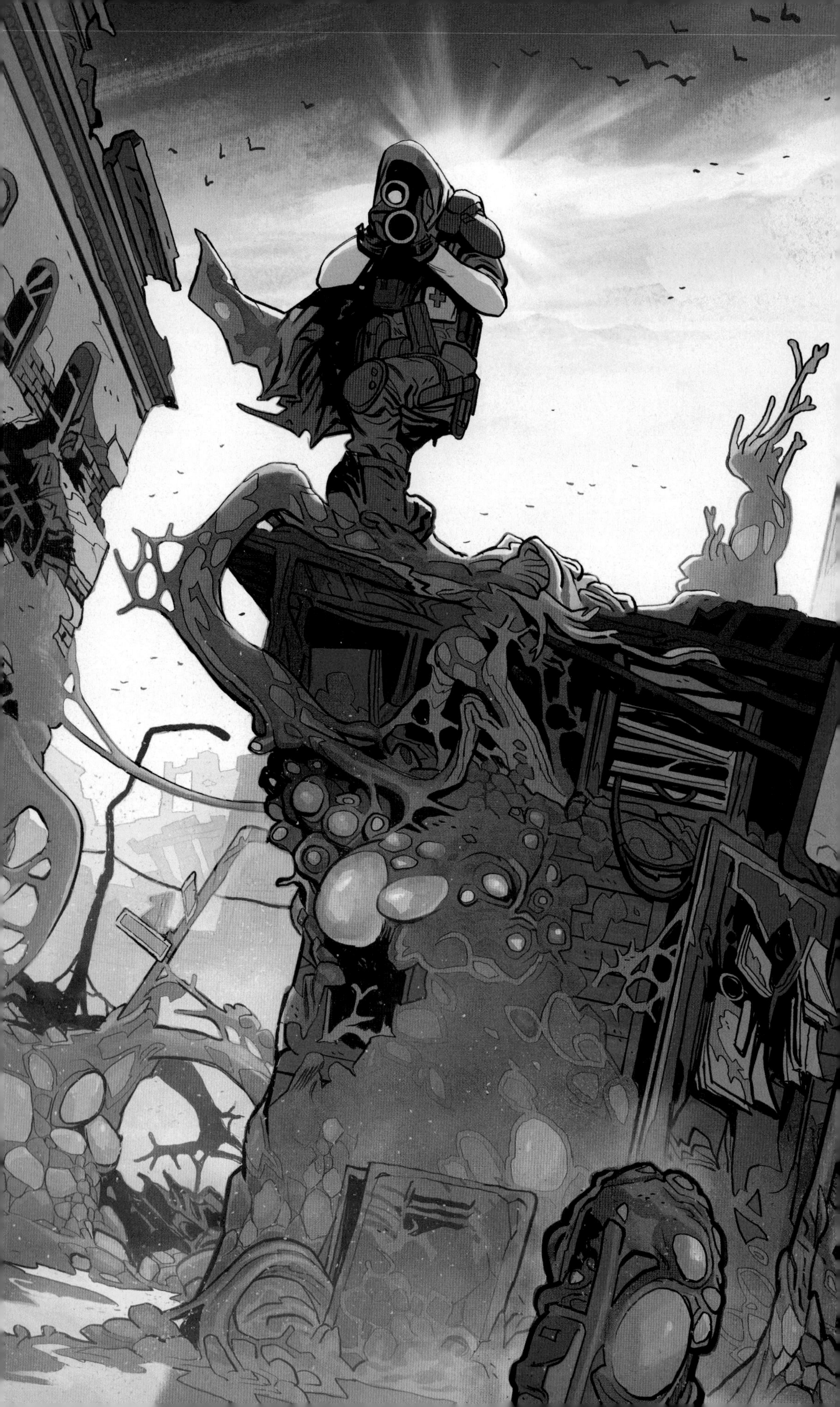

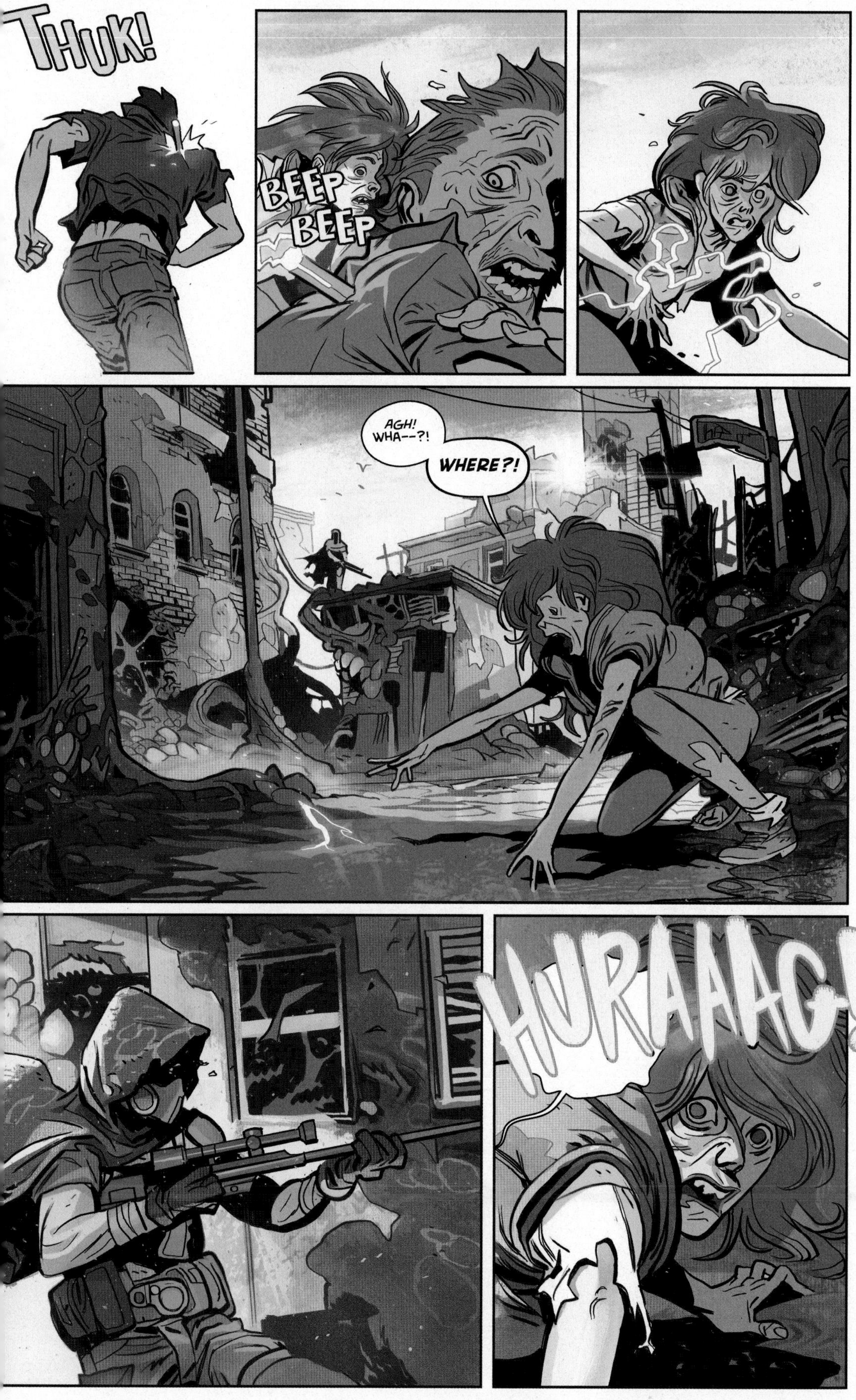
THUK!
BEEP
BEEP
AGH! WHA--?!
WHERE?!
HURAAAG!

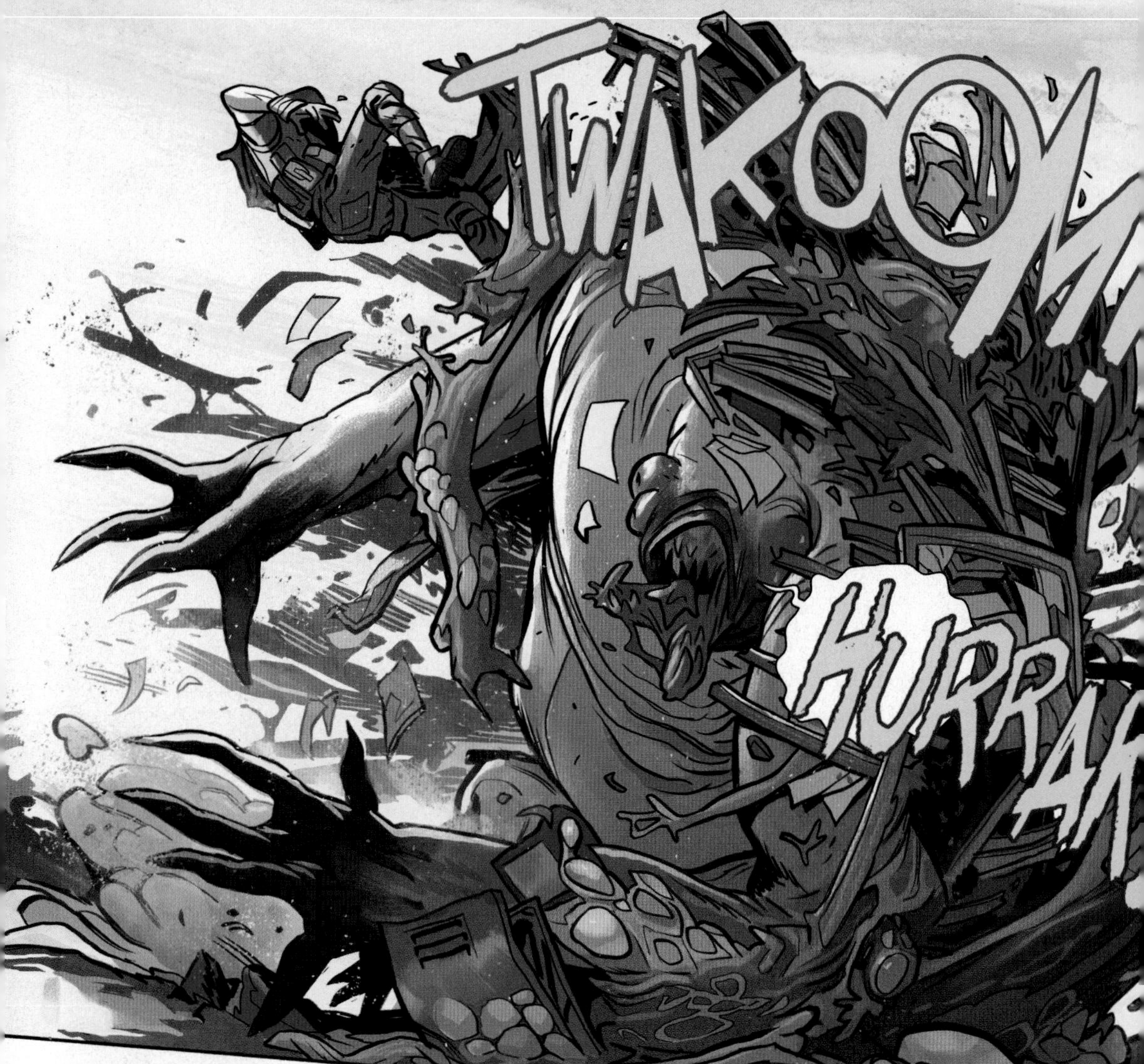
TWAKOOM
HURRAK

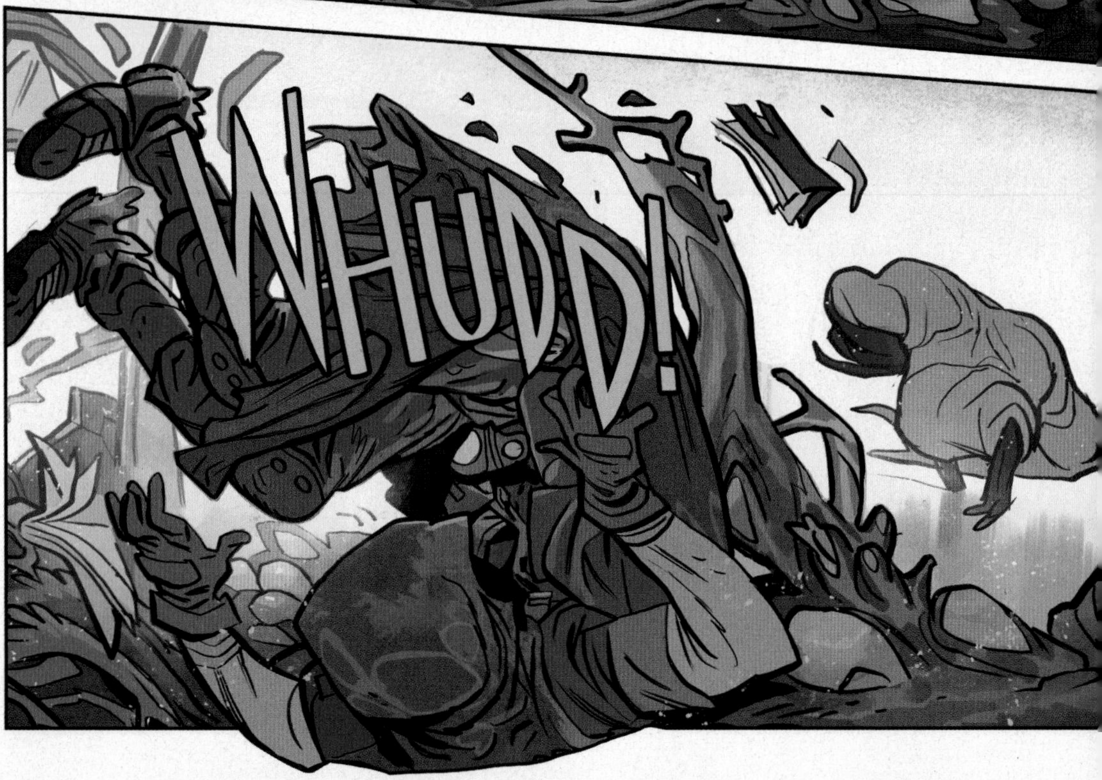
WHUDD!

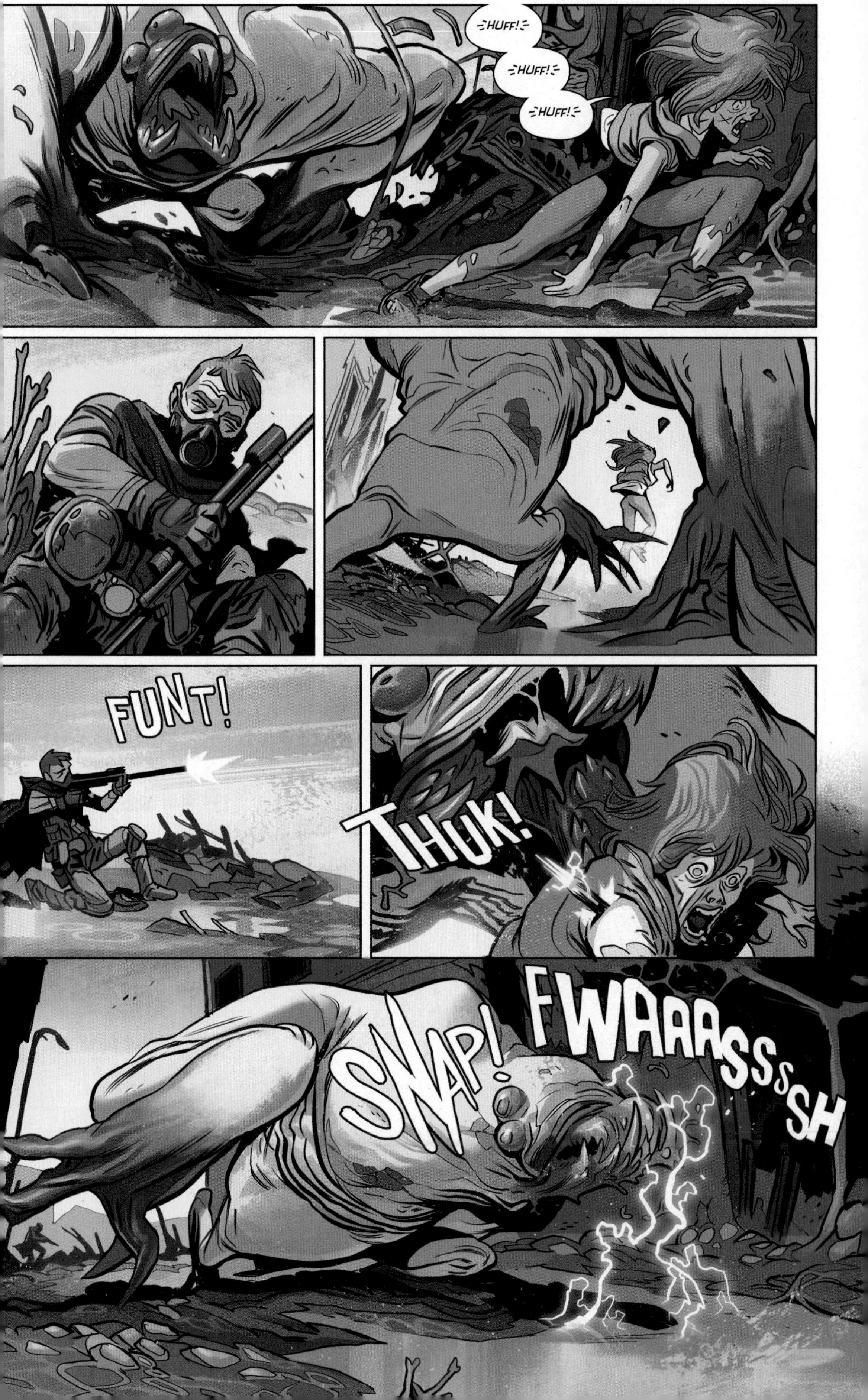
HUFF!
HUFF!
HUFF!
FUNT!
THUK!
SNAP!
FWAAASSSSH

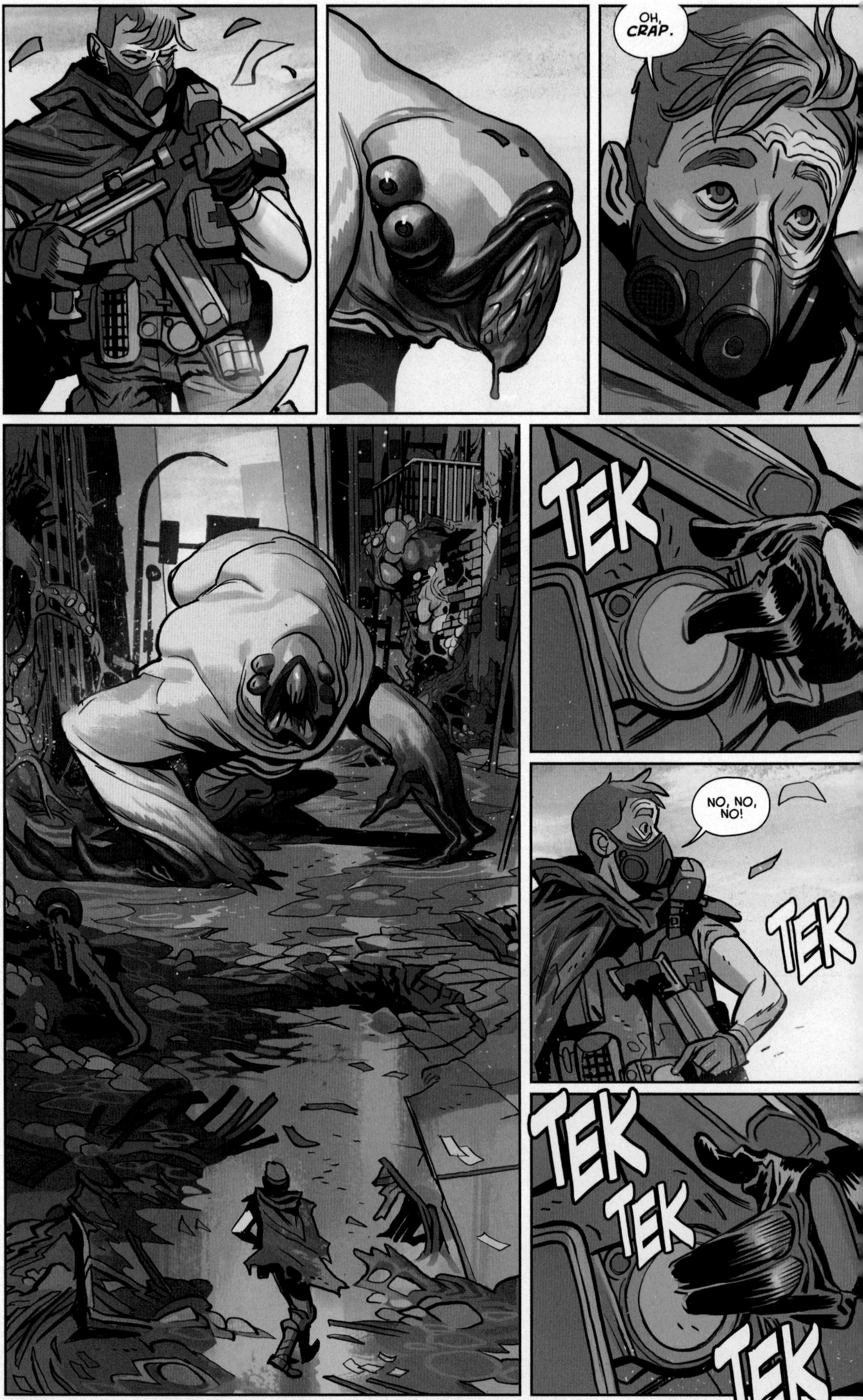
OH, CRAP.
TEK
NO, NO, NO!
TEK
TEK
TEK
TEK

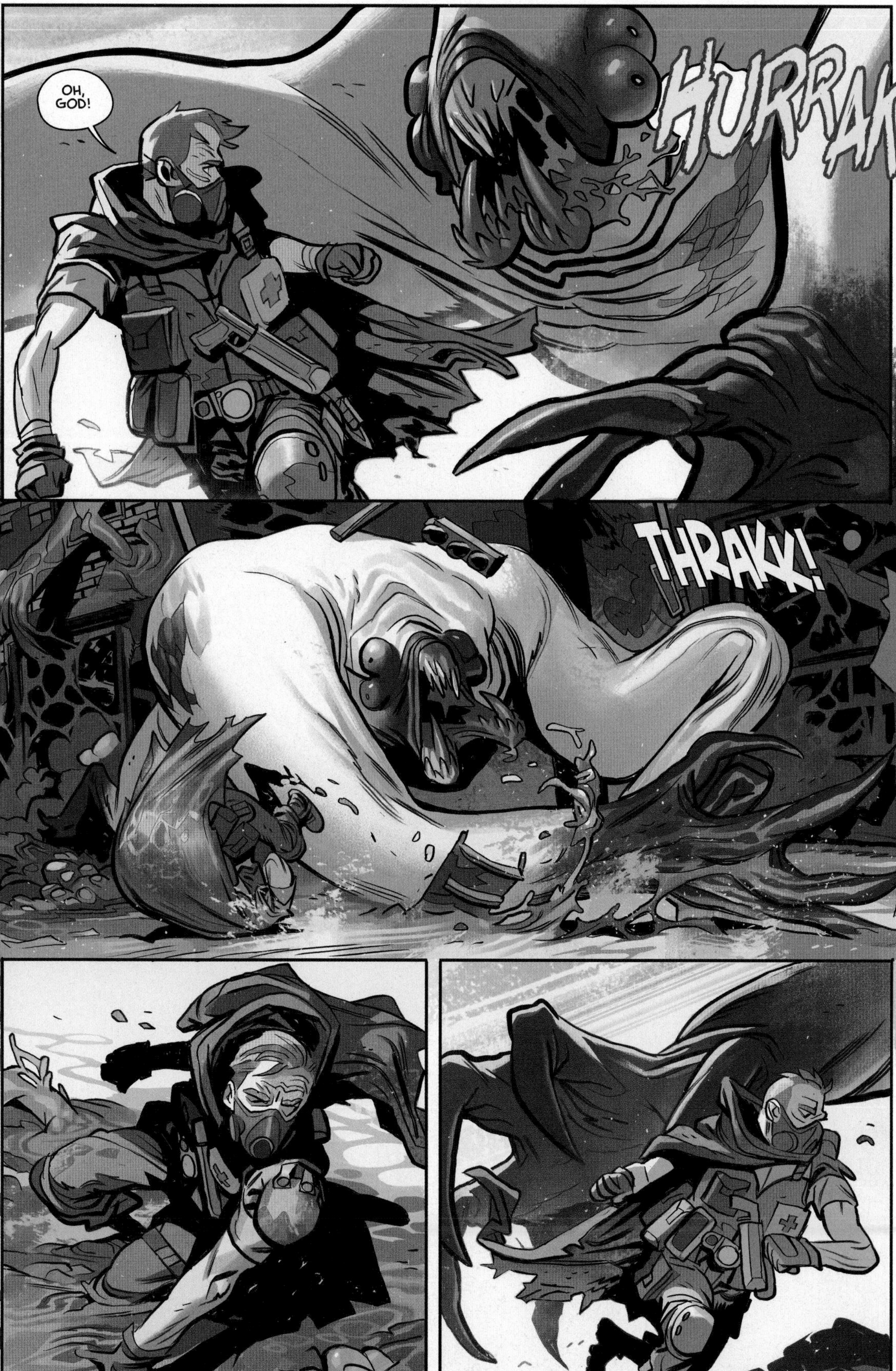
OH, GOD!
HURRAK!
THRAKK!

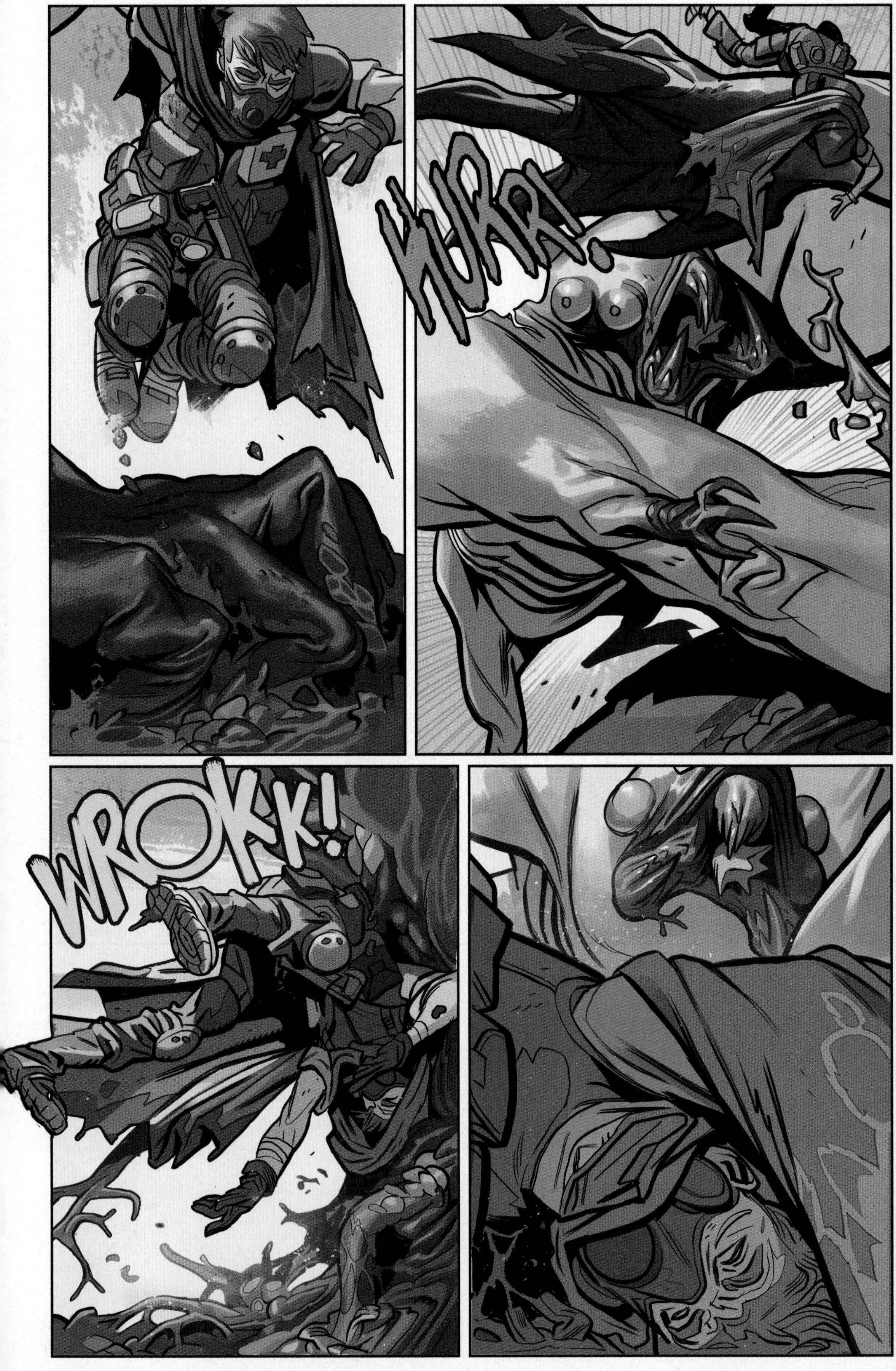
HURR!
WROKK!

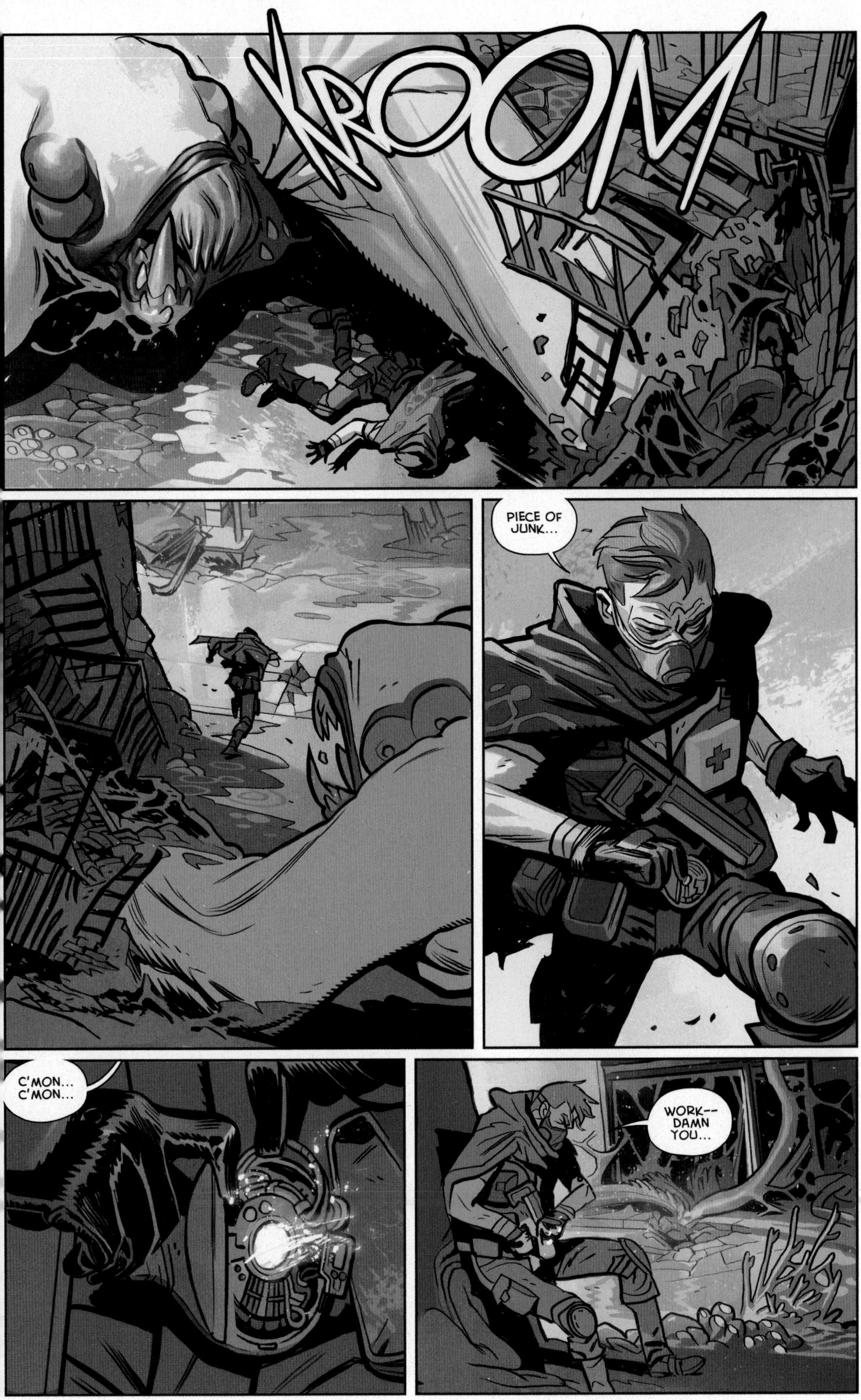
KROOM
PIECE OF JUNK...
C'MON... C'MON...
WORK-- DAMN YOU...

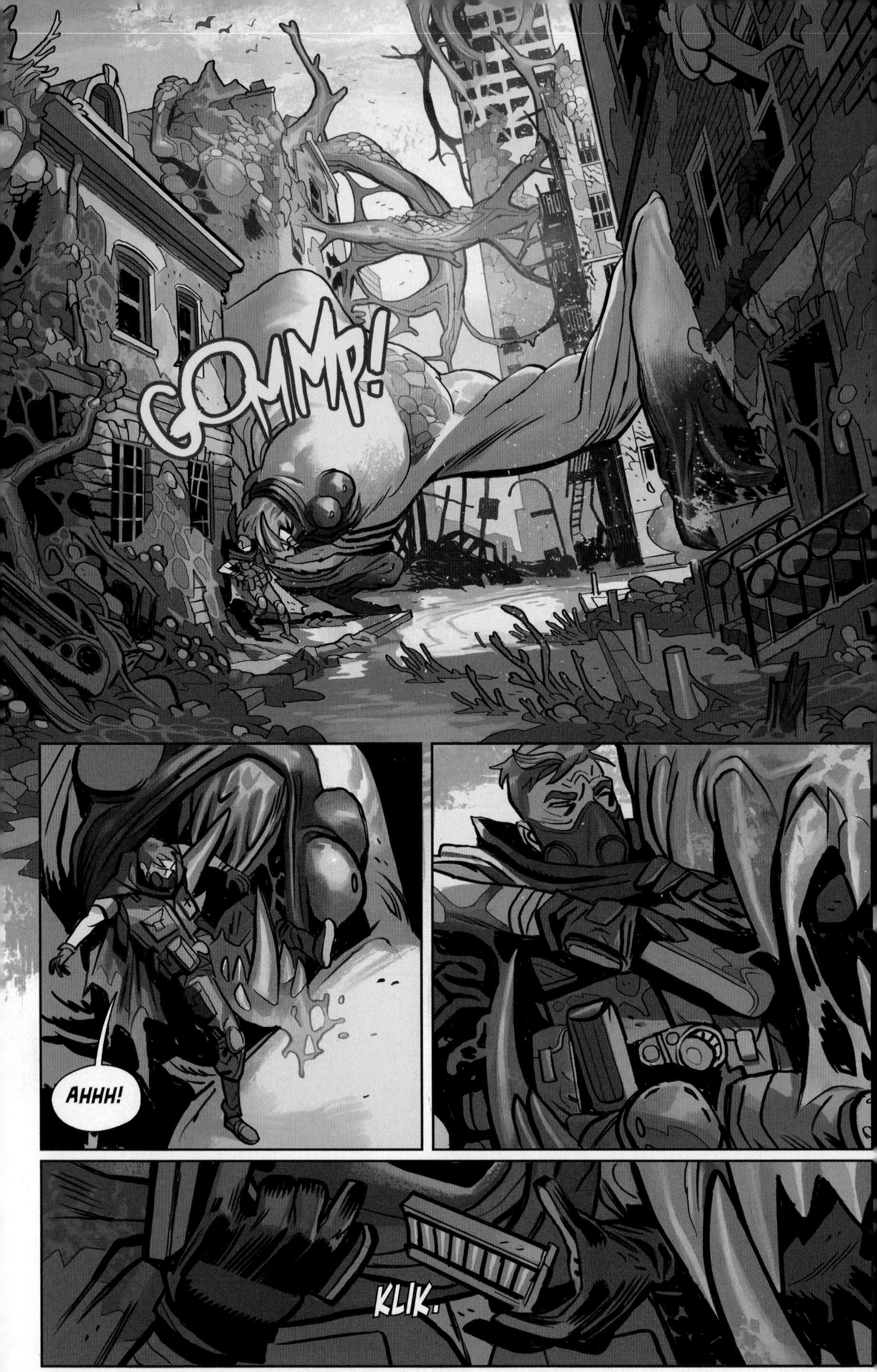
GOMMP!
AHHH!
KLIK.

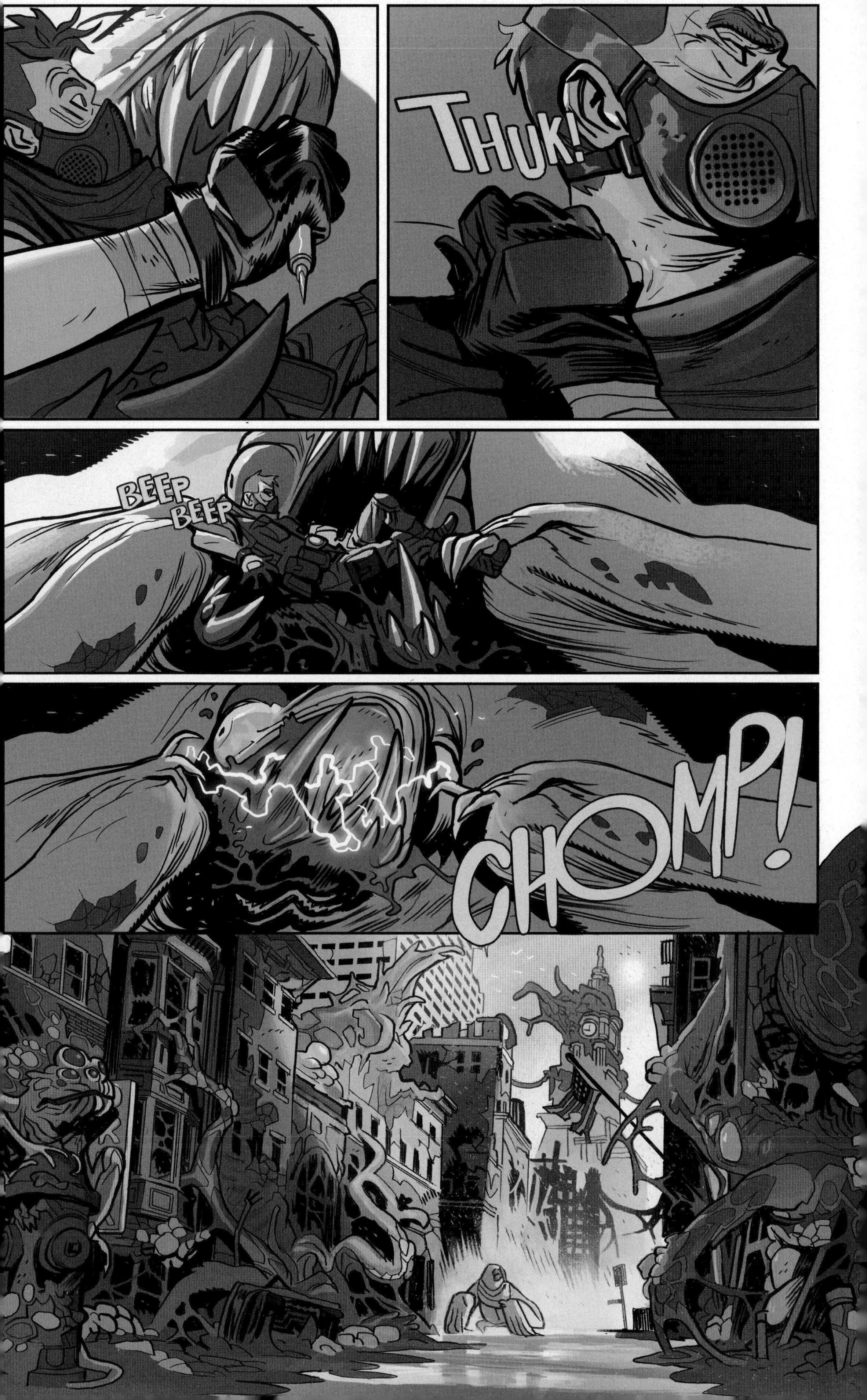
THUK!
BEEP
BEEP
CHOMP!

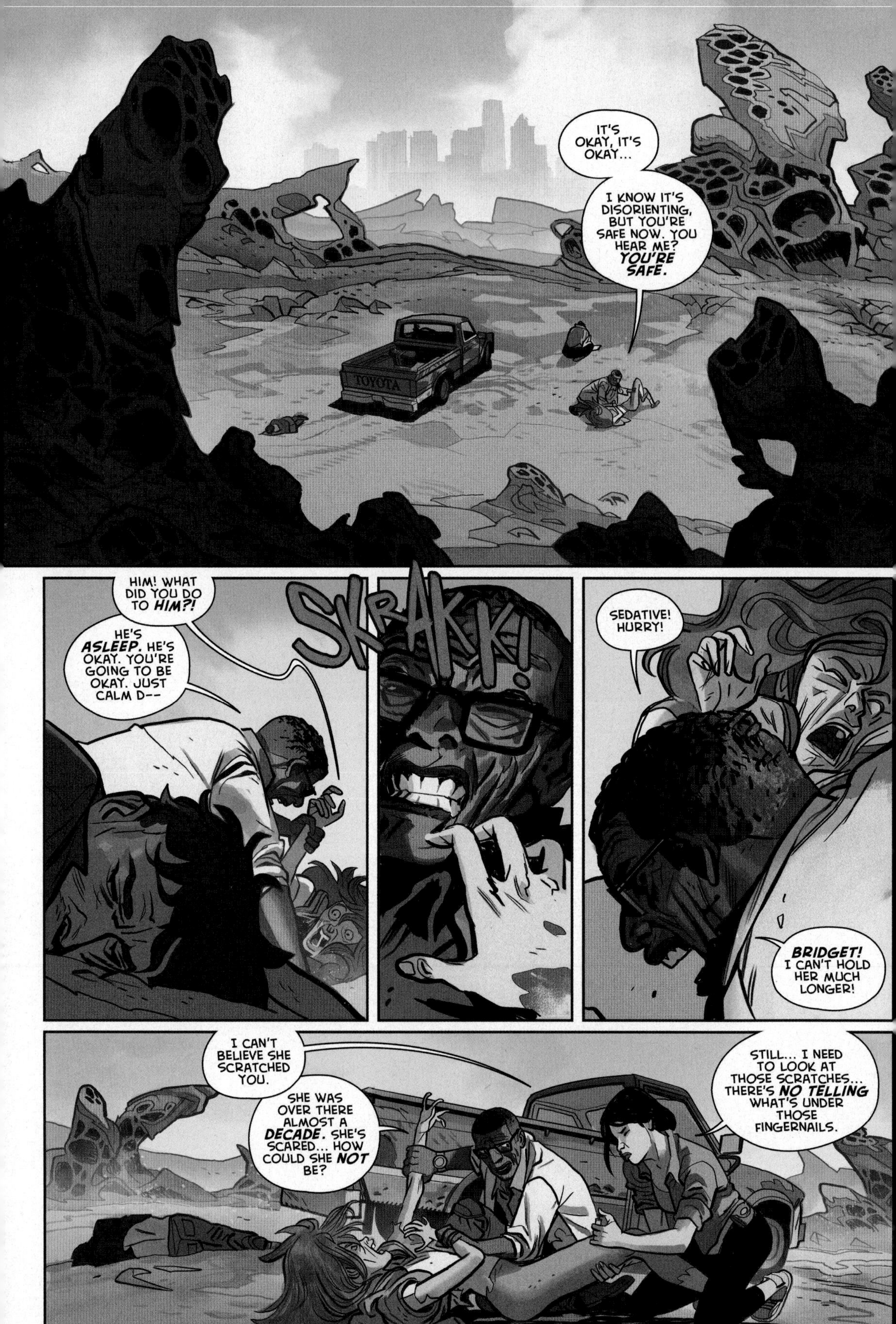
IT'S OKAY, IT'S OKAY...
I KNOW IT'S DISORIENTING, BUT YOU'RE SAFE NOW. YOU HEAR ME? YOU'RE SAFE.
TOYOTA
HIM! WHAT DID YOU DO TO HIM?!
HE'S ASLEEP. HE'S OKAY. YOU'RE GOING TO BE OKAY. JUST CALM D--
SKRAKK!
SEDATIVE! HURRY!
BRIDGET! I CAN'T HOLD HER MUCH LONGER!
I CAN'T BELIEVE SHE SCRATCHED YOU.
SHE WAS OVER THERE ALMOST A DECADE. SHE'S SCARED... HOW COULD SHE NOT BE?
STILL... I NEED TO LOOK AT THOSE SCRATCHES... THERE'S NO TELLING WHAT'S UNDER THOSE FINGERNAILS.

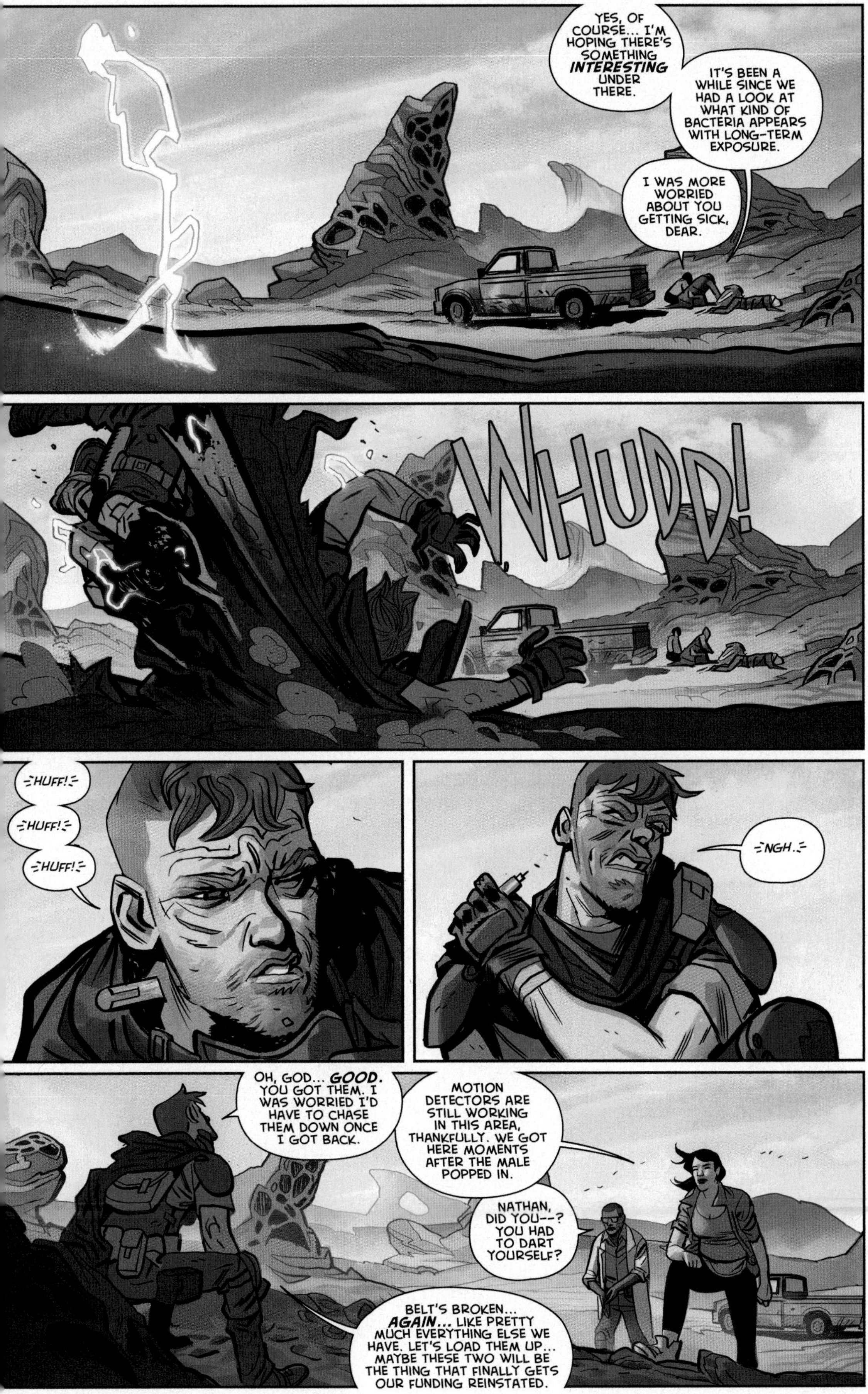
YES, OF COURSE... I'M HOPING THERE'S SOMETHING ***INTERESTING*** UNDER THERE.
IT'S BEEN A WHILE SINCE WE HAD A LOOK AT WHAT KIND OF BACTERIA APPEARS WITH LONG-TERM EXPOSURE.
I WAS MORE WORRIED ABOUT YOU GETTING SICK, DEAR.
WHUDD!
HUFF!
HUFF!
HUFF!
NGH.
OH, GOD... ***GOOD.*** YOU GOT THEM. I WAS WORRIED I'D HAVE TO CHASE THEM DOWN ONCE I GOT BACK.
MOTION DETECTORS ARE STILL WORKING IN THIS AREA, THANKFULLY. WE GOT HERE MOMENTS AFTER THE MALE POPPED IN.
NATHAN, DID YOU--? YOU HAD TO DART YOURSELF?
BELT'S BROKEN... ***AGAIN...*** LIKE PRETTY MUCH EVERYTHING ELSE WE HAVE. LET'S LOAD THEM UP... MAYBE THESE TWO WILL BE THE THING THAT FINALLY GETS OUR FUNDING REINSTATED.

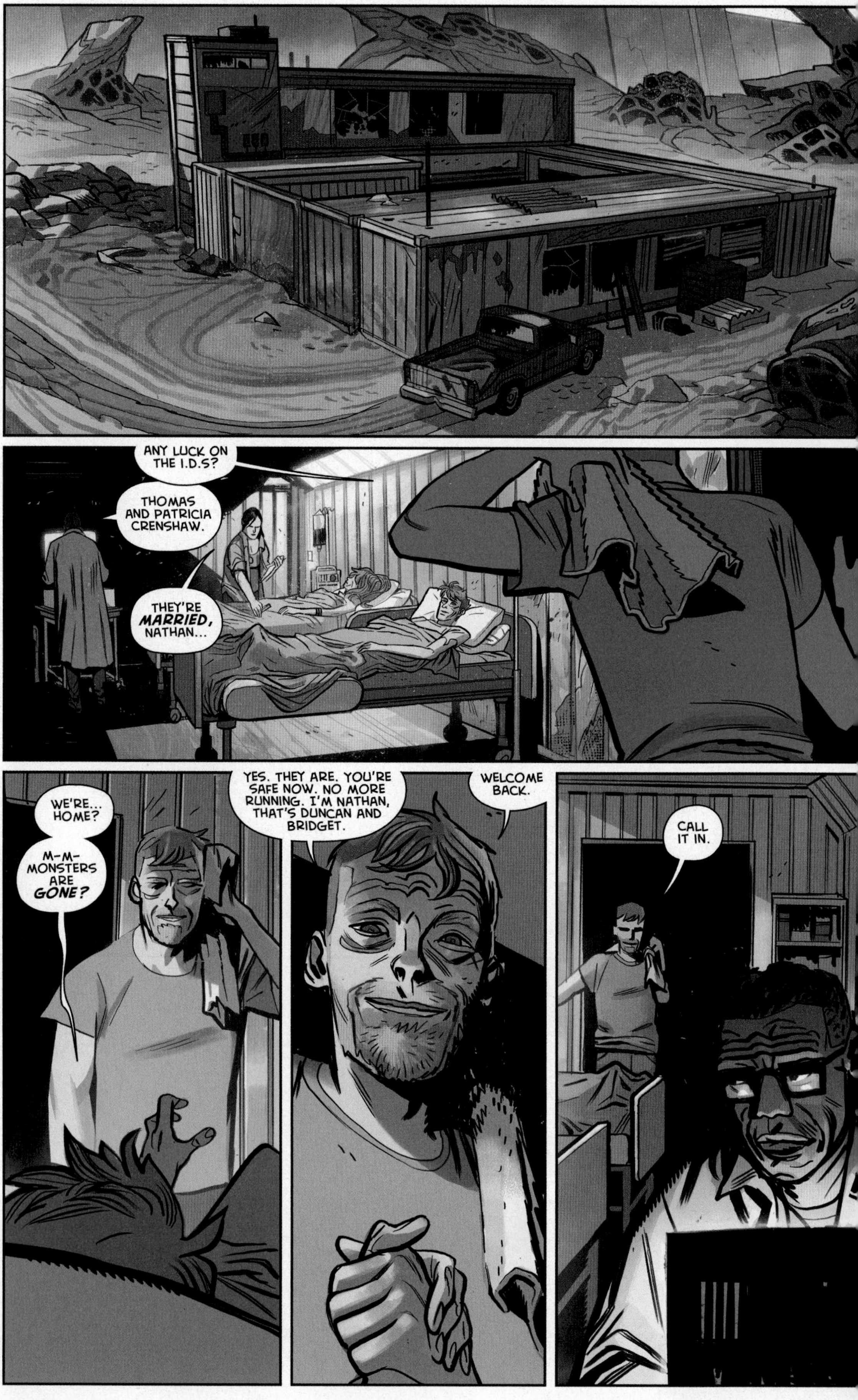
ANY LUCK ON THE I.D.S?
THOMAS AND PATRICIA CRENSHAW.
THEY'RE **MARRIED**, NATHAN...
WE'RE... HOME?
M-M-MONSTERS ARE **GONE?**
YES. THEY ARE. YOU'RE SAFE NOW. NO MORE RUNNING. I'M NATHAN, THAT'S DUNCAN AND BRIDGET.
WELCOME BACK.
CALL IT IN.

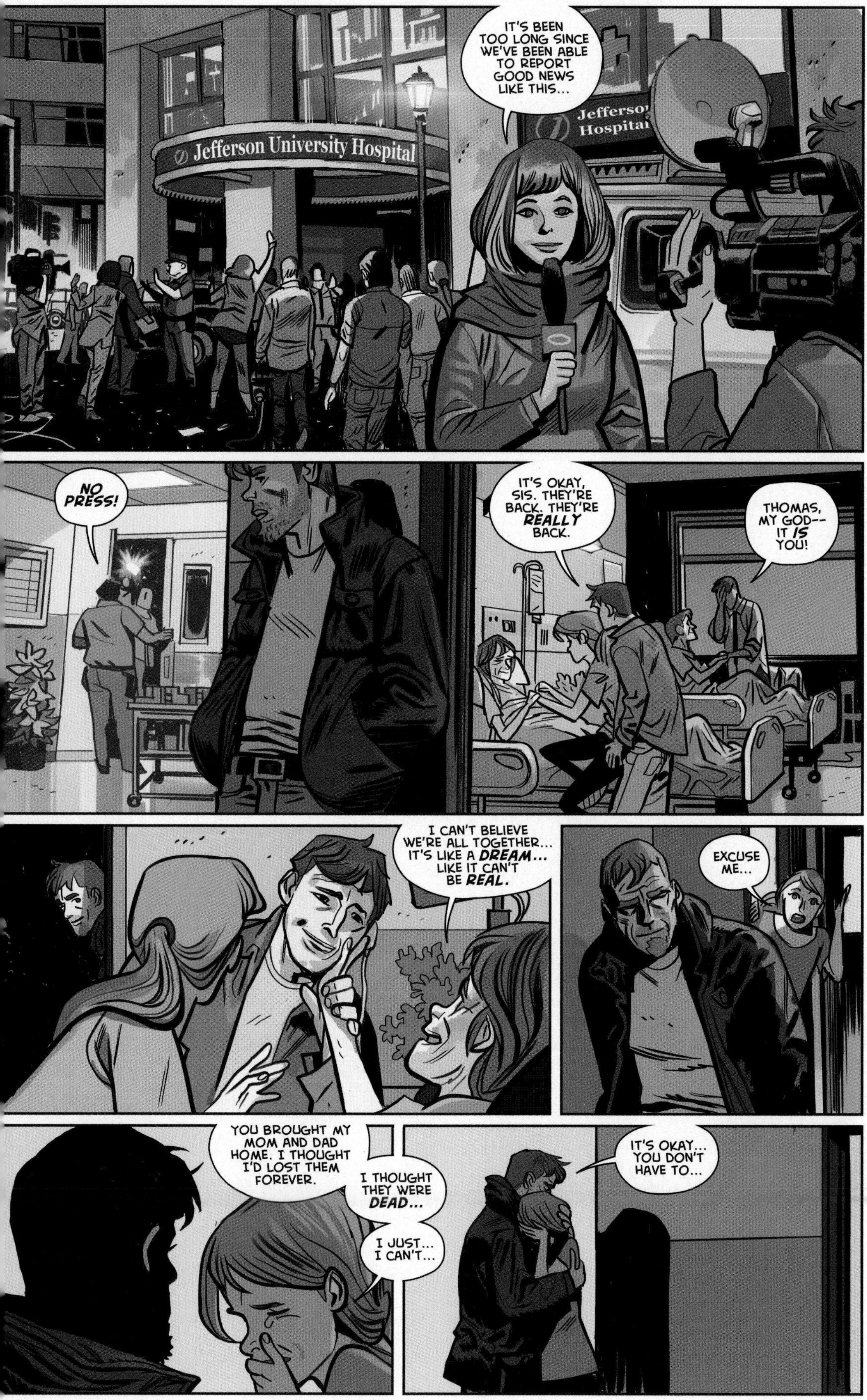
Jefferson University Hospital
IT'S BEEN TOO LONG SINCE WE'VE BEEN ABLE TO REPORT GOOD NEWS LIKE THIS...
Jefferson Hospital
NO PRESS!
IT'S OKAY, SIS. THEY'RE BACK. THEY'RE REALLY BACK.
THOMAS, MY GOD-- IT IS YOU!
I CAN'T BELIEVE WE'RE ALL TOGETHER... IT'S LIKE A DREAM... LIKE IT CAN'T BE REAL.
EXCUSE ME...
YOU BROUGHT MY MOM AND DAD HOME. I THOUGHT I'D LOST THEM FOREVER.
I THOUGHT THEY WERE DEAD...
I JUST... I CAN'T...
IT'S OKAY... YOU DON'T HAVE TO...

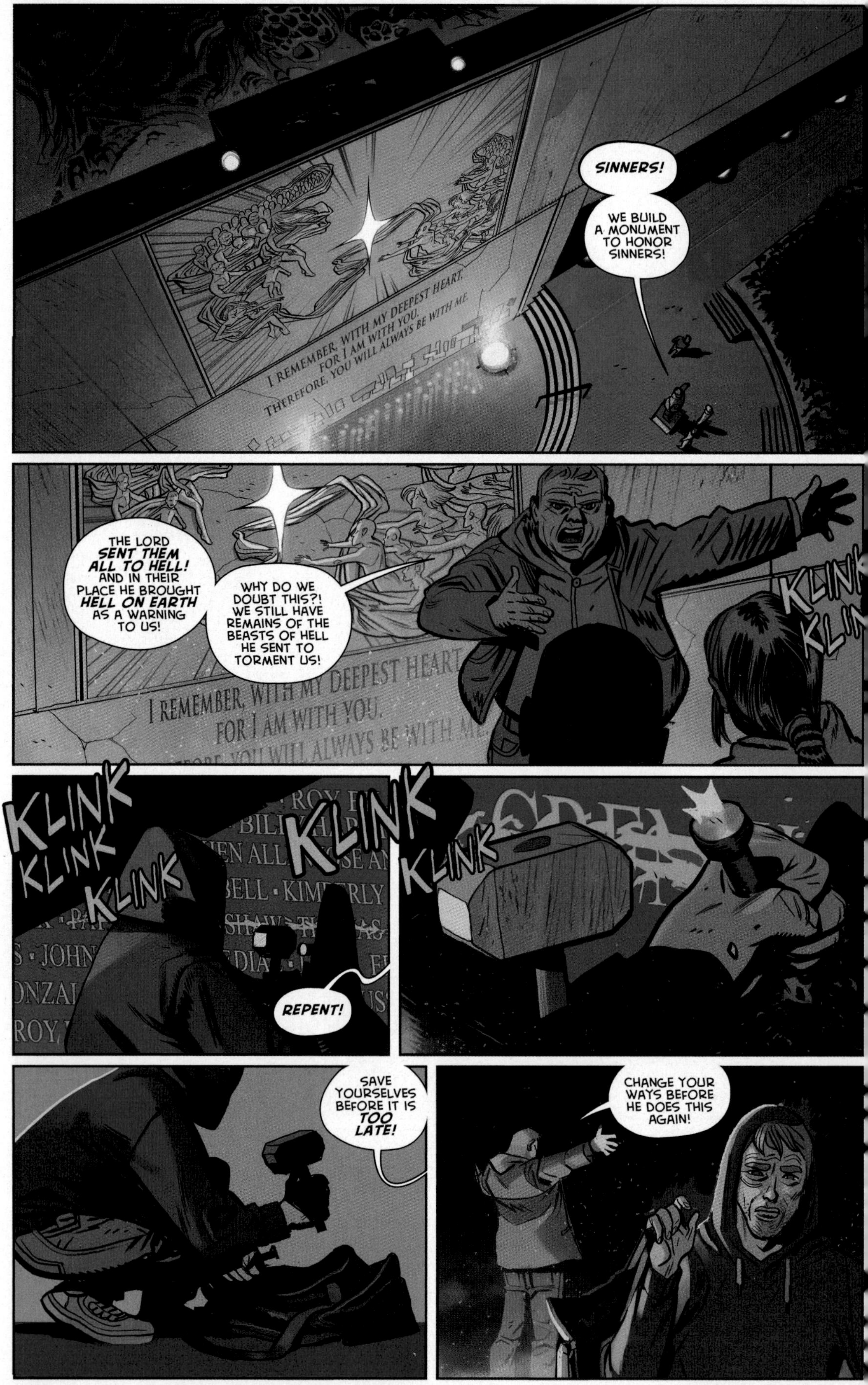
I REMEMBER, WITH MY DEEPEST HEART,
FOR I AM WITH YOU.
THEREFORE, YOU WILL ALWAYS BE WITH ME.
SINNERS!
WE BUILD A MONUMENT TO HONOR SINNERS!
THE LORD SENT THEM ALL TO HELL! AND IN THEIR PLACE HE BROUGHT HELL ON EARTH AS A WARNING TO US!
WHY DO WE DOUBT THIS?! WE STILL HAVE REMAINS OF THE BEASTS OF HELL HE SENT TO TORMENT US!
I REMEMBER, WITH MY DEEPEST HEART
FOR I AM WITH YOU.
KLINK KLINK
KLINK KLINK KLINK
KLINK
KLINK
REPENT!
SAVE YOURSELVES BEFORE IT IS TOO LATE!
CHANGE YOUR WAYS BEFORE HE DOES THIS AGAIN!

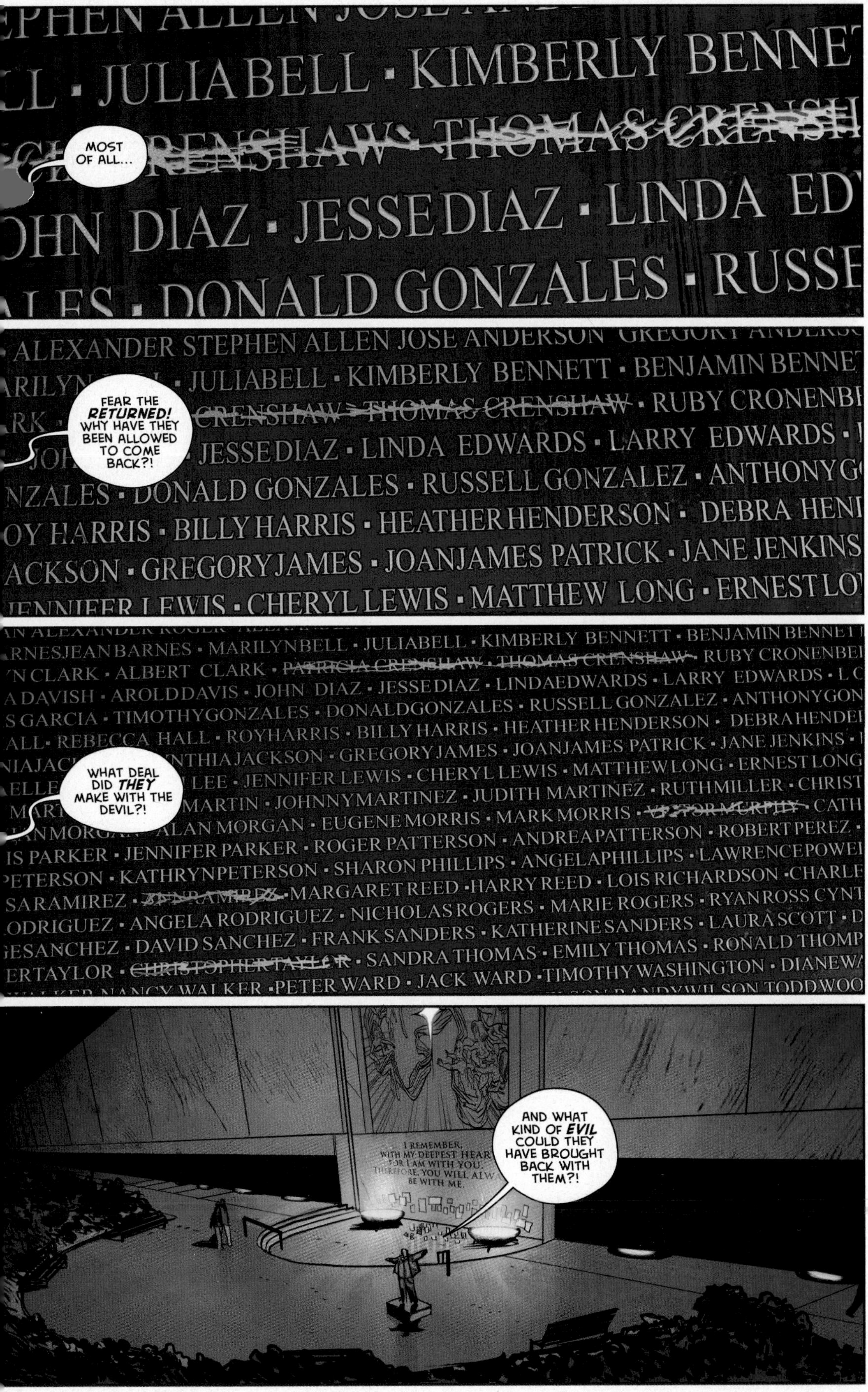
MOST OF ALL...
FEAR THE *RETURNED!* WHY HAVE THEY BEEN ALLOWED TO COME BACK?!
WHAT DEAL DID *THEY* MAKE WITH THE DEVIL?!
I REMEMBER, WITH MY DEEPEST HEART FOR I AM WITH YOU. THEREFORE, YOU WILL ALWA BE WITH ME.
AND WHAT KIND OF *EVIL* COULD THEY HAVE BROUGHT BACK WITH THEM?!

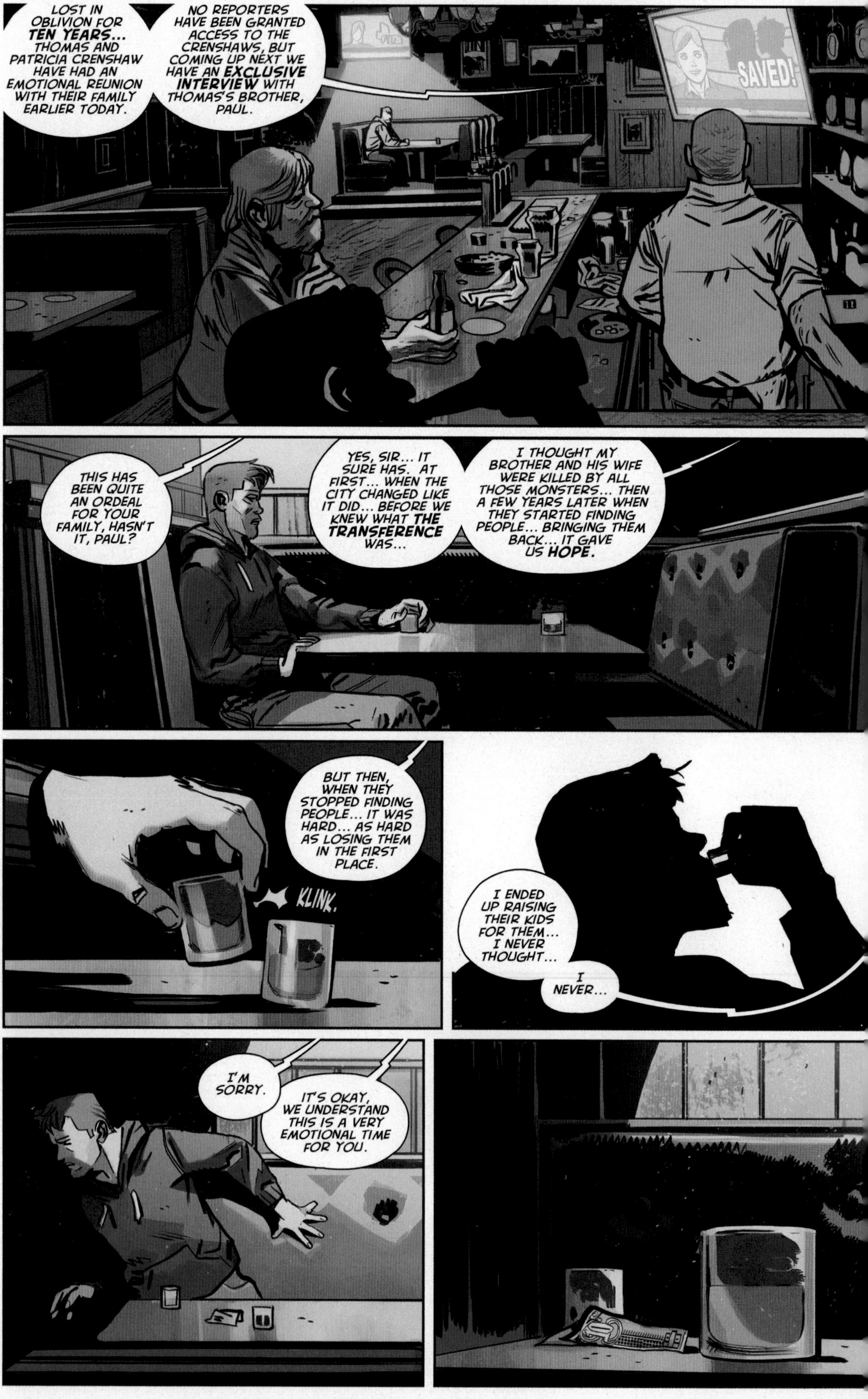
LOST IN OBLIVION FOR TEN YEARS... THOMAS AND PATRICIA CRENSHAW HAVE HAD AN EMOTIONAL REUNION WITH THEIR FAMILY EARLIER TODAY.
NO REPORTERS HAVE BEEN GRANTED ACCESS TO THE CRENSHAWS, BUT COMING UP NEXT WE HAVE AN EXCLUSIVE INTERVIEW WITH THOMAS'S BROTHER, PAUL.
SAVED!
THIS HAS BEEN QUITE AN ORDEAL FOR YOUR FAMILY, HASN'T IT, PAUL?
YES, SIR... IT SURE HAS. AT FIRST... WHEN THE CITY CHANGED LIKE IT DID... BEFORE WE KNEW WHAT THE TRANSFERENCE WAS...
I THOUGHT MY BROTHER AND HIS WIFE WERE KILLED BY ALL THOSE MONSTERS... THEN A FEW YEARS LATER WHEN THEY STARTED FINDING PEOPLE... BRINGING THEM BACK... IT GAVE US HOPE.
BUT THEN, WHEN THEY STOPPED FINDING PEOPLE... IT WAS HARD... AS HARD AS LOSING THEM IN THE FIRST PLACE.
KLINK.
I ENDED UP RAISING THEIR KIDS FOR THEM... I NEVER THOUGHT...
I NEVER...
I'M SORRY.
IT'S OKAY, WE UNDERSTAND THIS IS A VERY EMOTIONAL TIME FOR YOU.

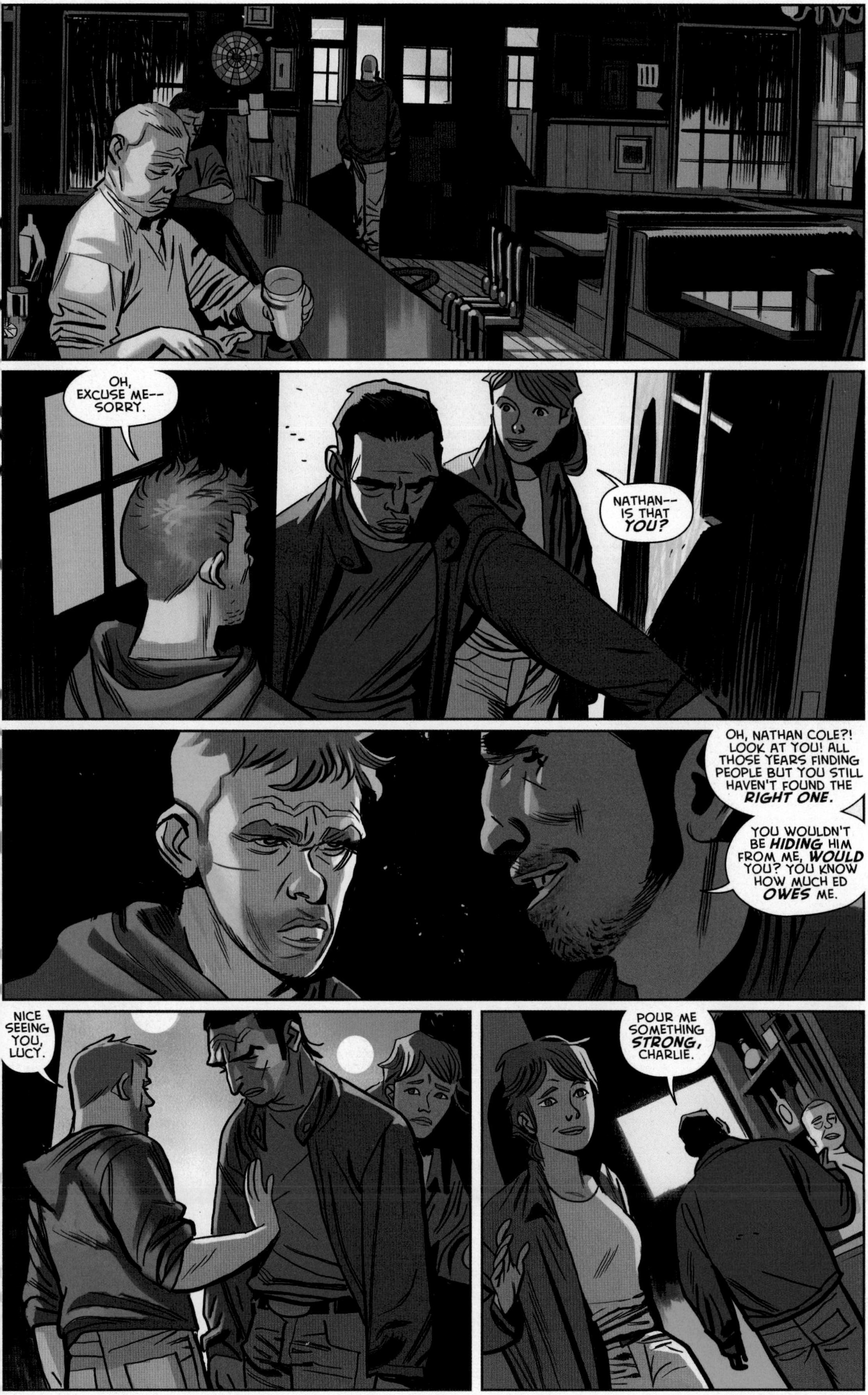
OH, EXCUSE ME-- SORRY.
NATHAN-- IS THAT YOU?
OH, NATHAN COLE?! LOOK AT YOU! ALL THOSE YEARS FINDING PEOPLE BUT YOU STILL HAVEN'T FOUND THE RIGHT ONE.
YOU WOULDN'T BE HIDING HIM FROM ME, WOULD YOU? YOU KNOW HOW MUCH ED OWES ME.
NICE SEEING YOU, LUCY.
POUR ME SOMETHING STRONG, CHARLIE.

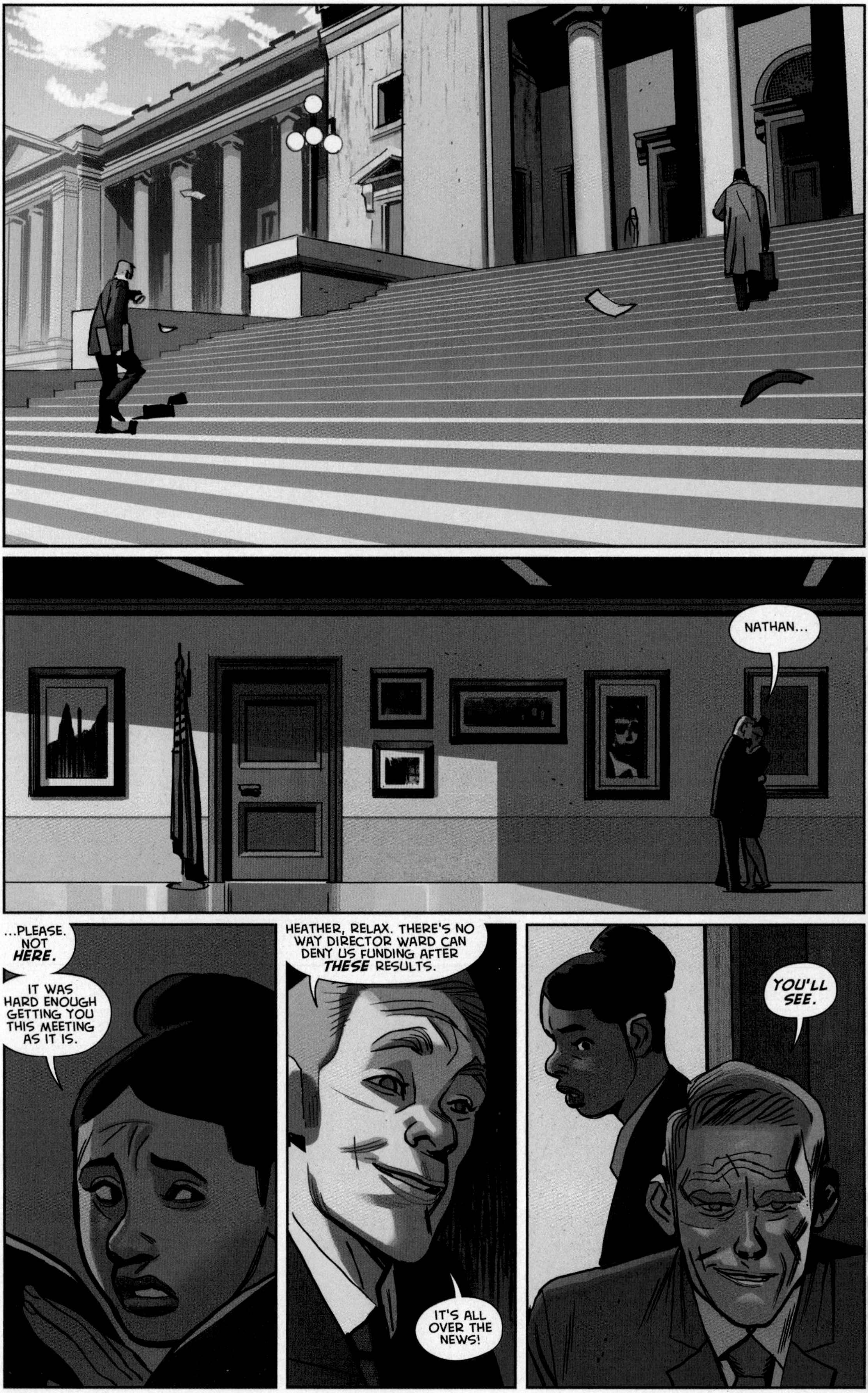
NATHAN...
...PLEASE. NOT HERE.
IT WAS HARD ENOUGH GETTING YOU THIS MEETING AS IT IS.
HEATHER, RELAX. THERE'S NO WAY DIRECTOR WARD CAN DENY US FUNDING AFTER THESE RESULTS.
IT'S ALL OVER THE NEWS!
YOU'LL SEE.

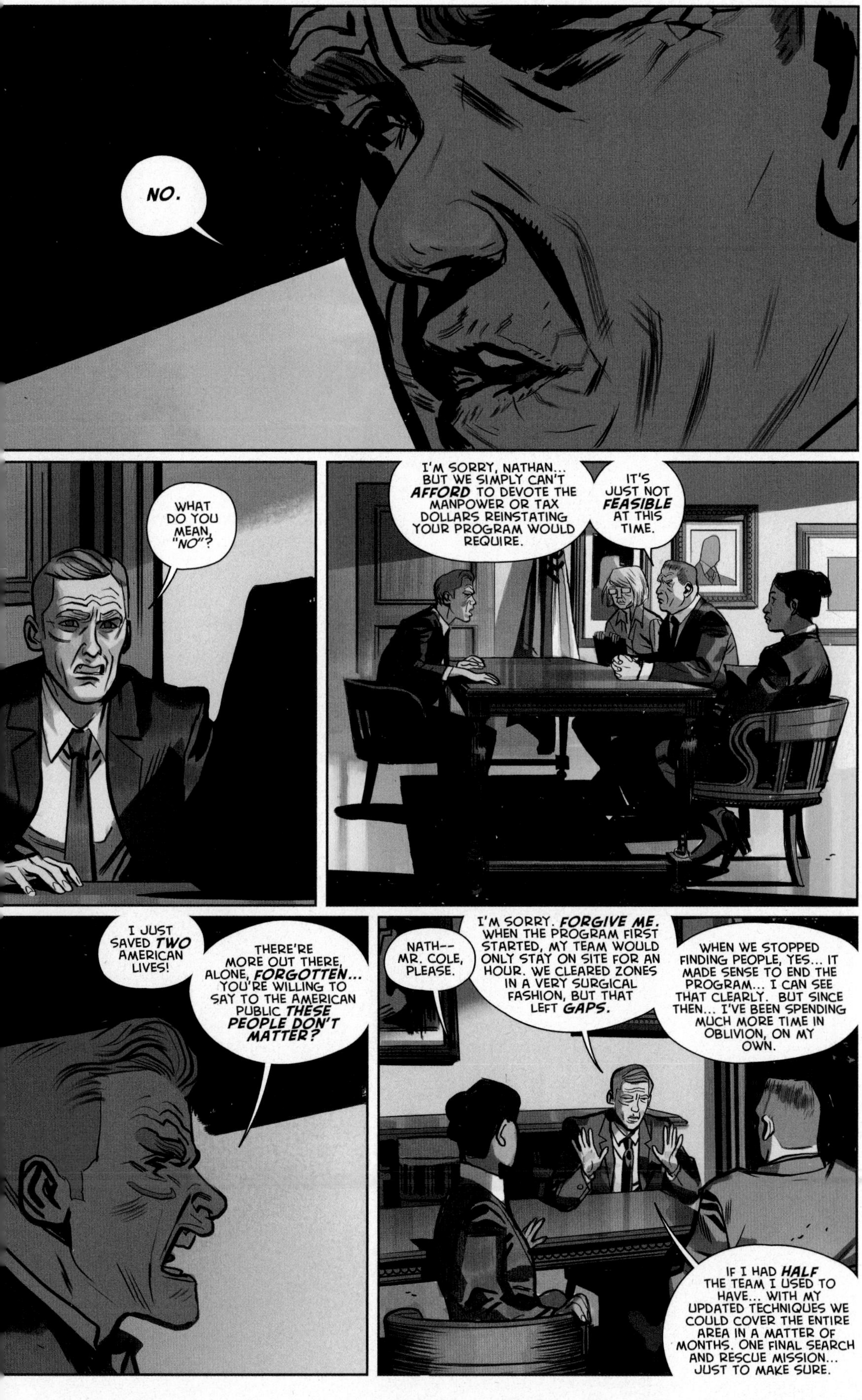
NO.
WHAT DO YOU MEAN, "NO"?
I'M SORRY, NATHAN... BUT WE SIMPLY CAN'T AFFORD TO DEVOTE THE MANPOWER OR TAX DOLLARS REINSTATING YOUR PROGRAM WOULD REQUIRE.
IT'S JUST NOT FEASIBLE AT THIS TIME.
I JUST SAVED TWO AMERICAN LIVES!
THERE'RE MORE OUT THERE, ALONE, FORGOTTEN... YOU'RE WILLING TO SAY TO THE AMERICAN PUBLIC THESE PEOPLE DON'T MATTER?
NATH-- MR. COLE, PLEASE.
I'M SORRY. FORGIVE ME. WHEN THE PROGRAM FIRST STARTED, MY TEAM WOULD ONLY STAY ON SITE FOR AN HOUR. WE CLEARED ZONES IN A VERY SURGICAL FASHION, BUT THAT LEFT GAPS.
WHEN WE STOPPED FINDING PEOPLE, YES... IT MADE SENSE TO END THE PROGRAM... I CAN SEE THAT CLEARLY. BUT SINCE THEN... I'VE BEEN SPENDING MUCH MORE TIME IN OBLIVION, ON MY OWN.
IF I HAD HALF THE TEAM I USED TO HAVE... WITH MY UPDATED TECHNIQUES WE COULD COVER THE ENTIRE AREA IN A MATTER OF MONTHS. ONE FINAL SEARCH AND RESCUE MISSION... JUST TO MAKE SURE.

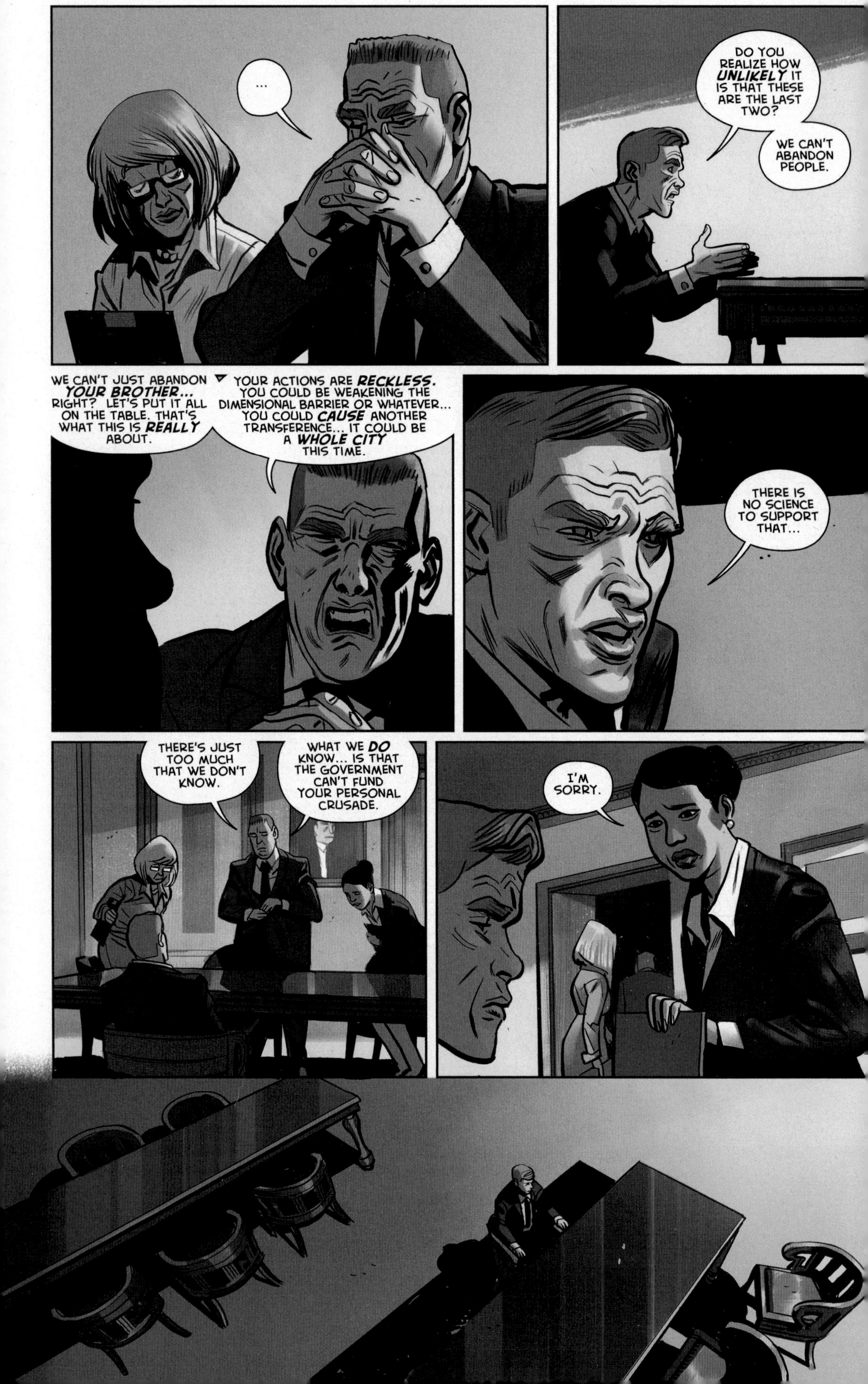
...
DO YOU REALIZE HOW UNLIKELY IT IS THAT THESE ARE THE LAST TWO?
WE CAN'T ABANDON PEOPLE.
WE CAN'T JUST ABANDON YOUR BROTHER... RIGHT? LET'S PUT IT ALL ON THE TABLE. THAT'S WHAT THIS IS REALLY ABOUT.
YOUR ACTIONS ARE RECKLESS. YOU COULD BE WEAKENING THE DIMENSIONAL BARRIER OR WHATEVER... YOU COULD CAUSE ANOTHER TRANSFERENCE... IT COULD BE A WHOLE CITY THIS TIME.
THERE IS NO SCIENCE TO SUPPORT THAT...
THERE'S JUST TOO MUCH THAT WE DON'T KNOW.
WHAT WE DO KNOW... IS THAT THE GOVERNMENT CAN'T FUND YOUR PERSONAL CRUSADE.
I'M SORRY.

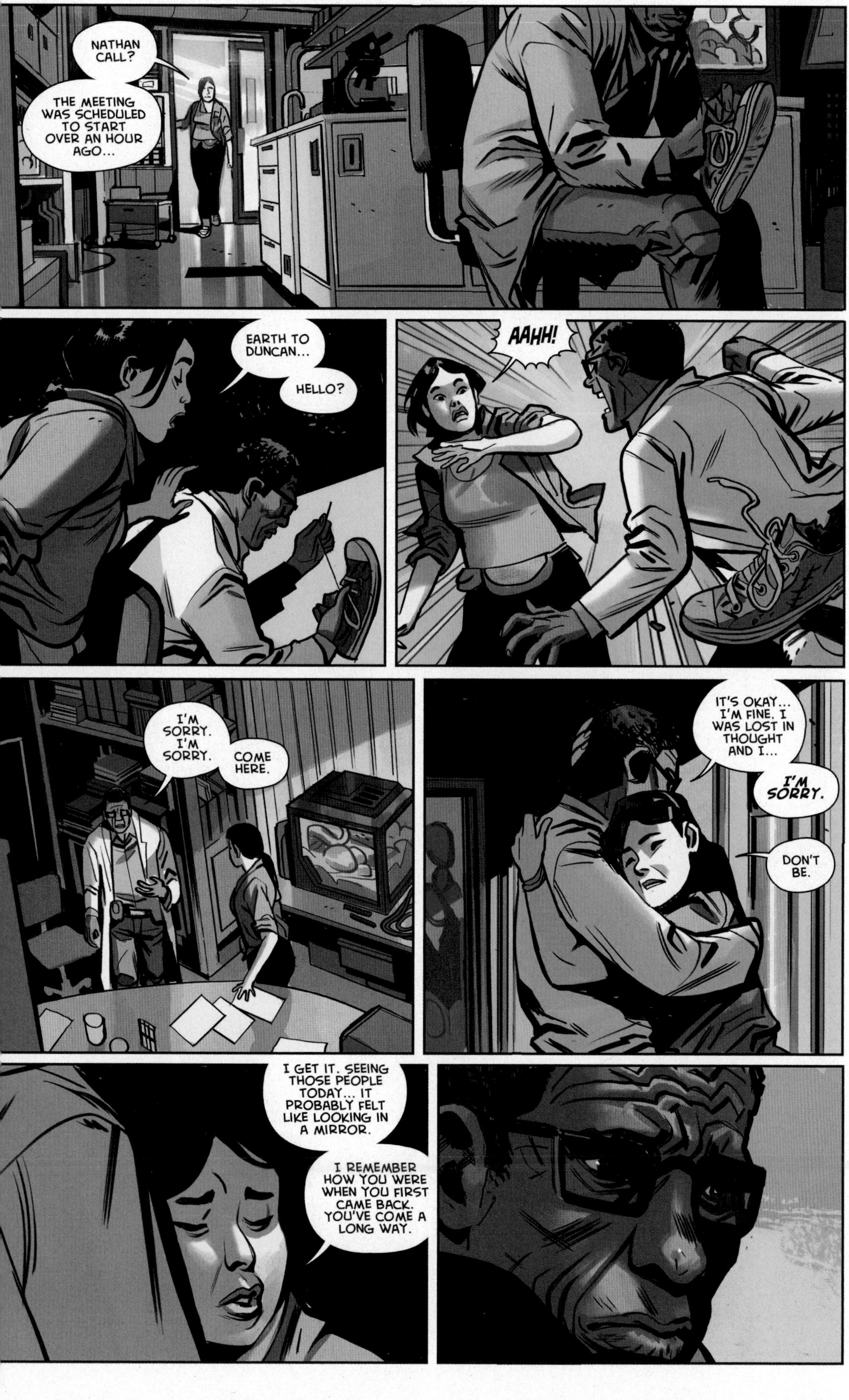
NATHAN CALL?
THE MEETING WAS SCHEDULED TO START OVER AN HOUR AGO...
EARTH TO DUNCAN...
HELLO?
AAHH!
I'M SORRY. I'M SORRY.
COME HERE.
IT'S OKAY... I'M FINE. I WAS LOST IN THOUGHT AND I...
I'M SORRY.
DON'T BE.
I GET IT. SEEING THOSE PEOPLE TODAY... IT PROBABLY FELT LIKE LOOKING IN A MIRROR.
I REMEMBER HOW YOU WERE WHEN YOU FIRST CAME BACK. YOU'VE COME A LONG WAY.

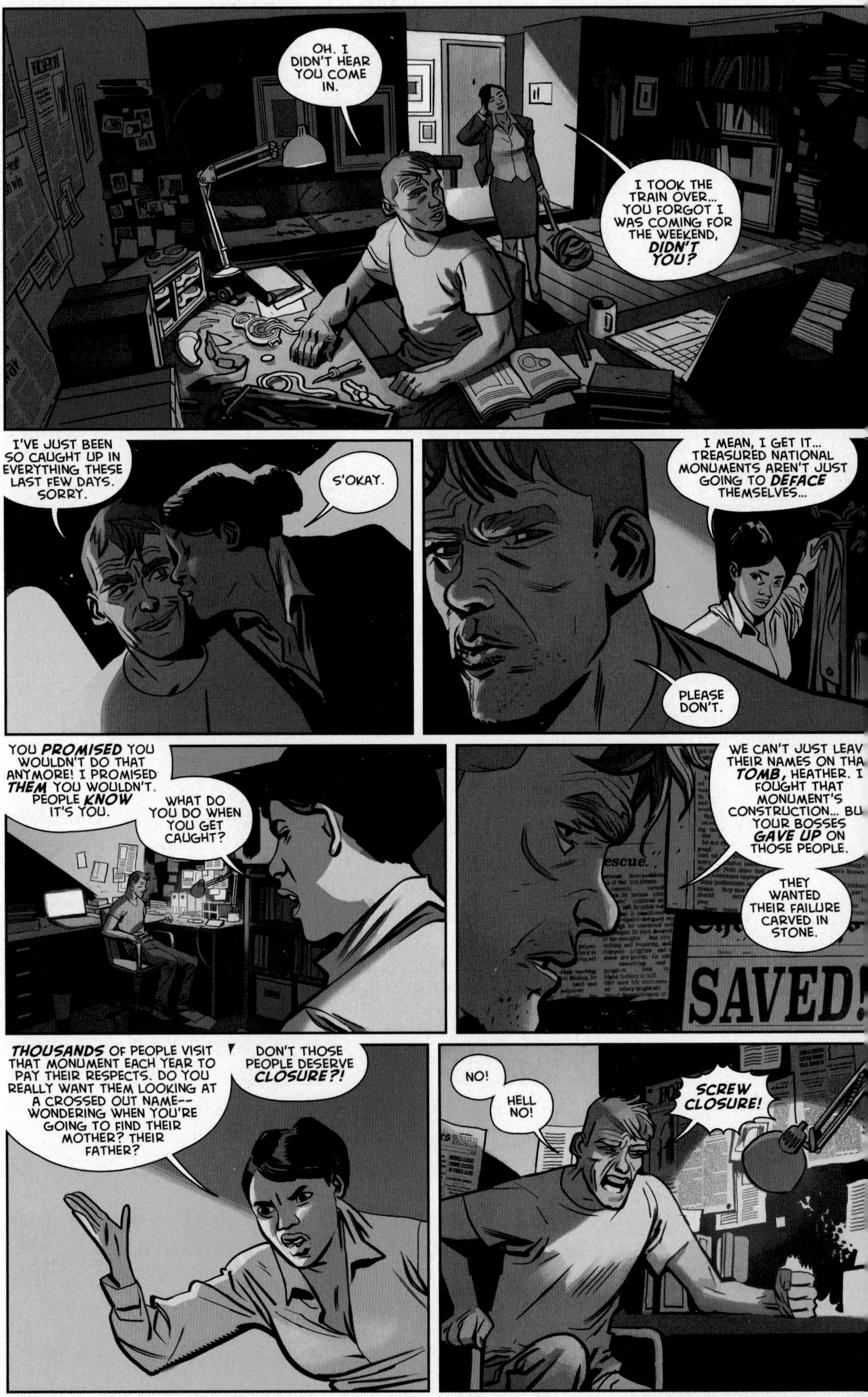
OH. I DIDN'T HEAR YOU COME IN.
I TOOK THE TRAIN OVER... YOU FORGOT I WAS COMING FOR THE WEEKEND, DIDN'T YOU?
I'VE JUST BEEN SO CAUGHT UP IN EVERYTHING THESE LAST FEW DAYS. SORRY.
S'OKAY.
I MEAN, I GET IT... TREASURED NATIONAL MONUMENTS AREN'T JUST GOING TO DEFACE THEMSELVES...
PLEASE DON'T.
YOU PROMISED YOU WOULDN'T DO THAT ANYMORE! I PROMISED THEM YOU WOULDN'T. PEOPLE KNOW IT'S YOU.
WHAT DO YOU DO WHEN YOU GET CAUGHT?
WE CAN'T JUST LEAV THEIR NAMES ON THA TOMB, HEATHER. I FOUGHT THAT MONUMENT'S CONSTRUCTION... BU YOUR BOSSES GAVE UP ON THOSE PEOPLE.
THEY WANTED THEIR FAILURE CARVED IN STONE.
SAVED!
THOUSANDS OF PEOPLE VISIT THAT MONUMENT EACH YEAR TO PAY THEIR RESPECTS. DO YOU REALLY WANT THEM LOOKING AT A CROSSED OUT NAME-- WONDERING WHEN YOU'RE GOING TO FIND THEIR MOTHER? THEIR FATHER?
DON'T THOSE PEOPLE DESERVE CLOSURE?!
NO!
HELL NO!
SCREW CLOSURE!

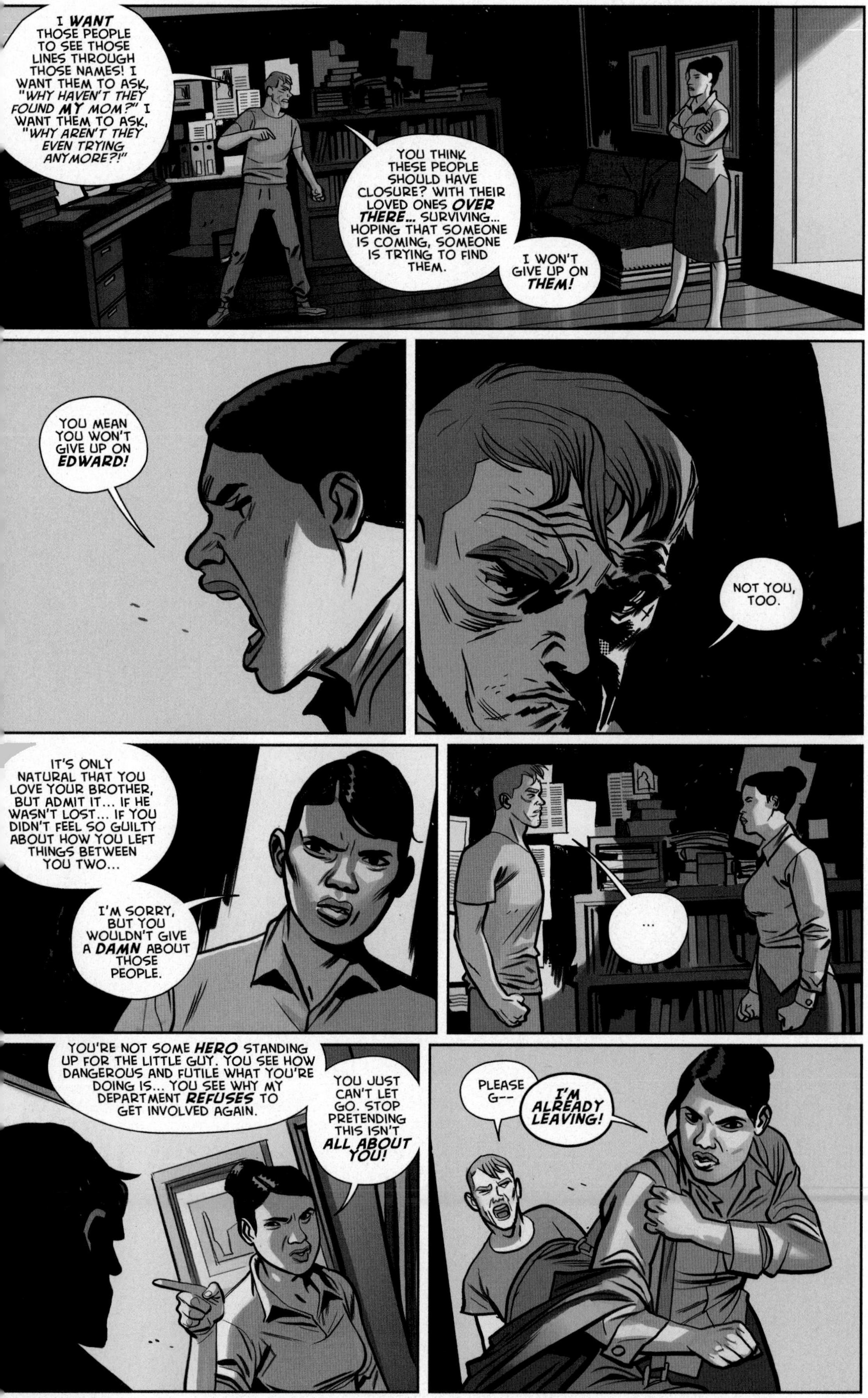
I WANT THOSE PEOPLE TO SEE THOSE LINES THROUGH THOSE NAMES! I WANT THEM TO ASK, "WHY HAVEN'T THEY FOUND MY MOM?" I WANT THEM TO ASK, "WHY AREN'T THEY EVEN TRYING ANYMORE?!"
YOU THINK THESE PEOPLE SHOULD HAVE CLOSURE? WITH THEIR LOVED ONES OVER THERE... SURVIVING... HOPING THAT SOMEONE IS COMING, SOMEONE IS TRYING TO FIND THEM.
I WON'T GIVE UP ON THEM!
YOU MEAN YOU WON'T GIVE UP ON EDWARD!
NOT YOU, TOO.
IT'S ONLY NATURAL THAT YOU LOVE YOUR BROTHER, BUT ADMIT IT... IF HE WASN'T LOST... IF YOU DIDN'T FEEL SO GUILTY ABOUT HOW YOU LEFT THINGS BETWEEN YOU TWO...
I'M SORRY, BUT YOU WOULDN'T GIVE A DAMN ABOUT THOSE PEOPLE.
...
YOU'RE NOT SOME HERO STANDING UP FOR THE LITTLE GUY. YOU SEE HOW DANGEROUS AND FUTILE WHAT YOU'RE DOING IS... YOU SEE WHY MY DEPARTMENT REFUSES TO GET INVOLVED AGAIN.
YOU JUST CAN'T LET GO. STOP PRETENDING THIS ISN'T ALL ABOUT YOU!
PLEASE G--
I'M ALREADY LEAVING!

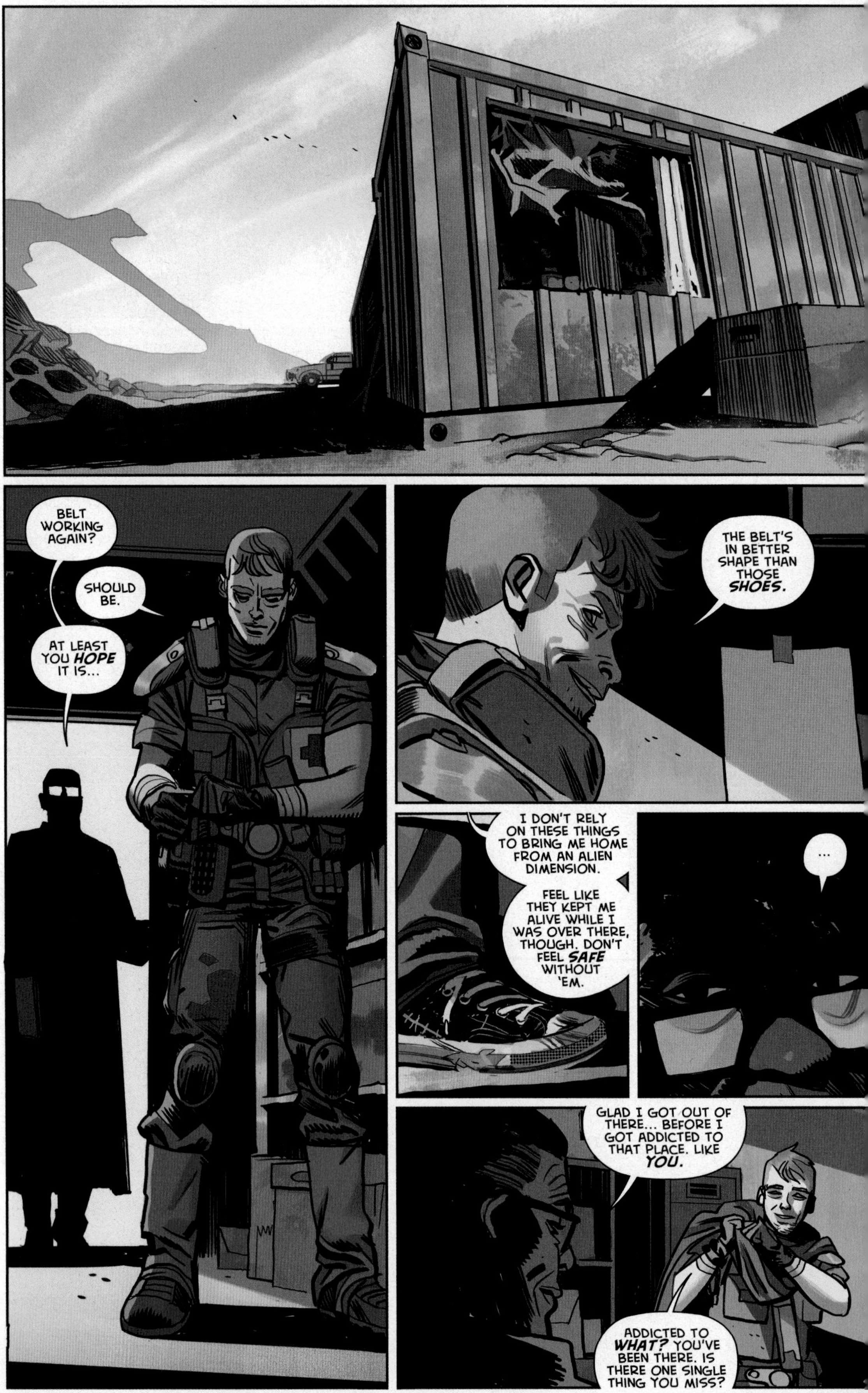
BELT WORKING AGAIN?
SHOULD BE.
AT LEAST YOU HOPE IT IS...
THE BELT'S IN BETTER SHAPE THAN THOSE SHOES.
I DON'T RELY ON THESE THINGS TO BRING ME HOME FROM AN ALIEN DIMENSION.
FEEL LIKE THEY KEPT ME ALIVE WHILE I WAS OVER THERE, THOUGH. DON'T FEEL SAFE WITHOUT 'EM.
...
GLAD I GOT OUT OF THERE... BEFORE I GOT ADDICTED TO THAT PLACE. LIKE YOU.
ADDICTED TO WHAT? YOU'VE BEEN THERE. IS THERE ONE SINGLE THING YOU MISS?

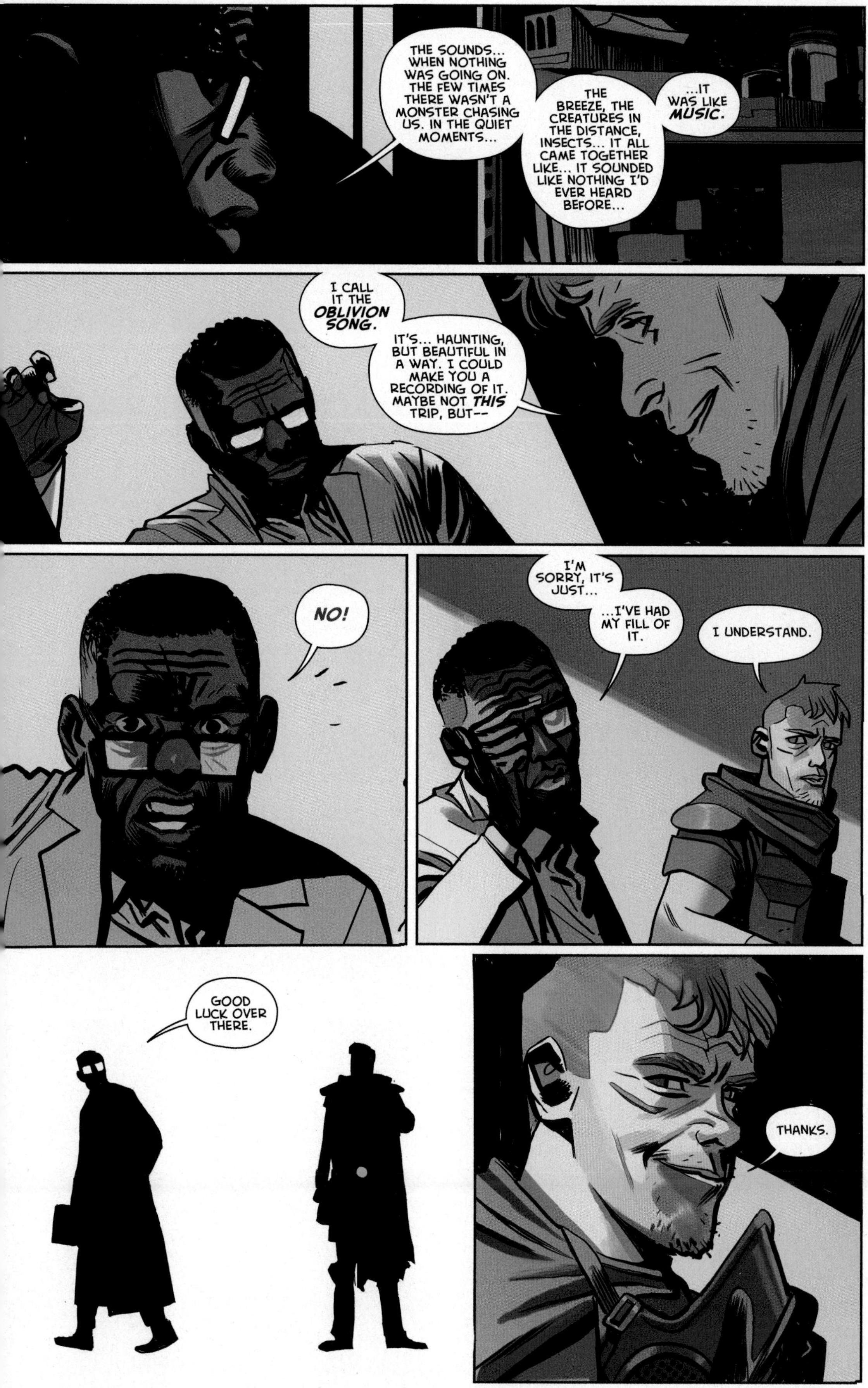
THE SOUNDS... WHEN NOTHING WAS GOING ON. THE FEW TIMES THERE WASN'T A MONSTER CHASING US. IN THE QUIET MOMENTS...
THE BREEZE, THE CREATURES IN THE DISTANCE, INSECTS... IT ALL CAME TOGETHER LIKE... IT SOUNDED LIKE NOTHING I'D EVER HEARD BEFORE...
...IT WAS LIKE MUSIC.
I CALL IT THE OBLIVION SONG.
IT'S... HAUNTING, BUT BEAUTIFUL IN A WAY. I COULD MAKE YOU A RECORDING OF IT. MAYBE NOT THIS TRIP, BUT--
NO!
I'M SORRY, IT'S JUST...
...I'VE HAD MY FILL OF IT.
I UNDERSTAND.
GOOD LUCK OVER THERE.
THANKS.

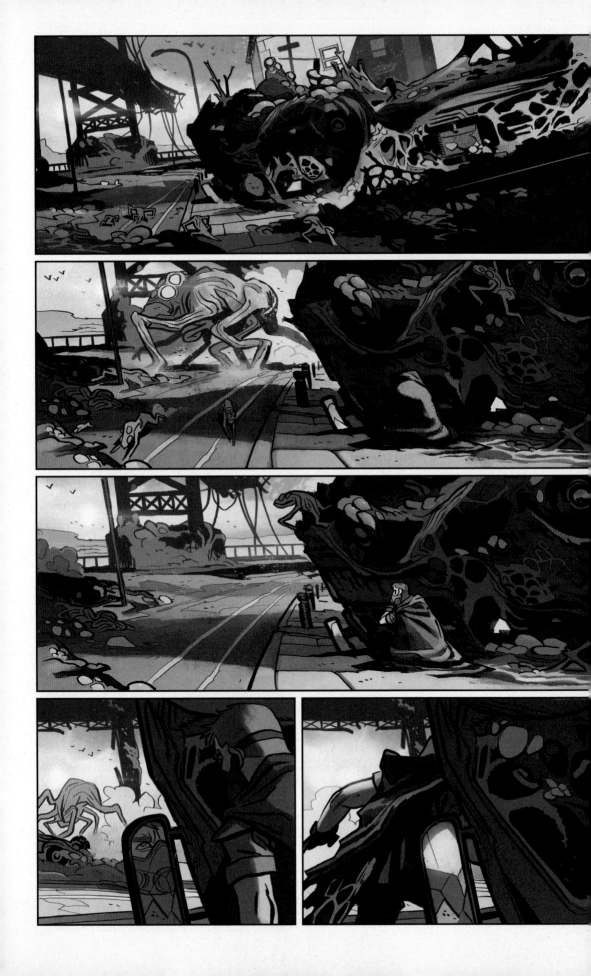

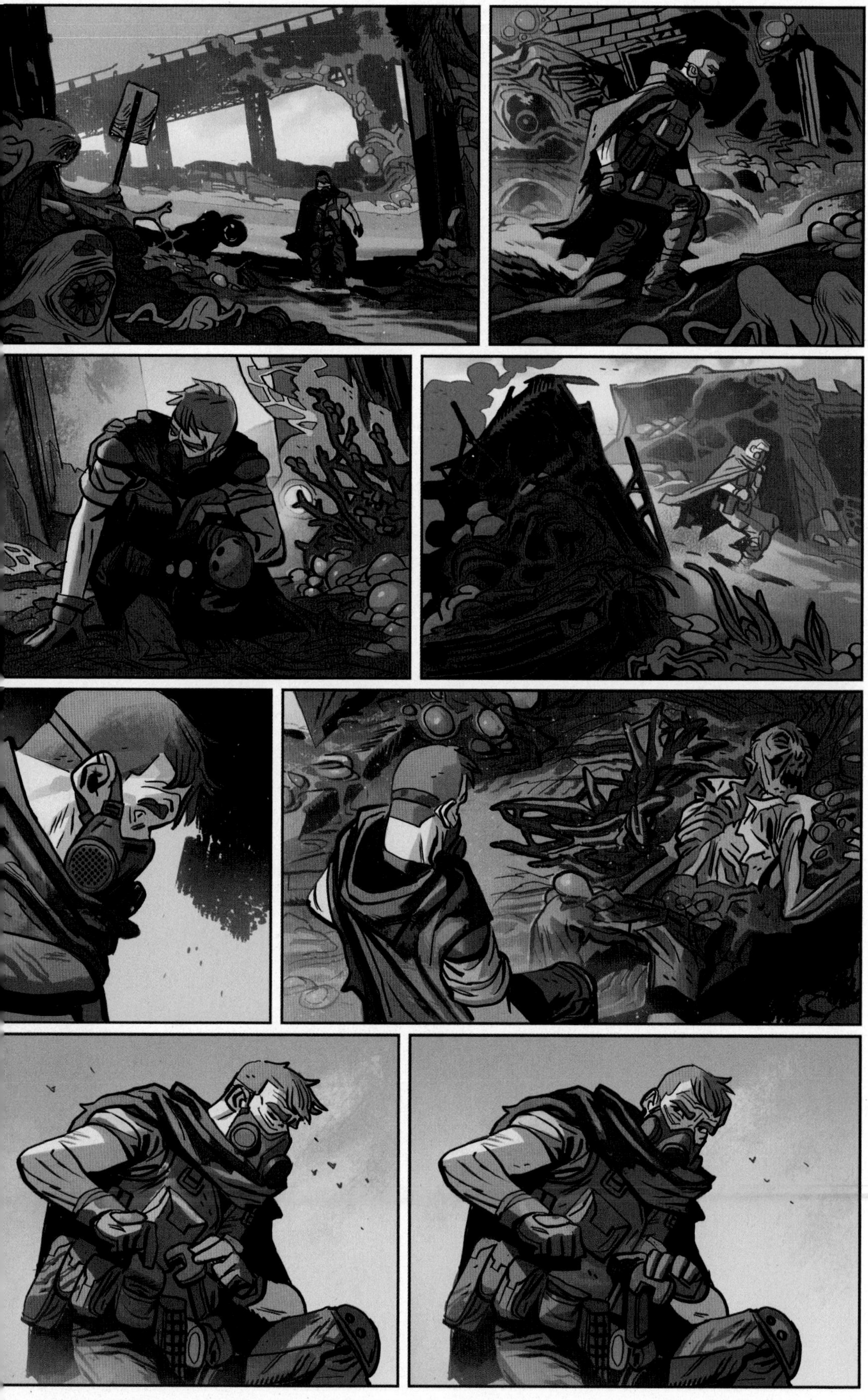

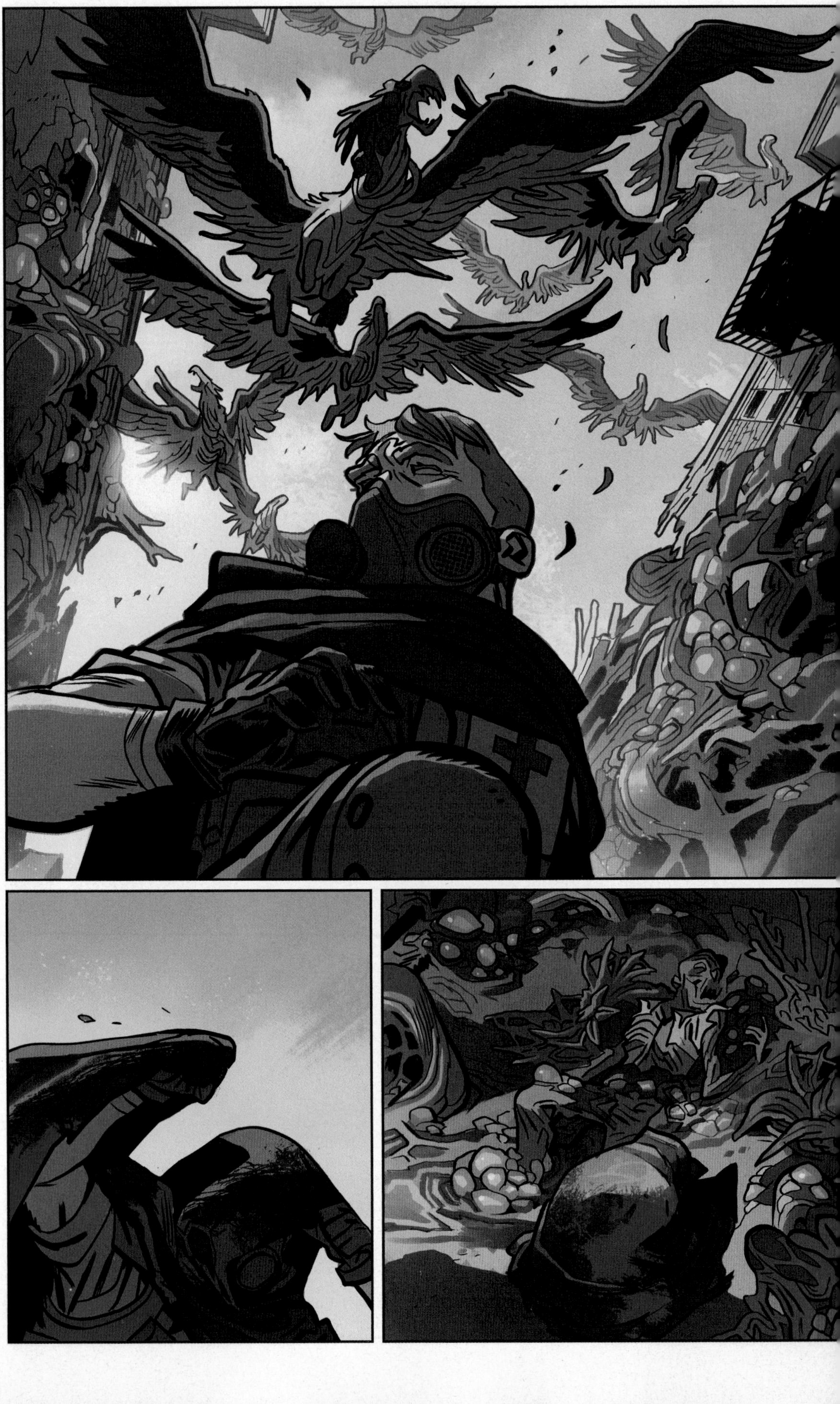

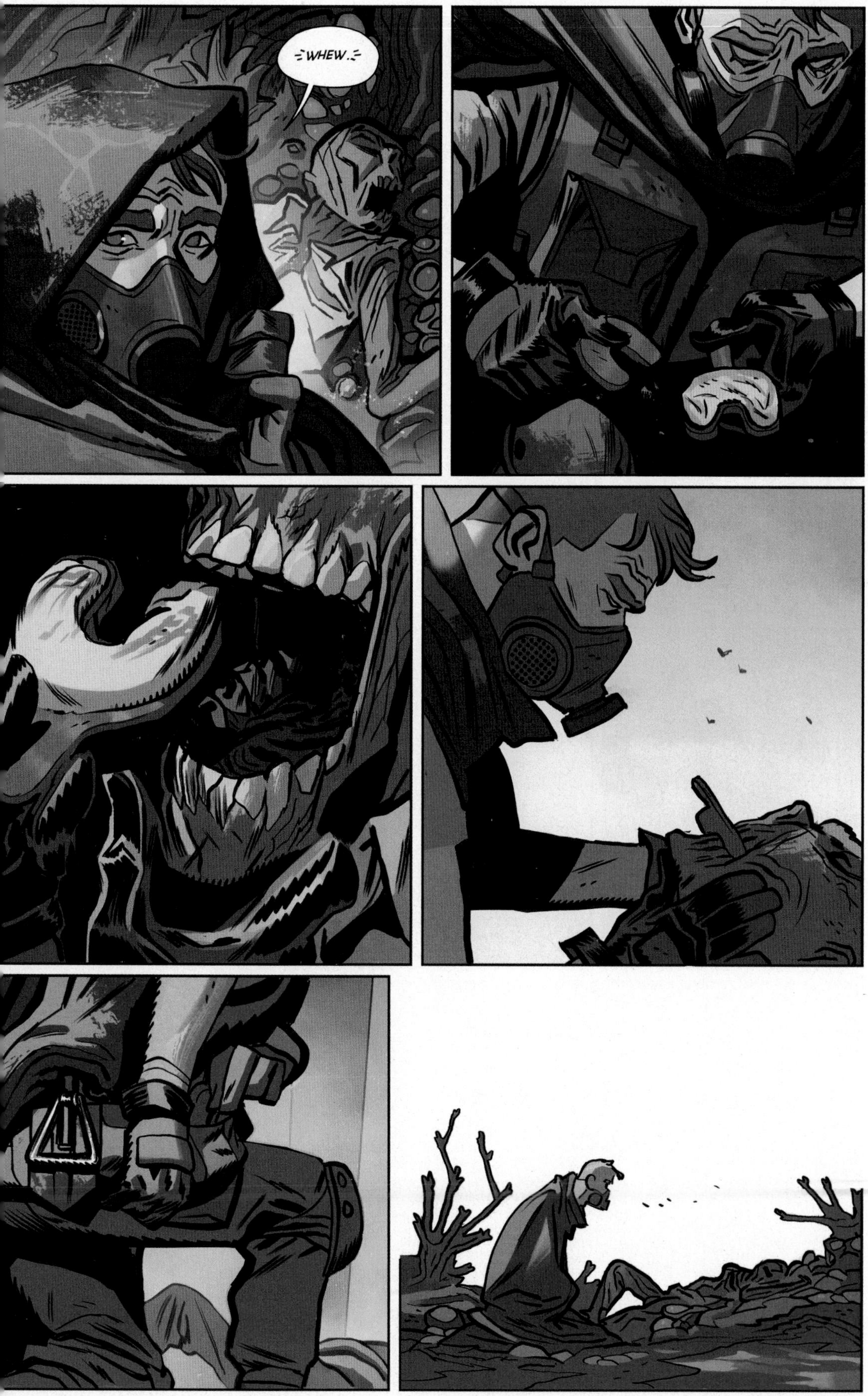
WHEW.

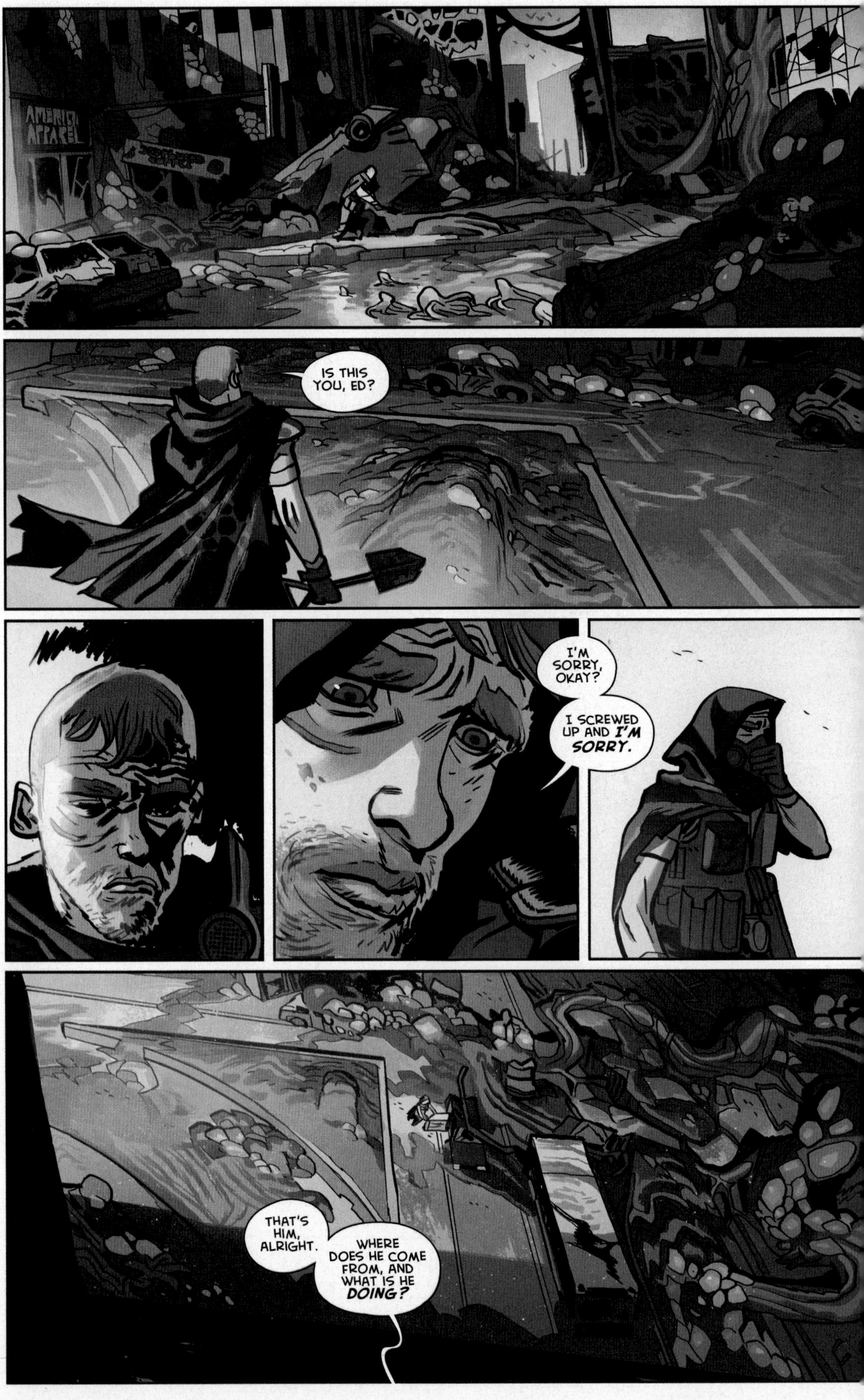
IS THIS YOU, ED?
I'M SORRY, OKAY?
I SCREWED UP AND I'M SORRY.
THAT'S HIM, ALRIGHT.
WHERE DOES HE COME FROM, AND WHAT IS HE DOING?

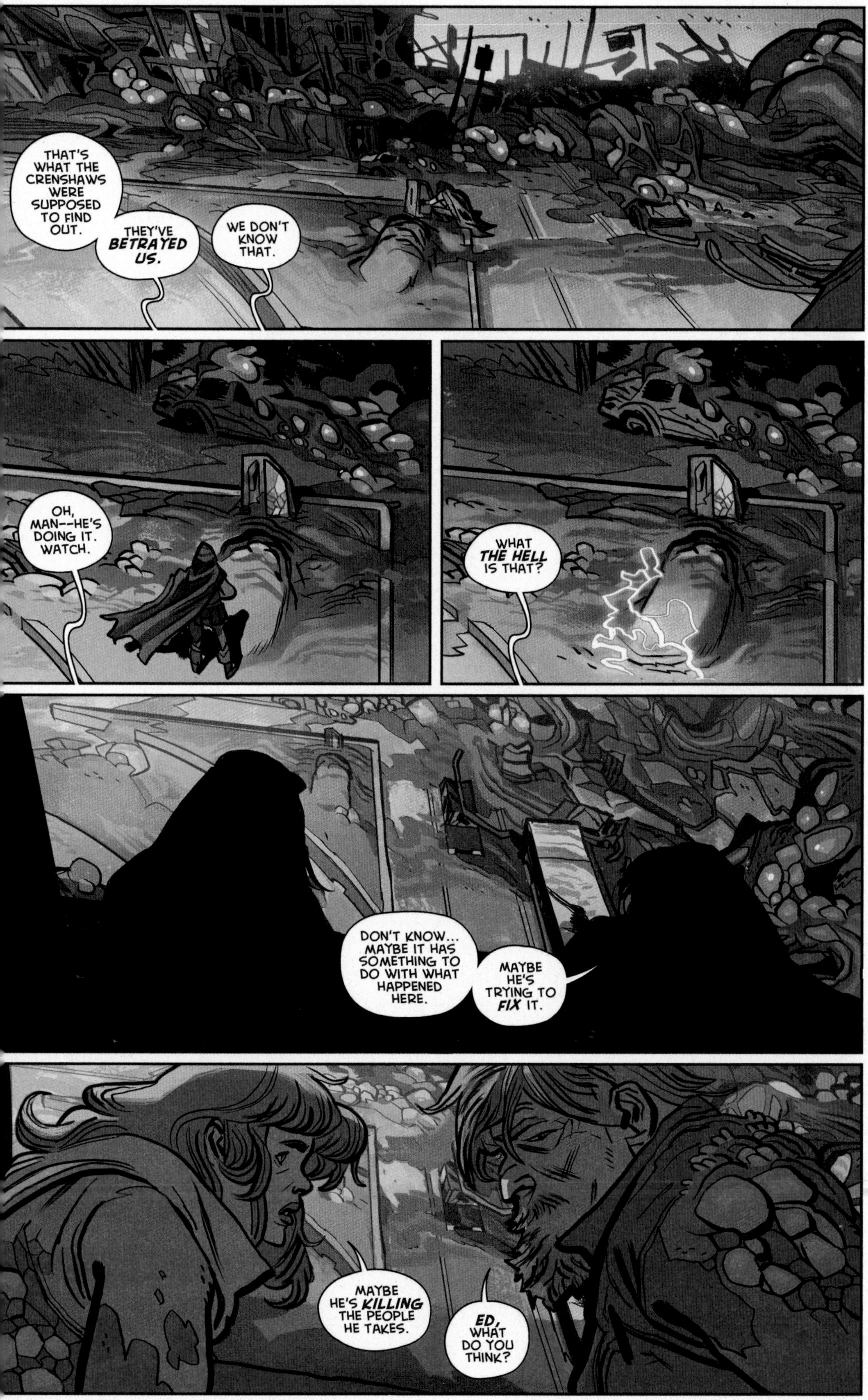

THAT'S WHAT THE CRENSHAWS WERE SUPPOSED TO FIND OUT.
THEY'VE BETRAYED US.
WE DON'T KNOW THAT.
OH, MAN--HE'S DOING IT. WATCH.
WHAT THE HELL IS THAT?
DON'T KNOW... MAYBE IT HAS SOMETHING TO DO WITH WHAT HAPPENED HERE.
MAYBE HE'S TRYING TO FIX IT.
MAYBE HE'S KILLING THE PEOPLE HE TAKES.
ED, WHAT DO YOU THINK?

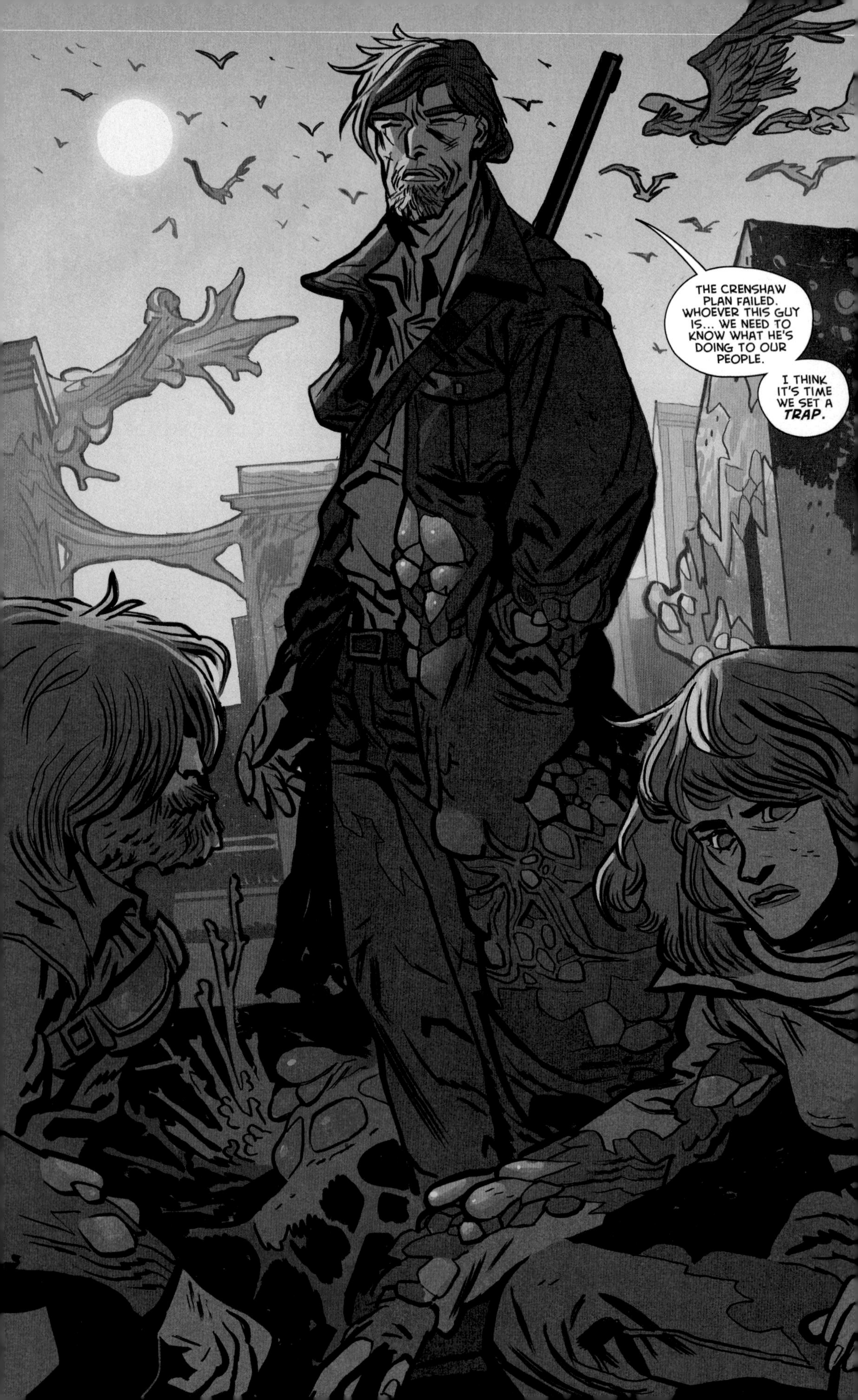
THE CRENSHAW PLAN FAILED. WHOEVER THIS GUY IS... WE NEED TO KNOW WHAT HE'S DOING TO OUR PEOPLE.
I THINK IT'S TIME WE SET A *TRAP*.

OBLIVION SONG ™

SEND MAIL TO
OBLIVIONSONG@SKYBOUND.COM

o o o o o o o o o o o o o

Let me tell you something you should already know about me at this point: I love doing new things. To me, nothing is more exciting than diving into a new world, starting off a new journey and getting to know new characters. It's the thing that keeps me creatively driven enough to write four thousand issues of THE WALKING DEAD. That long run doesn't happen without me constantly stretching my legs on something new.

Which brings us to the book you now hold in your hands, OBLIVION SONG.

I got the initial nugget for this idea nearly a decade ago. That idea would grow and evolve and change (and I believe improve) over the years as I'd add new elements and see it in new angles. The opening scene of this issue is something I'd think over often as I was drifting off to sleep, or staring at the back of a seat on an airplane. This soldier with his malfunctioning belt having to stab himself with his own magic bullet to escape the jaws of an unknown creature. I would often wonder when I was going to get around to telling that story... what was I waiting for?

I was waiting for Lorenzo De Felici.

As with most great things in my life, I owe Cory Walker for the discovery of Lorenzo. Cory scours the internet for the best of art things, and had tipped me off to Lorenzo's online portfolio a number of years ago. This led to me essentially cyberstalking the poor guy as I'd wait for his new posts, and I'd often spend a few minutes here or there scrolling back through his archive of art while I was supposed to be looking at a monitor on set or writing a letters column or something.

I eventually found a window of time to start something new, and built up the nerve to contact Lorenzo. From there that nameless soldier became Nathan Cole and that unknown creature took shape and the dystopian landscape I was exploring became Oblivion and the series we were working on became OBLIVION SONG. Creating this series with Lorenzo has been an amazing experience. His creativity knows no bounds. His work, along with colorist Annalisa Leoni, will continue to astound you month after month. Just you wait.

With this series, we're going to be telling a big story that is just going to get bigger as we go along. The plan is by the time you're reading issue #30, this will be a very different book, dealing with a much larger scope and scale than we currently are. But, as we take little steps in that direction from issue to issue, we'll grow into those stories organically, so you'll just be along for the ride. We're also planning on keeping things pretty fast-paced. So, there's going to be a lot of mystery and intrigue to this book, but you won't have to wait too long for questions to get answered and new questions to be presented.

More good news for comic fans: we've been working on this series for a long time in secret, so as this issue hits the shelves, we should be starting issue... #13. Yeah, that's right, we're a year ahead of schedule. Having been in comics for nearly two decades (oh, god), I've finally learned that the monthly grind is no joke, and to do a series right you need to have the breathing room to dig in and make things special. So that's what we're doing here. So don't expect any of those pesky delays you may have come to expect from other titles (some by me, sadly).

So, thank you, from the bottom of my heart, for being an adventurous reader and trying something new. I hope you grow to love Nathan Cole and the rest of the cast as much as we do. And, trust me, no matter where you think this story is going... you're probably wrong.

Buckle up, things are about to get awesome.

-Robert Kirkman
Backwoods, CA
February 2018

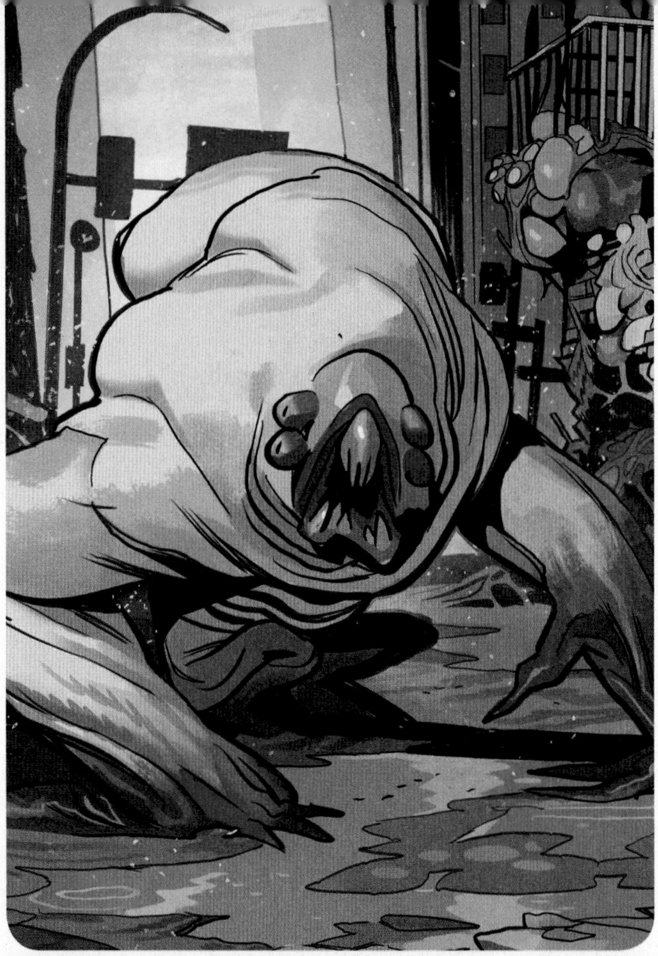

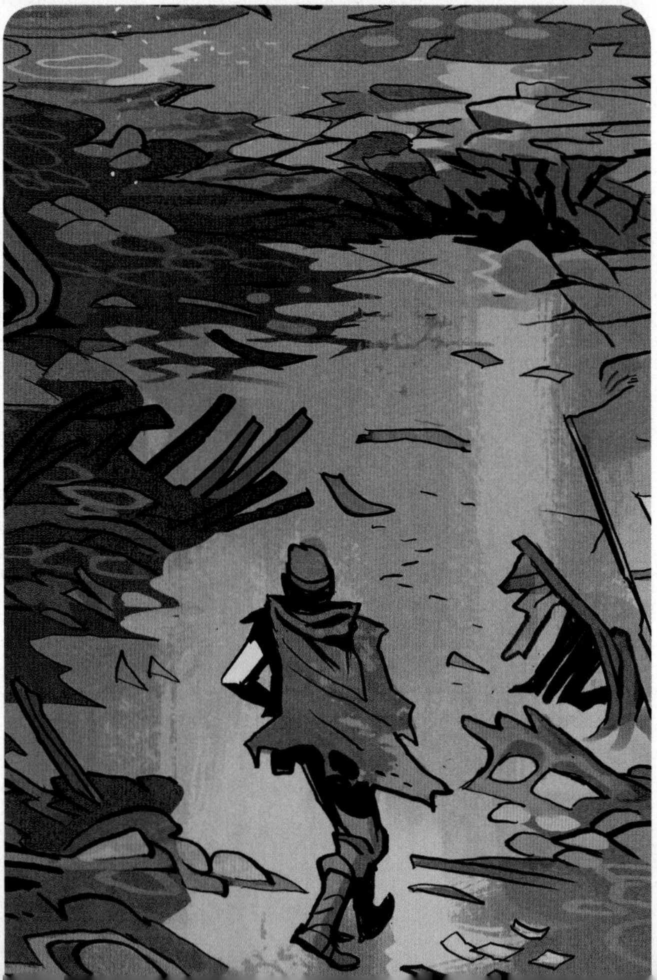

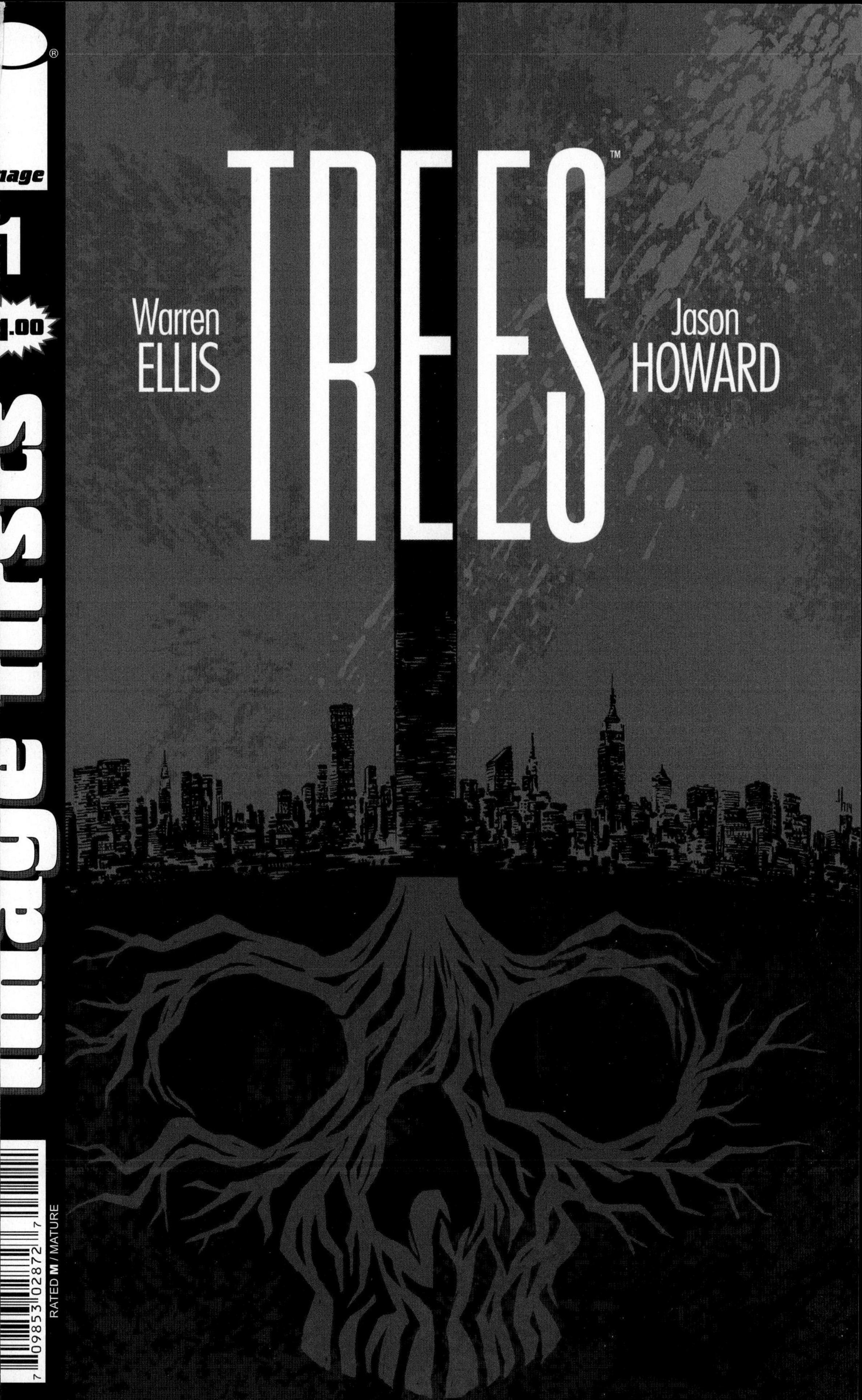

image firsts
1
TREES™
Warren
ELLIS
Jason
HOWARD
RATED M / MATURE

TREES

WARREN ELLIS
writer

JASON HOWARD
artist

FONOGRAFIKS
letterer

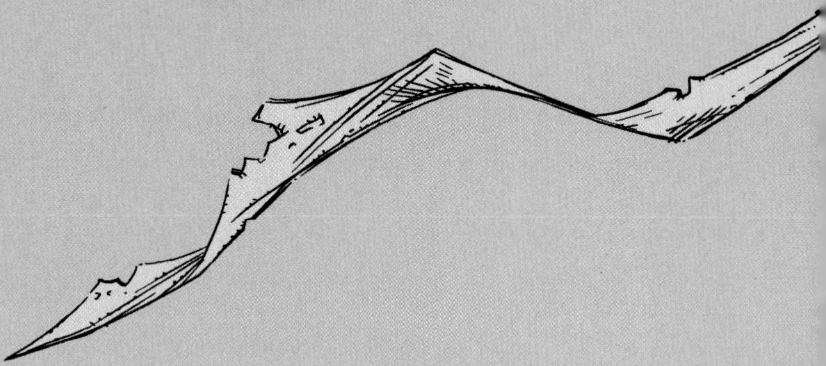

imagecomics.com

IMAGE COMICS, INC.

Robert Kirkman CHIEF OPERATING OFFICER · Erik Larsen CHIEF FINANCIAL OFFICER · Todd McFarlane PRESIDENT

Marc Silvestri CHIEF EXECUTIVE OFFICER · Jim Valentino VICE PRESIDENT

Eric Stephenson PUBLISHER/CHIEF CREATIVE OFFICER · Jeff Boison DIRECTOR OF PUBLISHING PLANNING & BOOK TRADE SALES

Chris Ross DIRECTOR OF DIGITAL SALES · Jeff Stang DIRECTOR OF DIRECT MARKET SALES · Kat Salazar DIRECTOR OF PR & MARKETING

Drew Gill ART DIRECTOR · Heather Doornink PRODUCTION DIRECTOR · Nicole Lapalme CONTROLLER

imagecomics.com

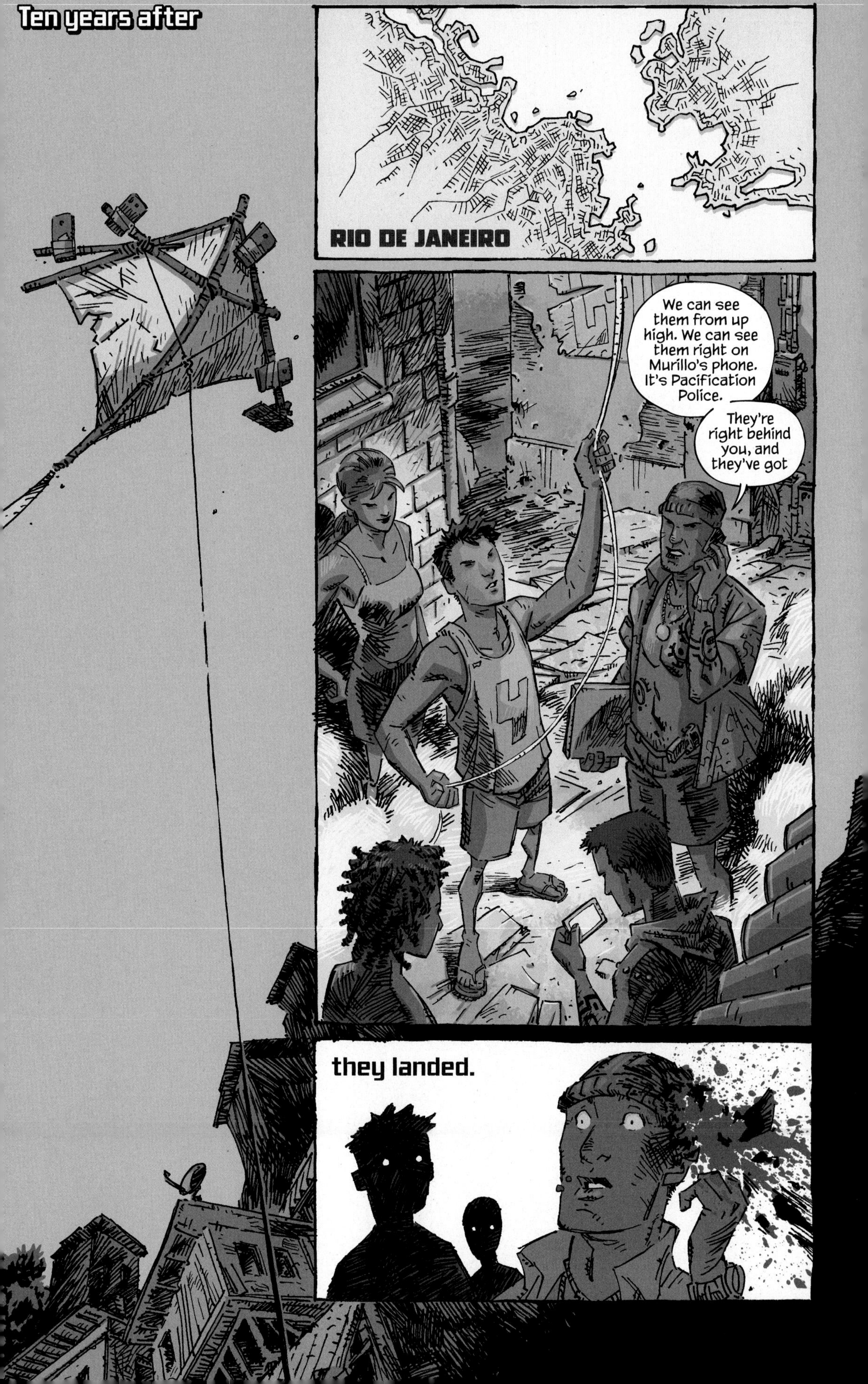
Ten years after
RIO DE JANEIRO
We can see them from up high. We can see them right on Murillo's phone. It's Pacification Police.
They're right behind you, and they've got
they landed.

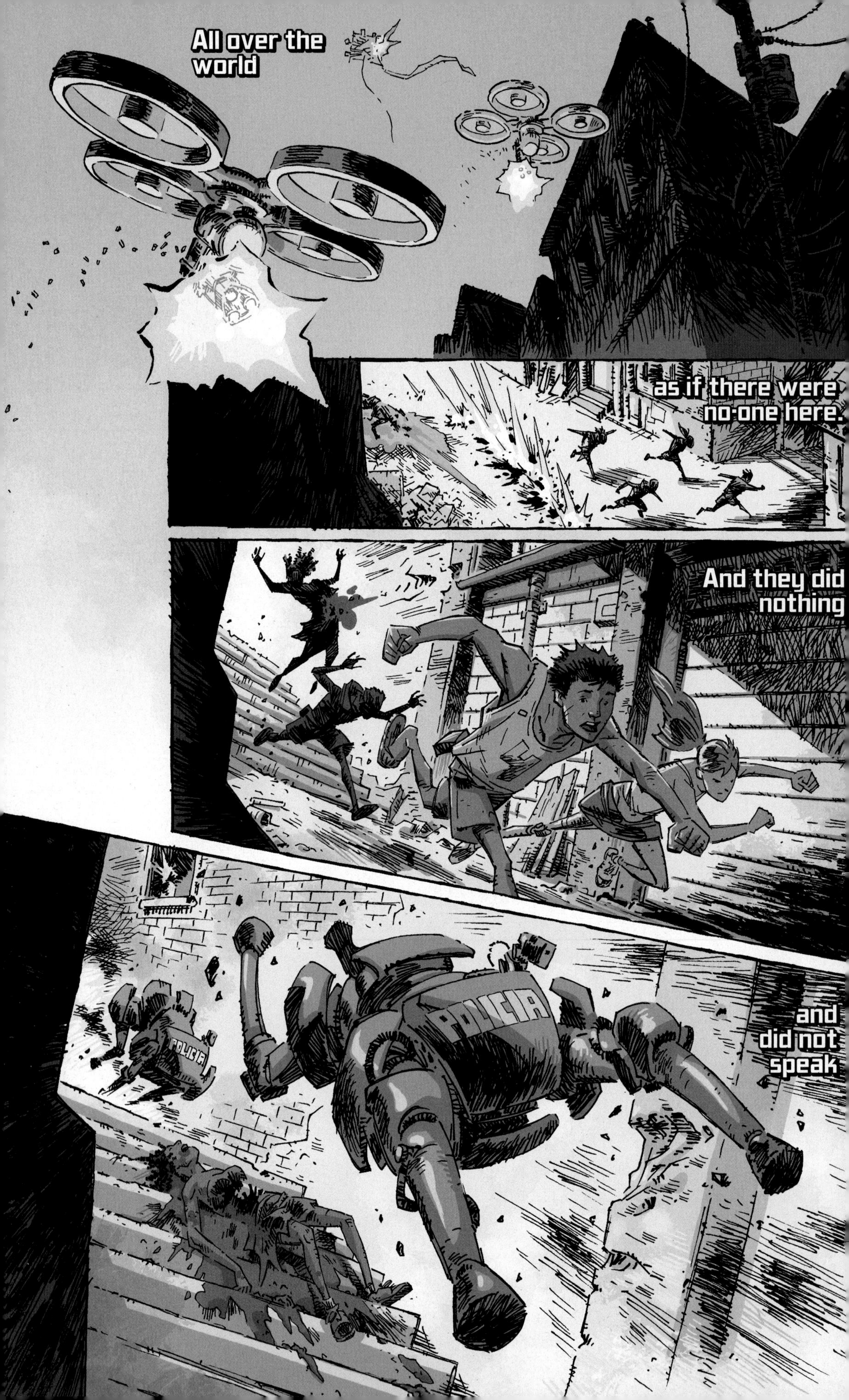
All over the world
as if there were no-one here.
And they did nothing
and did not speak
POLICIA
POLICIA

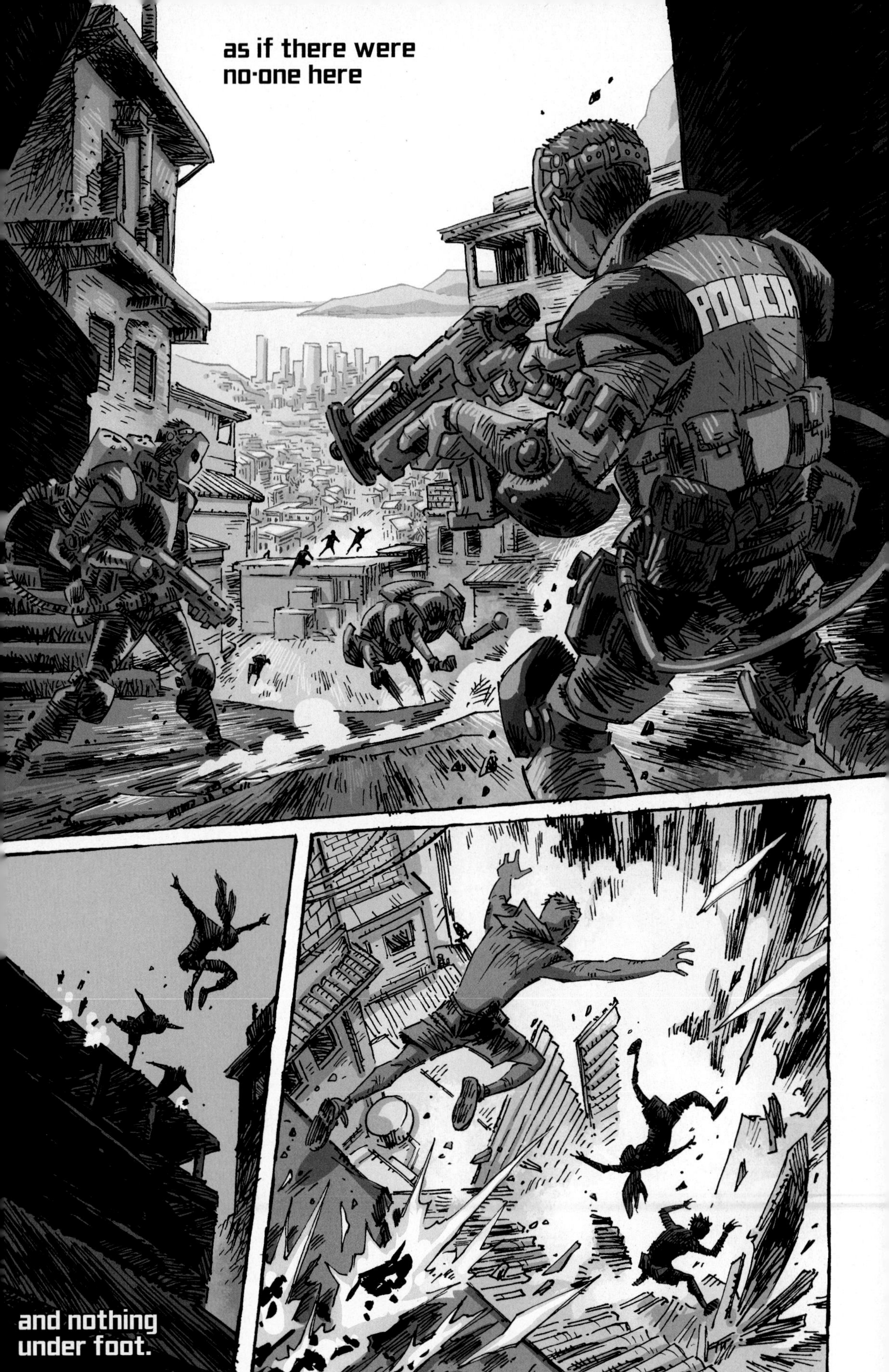
as if there were
no-one here
POLICIA
and nothing
under foot.

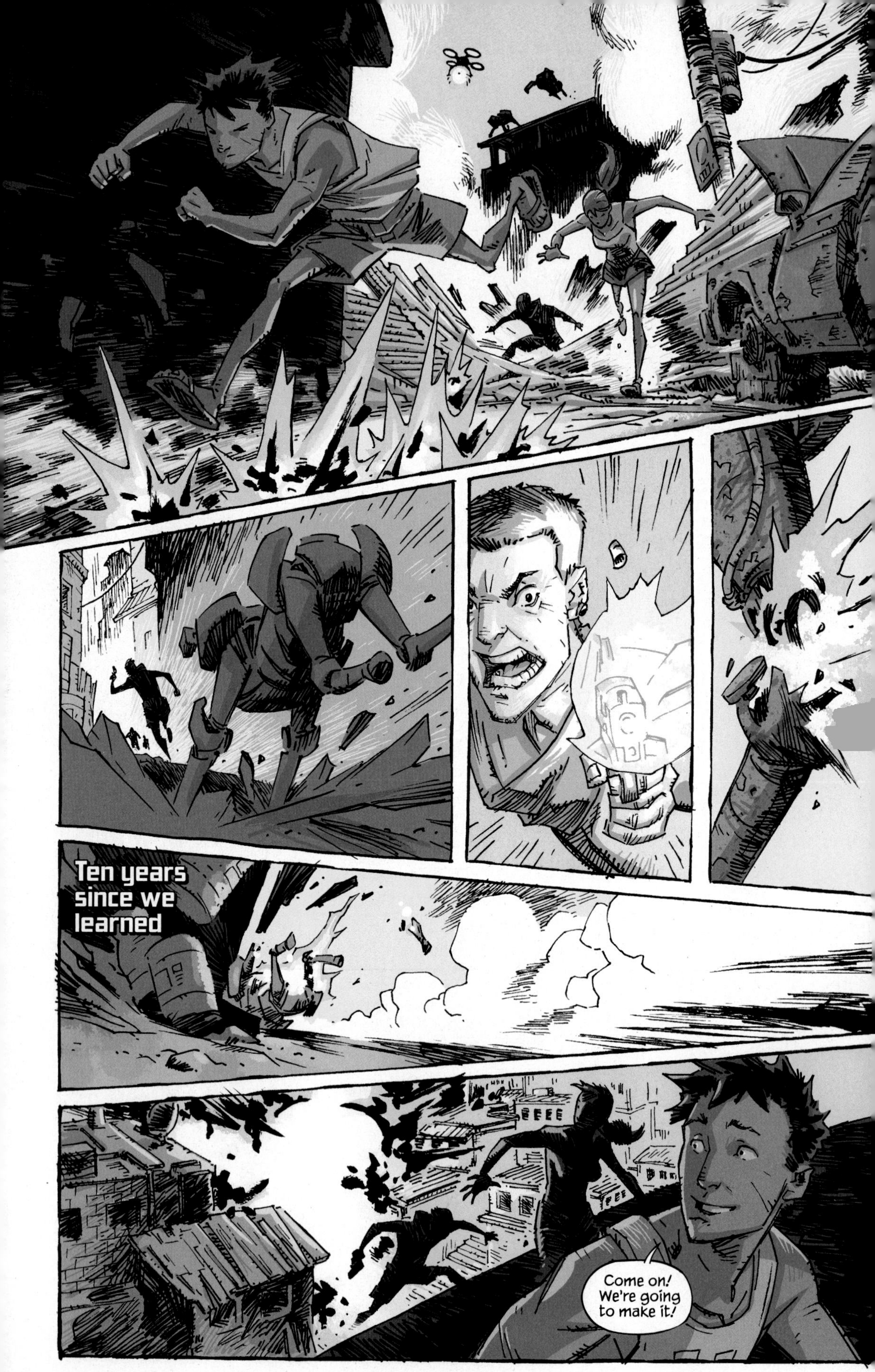
Ten years since we learned
Come on! We're going to make it!

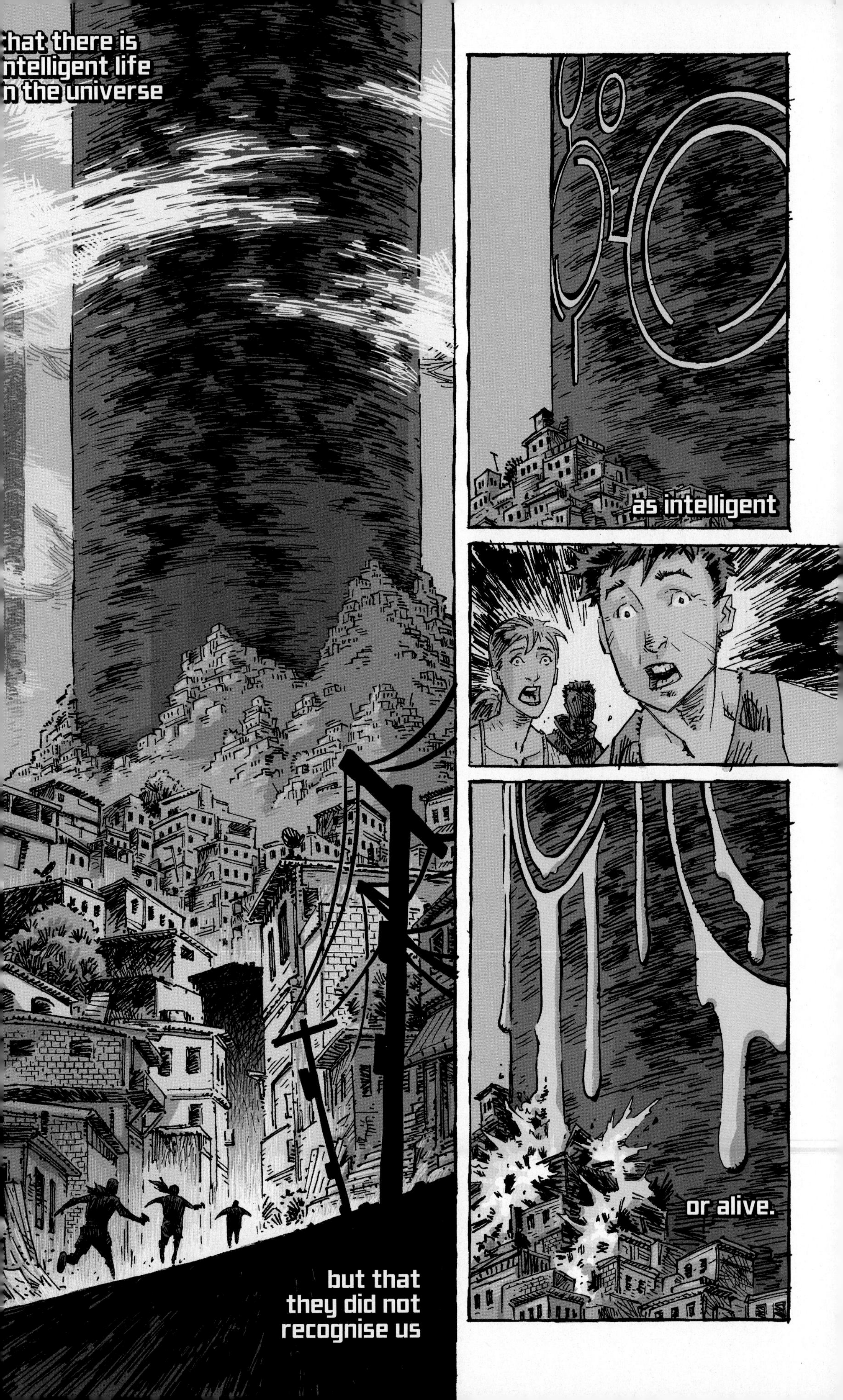
:hat there is
ntelligent life
n the universe
but that
they did not
recognise us
as intelligent
or alive.

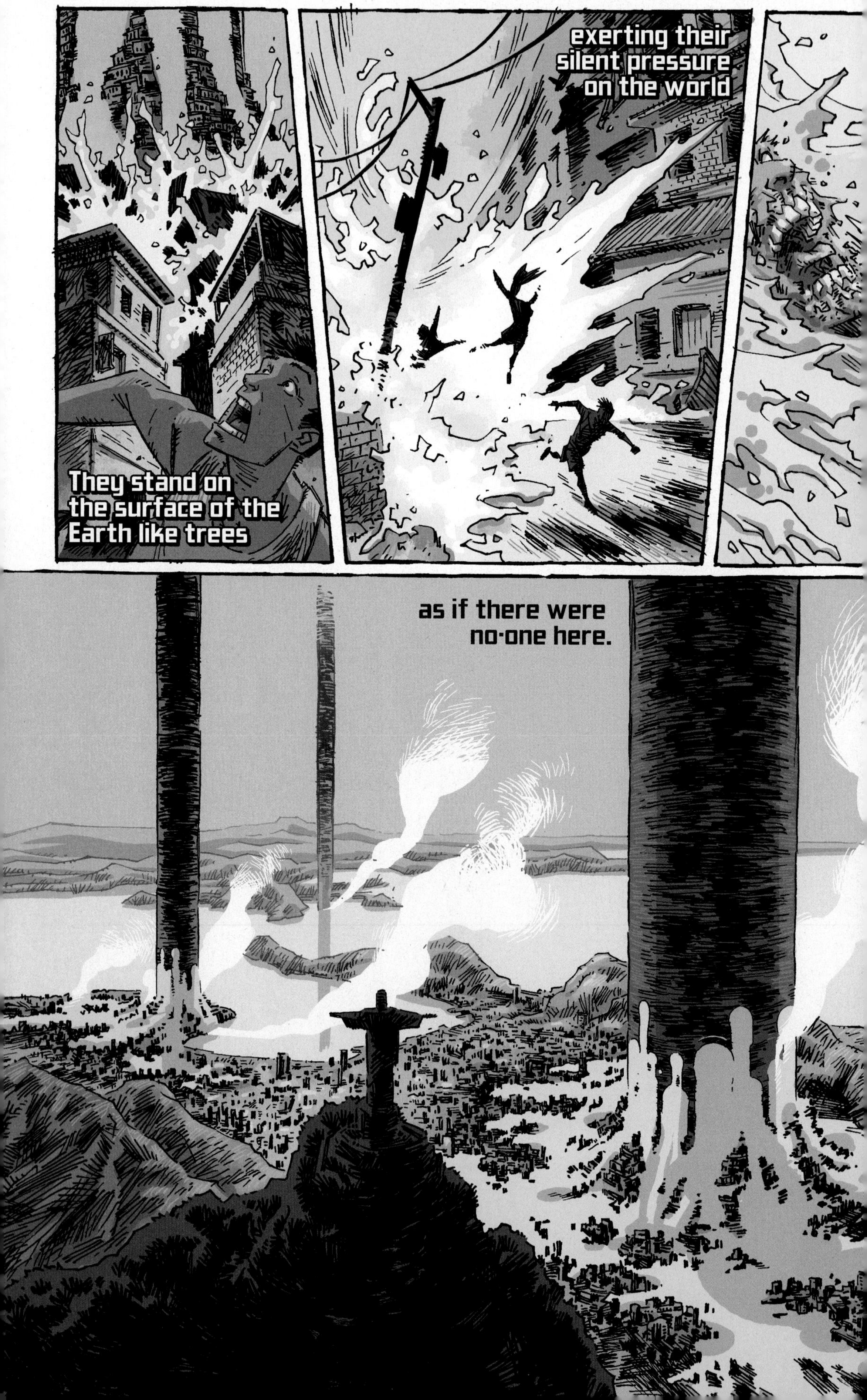
They stand on
the surface of the
Earth like trees
exerting their
silent pressure
on the world
as if there were
no-one here.

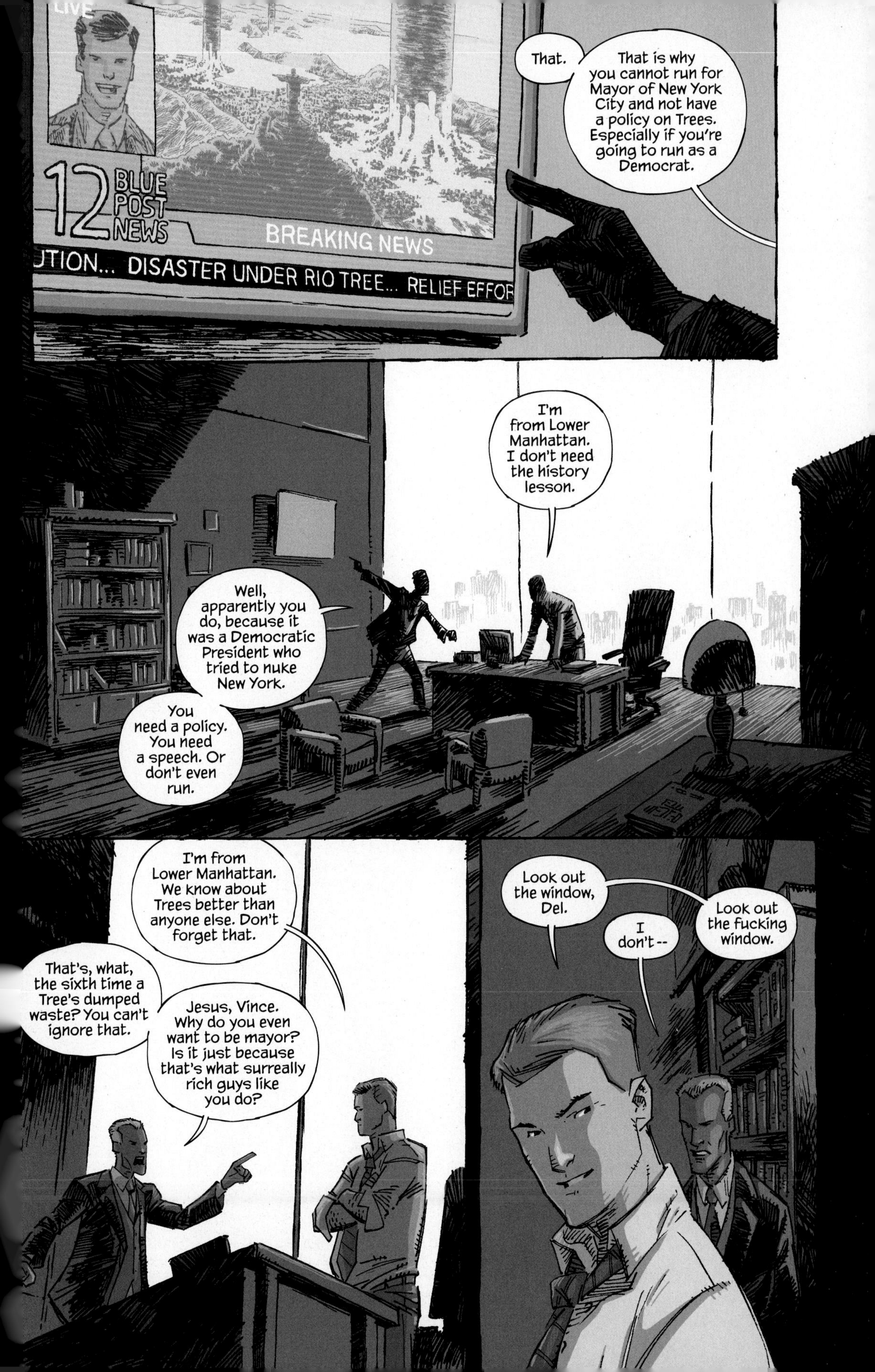
LIVE
12 BLUE POST NEWS
BREAKING NEWS
UTION... DISASTER UNDER RIO TREE... RELIEF EFFOR
That.
That is why you cannot run for Mayor of New York City and not have a policy on Trees. Especially if you're going to run as a Democrat.
I'm from Lower Manhattan. I don't need the history lesson.
Well, apparently you do, because it was a Democratic President who tried to nuke New York.
You need a policy. You need a speech. Or don't even run.
I'm from Lower Manhattan. We know about Trees better than anyone else. Don't forget that.
That's, what, the sixth time a Tree's dumped waste? You can't ignore that.
Jesus, Vince. Why do you even want to be mayor? Is it just because that's what surreally rich guys like you do?
Look out the window, Del.
I don't --
Look out the fucking window.

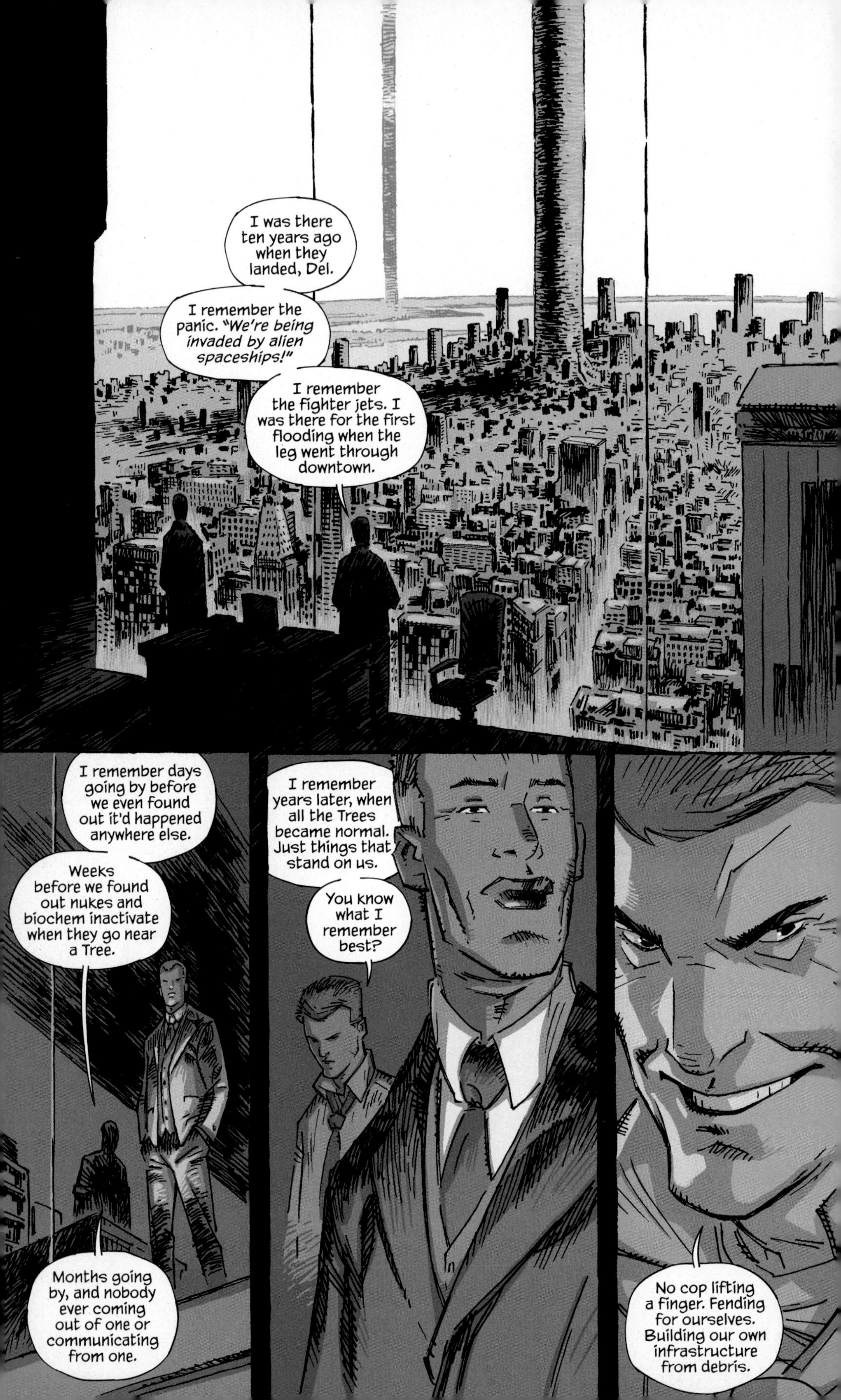
I was there ten years ago when they landed, Del.
I remember the panic. *"We're being invaded by alien spaceships!"*
I remember the fighter jets. I was there for the first flooding when the leg went through downtown.
I remember days going by before we even found out it'd happened anywhere else.
Weeks before we found out nukes and biochem inactivate when they go near a Tree.
Months going by, and nobody ever coming out of one or communicating from one.
I remember years later, when all the Trees became normal. Just things that stand on us.
You know what I remember best?
No cop lifting a finger. Fending for ourselves. Building our own infrastructure from debris.

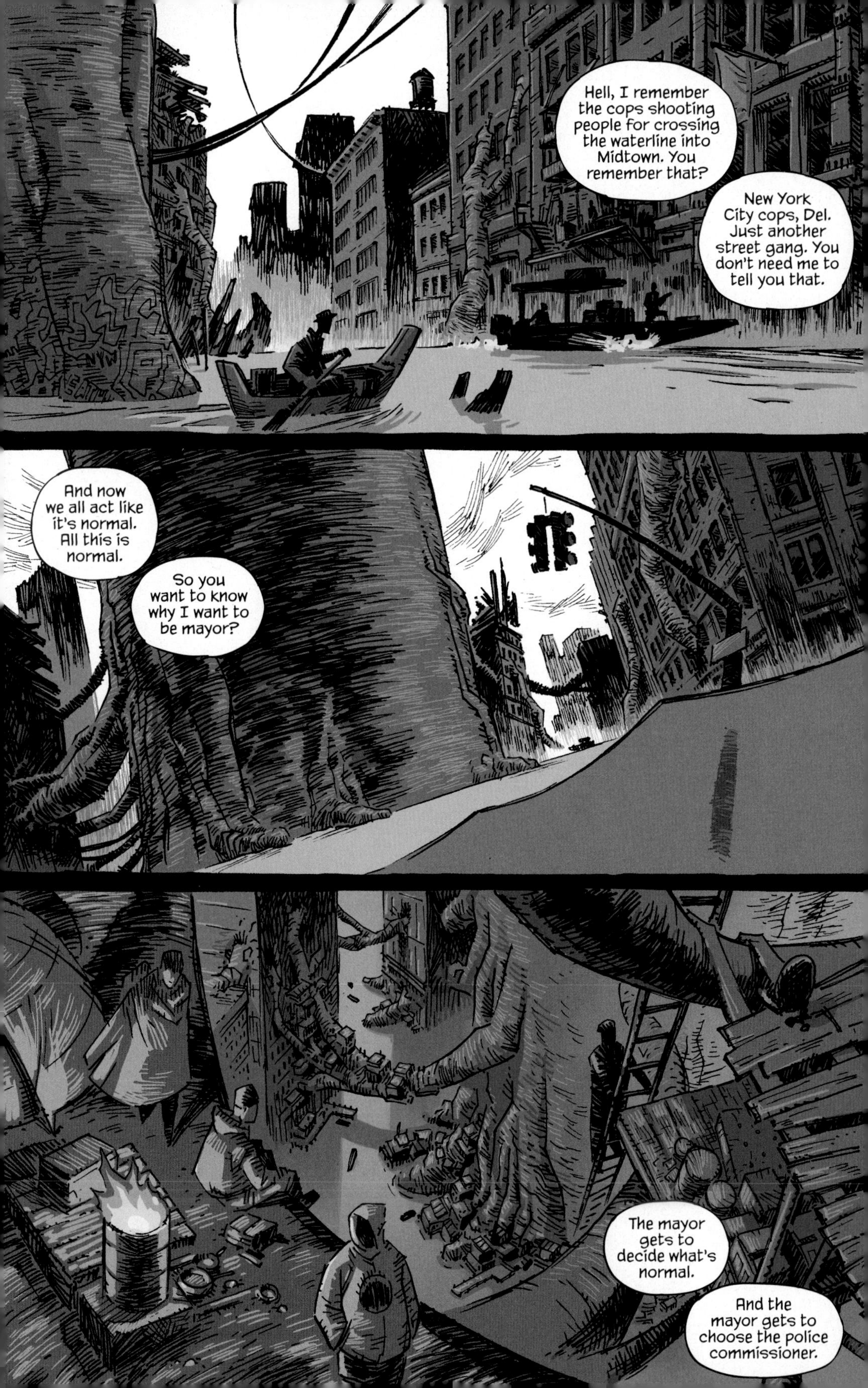
Hell, I remember the cops shooting people for crossing the waterline into Midtown. You remember that?
New York City cops, Del. Just another street gang. You don't need me to tell you that.
And now we all act like it's normal. All this is normal.
So you want to know why I want to be mayor?
The mayor gets to decide what's normal.
And the mayor gets to choose the police commissioner.

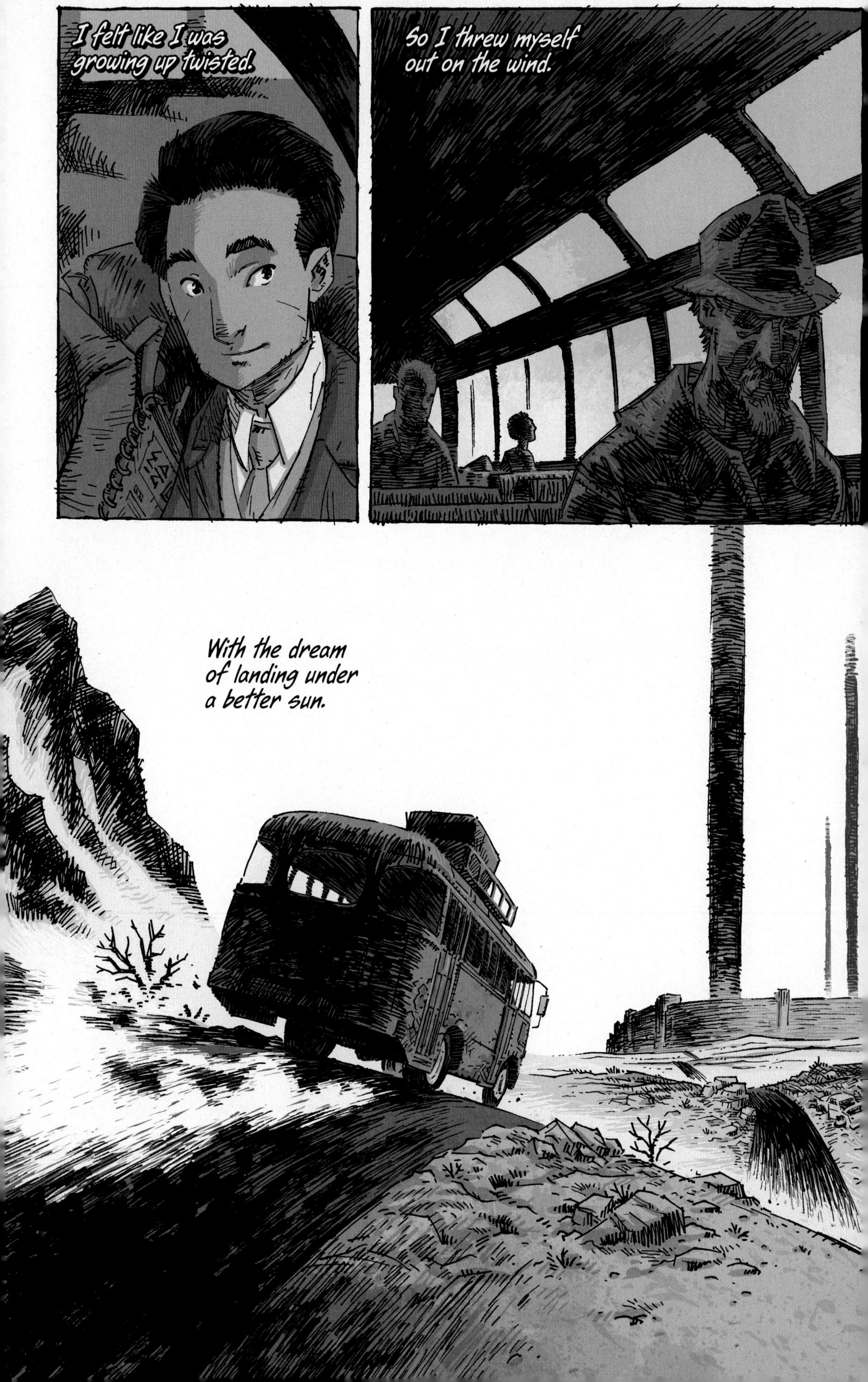
I felt like I was growing up twisted.
So I threw myself out on the wind.
With the dream of landing under a better sun.

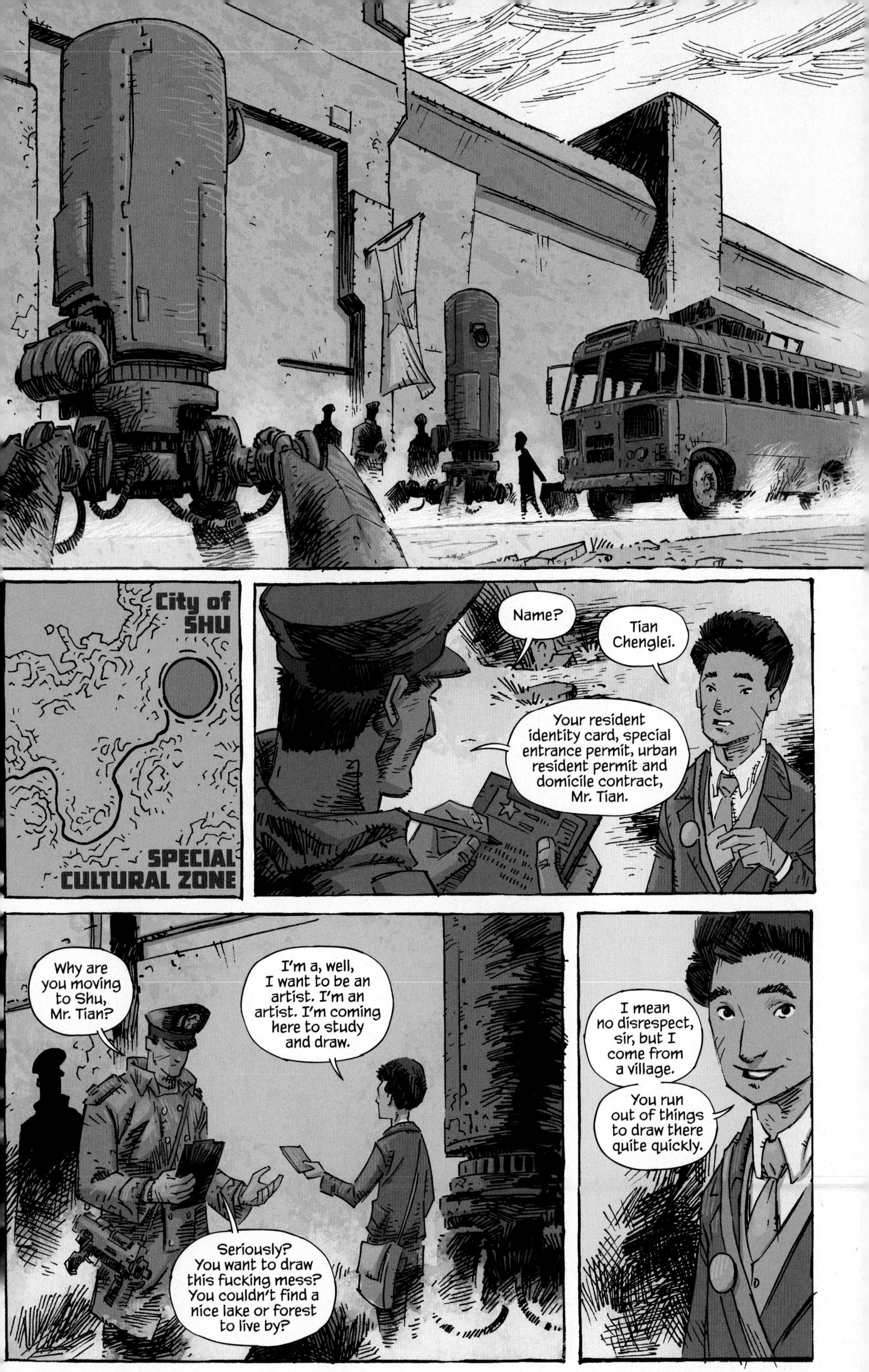
City of SHU
SPECIAL CULTURAL ZONE
Name?
Tian Chenglei.
Your resident identity card, special entrance permit, urban resident permit and domicile contract, Mr. Tian.
Why are you moving to Shu, Mr. Tian?
I'm a, well, I want to be an artist. I'm an artist. I'm coming here to study and draw.
Seriously? You want to draw this fucking mess? You couldn't find a nice lake or forest to live by?
I mean no disrespect, sir, but I come from a village.
You run out of things to draw there quite quickly.

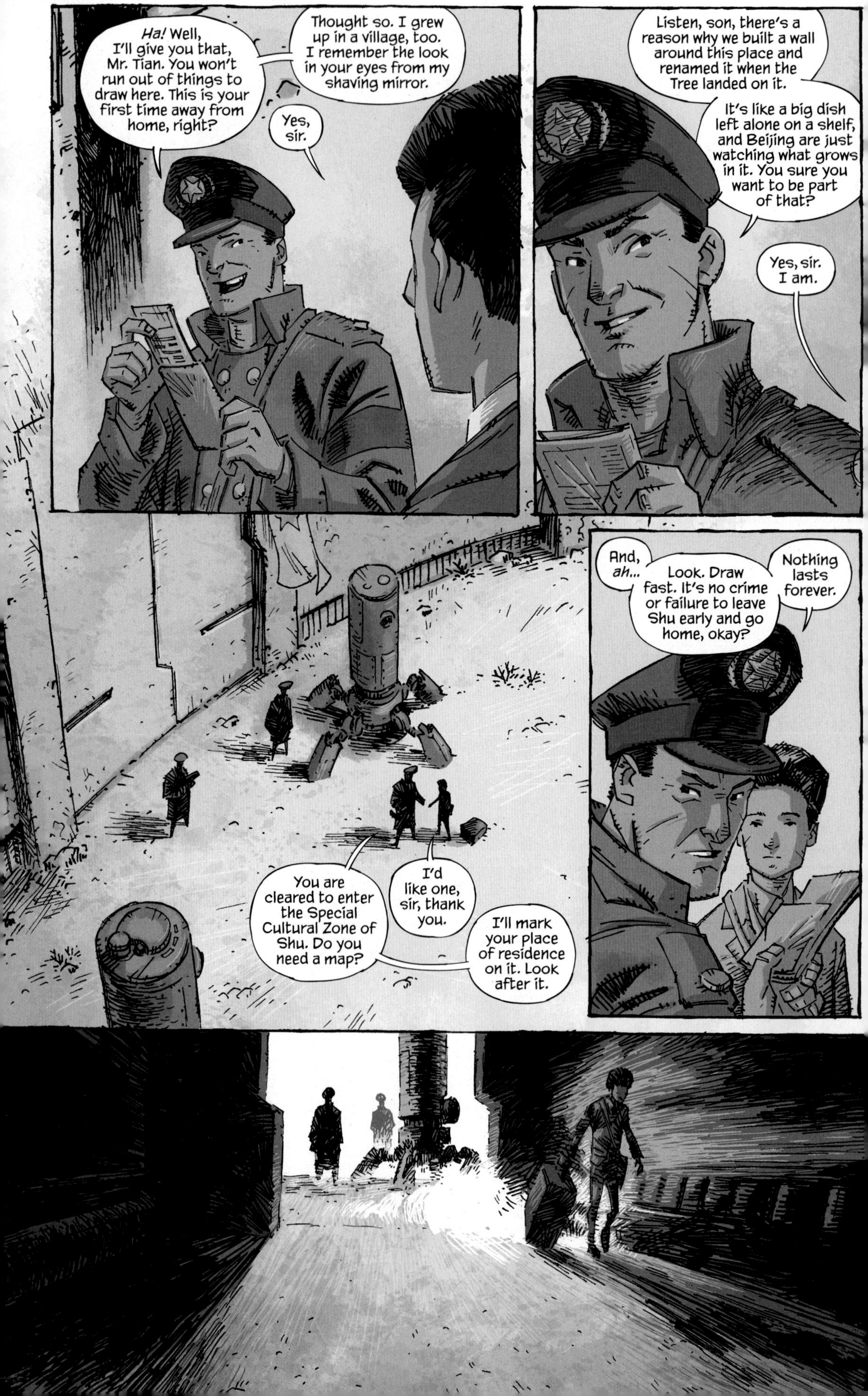

Ha! Well, I'll give you that, Mr. Tian. You won't run out of things to draw here. This is your first time away from home, right?
Yes, sir.
Thought so. I grew up in a village, too. I remember the look in your eyes from my shaving mirror.
Listen, son, there's a reason why we built a wall around this place and renamed it when the Tree landed on it.
It's like a big dish left alone on a shelf, and Beijing are just watching what grows in it. You sure you want to be part of that?
Yes, sir. I am.
You are cleared to enter the Special Cultural Zone of Shu. Do you need a map?
I'd like one, sir, thank you.
I'll mark your place of residence on it. Look after it.
And, ah...
Look. Draw fast. It's no crime or failure to leave Shu early and go home, okay?
Nothing lasts forever.

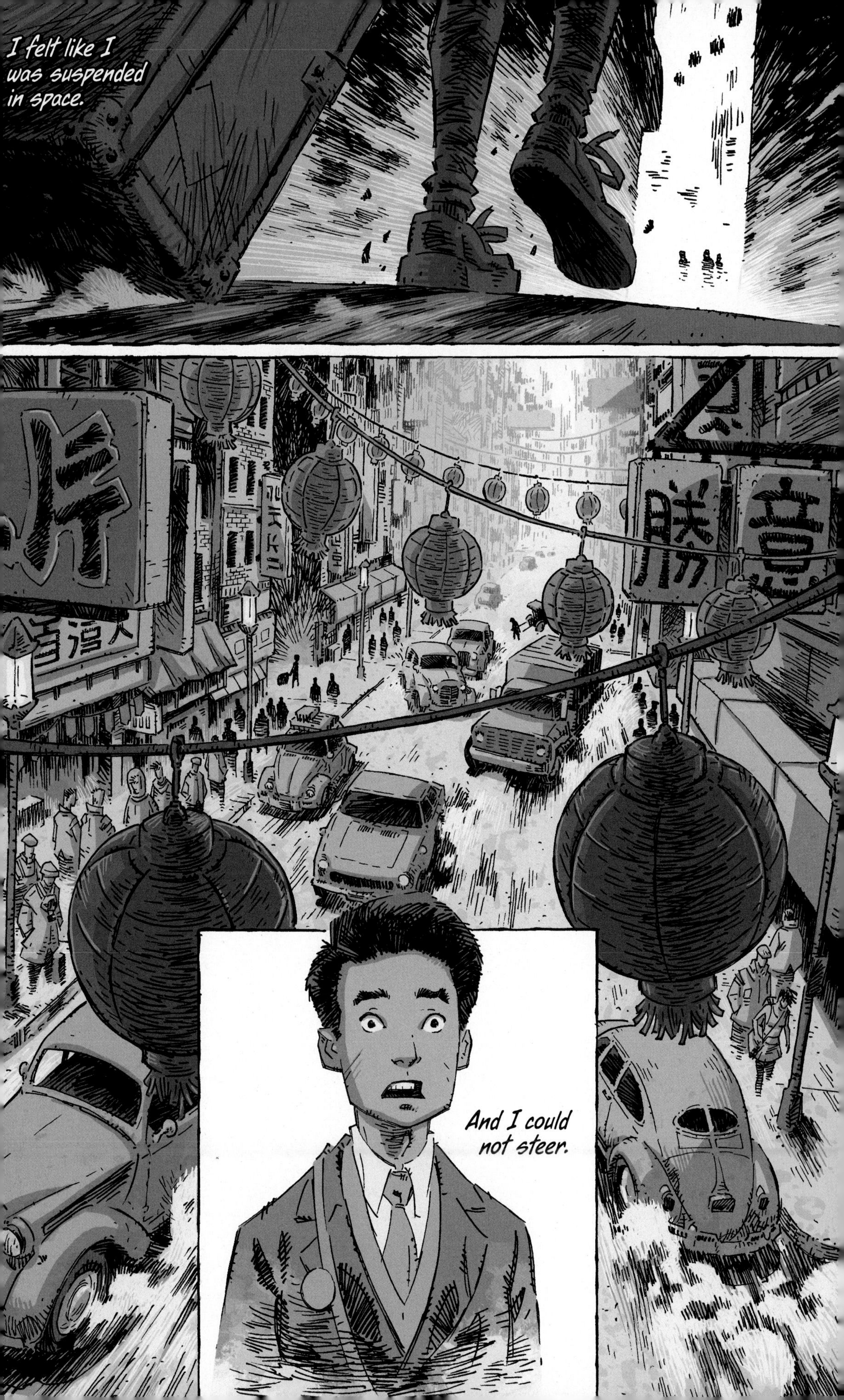
I felt like I was suspended in space.
And I could not steer.

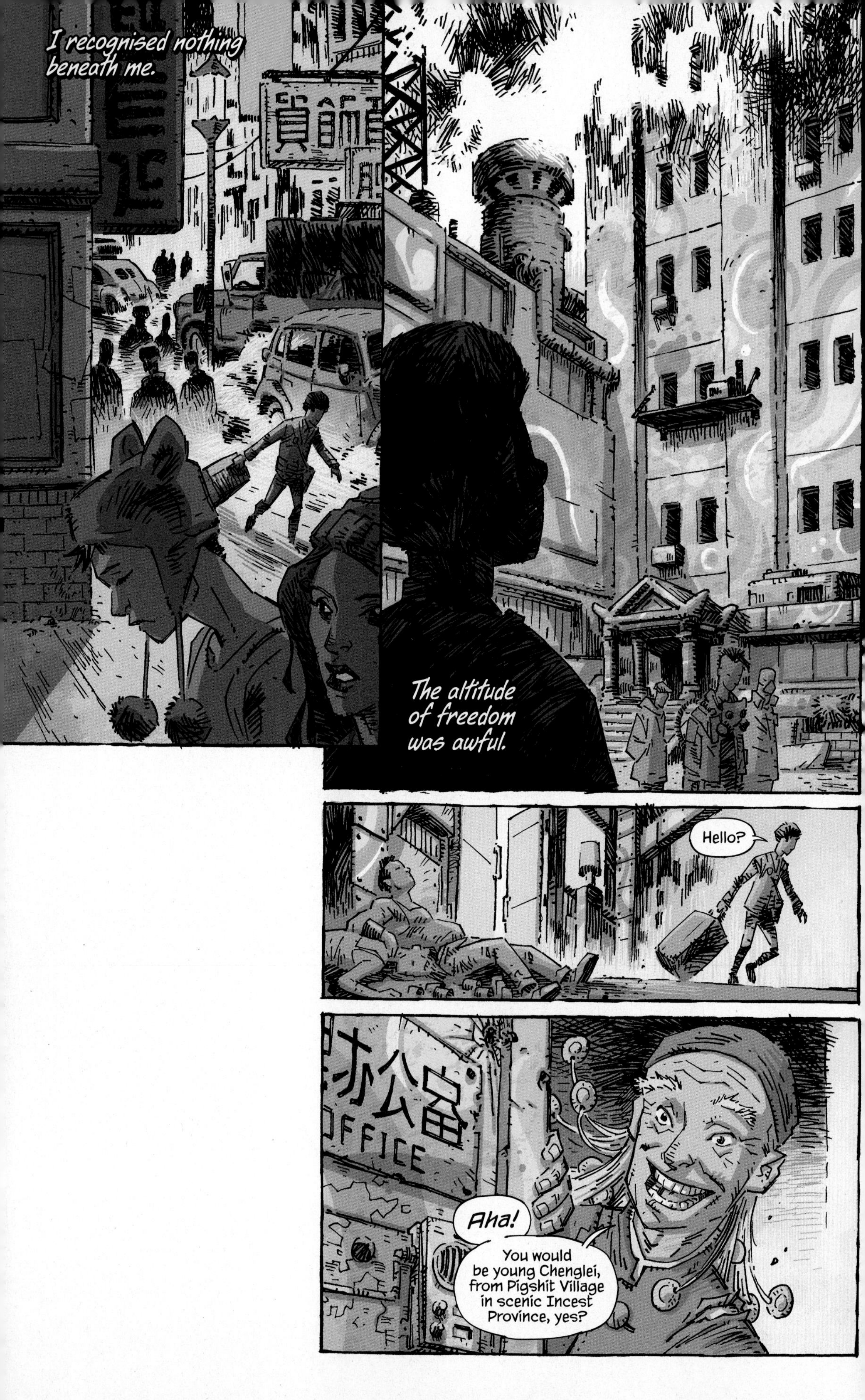
I recognised nothing beneath me.
The altitude of freedom was awful.
Hello?
Aha!
You would be young Chenglei, from Pigshit Village in scenic Incest Province, yes?
OFFICE

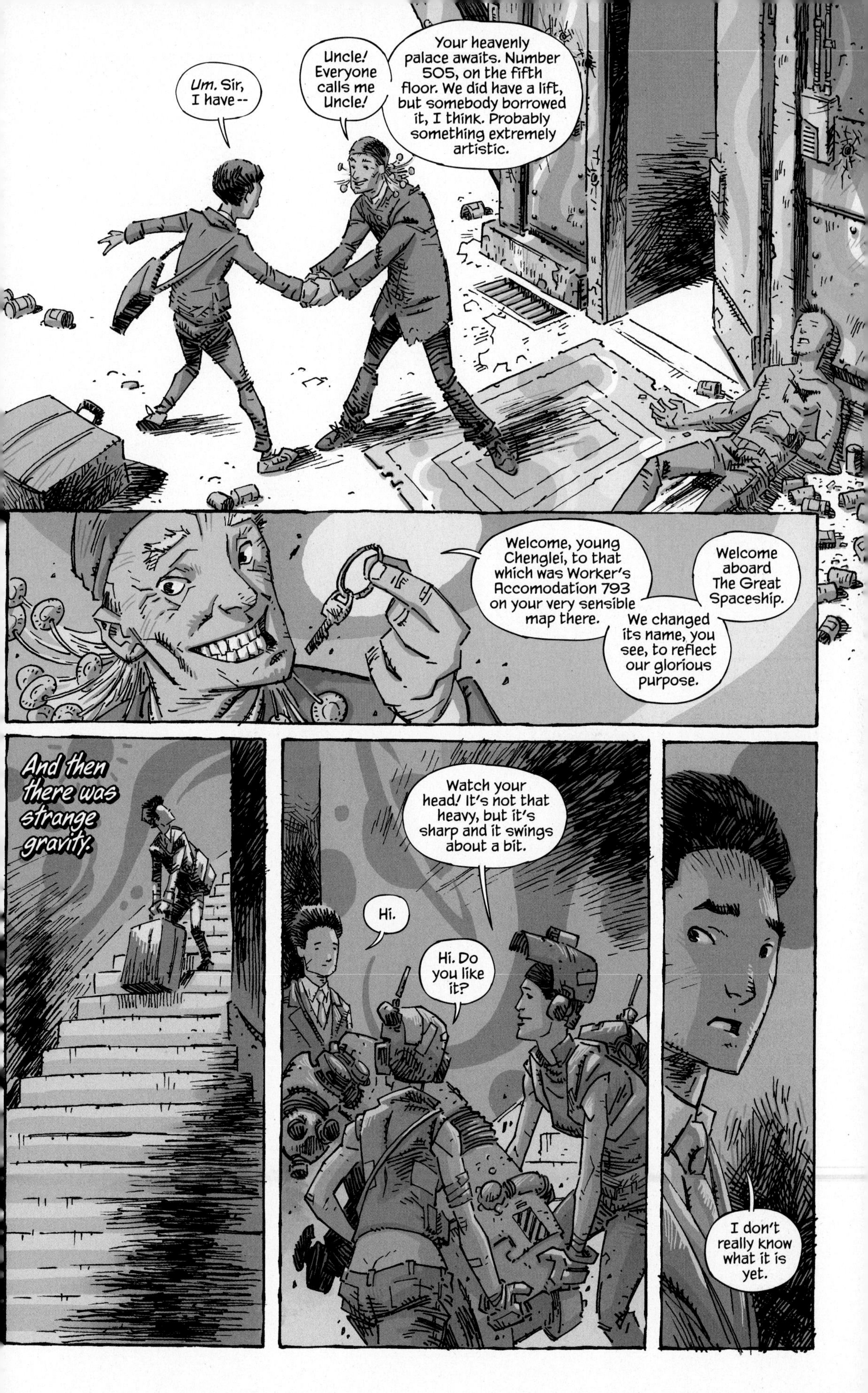
Um. Sir, I have --
Uncle! Everyone calls me Uncle!
Your heavenly palace awaits. Number 505, on the fifth floor. We did have a lift, but somebody borrowed it, I think. Probably something extremely artistic.
Welcome, young Chenglei, to that which was Worker's Accomodation 793 on your very sensible map there.
Welcome aboard The Great Spaceship.
We changed its name, you see, to reflect our glorious purpose.
And then there was strange gravity.
Watch your head! It's not that heavy, but it's sharp and it swings about a bit.
Hi.
Hi. Do you like it?
I don't really know what it is yet.

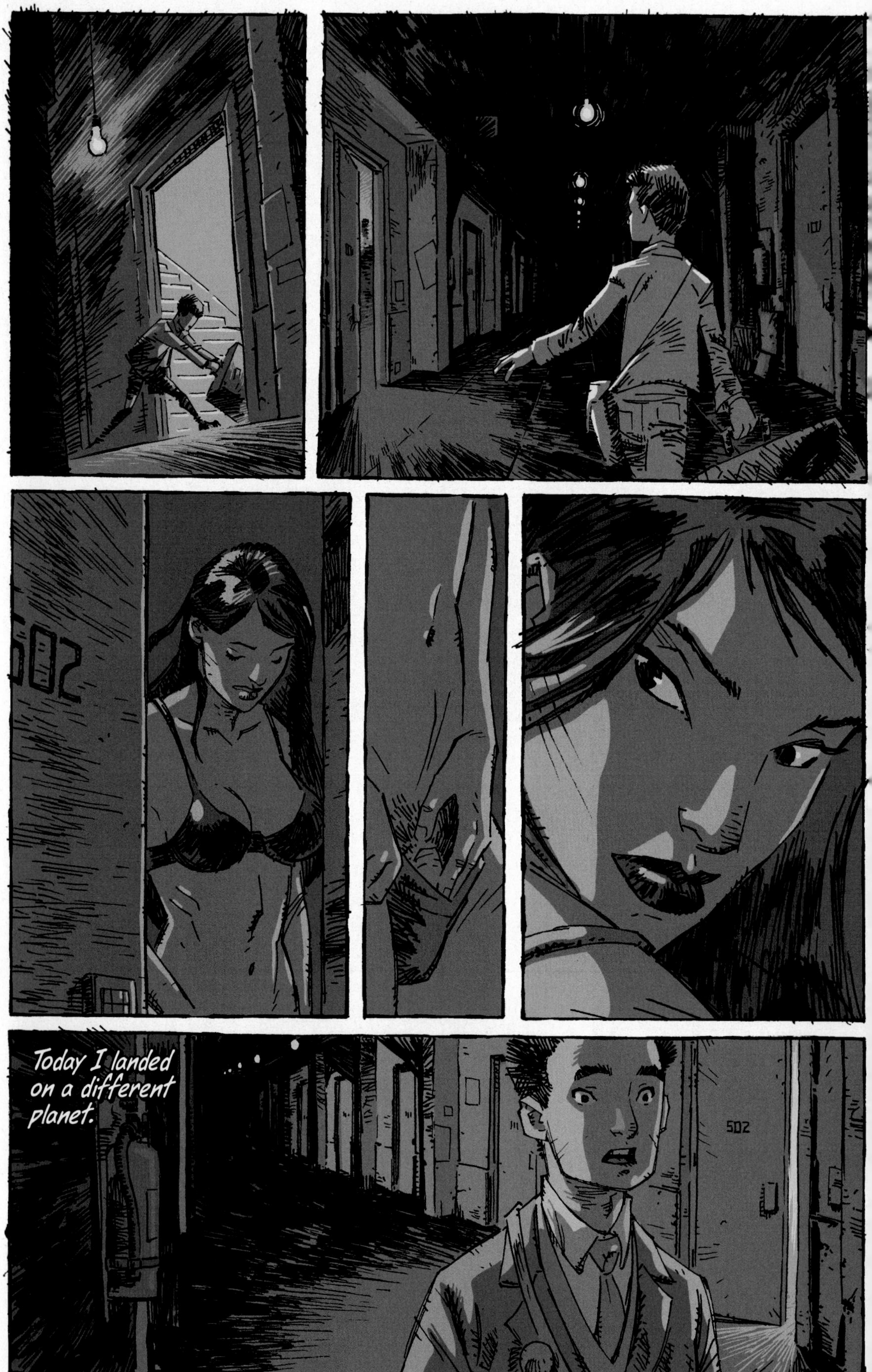
502
Today I landed on a different planet.
502

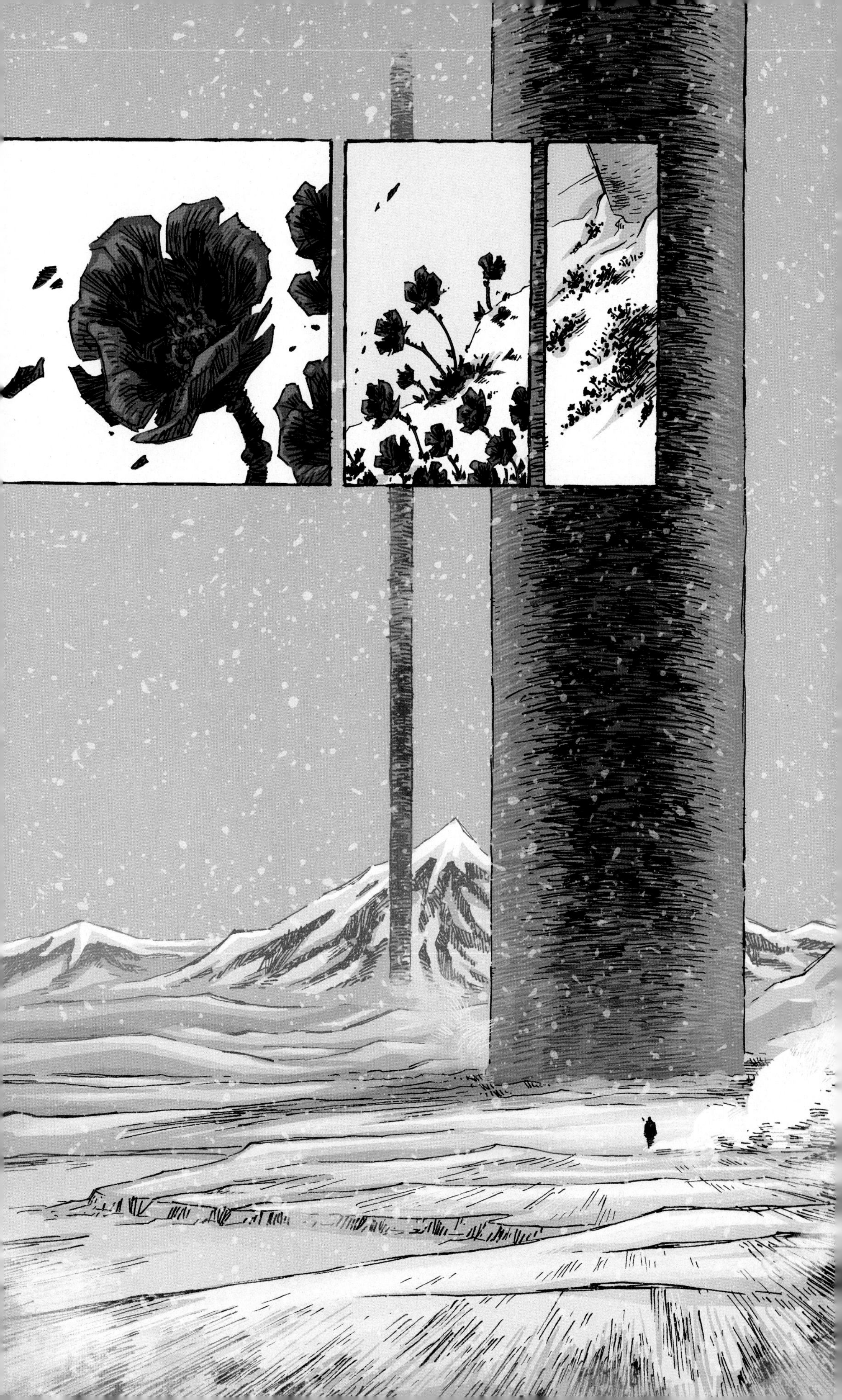

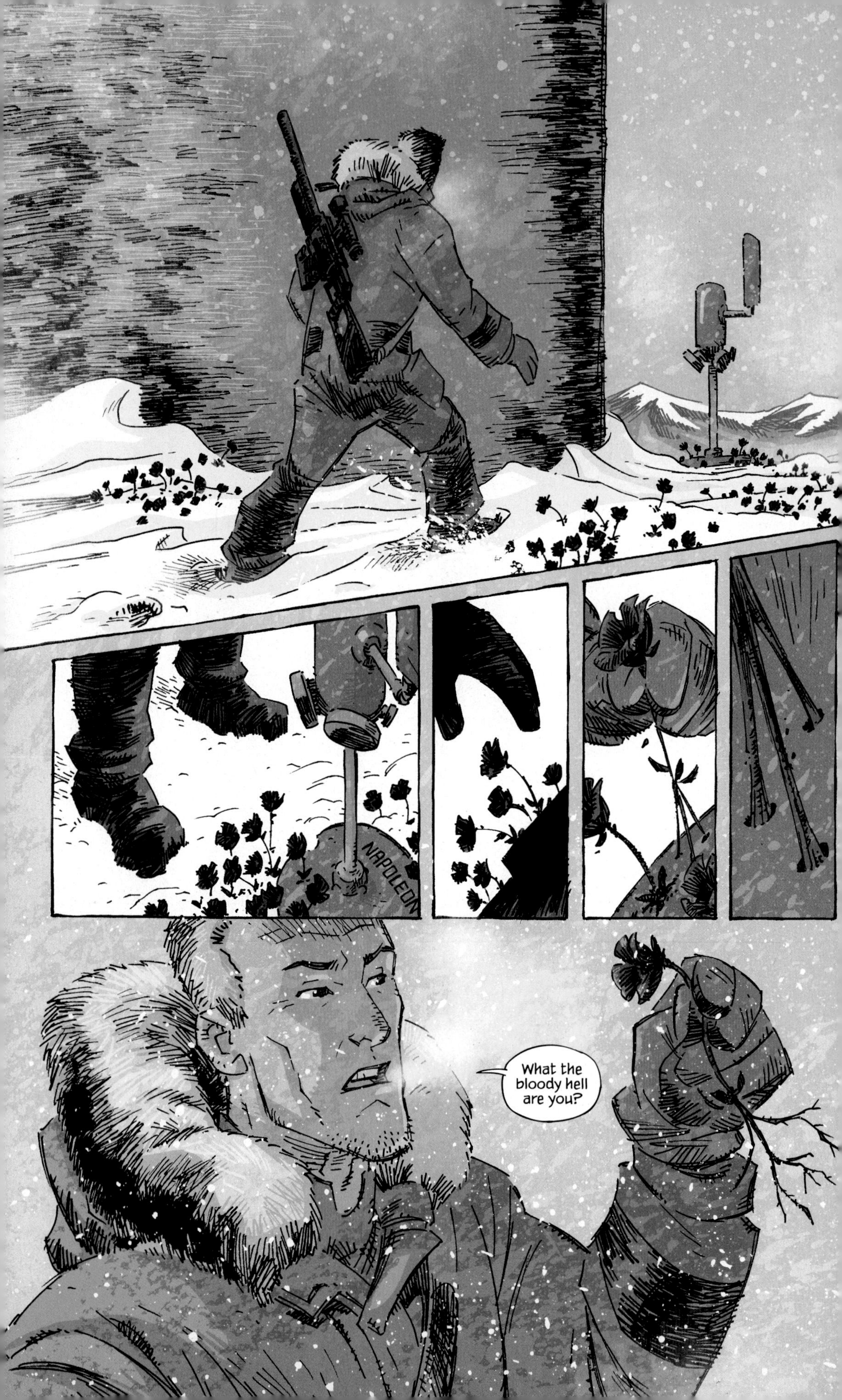
NAPOLEON
What the bloody hell are you?

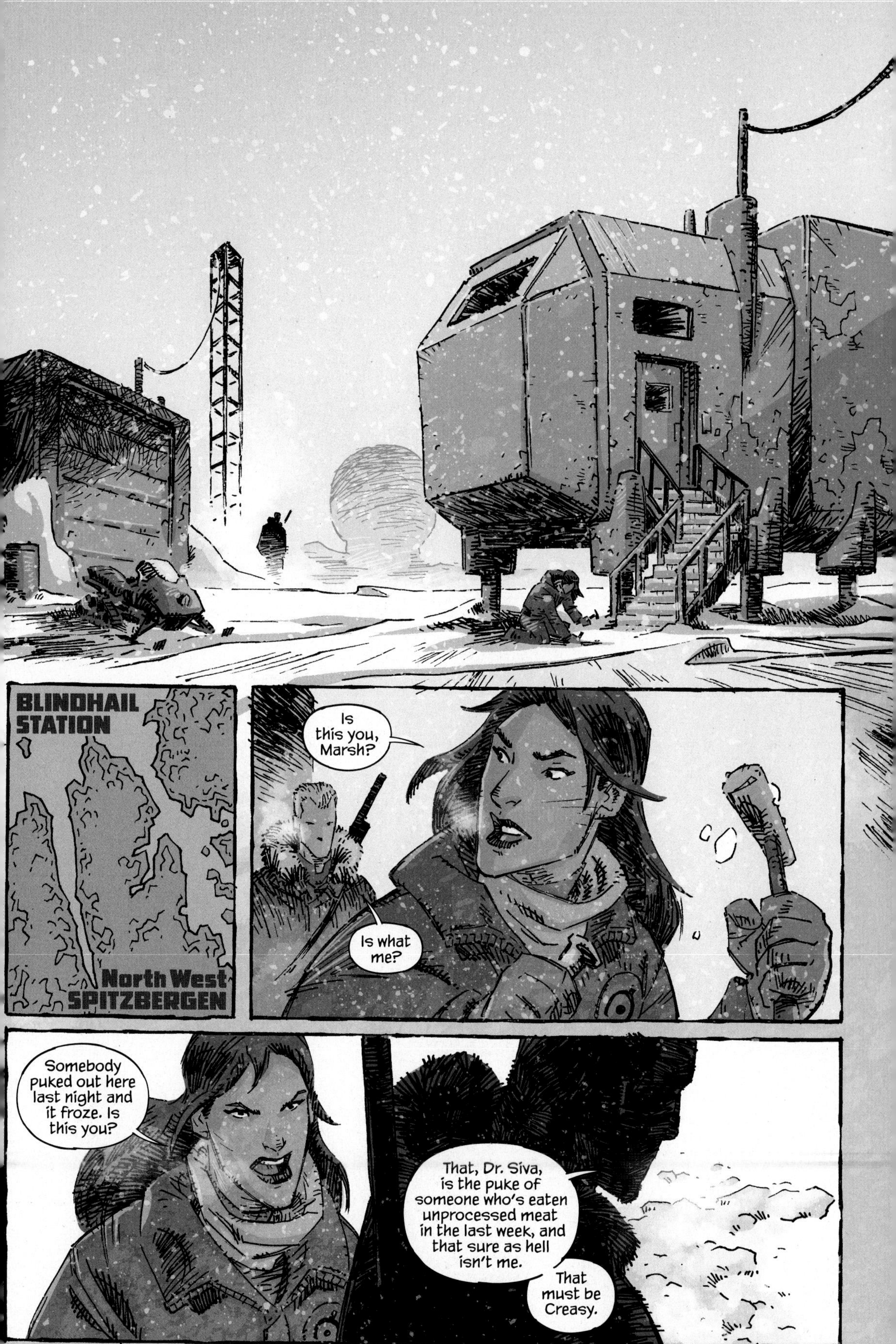
BLINDHAIL STATION
North West SPITZBERGEN
Is this you, Marsh?
Is what me?
Somebody puked out here last night and it froze. Is this you?
That, Dr. Siva, is the puke of someone who's eaten unprocessed meat in the last week, and that sure as hell isn't me.
That must be Creasy.

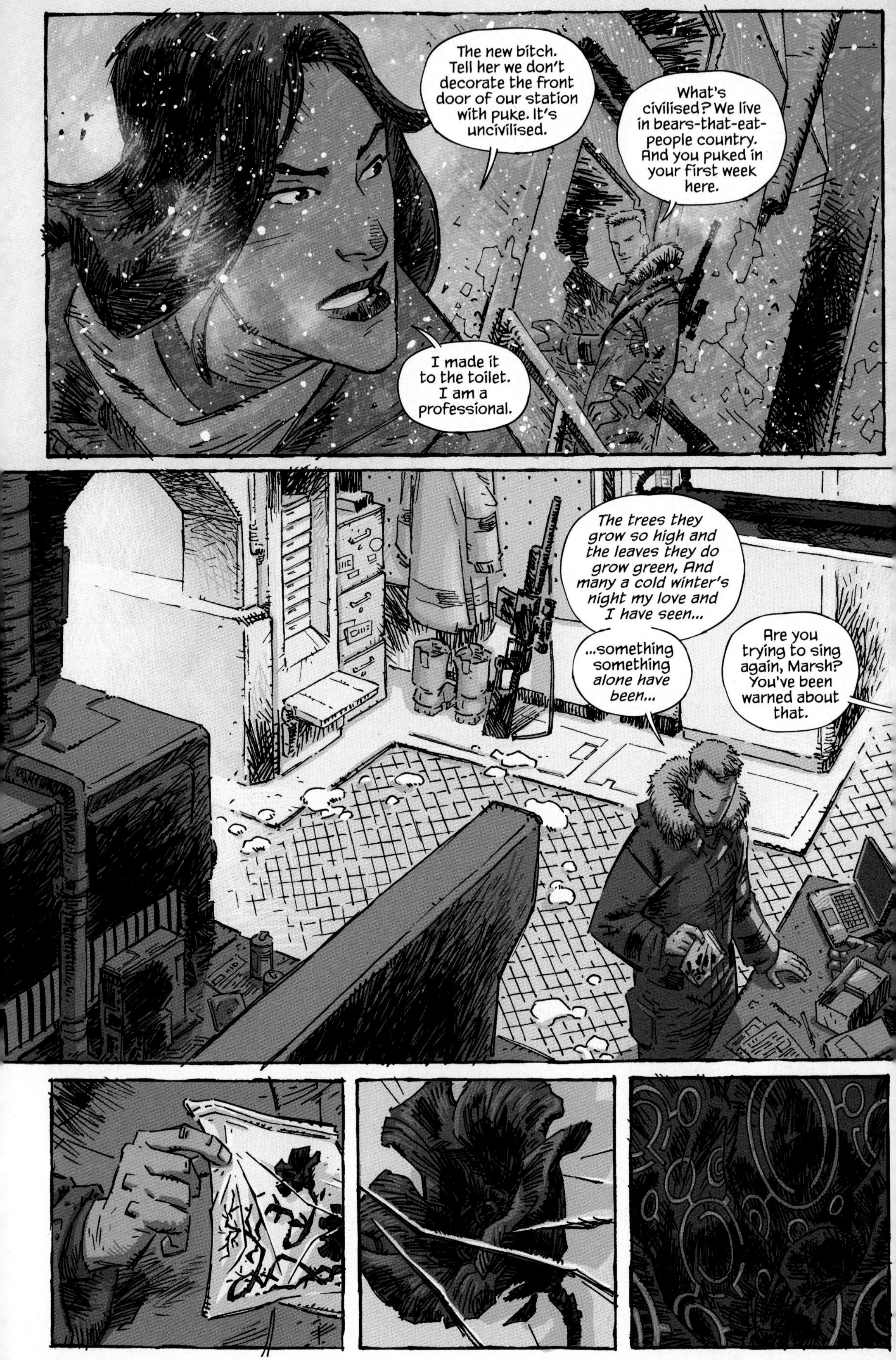
The new bitch. Tell her we don't decorate the front door of our station with puke. It's uncivilised.
What's civilised? We live in bears-that-eat-people country. And you puked in your first week here.
I made it to the toilet. I am a professional.
The trees they grow so high and the leaves they do grow green, And many a cold winter's night my love and I have seen...
...something something alone have been...
Are you trying to sing again, Marsh? You've been warned about that.

ALL THIS IS NORMAL

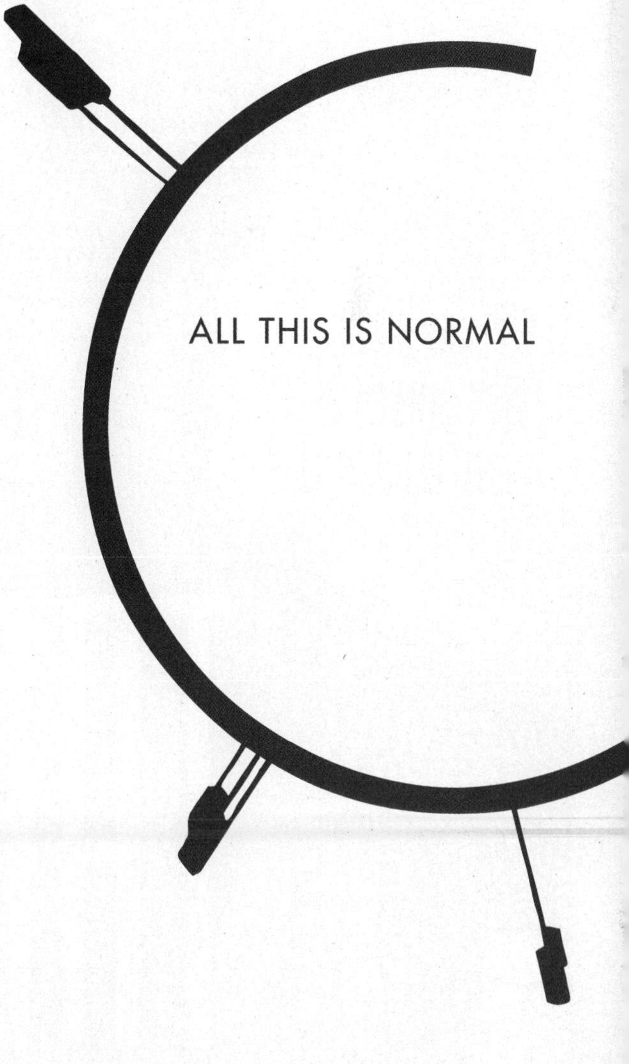

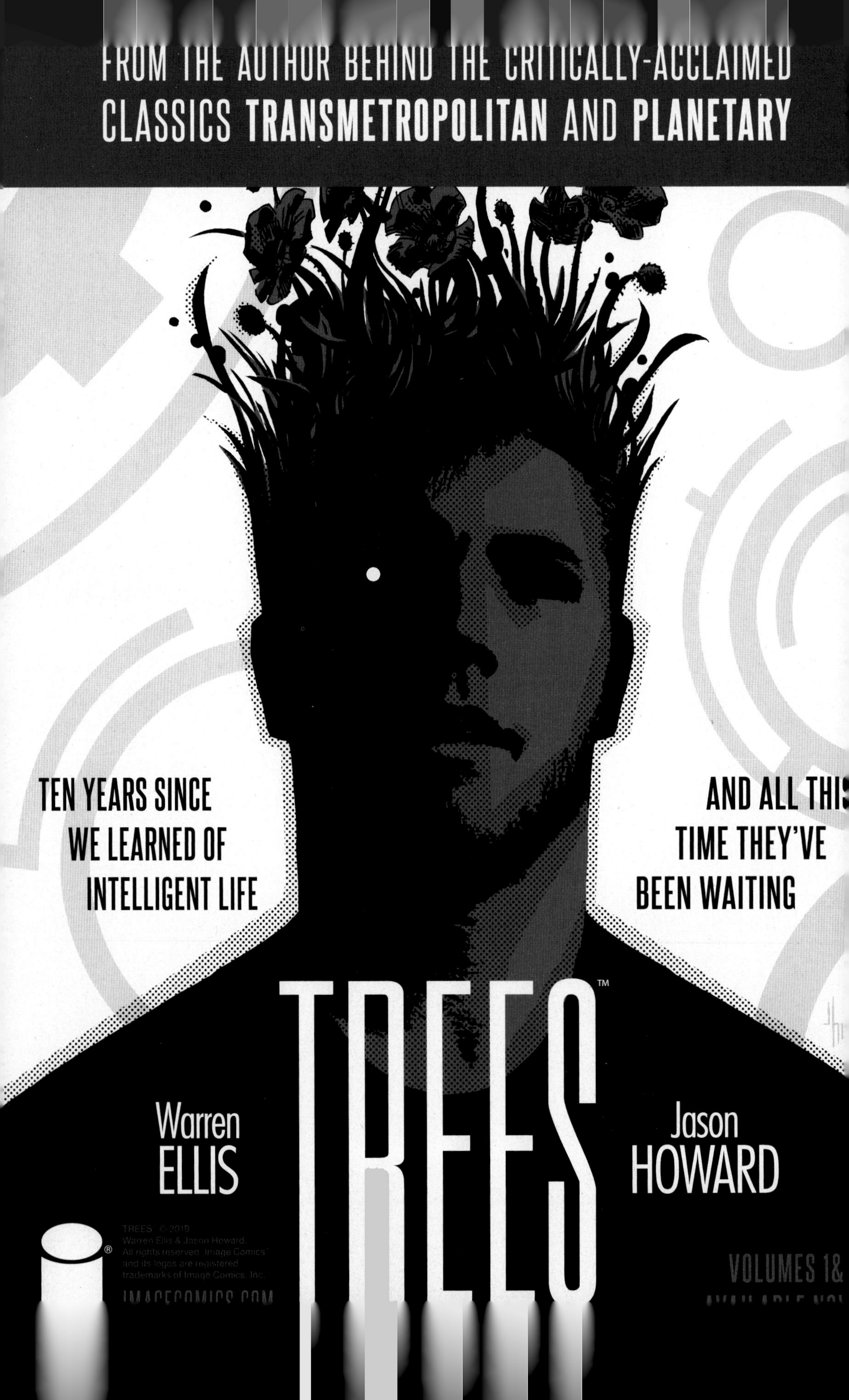

FROM THE AUTHOR BEHIND THE CRITICALLY-ACCLAIMED
CLASSICS TRANSMETROPOLITAN AND PLANETARY
TEN YEARS SINCE
WE LEARNED OF
INTELLIGENT LIFE
AND ALL THI
TIME THEY'VE
BEEN WAITING
TREES™
Warren
ELLIS
Jason
HOWARD
TREES™ © 2019
Warren Ellis & Jason Howard.
All rights reserved. Image Comics™
and its logos are registered
trademarks of Image Comics, Inc.
VOLUMES 1&

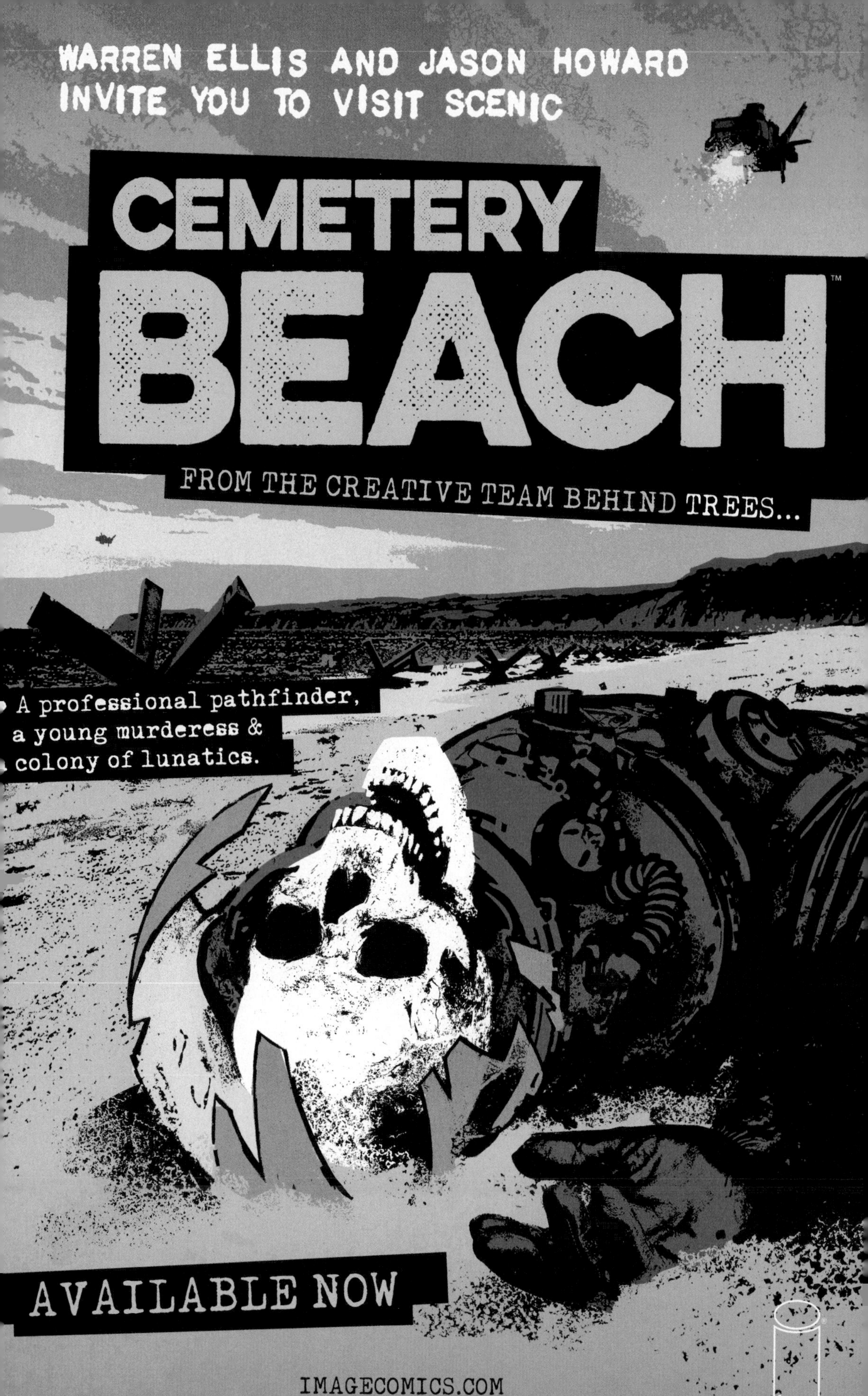

WARREN ELLIS AND JASON HOWARD
INVITE YOU TO VISIT SCENIC
CEMETERY BEACH™
FROM THE CREATIVE TEAM BEHIND TREES...
A professional pathfinder,
a young murderess &
colony of lunatics.
AVAILABLE NOW
IMAGECOMICS.COM
image

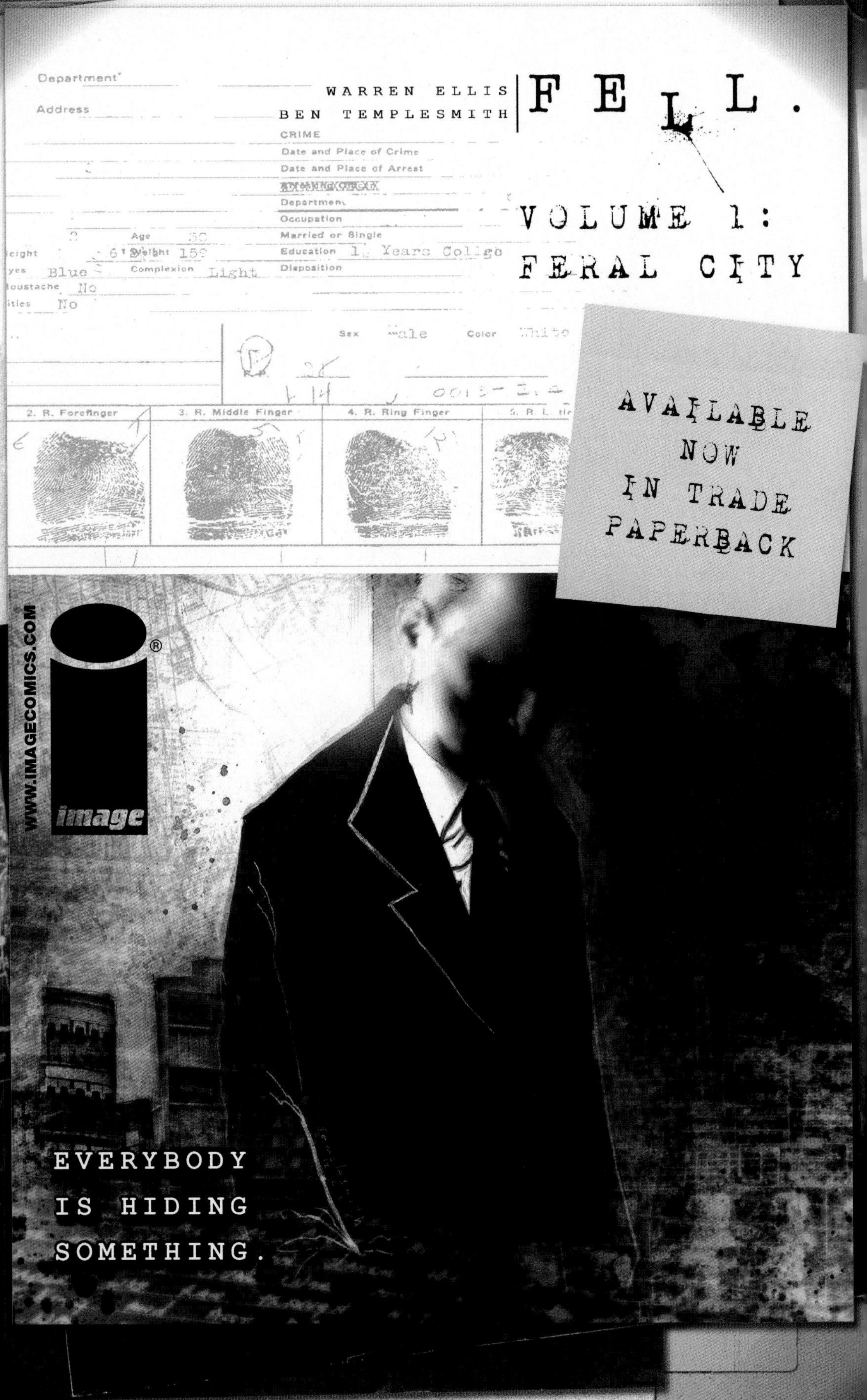

WARREN ELLIS
BEN TEMPLESMITH
FELL.
VOLUME 1:
FERAL CITY
AVAILABLE NOW IN TRADE PAPERBACK
WWW.IMAGECOMICS.COM
image
EVERYBODY IS HIDING SOMETHING.

ELLIS • SHALVEY • BELLAIRE

THE WORLD HAS BEEN POISONED TO DEATH

INJECTION™

FROM THE CREATORS OF MOON KNIGHT: FROM THE DEAD

VOLUMES 1-3 & HARDCOVER EDITION

AVAILABLE NOW

IMAGECOMICS.COM

FOLLOW #IMAGECOMICS

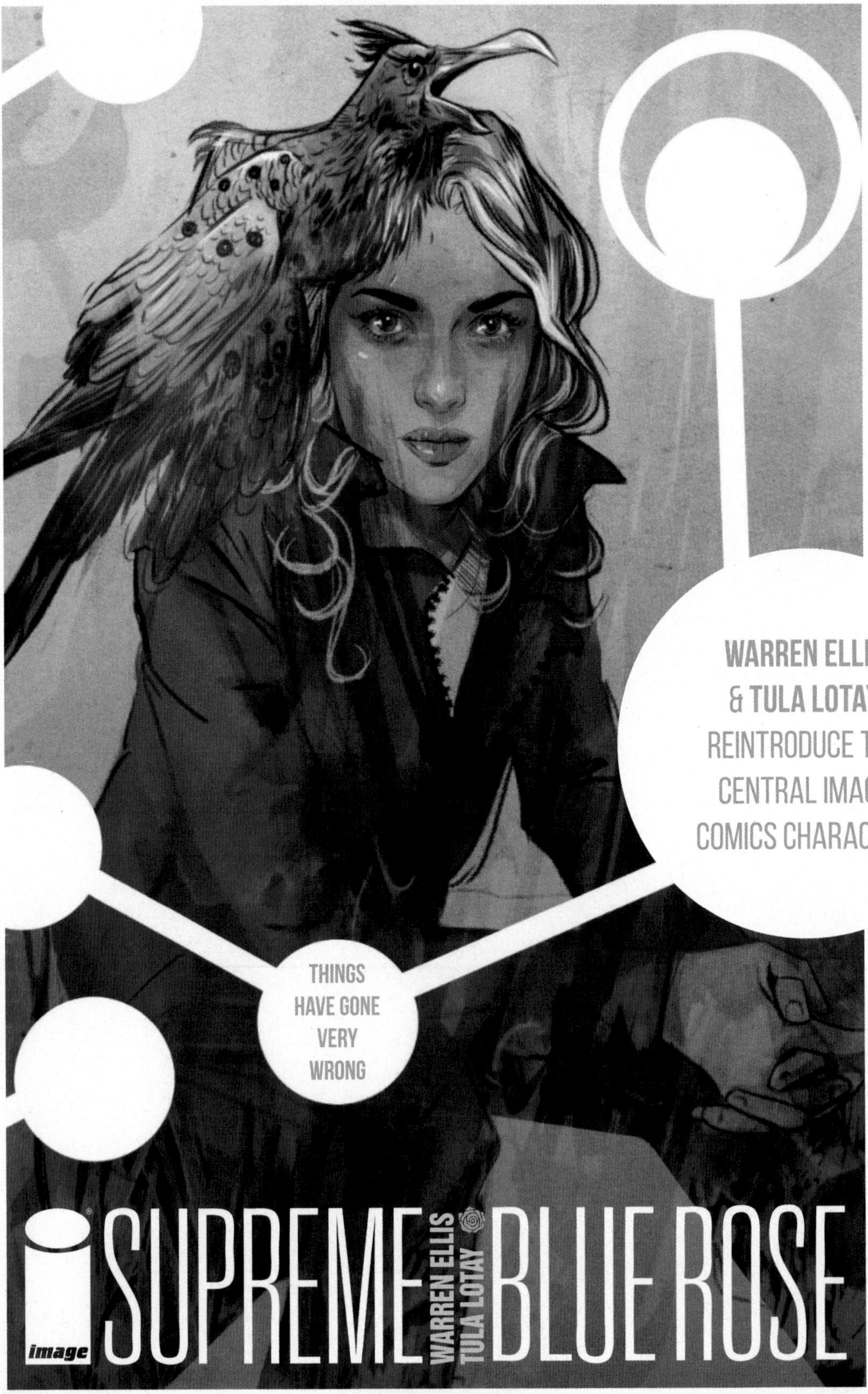
WARREN ELLIS
& TULA LOTAY
REINTRODUCE THE
CENTRAL IMAGE
COMICS CHARACTE
THINGS
HAVE GONE
VERY
WRONG
image
SUPREME
WARREN ELLIS
TULA LOTAY
BLUE ROSE

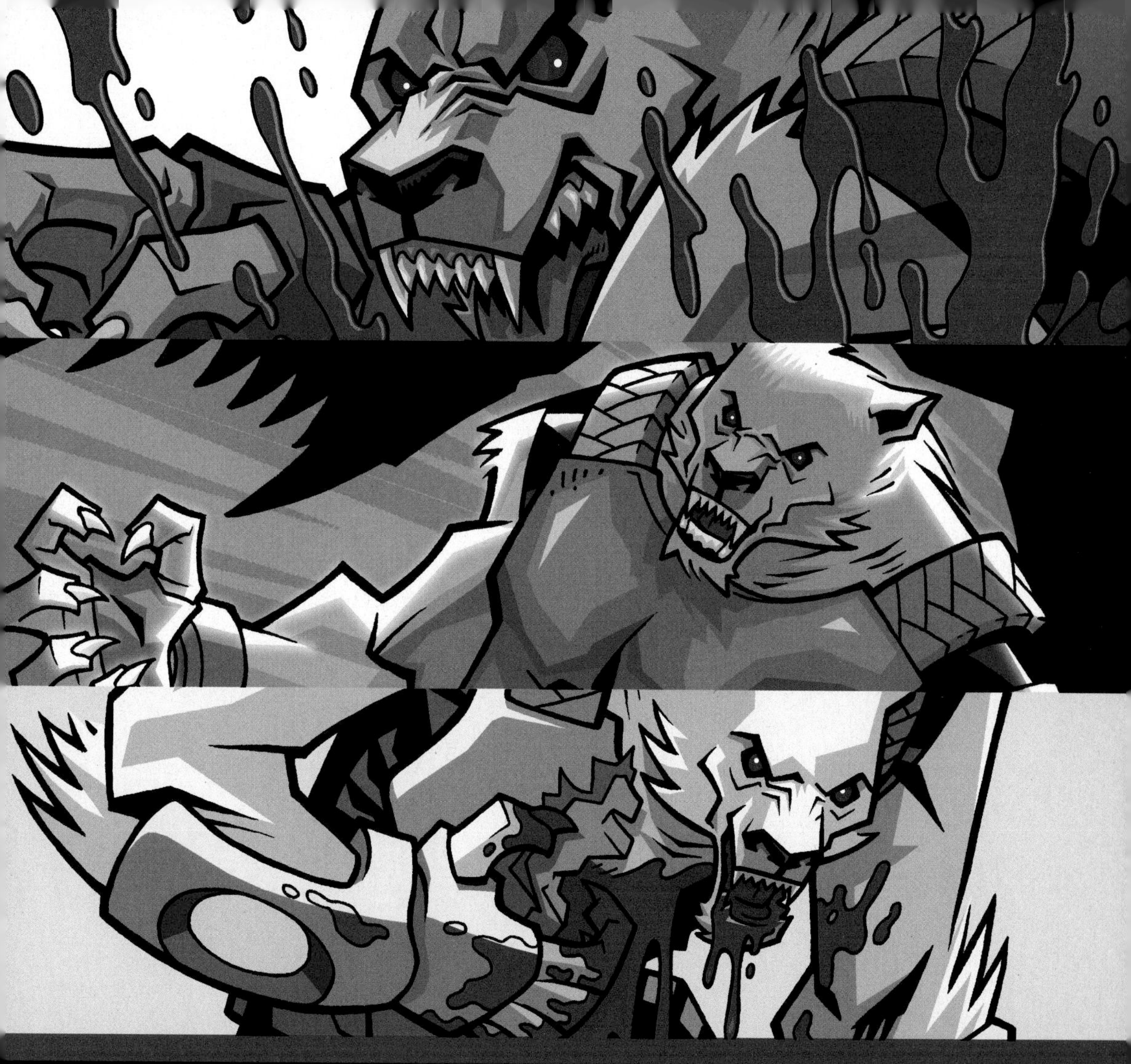

GALAXIES OF POSSIBILITIES

THE **IMAGINATION** HAS **NO LIMITS** IN THESE

SCIENCE FICTION
— COMICS —

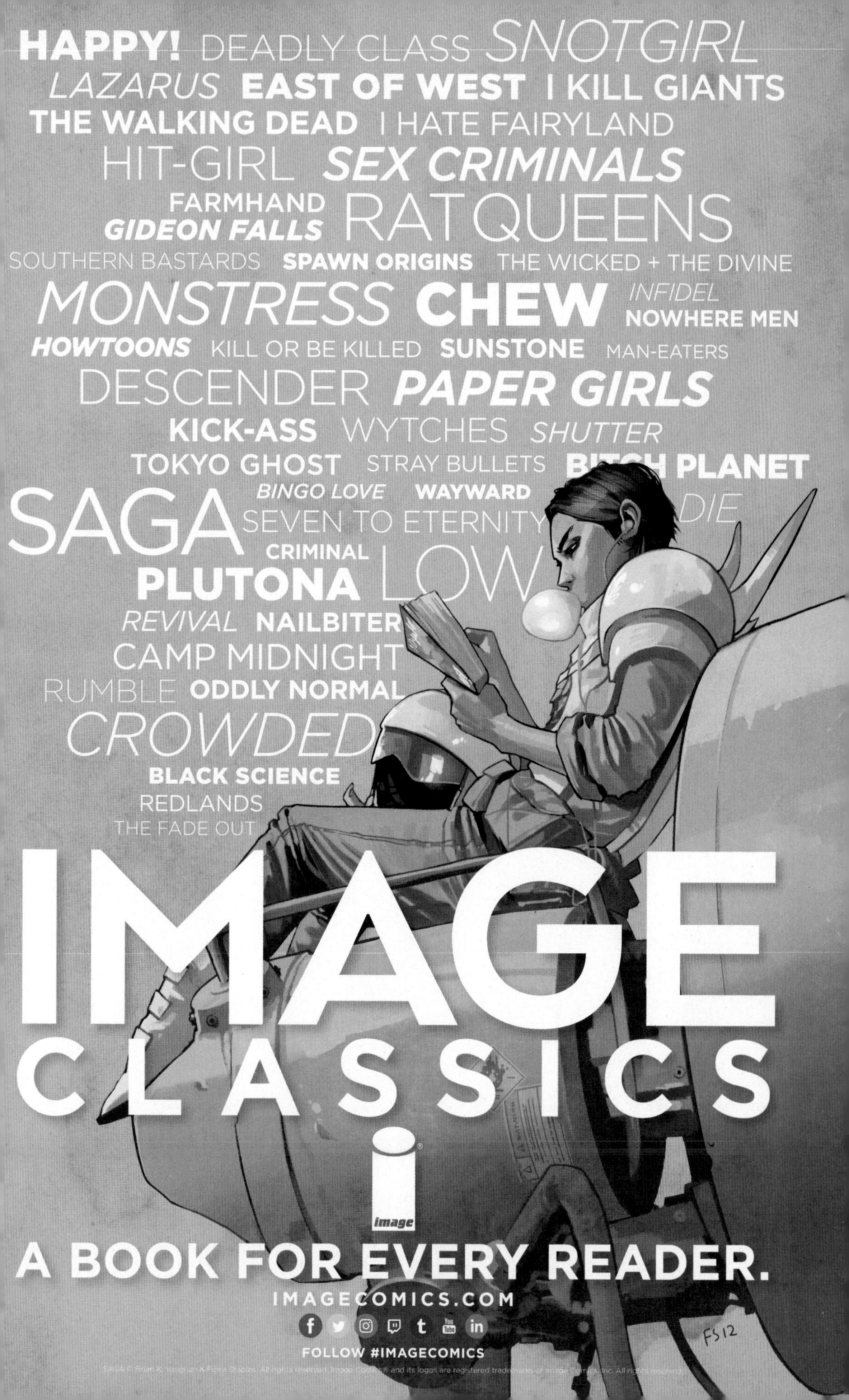
HAPPY! DEADLY CLASS SNOTGIRL
LAZARUS EAST OF WEST I KILL GIANTS
THE WALKING DEAD I HATE FAIRYLAND
HIT-GIRL SEX CRIMINALS
FARMHAND
GIDEON FALLS
RAT QUEENS
SOUTHERN BASTARDS SPAWN ORIGINS THE WICKED + THE DIVINE
MONSTRESS CHEW INFIDEL
NOWHERE MEN
HOWTOONS KILL OR BE KILLED SUNSTONE MAN-EATERS
DESCENDER PAPER GIRLS
KICK-ASS WYTCHES SHUTTER
TOKYO GHOST STRAY BULLETS BITCH PLANET
BINGO LOVE WAYWARD
SAGA SEVEN TO ETERNITY DIE
CRIMINAL
PLUTONA LOW
REVIVAL NAILBITER
CAMP MIDNIGHT
RUMBLE ODDLY NORMAL
CROWDED
BLACK SCIENCE
REDLANDS
THE FADE OUT
IMAGE CLASSICS
image
A BOOK FOR EVERY READER.
IMAGECOMICS.COM
FOLLOW #IMAGECOMICS
FS12
SAGA © Brian K. Vaughan & Fiona Staples. All rights reserved. Image Comics® and its logos are registered trademarks of Image Comics, Inc. All rights reserved.

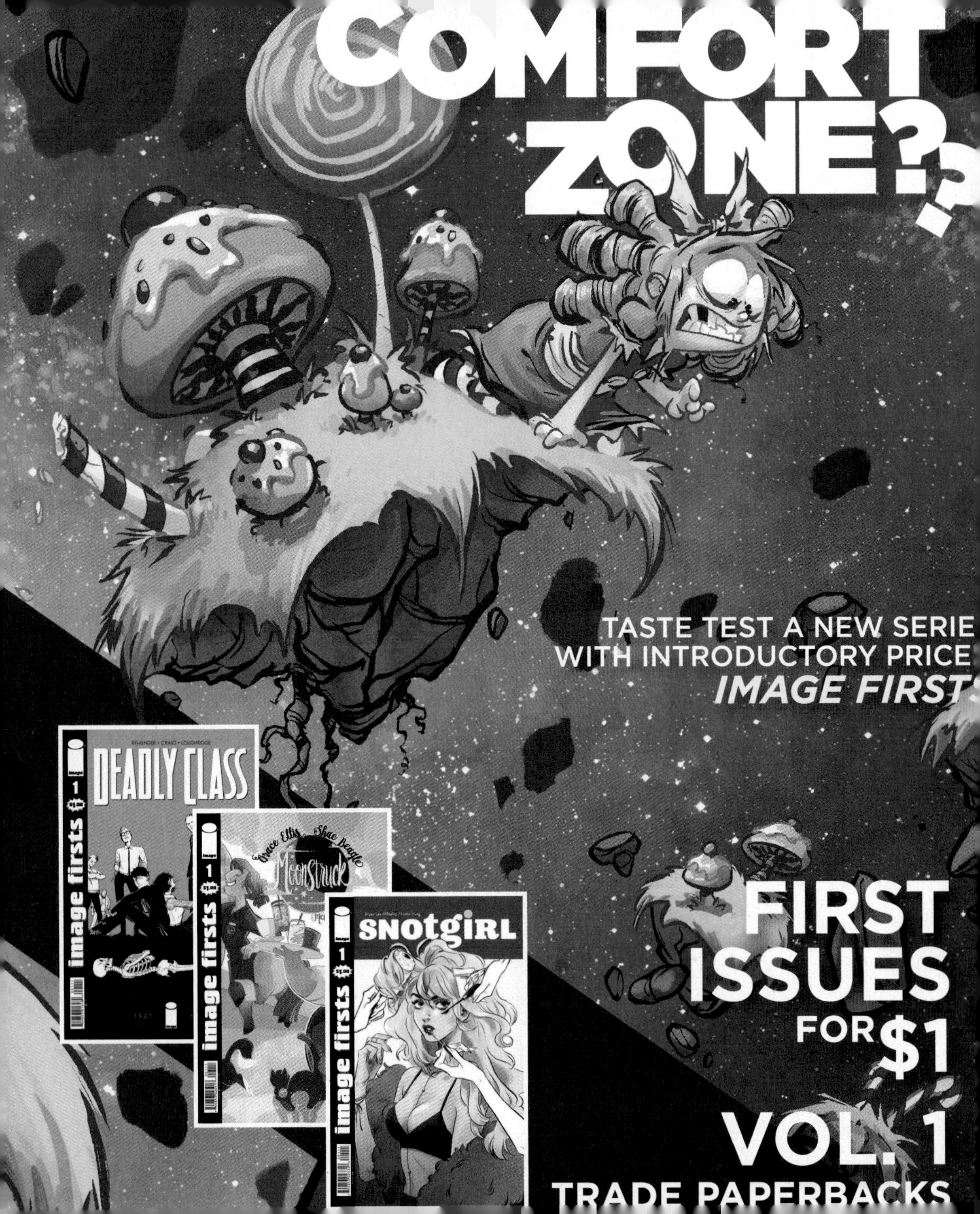
COMFORT ZONE??
TASTE TEST A NEW SERIE
WITH INTRODUCTORY PRICE
IMAGE FIRST
DEADLY CLASS
image firsts
1
Grace Ellis
Shae Beagle
Moonstruck
image firsts
1
SNOTGIRL
image firsts
1
FIRST ISSUES FOR $1
VOL. 1
TRADE PAPERBACKS

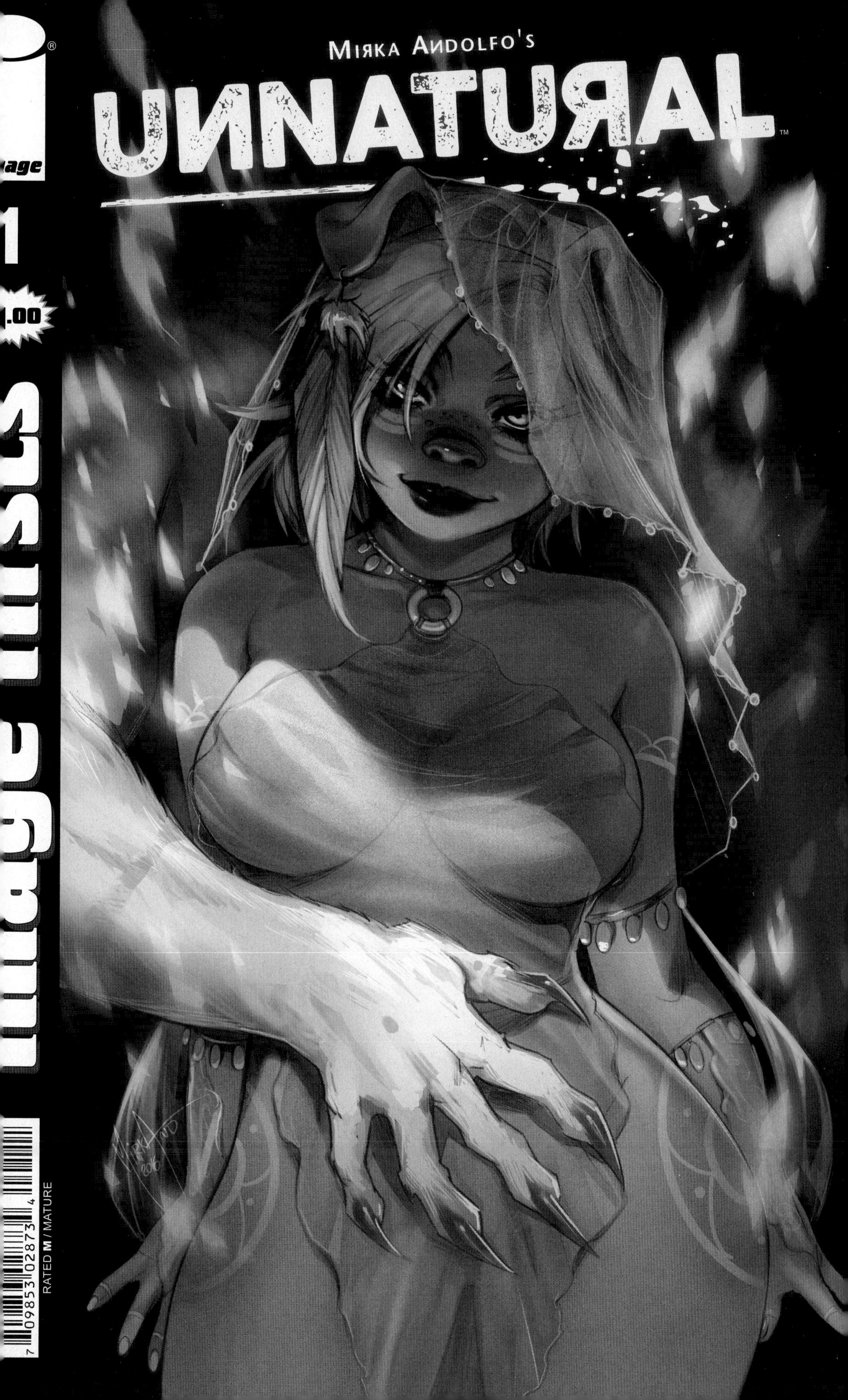

MIRKA ANDOLFO'S
UNNATURAL
1
.00
RATED M / MATURE

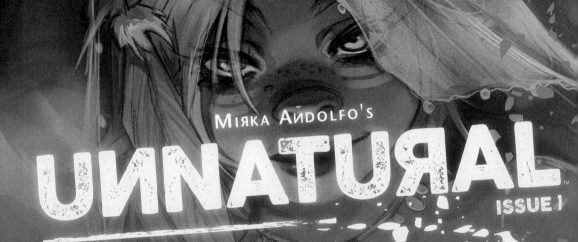

MIRKA ANDOLFO'S
UNNATURAL™
ISSUE 1

writer, artist and colorist
MIRKA ANDOLFO

colors assistant
GIANLUCA PAPI
(ARANCIA STUDIO)

lettering and production
FABIO AMELIA
(ARANCIA STUDIO)

translation from italian
ARANCIA STUDIO

cover artist
MIRKA ANDOLFO

editors
DIEGO MALARA
MARCO RICOMPENSA

design
ALESSANDRO GUCCIARDO
FABIO AMELIA

IMAGE FIRSTS: UNNATURAL #1, August 2019. Published by Image Comics, Inc. Office of publication: 2701 NW Vaughn St., Suite 780, Portland, OR 97210. Printed in the USA. For information regarding the CPSIA on this printed material call: 203-595-3636. For international rights, contact: foreignlicensing@imagecomics.com.

UNNATURAL (CONTRO NATURA) is a **PANINI COMICS**, Italy original production. Managing Director: **Aldo H Sallustro**, Publishing and Licensing Director: **Marco M. Lupoi**, Publishing Manager: **Sara Mattioli**, Editorial Coordinator: **Diego Malara**, Licensing manager: **Annalisa Califano**, Licensing consultant: **Serena Varani**.

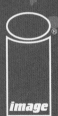

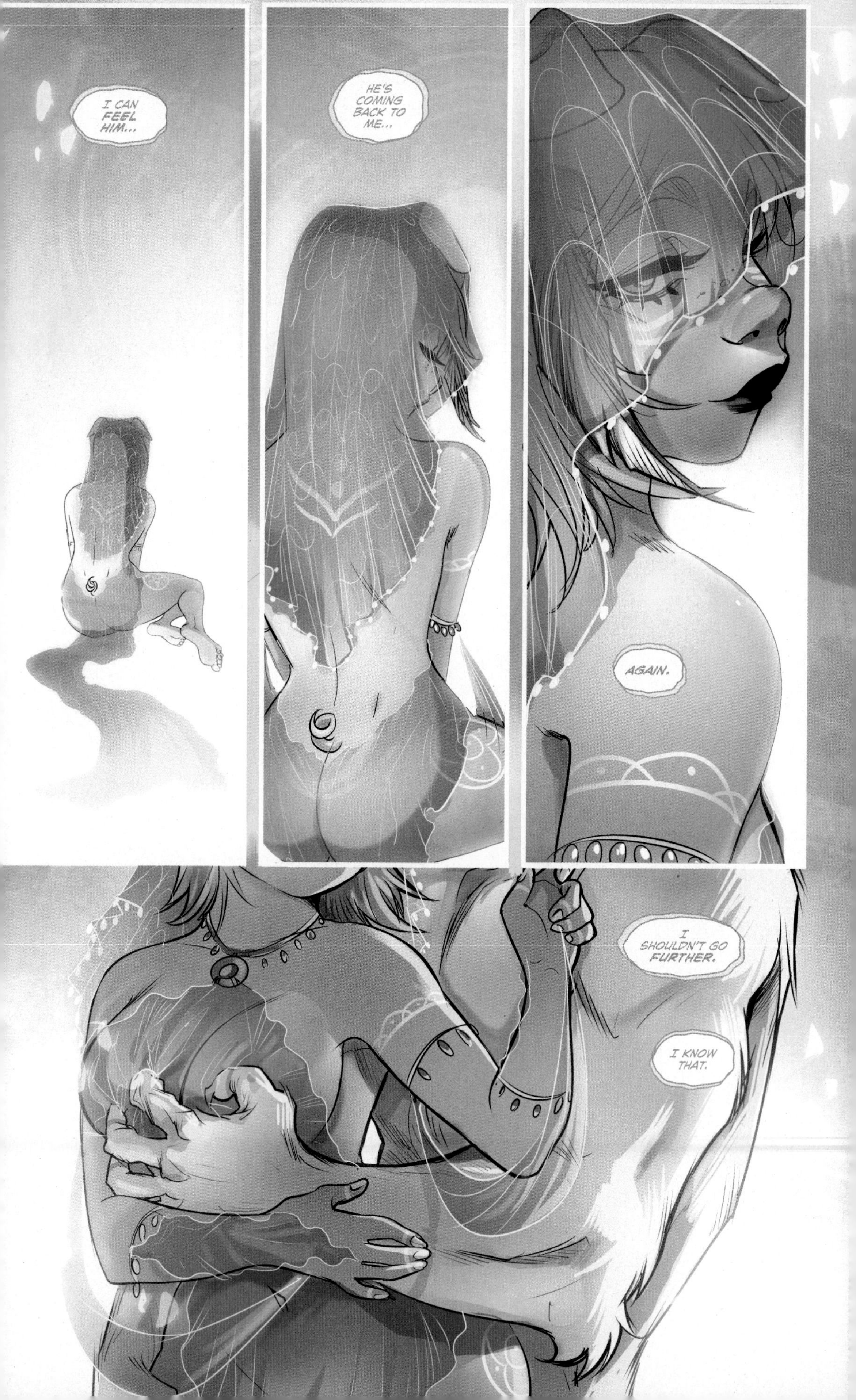
I CAN FEEL HIM...
HE'S COMING BACK TO ME...
AGAIN.
I SHOULDN'T GO FURTHER.
I KNOW THAT.

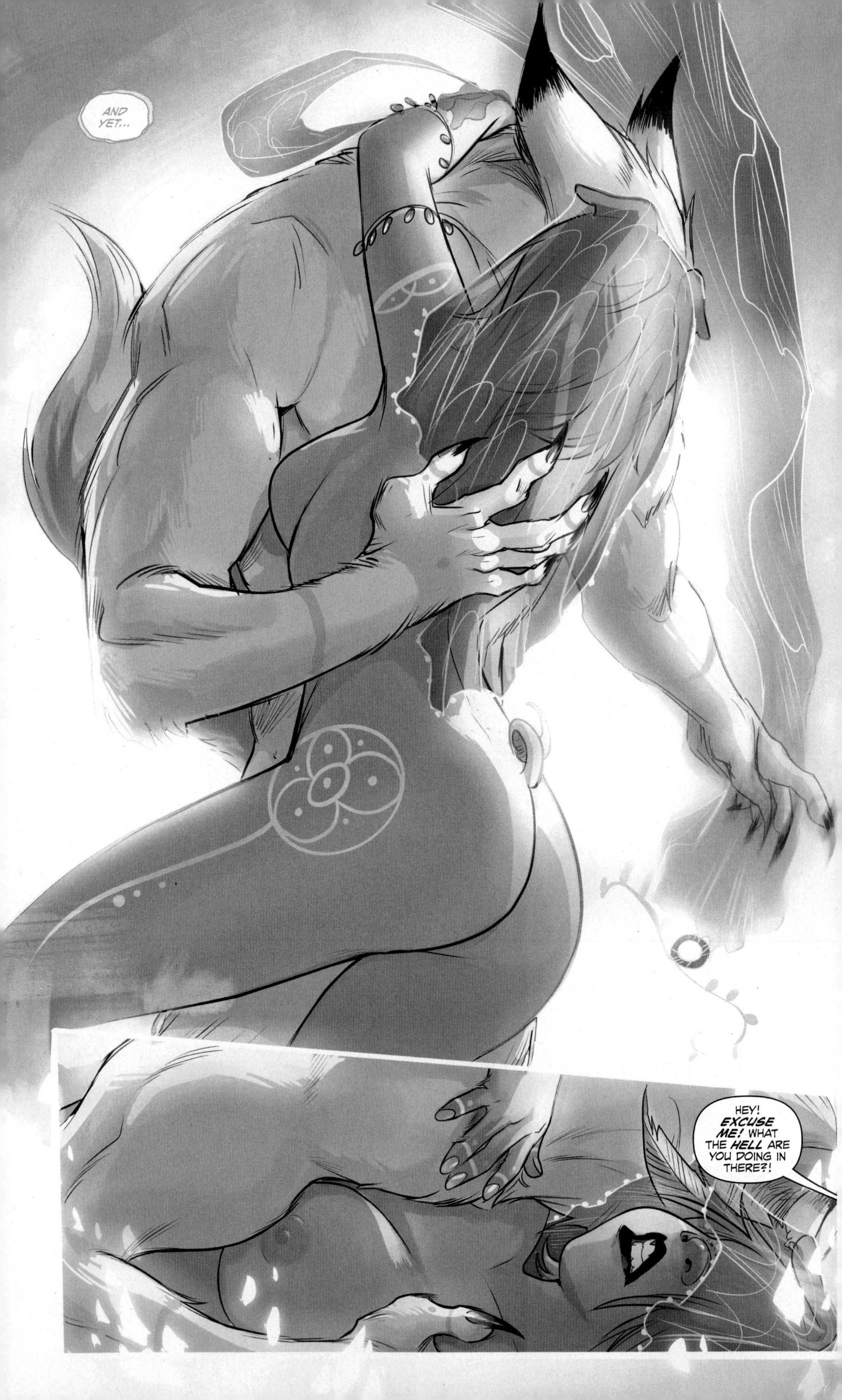
AND YET...
HEY! EXCUSE ME! WHAT THE HELL ARE YOU DOING IN THERE?!

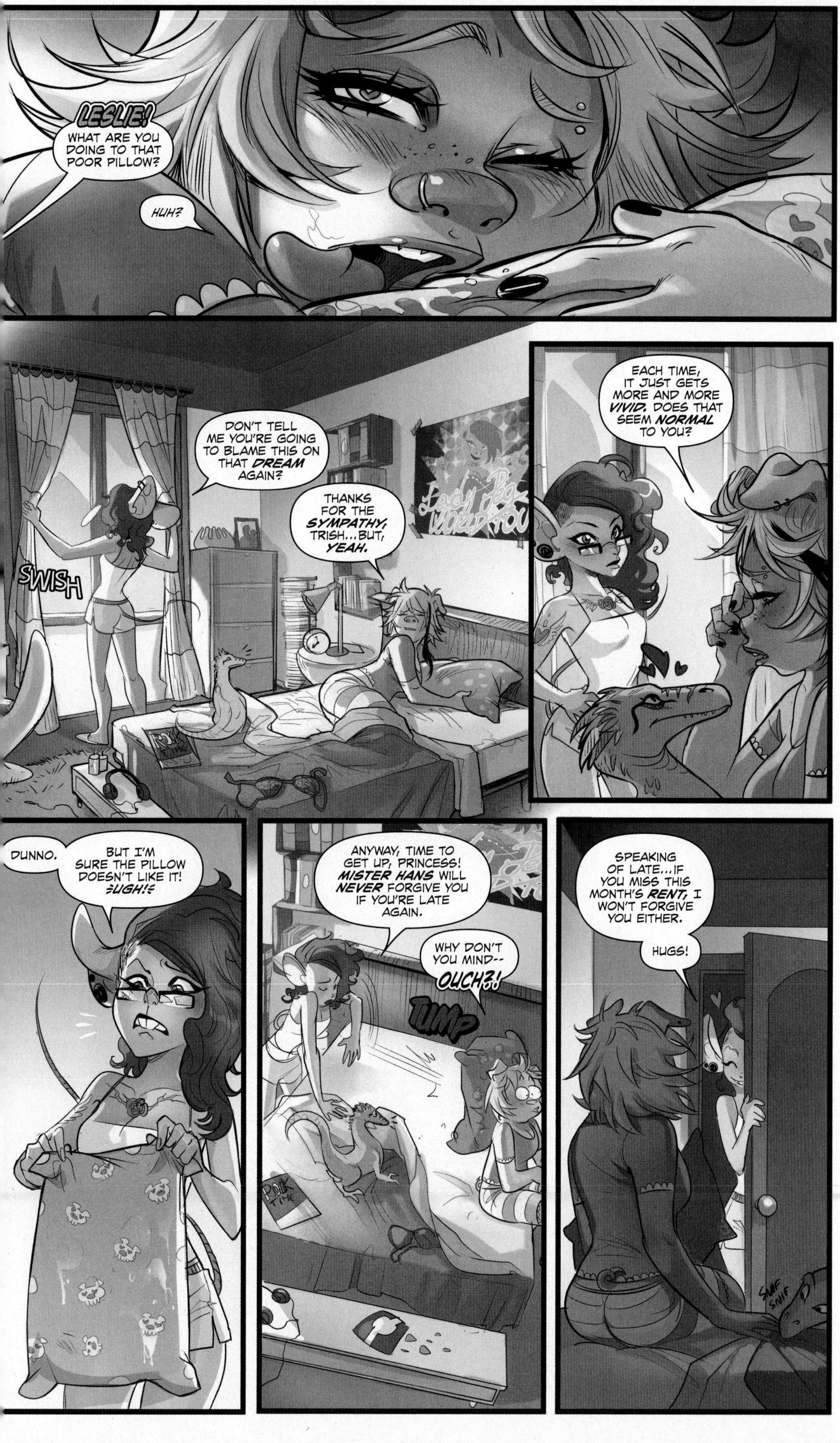

LESLIE!
WHAT ARE YOU DOING TO THAT POOR PILLOW?
HUH?
DON'T TELL ME YOU'RE GOING TO BLAME THIS ON THAT DREAM AGAIN?
SWISH
THANKS FOR THE SYMPATHY, TRISH...BUT, YEAH.
EACH TIME, IT JUST GETS MORE AND MORE VIVID. DOES THAT SEEM NORMAL TO YOU?
DUNNO.
BUT I'M SURE THE PILLOW DOESN'T LIKE IT! =UGH!=
ANYWAY, TIME TO GET UP, PRINCESS! MISTER HANS WILL NEVER FORGIVE YOU IF YOU'RE LATE AGAIN.
WHY DON'T YOU MIND--
OUCH?!
TUMP
SPEAKING OF LATE...IF YOU MISS THIS MONTH'S RENT, I WON'T FORGIVE YOU EITHER.
HUGS!

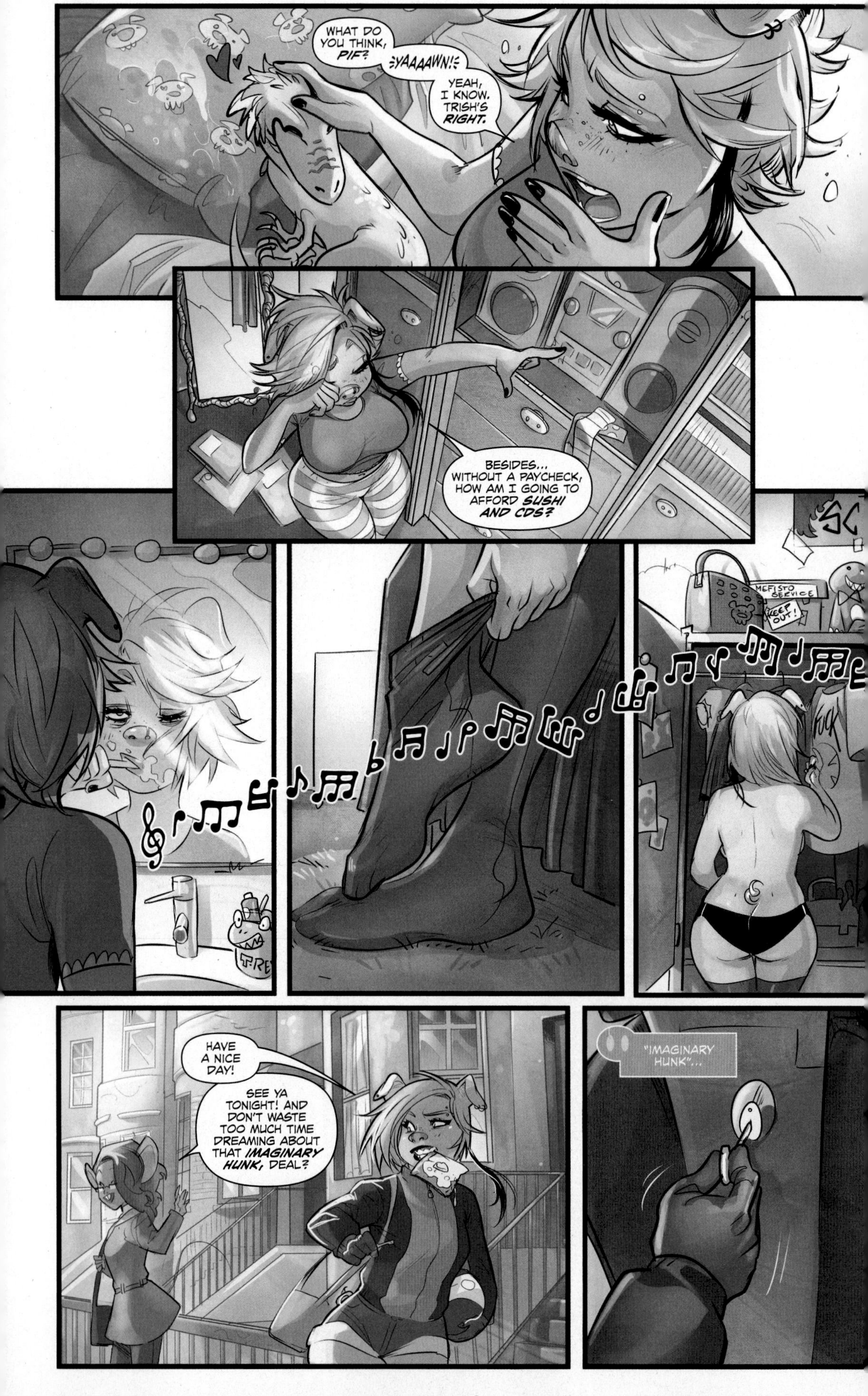
WHAT DO YOU THINK, PIF?
:YAAAAWN!:
YEAH, I KNOW. TRISH'S RIGHT.
BESIDES... WITHOUT A PAYCHECK, HOW AM I GOING TO AFFORD SUSHI AND CDS?
MEFISTO SERVICE
KEEP OUT!
T-REX
HAVE A NICE DAY!
SEE YA TONIGHT! AND DON'T WASTE TOO MUCH TIME DREAMING ABOUT THAT IMAGINARY HUNK, DEAL?
"IMAGINARY HUNK"...

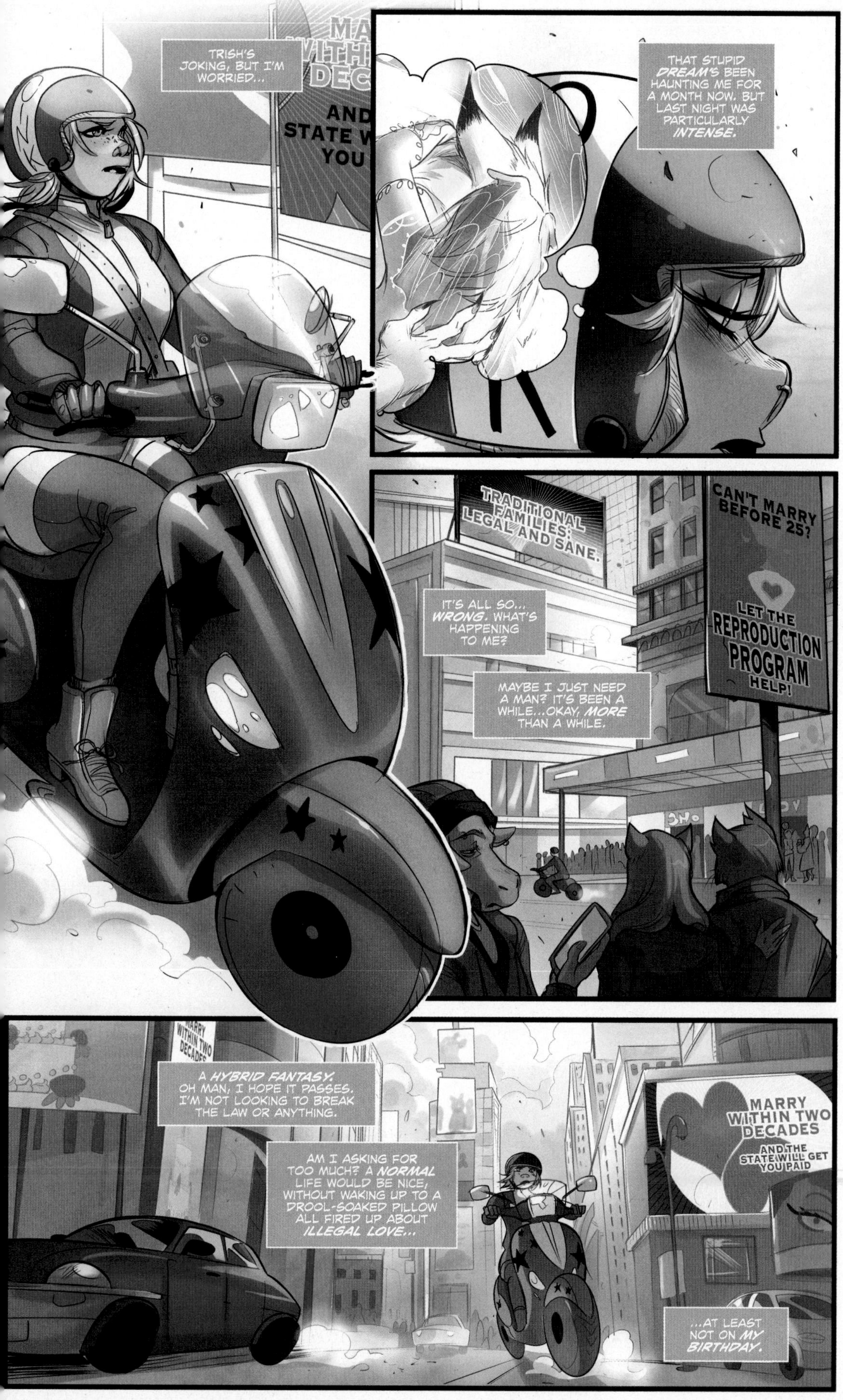
MA... WITH... DEC...
AND... STATE W... YOU...
TRISH'S JOKING, BUT I'M WORRIED...
THAT STUPID DREAM'S BEEN HAUNTING ME FOR A MONTH NOW. BUT LAST NIGHT WAS PARTICULARLY INTENSE.
TRADITIONAL FAMILIES: LEGAL AND SANE.
CAN'T MARRY BEFORE 25?
LET THE REPRODUCTION PROGRAM HELP!
IT'S ALL SO... WRONG. WHAT'S HAPPENING TO ME?
MAYBE I JUST NEED A MAN? IT'S BEEN A WHILE...OKAY, MORE THAN A WHILE.
MARRY WITHIN TWO DECADES
A HYBRID FANTASY. OH MAN, I HOPE IT PASSES. I'M NOT LOOKING TO BREAK THE LAW OR ANYTHING.
AM I ASKING FOR TOO MUCH? A NORMAL LIFE WOULD BE NICE, WITHOUT WAKING UP TO A DROOL-SOAKED PILLOW ALL FIRED UP ABOUT ILLEGAL LOVE...
MARRY WITHIN TWO DECADES
AND THE STATE WILL GET YOU PAID
...AT LEAST NOT ON MY BIRTHDAY.

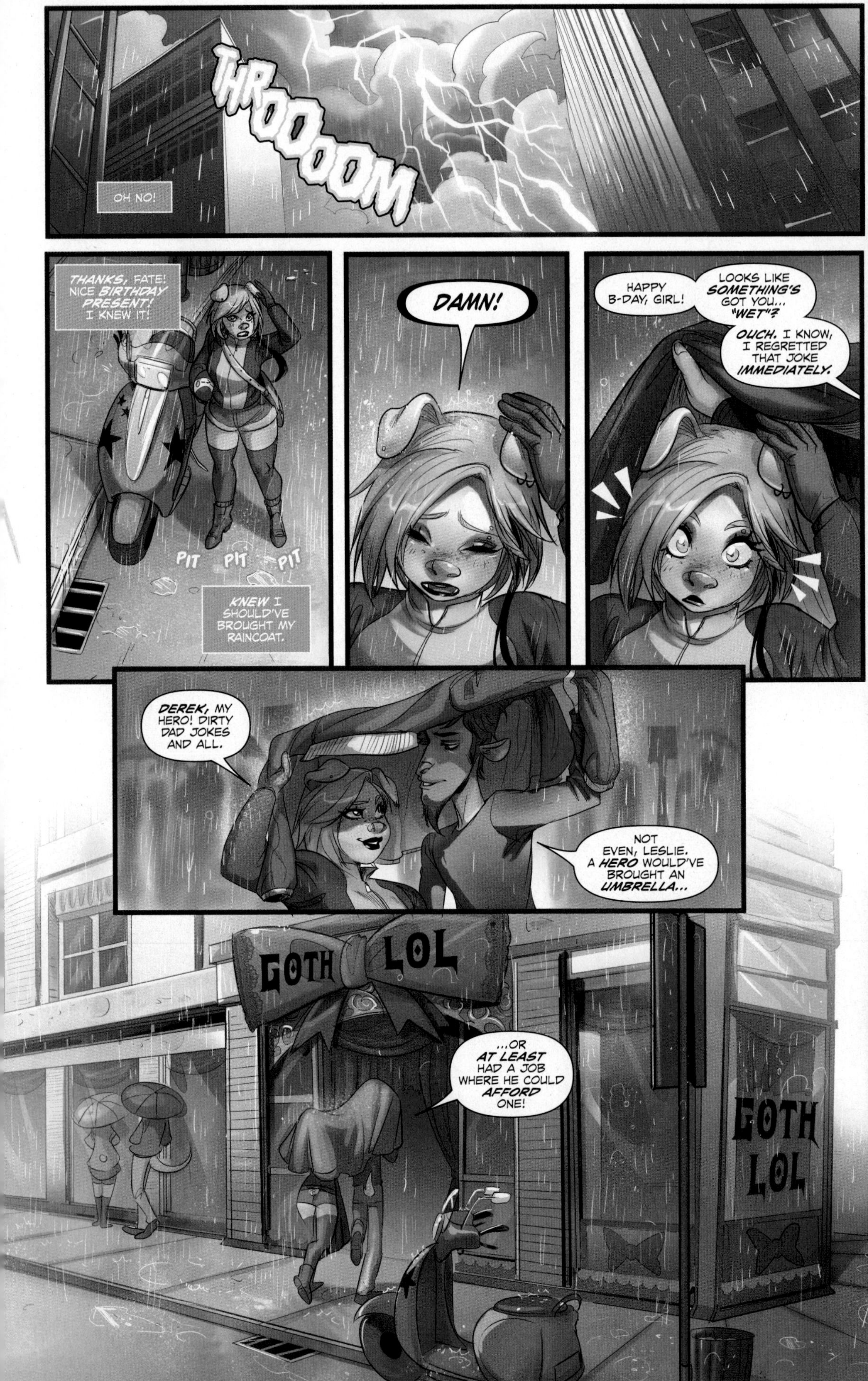
THROOOOOM
OH NO!
THANKS, FATE! NICE BIRTHDAY PRESENT! I KNEW IT!
PIT PIT PIT
KNEW I SHOULD'VE BROUGHT MY RAINCOAT.
DAMN!
HAPPY B-DAY, GIRL!
LOOKS LIKE SOMETHING'S GOT YOU... "WET"?
OUCH. I KNOW, I REGRETTED THAT JOKE IMMEDIATELY.
DEREK, MY HERO! DIRTY DAD JOKES AND ALL.
NOT EVEN, LESLIE. A HERO WOULD'VE BROUGHT AN UMBRELLA...
GOTH LOL
...OR AT LEAST HAD A JOB WHERE HE COULD AFFORD ONE!
GOTH LOL

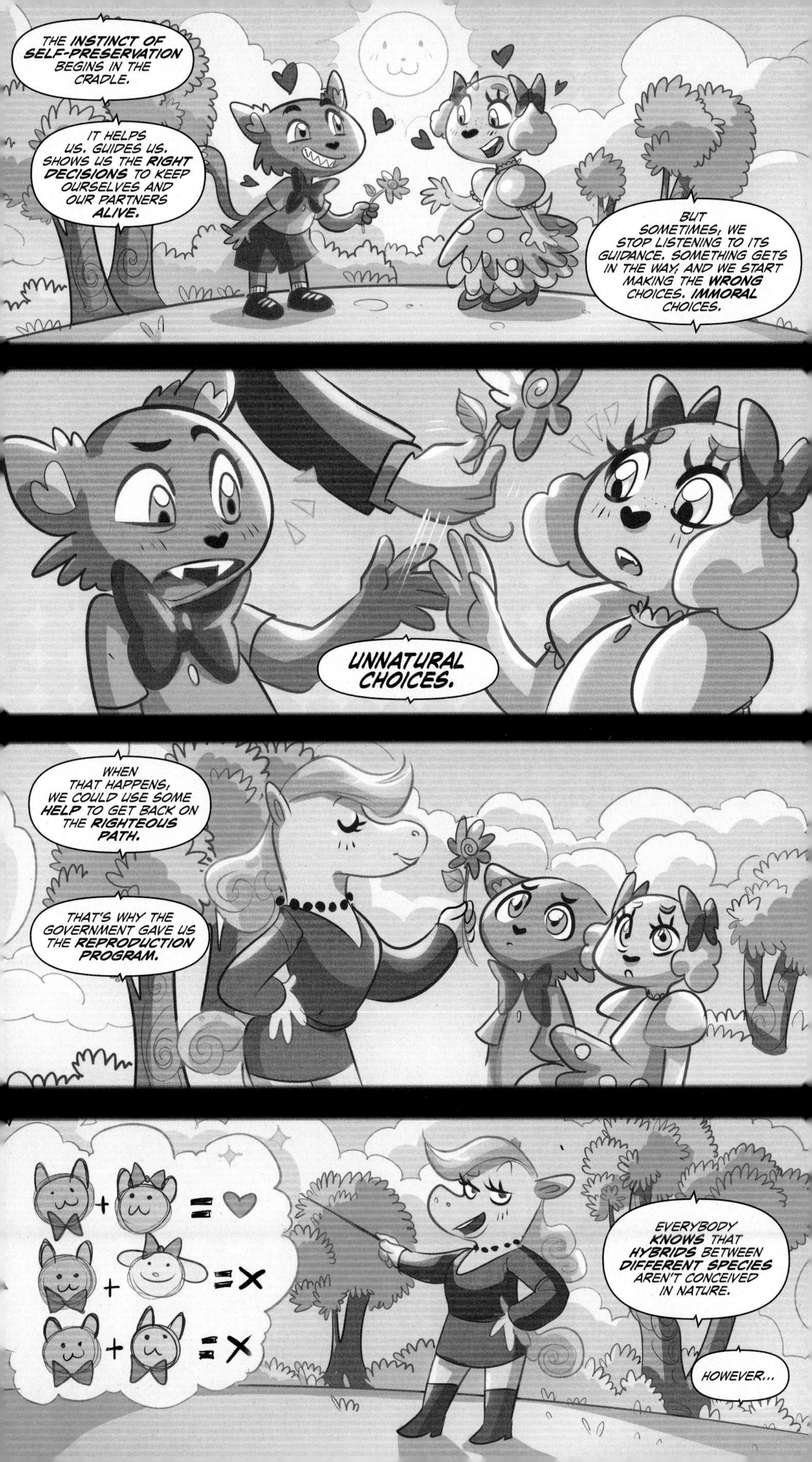
THE INSTINCT OF SELF-PRESERVATION BEGINS IN THE CRADLE.
IT HELPS US. GUIDES US. SHOWS US THE RIGHT DECISIONS TO KEEP OURSELVES AND OUR PARTNERS ALIVE.
BUT SOMETIMES, WE STOP LISTENING TO ITS GUIDANCE. SOMETHING GETS IN THE WAY, AND WE START MAKING THE WRONG CHOICES. IMMORAL CHOICES.
UNNATURAL CHOICES.
WHEN THAT HAPPENS, WE COULD USE SOME HELP TO GET BACK ON THE RIGHTEOUS PATH.
THAT'S WHY THE GOVERNMENT GAVE US THE REPRODUCTION PROGRAM.
EVERYBODY KNOWS THAT HYBRIDS BETWEEN DIFFERENT SPECIES AREN'T CONCEIVED IN NATURE.
HOWEVER...

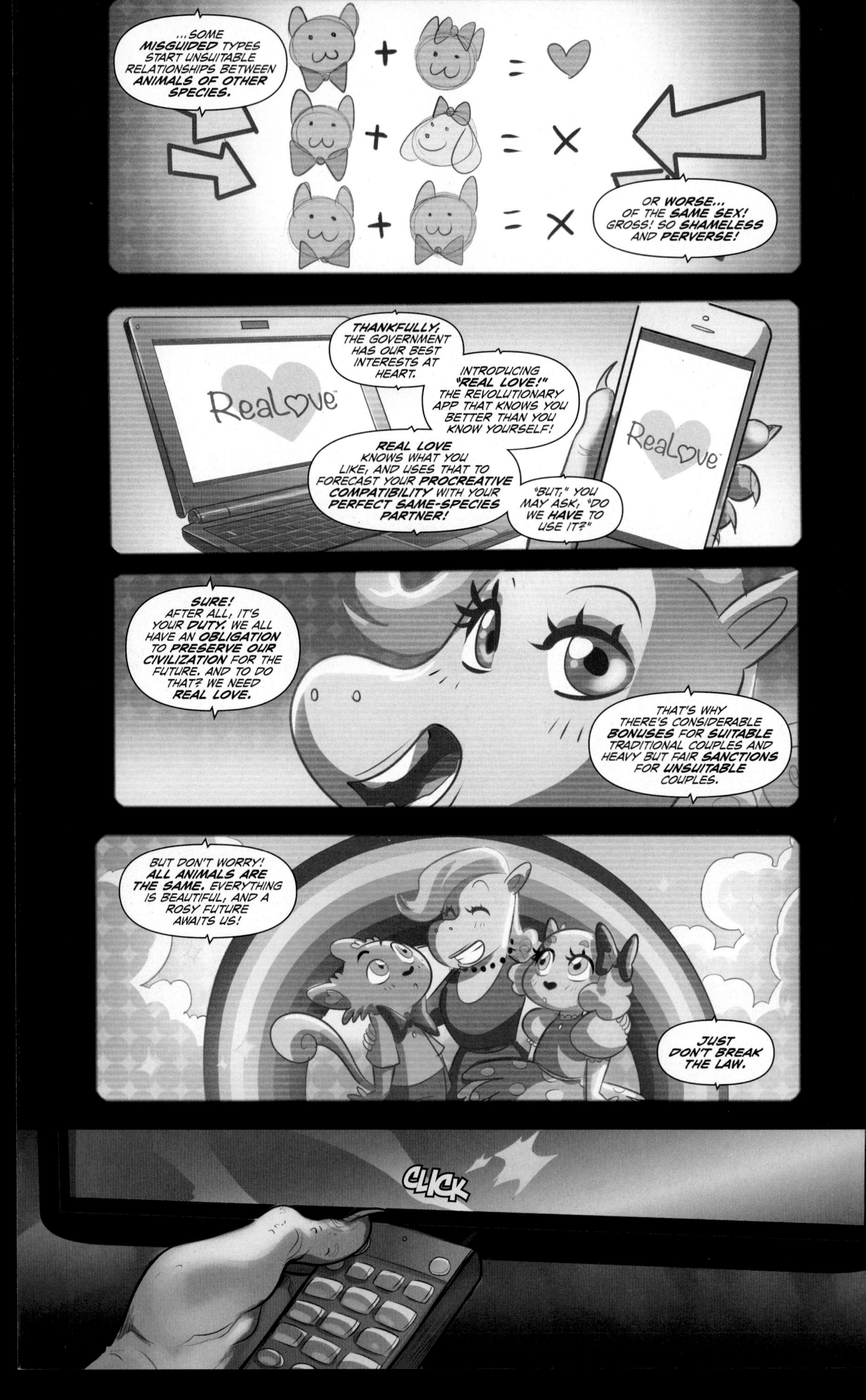
...SOME MISGUIDED TYPES START UNSUITABLE RELATIONSHIPS BETWEEN ANIMALS OF OTHER SPECIES.
OR WORSE... OF THE SAME SEX! GROSS! SO SHAMELESS AND PERVERSE!
THANKFULLY, THE GOVERNMENT HAS OUR BEST INTERESTS AT HEART.
RealLove™
INTRODUCING "REAL LOVE!" THE REVOLUTIONARY APP THAT KNOWS YOU BETTER THAN YOU KNOW YOURSELF!
RealLove™
REAL LOVE KNOWS WHAT YOU LIKE, AND USES THAT TO FORECAST YOUR PROCREATIVE COMPATIBILITY WITH YOUR PERFECT SAME-SPECIES PARTNER!
"BUT," YOU MAY ASK, "DO WE HAVE TO USE IT?"
SURE! AFTER ALL, IT'S YOUR DUTY. WE ALL HAVE AN OBLIGATION TO PRESERVE OUR CIVILIZATION FOR THE FUTURE. AND TO DO THAT? WE NEED REAL LOVE.
THAT'S WHY THERE'S CONSIDERABLE BONUSES FOR SUITABLE TRADITIONAL COUPLES AND HEAVY BUT FAIR SANCTIONS FOR UNSUITABLE COUPLES.
BUT DON'T WORRY! ALL ANIMALS ARE THE SAME. EVERYTHING IS BEAUTIFUL, AND A ROSY FUTURE AWAITS US!
JUST DON'T BREAK THE LAW.
CLICK

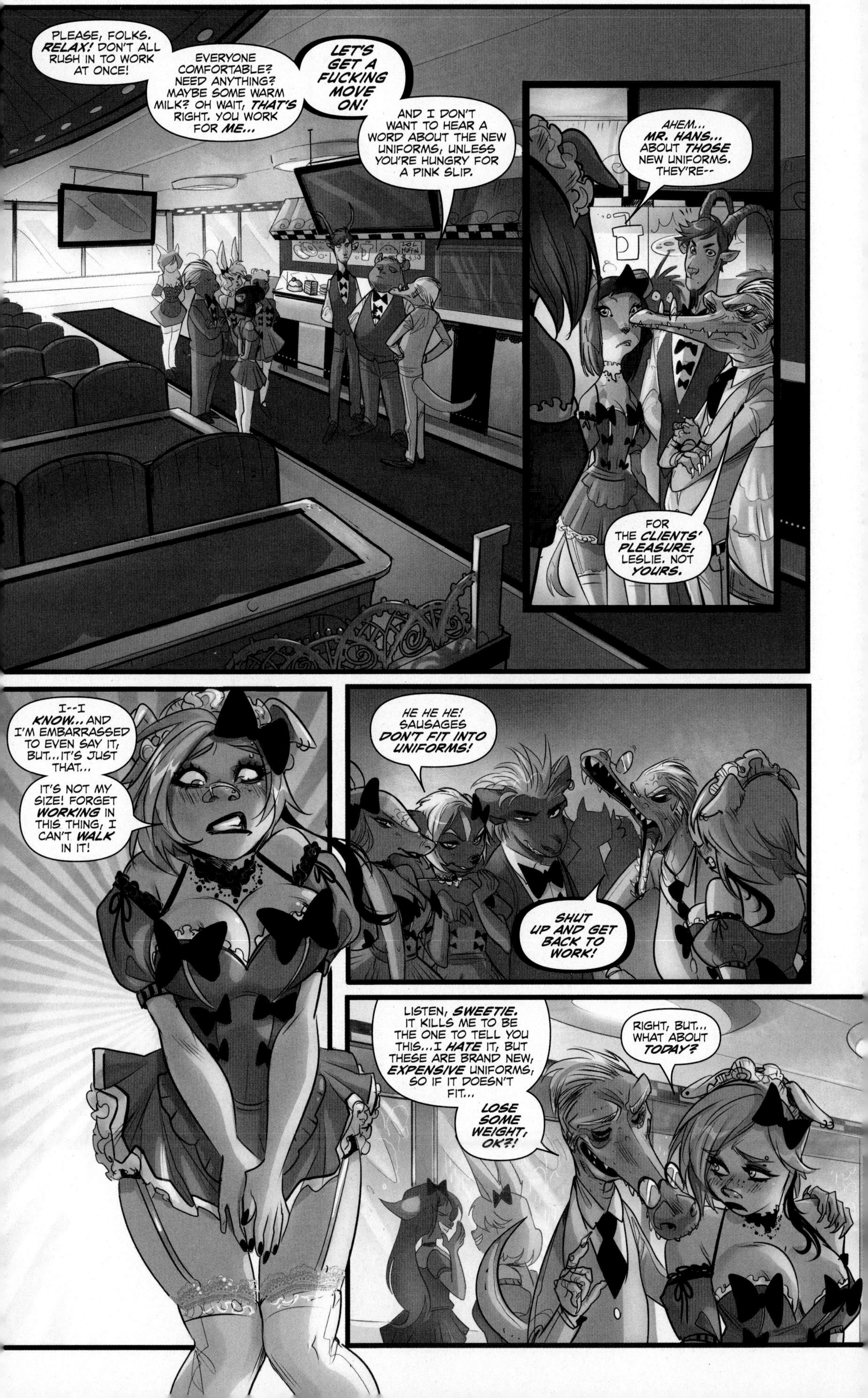
PLEASE, FOLKS. RELAX! DON'T ALL RUSH IN TO WORK AT ONCE!
EVERYONE COMFORTABLE? NEED ANYTHING? MAYBE SOME WARM MILK? OH WAIT, THAT'S RIGHT. YOU WORK FOR ME...
LET'S GET A FUCKING MOVE ON!
AND I DON'T WANT TO HEAR A WORD ABOUT THE NEW UNIFORMS, UNLESS YOU'RE HUNGRY FOR A PINK SLIP.
AHEM... MR. HANS... ABOUT THOSE NEW UNIFORMS. THEY'RE--
FOR THE CLIENTS' PLEASURE, LESLIE. NOT YOURS.
I--I KNOW... AND I'M EMBARRASSED TO EVEN SAY IT, BUT... IT'S JUST THAT...
IT'S NOT MY SIZE! FORGET WORKING IN THIS THING, I CAN'T WALK IN IT!
HE HE HE! SAUSAGES DON'T FIT INTO UNIFORMS!
SHUT UP AND GET BACK TO WORK!
LISTEN, SWEETIE. IT KILLS ME TO BE THE ONE TO TELL YOU THIS... I HATE IT, BUT THESE ARE BRAND NEW, EXPENSIVE UNIFORMS, SO IF IT DOESN'T FIT...
LOSE SOME WEIGHT, OK?!
RIGHT, BUT... WHAT ABOUT TODAY?

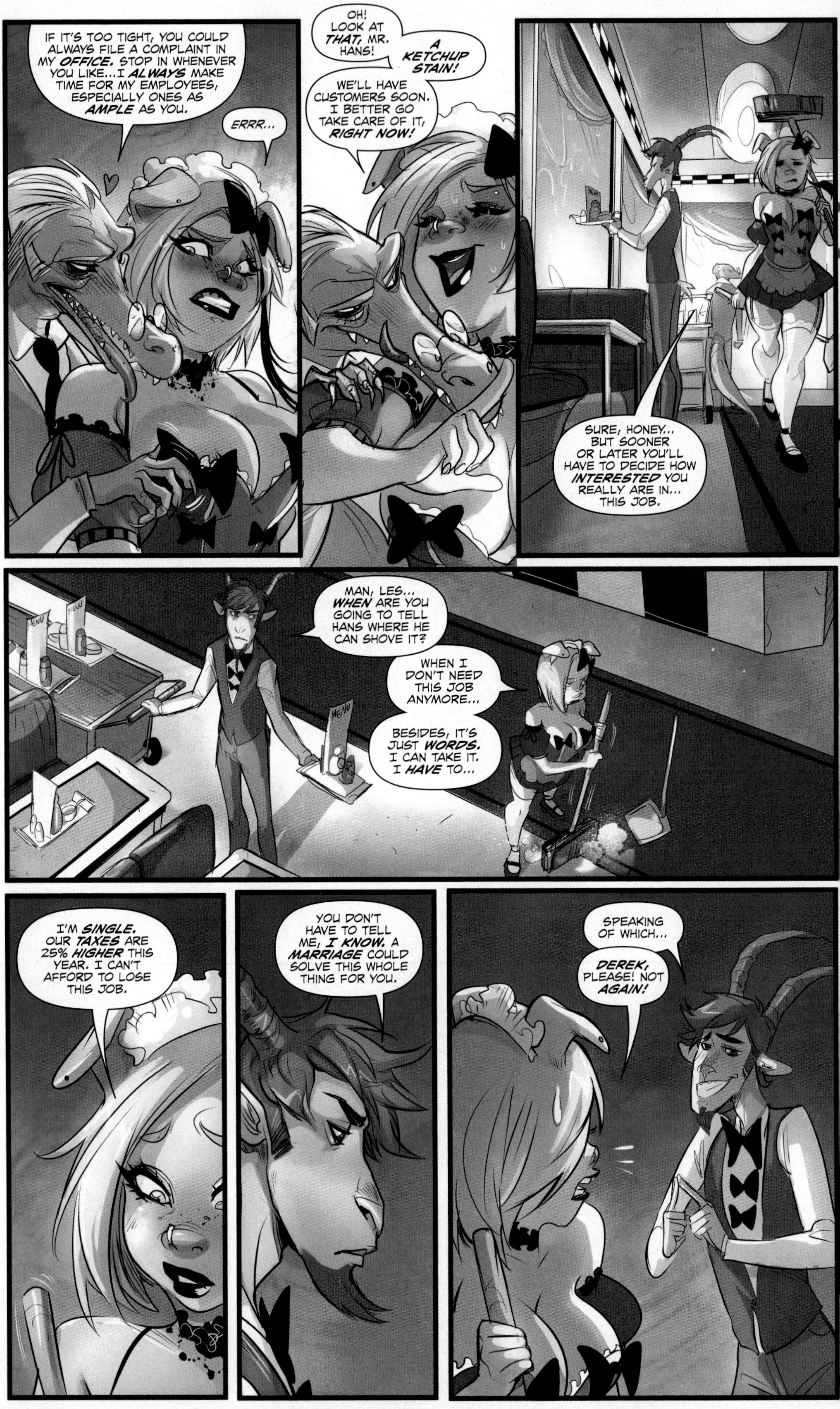
IF IT'S TOO TIGHT, YOU COULD ALWAYS FILE A COMPLAINT IN MY OFFICE. STOP IN WHENEVER YOU LIKE...I ALWAYS MAKE TIME FOR MY EMPLOYEES, ESPECIALLY ONES AS AMPLE AS YOU.
ERRR...
OH! LOOK AT THAT, MR. HANS!
A KETCHUP STAIN!
WE'LL HAVE CUSTOMERS SOON. I BETTER GO TAKE CARE OF IT, RIGHT NOW!
SURE, HONEY... BUT SOONER OR LATER YOU'LL HAVE TO DECIDE HOW INTERESTED YOU REALLY ARE IN... THIS JOB.
MAN, LES... WHEN ARE YOU GOING TO TELL HANS WHERE HE CAN SHOVE IT?
WHEN I DON'T NEED THIS JOB ANYMORE...
BESIDES, IT'S JUST WORDS. I CAN TAKE IT. I HAVE TO...
I'M SINGLE. OUR TAXES ARE 25% HIGHER THIS YEAR. I CAN'T AFFORD TO LOSE THIS JOB.
YOU DON'T HAVE TO TELL ME, I KNOW. A MARRIAGE COULD SOLVE THIS WHOLE THING FOR YOU.
SPEAKING OF WHICH...
DEREK, PLEASE! NOT AGAIN!

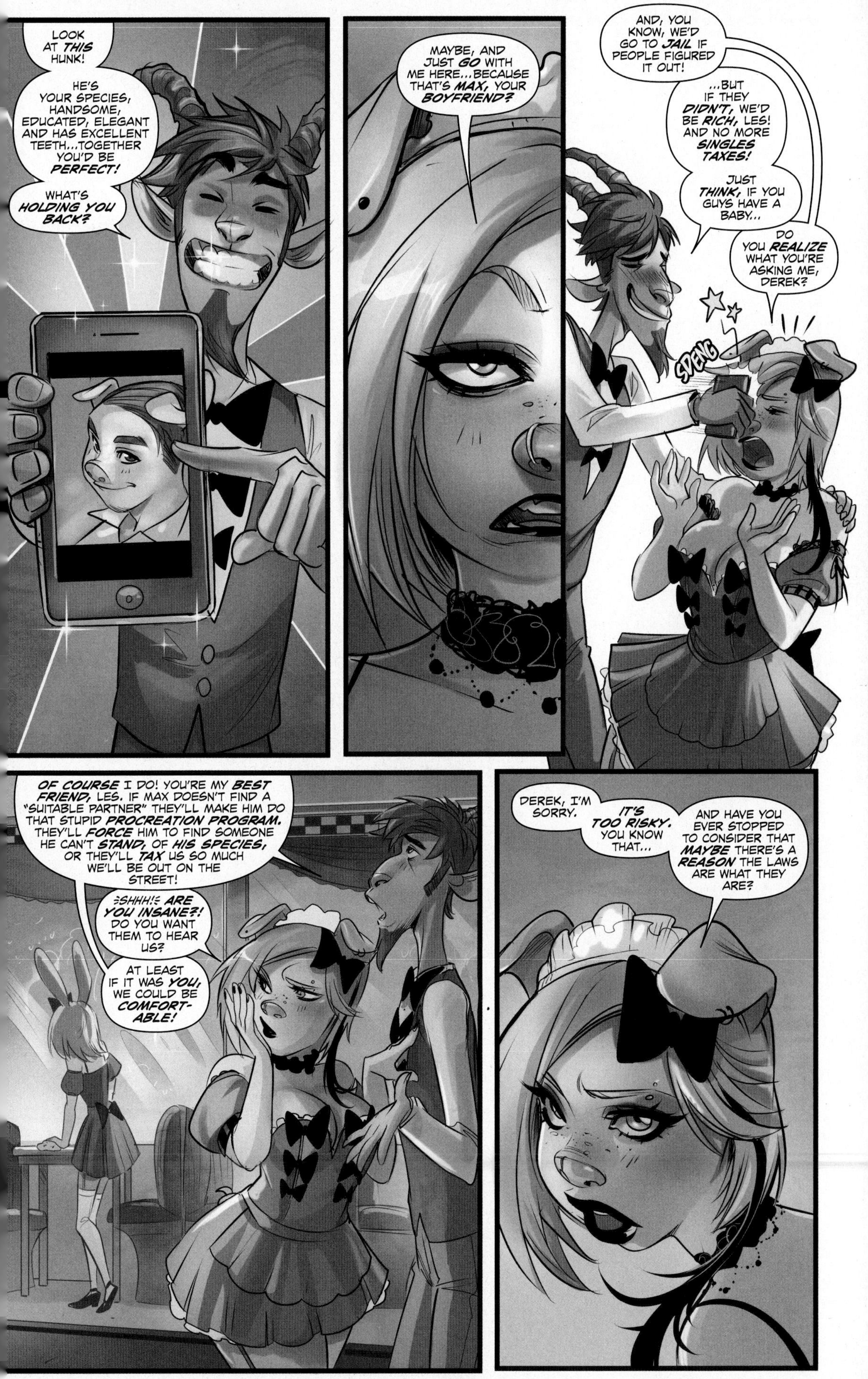

LOOK AT THIS HUNK!
HE'S YOUR SPECIES, HANDSOME, EDUCATED, ELEGANT AND HAS EXCELLENT TEETH...TOGETHER YOU'D BE PERFECT!
WHAT'S HOLDING YOU BACK?
MAYBE, AND JUST GO WITH ME HERE...BECAUSE THAT'S MAX, YOUR BOYFRIEND?
AND, YOU KNOW, WE'D GO TO JAIL IF PEOPLE FIGURED IT OUT!
...BUT IF THEY DIDN'T, WE'D BE RICH, LES! AND NO MORE SINGLES TAXES!
JUST THINK, IF YOU GUYS HAVE A BABY...
SPENG
DO YOU REALIZE WHAT YOU'RE ASKING ME, DEREK?
OF COURSE I DO! YOU'RE MY BEST FRIEND, LES. IF MAX DOESN'T FIND A "SUITABLE PARTNER" THEY'LL MAKE HIM DO THAT STUPID PROCREATION PROGRAM. THEY'LL FORCE HIM TO FIND SOMEONE HE CAN'T STAND, OF HIS SPECIES, OR THEY'LL TAX US SO MUCH WE'LL BE OUT ON THE STREET!
SHHH! ARE YOU INSANE?! DO YOU WANT THEM TO HEAR US?
AT LEAST IF IT WAS YOU, WE COULD BE COMFORT-ABLE!
DEREK, I'M SORRY.
IT'S TOO RISKY. YOU KNOW THAT...
AND HAVE YOU EVER STOPPED TO CONSIDER THAT MAYBE THERE'S A REASON THE LAWS ARE WHAT THEY ARE?

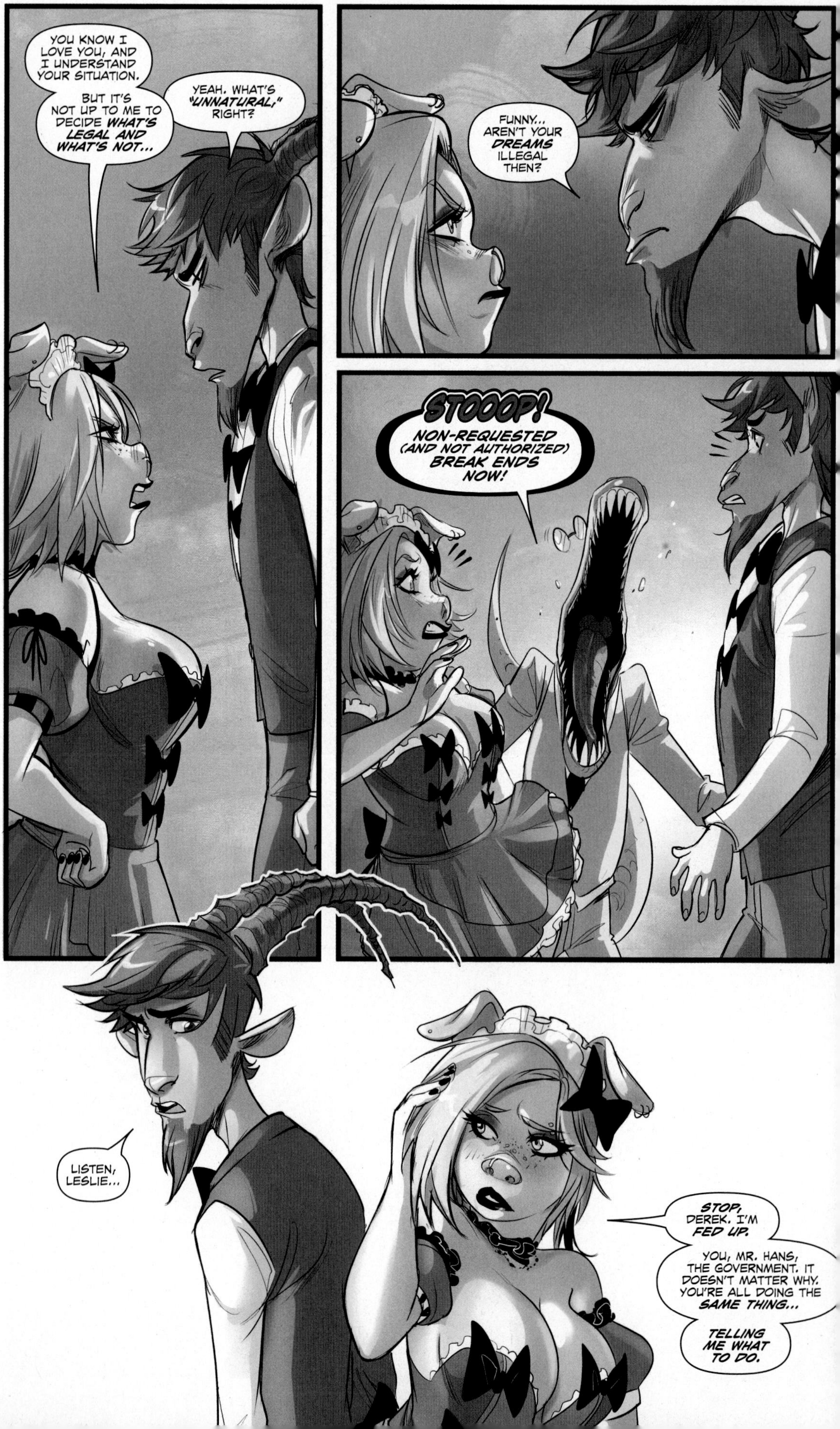
YOU KNOW I LOVE YOU, AND I UNDERSTAND YOUR SITUATION.
BUT IT'S NOT UP TO ME TO DECIDE WHAT'S LEGAL AND WHAT'S NOT...
YEAH. WHAT'S "UNNATURAL," RIGHT?
FUNNY... AREN'T YOUR DREAMS ILLEGAL THEN?
STOOOP!
NON-REQUESTED (AND NOT AUTHORIZED) BREAK ENDS NOW!
LISTEN, LESLIE...
STOP, DEREK. I'M FED UP.
YOU, MR. HANS, THE GOVERNMENT. IT DOESN'T MATTER WHY. YOU'RE ALL DOING THE SAME THING...
TELLING ME WHAT TO DO.

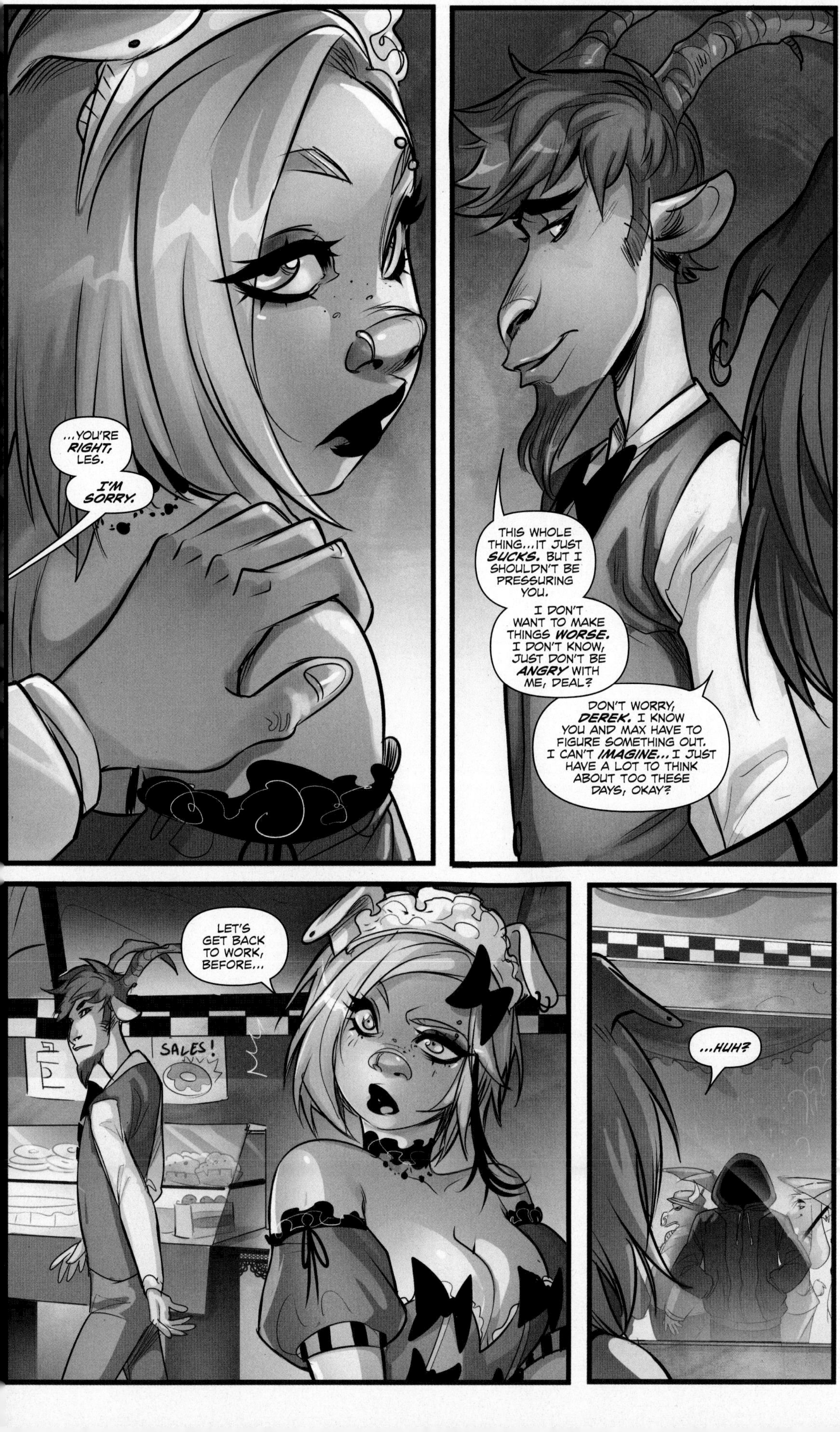

...YOU'RE RIGHT, LES.
I'M SORRY.
THIS WHOLE THING... IT JUST SUCKS. BUT I SHOULDN'T BE PRESSURING YOU.
I DON'T WANT TO MAKE THINGS WORSE. I DON'T KNOW, JUST DON'T BE ANGRY WITH ME, DEAL?
DON'T WORRY, DEREK. I KNOW YOU AND MAX HAVE TO FIGURE SOMETHING OUT. I CAN'T IMAGINE... I JUST HAVE A LOT TO THINK ABOUT TOO THESE DAYS, OKAY?
LET'S GET BACK TO WORK, BEFORE...
SALES!
...HUH?

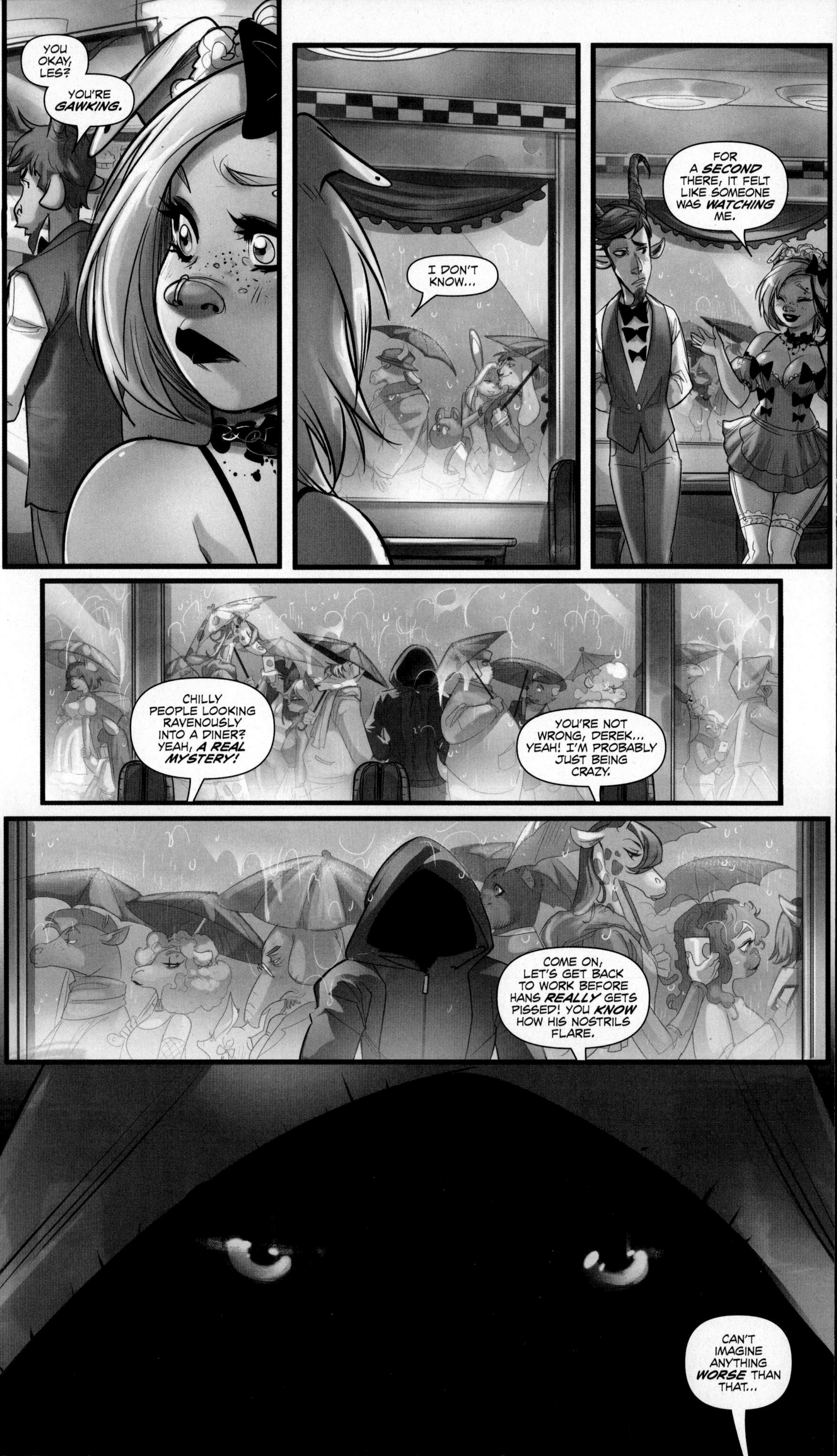
YOU OKAY, LES?
YOU'RE GAWKING.
I DON'T KNOW...
FOR A SECOND THERE, IT FELT LIKE SOMEONE WAS WATCHING ME.
CHILLY PEOPLE LOOKING RAVENOUSLY INTO A DINER? YEAH, A REAL MYSTERY!
YOU'RE NOT WRONG, DEREK... YEAH! I'M PROBABLY JUST BEING CRAZY.
COME ON, LET'S GET BACK TO WORK BEFORE HANS REALLY GETS PISSED! YOU KNOW HOW HIS NOSTRILS FLARE.
CAN'T IMAGINE ANYTHING WORSE THAN THAT...

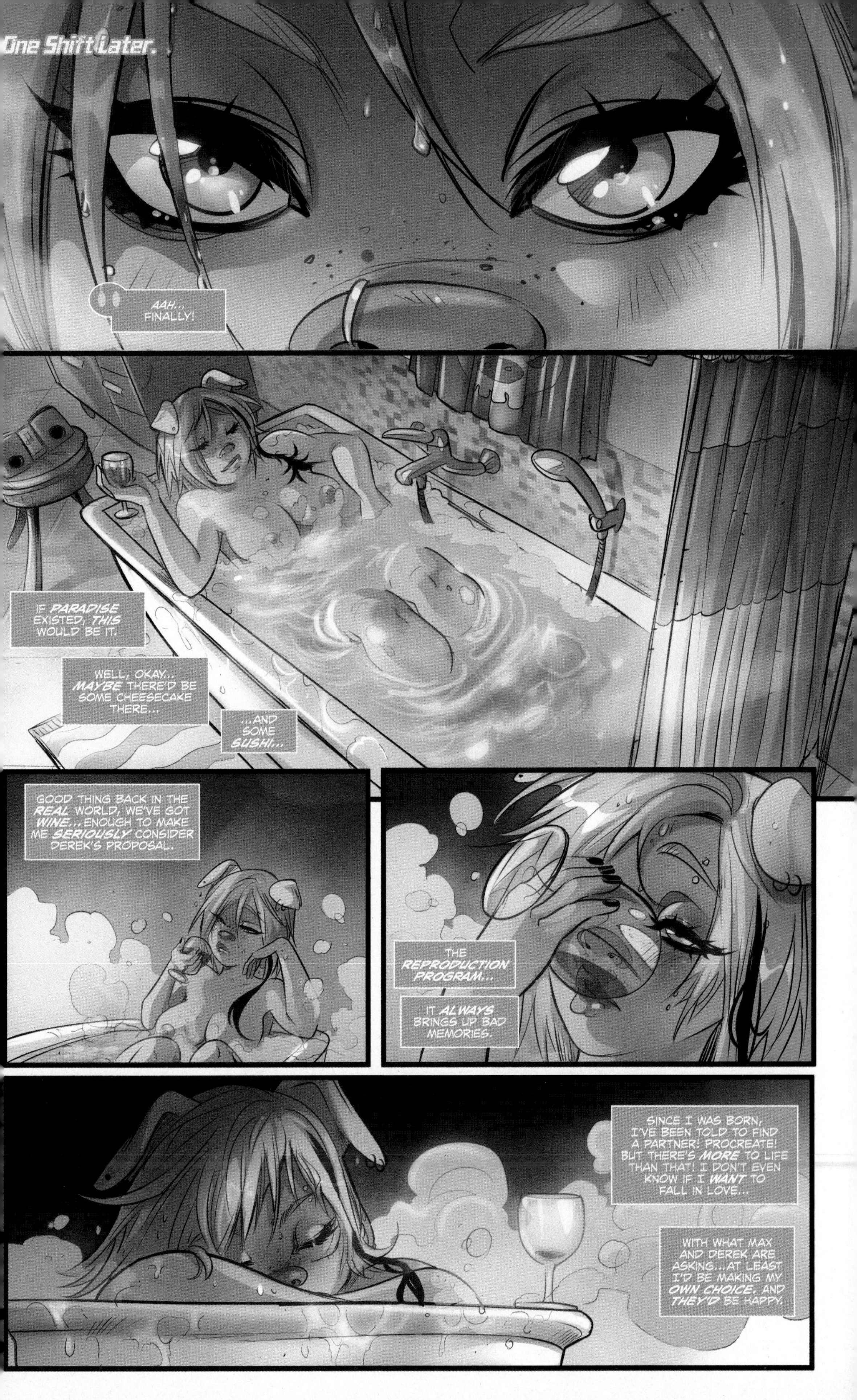
One Shift Later.
AAH... FINALLY!
IF PARADISE EXISTED, THIS WOULD BE IT.
WELL, OKAY... MAYBE THERE'D BE SOME CHEESECAKE THERE...
...AND SOME SUSHI...
GOOD THING BACK IN THE REAL WORLD, WE'VE GOT WINE... ENOUGH TO MAKE ME SERIOUSLY CONSIDER DEREK'S PROPOSAL.
THE REPRODUCTION PROGRAM...
IT ALWAYS BRINGS UP BAD MEMORIES.
SINCE I WAS BORN, I'VE BEEN TOLD TO FIND A PARTNER! PROCREATE! BUT THERE'S MORE TO LIFE THAN THAT! I DON'T EVEN KNOW IF I WANT TO FALL IN LOVE...
WITH WHAT MAX AND DEREK ARE ASKING... AT LEAST I'D BE MAKING MY OWN CHOICE. AND THEY'D BE HAPPY.

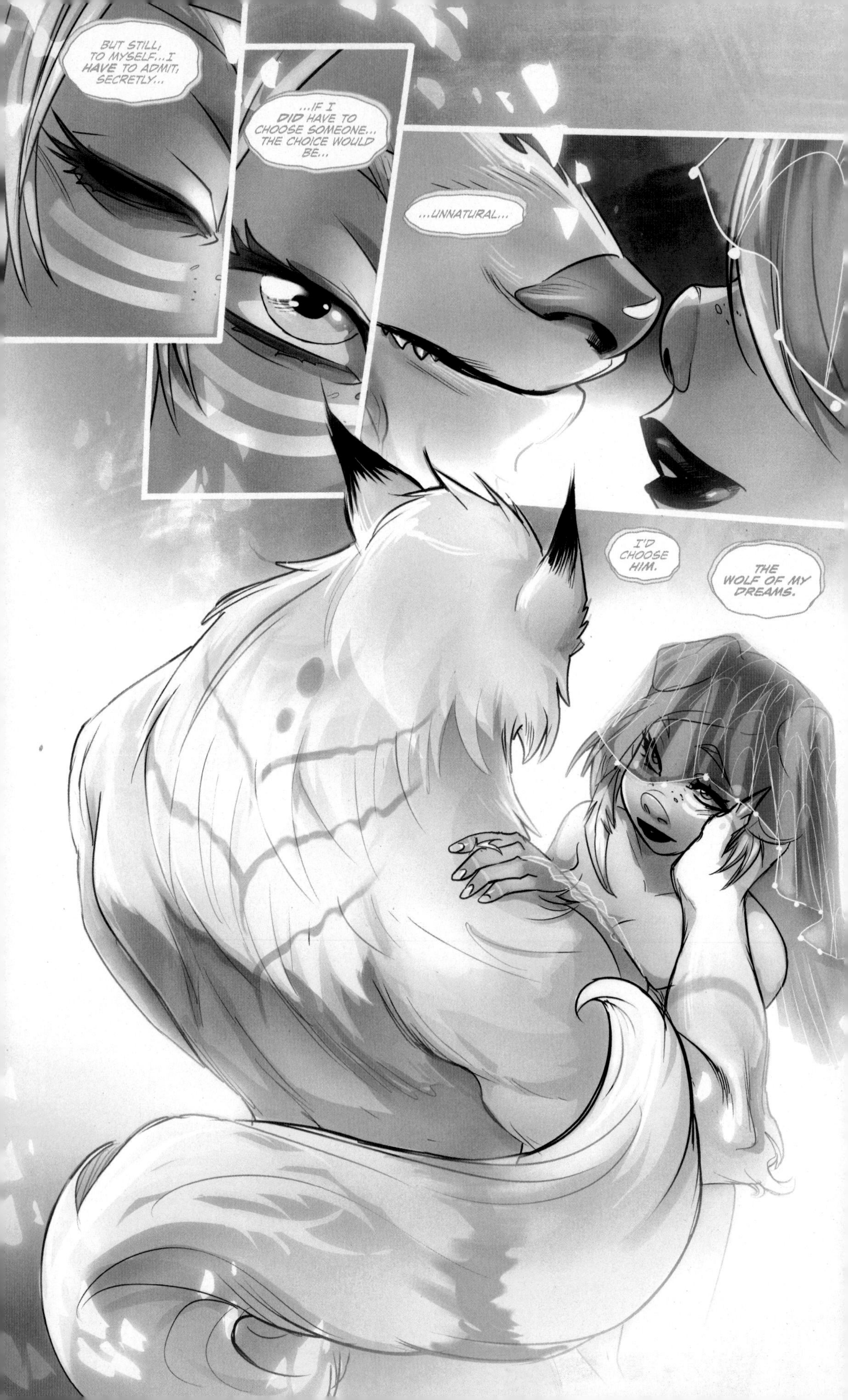
BUT STILL, TO MYSELF... I HAVE TO ADMIT, SECRETLY...
...IF I DID HAVE TO CHOOSE SOMEONE... THE CHOICE WOULD BE...
...UNNATURAL...
I'D CHOOSE HIM.
THE WOLF OF MY DREAMS.

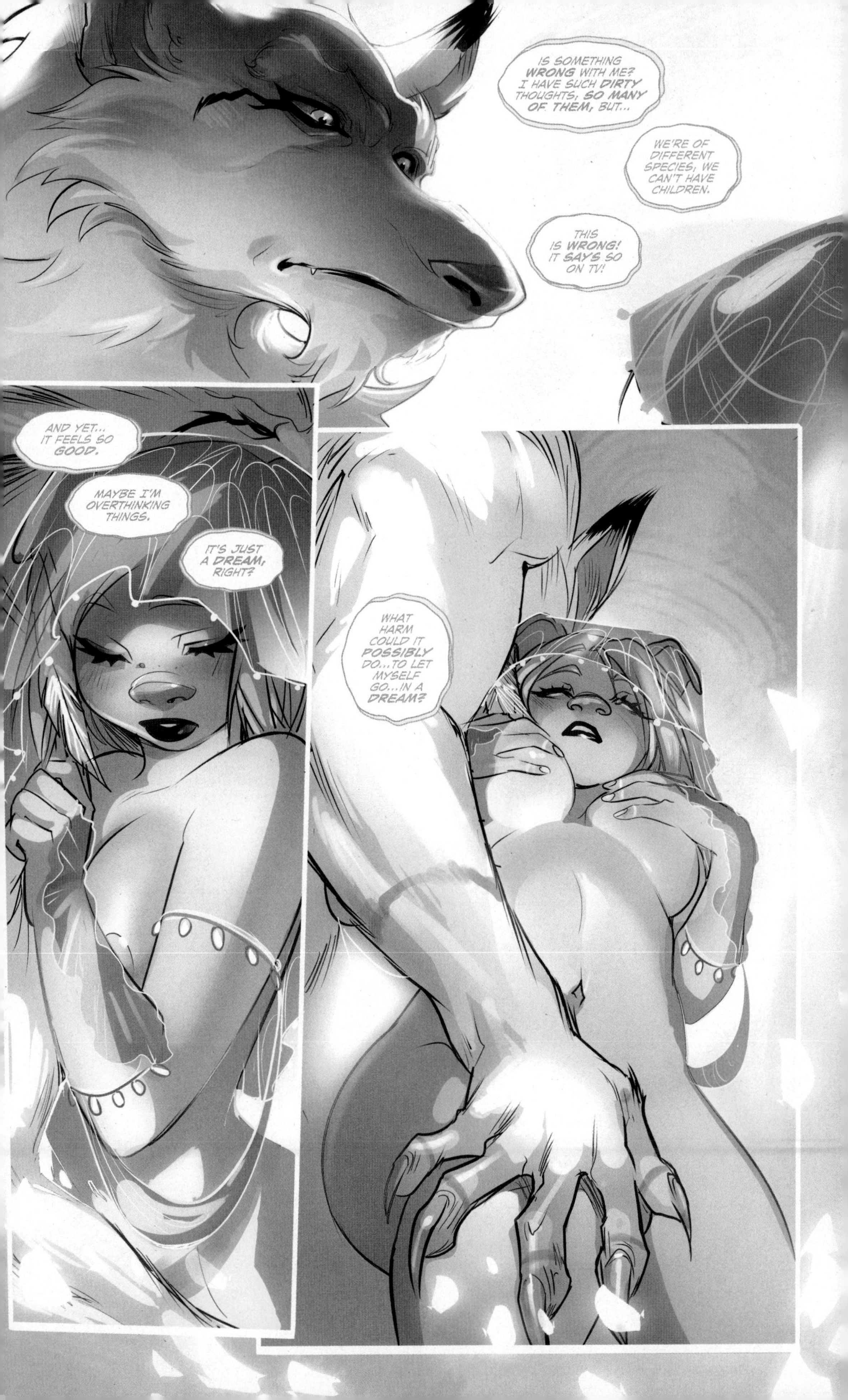

IS SOMETHING WRONG WITH ME? I HAVE SUCH DIRTY THOUGHTS, SO MANY OF THEM, BUT...
WE'RE OF DIFFERENT SPECIES; WE CAN'T HAVE CHILDREN.
THIS IS WRONG! IT SAYS SO ON TV!
AND YET... IT FEELS SO GOOD.
MAYBE I'M OVERTHINKING THINGS.
IT'S JUST A DREAM, RIGHT?
WHAT HARM COULD IT POSSIBLY DO...TO LET MYSELF GO...IN A DREAM?

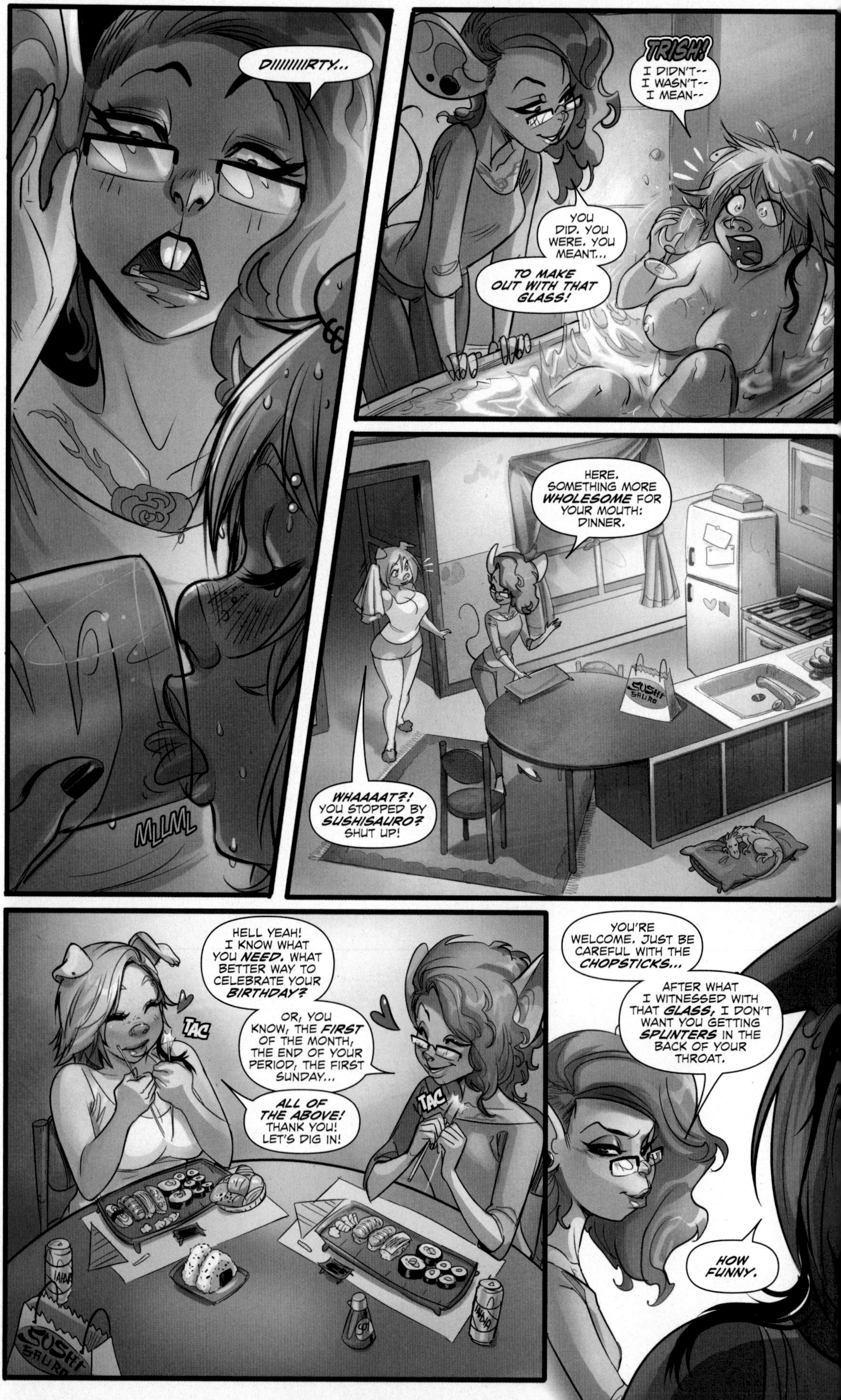
DIIIIIIIRTY...
MLLML
TRISH!
I DIDN'T-- I WASN'T-- I MEAN--
YOU DID. YOU WERE. YOU MEANT...
TO MAKE OUT WITH THAT GLASS!
HERE. SOMETHING MORE WHOLESOME FOR YOUR MOUTH: DINNER.
SUSHI SAURO
WHAAAAT?! YOU STOPPED BY SUSHISAURO? SHUT UP!
HELL YEAH! I KNOW WHAT YOU NEED. WHAT BETTER WAY TO CELEBRATE YOUR BIRTHDAY?
OR, YOU KNOW, THE FIRST OF THE MONTH, THE END OF YOUR PERIOD, THE FIRST SUNDAY...
ALL OF THE ABOVE! THANK YOU! LET'S DIG IN!
TAC
TAC
SUSHI SAURO
YOU'RE WELCOME. JUST BE CAREFUL WITH THE CHOPSTICKS...
AFTER WHAT I WITNESSED WITH THAT GLASS, I DON'T WANT YOU GETTING SPLINTERS IN THE BACK OF YOUR THROAT.
HOW FUNNY.

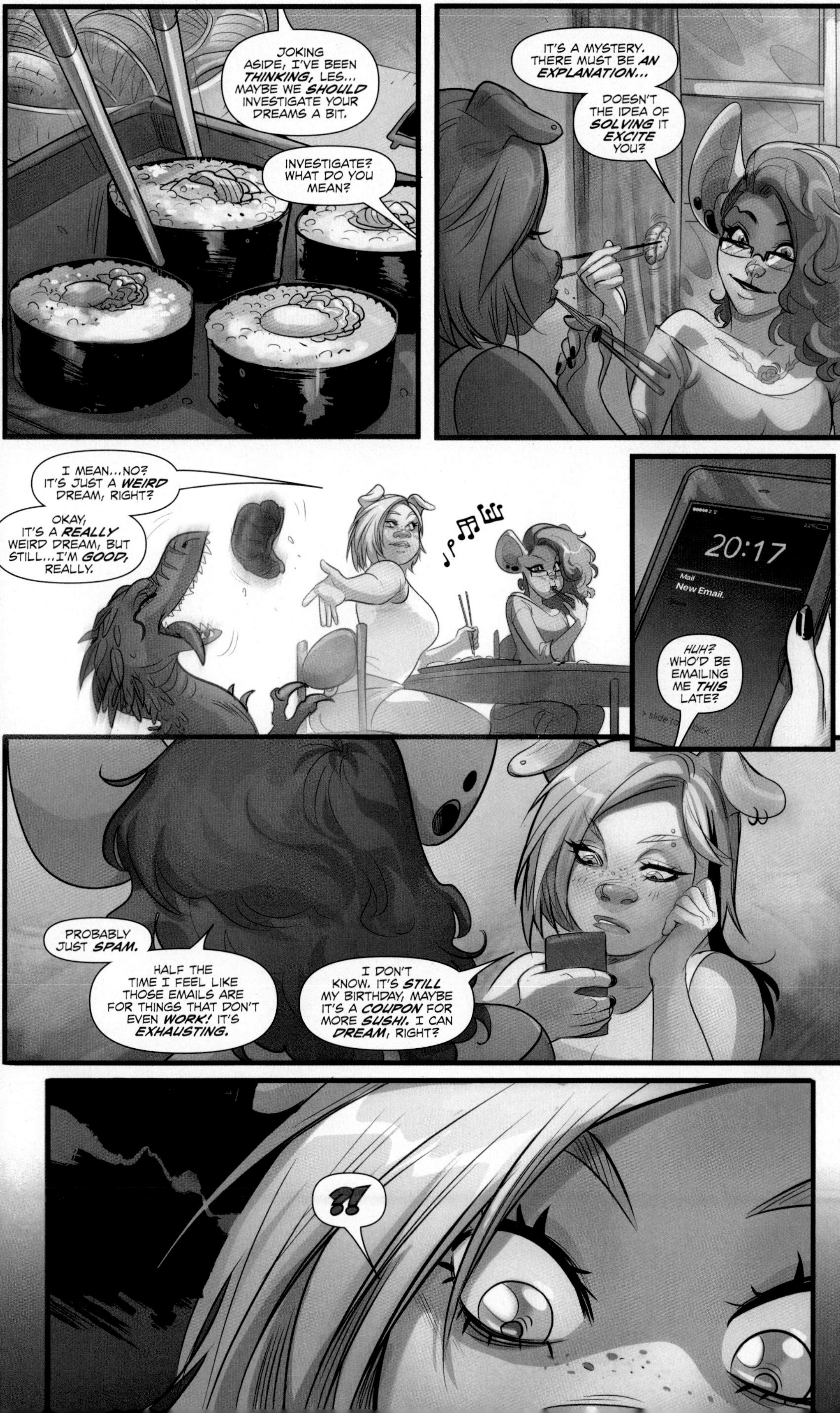
JOKING ASIDE, I'VE BEEN THINKING, LES... MAYBE WE SHOULD INVESTIGATE YOUR DREAMS A BIT.
INVESTIGATE? WHAT DO YOU MEAN?
IT'S A MYSTERY. THERE MUST BE AN EXPLANATION...
DOESN'T THE IDEA OF SOLVING IT EXCITE YOU?
I MEAN...NO? IT'S JUST A WEIRD DREAM, RIGHT?
OKAY, IT'S A REALLY WEIRD DREAM, BUT STILL...I'M GOOD, REALLY.
20:17
Mail
New Email.
HUH? WHO'D BE EMAILING ME THIS LATE?
PROBABLY JUST SPAM.
HALF THE TIME I FEEL LIKE THOSE EMAILS ARE FOR THINGS THAT DON'T EVEN WORK! IT'S EXHAUSTING.
I DON'T KNOW. IT'S STILL MY BIRTHDAY. MAYBE IT'S A COUPON FOR MORE SUSHI. I CAN DREAM, RIGHT?
?!

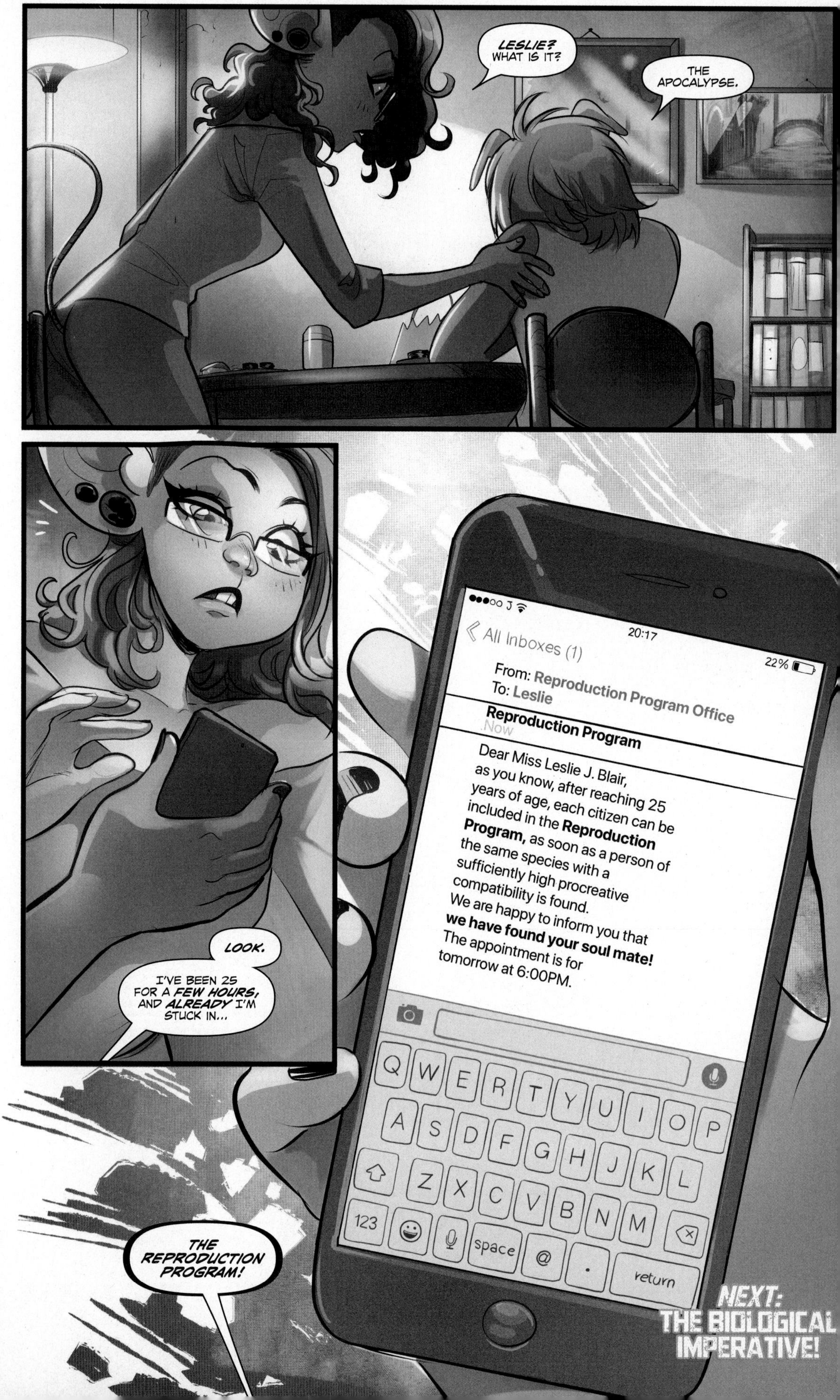
LESLIE? WHAT IS IT?
THE APOCALYPSE.
LOOK.
I'VE BEEN 25 FOR A FEW HOURS, AND ALREADY I'M STUCK IN...
All Inboxes (1)
20:17
22%
From: Reproduction Program Office
To: Leslie
Reproduction Program
Now
Dear Miss Leslie J. Blair, as you know, after reaching 25 years of age, each citizen can be included in the Reproduction Program, as soon as a person of the same species with a sufficiently high procreative compatibility is found. We are happy to inform you that we have found your soul mate! The appointment is for tomorrow at 6:00PM.
THE REPRODUCTION PROGRAM!
NEXT: THE BIOLOGICAL IMPERATIVE!

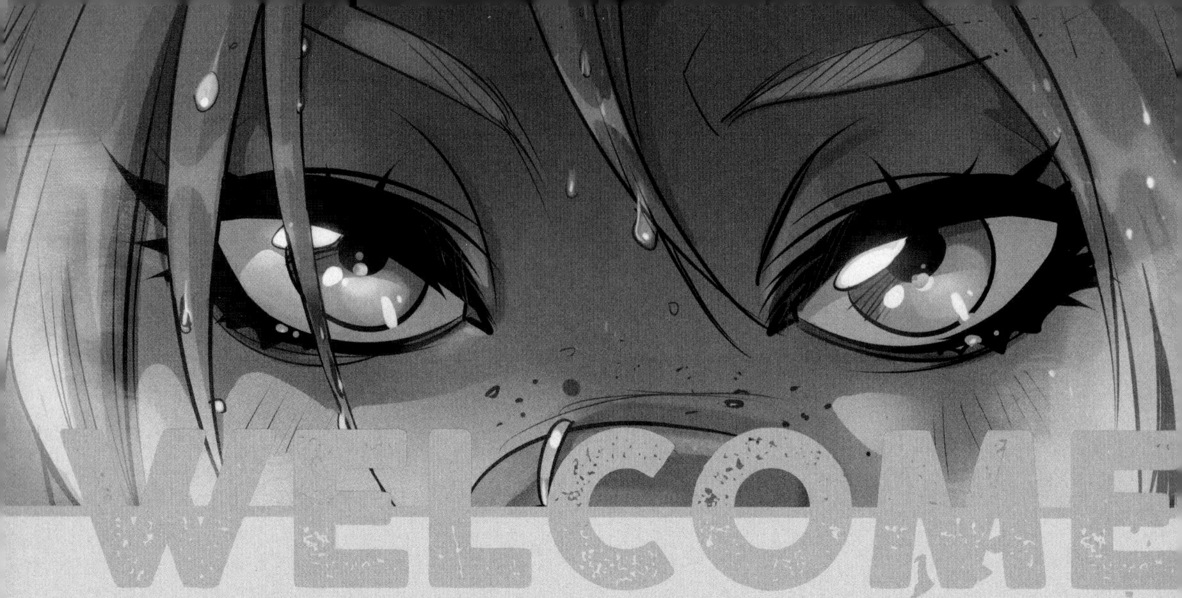
WELCOME

WELCOME TO THE UNNATURAL WORLD!

What you have in your hands is the first issue of my most recent series, published for the first time in English. It was originally published in 2016 in Italy by Panini Comics (and all the guys at Panini deserve all my thankfulness), under the name of *"Contro Natura."* It is not so common to see an Italian creator-owned comic book published in the US, so I can't say how honored – and grateful to the Image Comics editorial team – I am.

Well, let me say something about the book you're going to explore in the next 11 issues: Leslie's world is a "complicated" world, and, in some respects, it's not so different from ours… The fantasy side you're going to discover is more mysterious than what you can imagine. Leslie, in the end, is a simple, common girl (ok, except she's a piggy girl): she has a boring life, she is like me and many other girls all over the world. But the message she got on the very last page of this issue is going to totally change her life. How will she react to everything that's happening?

I hope that, issue after issue, you will feel the desire to discover a little bit more about her, her friends and the strange and terrible situation that they live in. And above all, I hope you see the passion that moved me, from the first page of the first issue to the end. I hope you'll love Les even just a tiny bit as much as I adore her, and I hope you'll join "Team Leslie." ♥

MIRKA

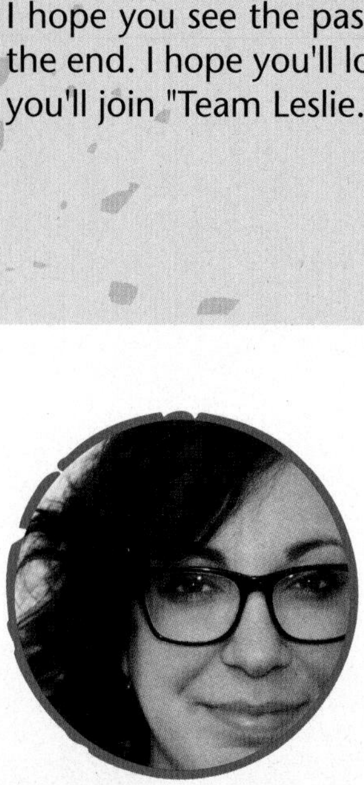

Mirka Andolfo is an Italian creator, working as an artist at DC Comics (*Harley Quinn*, *Wonder Woman*, *DC Bombshells*), Vertigo and Young Animal. She has drawn comics at Marvel, Dynamite and Aspen Comics. As a creator, *Unnatural* (published so far in Italy, Germany, Spain, Poland, Mexico) is her second book, after *Sacro/Profano* (published in Italy, France, Belgium, Netherlands, Spain, Germany and Serbia). You can reach Mirka on her social media channels and on her upcoming website: *mirkand.eu*

f mirkand.works @Mirkand @mirkand89

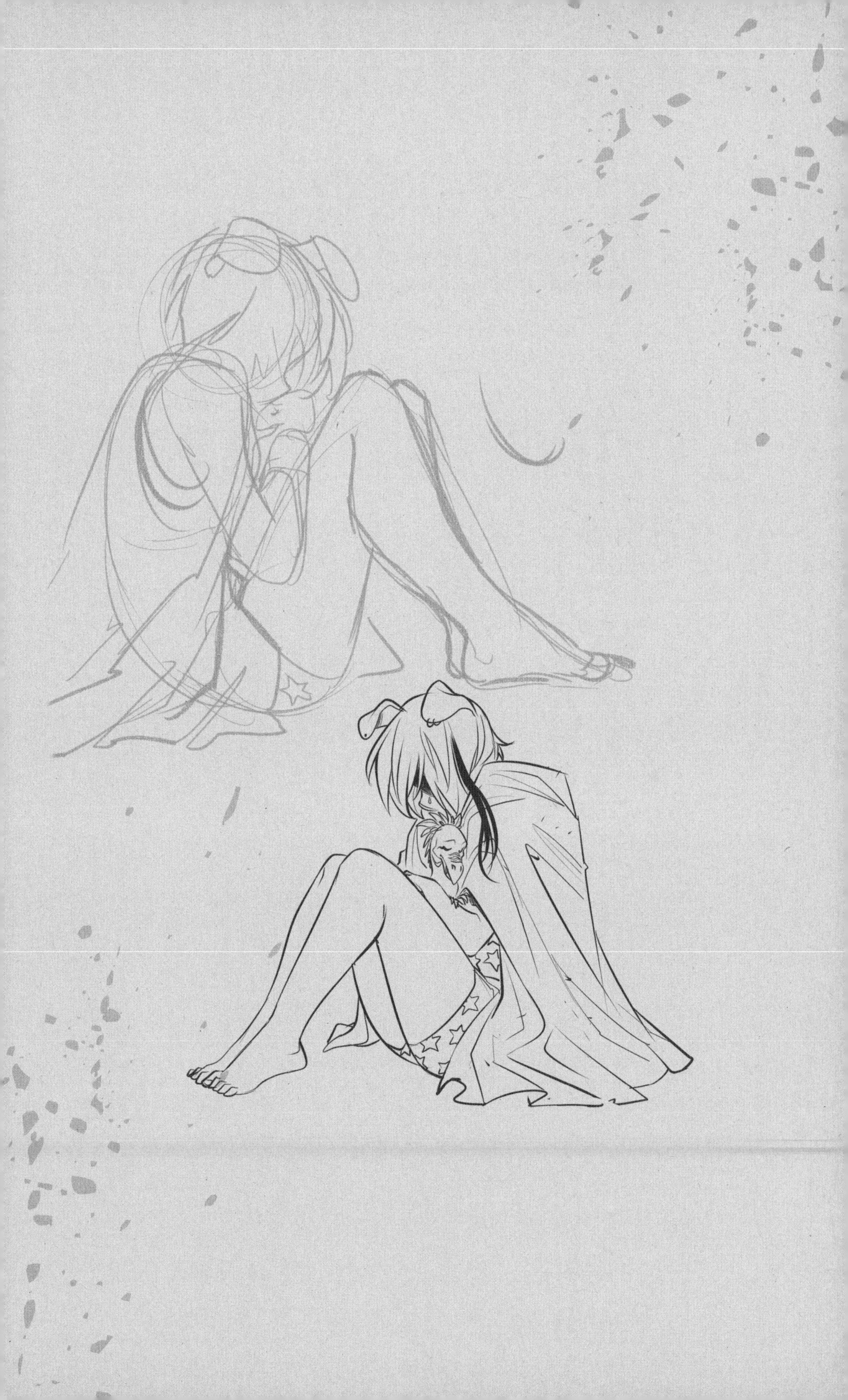

NEXT ISSUE

In a world where love is a government-imposed duty, Leslie is forced to face her most dreaded fear: the infamous Reproduction Program date night!

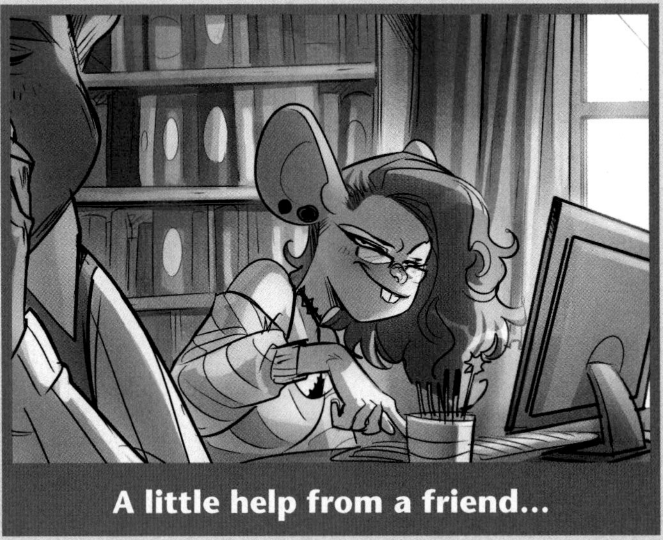
A little help from a friend...

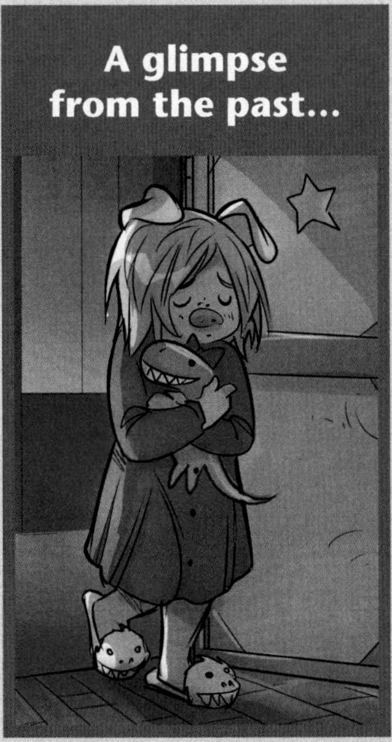
A glimpse from the past...

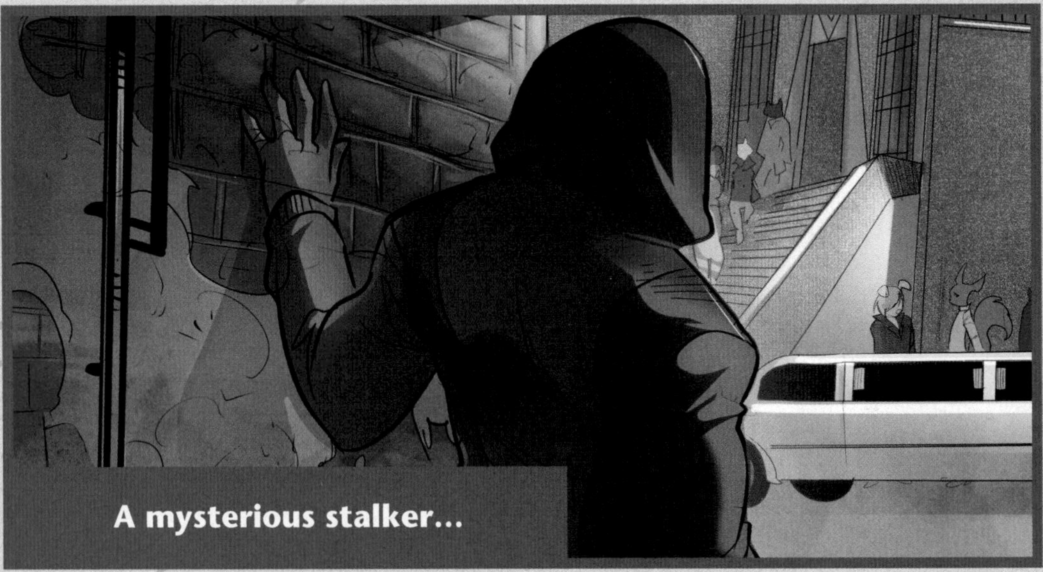
A mysterious stalker...

Will she comply or will she be forever marked as UNNATURAL?

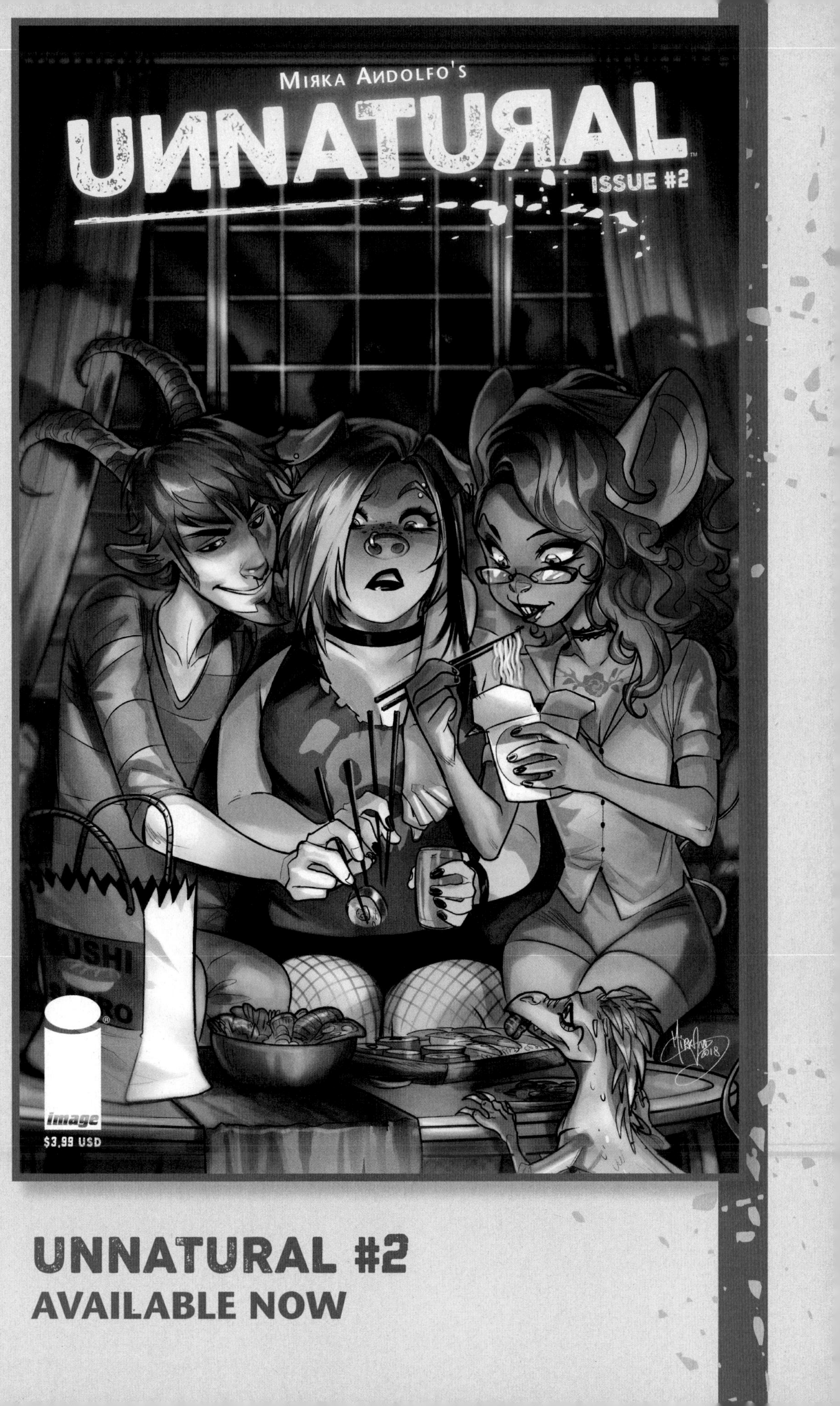
MIRKA ANDOLFO'S
UNNATURAL
ISSUE #2
SUSHI
RO
image
$3.99 USD

UNNATURAL #2
AVAILABLE NOW

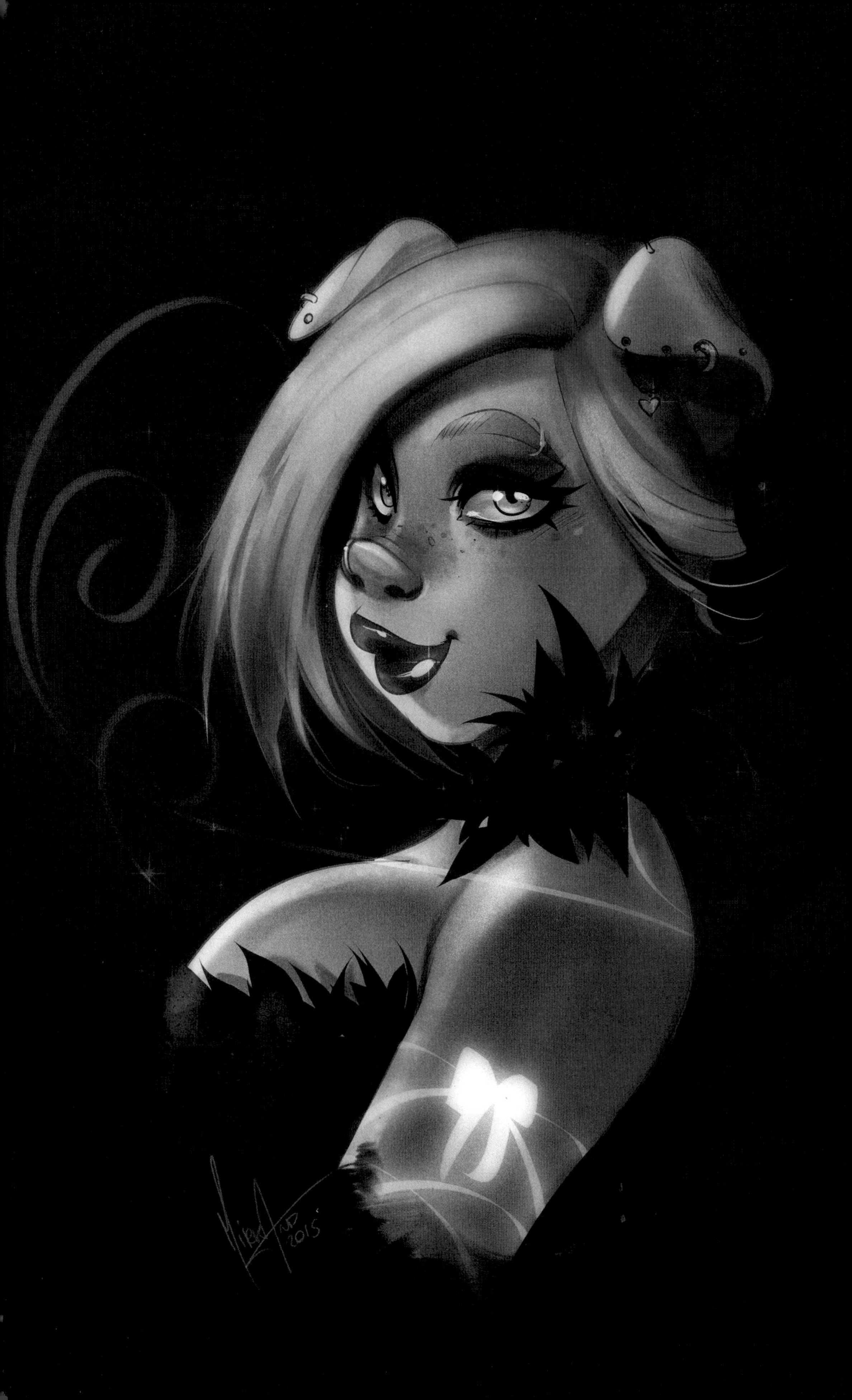

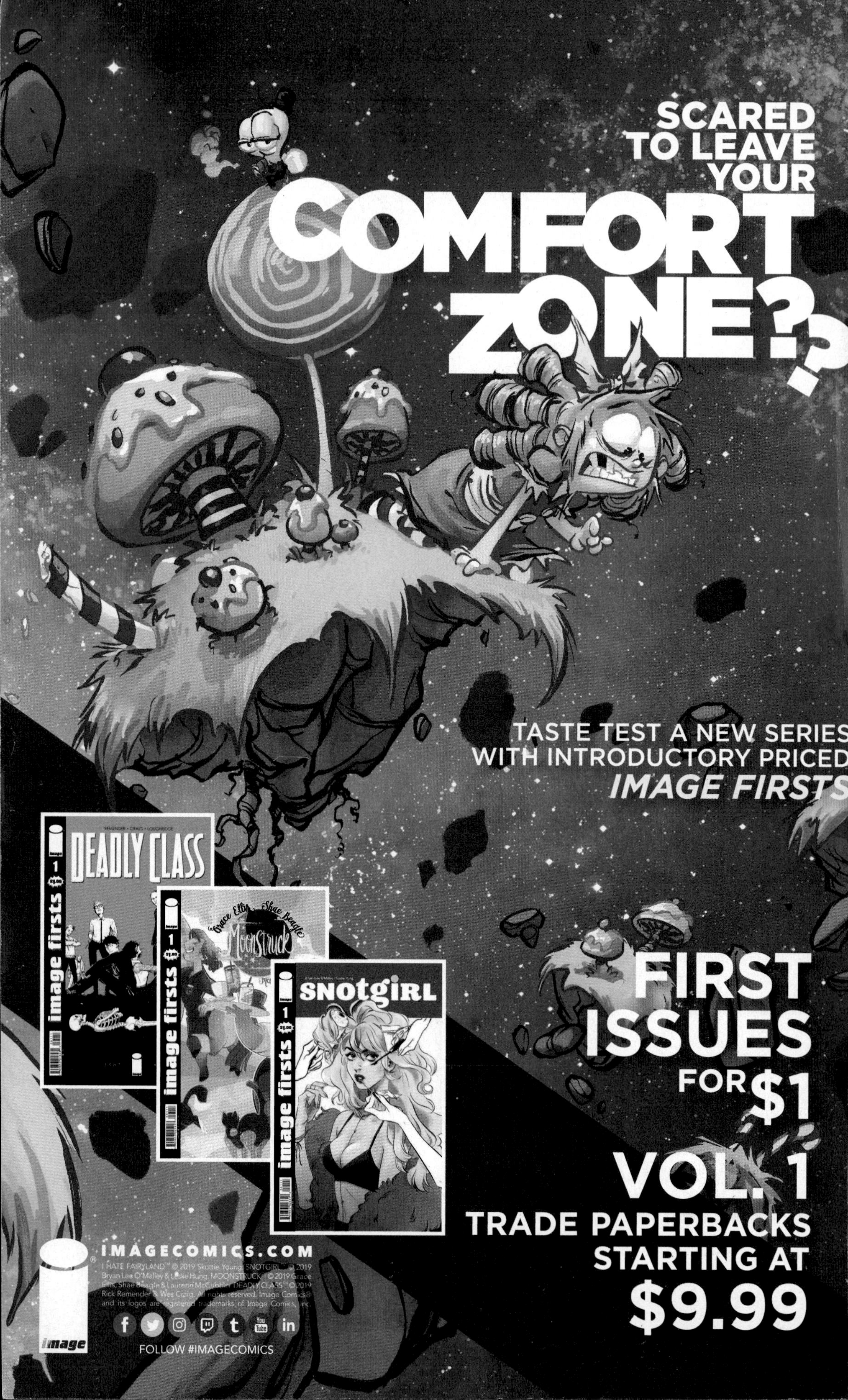
SCARED TO LEAVE YOUR
COMFORT ZONE?
TASTE TEST A NEW SERIES WITH INTRODUCTORY PRICED
IMAGE FIRSTS
DEADLY CLASS
image firsts
Moonstruck
image firsts
SNOTGIRL
image firsts
FIRST ISSUES FOR $1
VOL. 1 TRADE PAPERBACKS STARTING AT $9.99
IMAGECOMICS.COM
I HATE FAIRYLAND™ © 2019 Skottie Young. SNOTGIRL™ © 2019 Bryan Lee O'Malley & Leslie Hung. MOONSTRUCK™ © 2019 Grace Ellis, Shae Beagle & Laurenn McCubbin. DEADLY CLASS™ © 2019 Rick Remender & Wes Craig. All rights reserved. Image Comics® and its logos are registered trademarks of Image Comics, Inc.
FOLLOW #IMAGECOMICS